We Believe

We Believe

Creeds, Catechisms, and Confessions of Faith

LIGONIER MINISTRIES

We Believe: Creeds, Catechisms, and Confessions of Faith
© 2023 by Ligonier Ministries

Published by Ligonier Ministries
421 Ligonier Court, Sanford, FL 32771
Ligonier.org

Printed in China
Amity Printing Company
0000124
First edition, second printing

ISBN 978-1-64289-450-9 (Hardcover)
ISBN 978-1-64289-451-6 (ePub)

Cover design: Metaleap Creative
Berglandschap met herders, Nicolas Perelle, 1613–1695
Interior design and typeset: Katherine Lloyd, The DESK

Belgic Confession, Heidelberg Catechism, Canons of Dort adapted from Doctrinal Standards as found in *Psalter Hymnal* (© 1987, 1988, Faith Alive Christian Resources/Christian Reformed Church in North America; Doctrinal Standards translations © 1985, 1986, 1988). Used by permission. All rights reserved worldwide.

Scots Confession and First and Second Helvetic Confessions taken from *Reformed Confessions of the 16th and 17th Centuries in English Translation* (© 2014 by James T. Dennison Jr.). Used by permission of Reformation Heritage Books. All rights reserved.

Westminster Standards taken from *The Confession of Faith and Catechisms of the Orthodox Presbyterian Church with Proof Texts* (© 2005, 2007, 2021). Used by permission of the Committee on Christian Education of the Orthodox Presbyterian Church. All rights reserved.

Apostles' Creed, Niceno-Constantinopolitan Creed, Luther's Small Catechism, Augsburg Confession, French Confession of Faith, and elements of the Savoy Declaration taken from Philip Schaff, *The Creeds of Christendom, with a History and Critical Notes* (1882). Public domain.

Definition of Chalcedon taken from T. Herbert Bindley, *The Oecumenical Documents of the Faith* (1899). Public domain.

Geneva Catechism taken from Elijah Waterman, *The Catechism of the Church of Geneva by the Rev. John Calvin* (1815). Public domain.

Thirty-Nine Articles taken from B.J. Kidd, *The Thirty-nine Articles: Their History and Explanation* (1905). Public domain.

Second London Baptist Confession of Faith taken from W.J. McGlothlin, *The Baptist Confessions of Faith* (1911). Public domain.

Library of Congress Control Number: 2022935516

Contents

Permissions

Ligonier Ministries would like to express our gratitude to the following for permission to reprint versions of select creeds, catechisms, and confessions:

The Christian Reformed Church in North America and the United Reformed Churches of North America for the use of the Belgic Confession, Heidelberg Catechism, and Canons of Dort from the *Psalter Hymnal* (© 1987, 1988, Faith Alive Christian Resources/CRCNA), with adaptations as found on the URCNA.org website.

The Committee on Christian Education of the Orthodox Presbyterian Church for the use of the Westminster Confession of Faith, Westminster Larger Catechism, and Westminster Shorter Catechism with proof texts.

James T. Dennison Jr. and Reformation Heritage Books for the use of the Scots Confession, the First Helvetic Confession, and the Second Helvetic Confession as found in *Reformed Confessions of the 16th and 17th Centuries in English Translation*.

Introduction

Why Creeds and Confessions?

Sola Scriptura—this rallying cry of the Protestant Reformation sounded forth during that great sixteenth-century awakening when the Holy Spirit moved God's people to return to Scripture and cast off the many unbiblical traditions of men that had been imposed by the Roman Catholic Church. Returning to divine revelation as the final and only infallible rule of faith, the Reformers and their heirs recovered the biblical gospel that had been all but lost under what had been added to Scripture over the centuries. Yet while the Reformers are known for what they cast aside, we must not overlook what they kept. In returning to the Scriptures, they set aside not all church traditions but only the ones that contradicted God's Word. Traditions faithful to Scripture and that stood as sound expositions of the biblical teaching were kept. Preeminent among these were the ecumenical creeds and confessions of the faith such as the Nicene Creed and the Definition of Chalcedon.

The Reformers kept these statements of faith and others because they are faithful summaries of the Bible's teaching on key doctrines of the faith. At their best, creeds and confessions serve the purpose of summarizing what the church believes Scripture to teach, helping believers to know biblical doctrine, to discern false teaching, and to instruct others in the deep matters of God's Word. While creeds and confessions do not take the place of Scripture and while they operate in submission to Scripture, time-tested creeds and confessions provide invaluable guidance to us as we seek to believe what God has revealed and only what God has revealed.

Everyone, in fact, has a creed or a confession that summarizes what he believes about essential matters of the faith. Even the statements "No creed but Christ" or "No confession but the Bible" are themselves creeds and confessions that communicate core convictions. Moreover, the minute we start trying to relate one part of biblical teaching to another part, we are starting to form a creed.

Creeds are so important that we find basic creeds even in the Bible itself. The Shema of Deuteronomy 6:4 is the fundamental creedal statement of biblical monotheism. Throughout the Epistles we find core summaries of the person and work of Christ that were likely recited or sung in the Apostolic Church. Philippians 2:5–11 summarizes the biblical teaching on the incarnation of the Son of God. First Timothy 3:16 masterfully encapsulates the work of Christ. These examples and others show us that summarizing and declaring our faith is a historical and biblical practice.

Protestant Creeds and the Purpose of This Work

From the start, Protestants put into creedal, confessional, and catechetical form their convictions regarding what the Bible teaches, both to instruct their people and to explain their differences with the theological views of the Roman Catholic Church. Martin Luther wrote both a large catechism and a small catechism that summarize essential teachings on faith and practice by expositing the Apostles' Creed, the Ten Commandments, and the Lord's Prayer. Perhaps the most significant early Protestant confession is the Augsburg Confession, presented to Emperor Charles V at the Diet of Augsburg as a summary of Lutheran beliefs and where they differed from both Roman Catholicism and the teaching of the Anabaptists. To this day, the Augsburg Confession remains the fundamental confession of the Lutheran tradition.

Throughout the sixteenth century, Reformed Protestants, who held sway in the Church of England, in Geneva, and elsewhere composed many different creeds, confessions, and catechisms including the Thirty-Nine Articles of Religion, the Heidelberg Catechism, and the Belgic Confession. The Thirty-Nine Articles continue to guide the Anglican Communion, while the Heidelberg Catechism and the Belgic Confession are two of the Three Forms of Unity that are the confessional foundation of the Dutch Reformed Churches. A host of other Reformed confessions written during the same period continue to serve the churches of the Reformed tradition.

One of the most important of the Reformed Confessions, the Canons of Dort, is the third of the Three Forms of Unity and has served to unite Christians from many different traditions who hold to a Reformed understanding of God's grace in salvation. A high point of Reformed confessionalism is represented by the Westminster Standards, written in the middle of the seventeenth century to reform the Church of England but which has subsequently been adopted by Presbyterians the world over.

This work is a collection of the aforementioned creeds, confessions, and catechisms and several others, providing the church a one-volume resource containing the most significant Protestant statements of faith ever formulated. This volume is offered to help Christians better understand the distinctions and commonalities among different Protestant traditions as well as to become better grounded in the faith once delivered to the saints.

1

Apostles' Creed

(SECOND CENTURY)

The Apostles' Creed is one of the earliest and most important statements of belief produced by the Christian church. Its present form is believed to have originated in Gaul (modern-day France) during the fifth century. It was likely based on an earlier creed from the second century known as the Old Roman Symbol, which was somewhat shorter and simpler. By the eighth century, the Apostles' Creed gained wide use in liturgical contexts as a brief and faithful summary of Christian belief.

The name of the creed comes from an early belief that it was written by Jesus' Apostles, with each Apostle writing one of the twelve articles of the creed. Over time, the name came simply to reflect the acknowledgment that the creed summarizes the teaching of the Apostles as they had received it from Christ Himself.

The creed teaches the basics of the Christian faith: the Trinity; the virgin birth, death, burial, resurrection, ascension, and return of Christ; the holy and universal church, the forgiveness of sin; and the bodily resurrection. Knowing these basics provides a good starting point for understanding Christianity and for differentiating it from other religions.

Apostles' Creed

I believe in God the Father, Almighty,
Maker of heaven and earth;

And in Jesus Christ, His only begotten Son, our Lord;
Who was conceived by the Holy Ghost,
Born of the virgin Mary;
Suffered under Pontius Pilate,
Was crucified, dead, and buried;
He descended into hell.
The third day He arose again from the dead;
He ascended into heaven;
And sitteth on the right hand of God the Father Almighty;
From thence He shall come to judge the quick and the dead.

I believe in the Holy Ghost;
The holy catholic[1] church; the communion of saints;
The forgiveness of sins;
The resurrection of the body;
And the life everlasting. Amen.

---

1   The word "catholic" refers to the universal church.

2

Niceno-Constantinopolitan Creed

(325/381)

In the early fourth century, the teachings of a North African presbyter named Arius began to cause controversy in the church of Alexandria. Reportedly disturbed by a sermon preached by the orthodox bishop Alexander on the relationship between the Father and the Son that Arius understood as proclaiming Sabellianism (a form of modalism, the belief that the Father, Son, and Spirit are merely different modes of the one God), Arius argued that if the Son is begotten, then He must have had a beginning. He famously declared, "There was a time when the Son was not."

Alexander exiled Arius, who received support from various leaders in the church. The controversy soon spread, prompting Emperor Constantine I to call a church council to decide the issue. The First Council of Nicaea, held in 325 in modern-day Turkey, was attended by more than three hundred bishops from across the Roman Empire. It became known as the first ecumenical—representing all the churches—council of the post-Apostolic church. The orthodox party—led by Alexander and supported by Athanasius of Alexandria—prevailed, with the council affirming the full deity of the Son by concluding that He is *homoousios* (of one substance) with the Father, rather than *homoiousios* (of like substance) or *heteroousios* (of different substance).

Arianism did not die, however. In the East, it was largely suppressed by 381, when the First Council of Constantinople revised and expanded the Nicene Creed, giving us the form we know today (and leading to the creed's often being called the Niceno-Constantinopolitan Creed). But Arianism continued to be taught over the following centuries, especially among the Goths who invaded the Western empire beginning in the fourth century. It died out in the West for the most part by the eighth century, though later groups have held Arian-like beliefs.

Niceno-Constantinopolitan Creed

We believe in one God, the Father Almighty, Maker of heaven and earth, of all things visible and invisible.

And in one Lord Jesus Christ, the only-begotten Son of God, begotten of His Father before all worlds; God of God, Light of Light, very God of very God; begotten, not made, being of one substance with the Father, by whom all things were made. Who, for us men and for our salvation, came down from heaven, and was incarnate by the Holy Spirit of the virgin Mary, and was made man; and was crucified also for us under Pontius Pilate; He suffered and was buried; and the third day He rose again, according to the Scriptures; and ascended into heaven, and is seated at the right hand of the Father; and He shall come again, with glory, to judge both the living and the dead; whose kingdom shall have no end.

And we believe in the Holy Spirit, the Lord and Giver of Life; who proceeds from the Father and the Son; who with the Father and the Son together is worshiped and glorified; who spoke by the prophets. And we believe in one holy catholic[1] and apostolic church. We acknowledge one baptism for the remission of sins; and we look for the resurrection of the dead, and the life of the world to come. Amen.

---

1   The word "catholic" refers to the universal church.

3

Definition of Chalcedon

(451)

By the end of the fourth century, the church had largely settled the question of our Savior's divinity, but debate continued regarding the relationship of the deity of Christ to the humanity of Christ. Everyone agreed that Christ is in some sense both divine and human, but there was disagreement about how Jesus could be both God and man.

These disagreements led to the Council of Chalcedon in 451. The council repudiated two errors especially: Nestorianism, which taught that the divine and human in Christ are two persons rather than two natures in one person; and Eutychianism, which taught that in the person of Christ there is really only one nature, a divine-human mixture.

Chalcedon produced the standard orthodox definition of the person of Christ, which says that in the one person of Christ are perfectly united the divine nature and a human nature, and that this union is without confusion, mixture, separation, or division, each nature retaining its own attributes. This is what is called the hypostatic union: Christ is one person with two natures. The Definition of Chalcedon does not spell out this union in every detail, but it gives parameters to preserve the biblical witness. Because each nature retains its own attributes, Christ is truly human and truly divine. He is not one at the expense of the other, and because these natures are not confused or mixed, He is not a third kind of being, neither truly human nor truly divine. The natures are united in one person without separation or division, so Christ is a single person or subject.

Definition of Chalcedon

The holy, great, and ecumenical synod, by the grace of God and the command of our most orthodox and Christ-loving Emperors, Marcian and Valentenian Augusti, assembled in the metropolis of Chalcedon, in the Bithynian province, in the martyry of the holy and nobly triumphant martyr Euphemia, hath decreed as follows:

Our Lord and Savior Jesus Christ, confirming the knowledge of the faith to His disciples, said, "My peace I leave with you, My peace I give to you," to the end that no one should differ from his neighbor in the doctrines of orthodoxy, but that the proclamation of the truth should be shown forth equally by all.

But since the evil one ceaseth not, by means of his own tares, to supplant the seeds of orthodoxy, and ever inventeth something new against the truth, therefore the Lord, in His wonted care for the human race, excited to zeal this orthodox and most faithful emperor, and called together to Himself the chiefs of the priesthood from all parts, in order that, by the action of the grace of Christ the Lord of us all, we might remove every noxious element from the sheep of Christ, and enrich them with the fresh herbage of the truth.

And this, in fact, we have accomplished, having by a unanimous vote driven away the dogmas of error, and having renewed the undeviating creed of the fathers, proclaiming to all the symbol of the three hundred and eighteen; and, in addition, accepting as our own fathers those who received that statement of orthodoxy—we mean the one hundred and fifty who subsequently met together in great Constantinople, and themselves set their seal to the same creed.

Therefore (preserving the order and all the decrees concerning the faith passed by the holy synod held formerly at Ephesus, the leaders of which were Caelestine of Rome and Cyril of Alexandria of most holy memory) we decree that the exposition of the right and blameless faith of the three hundred and eighteen holy and blessed fathers, assembled in Nicaea, in the time of the

Emperor Constantine of orthodox memory, be preeminent; and moreover, the definitions made by the one hundred and fifty holy fathers in Constantinople, for the removal of the heresies then rife, and for the confirmation of the same catholic and apostolic faith, remain valid.

The symbol of the three hundred and eighteen:

"We believe in One God the Father All-sovereign, Maker of all things visible and invisible:

"And in One Lord Jesus Christ, the Son of God, begotten from the Father, only-begotten, that is, from the essence of the Father; God from God, Light from Light, very God from very God; begotten, not made; co-essential with the Father; through whom all things were made [both in heaven and in earth]; who for us men and for our salvation came down from the heavens, and was incarnate of the Holy Spirit and the Virgin Mary, and lived as man; was crucified also for us under Pontius Pilate, and suffered, and was buried, and rose the third day according to the Scriptures, and ascended into the heavens; and sitteth on the right hand of the Father, and again cometh with glory to judge the quick and the dead, of whose kingdom there shall be no end:

"And in the Spirit, holy, sovereign, and life-giving.

"But those who say, 'Once He was not,' and 'Before He was begotten He was not,' and that 'He was made out of nothing,' or who say that 'the Son of God is of a different hypostasis or essence,' or 'mutable' or 'changeable'; these the catholic and apostolic church anathematizes."

The symbol of the one hundred and fifty:

"We believe in One God the Father All-sovereign, Maker of heaven and earth, and of all things visible and invisible:

"And in One Lord Jesus Christ, the only-begotten Son of God, begotten of the Father before all worlds; Light from Light, very God from very God; begotten, not made; co-essential with the Father; through whom all things were made; who for us men and for our salvation came down from the heavens, and was incarnate of the Holy Spirit and the Virgin Mary, and lived as man; was crucified also for us under Pontius Pilate, and suffered, and was buried and rose the third day according to the Scriptures; and ascended into the heavens, and sitteth on the right hand of the Father; and cometh again with glory to judge both the quick and the dead, of whose kingdom there shall be no end:

"And in the Spirit, holy, sovereign, and life-giving, who proceedeth from the Father; who with the Father and the Son is together worshiped and glorified; who spake by the prophets:

"In one holy catholic and apostolic church:

"We acknowledge one baptism for the remission of sins:

"We look for a resurrection of the dead, and a life of the world to come. Amen."

Although this wise and saving symbol of the divine grace would have been sufficient for complete knowledge and confirmation of orthodoxy, for it both teaches the perfect doctrine concerning the Father and the Son and the Holy Spirit, and sets forth the incarnation of the Lord to those who receive it faithfully; yet, forasmuch as those who attempt to set aside the preaching of the truth have produced foolish utterances through their own heresies, some daring to corrupt the mystery of the Lord's incarnation for us, and denying the title "Theotokos" to the virgin; others introducing a confusion and mixture, shamelessly imagining too the nature of the flesh and of the Godhead to be one, and absurdly maintaining that the divine nature of the only-begotten is by this confusion passible; therefore the present holy, great, and ecumenical synod, being minded to exclude all their machinations against the truth, and affirming the doctrine as unchangeable from the first, hath decreed primarily that the creed of the three hundred and eighteen holy fathers should remain inviolate; and, on account of those who contend against the Holy Spirit, it ratifies the teaching subsequently set forth by the one hundred and fifty holy fathers assembled in the imperial city concerning the essence of the Spirit, which they made known to all; not as adducing anything left lacking by their predecessors, but making distinct by scriptural testimonies their conception concerning the Holy Spirit against those who were trying to set aside His sovereignty; and, on account of those who attempt to corrupt the mystery of the incarnation, and who shamelessly pretend that He who was born of the holy Mary was a mere man, it hath received the synodical epistles of the blessed Cyril, pastor of the church of Alexandria, to Nestorius and to the Easterns, as being agreeable thereto, for the refutation of the wild notions of Nestorius and for the instruction of those who in pious zeal desire to understand the saving symbol. To these also it hath suitably united, for the confirmation of the right doctrines, the epistle of the prelate of the great and older Rome, the most blessed and most holy Archbishop Leo, which was written to the saintly Archbishop Flavian for the exclusion of the wrong opinion of Eutyches, inasmuch as it agrees with the confession of the great Peter, and is a common pillar against the heterodox.

For the synod opposes those who presume to rend the mystery of the incarnation into a duality of sons; and it expels from the company of the priests those who dare to say that the Godhead of the only-begotten is passible, and it withstands those who imagine a mixture or confusion of the two natures of Christ, and it drives away those who fancy that the form of a servant, taken by Him of us, is of a heavenly or any other essence; and it anathematizes those who imagine two natures of the Lord before the union, but fashion anew one nature after the union.

Following, then, the holy fathers, we all unanimously teach that our Lord Jesus Christ is to us one and the same Son, the self-same perfect in Godhead, the self-same perfect in manhood; truly God and truly man; the self-same of a rational soul and body; coessential with the Father according to the Godhead, the self-same co-essential with us according to the manhood; like us in all things, sin apart; before the ages begotten of the Father as to the Godhead, but in the last days, the self-same, for us and for our salvation (born) of Mary the Virgin Theotokos as to the manhood; one and the same Christ, Son, Lord, only-begotten; acknowledged in two natures unconfusedly, unchangeably, indivisibly, inseparably; the difference of the natures being in no way removed because of the union, but rather the properties of each nature being preserved, and (both) concurring into one person and one hypostasis; not as though He were parted or divided into two persons, but one and the self-same Son and only-begotten God, Word, Lord, Jesus Christ; even as from the beginning the prophets have taught concerning Him, and as the Lord Jesus Christ Himself hath taught us, and as the symbol of the fathers hath handed down to us.

These things having been defined by us with all possible accuracy and care, the holy and ecumenical synod hath decreed that it is unlawful for any one to present, write, compose, devise, or teach to others any other creed; but that those who dare either to compose another creed, or to bring forward or teach or deliver another symbol to those wishing to turn to the full knowledge of the truth from paganism or from Judaism, or from heresy of any kind whatsoever, that such persons, if bishops or clerics, shall be deposed, the bishops from the episcopate and clerics from the clerical office, and, if monks or laics, they shall be anathematized.

4

Athanasian Creed

(FIFTH CENTURY)

In 325, the Council of Nicaea met to deal with the Arian controversy, but it did not put the controversy to rest. The council affirmed the biblical teaching on Christ by declaring that He is *homoousios* (of one substance) with the Father. Arianism, however, continued to enjoy support from church leaders and even emperors.

Athanasius became bishop of Alexandria in 328 and affirmed the orthodox doctrine of Nicaea. He faced great personal risk in doing so. Constantine I, the emperor who had called the Council of Nicaea, banished Athanasius for refusing to admit Arius back into the church. After Constantine's death, his son Constantius banished Athanasius from his post several times as punishment for teaching against Arianism. Athanasius found his life in danger quite often as he held to the biblical teaching that Jesus is God. Because of his stand, it is said that the epitaph on Athanasius' grave read *Athanasius contra mundum*, or, "Athanasius against the world."

Athanasius almost certainly did not write the creed that bears his name; it was likely written in the fifth century or perhaps as late as the seventh century, eras when the church continued to battle Arianism and new threats such as Nestorianism and Eutychianism. But the creed pays homage to this courageous church leader by affirming the doctrines for which he fought.

Athanasian Creed

Whoever desires to be saved should above all hold to the catholic faith.

Anyone who does not keep it whole and unbroken will doubtless perish eternally.

Now this is the catholic faith:

That we worship one God in Trinity and the Trinity in unity,
neither confounding their persons nor dividing the essence.
>   For the person of the Father is a distinct person,
>   the person of the Son is another, and that of the Holy Spirit still
>   another.
>   But the divinity of the Father, Son, and Holy Spirit is one,
>   the glory equal, the majesty coeternal.

Such as the Father is, such is the Son and such is the Holy Spirit.
>   The Father is uncreated,
>   the Son is uncreated,
>   the Holy Spirit is uncreated.

>   The Father is immeasurable,
>   the Son is immeasurable,
>   the Holy Spirit is immeasurable.

>   The Father is eternal,
>   the Son is eternal,
>   the Holy Spirit is eternal.

>>   And yet there are not three eternal beings;
>>   there is but one eternal being.
>>   So too there are not three uncreated or immeasurable beings;
>>   there is but one uncreated and immeasurable being.

Similarly, the Father is almighty,
    the Son is almighty,
    the Holy Spirit is almighty.
    Yet there are not three almighty beings;
    there is but one almighty being.

Thus, the Father is God,
    the Son is God,
    the Holy Spirit is God.
        Yet there are not three gods;
        there is but one God.

Thus, the Father is Lord,
    the Son is Lord,
    the Holy Spirit is Lord.
        Yet there are not three lords;
        there is but one Lord.

Just as Christian truth compels us
to confess each person individually
as both God and Lord,
so catholic religion forbids us
to say that there are three gods or lords.

The Father was neither made nor created nor begotten from anyone.
The Son was neither made nor created; he was begotten from the Father
    alone.
The Holy Spirit was neither made nor created nor begotten;
he proceeds from the Father and the Son.

Accordingly, there is one Father, not three fathers;
there is one Son, not three sons;
there is one Holy Spirit, not three holy spirits.

None in this Trinity is before or after,
none is greater or smaller;
in their entirety the three persons
are coeternal and coequal with each other.

19

So in everything, as was said earlier,
the unity in Trinity, and the Trinity in unity,
is to be worshipped.

Anyone then who desires to be saved
should think thus about the Trinity.

But it is necessary for eternal salvation
that one also believe in the incarnation
of our Lord Jesus Christ faithfully.

Now this is the true faith:

That we believe and confess
that our Lord Jesus Christ, God's Son,
is both God and man, equally.

He is God from the essence of the Father,
begotten before time;
and he is man from the essence of his mother,
born in time;
completely God, completely man,
with a rational soul and human flesh;
equal to the Father as regards divinity,
less than the Father as regards humanity.

Although he is God and man,
yet Christ is not two, but one.
He is one, however,
not by his divinity being turned into flesh,
but by God's taking humanity to himself.
He is one,
certainly not by the blending of his essence,
but by the unity of his person.
For just as one man is both rational soul and flesh,
so too the one Christ is both God and man.

He suffered for our salvation;
he descended to hell;

he arose from the dead on the third day;
he ascended to heaven;
he is seated at the Father's right hand;
from there he will come to judge the living and the dead.
At his coming all people will arise bodily
and give an accounting of their own deeds.
Those who have done good will enter eternal life,
and those who have done evil will enter eternal fire.

This is the catholic faith:
That one cannot be saved without believing it firmly and faithfully.

5

Luther's Small Catechism

(1529)

Martin Luther is well known for his role in sparking the movement that came to be known as the Protestant Reformation. His posting of the Ninety-Five Theses in 1517 set the Reformation in motion, leading to a dramatic showdown with the secular and religious authorities of his day at the Diet of Worms in 1521.

But what is often not appreciated about Luther is his pastoral heart. Luther was not just a theologian and professor; he was also a priest with pastoral oversight over people, and as part of his duties he regularly preached and administered the sacraments. The Ninety-Five Theses attacked the selling of indulgences, and they did so in part out of Luther's concern that his parishioners were spending their hard-earned money on trifles that conferred no spiritual benefit. They were, in short, being deceived and exploited. Luther would leave the Roman Catholic priesthood, but he remained a pastor as the Reformation reshaped the church's understanding of the pastoral role according to Scripture.

Luther's pastoral heart is on display also in his Small Catechism. Here we see Luther's concern that the people of the church—and especially children—know, understand, and love the Christian faith. To this end, the catechism explores the Ten Commandments, the Apostles' Creed, the Lord's Prayer, and the sacraments.

Luther's Small Catechism

PART I
THE TEN COMMANDMENTS

As they should be clearly and simply explained to every household by the head of the family.

The First Commandment

Thou shalt have no other gods.

What does this mean? Answer:

We should fear and love God, and trust in him, above all things.

The Second Commandment

Thou shalt not take the name of thy God in vain.

What does this mean? Answer:

We should so fear and love God as not to curse, swear, conjure, lie, or deceive, by his name; but call upon it in every time of need, pray, praise, and give thanks.

The Third Commandment

Thou shalt keep holy the Sabbath day.

What does this mean? Answer:

We should so fear and love God as not to despise preaching and his Word, but deem it holy, and willingly hear and learn it.

The Fourth Commandment

Thou shalt honor thy father and thy mother.

What does this mean? Answer:

We should so fear and love God as not to despise nor provoke our parents and rulers, but honor, serve, obey, love, and esteem them.

The Fifth Commandment

Thou shalt not kill.

What does this mean? Answer:

We should so fear and love God as not to do our neighbor any injury or harm in his body, but help and befriend him in all bodily troubles.

The Sixth Commandment

Thou shalt not commit adultery.

What does this mean? Answer:

We should so fear and love God as to be chaste and pure in our words and deeds, and that husband and wife should love and honor each other.

The Seventh Commandment

Thou shalt not steal.

What does this mean? Answer:

We should so fear and love God as not to take our neighbor's money or property, nor get it by false ware or dealing, but help him to improve and protect his property and livelihood.

The Eighth Commandment

Thou shalt not bear false witness against thy neighbor.

What does this mean? Answer:

We should so fear and love God as not to belie, betray, or slander our neighbor, nor injure his character, but defend him, speak well of him, and make the best of all he does.

The Ninth Commandment

Thou shalt not covet thy neighbor's house.

What does this mean? Answer:

We should so fear and love God as not to try to defraud our neighbor of his inheritance or home, nor obtain it under pretext of a legal right, but aid and assist him to keep it.

The Tenth Commandment

Thou shalt not covet thy neighbor's wife, nor his man-servant, nor his maid-servant, nor his cattle, nor any thing that is his own.

What does this mean? Answer:

We should so fear and love God as not to detach, extort, or alienate from our neighbor his wife, servants, or cattle, but induce them to stay and do their duty.

What does God say about all these Commandments?

He says this: "I the Lord thy God am a jealous God, visiting the iniquity of the fathers upon the children unto the third and fourth generation of them that hate me, and showing mercy unto thousands of them that love me and keep my commandments."

What does this mean? Answer:

God threatens to punish all who transgress these Commandments: we should, therefore, fear his anger, and do nothing against such Commandments. But he promises grace and every blessing to all who keep them: we should, therefore, love and trust in him, and gladly obey his Commandments.

PART II
THE CREED

As it should be clearly and simply explained to every household by the head of the family.

The First Article: Of Creation

I believe in God the Father Almighty, Maker of heaven and earth.

What does this mean? Answer:

I believe that God has created me and all that exists; that he has given and still preserves to me body and soul, eyes, ears, and all my limbs, my reason and all my senses; and also clothing and shoes, food and drink, house and home, wife and child, land, cattle, and all my property; that he provides me richly and daily with all the necessaries of life, protects me from all danger, and preserves and guards me against all evil; and all this out of pure paternal, divine goodness and mercy, without any merit or worthiness of mine; for all which I am in duty bound to thank, praise, serve, and obey him. This is most certainly true.

The Second Article: Of Redemption

And in Jesus Christ his only Son, our Lord; who was conceived by the Holy Ghost, born of the Virgin Mary; suffered under Pontius Pilate; was crucified, dead, and buried; he descended into hell; the third day he rose again from the dead; he ascended into heaven, and sitteth on the right hand of God the Father Almighty; from thence he shall come to judge the quick and the dead.

What does this mean? Answer:

I believe that Jesus Christ, true God, begotten of the Father from eternity, and also true man, born of the Virgin Mary, is my Lord; who has redeemed me, a lost and condemned man, secured and delivered me [even] from all sins, from death, and from the power of the devil, not with gold or silver, but with his holy, precious blood, and with his innocent sufferings and death; in order that I might be his own, live under him in his kingdom, and serve him in everlasting righteousness, innocence, and blessedness, even as he is risen from the dead, and lives and reigns forever. This is most certainly true.

The Third Article: Of Sanctification

I believe in the Holy Ghost; one holy Christian Church; the Communion of Saints; the Forgiveness of Sins; the Resurrection of the Body; and the Life Everlasting. Amen.

What does this mean? Answer:

I believe that I can not, by my own reason or strength, believe in Jesus Christ my Lord, or come to him; but the Holy Ghost has called me through the Gospel, enlightened me by his gifts, and sanctified and preserved me in the true faith; just as he calls, gathers, enlightens, and sanctifies the whole Christian Church on earth, and preserves it in union with Jesus Christ in the one true faith; in which Christian Church he daily forgives richly all my sins, and the sins of all believers; and will raise up me and all the dead at the last day, and will grant everlasting life to me and to all who believe in Christ. This is most certainly true.

PART III
THE LORD'S PRAYER

As it should be clearly and simply explained to every household by the head of the family.

The Address
Our Father, who art in heaven.

What does this mean? Answer:

God would thereby affectionately encourage us to believe that he is truly our Father, and that we are truly his children, so that we may cheerfully and with all confidence pray to him, even as dear children ask their dear father.

The First Petition
Hallowed be thy name.

What does this mean? Answer:

The name of God is indeed in itself holy; but we pray in this petition that it may be hallowed also by us.

How can this be done? Answer:

When the Word of God is taught in its truth and purity, and we, as the children of God, lead holy lives accordingly. To this may our blessed Father in heaven help us! But whoever teaches and lives otherwise than as God's Word teaches, profanes the name of God among us. From this preserve us, heavenly Father!

The Second Petition
Thy kingdom come.

What does this mean? Answer:

The kingdom of God comes indeed of itself, without our prayer; but we pray in this petition that it may come also to us.

How can this be done? Answer:

When our heavenly Father gives us his Holy Spirit, so that by his grace we believe his holy Word, and live a godly life here in time, and hereafter in eternity.

The Third Petition

Thy will be done on earth, as it is in heaven.

What does this mean? Answer:

God's good, gracious will is done indeed without our prayer; but we pray in this petition that it may be done also by us.

How can this be done? Answer:

When God breaks and brings to naught every evil counsel and will which would hinder us from hallowing the name of God, and prevent his kingdom from coming to us (such as the will of the devil, of the world, and of our own flesh); but makes us strong and steadfast in his Word and faith even unto our end: this is his gracious, good will.

The Fourth Petition

Give us this day our daily bread.

What does this mean? Answer:

God gives indeed, without our prayer, even to the wicked their daily bread; but we pray in this petition that he would make us sensible [of his benefits] and enable us to receive our daily bread with thanksgiving.

What is, then, our daily bread? Answer:

All that pertains to the nourishment and needs of the body, as drink, food, clothing, shoes, house, home, land, cattle, money, property, pious husband or wife, pious children, pious servants, pious and faithful rulers, good government, good seasons, peace, health, education, honor, good friends, trusty neighbors, and the like.

The Fifth Petition

And forgive us our debts, as we forgive our debtors.

What does this mean? Answer:

We pray in this petition that our Father in heaven would not look upon our sins, nor on account of them deny our request; for we are not worthy of any thing for which we pray, and have not merited it; but that he would grant us all things through grace; for we daily sin much, and deserve nothing but punishment. We will, therefore, also on our part, heartily forgive and willingly do good to those who sin against us.

The Sixth Petition

And lead us not into temptation.

What does this mean? Answer:

God indeed tempts no one, but we pray in this petition that God would so guard and preserve us that the devil, the world, and our own flesh may not deceive us, nor lead us into misbelief, despair, and other great shame and vice; and that, though we may be thus tempted, we may nevertheless finally prevail and gain the victory.

The Seventh Petition

But deliver us from evil.

What does this mean? Answer:

We pray in this petition, as in a summary, that our Father in heaven may deliver us from all manner of evil—in body or soul, property or honor—and, at last, when our time comes, may grant us a happy end, and graciously take us from this world of sorrow to himself in heaven.

The Closing

Amen.

What does this mean? Answer:

That I should be sure that such petitions are pleasing to our Father in heaven, and are heard by him; for he himself has commanded us thus to pray, and has promised that he will hear us. Amen, Amen: that is, Yea, yea, so shall it be.

PART IV

THE SACRAMENT OF HOLY BAPTISM

As it should be clearly and simply explained to every household by the head of the family.

I.

What is Baptism?

Baptism is not simply common water, but it is the water comprehended in God's command, and connected with God's Word.

What is that Word of God?

It is that which our Lord Christ speaks in the last chapter of Matthew [28:19]: *"Go ye [into all the world], and teach all nations, baptizing them in the name of the Father, and of the Son, and of the Holy Ghost."*

II.

What does Baptism give, or of what use is it?

It worketh forgiveness of sins, delivers from death and the devil, and gives everlasting salvation to all who believe, as the Word and promise of God declare.

What are such words and promises of God?

Those which our Lord Christ speaks in the last chapter of Mark: *"He that believeth and is baptized, shall be saved; but he that believeth not, shall be damned."*

III.

How can water do such great things?

It is not water, indeed, that does it, but the Word of God which is with and in the water, and faith, which trusts in the Word of God in the water. For without the Word of God the water is nothing but water, and no baptism; but with the Word of God it is a baptism—that is, a gracious water of life and a washing of regeneration in the Holy Ghost, as St. Paul says, Titus, third chapter [3:5–8]: *"By the washing of regeneration, and renewing of the Holy Ghost, which he shed on us abundantly through Jesus Christ our Saviour; that being justified by his grace, we should be made heirs according to the hope of eternal life."* This is certainly true. [Or, *"This is a faithful saying,"* ver. 8.]

IV.

What does such baptizing with water signify?

It signifies that the old Adam in us is to be drowned by daily sorrow and repentance, and perish with all sins and evil lusts; and that the new man should daily come forth again and rise, who shall live before God in righteousness and purity forever.

Where is it so written?

St. Paul, in the 6th chapter of Romans, says: *"We are buried with Christ by baptism into death; that like as he was raised up from the dead by the glory of the Father, even so we also should walk in newness of life."*

PART V

**HOW THE UNLEARNED SHOULD BE
TAUGHT TO CONFESS**

What is confession?

Confession comprehends two parts: one, that we confess our sins; the other, that we receive absolution or forgiveness from the father confessor, as from God himself, in no wise doubting, but firmly believing that our sins are thereby forgiven before God in heaven.

What sins should we confess?

Before God we should accuse ourselves of all manner of sins, even of those which we do not ourselves perceive; as we do in the Lord's Prayer. But to the confessor we should confess those sins only which we know and feel in our hearts.

Which are these?

Here consider your condition, according to the Ten Commandments, whether you are a father or mother, a son or daughter, a master or mistress, a man-servant or maid-servant; whether you have been disobedient, unfaithful, lazy, angry, unchaste, spiteful; whether you have injured any one by words or deeds; whether you have stolen, neglected, or wasted any thing, or done any harm.

Show me a short way to confess.

Speak thus to the confessor:

Worthy, dear sir, I beseech you to hear my confession, and absolve me for God's sake.

Say:

I, poor sinner, confess before God that I am guilty of all manner of sin; in particular I confess before you that I am a man-servant, maid-servant, etc.; but, alas! I serve my master unfaithfully, for I have not done what they told me; I have moved them to anger and to cursing, have neglected my duty, and let things go to waste; I have also been immodest in words and deeds, have quarreled with my equals, have grumbled and sworn at my wife, etc. For all this I am sorry, and plead for mercy; I will do so no more.

A master or mistress should say thus:

In particular I confess before you, that I have not brought up my child, household, and wife to the glory of God; I have cursed, have set a bad example with unchaste words and actions, have injured my neighbor, have slandered, overcharged, given spurious goods and short measure.

[And so on with any thing he has done contrary to the commands of God, and to his position, etc. If, however, the conscience of any one of you is not troubled with such or greater sins, do not worry, or hunt up, or invent other sins, and thereby make a torture out of confession, but mention one or two you know of. Thus:]

In particular, I confess that I have once sworn; also, I have once used improper language, once neglected some duty, etc.

[And then stop. But if you should know of no sin (which, however, is hardly possible), then mention none in particular, but receive absolution after the general confession which you make to God before the confessor.]

Then shall the father confessor say:

God be merciful unto thee, and strengthen thy faith. Amen.

Further:

Dost thou believe that my forgiveness is the forgiveness of God?

Answer:

Yes, dear sir.

Then let him say:

As thou believest, so be it unto thee. And I, by command of our Lord Jesus Christ, forgive thee thy sins in the name of the Father, and of the Son, and of the Holy Ghost. Amen.

Depart in peace.

[Those, however, who are much troubled in conscience, or who are in distress or temptation, a father confessor will know how to comfort with Scripture passages, and stir up to faith. This is only a general method of confession for the unlearned.]

PART VI
THE SACRAMENT OF THE ALTAR

As it should be clearly and simply explained to every household by the head of the family.

What is the Sacrament of the Altar?

It is the true body and blood of our Lord Jesus Christ, under the bread and wine, given unto us Christians to eat and to drink, as it was instituted by Christ himself.

Where is it so written?

The holy Evangelists, Matthew, Mark, and Luke, together with St. Paul, write thus: *"Our Lord Jesus Christ, the same night in which he was betrayed, took bread; and when he had given thanks, he brake it, and gave it to the disciples, and said, Take, eat; this is my body, which is given for you; this do, in remembrance of me.*

"After the same manner also he took the cup, when he had supped, gave thanks, and gave it to them, saying, Drink ye all of it: this cup is the New Testament in my blood, which is shed for you, for the remission of sins: this do ye, as oft as ye drink it, in remembrance of me."

What is the use, then, of such eating and drinking?

It is pointed out to us in the words: *"Given, and shed for you, for the remission of sins."* Namely, through these words, the remission of sins, life and salvation are given us in the Sacrament: for where there is remission of sins, there are also life and salvation.

How can bodily eating and drinking do such great things?

Eating and drinking, indeed, do not do them, but the words which stand here: *"Given, and shed for you, for the remission of sins."* Which words, besides the bodily eating and drinking, are the main point in the sacrament; and he who believes these words has that which they declare and mean, namely, forgiveness of sins.

Who, then, receives this Sacrament worthily?

Fasting and bodily preparation are, indeed, a good external discipline; but he is truly worthy and well prepared who has faith in these words: *"Given, and shed for you, for the remission of sins."* But he who does not believe these words, or who doubts, is unworthy and unfit, for the words *"for you"* require truly believing hearts.

6

Augsburg Confession

(1530)

The Protestant Reformation was not only a religious movement but also a political one. As it spread across Germany, the various princes of the disparate German states—at that time constituent parts of the Holy Roman Empire—had to reckon with the changes that the Reformation was bringing to society. Change is often not welcome, for change brings upheaval—a tendency that was demonstrated in the German Peasants' War of 1524–25.

Emperor Charles V soon decided it was time to end the religious strife that was roiling his empire. To that end, he convoked the Diet of Augsburg in 1530, which had as one of its aims the achievement of religious and political unity so that the Christian empire could meet the threat of the Muslim Ottoman Empire.

The Lutheran princes and theologians, led by Luther's friend Philip Melanchthon, drafted the Augsburg Confession as a summary of the beliefs of the Reformation and as an attempt to find common ground with the Roman Catholic Church in the historic beliefs of Christianity. Tensions continued between the Lutheran and Roman Catholic sides, however, and it was not until 1555 with the Peace of Augsburg that Charles acknowledged the legitimacy of Protestantism in the empire.

Augsburg Confession

CONFESSION OF FAITH

Presented to the Invincible Emperor Charles V., Cæsar Augustus, at the Diet of Augsburg, Anno Domini MDXXX.

I will speak of thy testimonies also before kings, and will not be ashamed. —Psalm 119:46.

PREFACE TO THE EMPEROR CHARLES V

Most Invincible Emperor, Cæsar Augustus, Most Clement Master: Inasmuch as Your Imperial Majesty has summoned a Convention of the Empire at Augsburg, to deliberate in regard to aid against the Turk, the most atrocious, the hereditary, and ancient enemy of the Christian name and religion, in what way, to wit, resistance might be made to his rage and assaults, by protracted and perpetual preparation for war: Because, moreover, of dissensions in the matter of our holy religion and Christian faith, and in order that in this matter of religion the opinions and judgments of diverse parties may be heard in each other's presence, may be understood and weighed among one another, in mutual charity, meekness, and gentleness, that those things which in the writings on either side have been handled or understood amiss, being laid aside and corrected, these things may be harmonized and brought back to the one simple truth and Christian concord; so that hereafter the one unfeigned and true religion may be embraced and preserved by us, so that as we are subjects and soldiers of the one Christ, so also, in unity and concord, we may live in the one Christian Church: And inasmuch as we, the Elector and Princes, whose names are subscribed, together with others who are conjoined with us, in common with other Electors, and Princes, and States, have been called to the aforenamed Diet,—we have, in order to render most humble obedience to the Imperial Mandate, come early to Augsburg, and, with no desire to boast, would state that we were among the very first to be present.

When, therefore, Your Imperial Majesty, among other things, has also at Augsburg, at the very beginning of these sessions, caused the proposition to be made to the Princes and States of the Empire, that each of the States of the Empire, in virtue of the Imperial Edict, should propose and offer in the German and in the Latin language its opinion and decision; after discussion on Wednesday we replied to Your Imperial Majesty, that on the following Friday we would offer on our part the Articles of our Confession:

Wherefore, in order that we may do homage to the will of Your Imperial Majesty, we now offer in the matter of religion the Confession of our preachers and of ourselves, the doctrine of which, derived from the Holy Scriptures and pure Word of God, they have to this time set forth in our lands, dukedoms, domains, and cities, and have taught in the churches. If the other Electors, Princes, and States of the Empire, should in similar writings, to wit, in Latin and German, according to the aforementioned Imperial proposition, produce their opinions in this matter of religion: we here, in the presence of Your Imperial Majesty, our most Clement Lord, offer ourselves, prepared, in conjunction with the Princes and our friends already designated, to compare views in a kindly manner in regard to mode and ways which may be available, so that, as far as may honorably be done, we may agree, and the matter between us of both parts being peacefully discussed, with no hateful contention, by God's help the dissension may be removed, and brought back to one true accordant religion (as we are all subjects and soldiers under one Christ, so also we ought to confess one Christ, in accordance with the tenor of the decree of Your Imp. M.), and all things should be brought back to the truth of God, which with most fervent prayers we beseech God to grant.

But if, as regards the rest of the Electors, Princes, and States, those of the other party, this treatment of the matter of religion, in the manner in which Your Imperial Majesty has wisely thought fit it should be conducted and treated, to wit, with such a mutual presentation of writings and calm conference between us, should not go on, nor be attended by any result; yet shall we leave a clear testimony that in no manner do we evade any thing which can tend to promote Christian concord (any thing which God and a good conscience allow); and this Your Imperial Majesty and the other Electors and States of the Empire, and all who are moved by a sincere love of religion and concern for it, all who are willing to give an equitable hearing in this matter, will kindly gather and understand from the Confession of ourselves and of ours.

Since, moreover, Your Imperial Majesty has not once only, but repeatedly signified to the Electors, Princes, and other States of the Empire; and at the Diet of Spires, which was held in the year of our Lord 1526, caused to be recited and publicly proclaimed, in accordance with the form of Your Imperial instruction and commission given and prescribed: That Your Imperial Majesty in this matter of religion for certain reasons, stated in the name of Your Majesty, was not willing to determine, nor was able to conclude touching any thing, but that Your Imperial Majesty would diligently endeavor to have the Roman Pontiff, in accordance with his office, to assemble a General Council; as also the same matter was more amply set forth a year ago in the last public Convention, which was held at spires, where through His Highness Ferdinand, King of Bohemia and Hungary, our friend and clement Lord, afterward through the Orator and the Imperial Commissioners, Your Imperial Majesty, among other propositions, caused these to be made: that your Imperial Majesty had known and pondered the resolution to convene a Council, formed by the Representatives of Your Imperial Majesty in the Empire, and by the Imperial President and Counselors, and by the Legates of other States convened at Ratisbon, and this Your Imperial Majesty also judged that it would be useful to assemble a Council; and because the matters which were to be adjusted at this time between Your Imperial Majesty and the Roman Pontiff were approaching agreement and Christian reconciliation, Your Imperial Majesty did not doubt that, but that the Pope could be induced to summon a General Council: Wherefore Your Imperial Majesty signified that Your Imperial Majesty would endeavor to bring it to pass that the Chief Pontiff, together with Your Imperial Majesty, would consent at the earliest opportunity to issue letters for the convening of such a General Council.

In the event, therefore, that in this matter of religion the differences between us and the other party should not be settled in friendship and love, we here present ourselves before Your Imperial Majesty in all obedience, as we have done before, ready to appear and to defend our cause in such a general, free, and Christian Council, concerning the convening of which there has been concordant action and a determination by agreeing votes on the part of the Electors, Princes, and the other States of the Empire, in all the Imperial Diets which have been held in the reign of Your Imperial Majesty. To this Convention of a General Council, as also to Your Imperial Majesty, we have in the due method and legal form before made our protestation and appeal in this greatest and gravest of matters. To which appeal both to Your Imperial Majesty and a Council we still adhere; nor do we intend, nor would it be possible for us to forsake it by this or any other document, unless the matter between us and the other party should, in accordance with the tenor of the latest Imperial citation, be adjusted, settled, and brought to Christian concord, in friendship and love; concerning which appeal we here also make our solemn and public protest.

PART FIRST
CHIEF ARTICLES OF FAITH
ART. I.—OF GOD

The churches, with common consent among us, do teach that the decree of the Nicene Synod concerning the unity of the divine essence and of the three persons is true, and without doubt to be believed: to wit, that there is one divine essence which is called and is God, eternal, without body, indivisible [without part], of infinite power, wisdom, goodness, the Creator and Preserver of all things, visible and invisible; and that yet there are three persons of the same essence and power, who also are coeternal, the Father, the Son, and the Holy Ghost. And they use the name of person in that signification in which the ecclesiastical writers [the Fathers] have used it in this cause, to signify, not a part or qualify in another, but that which properly subsists.

They condemn all heresies which have sprung up against this Article, as the Manichees, who set down two principles, good and evil; in the same manner the Valentinians, Arians, Eunomians, Mohammedans, and all such like. They condemn also the Samosatenes, old and new; who, when they earnestly contend that there is but one person, do craftily and wickedly trifle, after the manner of rhetoricians, about the Word and Holy Ghost, that they are not distinct persons, but that the Word signifieth a vocal word, and the Spirit a motion created in things.

ART. II.—OF ORIGINAL SIN

Also they teach that, after Adam's fall, all men begotten after the common course of nature are born with sin; that is, without the fear of God, without trust in him, and with fleshly appetite; and that this disease, or original fault, is truly sin, condemning and bringing eternal death now also upon all that are not born again by baptism and the Holy Spirit.

They condemn the Pelagians, and others, who deny this original fault to be sin indeed; and who, so as to lessen the glory of the merits and benefits of Christ, argue that a man may, by the strength of his own reason, be justified before God.

ART. III.—OF THE SON OF GOD

Also they teach that the Word, that is, the Son of God, took unto him man's nature in the womb of the blessed Virgin Mary, so that there are two natures, the divine and the human, inseparably joined together in unity of person; one Christ, true God and true man: who was born of the Virgin Mary, truly suffered, was crucified, dead, and buried, that he might reconcile the Father unto us, and might be a sacrifice, not only for original guilt, but also for all actual sins of men.

The same also descended into hell, and truly rose again the third day. Afterward he ascended into the heavens, that he might sit at the right hand of the Father; and reign forever, and have dominion over all creatures; might sanctify those that believe in him, by sending the Holy Spirit into their hearts, who shall rule [sanctify, purify, strengthen], comfort, and quicken them, and shall defend them against the devil, and the power of sin.

The same Christ shall openly come again, to judge the quick and the dead, according as the Apostles' Creed declareth these and other things.

ART. IV.—OF JUSTIFICATION

Also they teach that men can not be justified [obtain forgiveness of sins and righteousness] before God by their own powers, merits, or works; but are justified freely [of grace] for Christ's sake through faith, when they believe that they are received into favor, and their sins forgiven for Christ's sake, who by his death hath satisfied for our sins. This faith doth God impute for righteousness before him. Rom. 3 and 4.

ART. V.—OF THE MINISTRY OF THE CHURCH

For the obtaining of this faith, the ministry of teaching the Gospel and administering the Sacraments was instituted.

For by the Word and Sacraments, as by instruments, the Holy Spirit is given: who worketh faith, where and when it pleaseth God, in those that hear the Gospel, to wit, that God, not for our merit's sake, but for Christ's sake, doth justify those who believe that they for Christ's sake are received into favor.

They condemn the Anabaptists and others, who imagine that the Holy Spirit is given to men without the outward word, through their own preparations and works.

ART. VI.—OF NEW OBEDIENCE

Also they teach that this faith should bring forth good fruits, and that men ought to do the good works commanded of God, because it is God's will, and not on any confidence of meriting justification before God by their works.

For remission of sins and justification is apprehended by faith, as also the voice of Christ witnesseth: "When ye have done all these things, say, We are unprofitable servants."

The same also do the ancient writers of the Church teach; for Ambrose saith: "This is ordained of God, that he that believeth in Christ shall be saved, without works, by faith alone, freely receiving remission of sins."

ART. VII.—OF THE CHURCH

Also they teach that one holy Church is to continue forever. But the Church is the congregation of saints [the assembly of all believers], in which the Gospel is rightly taught [purely preached] and the Sacraments rightly administered [according to the Gospel].

And unto the true unity of the Church, it is sufficient to agree concerning the doctrine of the Gospel and the administration of the Sacraments. Nor is it necessary that human traditions, rites, or ceremonies instituted by men should be alike every where, as St. Paul saith: "There is one faith, one baptism, one God and Father of all."

ART. VIII. — WHAT THE CHURCH IS

Though the Church be properly the congregation of saints and true believers, yet seeing that in this life many hypocrites and evil persons are mingled with it, it is lawful to use the Sacraments administered by evil men, according to the voice of Christ (Matt. 23:2): "The Scribes and the Pharisees sit in Moses' seat," and the words following. And the Sacraments and the Word are effectual, by reason of the institution and commandment of Christ, though they be delivered by evil men.

They condemn the Donatists and such like, who denied that it was lawful to use the ministry of evil men in the Church, and held that the ministry of evil men is useless and without effect.

ART. IX. — OF BAPTISM

Of Baptism they teach that it is necessary to salvation, and that by Baptism the grace of God is offered, and that children are to be baptized, who by Baptism, being offered to God, are received into God's favor.

They condemn the Anabaptists who allow not the Baptism of children, and affirm that children are saved without Baptism.

ART. X. — OF THE LORD'S SUPPER

Of the Supper of the Lord they teach that the [true] body and blood of Christ are truly present [under the form of bread and wine], and are [there] communicated to those that eat in the Lord's Supper [and received]. And they disapprove of those that teach otherwise [wherefore also the opposite doctrine is rejected].

ART. XI. — OF CONFESSION

Concerning confession, they teach that private absolution be retained in the churches, though enumeration of all offenses be not necessary in confession. For it is impossible; according to the Psalm: "Who can understand his errors?"

ART. XII. — OF REPENTANCE

Touching repentance, they teach that such as have fallen after baptism may find remission of sins, at what time they are converted [whenever they come to repentance], and that the Church should give absolution unto such as return to repentance.

Now repentance consisteth properly of these two parts: One is contrition; or terrors stricken into the conscience through the acknowledgment of sin; the other is faith, which is conceived by the Gospel, or absolution, and doth believe that for Christ's sake sins be forgiven, and comforteth the conscience, and freeth it from terrors. Then should follow good works, which are fruits of repentance.

They condemn the Anabaptists, who deny that men once justified can lose the Spirit of God, and do contend that some men may attain to such a perfection in this life that they can not sin. [Here are rejected those who teach that those who have once been holy can not fall again.] The Novatians are also condemned, who would not absolve such as had fallen after baptism, though they returned to repentance. They also that do not teach that remission of sins is obtained by faith, and who command us to merit grace by satisfactions, are rejected.

ART. XIII.—OF THE USE OF SACRAMENTS

Concerning the use of the Sacraments, they teach that they were ordained, not only to be marks of profession among men, but rather that they should be signs and testimonies of the will of God towards us, set forth unto us to stir up and confirm faith in such as use them. Therefore men must use Sacraments so as to join faith with them, which believes the promises that are offered and declared unto us by the Sacraments.

Wherefore they condemn those that teach that the Sacraments do justify by the work done, and do not teach that faith which believes the remission of sins is requisite in the use of Sacraments.

ART. XIV.—OF ECCLESIASTICAL ORDERS

Concerning Ecclesiastical Orders [Church Government], they teach that no man should publicly in the Church teach, or administer the Sacraments, except he be rightly called [without a regular call].

ART. XV.—OF ECCLESIASTICAL RITES

Concerning Ecclesiastical rites [made by men], they teach that those rites are to be observed which may be observed without sin, and are profitable for tranquillity and good order in the Church; such as are set holidays, feasts, and such like. Yet concerning such things, men are to be admonished that consciences are not to be burdened as if such service were necessary to salvation.

They are also to be admonished that human traditions, instituted to pro-pitiate God, to merit grace, and make satisfaction for sins, are opposed to the Gospel and the doctrine of faith. Wherefore vows and traditions concerning foods and days, and such like, instituted to merit grace and make satisfaction for sins, are useless and contrary to the Gospel.

ART. XVI.—OF CIVIL AFFAIRS

Concerning civil affairs, they teach that such civil ordinances as are lawful are good works of God; that Christians may lawfully bear civil office, sit in judg-ments, determine matters by the imperial laws, and other laws in present force, appoint just punishments, engage in just war, act as soldiers, make legal bar-gains and contracts, hold property, take an oath when the magistrates require it, marry a wife, or be given in marriage. They condemn the Anabaptists who forbid Christians these civil offices. They condemn also those that place the perfection of the Gospel, not in the fear of God and in faith, but in forsak-ing civil offices, inasmuch as the Gospel teacheth an everlasting righteousness of the heart. In the mean time, it doth not disallow order and government of commonwealths or families, but requireth especially the preservation and maintenance thereof, as of God's own ordinances, and that in such ordinances we should exercise love. Christians, therefore, must necessarily obey their magistrates and laws, save only when they command any sin; for then they must rather obey God than men (Acts 5:29).

ART. XVII.—OF CHRIST'S RETURN TO JUDGMENT

Also they teach that, in the consummation of the world [at the last day], Christ shall appear to judge, and shall raise up all the dead, and shall give unto the godly and elect eternal life and everlasting joys; but ungodly men and the devils shall he condemn unto endless torments.

They condemn the Anabaptists who think that to condemned men and the devils shall be an end of torments. They condemn others also, who now scatter Jewish opinions, that, before the resurrection of the dead, the godly shall occupy the kingdom of the world, the wicked being every where suppressed [the saints alone, the pious, shall have a worldly kingdom, and shall exterminate all the godless].

ART. XVIII.—OF FREE WILL

Concerning free will, they teach that man's will hath some liberty to work a civil righteousness, and to choose such things as reason can reach unto; but that it hath no power to work the righteousness of God, or a spiritual righteousness, without the Spirit of God; because that the natural man receiveth not the things of the Spirit of God (1 Cor. 2:14). But this is wrought in the heart when men do receive the Spirit of God through the Word.

These things are in as many words affirmed by St. Augustine, *Hypognosticon*, lib. iii.: "We confess that there is in all men a free will, which hath indeed the judgment of reason; not that it is thereby fitted, without God, either to begin or to perform any thing in matters pertaining to God, but only in works belonging to this present life, whether they be good or evil. By good works, I mean those which are of the goodness of nature; as to will to labor in the field, to desire meat or drink, to desire to have a friend, to desire apparel, to desire to build a house, to marry a wife, to nourish cattle, to learn the art of divers good things, to desire any good thing pertaining to this present life; all which are not without God's government, yea, they are, and had their beginning from God and by God. Among evil things, I account such as these: to will to worship an image; to will manslaughter, and such like."

They condemn the Pelagians and others, who teach that by the powers of nature alone, without the Spirit of God, we are able to love God above all things; also to perform the commandments of God, as touching the substance of our actions. For although nature be able in some sort to do the external works (for it is able to withhold the hands from theft and murder), yet it can not work the inward motions, such as the fear of God, trust in God, chastity, patience, and such like.

ART. XIX.—OF THE CAUSE OF SIN

Touching the cause of sin, they teach that, although God doth create and preserve nature, yet the cause of sin is the will of the wicked; to wit, of the devil and ungodly men; which will, God not aiding, turneth itself from God, as Christ saith: "When he speaketh a lie, he speaketh of his own" (John 8:44).

ART. XX. — OF GOOD WORKS

Ours are falsely accused of forbidding good works. For their writings extant upon the Ten Commandments, and others of the like argument, do bear witness that they have to good purpose taught concerning every kind of life, and its duties; what kinds of life, and what works in every calling, do please God. Of which things preachers in former times taught little or nothing: only they urged certain childish and needless works; as, keeping of holidays, set fasts, fraternities, pilgrimages, worshiping of saints, the use of rosaries, monkery, and such like things. Whereof our adversaries having had warning, they do now unlearn them, and do not preach concerning these unprofitable works, as they were wont. Besides, they begin now to make mention of faith, concerning which there was formerly a deep silence. They teach that we are not justified by works alone; but they conjoin faith and works, and say we are justified by faith and works. Which doctrine is more tolerable than the former one, and can afford more consolation than their old doctrine.

Whereas, therefore, the doctrine of faith, which should be the chief one in the Church, hath been so long unknown, as all men must needs grant, that there was the deepest silence about the righteousness of faith in their sermons, and that the doctrine of works was usual in the churches; for this cause our divines did thus admonish the churches:

First, that our works can not reconcile God, or deserve remission of sins, grace, and justification at his hands, but that these we obtain by faith only, when we believe that we are received into favor for Christ's sake, who alone is appointed the Mediator and Propitiatory, by whom the Father is reconciled. He, therefore, that trusteth by his works to merit grace, doth despise the merit and grace of Christ, and seeketh by his own power, without Christ, to come unto the Father; whereas Christ hath said expressly of himself, "I am the way, the truth, and the life" (John 14:6).

This doctrine of faith is handled by Paul almost every where: "By grace ye are saved through faith, and that not of yourselves: it is the gift of God, not of works" (Eph. 2:8–9). And lest any here should cavil, that we bring in a new-found interpretation, this whole cause is sustained by testimonies of the Fathers. Augustine doth in many volumes defend grace, and the righteousness of faith, against the merit of works. The like doth Ambrose teach in his book, *De Vocatione Gentium*, and elsewhere; for thus he saith of the calling of the

Gentiles: "The redemption made by the blood of Christ would be of small account, and the prerogative of man's works would not give place to the mercy of God, if the justification which is by grace were due to merits going before; so as it should not be the liberality of the giver, but the wages or hire of the laborer."

This doctrine, though it be contemned of the unskillful, yet godly and fearful consciences find by experience that it bringeth very great comfort: because that consciences can not be quieted by any works, but by faith alone, when they believe assuredly that they have a God who is propitiated for Christ's sake; as St. Paul teacheth, "Being justified by faith, we have peace with God" (Rom. 5:1). This doctrine doth wholly belong to the conflict of a troubled conscience; and can not be understood, but where the conscience hath felt that conflict. Wherefore, all such as have had no experience thereof, and all that are profane men, who dream that Christian righteousness is naught else but a civil and philosophical righteousness, are poor judges of this matter.

Formerly men's consciences were vexed with the doctrine of works; they did not hear any comfort out of the Gospel. Whereupon conscience drove some into the desert, into monasteries, hoping there to merit grace by a monastical life. Others devised other works, whereby to merit grace, and to satisfy for sin. There was very great need, therefore, to teach and renew this doctrine of faith in Christ; to the end that fearful consciences might not want comfort, but might know that grace, and forgiveness of sins, and justification, are received by faith in Christ.

Another thing, which we teach men, is that in this place the name of FAITH doth not only signify a knowledge of the history, which may be in the wicked, and in the devil, but that it signifieth a faith which believeth, not only the history, but also the effect of the history; to wit, the article of remission of sins; namely, that by Christ we have grace, righteousness, and remission of sins. Now he that knoweth that he hath the Father merciful to him through Christ, this man knoweth God truly; he knoweth that God hath a care of him; he loveth God, and calleth upon him; in a word, he is not without God, as the Gentiles are. For the devils and the wicked can never believe this article of the remission of sins; and therefore they hate God as their enemy; they call not upon him, they look for no good thing at his hands. After this manner doth Augustine admonish the reader touching the name of Faith, and teacheth that this word Faith is taken in Scriptures, not for such a knowledge as is in the wicked, but for a trust, which doth comfort and lift up disquieted minds.

Moreover, ours teach that it is necessary to do good works; not that we may trust that we deserve grace by them, but because it is the will of God that we should do them. By faith alone is apprehended remission of sins and grace. And because the Holy Spirit is received by faith, our hearts are now renewed, and so put on new affections, so that they are able to bring forth good works. For thus saith Ambrose: "Faith is the begetter of a good will and of good actions." For man's powers, without the Holy Spirit, are full of wicked affections, and are too weak to perform any good deed before God. Besides, they are in the devil's power, who driveth men forward into divers sins, into profane opinions, and into heinous crimes; as was to be seen in the philosophers, who, assaying to live an honest life, could not attain unto it, but were defiled with many heinous crimes. Such is the weakness of man, when he is without faith and the Holy Spirit, and hath no other guide but the natural powers of man.

Hereby every man may see that this doctrine is not to be accused, as forbidding good works; but rather is much to be commended, because it showeth after what sort we must do good works. For without faith the nature of man can by no means perform the works of the First or Second Table. Without faith, it can not call upon God, hope in God, bear the cross; but seeketh help from man, and trusteth in man's help. So it cometh to pass that all lusts and human counsels bear sway in the heart so long as faith and trust in God are absent.

Wherefore, also, Christ saith, "Without me ye can do nothing" (John 15:5), and the Church singeth, "Without thy power is naught in man, naught that is innocent."

ART. XXI. —OF THE WORSHIP OF SAINTS

Touching the worship of saints, they teach that the memory of saints may be set before us, that we may follow their faith and good works according to our calling; as the Emperor may follow David's example in making war to drive away the Turks from his country; for either of them is a king. But the Scripture teacheth not to invocate saints, or to ask help of saints, because it propoundeth unto us one Christ the Mediator, Propitiatory, High-Priest, and Intercessor. This Christ is to be invocated, and he hath promised that he will hear our prayers, and liketh this worship especially, to wit, that he be invocated in all afflictions. "If any man sin, we have an advocate with God, Jesus Christ the righteous" (1 John 2:1).

This is about the sum of doctrine among us, in which can be seen that there is nothing which is discrepant with the Scriptures, or with the Church Catholic, or even with the Roman Church, so far as that Church is known from writers [the writings of the Fathers]. This being the case, they judge us harshly who insist that we shall be regarded as heretics. But the dissension is concerning certain [traditions and] abuses, which without any certain authority have crept into the churches; in which things, even if there were some difference, yet would it be a becoming lenity on the part of the bishops that, on account of the Confession which we have now presented, they should bear with us, since not even the Canons are so severe as to demand the same rites every where, nor were the rites of all churches at any time the same. Although among us in large part the ancient rites are diligently observed. For it is a calumnious falsehood, that all the ceremonies, all the things instituted of old, are abolished in our churches. But the public complaint was that certain abuses were connected with the rites in common use. These, because they could not with good conscience be approved, have to some extent been corrected.

PART SECOND
ARTICLES IN WHICH ARE RECOUNTED THE ABUSES WHICH HAVE BEEN CORRECTED

Inasmuch as the churches among us dissent in no article of faith from [the holy Scriptures, or] the Church Catholic [the Universal Christian Church], and only omit a few of certain abuses, which are novel [in part have crept in with time, in part have been introduced by violence], and, contrary to the purport of the Canons, have been received by the fault of the times, we beg that Your Imperial Majesty would clemently hear both what ought to be changed and what are the reasons that the people ought not to be forced against their consciences to observe those abuses.

Nor should Your Imperial Majesty have faith in those who, that they may inflame the hatred of men against us, scatter amazing slanders among the people. In this way, the minds of good men being angered at the beginning, they gave occasion to this dissension, and by the same art they now endeavor to increase the discords. For beyond doubt your Imperial Majesty will find that the form, both of doctrines and of ceremonies, among us is far more tolerable than that which these wicked and malicious men describe. The truth, moreover, can not be gathered from common rumors and the reproaches of enemies. But it is easy to judge this, that nothing is more profitable to preserve the dignity of ceremonies and to nurture reverence and piety among the people than that the ceremonies should be rightly performed in the churches.

ART. I. — OF BOTH KINDS [IN THE LORD'S SUPPER]

Both kinds of the Sacrament in the Lord's Supper are given to the laity, because that this custom hath the commandment of the Lord: "Drink ye all of this" (Matt. 26:27); where Christ doth manifestly command concerning the cup that all should drink. And that no man might cavil that this doth only pertain to the priests, the example of Paul to the Corinthians witnesseth that the whole Church did use both kinds in common (1 Cor. 11:28). And this custom remained a long time in the Church; neither is it certain when or by what authority it was changed; although the Cardinal de Cusa relates when it was approved. [And this custom remained a long time in the churches, as may be proved from history and the writings of the Fathers.] Cyprian in certain places doth witness that the blood was given to the people; the same thing doth Jerome testify, saying, "The priests do minister the Eucharist, and communicate the blood of Christ to the people." Nay, Pope Gelasius commandeth that the Sacrament be not divided (*Dist. II., De Consecr. Cap. Comperimus*). Only a custom, not thus ancient, doth otherwise. But it is manifest that a custom, brought in contrary to the commandments of God, is not to be approved, as the Canons do witness (*Dist. VIII., Cap. Veritate*) with the words which follow. Now this custom has been received, not only against the Scripture, but also against the ancient Canons and the example of the Church.

ART. II. — OF THE MARRIAGE OF PRIESTS

There was a common complaint of the examples of such priests as were not continent. For which cause Pope Pius is reported to have said, that "there were certain causes for which marriage was forbidden to priests, but there were many weightier causes why it should be permitted again;" for so Platina writeth. Whereas, therefore, the priests among us seek to avoid these public offenses, they have married wives, and have taught that it is lawful for them to enter into marriage. First, because that Paul saith, "To avoid fornication, let every man have his wife;" again, "It is better to marry than to burn" (1 Cor. 7:2, 9). Secondly, Christ saith, "All men can not receive this word" (Matt. 19:11); where he showeth that all men are not fit for a single life, because that God created man kind male and female (Gen. 1:28). Nor is it in man's power, without a special gift and work of God, to alter his creation. Therefore such as are not meet for a single life ought to contract marriage. For no law of man, no vow, can take away the commandment of God and his ordinance. By these reasons the priests do prove that they may lawfully take wives. And it is well known that in the ancient churches priests were married. For Paul saith, "That a bishop must be chosen which is a husband" (1 Tim. 3:2). And in Germany, not until about four hundred years ago, were the priests by violence compelled to live a single life; who then were so wholly bent against the matter, that the Archbishop of Mentz, being about to publish the Pope of Rome's decree to that effect, was almost murdered in a tumult by the priests in their anger. And the matter was handled so rudely, that not only were marriages forbidden for the time to come, but also such as were then contracted were broken asunder, contrary to all laws divine and human, contrary to the Canons themselves, that were before made not only by Popes, but also by most famous Councils. And seeing that, as the world decayeth, man's nature by little and little waxeth weaker, it is well to look to it, that no more vices do overspread Germany. Furthermore, God ordained marriage to be a remedy for man's infirmity. The Canons themselves do say that the old rigor is now and then in latter times to be released because of the weakness of men. Which it were to be wished might be done in this matter also. And if marriage be forbidden any longer, the churches may at length want pastors.

Seeing, then, that there is a plain commandment of God; seeing the use of the Church is well known; seeing that impure single life bringeth forth very many offenses, adulteries, and other enormities worthy to be punished by the godly magistrate, it is a marvel that greater cruelty should be showed in no other thing than against the marriage of priests. God hath commanded to honor marriage; the laws in all well-ordered commonwealths, even among the heathen, have adorned marriage with very great honors. But now men are cruelly put to death, yea, and priests also, contrary to the mind of the Canons, for no other cause but marriage. Paul calleth that "a doctrine of devils" which forbiddeth marriage (1 Tim. 4:1, 3); which may now very well be seen, since the forbidding of marriage is maintained by such punishments.

But as no law of man can take away the law of God, no more can any vow whatsoever. Therefore Cyprian also giveth counsel, that those women should marry who do not keep their vowed chastity. His words are these, in the 1st Book, the 2d Epistle: "If they will not or are not able to endure, it is far better they should marry than that they should fall into the fire by their importunate desires. In any wise let them give no offense to their brethren or sisters." Yea, even the Canons show some kind of justice towards such as before their ripe years did vow chastity, as hitherto the use hath for the most part been.

ART. III. — OF THE MASS

Our churches are wrongfully accused to have abolished the Mass. For the Mass is retained still among us, and celebrated with great reverence; yea, and almost all the ceremonies that are in use, saving that with the things sung in Latin we mingle certain things sung in German at various parts of the service, which are added for the people's instruction. For therefore alone we have need of ceremonies, that they may teach the unlearned.

This is not only commanded by St. Paul, to use a tongue that the people understand (1 Cor. 14:9), but man's law hath also appointed it. We accustom the people to receive the Sacrament together, if so any be found fit thereunto; and that is a thing that doth increase the reverence and due estimation of the public ceremonies. For none are admitted, except they be first proved. Besides, we put men in mind of the worthiness and use of the Sacrament, how great comfort it bringeth to timid consciences; that they may learn to believe God, and to look for and crave all good things at his hands.

This worship doth please God; such a use of the Sacrament doth nourish piety towards God. Therefore it seemeth not that Masses be more religiously celebrated among our adversaries than with us.

But it is evident that of long time this hath been the public and most grievous complaint of all good men, that Masses are basely profaned, being used for gain. And it is not unknown how far this abuse hath spread itself in all churches; of what manner of men Masses are used, only for a reward, or for wages; and how many do use them against the prohibition of the Canons. But Paul doth grievously threaten those who treat the Lord's Supper unworthily, saying, "He that eateth this bread or drinketh this cup of the Lord unworthily, shall be guilty of the body and blood of the Lord" (1 Cor. 11:27). Therefore, when the priests among us were admonished of this sin, private Masses were laid aside among us, seeing that for the most part there were no private Masses but only for lucre's sake. Neither were the bishops ignorant of these abuses, and if they had amended them in time, there had now been less of dissensions. Heretofore, by their dissembling, they suffered much corruption to creep into the Church; now they begin, though it be late, to complain of the calamities of the Church; seeing that this tumult was raised up by no other mean than by those abuses, which were so evident that they could no longer be tolerated. There were many dissensions, concerning the Mass, concerning the Sacrament. And perhaps the world is punished for so long a profaning of Masses, which they, who both could and ought to have amended it, have so many years tolerated in the churches. For in the Ten Commandments it is written, "He that taketh in vain the name of the Lord shall not be held guiltless" (Ex. 20:7). And from the beginning of the world there neither was nor is any divine thing which seems so to have been employed for gain as the Mass.

There was added an opinion, which increased private Masses infinitely: to wit, that Christ by his passion did satisfy for original sin, and appointed the Mass, wherein an oblation should be made for daily sins, both mortal and venial. Hereupon a common opinion was received, that the Mass is a work that taketh away the sins of the quick and the dead, and that for the doing of the work. Here men began to dispute, whether one Mass said for many were of as great force as particular Masses said for particular men. This disputation hath brought forth that infinite multitude of Masses. Our preachers have admonished concerning these opinions that they do depart from the holy Scriptures, and diminish the glory of the passion of Christ. For the passion of Christ was an oblation and satisfaction, not only for original sin, but also for all other sins; as it is written in the Epistle to the Hebrews (10:10): "We are sanctified by the oblation of Jesus Christ once made;" also, "By one oblation he hath perfected forever them that are sanctified" (Heb. 10:14). The Scripture also teacheth that we are justified before God through faith in Christ, when we believe that our sins are forgiven for Christ's sake. Now, if the Mass do take away the sins of the quick and the dead, even for the work's sake that is done, then justification cometh by the work of Masses, and not by faith; which the Scripture can not endure. But Christ commandeth us "to do it in remembrance of himself" (Luke 22:19), therefore the Mass has been instituted that faith in them which use the Sacrament may remember what benefits it receiveth by Christ, and that it may raise and comfort the fearful conscience. For this is to remember Christ, to wit, to remember his benefits, and to feel and perceive that they be indeed imparted unto us. Nor is it sufficient to call to mind the history; because that the Jews also and the wicked can do. Therefore the Mass must be used to this end, that there the Sacrament may be reached unto them that have need of comfort; as Ambrose saith, "Because I do always sin, therefore I ought always to receive the medicine."

And seeing that the Mass is such a communion of the Sacrament, we do observe one common Mass every holy day, and on other days, if any will use the Sacrament, at which times it is offered to them that desire it. Neither is this custom newly brought into the Church. For the ancients, before Gregory's time, make no mention of any private Mass; of the common Mass they speak much. Chrysostom saith that "the priest doth daily stand at the altar, and call some unto the Communion, and put back others." And by the ancient Canons it is evident that some one did celebrate the Mass, of whom the other elders and deacons did receive the body of the Lord. For so the words of the Nicene Canon do sound: "Let the deacons in their order, after the elders, receive the holy Communion of a bishop, or of an elder." And Paul, concerning the Communion, commandeth, "that one tarry for another" (1 Cor. 11:33), that so there may be a common participation.

Seeing, therefore, that the Mass amongst us hath the example of the Church, out of the Scripture, and the Fathers, we trust that it can not be disapproved; especially since our public ceremonies are kept, the most part, like unto the usual ceremonies; only the number of Masses is not alike, the which, by reason of very great and manifest abuses, it were certainly far better to be moderated. For in times past also, in the churches whereunto was greatest resort, it was not the use to have Mass said every day, as the Tripartite History, lib. ix. cap. 38, doth witness. "Again," saith it, "in Alexandria, every fourth and sixth day of the week, the Scriptures are read, and the doctors do interpret them; and all other things are done also, except only the celebration of the Eucharist."

ART. IV.—OF CONFESSION

Confession is not abolished in our churches. For it is not usual to communicate the body of our Lord, except to those who have been previously examined and absolved. And the people are taught most carefully concerning the faith required to absolution, about which before these times there has been a deep silence. Men are taught that they should highly regard absolution, inasmuch as it is God's voice, and pronounced by God's command.

The power of the keys is honored, and mention is made how great consolation it brings to terrified consciences, and that God requires faith that we believe that absolution as a voice sounding from heaven, and that this faith in Christ truly obtains and receives remission of sins.

Aforetime satisfactions were immoderately extolled; of faith, and the merit of Christ, and justification by faith, no mention was made. Wherefore on this point our churches are by no means to be blamed. For this even our adversaries are compelled to concede in regard to us, that the doctrine of repentance is most diligently treated and laid open by us.

But of Confession our churches teach that the enumeration of sins is not necessary, nor are consciences to be burdened with the care of enumerating all sins, inasmuch as it is impossible to recount all sins, as the Psalm (19:12) testifies: "Who can understand his errors?" So also Jeremiah (17:9): "The heart is deceitful above all things, and desperately wicked. Who can know it?" But if no sins were remitted except what were recounted, consciences could never find peace, because very many sins they neither see nor can remember.

The ancient writers also testify that the enumeration is not necessary. For in the Decrees Chrysostom is cited, who speaks thus: "I do not say to thee that thou shouldst discover thyself in public, or accuse thyself before others, but I would have thee obey the prophet when he says: 'Reveal thy way unto the Lord.' Therefore with prayer confess thy sins before God the true Judge. Pronounce thine errors, not with the tongue, but with the memory of thy conscience." And the Gloss (*Of Repentance*, Dist. V., Chap. *Consideret*), admits that Confession is of human right only [is not commanded in Scripture, but has been instituted by the Church].

Nevertheless, on account of the very great benefit of absolution, as well as for other uses to the conscience, confession is retained among us.

ART. V.—OF THE DISTINCTION OF MEATS, AND OF TRADITIONS

It hath been a general opinion, not of the people alone, but also of such as are teachers in the churches, that the differences of meats, and such like human traditions, are works available to merit grace, and are satisfactions for sins. And that the world thus thought is apparent by this—that daily new ceremonies, new orders, new holidays, new fasts, were appointed; and the teachers in the churches did exact these works as a service necessary to deserve grace; and they did greatly terrify men's consciences, if aught were omitted.

Of this persuasion concerning traditions many disadvantages have followed in the Church. For first the doctrine of grace is obscured by it, and also the righteousness of faith, which is the principal part of the Gospel, and which it behooveth most of all to stand forth and to have the pre-eminence in the Church, that the merit of Christ may be well known, and faith, which believeth that sins are remitted for Christ's sake, may be exalted far above works. For which cause also Paul lays much stress on this point: he removeth the law and human traditions, that he may show that the righteousness of Christ is a far other thing than such works as these be, namely, a faith, which believeth that sins are freely remitted for Christ's sake. But this doctrine of Paul is almost wholly smothered by traditions, which have bred an opinion, that, by making difference in meats, and such like services, a man should merit grace and justification. In their doctrine of repentance there was no mention of faith; only these works of satisfaction were spoken of: repentance seemed to consist wholly in these.

Secondly, these traditions obscured the commandments of God, because traditions were preferred far above the commandments of God. All Christianity was thought to be an observation of certain holidays, rites, fasts, and attire. These observations were in possession of a most goodly title, that they were the spiritual life and the perfect life. In the mean time God's commandments, touching every man's calling, were of small estimation: that the father brought up his children, that the mother nurtured them, that the prince governed the commonwealth. These were reputed worldly affairs, and imperfect, and far inferior to those glittering observances. And this error did greatly torment pious consciences, which were grieved that they were held by an imperfect kind of life, in marriage, in magistracy, or in other civil functions. They had the monks, and such like, in admiration, and falsely imagined that the observances of these men were more grateful to God than their own.

Thirdly, traditions brought great danger to men's consciences, because it was impossible to keep all traditions, and yet men thought the observation of them to be necessary services. Gerson writeth that "many fell into despair, and some murdered themselves, because they perceived that they could not keep the traditions;" and all this while they never heard the comfort of the righteousness of faith, or of grace. We see the Summists and Divines gather together the traditions, and seek qualifications of them, to unburden men's consciences; and yet all will not serve, but meantime they bring more snares upon the conscience. The schools and pulpits have been so busied in gathering together the traditions, that they had not leisure to touch the Scripture, and to seek out a more profitable doctrine—of faith, of the cross, of hope, of the dignity of civil affairs, of the comfort of conscience in arduous trials. Wherefore Gerson and some other Divines have made grievous complaints, that they were hindered by these strifes about traditions, so that they could not be occupied in some better kind of doctrine. And Augustine forbiddeth that men's consciences should be burdened with observations of this kind, and doth very prudently warn Januarius to know that they are to be observed as things indifferent; for he so speaketh.

Wherefore our ministers must not be thought to have touched this matter rashly, or from hatred of the bishops, as some do falsely surmise. There was great need to admonish the churches of those errors, which did arise from mistaking of traditions; for the Gospel compelleth men to urge the doctrine of grace and of the righteousness of faith in the Church; which yet can never be understood if men suppose that they can merit remission of sins and justification by observances of their own choice. Thus, therefore, they teach us that we can not merit grace or justification by the observation of man's traditions; and therefore we must not think that such observations are necessary service.

Hereunto they add testimonies out of the Scriptures. Christ excuseth his Apostles who kept not the received tradition (which yet seemed to be about a matter not unlawful, but indifferent, and to have some affinity with the baptisms of the law), and saith, "They worship me in vain with the commandments of men" (Matt. 15:9). Christ, therefore, exacteth no unprofitable service. And a little after, he addeth: "Whatsoever entereth in at the mouth defileth not the man" (v. 11). So also (Paul): "The kingdom of God is not meat and drink" (Rom. 15:17). "Let no man judge you in meat or drink, or in respect of the Sabbath-days, or of a holiday" (Col. 2:16). Again: "If ye be dead with Christ from the rudiments of the world, why, as though ye lived in the world, are ye subject to traditions: Touch not, taste not, handle not?" (vv. 20–21).

Peter saith, "Why tempt ye God, laying a yoke upon the necks of the disciples, which neither we nor our fathers were able to bear? But we believe that through the grace of the Lord Jesus Christ we shall be saved, even as they" (Acts 15:10–11). Here Peter forbiddeth to burden the consciences with many rites, whether they be of Moses' or of any others' appointing. And he (Paul) calleth the forbidding of meats "a doctrine of devils" (1 Tim. 4:1), because that it is against the Gospel to appoint or do such works, to the end that by them we may merit grace or justification, or as though Christianity could not exist without such service.

Here our adversaries object against us, that our ministers hinder all good discipline and mortification of the flesh, as Jovinian did. But the contrary may be seen by our men's writings. For they have always taught, touching the cross, that Christians ought to bear afflictions. This is the true, earnest, and unfeigned mortification, to be exercised with divers afflictions, and to be crucified with Christ. Moreover they teach that every Christian must so by bodily discipline, or bodily exercises and labor, exercise and keep himself under, that plenty and sloth do not stimulate him to sin; not that he may by such exercises merit grace, or satisfy for sins. And this corporal discipline should be used always, not only on a few and set days; according to the commandment of Christ: "Take heed lest your hearts be overcharged with surfeiting" (Luke 21:34). Again: "This kind (of devils) goeth not out but by prayer and fasting" (Matt. 17:21). And Paul saith, "I keep under my body, and bring it into subjection" (1 Cor. 9:27), where he plainly showeth that he did therefore chastise his body; not that by that discipline he might merit remission of sins, but that his body might be apt and fit for spiritual things, and to do his duty according to his calling. Therefore we do not condemn fasts themselves, but the traditions which prescribe certain days and certain meats, with danger to the conscience, as though such works as these were a necessary service.

Yet most of the traditions are observed among us which tend unto this end, that things may be done orderly in the Church; as, namely, the order of Lessons in the Mass and the chiefest holidays. But, in the mean time, men are admonished that such a service doth not justify before God, and that it is not to be supposed there is sin in such things, if they be left undone, without scandal. This liberty in human rites and ceremonies was not unknown to the Fathers. For in the East they kept Easter at another time than they did in Rome; and when they of Rome accused the East of schism for this diversity, they were admonished by others that such customs need not be alike every where. And Irenæus saith: "The disagreement about fasting doth not break off the agreement of faith." Besides, Pope Gregory, in the 12th Distinction, intimates that such diversity doth not hurt the unity of the Church; and in the *Tripartite History*, lib. 9, many examples of dissimilar rites are gathered together, and these words are there rehearsed: "The mind of the Apostles was, not to give precepts concerning holidays, but to preach godliness and a holy life [faith and love]."

ART. VI.—OF MONASTIC VOWS

What is taught among us touching the Vows of Monks will be better understood if one call to mind what was the state of monasteries, and how many things were every day committed in the monasteries contrary to the Canons. In Augustine's time cloister-fraternities were free; but afterwards, when discipline was corrupted, vows were every where laid upon them, that, as it were in a newly devised prison, the discipline might be restored again.

Over and besides vows, many other observances by little and little were added. And these bands and snares were cast upon many, before they came to ripe years, contrary to the Canons.

Many through error fell into this kind of life unawares, who, though they wanted not years, yet they wanted discretion to judge of their strength and ability. They who were once got within these nets were constrained to abide in them, though, by the benefit of the Canons, some might be set at liberty. And that fell out rather in the monasteries of nuns than of monks; although the weaker sex ought more to have been spared.

This rigor and severity displeased many good men heretofore, when they saw young maids and young men thrust into monasteries, there to get their living. They saw what an unhappy issue this counsel had, what offenses it bred, and what snares it laid upon consciences. They were grieved that the authority of the Canons was wholly neglected and contemned in a thing most dangerous.

To all these evils there was added such a persuasion concerning vows, as, it is well known, did in former times displease the monks themselves, if any of them were somewhat wiser than the rest. They taught that vows were equal to baptism; they taught that by this kind of life they merited remission of sins and justification before God; yea, they added that the monk's life did not only merit righteousness before God, but more than that, because it observed not only the commandments, but also the counsels of the Gospel. And thus they taught that the monk's profession was better than baptism; that the monk's life did merit more than the life of magistrates, of pastors, and such like, who, in obedience to God's commandment, followed their calling without any such religions of man's making.

None of these things can be denied: they are to be seen in their writings.

What occurred afterwards in the monasteries? In old time they were schools for the study of sacred letters, and other branches of knowledge, which were profitable to the Church; and thence were pastors and bishops taken: but now the case is altered. It is needless to rehearse what is notorious. In old time they came together into such places to learn; but now they feign that it is a kind of life taken up to merit remission of sins and justification; yea, they say it is a state of perfection, and prefer it to all other kinds of life, the kinds that God ordained.

We have therefore mentioned these things, not to excite odium, exaggerating nothing, to the end that the doctrine of our churches touching this matter might be understood.

First, concerning such as contract marriage, thus they teach among us: that it is lawful for any to marry that are not adapted for a single life; forasmuch as vows can not take away God's ordinance and commandment. The commandment of God is, "To avoid fornication, let every man have his own wife" (1 Cor. 7:2). And not only the commandment, but also the creation and ordinance of God, compelleth such unto marriage as without the special work of God are not exempted; according to that saying, "It is not good for man to be alone" (Gen. 2:18). They, therefore, that are obedient to this commandment and ordinance of God do not sin.

What can be said against these things? Let a man exaggerate the bond of a vow as much as he will, yet can he never bring to pass that the vow shall take away God's commandment. The Canons teach, "that in every vow the right of the superior is excepted:" much less, therefore, can these vows, which are contrary to God's commandment, be of force.

If so be that the obligation of vows has no causes why it might be changed, then could not the Roman Pontiffs have dispensed therewith. For neither is it lawful for man to disannul that bond which doth simply belong to the law of God. But the Roman Pontiffs have judged very prudently, that in this obligation there must equity be used; therefore they often, as we read, have dispensed with vows. The history of the King of Arragon, being called back out of a monastery, is well known; and there are examples in our own time.

Secondly, why do our adversaries exaggerate the obligation or the effect of the vow; when in the mean time they speak not a word of the very nature of a vow, that it ought to be in a thing possible, ought to be voluntary, and taken up of a man's own accord, and with deliberation? But it is not unknown how far perpetual chastity is in the power of a man. And how many a one amongst them is there that doth vow of his own accord and well advised? Maidens and youths, before they know how to judge, are persuaded, yea, sometimes also compelled to vow.

Wherefore it is not meet to dispute so rigorously of the obligation, seeing that all men confess that it is against the nature of a vow, that it is not done of a man's own accord, nor advisedly.

The Canons for the most part disannul vows which are made before fifteen years of age; because that before one come to that age there seemeth not to be so much judgment that determination may be made concerning a perpetual life. Another Canon, permitting more to the weakness of men, doth add some years more; for it forbiddeth a vow to be made before one be eighteen years of age. But which of these shall we follow? The greatest part have this excuse for forsaking monasteries, because most of them vowed before they came to this age.

Last of all, even though the breaking of a vow were to be reprehended, yet it seems not to follow directly that the marriages of such persons are to be dissolved. For Augustine, in his 27th quest. 1st chap. *Of Marriages*, doth deny that they ought to be dissolved; and his authority is not lightly to be esteemed, although others afterwards have thought otherwise.

And although the commandment of God touching wedlock doth free most men from vows; yet our teachers do also bring another reason concerning vows, to show that they are void: because that all the worship of God, instituted of men without the commandment of God, and chosen to merit remission of sins and justification, is wicked; as Christ saith: "In vain they do worship me, teaching for doctrines the commandments of men" (Matt. 15:9). And Paul doth every where teach that righteousness is not to be sought of our own observances, and services which are devised by men; but that it cometh by faith to those that believe that they are received into favor by God for Christ's sake.

But it is evident that the monks did teach that these counterfeited religions satisfy for sins, and merit grace and justification. What else is this than to detract from the glory of Christ, and to obscure and deny the righteousness of faith? Wherefore it followeth that these common vows were wicked services, and are therefore void. For a wicked vow, and that which is made against the commandments of God, is one of no force; neither, as the Canon saith, ought a vow to be a bond of iniquity.

Paul saith, "Christ is become of no effect unto you, whosoever of you are justified by the law; ye are fallen from grace" (Gal. 5:4). They, therefore, who wish to be justified by vows, are made void of Christ, and fall from grace. For they also who attribute justification to their vows, attribute to their own works what properly belongs to the glory of Christ. Nor truly can it be denied that the monks taught that they are justified by their vows and observances, and merit the remission of sins; nay, they invented yet greater absurdities, and said they could transfer their good works to others. If any man wished to expand these things, so as to excite odium, how many things might he rehearse whereof the monks themselves are now ashamed!

Moreover, they would persuade men that these invented religious orders are a state of Christian perfection. Or is this not attributing justification to works? It is no light offense in the Church to propound unto the people a certain service devised by men, without the commandment of God, and to teach that such a service doth justify men; because that the righteousness of faith, which ought especially to be taught in the Church, is obscured when those marvelous religions of angels, the pretense of poverty and humility, and of celibacy, are cast before men's eyes.

Moreover, the commandments of God, and the true worship of God, are obscured when men hear that monks alone are in that state of perfection; because that Christian perfection is this, to fear God sincerely, and again, to conceive great faith, and to trust assuredly that God is pacified towards us, for Christ's sake; to ask, and certainly to look for, help from God in all our affairs, according to our calling; and outwardly to do good works diligently, and to attend to our vocation. In these things doth true perfection and the true worship of God consist: it doth not consist in singleness of life, in beggary, or in vile apparel.

The people doth also conceive many pernicious opinions from these false commendations of the monastic life. They hear celibacy praised above measure; therefore with offense of conscience they live in marriage. They hear that mendicants only are perfect; therefore with offense of conscience they keep their possessions, and buy and sell. They hear that the Gospel only giveth counsel not to take revenge; therefore some in private life are not afraid to avenge themselves; for they hear that it is a counsel, not a commandment. Others do think that all magistracy and civil offices are unworthy Christian men.

We read examples of men who, forsaking wedlock, and leaving the government of the commonwealth, have hid themselves in monasteries. This they called flying out of the world, and seeking a kind of life which is more acceptable to God: neither did they see that God is to be served in those commandments which he himself hath delivered, not in the commandments which are devised by men. That is a good and perfect kind of life which hath the commandment of God for it. It is necessary to admonish men of these things. And before these times Gerson did reprehend this error of the monks concerning perfection; and witnesseth, that in his time this was a new saying, that the monastical life is a state of perfection.

Thus many wicked opinions do cleave fast unto vows: as that they merit remission of sins and justification, that they are Christian perfection, that they do keep the counsels and commandments, that they have works of supererogation. All these things (seeing they be false and vain) do make vows to be of none effect.

ART. VII.—OF ECCLESIASTICAL POWER

There have been great controversies touching the power of Bishops; in which many have incommodiously mingled together the Ecclesiastical power and the power of the sword. And out of this confusion there have sprung very great wars and tumults, while that the Pontiffs, trusting in the power of the keys, have not only appointed new kinds of service, and burdened men's consciences by reserving of cases, and by violent excommunications; but have also endeavored to transfer worldly kingdoms from one to another, and to despoil emperors of their power and authority.

These faults did godly and learned men long since reprehend in the Church; and for that cause our teachers were compelled, for the comfort of men's consciences, to show the difference between the ecclesiastical power and the power of the sword. And they have taught that both of them, because of God's commandment, are dutifully to be reverenced and honored, as the chiefest blessings of God upon earth.

Now their judgment is this: that the power of the keys, or the power of the Bishops, by the rule of the Gospel, is a power or commandment from God, of preaching the Gospel, of remitting or retaining sins, and of administering the Sacraments. For Christ doth send his Apostles with this charge: "As the Father hath sent me, even so send I you. Receive ye the Holy Ghost: whosoever sins ye remit, they are remitted unto them; and whosoever sins ye retain, they are retained" (John 20:21–23). "Go, and preach the Gospel to every creature," etc. (Mark 16:15).

This power is put in execution only by teaching or preaching the Word and administering the Sacraments, either to many or to single individuals, in accordance with their call. For thereby not corporal things, but eternal, are granted; as an eternal righteousness, the Holy Ghost, life everlasting. These things can not be got but by the ministry of the Word and of the Sacraments, as Paul saith, "The Gospel is the power of God to salvation to every one that believeth" (Rom. 1:16).

Seeing, then, that the ecclesiastical power concerneth things eternal, and is exercised only by the ministry of the Word, it hindereth not the political government any more than the art of singing hinders political government. For the political administration is occupied about other matters than is the Gospel. The magistracy defends not the minds, but the bodies, and bodily things, against manifest injuries; and coerces men by the sword and corporal punishments, that it may uphold civil justice and peace.

Wherefore the ecclesiastical and civil powers are not to be confounded. The ecclesiastical power hath its own commandment to preach the Gospel and administer the Sacraments. Let it not by force enter into the office of another; let it not transfer worldly kingdoms; let it not abrogate the magistrates' laws; let it not withdraw from them lawful obedience; let it not hinder judgments touching any civil ordinances or contracts; let it not prescribe laws to the magistrate touching the form of the republic; as Christ saith, "My kingdom is not of this world" (John 18:36). Again, "Who made me a judge or a divider over you?" (Luke 12:14). And Paul saith, "Our conversation [citizenship] is in heaven" (Phil. 3:20). "The weapons of our warfare are not carnal, but mighty through God, casting down imaginations," etc. (2 Cor. 10:4). In this way do our teachers distinguish between the duties of each power one from the other, and do warn all men to honor both powers, and to acknowledge both to be the [highest] gift and blessing of God.

If so be that the Bishops have any power of the sword, they have it not as Bishops by the commandment of the Gospel, but by man's law given unto them of kings and emperors, for the civil government of their goods. This, however, is a kind of function diverse from the ministry of the Gospel.

Therefore, when the question touches the jurisdiction of Bishops, government must be distinguished from ecclesiastical jurisdiction. Again, by the Gospel, or, as they term it, by divine right, Bishops, as Bishops—that is, those who have the administration of the Word and Sacraments committed to them—have no other jurisdiction at all, but only to remit sin, also to take cognizance of [to judge in regard to] doctrine, and to reject doctrine inconsistent with the Gospel, and to exclude from the communion of the Church, without human force, but by the Word [of God], those whose wickedness is known. And herein of necessity the churches ought by divine right to render obedience unto them; according to the saying of Christ, "He that heareth you heareth me" (Luke 10:16).

But when they teach or determine any thing contrary to the Gospel, then have the churches a commandment of God, which forbiddeth obedience to them: "Beware of false prophets" (Matt. 7:15). "If an angel from heaven preach any other Gospel, let him be accursed" (Gal. 1:8). "We can not do any thing against the truth, but for the truth" (2 Cor. 13:8). Also, "This power is given us to edify, and not to destroy" (2 Cor. 13:10). So do the Canons command (II. Quæst. 7, Cap. Sacerdotes, and Cap. Oves). And Augustine, in his Treatise against Petilian's Epistle, saith, "Neither must we subscribe to

Catholic Bishops, if they chance to err, or determine any thing contrary to the canonical divine Scriptures."

If so be that they have any other power or jurisdiction, in hearing and understanding certain cases, as, namely, of Matrimony, and Tithes, etc., they hold it by human right. But when the ordinaries fail [to attend to this office], princes are constrained, whether they wish to do so or not, to declare the law to their subjects, for maintaining of peace.

Besides these things, there is a controversy whether Bishops or Pastors have power to institute ceremonies in the Church, and to make laws concerning meats, and holidays, and degrees, or orders of ministers, etc. They that ascribe this power to the Bishops allege this testimony for it: "I have yet many things to say unto you, but ye can not bear them now; but when that Spirit of truth shall come, he shall teach you all truth" (John 16:12–13). They allege also the examples of the Apostles, who commanded to abstain from blood, and that which was strangled (Acts 15:29). They allege the change of the Sabbath into the Lord's day, contrary, as it seemeth, to the Decalogue; and they have no example more in their mouths than the change of the Sabbath. They will needs have the Church's power to be very great, because it hath dispensed with a precept of the Decalogue.

But of this question ours do thus teach: that the Bishops have no power to ordain any thing contrary to the Gospel, as was showed before. The same also do the Canons teach: Distinct. 9. Moreover, it is against the Scripture to ordain or require the observation of any traditions, to the end that we may merit remission of sins, and satisfy for sins by them. For the glory of Christ's merit suffers when we seek by such observances to merit justification. And it is very apparent, that through this persuasion traditions grew into an infinite number in the Church. In the mean while, the doctrine concerning faith, and the righteousness of faith, was quite suppressed, for thereupon there were new holidays made, new fasts appointed, new ceremonies, new worships for saints, instituted; because that the authors of such things supposed by these works to merit grace. After the same manner heretofore did the Penitential Canons increase, whereof we still see some traces in satisfactions.

Moreover, the authors of traditions do contrary to the command of God when they find matters of sin in foods, in days, and like things, and burden the Church with the servitude of the law, as if there ought to be among Christians, in order to merit justification, a service like the Levitical, the ordination of which God has committed to the Apostles and Bishops. For this some of them write, and the Pontiffs in some measure seem to be misled by the example of the Law of Moses. From hence are those burdens, that it is mortal sin, even without offense to others, to do manual labor on the festivals, that it is a mortal sin to omit the Canonical Hours, that certain foods defile the conscience, that fastings are works which appease God; that sin, in a reserved case, can not be pardoned, but by the authority of him that reserved it; whereas the Canons speak only of reserving of ecclesiastical penalty, and not of the reserving of the fault.

Whence, then, have the Bishops power and authority of imposing these traditions upon the churches, for the ensnaring of men's consciences, when Peter forbids (Acts 15:10) "to put a yoke upon the neck of the disciples," and St. Paul says (2 Cor. 13:10) that the power given him was to edification, not to destruction? Why, therefore, do they increase sins by these traditions?

For there are divers clear testimonies which prohibit the making of such traditions, either to merit grace, or as things necessary to salvation. Paul saith to the Colossians, "Let no man judge you in meat, or in drink, or in respect of a holiday, or of the new moon, or of the Sabbath days" (Col. 2:16). Again, "If ye be dead with Christ from the rudiments of the world, why, as though living in the world, are ye subject to ordinances (Touch not, taste not, handle not; which all are to perish with the using) after the commandments and doctrines of men? which things indeed have a show of wisdom" (Col. 2:20–23). And to Titus he doth plainly forbid traditions; for he saith, "Not giving heed to Jewish fables, and to commandments of men, that turn from the truth" (Titus 1:14). And Christ saith of them which urge traditions, "Let them alone; they be blind leaders of the blind" (Matt. 15:14). And he condemneth such services: "Every plant which my heavenly Father hath not planted shall be rooted up" (v. 13).

If Bishops have authority to burden the churches with innumerable traditions, and to snare men's consciences, why doth the Scripture so oft forbid to make and to listen to traditions? Why doth it call them the doctrines of devils? (1 Tim. 4:1.) Hath the Holy Ghost warned us of them to no purpose?

It remaineth, then, that (seeing ordinances, instituted as necessary, or with the opinion of meriting grace, are repugnant to the Gospel) it is not lawful for any Bishops to institute or exact such worship. For it is necessary that the doctrine of Christian liberty should be maintained in the churches [Christendom]; that the bondage of the law is not necessary unto justification, as it is written to the Galatians: "Be not entangled again with the yoke of bondage" (Gal. 5:1). It is necessary that the chiefest point of all the Gospel should be holden fast, that we do freely obtain grace, by faith in Christ, not because of certain observances, or of services devised by men.

What is, then, to be thought of the Lord's day, and of like rites of temples? Hereunto they [ours] answer, that it is lawful for Bishops or Pastors to make ordinances, whereby things may be done in order in the Church; not that by them we may merit grace, or satisfy for sins, or that men's consciences should be bound to esteem them as necessary services, and think that they sin when they violate them, without the offense of others. So Paul ordained, "that women should cover their heads in the congregation" (1 Cor. 11:6); "that the interpreters of Scripture should be heard in order in the Church" (1 Cor. 14:27), etc.

Such ordinances it behooveth the churches to keep for charity and quietness' sake, so that one offend not another, that all things may be done in order, and without tumult in the churches (1 Cor. 14:40; Phil. 2:14), but so that consciences be not burdened, so as to account them as things necessary to salvation, and think they sin when they violate them, without offense of others; as no one would say that a woman sins if she went into public with her head uncovered, provided it were without the offense of men.

Such is the observation of the Lord's day, of Easter, of Pentecost, and like holidays and rites. For they that think that the observation of the Lord's day was appointed by the authority of the Church, instead of the Sabbath, as necessary, are greatly deceived. The Scripture, which teacheth that all the Mosaical ceremonies can be omitted after the Gospel is revealed, has abrogated the Sabbath. And yet, because it was requisite to appoint a certain day, that the people might know when they ought to come together, it appears that the [Christian] Church did for that purpose appoint the Lord's day: which for this cause also seemed to have been pleasing, that men might have an example of Christian liberty, and might know that the observation, neither of the Sabbath, nor of another day, was of necessity.

There are certain marvelous disputations touching the changing of the law, and the ceremonies of the new law, and the change of the Sabbath:

which all arose from the false persuasion, that there should be a service in the Church, like to the Levitical; and that Christ committed to the Apostles and Bishops the devising new ceremonies, which should be necessary to salvation. These errors crept into the Church, when the righteousness of faith was not plainly enough taught. Some dispute that the observation of the Lord's day is not indeed of the law of God, but as it were of the law of God; and touching holidays, they prescribe how far it is lawful to work in them. What else are such disputations but snares for men's consciences? For though they seek to moderate traditions, yet the equity of them can never be perceived so long as the opinion of necessity remaineth; which must needs remain, where the righteousness of faith and Christian liberty are not known.

The Apostles commanded "to abstain from blood" (Acts 15:20). Who observeth that nowadays? And yet they do not sin that observe it not. For the Apostles themselves would not burden men's consciences with such a servitude; but they forbade it for a time, because of scandal. For in the decree, the will of the Gospel is always to be considered.

Scarcely any Canons are precisely kept; and many grow out of use daily, yea, even among them that do most busily defend traditions. Neither can there be sufficient care had of men's consciences, except this equity be kept, that men should know that such rites are not to be observed with any opinion of necessity, and that men's consciences are not hurt, though traditions grow out of use.

The Bishops might easily retain lawful obedience, if they would not urge men to observe such traditions as can not be kept with a good conscience. Now they command single life; and they admit none, except they will swear not to teach the pure doctrine of the Gospel. The churches do not desire of the Bishops that they would repair peace and concord with the loss of their honor (which yet good pastors ought to do): they only desire that they would remit unjust burdens, which are both new and received contrary to the custom of the Catholic [Christian Universal] Church. It may well be that some constitutions had some probable reasons when they began, which yet will not agree to latter times. It is evident that some were received through error. Wherefore it were a matter for the pontifical gentleness to mitigate them now; for such a change would not overthrow the unity of the Church. For many human traditions have been changed in time, as the Canons themselves declare. But if it can not be obtained that those observances may be relaxed which can not be kept without sin, then must we follow the Apostles' rule, which willeth "to obey God rather than men" (Acts 5:29).

Peter forbiddeth Bishops to be lords, and to be imperious over the churches (1 Peter 5:3). Now our meaning is not to have rule taken from the Bishops; but this one thing only is requested at their hands, that they would suffer the Gospel to be purely taught, and that they would relax a few observances, which can not be held without sin. But if they will remit none, let them look how they will give account to God for this, that by their obstinacy they afford cause of schism [division and schism, which it were yet fit they should aid in avoiding].

CONCLUSION

These are the principal articles which seem to be matters of controversy. For although we might speak of more abuses, yet that we may avoid undue length we have embraced a few, whereby it is easy to judge of the others. Great have been the complaints about indulgences, about pilgrimages, about the abuse of excommunication. The parishes have been vexed in manifold ways by the *stationarii*. Endless contentions have arisen between the pastors and the monks about parochial law, about confession, about burials, about sermons on extraordinary occasions, and about other things without number. Things of this sort we pass over, that those which are chief in this matter, being briefly set forth, may more easily be noted. Nor has any thing been here said or adduced for the purpose of casting reproach on any one. Those things only have been enumerated which it seemed necessary to say, that it might be understood that in doctrine and ceremonials among us there is nothing received contrary to Scripture or to the Catholic [Universal Christian] Church, inasmuch as it is manifest that we have diligently taken heed that no new and godless doctrines should creep into our churches.

In accordance with the Edict of His Imperial Majesty, we wish to present these articles above written, in which is our Confession, and in which is seen a summary of the doctrine of those who teach among us. If any thing be lacking in this Confession, we are prepared, God willing, to present ampler information, in accordance with the Scriptures.

Your Imperial Majesty's
most faithful and humble,

John, Duke of Saxony, Elector.
George, Margrave of Brandenburg.
Ernest, Duke of Luneburg.
Philip, Landgrave of Hesse.
John Frederick, Duke of Saxony.
Francis, Duke of Luneburg.
Wolfgang, Prince of Anhalt.
Senate and Magistracy of Nuremberg.
Senate of Reutlingen.

7

First Helvetic Confession

(1536)

The First Helvetic Confession is also known as the Second Confession of Basel, after the earlier confession of 1534. It was an attempt to unite the Lutheran and Swiss Reformed branches of the Reformation.

A league of seven Swiss cities called for a conference in Basel 1536 in an attempt to find common ground with the Lutherans—especially on the controversy over the Lord's Supper. Martin Luther maintained the bodily presence of Christ in the supper, though not in the sense that the elements actually transform into Christ's body and blood. The Swiss, following Huldrych Zwingli—who famously disputed with Luther at the Marburg Colloquy in 1529—asserted that the supper is a bare memorial to the death of Christ.

Ultimately, the confession—drafted by a team that included Heinrich Bullinger—failed to achieve its goal of uniting the Lutherans and Swiss Reformed. It did, however, bring the German-speaking Swiss into greater union and informed Bullinger's creation of its successor document in 1562.

First Helvetic Confession

Summary and General Confession of Faith of the Churches throughout Switzerland

1. Of Holy Scripture

Canonical Scripture is the Word of God, given by the Holy Spirit, and published to the world by the prophets and apostles, the most perfect and ancient philosophy; it alone perfectly contains all godliness [and] all reasonable manner of life. (2 Peter 1; 2 Tim. 3)

2. Of the Interpretation of Scripture

The interpretation of this [holy Scripture] ought to be sought out of itself, so that it is to be its own interpreter, guided by the rule of love and faith. (John 5; Rom. 12; 1 Cor. 13)

3. Of the Ancient Fathers

From which sort of interpretation, so far as the holy fathers have not departed from it, not only do we receive them as interpreters of the Scripture, but we honor them as chosen instruments of God.

4. Of Human Traditions

As to the rest concerning the traditions of men, howsoever much attractive and accepted, whatsoever withdraws us [from the Scriptures], of such we answer with the saying of the Lord, "They worship me in vain teaching the doctrines of man." (Matt. 15; Isa. 29; Titus 1; 1 Tim. 4)

5. The Objective of Scripture

The principal intent of all canonical Scripture is that God wishes to be good to mankind, and that He has declared that benevolence through Christ, His only Son. This kindness comes to us and is received by faith alone, but this faith is effective through love for our neighbors. (Gen. 3; John 3; Eph. 2)

6. God

Concerning God, we believe thus: that He is almighty, being one in substance and three in persons. Who as He created by His Word (that is His Son) all things of nothing, so by His providence He governs, preserves, and nourishes truly, righteously, and most wisely all things. (Deut. 6; Matt. 28; Gen. 1; Acts 17)

7. Man and His Powers

Man, who is the most perfect image of God on earth and holds the title of honor among all the visible creatures, is made of soul and body, of which the body is mortal, the soul immortal. When he was created holy by God, through his own fault he fell into sin, drew with him into the same ruin the whole human race, and subjected them to the same punishable calamity. (Gen. 3; Rom. 5)

8. Original Sin

Therefore, this pestiferous infection, which they call "original," has spread through the whole human race, so that by no work (man being the child of wrath and enemy of God) could he be cured except by a divine one through Christ. For if there is any fruit of good that remains in man, he turns to that which is worse, being constantly weakened by his vices. For the power of evil overcomes us and neither allows us to follow reason nor to exercise the divine quality of our mind. (Eph. 2; Ps. 51 [50]; Rom. 8)

9. Free Will

Wherefore we indeed attribute to man free will, as we who experience knowing and wanting to do good and evil; to be sure, we are able to do evil willingly, but we are not able to embrace and follow good (except as we are illuminated by the grace of Christ and moved by His Spirit). For God is the one who works in us both to will and to perform according to His good pleasure. Also our salvation comes from God, but from ourselves comes perdition. (Phil. 2; Hos. 13)

10. The Eternal Counsel of God concerning the Renewal of Man

Thus through his fault, man was given over to damnation and incurred just indignation; nevertheless, God the Father never ceased to care for him. This is manifest from the first promises, and the whole law (which stirs up but does not extinguish sin), and from Christ who was ordained and appointed for that purpose. (Eph. 1; Rom. 7)

11. Jesus Christ and That Which Is through Christ

This Christ, the very Son of God, both true God and true man, was made our brother, when at the appointed time He assumed a complete, uniform human nature, that is, soul and body, maintaining in the one and undivided person, two yet unmixed natures, so that He might restore us who are dead to life and make us joint heirs of God. (Luke 1; Gal. 4; John 16; Heb. 2)

This most holy flesh, by union with the divinity, like us in all things (sin only excepted because it was necessary for Him to be an unblemished sacrifice), taken from the intact virgin Mary by the cooperation of the Holy Spirit, He handed over to death to wash away all our sin. (Heb. 5; Luke 2; 1 John 2)

In order that He might be a full and perfect hope to our faith and confidence of immortality, He set his own flesh, being raised from the dead, at the right hand of His almighty Father in heaven. (1 Cor. 15; Acts 1)

There He sits having triumphed over death, sin, and all the infernal powers, our victor and leader, and our Head and true High Priest. He defends and pleads our cause perpetually, until He will renew us to that likeness in which we were created. (Eph. 1; Rom. 8; Eph. 4)

From thence we expect He is coming at the end of all ages to be our true and righteous Judge, and shall pronounce sentence on all flesh, who will previously be raised up to judgment and that the godly shall be carried and conducted above the heavens, but the ungodly shall He condemn both body and soul to the eternal destruction of damnation. (Dan. 7; John 5)

Who, as He is our only Mediator, Intercessor, Sacrifice, High Priest and Lord, and our King, we thus acknowledge and confess with the whole heart that this one alone is our reconciliation, redemption, sanctification, expiation, wisdom, protection, our only judicial assertion that we are free. We utterly reject all other means of our life and salvation except this Christ alone. (1 Tim. 2; Heb. [7]; Rom. 3; 1 Cor. 1)

12. The Aim of Evangelical Doctrine

And, therefore, in the whole of evangelical doctrine, it ought to be announced first and foremost that we are only saved by the mercy of God and merit of Christ. So that men may understand how great a work they possess, their sins should always be clearly made known to them by the law and the death of Christ. (1 Tim. 1; Rom. 5)

13. A Christian and His Duty

But we obtain these divine benefits, and the true sanctification of the Spirit of God, merely by faith, the gift of God and by no means by any power or merits of ours. (Eph. 2)

14. Concerning Faith

This faith is a certain and undoubted substance and apprehension of all things hoped for from the benevolence of God. It arises out of love itself and afterwards is clearly the fruit of all virtues. Yet notwithstanding, we attribute nothing to these duties, even though from the pious, yet we attribute them simply to justification and the saving portion of the grace of God.

And this is the only true worship of God—faith most pregnant of works, faith I say with no confidence in the works. (Mic. 6)

15. The Church

And from such stones, upon this living rock, the Church is constructed by this building upon (*inedificatis*); and we hold it to be the holy gathering of all the saints, and the immaculate bride of Christ, whom Christ washes and purifies by His blood, and finally establishes and hands over to His Father without spot and wrinkle.

Which since indeed it is known only to the eyes of God, yet by certain external rites, instituted by Christ Himself and by the Word of God, for instance by public and legitimate discipline, not only is it discerned and known, but it is also so constituted that no one may be reckoned to be in it without these things (except by a singular privilege of God). (1 Peter 2; Matt. 16; Eph. 5; Mark 16; Matt. 28; Acts 8–10)

16. Of the Ministry of the Word

And for this reason, we confess that the ministers of the church are fellow workers of God (which Paul also acknowledges), by whom He ministers both knowledge of Himself, and remission of sins, converts men to Himself, raising them up, comforts them, and alarms and judges them. Yet we ascribe all the virtue and efficacy in these things to the Lord, the ministering nevertheless to the ministers. For it is certain that this power and efficacy is not tied to any creature, but is dispensed freely by the graciousness of God to those to whom He wishes. (1 Cor. 3; John 20; Luke 1; 1 Cor. 14)

17. The Power of the Church

Moreover, the authority of the Word itself, and the shepherding of the Lord's flock, which properly is "the power of the keys," prescribes to all both high as well as low, that they are to be most holy and irreproachable. It should be entrusted for instance either by the calling of God or by the certain and experienced suffrage of the church, only to those elected to the ministry. (Matt. 16; John 20; Jer. 1; 1 Thess. 4; Acts 13)

18. The Election of Ministers

For this function should be granted to no one who is not both skilled in the divine law and of blameless life, and by a singular study of the name of Christ has been prepared and adjudged a minister of the church; and by those to whom that business has been entrusted by the Christian magistrate in the name of the church.

Who when he is truly chosen by God, nevertheless is rightly approved by the vote of the church and the laying on of hands by the elders. (1 Tim. 3; Luke 12; Acts 1; Titus 1)

19. Who Is Pastor

Christ himself alone is the true Head and Pastor of His Church. He gives pastors and teachers to His Church, who, in the visible church, rightly use the legitimate power of the keys thus entrusted to them. Hence we acknowledge them [as] pastors in name only, least of all a Roman head. (John 10; Eph. 1, 4–5; John 21)

20. The Duties of Ministers

The chief function of this office is to preach repentance and remission of sins through Christ, to pray incessantly for the people, to pay attention tirelessly to godly study and to the Word of God, and also with the Word of God as with the sword of the Spirit, to always pursue and cripple Satan with a deadly hatred by all kinds of skill; indeed to defend the sound citizens of Christ.

Moreover, [the function of this office is] to warn the vicious, to censure, [and] to also restrain those raging for a long time against the church (that is, the confederation of Christ by common and pious agreement); with all authority, either to eject and make them known publicly, or meanwhile to amend by another suitable reason, until they have a change of heart and are saved. For this returns the depraved to the church of the citizens of Christ, if converted in soul and inclination (to which all of this discipline tends), he confesses acknowledging his error, also immediately seeks healthy correction and revives the fresh study of godliness in all the pious. (Luke 24; Jer. 11; Acts 6; 1 Tim. 4; Eph. 6; 2 Tim. 4; Ezek. 34; 1 Cor. 5; 2 Thess. 3)

21. Of the Power and Efficacy of the Sacraments

There are two signs which are called "sacraments," baptism and the Eucharist. These are symbols of hidden things, not bare signs, but they are composed of the signs and things together. For in baptism, the water is the sign, but the thing itself is regeneration and adoption into the people of God. In the Eucharist, the bread and the wine are signs, but the thing is the sharing of the body of the Lord, salvation and remission of sins having been procured. Indeed, as the signs are received through the mouth of the body, so the spiritual things [are received] by faith. For in the things themselves is the entire benefit of the sacraments.

Hence we affirm that the sacraments are not only a certain distinguishing mark of Christian fellowship, but are also symbols of the divine grace of God, by which the ministers work with the Lord to the end that what He promises is offered and effected, yet nevertheless just as has been said of the ministry of the Word, all the power of salvation is ascribed to the Lord only.

22. Baptism

To be sure baptism is from the institution of the Lord, the laver of regeneration, which the Lord exhibits to His elect, by a visible sign through the ministry of the church (as has been explained above).

In this holy laver, we bathe our infants for the reason that it is wrong to cast away from us (we who are the people of God) those born to the company of the people of God, not only designated this way by the divine voice, especially as their election has often piously been taken for granted. (Titus 3; Acts 10; Gen. 17; 1 Cor. 7; Luke 18)

23. The Eucharist

But the mystical supper is that in which the Lord offers His body and His blood, that is, His own self truly to His own, for this purpose, that He might live more and more in them and they in Him. Not that the body and blood of the Lord are either joined naturally to the bread and wine, or included locally in them, or placed in them by any carnal presence. But from the institution of the Lord, the bread and wine are symbols, by which from the Lord Himself by the ministry of the church, the true sharing of His body and blood is exhibited, not in the perishable food of the stomach, but in the nourishment of eternal life. (Matt. 26; John 6, 14; 1 Cor. 10)

And this sacred food we use often for this reason, because through the remembrance of it, we behold with the eye of faith the death and blood of the crucified one. We remember our salvation, not without a taste of the heavenly life, and a true sense of life eternal. Reflecting with inexpressible sweetness, we are refreshed by this spiritual, living, and eternal nourishment. And with indescribable words of joy, we exult exceedingly on account of the life which we have found. Wholly and with all our strength, we pour out thanksgiving for such a wonderful benefit of Christ toward us.

Therefore, it is greatly undeserved that some suppose that we attribute little value to the sacred symbols. For they are holy and honorable things because instituted and upheld by Christ our High Priest, exhibiting the things signified in their own manner as we have said, a testimony to the things exhibited, representing such difficult things, and by a certain wonderful correspondence of the things signified, an analogy shining the brightest light on these mysteries. They furnish help and support to faith itself, and finally they bind us together after the manner of an oath on account of Christ our Head and the church having admitted us to sacred rites. In so godly a way do we think with regard to the sacred symbols. But we attribute the power and strength of quickening and sanctifying to Him forever who is life, to whom be praise for ever and ever. Amen.

24. The Sacred Assembly

Moreover, we are of the opinion that the sacred assembly is celebrated thus, as before all things the Word of God is preached in public to the people daily, the hidden things of the Scriptures are drawn out and expounded daily by trustworthy ministers, celebrating the sacred Eucharist, the faith of the pious then being exercised, prayers continually offered for all men [and] for the necessities of all men. But the rest of the ceremonies we remove far away from our sacred assembly as tedious, useless, and innumerable, [such as] vessels, curtains, garments, lights, altars, gold, silver, insofar as they serve to pervert religion, especially idols and images that are set up for worship and a stumbling block, and all such profane things. (1 Tim. 2; 1 Cor. 14; Ex. 10; John 5; Isa. 40)

25. Of Heretics and Schismatics

Also we prevent from approaching as many as deviate from the sacred fellowship of the church, [who] either bring in or follow strange doctrines. In which evil the Catabaptists since the beginning continue to labor today. Who if they obstinately do not comply with the warnings of the church and Christian instruction, are in our judgment to be bridled by the magistrate, lest by their contagion they infect the flock of God.

26. Of Things Indifferent

The things that are called and are properly indifferent, although a godly man may use freely everywhere and at all times; nevertheless, he is to use them according to knowledge and from love, namely to the edification of all. (Rom. 14; 1 Cor. 3)

27. Concerning the Magistrate

Since every magistrate is from God, his principal duty (unless he prefers to exercise tyranny) is to defend and look after religion by curbing all blasphemy, and just as the prophet teaches from the Word of God, to perform it vigorously. By which to be sure in part especially these keep watch that the clear Word of God may be preached purely and sincerely, and truly to the people, not shutting any man out from gospel truth. Afterwards he will pay attention that all the youth and teens among the citizens may be guided with a correct and proper foundation and discipline, the ministers of the church may have a just provision, and the poor solicitous care. For to this end ecclesiastical authorities watch. Finally, to judge the people according to equitable laws: to protect the public peace; to cherish the republic, to fine the guilty for their crimes reckoning with their powers in the body politic [and] in conduct. Which serves reverence since it pays the debt to God.

This we know (if we have been set free in Christ) that both in the body and in all our faculties, we also ought to be obedient by the zeal of the spirit, with holy [and] true faith (as long as the rule of Him for whose sake we revere this, they do not oppose openly).

28. Of Holy Matrimony

We think marriage is fitting in all men and elsewhere not repugnant to the life of divine calling, nor holy orders. For as the church consecrates and sanctions the solemn rites by exhortation and prayer, so the magistrate tends to it so that it may worthily be kept and maintained, unless it is dissolved by a just cause.

Hence that monastic celibacy and the impure chastity of them (whom they call spiritual ones), and this whole idle kind of life, by the abominable fiction of human superstitions, we cast far away [as] repugnant equally both to the church and the commonwealth.

(Translated by James T. Dennison Jr.)

8

Geneva Catechism

(1542)

John Calvin hadn't meant to be a pastor in Geneva. After fleeing and moving to Basel, Switzerland, where he wrote his *Institutes of the Christian Religion*, Calvin passed through Geneva in 1536 on his way to Strasbourg. Geneva had recently left Roman Catholicism and joined the Reformation cause, but the citizens there were in desperate need of sound biblical teaching. A church leader named William Farel challenged Calvin, telling him that God would curse his work if he left the church in Geneva in such dire need. Terrified, Calvin acquiesced.

But tensions with the city leaders soon marked Calvin's ministry in Geneva. The situation reached a breaking point on Easter Sunday 1538, when Calvin refused to administer the Lord's Supper to certain leading residents who were known to be in open sin. The council ordered Calvin and Farel to leave. Calvin went on to Strasbourg before the Geneva city council entreated him to return in 1541.

As part of his ministry in Geneva, Calvin wrote catechisms to train his people: the first in 1537, the second in 1538, and the third in 1542 (in French, followed by a Latin version in 1545). The final catechism enjoyed wide use in Switzerland and Scotland before it was supplanted by the Heidelberg Catechism and the Westminster Shorter Catechism.

Catechism of the Church of Geneva

I. THE DOCTRINES OF FAITH

Q. 1. Minister. What is the chief end of man?

A. Child. It is to know God his Creator.

2. M. What reason have you for this answer?

C. Because God has created us, and placed us in this world, that he may be glorified in us. And it is certainly right, as he is the author of our life, that it should advance his glory.

3. M. What is the chief good of man?

C. It is the same thing.

4. M. Why do you account the knowledge of God, the chief good?

C. Because without it, our condition is more miserable than that of any of the brute creatures.

5. M. From this then we clearly understand, that nothing more unhappy can befall man than not to glorify God.

C. It is so.

6. M. What is the true and correct knowledge of God?

C. When he is so known, that the honour, which is his due, is rendered to him.

7. M. What is the true method of rendering him due honour?

C. It is to put our whole trust in him; to serve him by obedience to his will, all our life; to call upon him in all our necessities, seeking in him salvation, and every good thing which can be desired; and finally, to acknowledge, both in the heart and with the mouth, that he is the sole author of all blessings.

8. M. But that we may discuss these things in order, and explain them more fully: Which is the first head of your division?

C. That we should place our whole confidence in God.

9. M. How is that to be done?

C. By acknowledging him, Almighty and perfectly good.

10. M. Is this sufficient?

C. By no means.

11. M. Why not?

C. Because we do not deserve that he should exert his power for our assistance, or manifest his goodness for our benefit.

12. M. What more is needful?

C. That each one of us be fully convinced that God loves him, and that he is willing to be to him a Father and a Saviour.

13. M. But how will that be evident to us?

C. Truly from his word, in which he declares to us his mercy, and testifies his love for us, in Christ.

14. M. The foundation and beginning of confidence in God is then, the knowledge of him in Christ?

C. Entirely.

15. M. Now I would hear from you, in a few words, the sum of this knowledge?

C. It is contained in the Confession of Faith, or rather Formula of Confession, which all Christians have always held in general among themselves. It is commonly called the Symbol of the Apostles, which has been received from the beginning of the Church among all the pious; and which was either taken from the mouth of the Apostles, or faithfully collected from their writings.

16. M. Repeat it.

C. *I believe in God the Father Almighty, Maker of Heaven and earth: and in Jesus Christ, his only Son, our Lord; who was conceived by the Holy Ghost, born of the virgin Mary; suffered under Pontius Pilate, was crucified, dead, and buried; He descended into Hell; the third day he arose from the dead; ascended into Heaven, and sitteth at the right hand of God the Father Almighty; from thence he shall come to judge the living and the dead. I believe in the Holy Ghost: the Holy Catholic Church: the communion of Saints: the forgiveness of sins: the resurrection of the body, and the life everlasting. Amen.*

17. M. That each head may be understood, into how many parts shall we divide this Confession?

C. Into four principal ones.

18. M. What are they?

C. The first respects God, the Father: the second, Jesus Christ, his Son, which embraces also the whole subject of man's redemption: the third, the Holy Spirit: and the fourth, the Church, and the benefits of God towards it.

19. M. Since there is but one God, why do you name three; the Father, the Son, and the Holy Spirit?

C. Because, in the one substance of God, we must consider the Father, as the beginning and origin or first cause of all things; then the Son, who is his eternal wisdom; and lastly the Holy Spirit, as the power of God, spread abroad through all things, which yet perpetually dwells in him.

20. M. You mean then, that there is no absurdity, although we determine that these three distinct persons are in the one Godhead; and that God is not therefore divided.

C. It is so.

21. M. Recite the first part of the Creed.

C. *I believe in God the Father Almighty, Creator of Heaven and Earth.*

22. M. Why do you call him, *Father*?

C. Chiefly as it respects Jesus Christ, who is the eternal word of God begotten of him from eternity; and sent into this world and declared to be his Son. From hence also we understand, that since God is the Father of Jesus Christ, he is a Father to us also.

23. M. In what sense do you give him the name of *Almighty*?

C. Not in this manner, that he should have power and not exercise it; but that he holds all things under his hand and management; to govern the world by his Providence; to order it after his own will; and to command all creatures as it pleaseth him.

24. M. You do not then imagine an idle power of God; but you consider him to be one, who has always a hand prepared for operation, so that nothing is done but by him and his appointment.

C. It is so.

25. M. Why do you add, *Maker* or *Creator of Heaven and Earth*?

C. In as much as he has made himself known to us by his works;[1] in which also he is to be sought by us. For our understandings are not capable of comprehending his essence. The world itself, therefore, is as it were a glass, in which we may discern him as far as it is for our benefit to know him.

26. M. By *heaven and earth*, do you not understand the whole creation?

C. Yes, truly. These two words include all things that exist in heaven and in earth.

27. M. But why do you call God Creator only, since it is much more excellent to *guard* and *preserve* the Creation in its order, than to have once created?

C. It is not indeed so much as intimated, by this expression, that God at once created his works, so that he might cast off the care of them afterwards; but it

---

1   Rom. 1:20.

is rather to be accounted, that as he framed the world in the beginning, so he still preserves it; and that the earth and all other things abide, only as they are preserved by his power and management. Besides, as he upholds all things by his hand, it is evident that he is the supreme Moderator and Lord of all. Since then he is the Creator of heaven and earth, it becomes us to understand him to be the One, who by his wisdom, power, and goodness, governs the whole course and order of nature; who is alike the author of the rain and the drouth, of the hail and other tempests, and of fair weather; who makes the earth fruitful by his bounty, and by withdrawing his hand, again renders it barren; from whom alike come health and disease; to whose dominion, all things are subject, and to whose will, all things are obedient.

28. M. What then shall I think of devils and wicked men? Shall I say that these also are in subjection to him?

C. Although God doth not influence them by his Spirit; yet he restrains them by his power, as with a bridle, that they cannot move themselves, except as he permits.—Moreover, he makes them the servants of his will, so that they are constrained to pursue, unwillingly and without their intention, his pleasure.

29. M. What benefit do you derive from the knowledge of this subject?

C. Very great. For it would go ill with us, if any thing was permitted to devils and wicked men, without the will of God. In that case, knowing ourselves exposed to their perverseness, the tranquillity of our minds would be destroyed. But now we rest in safety, believing them to be curbed by the will of God, and held in by restraint, so that they can do nothing but by his permission and especially since God presents himself to us as our guardian and defender.

30. M. Now let us proceed to the second part.

C. That is—*To believe in Jesus Christ, his only Son, our Lord.*

31. M. What is summarily contained in this?

C. That the Son of God is our Saviour; and at the same time it explains the manner in which he has redeemed us from death, and obtained *life* for us.

32. M. What is the meaning of the name, *Jesus*, by which you call him?

C. That name in Greek signifies *Saviour*. The Latins have no proper name, by which its force can be well expressed. Therefore the word Saviour was commonly received. Besides, the Angel gave this appellation to the Son of God by the command of God himself.[2]

33. M. Is this of any more weight, than if men had given it to him?

C. Altogether: For since God would have him so called he must of necessity be truly what he is called.

34. M. What then does the word, *Christ*, signify?

C. By this title, his office is still better expressed. For it signifies, that he was anointed, for a Prophet, Priest, and King.

35. M. How do you know that?

C. Because the Scriptures apply anointing to these three uses; and also often ascribe to Christ, these three offices, which we mentioned.

36. M. With what kind of oil was he anointed?

C. Not with visible; not with such as was used in the consecration of ancient Kings, Priests, and Prophets, but with more excellent: That is by the grace of the Holy Spirit, which is the substance represented by that external anointing.

37. M. What is the nature of that kingdom of his, of which you speak?

C. It is spiritual, as it is governed by the word and Spirit of God; which bring with them righteousness and life.

38. M. What is the nature of his Priesthood?

C. It is the office and prerogative of standing in the presence of God, for obtaining his favour, and for appeasing his wrath, by the oblation of a sacrifice, which is acceptable to him.

---

2   Matt. 1:21.

39. M. In what sense, do you call Christ a Prophet?

C. Because when he came into the world, he declared himself the Ambassador of the Father, and the Interpreter of his will among men. And for this purpose, that having fully explained the will of the Father, he might put an end to all revelations and prophecies.

40. M. But do you receive any benefit from this?

C. Truly all these things have no other object, but our good. For Christ was endowed with those things of the Father that he might impart them to us, and that we all might partake of his fulness.

41. M. Explain this to me a little more fully.

C. He was filled with the Holy Spirit, and enriched with all the fulness of its gifts, that he might impart them to us, and to each one, according to the measure, which the Father knew to be expedient for us. Thus from him, as the one only fountain, we draw whatever we have of spiritual good.

42. M. What does his kingly office profit us?

C. By it we are enabled to live pious and holy lives in liberty of conscience; are endowed with his spiritual riches; and also armed with that power which enables us to overcome the flesh, the world, sin, and the devil, those perpetual enemies of our souls.

43. M. What purpose does the Priesthood of Christ answer?

C. Chiefly as by this means, he is our Mediator, who reconciles us to the Father; and also that a way is opened for us to the Father, that we may come into his presence with confidence, and offer ourselves and all that is ours to him for a sacrifice. And hence, you may understand in what manner he makes us his, by his Priesthood.

44. M. The prophetic office still remains?

C. As the office of master was bestowed upon the Son of God for his people; the end is that he might illuminate them in the true knowledge of the Father, instruct them in the truth, and make them the family-disciples of God.

45. M. This then is the conclusion of all you have said: The name, Christ, comprehends three offices, which the Father conferred on the Son, that he might abundantly communicate their power and fruit unto his own.

C. It is so.

46. M. Why do you call him *the only Son of God*, since God distinguishes us all, by that appellation?

C. Because, if we are the sons of God, we have it not from nature; but only from grace and adoption, does God hold us in that condition. But the Lord Jesus, who is begotten of the substance of the Father, and is of the same essence with him, is by the best right called the only Son of God; since he alone is so, by nature.[3]

47. M. You understand, then, that this honour is due to him by the right of nature, and is personally his own; but it is communicated to us by gratuitous kindness, in as much as we are his members.

C. Entirely. Therefore in respect to this communication, he is called the first born among many brethren.[4]

48. M. In what sense do you understand him to be *our Lord*?

C. As he is appointed by the Father, that he might have us under his dominion; that he should administer the kingdom of God in heaven and on earth, and should be the head of angels, and of believers.

49. M. What is meant by that which follows?

C. It shows the manner in which the Son is anointed by the Father, that he should be our Saviour; namely, that having taken our flesh, he performed all those things which were necessary for our salvation, as they have been here declared.

50. M. What do you mean by these two sentences: *Who was conceived of the Holy Ghost, born of the Virgin Mary*?

C. That he was formed by the miraculous and secret power of the Holy Spirit, in the womb of the Virgin, of her substance, that he should be the true seed of David, as was foretold by the Prophets.[5]

---

3   John 1:1; Eph. 1:3; Heb. 1:1.
4   Rom. 8:29; Col. 1:15, 18.
5   Ps. 132:11; Matt. 1:1; Luke 1:32.

51. M. Was it then needful that he should put on our flesh?

C. Certainly, because it was necessary that man's disobedience to God should be expiated also in human nature. Nor indeed otherwise would he have been our Mediator, to accomplish the reconciliation of men with God.[6]

52. M. You say then that it behoved Christ to be made man, so that, as in our person, he might fulfil the office of our Saviour.

C. So I think; for it is necessary for us to recover in him, whatever is wanting in ourselves; which cannot otherwise be done.

53. M. But why was his generation effected by the Holy Spirit, and not rather in the common and usual manner?

C. In as much as the seed of man is wholly corrupted, it became the office of the Holy Spirit to interpose in the generation of the Son of God, lest he should be affected by that contagion, and that he might be endowed with the most perfect purity.

54. M. Hence then we learn, that he who is to sanctify others should be free from every blemish, endowed from the womb with original purity, entirely consecrated to God, and undefiled with any corruption of the human race.

C. So I understand it.

55. M. Why do you pass immediately from his birth to his death, omitting the whole history of his life?

C. Because the Creed here treats only of those points which are the chief things of our redemption, and which contain in them as it were, its substance.

56. M. But why do you not say, in one word, *that he was dead*, without adding, the name of Pontius Pilate, under whom he suffered?

C. That not only respects the truth of the history, but proves also, that his death was inflicted by a judicial sentence.

---

6   Rom. 3:25; 1 Tim. 2:5; Heb. 4:7, 15.

57. M. Explain this more fully.

C. He died that he might bear the punishment due to us, and in this manner deliver us from it. But as we all, as we were sinners, were exposed to the judgment of God, that he might suffer it in our stead, he was pleased to place himself before an earthly judge, and to be condemned by his mouth, so that we might be absolved before the throne of the heavenly Judge.

58. M. But Pilate pronounced him innocent, therefore he was not condemned as a malefactor.[7]

C. It becomes us to observe both these points. For thus the judge gives the testimony of his innocence, that it might be witnessed, that he suffered not for his own sins, but for ours; yet, at the same time, he was condemned, in solemn form, by the same sentence, that it might be manifest, that by undergoing, as our substitute, the punishment which we merited, he might deliver us from it.

59. M. It is well said. For if he had been a sinner, he would not have been a fit surety for suffering the punishment of the sins of others. Yet that his condemnation might be accounted to us for absolution, it became him to be numbered among malefactors.

C. So I understand it.

60. M. As to his being *crucified*, has this any thing of more moment, than if he had suffered any other kind of death?

C. Yes, as the Apostle informs, when he says, *That he was hanged on a tree*, that by bearing our curse in himself, we might be delivered from it. For that kind of death was accursed of God.[8]

61. M. What? Is not reproach fixed on the Son of God, when he is said to be subjected to a curse, even in the sight of God?

C. By no means; for by receiving it, he abolished it: nor did he cease, at that time, to be blessed, when he enriched us with his benefits.

---

7 Matt. 27:24.
8 Gal. 3:13; Deut. 21:23.

62. M. Proceed.

C. Since death was a punishment laid upon man, on account of sin, the Son of God endured it, and by enduring conquered it. And that it might be more fully manifested, that he endured a real death, he would be placed in a tomb, like other men.

63. M. But it does not appear that we derive any advantage from this victory, since we all die.

C. That is no objection; for death is nothing now to believers, but a passage to a better life.

64. M. Hence it follows, that death is no more to be dreaded as a formidable thing: but we must follow Christ our Leader with an intrepid mind, who, as he did not himself perish in death, will not suffer us to perish.

C. So we must do.

65. M. What is to be understood, as to what is immediately added concerning *his descent into hell*?

C. That he not only suffered a natural death, which is the separation of soul and body, but also the pains of death; as Peter calls them:[9] and by this phrase I understand those dreadful agonies, by which his soul was straitened.

66. M. Relate to me the cause and manner of this suffering.

C. As he placed himself before the tribunal of God, that he might make satisfaction for sinners, it became him to be tortured with horrible distress of soul, as if he was forsaken of God—nay as if he was hated of God. *He was in these pains*, when he cried to his Father, MY GOD, MY GOD, WHY HAST THOU FORSAKEN ME!

67. M. Was the Father then displeased with him?

C. By no means; but he exercised this severity towards him, that it might be fulfilled which was spoken by Isaiah the Prophet—"He was wounded for our transgressions, he was bruised for our iniquities."[10]

---

9   Acts 2:24.
10 Isa. 53:4–5.

68. M. Since he is God, how could he be seized with this kind of horror, as if he was forsaken of God?

C. We must consider that he was reduced to this necessity, according to the affections of his human nature. And that this might be done, his Divinity in the mean time retired, that is, did not exert its power.

69. M. But how, again, can it be, that Christ, who is the Saviour of the world, should be subjected to this condemnation.

C. He did not so submit to it as to remain under it. For he was not so seized by those horrors, which have been mentioned, as to be overcome by them, but rather struggling with the power of hell, he subdued and destroyed it.

70. M. Hence we learn, what is the difference between the torment of conscience, which he sustained, and that by which sinners are tortured, who are pursued by the hand of an offended God. For what in him was temporary, in them is eternal; and what in him was only the piercing of a needle's point, is in them a deadly sword wounding to the heart.

C. So it is. For the Son of God, in the midst of these pains, did not cease to hope in the Father; but sinners, condemned by the judgment of God, rush into desperation, rage against him, and press on even to open blasphemies.

71. M. Are we able to learn from hence, what fruit believers derive from the death of Christ?

C. Yes. And first, we perceive him to be a sacrifice, by which he expiated our sins before God; and thus the wrath of God being appeased, he brought us back into favour with him. Secondly, that his blood is a fountain, in which our souls are purged from all pollution. Lastly, that by his death our sins are so blotted out, that they shall not come into remembrance before God; and thus the hand writing, which held us as guilty, is erased and abolished.

72. M. Does the death of Christ bring no other benefit to us?

C. Yes truly. For by its efficacy (if indeed we are the true members of Christ) our old man is crucified; the body of sin is so destroyed, that the depraved lusts of the flesh reign no more in us.

73. M. Proceed to other things.

C. It follows—*The third day he arose again from the dead*. By which he proved himself, the conqueror of sin and death.—For by his resurrection, he swallowed up death, broke the bonds of Satan, and reduced his whole power to nothing.

74. M. How manifold are the benefits which we derive from his resurrection?

C. Three fold. By it, righteousness is obtained for us: It is a sure pledge of our resurrection to a glorious immortality: And by its power, we are even now raised to newness of life, that we may live in pure and holy obedience to the will of God.[11]

75. M. Let us attend to the next point.

C. *He ascended into Heaven.*

76. M. Did he so ascend into heaven, that he is no more on earth?

C. Yes truly. For after he had finished all those things, commanded him of his Father, and which were requisite for our salvation, there was no occasion why he should be longer conversant on earth.

77. M. What benefit do we derive from this ascension?

C. The fruit is two fold. For in as much as Christ has entered into heaven in our name, as he descended to the earth for our sakes, he has opened to us also that door, which, on account of sin, was before shut. Secondly, he appears in the presence of God, as our Intercessor and Advocate.

78. M. But has he, by ascending to heaven, so departed, as to be no more with us?

C. By no means. For he promised, that he would be with us even to the end of the world.

79. M. But by his dwelling with us, are we to understand his bodily presence?

C. No. For the manner in which his body is received into heaven, is one thing; and the presence of his power which is diffused every where, is another.

---

11 Rom. 4:25; 1 Cor. 15:22; Rom. 6:4.

80. M. In what sense do you say that *he sits at the right hand of God the Father*?

C. These words signify, that the Father has given to him the dominion of heaven and earth, that he should govern all things.[12]

81. M. What do you understand by this right hand and by this sitting?

C. It is a similitude taken from earthly Princes, who are accustomed to place, at their right hand, those who act as their ministers.

82. M. Do you mean the same thing, as that which Paul declares: viz. That Christ is constituted head over all things to the Church, and being exalted above all principalities, he hath obtained a name which is above every name?[13]

C. Yes, it is so.

83. M. Let us pass to that which follows.

C. *From thence he shall come to judge the quick and the dead.* The meaning of which words is, that he will as openly come from heaven, to judge the world, as he was seen to ascend into heaven.[14]

84. M. As the day of judgment will not be till the end of the world, how do you say that there will be some of mankind remaining; as it is appointed unto all men once to die.[15]

C. Paul answers this question, when he says that those who are then alive shall be made new by a sudden change, that the corruption of the flesh being put off, they may put on incorruption.[16]

85. M. You understand then that this change will be the same to them, as death; as it will be the abolishing of the first nature, and the beginning of a new life.

C. So I understand it.

---

12 Matt. 28:20.
13 Eph. 1:22; Phil. 2:9.
14 Acts 1:11.
15 Heb. 9:27.
16 1 Cor. 15:5; 1 Thess. 4:7.

86. M. May not our minds receive consolation from this, that Christ is one day to be the Judge of the world?

C. Yes, singular consolation. For by this we certainly know that he will come, for our salvation.

87. M. We should not then so fear this judgment, as to have it fill us with dread.

C. By no means. For we shall then stand before the tribunal of the Judge, who is also our Advocate; and who will receive us into his confidence and charge.

88. M. Let us now come to the third part.

C. That is concerning Faith *in the Holy Spirit.*

89. M. Of what use is that to us?

C. Truly in this respect, that we may know, that as God has redeemed and saved us by his Son, so he will make us partakers of this redemption and salvation by the Holy Spirit.

90. M. In what manner?

C. In as much as we have cleansing by the blood of Christ; so it is necessary, that our consciences be sprinkled with it, that they may be purified.[17]

91. M. This requires a more clear exposition.

C. I understand, that the Holy Spirit, dwelling in our hearts, operates so that we may experience the power of Christ. For it is by the illumination of the Holy Spirit that we understand the benefits we derive from Christ; by his persuasion they are sealed in our hearts; and he prepares in us a place for them; he also regenerates us and makes us new creatures. Therefore, whatever gifts are offered us in Christ, we receive by the power of the Spirit.[18]

92. M. Let us proceed.

C. The fourth part follows in which we profess to believe in the *Holy Catholick Church.*

17 1 Peter 1:2; 1 John 1:7.
18 Rom. 8:11; Eph. 1:13.

93. M. What is the Church?

C. The body and society of believers, whom God has predestinated unto eternal life.

94. M. Is this article necessary to be believed?

C. Yes, truly, unless we would render the death of Christ without effect, and account all that we have said, for nothing. For this is the sole purpose of all, that there should be a Church.

95. M. You understand then, that the cause of salvation has been hitherto treated of, and its foundation shown, when you explained, that we were received into the favour of God, by the merits and intercession of Christ; and that this grace is confirmed in us by the power of the Holy Spirit. But now the effect of all these is to be unfolded, so that from the very subject itself, Faith may be more firmly established.

C. It is so.

96. M. But why do you call the Church Holy?

C. Because those whom God elects, he justifies, and purifies in holiness and innocence of life, to make his glory shine forth in them. And this is what Paul means, when he says, that Christ sanctified the Church, which he redeemed, that it might be glorious and pure from every spot.[19]

97. M. What do you mean by the epithet Catholick or universal?

C. By that we are taught, that as there is one head of all believers, so it becomes all to be united in one body, that there may be one Church and no more, spread throughout all the world.[20]

98. M. What is the meaning of what is next added, *the communion of saints*?

C. This is laid down, to express more clearly the unity which is among the members of the Church. At the same time, it intimates, that whatever benefits

---

19 Rom. 8:30; Eph. 5:25.
20 Eph. 4:15; 1 Cor. 12:12.

God bestows on the Church, respect the common good of all, as all have a communion among themselves.

99. M. But is this holiness, which you attribute to the Church, already perfect?

C. Not yet, not so long, indeed, as it is militant in this world. For it will always labour under infirmities; nor will it ever be entirely purified from the remains of corruption, until it shall be completely united to Christ its head, by whom it is sanctified.

100. M. Can this Church be otherwise known, than as it is discerned by Faith?

C. There is indeed a visible Church of God, which he has designated to us by certain signs and tokens; but we now treat expressly of the congregation of those, whom he has elected to salvation. But this is neither known by signs, nor at any time discerned by the eyes.

101. M. What article follows next?

C. *I believe the forgiveness of sins.*

102. M. What does the word *forgiveness* signify?

C. That God, by his gratuitous goodness, will pardon and remit the sins of believers, so that they shall neither come into judgment, nor have punishment exacted of them.

103. M. Hence it follows, that we can by no means merit, by personal satisfactions, that pardon of sins, which we obtain from the Lord.

C. It is true. For Christ alone, by suffering the penalty, has finished the satisfaction. As to ourselves, we have nothing at all, which we can offer to God as a compensation; but we receive the benefit of pardon from his pure goodness and liberality.

104. M. Why do you connect forgiveness of sins with the Church?

C. Because no one obtains it, only as he is first united to the people of God, and perseveringly cherishes this union with the body of Christ even to the end; and in that manner gives evidence, that he is a true member of the Church.

105. M. By this rule you determine, that there is no condemnation or destruction, except to those who are without the Church?

C. It is so. For from those who make a separation from the body of Christ, and by factions destroy its unity, all hope of salvation is cut off, in so far as they continue in this separation.

106. M. Recite the last article.

C. *I believe the resurrection of the body, and the life everlasting.*

107. M. For what purpose is this article of Faith put in the Confession?

C. To admonish us that our happiness is not to be placed in this world. The knowledge of this has a twofold advantage and use. By it we are taught, first, that this world is to be passed through by us, merely as strangers—that we may think continually of our departure, and not suffer our hearts to be entangled with earthly anxieties. And secondly, that we should not, in the mean time, despair in our minds, but patiently wait for those things which are as yet hidden and concealed from our eyes, being the fruits of grace, laid up for us in Christ, until the day of revelation.

108. M. What will be the order of this resurrection?

C. Those who were before dead will receive the same bodies in which they dwelt on earth; but endowed with a new quality, that is, to be no more obnoxious to death and corruption. But those who shall be living at that day, God will marvellously raise up with a sudden change.[21]

109. M. But will it be common at once to the just and the unjust?

C. There will be one resurrection of all; but the condition will be different: Some will be raised to salvation and glory; others to condemnation, and final misery.[22]

---

21 1 Cor. 15:53.
22 Matt. 25:46; John 5:29.

110. M. Why then is eternal life spoken of, in the Creed and no mention made of the wicked?

C. Because nothing is treated of in that summary but what relates to the consolation of pious minds: Therefore, those blessings only are considered which the Lord has prepared for his servants. For this reason nothing is said about the condition which awaits the wicked, whom we know to be aliens from the kingdom of God.

111. M. Since we hold the foundation on which Faith depends, it will be easy to infer from thence the definition of true Faith.

C. It is so, and thus we may define it—Faith is the certain and stable knowledge of the paternal benevolence of God towards us, according to his testimony in the Gospel; that he will be to us, for the sake of Christ, a Father and a Saviour.

112. Do we obtain that of ourselves, or do we receive it from God?

C. The scriptures teach us, that it is the special gift of God, and experience confirms the testimony.

113. M. Inform me what experience.

C. Truly, our understandings are too weak to comprehend that spiritual knowledge of God, which is revealed to us by Faith; and our hearts have too strong a propensity to distrust God, and to put a perverse confidence in ourselves or the creatures, for us to submit to him of our own mere motion. But the Holy Spirit makes us capable, by his own illumination, of understanding those things, which would otherwise very far exceed our capacity, and forms in us a sure persuasion, by sealing in our hearts the promises of salvation.

114. M. What benefit arises to us from this Faith, when we have once obtained it?

C. It justifies us before God, and by this justification makes us heirs of eternal life.

115. M. What? Are not men justified by good works, when by living an innocent and holy life, they study to approve themselves to God?

C. If any one could be found thus perfect, he might well be called just; but since we are all sinners, in many ways guilty before God, that worthiness which may reconcile us to him must be sought by us in some other way.

116. M. But are all the works of men so polluted, and of no value, that they deserve no favour with God?

C. In the first place, all those things which proceed from us, as they are properly called ours, are polluted, and therefore avail nothing, but to displease God, and be rejected by him.

117. M. You say then, that before we are born again, and created anew by the Spirit of God, we can do nothing but sin; as a corrupt tree brings forth only corrupt fruit.[23]

C. It is wholly so; for whatever appearance our works may have in the eyes of men, they are altogether evil, as long as the heart is corrupt; at which God especially looks.

118. M. Hence you infer, that we cannot, by any merits of our own, come before God and challenge his favour: but rather, in all our undertakings and pursuits, we expose ourselves to his wrath and condemnation.

C. So I think. Therefore it is of his mere mercy, and not from any respect to our works, that he freely embraces us in Christ, and holds us accepted, by accounting that righteousness of his, which is accepted by us, as our own; and not imputing our sins unto us.[24]

119. M. In what manner then do you say that we are justified by Faith?

C. When by a sure confidence of heart, we embrace the promises of the gospel, then we obtain possession of this righteousness.

---

23 Matt. 7:18.
24 Titus 3:5.

120. M. You mean this then: That this righteousness is so to be received by Faith as it is offered unto us, of God, in the gospel.

C. Yes.

121. M. But when God has once embraced us, are not those works acceptable to him, which we do by the influence of the Holy Spirit?

C. They please him so far as he freely renders them worthy by his own favour; but not from the merit of their own worthiness.

122. M. But since they proceed from the Holy Spirit, do they not merit his acceptance?

C. No, because they have always some mixture of pollution from the infirmity of the flesh, by which they are defiled.

123. M. Whence then, and in what way, do they become pleasing to God?

C. It is Faith alone which renders them acceptable: then we may rest assuredly on this confidence, that they shall not come to the sentence of the last trial, as God will not examine them by the rule of his severity; but covering their impurities and spots, by the purity of Christ, he will account them as if they were perfect.

124. M. Shall we understand from thence, that a Christian is justified by his works, after he is called of God, or that he can obtain by their merit, that he should be loved of God, whose love to us is eternal life?

C. By no means; but let us rather believe what is written, that no man living can be justified before God; and therefore we pray: Enter not into judgment with us.[25]

125. M. Must we then conclude, that the good works of believers are useless?

C. No, for God has promised a reward to them, both in this world and in the life to come. But this reward proceeds from the gratuitous love of God as from a fountain; as he first embraces us as sons; and then by blotting out

---

25 Ps. 143:2.

the remembrance of our sins, he follows with his favour those things which we do.

126. M. But can that righteousness be separated from good works; so that he who has that may be destitute of these?

C. This cannot be done. For to believe in Christ is to receive him as he offers himself to us. Now he not only promises to us deliverance from death, and reconciliation with God, but at the same time also, the grace of the Holy Spirit, by which we are regenerated in newness of life. It is necessary that these things be united together, unless we would divide Christ from himself.

127. M. It follows from this, that Faith is the root, from which all good works originate; and cannot, by any means, make us slothful about them.

C. It is true: And therefore the whole doctrine of the gospel is contained in these two points, *Faith and Repentance*.

128. M. What is Repentance?

C. It is a hatred of sin and a love of righteousness, proceeding from the fear of God; leading us to a denial and mortification of the flesh, so that we may give up ourselves to be governed by the Holy Spirit, and perform all the actions of our lives in obedience to the will of God.

129. M. But this last point was, in the division, laid down in the beginning, when you stated the true method of honouring God.

C. Yes, it was then observed, that the true and legitimate rule of glorifying God, was to obey his will.

130. M. How so?

C. Because the service which God approves is not that which we may please to feign to ourselves, but that which he has prescribed by his own counsel.

II. OF THE LAW

That is, of the Ten Commandments of God.
131. M. What rule of life has God given to us?

C. His Law.

132. M. What does that contain?

C. It is divided into two parts: The first contains four commandments, and the other six. Thus the whole law is summed up in ten commandments.

133. M. Who is the author of this division?

C. God himself, who delivered it to Moses written on two tables; and it is often declared to be comprised in ten commandments.[26]

134. M. What is the subject of the first table?

C. It treats of the duties of religion towards God.

135. M. What is the subject of the second table?

C. Our duties to men, and our conduct towards them.

136. M. Which is the first commandment?

C. *Hear, O Israel, I am the Lord thy God, which have brought thee out of the land of Egypt, out of the house of bondage. THOU SHALT HAVE NO OTHER GODS BEFORE ME.*[27]

137. M. Explain these words.

C. The first part is used as a preface to the whole law. For in calling himself the Lord or Jehovah, he establishes his right and authority to command. Next, by declaring himself our God, he would render his law acceptable to us. Lastly, these words also imply, that he is our Saviour; and as he distinguishes us by this privilege, it is just on our part that we present ourselves to him as his willing people.

138. M. But does not the deliverance from the bondage of Egypt respect peculiarly the people of Israel?

C. I confess it does, as to the work itself, but there is another kind of deliverance, which pertains equally to all men.—For he has delivered us all from the spiritual servitude of sin and the tyranny of the devil.

---

26 Ex. 24:12; 32:15; 34:1; Deut. 4:13; 10:4.
27 Ex. 20:2; Deut. 5:6.

139. M. Why does he remind us of that in the preface to his law?

C. To admonish us that we shall be guilty of the highest ingratitude, unless we entirely devote ourselves in obedience to him.

140. M. What is required in the first commandment?

C. That we should render to him the honour, in full, which is his due; without giving any part of it to another.

141. M. What is the peculiar honour, which must not be transferred to another?

C. To worship him; to place our whole trust in him; to pray to him; and, in a word, to ascribe to him all those things which belong to his Majesty.

142. M. What are we taught by these words, BEFORE ME?

C. That nothing is so hidden, as to be concealed from him; that he is the witness and judge of all our secret thoughts; and that he requires, not merely the honour of an external confession, but also the sincere devotion of the heart.

143. M. Which is the second commandment?

C. *Thou shalt not make unto thee, any graven image, or any likeness of any thing that is in heaven above, or that is in the earth beneath, or that is in the water under the earth; thou shalt not bow down thyself to them nor serve them.*

144. M. Does God wholly forbid the painting or sculpturing of any images?

C. He forbids only these two—The making of images, for the purpose of representing God, or for worshipping him.

145. M. Why is it forbidden to represent God, by a visible image?

C. Because there is nothing in him, who is an eternal and incomprehensible Spirit, that resembles a corporeal, corruptible, and inanimated figure.[28]

146. M. You judge it then to be dishonourable to his Majesty, to attempt to represent him thus.

C. Yes.

---

28 Deut. 4:15; Acts 27:29; Rom. 1:23.

147. M. What sort of worship is forbidden, by this commandment?

C. That we should address ourselves in prayer to a statue or image; or prostrate ourselves before it; or by kneeling, or any other signs, give honour to it, as though God therein would present himself to us.

148. M. It is not then to be understood that the commandment condemns painting and sculpturing; but only, that images are forbidden to be made for the purpose of seeking or worshipping God in them; or, what is the same thing, that we should worship them in honour of God, or by any means abuse them to superstition and idolatry.

C. It is so.

149. M. What is required in this commandment?

C. As in the first, God declared that he was alone to be adored and worshipped; so in this, he shows us the true form of worship, by which he would recall us from all superstition, and other depraved and corrupt forgeries.

150. M. Let us proceed.

C. He adds a sanction: *I am the Lord thy God, mighty and jealous, visiting the iniquity of the Fathers upon the Children unto the third and fourth generation of them that hate me.*

151. M. Why does he mention his power or might?

C. To show us, that he is able to vindicate his glory.

152. M. What does he indicate by the word *jealous*?

C. That he can endure no equal or partner; that having given himself to us by his own infinite goodness, so he will have us to be wholly his own. And it is the chastity of our souls, to be dedicated to him, and to cleave wholly to him: as on the other hand, they are said to be defiled with adultery, when they turn away from him, to superstition.

153. M. In what sense is it said—*visiting the iniquity of the Fathers upon the Children*?

C. That he may awaken in us greater terror, he not only threatens that he will take punishment of those who transgress; but that their offspring also shall be under a curse.

154. M. But is it consistent with the equity of God, to punish one for the fault of another?

C. If we consider the true state of mankind, the question will be solved. For by nature, we are all exposed to the curse; nor is there any reason that we should complain of God, when he leaves us in this condition. But as he proves his love towards the pious, by blessing their posterity; so he executes his vengeance upon the wicked, by withholding his blessing from their children.

155. M. Proceed to the rest.

C. That he may allure us by his kindness, he promises, that he will *show mercy, towards all, who love him and keep his commandments, to a thousand generations.*

156. M. Does this intimate that the obedience of a godly man shall be for the salvation of all his children, however wicked?

C. By no means; but in this manner, he would exhibit himself as extending his bounty, thus far, towards believers, that out of favour to them, he would show kindness to their offspring; not only by prospering their worldly affairs; but also by sanctifying their souls, that they should be numbered among his flock.

157. M. But this does not appear to be continually done.

C. I confess it: For as the Lord reserves this liberty to himself, to show mercy when he pleases to the children of the wicked; so he has not so restricted his favour to the offspring of believers, but that he casts off those, whom it seemeth him good, according to his own will; yet he so manages this, as to make it evident that the promise is not a vain and fallacious thing.[29]

158. M. Why does he mention a thousand generations, in showing mercy, and only three or four, in executing punishment?

C. That he may show himself more inclined to kindness and mercy, than he is to severity. As in another place, he testifies—That he is ready to forgive, but slow to anger.[30]

---

29 Rom. 9.
30 Ex. 34:6; Ps. 103:8; 145:8.

159. M. Which is the third commandment?

C. *Thou shalt not take the name of the Lord thy God in vain.*

160. M. What is forbidden in this commandment?

C. It forbids us, to abuse the name of God, not only by perjury; but by all unnecessary oaths.

161. M. May the name of God be at all lawfully used in oaths?

C. Yes truly, when introduced on a just occasion: First, in establishing the truth: Secondly, in matters of importance, for preserving mutual peace and charity among men.

162. M. Is it not then the sole purpose of this commandment, to forbid those oaths, by which the name of God is profaned and dishonoured?

C. This one object being proposed, it admonishes us generally never to introduce the name of God in public, unless with fear and reverence, and for his glory. For as it is holy, we must take heed, by all means, lest we should appear to treat it with contempt, or give to others the occasion of despising it.

163. M. How is this to be done?

C. If we think or speak of God or his works, we must do it, in a manner that will honour him.

164. M. What follows?

C. The threatening—*For the Lord will not hold him guiltless, who taketh his name in vain.*

165. M. Since God, in other places, declares that he will punish the transgressors of his law, what more is contained in this?

C. By this he would declare, how highly he estimates the glory of his name; that we may be the more careful to hold it in reverence when we see him prepared to take vengeance on any one, who profanes it.

166. M. Let us proceed to the fourth commandment.

C. *Remember the Sabbath day to keep it holy. Six days shalt thou labour, and do all thy work; but the seventh day is the Sabbath of the Lord thy God: in it thou shalt not do any work, thou, nor thy son, nor thy daughter, thy man servant, nor thy maid servant, nor thy cattle, nor the stranger, that is within thy gates. For in six days the Lord made heaven and earth, the sea and all that in them is, and rested the seventh day: wherefore the Lord blessed the Sabbath day and hallowed it.*

167. M. Does he command us to labour the six days, that we may rest the seventh?

C. Not simply; but permitting six days to the labours of men, he excepts the seventh, that it may be devoted to rest.

168. M. But does he forbid us any labour on that day?

C. This commandment has a distinct and peculiar reason. In so far as the observation of rest was a part of the ceremonial law; it was abrogated at the coming of Christ.

169. M. Do you say that this commandment respected the Jews only, and was therefore merely temporary?

C. Yes, so far as it was ceremonial.

170. M. What then? Is there any thing in it besides what is ceremonial?

C. Yes; it was given for three reasons.

171. M. State them to me.

C. To prefigure a spiritual rest: To preserve the polity of the Church: And for the relief of servants.

172. M. What do you understand by a spiritual rest?

C. When we rest from our own works, that God may perform his works in us.

173. M. How is that done?

C. When we crucify our flesh; that is, renounce our own understanding, that we may be governed by the Spirit of God.

174. M. Is it sufficient that this be done on the seventh day merely?

C. No, it must be done continually: For when we have once begun, we must proceed through the whole course of our life.

175. M. Why then is a particular day appointed to represent this rest?

C. It is not at all necessary that the figure should, in every point, agree with the substance: it is enough, if there is a resemblance according to the order of types.

176. M. Why is the seventh day appointed, rather than any other?

C. This number in scripture, designates perfection; therefore it is proper to determine its perpetuity. At the same time, it indicates that this spiritual rest can only be begun in this life; and that it will not be perfected until we depart from this world.

177. M. What does this mean, that the Lord exhorts us to rest as he himself rested?

C. When God had made an end of creating the world, in six days, he devoted the seventh to the contemplation of his works. And he proposes his own example, that he may excite us more diligently to the same work. For nothing is more earnestly to be sought, than that we may be conformed to his image.

178. M. Ought this meditation of the works of God to be continual, or is it enough to appoint one of the seven days, for that purpose?

C. It is our duty to be daily exercised in that work; but on account of our weakness, one day is especially appointed, and this is the ecclesiastical polity which I mentioned.

179. M. What is the order to be observed on that day?

C. That the people assemble to hear the doctrine of Christ; to unite in the public prayers; and to offer the confession of their Faith.

180. M. Now explain the point, that the Lord in this commandment had respect also to the relief of servants.

C. It requires that some relaxation be given to those who are under the authority of others. And besides, this also tends to preserve the civil government. For where one day is devoted to rest, each one becomes accustomed to pursue his labours more orderly the rest of the time.

181. M. Now let us see how far this commandment respects us.

C. As to the ceremonial part it was abolished, when its substance was manifested in Christ.

182. M. How?

C. For example; as our old man is crucified by the power of his death, and we are raised by his resurrection to newness of life.[31]

183. M. What then of this commandment remains for us?

C. That we should not neglect the holy institutions, which support the spiritual government of the Church: but especially that we frequent the sacred meetings, for hearing the word of God; for celebrating the ordinances; and for joining in the public prayers, according to their appointment.

184. M. But does this figure conduce nothing more to our advantage?

C. Yes truly; for it brings us back to its substance: To wit, that being engrafted into the body of Christ, and becoming his members, we must cease from trusting in our own works, and resign ourselves wholly to the government of God.

185. M. Let us pass to the second table.

C. Its beginning is—*Honour thy father and thy mother*—

186. M. What in this place is the meaning of the word *honour*?

C. That with modesty and humility, children should be submissive and obedient to their parents, and treat them with reverence; that they assist them in their necessities, and repay them their own labours. These three points comprehend the honour which is due to parents.

---

31 Col. 2:17; Rom. 6:6.

187. M. Proceed now.

C. A promise is annexed to the commandment—*That thy days may be long upon the land which the Lord thy God giveth thee.*

188. M. What is the meaning of this?

C. That those who render due honour to their parents shall, by the blessing of God, live long.

189. M. Since this life is filled with so many cares, why does God promise its long continuance, as a blessing?

C. However great are the miseries to which life is exposed; yet it is the blessing of God to believers, even on this one account, that it is a proof of his paternal favour, while he preserves and cherishes them here.

190. M. Does it follow on the other hand, that he who is snatched away from the world, prematurely and suddenly, is accursed of God?

C. By no means; but it rather happens, sometimes, as any one is beloved of God, so much the sooner he is removed from this life.

191. M. But in doing this how does God fulfil his promise?

C. Whatever of earthly good is promised of God, it becomes us to receive it under this condition, as far as it shall conduce to our spiritual benefit, and the salvation of our souls. For the order would be very preposterous, unless the good of the soul was always preferred.

192. M. What shall we say of those who are disobedient to their parents?

C. They will not only be punished in the last judgment; but in this life God will also punish their bodies, either in taking them away in the flower of their age, or by some ignominious death, or by other means.

193. M. But does not the promise speak expressly of the land of Canaan?

C. It does so far as it respects the Israelites; but the promise reaches farther, and should be extended to us. For in whatever region we dwell, as the earth is the Lord's, he assigns it to us for a possession.[32]

---

32 Pss. 24:1; 85:5; 115:16.

194. M. What is there more required in this commandment?

C. Although the words express only father and mother, yet all those are to be included, who are in authority over us; when the same rule is applicable to them.

195. M. When is that?

C. It is when God raises them to a superiour degree of honour. For there is no authority of parents, or princes, or any rulers, no command, no honour, but what is derived from the appointment of God; because thus it pleases him to govern the world for his own glory.

196. M. Which is the sixth commandment?

C. *Thou shalt not kill.*

197. M. Does it forbid nothing but to commit murder?

C. Yes truly. For God, in this law, not only regulates the external actions, but also the affections of the heart, and these chiefly.

198. M. You seem to imply, that there is a kind of secret murder, which God here forbids us?

C. It is so. For anger, and hatred, and any revengeful desire of injuring, are accounted murder in the sight of God.

199. M. Are we sufficiently free from it, if we pursue no one with hatred?

C. By no means. In as much as the Lord, in condemning hatred, and forbidding us any thing which might be injurious to our neighbour's welfare, at the same time shows himself to demand this, that we love all men from the heart; and that we give diligence to defend and preserve their lives.

200. M. Which is the seventh commandment?

C. *Thou shalt not commit adultery.*

201. M. What is the sum of this commandment?

C. That fornication of every kind is accursed in the sight of God; and that unless we would provoke his wrath against ourselves we must diligently abstain from it.

202. M. What else does it require?

C. That the design of the Legislator be regarded; which, as we said, does not rest in the external action; but rather respects the affections of the heart.

203. M. What more then does it comprehend?

C. That as both our bodies and our souls are the temples of the Holy Spirit, therefore we should preserve them both chaste and pure: and also that we should modestly abstain not only from actual crimes, but even in our hearts, words, and gestures of body. Finally, that the body be kept free from all lascivious carriage, and the soul from every lust, that no part of us be defiled by the filth of impurity.[33]

204. M. Which is the eighth commandment?

C. *Thou shalt not steal.*

205. M. Does this only forbid those thefts which are punished by human laws or does it extend farther?

C. It embraces under the word *theft*, every kind of defrauding and circumventing, and all those evil arts by which we are intent to possess the goods of others. By it we are forbidden, either violently to seize on the goods of our neighbours, or by cunning or deceit to lay hands on them, or to endeavour to occupy them by any unjust means whatever.

206. M. Is it enough to abstain from the evil action, or is the intention also here forbidden?

C. It is. Since God is a spiritual Legislator, he wills that not only external theft be avoided; but also all those plans and counsels which at all injure others; and especially that selfishness, which seeks to grow rich by the misfortunes of our neighbours.

207. M. What is to be done, that we may obey this commandment?

C. Diligence must be given, that each one may safely possess his own.

---

33 1 Cor. 3:16; 6:19; 2 Cor. 6:16.

208. M. Which is the ninth commandment?

C. *Thou shalt not bear false witness against thy neighbour.*

209. M. Does this merely forbid perjury in courts, or in general, all false-hood against our neighbour?

C. Under this form of expression the whole doctrine is included: that we shall not by falsehood calumniate our neighbour; nor by our evil speaking and detraction destroy his reputation, or bring any damage to him in his estate.

210. M. But why is public perjury expressly forbidden?

C. That we might be struck with greater horror at this vice. And it implies that if any one become accustomed to evil speaking and backbiting, from that habit the descent to perjury is rapid.

211. M. Is it not the design of this commandment, to deter us not only from evil speaking, but also from evil suspicions, and uncandid and unjust judgments?

C. It condemns both according to the reason before given. *For that which is evil to do, before men, is even wicked to will before God.*

212. M. What is the sum of this commandment?

C. It forbids us to think evil of our neighbours, and to indulge any propensity to defame them: and on the other hand, God commands us to be endowed with equity and humanity, that we may be studious to think well of them as far as the truth will permit; and to preserve our estimation of them entire.

213. M. Which is the tenth commandment?

C. *Thou shalt not covet thy neighbour's house, thou shalt not covet thy neighbour's wife, nor his man servant, nor his maid servant, nor his ox, nor his ass, nor any thing that is thy neighbour's.*

214. M. Since, as you have said, the whole law is spiritual, and the preceding commandments are designed to restrain not only the external actions, but to correct also the affections of the mind; what more is there contained in this?

C. By the other precepts God would govern and restrain the will and affections; but in this, he imposes a law upon those thoughts which carry with them some degree of covetousness, although they do not ripen into an established determination.

215. M. Do you say that all even the least of those depraved desires, which seize upon believers, and come into their minds, are sins, even though they resist rather than assent to them?

C. It is surely evident, that all corrupt thoughts, although our consent is not added, proceed from the corruption of our nature: but this only I say, that by this commandment, those depraved desires are condemned, which stir up and please the heart of man, although they do not draw it to a firm and deliberate purpose.

216. M. Thus far then you understand, that not only are those evil affections in which men acquiesce and to which they become subject, forbidden; but also such strict integrity is required of us, that our minds must not admit any perverse desires, by which they might be stimulated to sin.

C. It is so.

217. M. Will you now give a short summary of the whole law?

C. Yes, it shall be done, in as much as we may sum it up in two heads: The first is, *Thou shalt love the Lord thy God with all thy heart, and with all thy mind, and with all thy strength.* The second is, *Thou shalt love thy neighbour as thyself.*

218. M. What is included in loving God?

C. To love him as God; that is, that he be acknowledged at once, as our Lord, our Father, and our Saviour. To the love of God, therefore, must be joined a reverence of him, obedience to his will, and that confidence which ought to be placed in him.

219. M. What do you understand by the whole heart, mind, and strength?

C. That ardour of affection, which leaves no place in us for any thoughts, desires, or endeavours, which are opposed to this love.

220. M. What is the meaning of the second head?

C. As we are by nature so prone to love ourselves, that this affection over-powers all others, so it becomes us to regulate the love of our neighbour in ourselves by this, that it may govern us in all respects, and be the rule of all our counsels and labours.

221. M. What do you understand by the word *neighbour*?

C. Not only kindred and friends, and those who are bound to us by some alliance, but those also who are unknown to us, and even our enemies.

222. M. But what connection have they with us?

C. They are certainly united to us by that bond, by which God binds together the whole race of men. And this is so sacred and inviolable, that it cannot be abolished by the wickedness of any one.

223. M. You say then, that if any one should hate us, this love is still his due; he is still our neighbour, and is so to be accounted by us; because the divine constitution stands inviolable, by which this relation between us is sanctioned.

C. It is so.

224. M. As the law declares the true manner of worshipping God, must we not live wholly according to his prescription?

C. Yes truly: but we all of us labour under such infirmity, that no one fulfils it, in all respects, as he ought.

225. M. Why then does God exact of us that perfection, which is above our ability?

C. He demands nothing above that excellence to which we are in duty bound. But only let us strive to reach that course of life, which his law prescribes, and although we should be at a distance from the mark, that is from perfection, the Lord will pardon us what is wanting.

226. M. Do you speak in this manner of all men, or only of believers?

C. He who is not yet regenerated by the Spirit of God, is not indeed qualified, to perform the least point of the law. Besides if we should grant some one to be found who should observe the law in some part, yet we could not from that determine that he complied with it fully in the sight of God. For he pronounces all those accursed, who do not fulfil all things contained in the law.[34]

227. M. Hence we must conclude, that as there are two sorts of men, so the office of the law is twofold.

C. Yes, for among unbelievers it effects nothing only as it precludes them from all excuse before God. And this is what Paul says, when he calls it the ministration of condemnation and death: towards believers it has a very different use.[35]

228. M. What use?

C. *First*, while they learn from it, that it is impossible for them to obtain justification by works, they are instructed in humility, which is the true preparation for seeking salvation in Christ. *Secondly*, That, in as much as the law demands of them more than they can perform, it excites them to seek strength of the Lord, and at the same time admonishes them of their constant guilt, lest they should presume to be proud. *Lastly*, It is to them like a bridle by which they are held, in the fear of God.[36]

229. M. Although then, in this earthly pilgrimage, we cannot satisfy the law, we must not account it superfluous that it demands of us such entire perfection; for it points out to us the mark at which we are to aim, the goal for which we are to contend: that each one of us may strive, with zealous assiduity, according to the measure of the grace given him, to conform his life to the highest rectitude, and to be still making continual progress.

C. So I think.

---

34 Deut. 27:26; Gal. 3:10.
35 Rom. 1:32; 2 Cor. 3:6.
36 Rom. 3:20; Gal. 2:16; 3:11; 4:5.

230. M. Have we not in the law a perfect rule of all righteousness?

C. We have, and God requires nothing more of us, than that we should follow it. But on the other hand, he accounts and rejects as corrupt, whatever we undertake beyond what he has prescribed. Nor does he hold any other sacrifice accepted but obedience.[37]

231. M. For what purpose then are so many admonitions, commands, and exhortations, constantly given by the prophets and apostles?

C. They are merely so many expositions of the law, which lead us by the hand to its obedience, and by no means draw us from it.

232. M. But does it command nothing concerning the callings of individuals?

C. As it commands us to render to each one his due, it is easy to collect from it what those personal duties are, which each one should perform, in his station and course of life. And those numerous expositions of each precept mentioned above, are repeatedly published in the scriptures. For what God summarily includes in a few words in these two tables of the law, is more fully and extensively illustrated in other parts of his word.

III. OF PRAYER

233. M. Having discoursed sufficiently concerning submission and obedience, which are the second part of the honour due to God, let us now treat of the third.

C. We called it Invocation, in as much as we betake ourselves to God in all our necessities.

234. M. Do you suppose that he alone is to be invoked?

C. Yes, for that is what he demands as the peculiar honour of his Godhead.

---

37 1 Sam. 14:22; Jer. 7:22.

235. M. If it is so, how is it lawful for us to implore the assistance of men?

C. The difference is very great in these two cases. For when we invoke God, we testify, that we look no where else for any blessing, and that our whole defence is placed entirely in him. However, he, at the same time, permits us to seek assistance from those to whom he has given the power to help us.

236. M. You say then, that when we invoke the true God we may betake ourselves to the help and support of men, provided we do not by any means put our trust in them; and that we must no otherwise ask their aid, but as they are endowed of God with the ability of being the ministers and dispensers of his favours, for our benefit.

C. It is so. And therefore whatever benefits we receive from them, we must consider as received from God; for the fact is that he bestows all those things upon us, by their agency.

237. M. But must we not give thanks to men, as often as they perform for us any office of kindness. For that is dictated by natural justice, and the law of humanity?

C. We must thank them, and for this sole reason, that God dignifies them with this honour, that those good things, which flow from the inexhaustible fountain of his fulness, are poured upon us as streams through their hands. By this method he binds us to them, and wills that we acknowledge the obligation. Therefore, he who does not shew himself grateful to men, in this way betrays also ingratitude to God.

238. M. May we conclude from hence that it is wicked to invoke either angels, or the holy servants of the Lord who have departed this life?

C. We may. For God has not assigned those services to the saints, that they should assist us. And as to the angels, although he uses their labours for our welfare, yet he will not have us pray to them.

239. M. You say, then, that whatever does not agree and fitly accord with the order instituted of God contravenes his will.

C. It is so, for it is a certain sign of unbelief, not to be contented with those things which God gives to us. If then we betake ourselves to the assistance of angels or departed saints, when God calls us to himself alone, if we transfer to them our confidence, which should rest entirely on him, we fall into idolatry; as we indeed impart among them, that which God challenges in full as belonging to himself alone.

240. M. Now let us treat of the nature of prayer. Is it enough in prayer to utter words, or does it require the understanding and the heart?

C. Words indeed are not always necessary; but true prayer can never be offered without the understanding and the heart.

241. M. By what argument will you prove this to me?

C. Since God is a spirit, and in other duties always demands the heart from men, so he especially does in prayer, in which they converse with him. Nor does he promise himself to be nigh unto any, but those who call upon him in truth: But on the other hand, he holds in abomination all those who pray in hypocrisy, and not from the heart.

242. M. All those prayers are then vain and ineffectual which are made by the mouth only.[38]

C. Not only so; but they are very displeasing to God.

243. M. What disposition does God require in prayer?

C. First, that we be sensible of our poverty and wretchedness; and that a sense of these should produce grief and anxiety of mind. Secondly, that we be animated with such a vehement and devout desire to obtain the favour of God, as may enkindle in us a spirit of ardent prayer.

244. M. Is that disposition natural to men, or do they derive it from the grace of God?

C. In this the assistance of God is necessary; for we are altogether stupid in both those points. And it is the Spirit of God, as Paul says, who excites in our minds those unutterable groans, and creates those desires which are required in prayer.[39]

---

38 Ps. 145:18; Isa. 29:13.
39 Rom. 8:25; Gal. 4:6.

245. M. Does this doctrine imply that we may sit down, and indifferently wait the motions of the Spirit, and that we have no occasion to stir up ourselves to prayer?

C. Not at all; but this is its tendency; that when we perceive ourselves to grow cold, sluggish, and indisposed to prayer, we should betake ourselves to God, and entreat that we may be awakened by the sharp convictions of the Holy Spirit, and thus be fitted for the duty of prayer.

246. M. You do not mean, however, that there is no use for the voice in prayer?

C. By no means; for the voice is often a help to elevate and guide the mind, that it may be restrained from wandering from God. Besides, as the tongue was created above the other members, to celebrate the glory of God, it is proper that its whole power should be devoted to this service. And besides, the ardour of devotion sometimes impels the tongue, without our intention, to utter itself in an audible voice.

247. M. If it is so, what profit do those have who pray in an unknown language, without understanding it themselves?

C. That is nothing else, than trifling with God; therefore such hypocrisy should be removed from Christians.

248. M. But when we pray, shall we do it at a venture, uncertain of success; or does it become us to be certainly persuaded that we shall be heard?

C. This should be the perpetual foundation of prayer; that we shall be heard, and shall obtain whatsoever we ask, as far as is conducive to our good. For this reason, Paul teaches that a right invocation of God flows from Faith: For no one ever, in a right manner, called upon God, unless he first rested with a sure confidence upon his goodness.

249. M. What then is the case with those who pray doubtingly, and are uncertain, whether they shall obtain any thing by prayer, or whether they shall be even heard of God?

C. Their prayers are vain and useless, as they are supported by no promise. For we are commanded to ask with an assured Faith, and the promise is added, that whatsoever we ask believing, we shall receive.[40]

250. M. But since we are, in so many respects, unworthy of his notice, how may we obtain this confidence, that we should presume to place ourselves in his presence?

C. First, we have the promises, by which it is clearly determined, that the consideration of our own worthiness is omitted. Secondly, if we are sons, his Spirit will animate and awaken us, that we shall betake ourselves familiarly to him as to a Father. And although we are as worms of the dust, and pressed with the consciousness of our sins; yet that we may not dread his glorious majesty, he proposes to us Christ, the Mediator, as the way in which we may approach him, with the confidence, that we shall obtain his favour.

251. M. You understand, then, that God is not to be approached, but in the name of Christ alone?

C. So I think; for he thus commands in express words; and the promise is added, that he will grant, through his intercession, that we shall obtain those things which we ask.

252. M. They are not then to be accused of rashness or arrogance who, relying on this Advocate, familiarly approach God, and propose him alone, both to God and themselves, as the way of acceptance?

C. By no means; for he who thus prays offers his prayers, as from the mouth of his Advocate, knowing that his prayer is assisted and commended through his intercession.[41]

253. M. Let us now consider what the prayers of believers ought to contain. Is it lawful to request of God any thing which enters our mind, or is some certain rule to be observed?

---

40 Matt. 21:22; Mark 11:24; James 1:6; Pss. 50:15; 91:15; 145:18; Isa. 30:19; 65:1; Jer. 29:12; Joel 2:32; Rom. 8:25; 10:13; 1 Tim. 2:5; 1 John 2:1; Heb. 4:14; John 14:14.
41 Rom. 8:15, 33.

C. It would be presumptuous, in prayer, to indulge our own inclinations and the will of the flesh; for we are too ignorant to determine what is best for ourselves, and we labour under those irregular appetites which it is necessary should be restrained with a bridle.

254. M. What then must be done?

C. It is our privilege that God has prescribed for us the correct form of praying; that we may follow him as if preceding our words, and guiding us by the hand.

255. M. What rule has he prescribed?

C. Ample and copious instruction on this subject is delivered to us in various parts of the scriptures. But that he might represent the object more clearly, he composed a formula, in which he has embraced and digested into a few heads, whatever it is lawful for us to ask of God, or that is for our benefit to obtain.

256. M. Rehearse it.

C. Our Lord Jesus Christ, being asked by his disciples in what manner they should pray, answered, when ye pray, say,—*Our Father, who art in Heaven; hallowed be thy name; thy kingdom come; thy will be done, on earth as it is in heaven: Give us this day, our daily bread: Forgive us our debts, as we forgive our debtors; and lead us not into temptation; but deliver us from evil: For thine is the kingdom, the power, and the glory, forever. Amen.*[42]

257. M. That we may better understand what it contains, let us divide it into heads.

C. It contains six parts: The three first respect only the glory of God, as their peculiar object. The others respect us and our welfare.

258. M. Is any thing then to be asked of God, from which no benefit is to be derived to ourselves?

C. He so orders all things from his infinite goodness, that whatever is for his glory is beneficial also to us. Therefore, when his name is sanctified, he causes

---

42 Matt. 6:9; Luke 11:2.

it to turn to our sanctification. His kingdom cannot come, but that we are, in some manner, partakers of its privileges. But in praying for all these things, it is our duty, passing by all advantage to ourselves, to regard his glory alone.

259. M. Truly, according to this doctrine, these three petitions are also connected with our benefit. And yet we ought to aim at no other end, than this, that the name of God may be glorified.

C. It is so, and in like manner the glory of God is to be regarded by us, in the other three; although these are peculiarly designed for them who pray for those things which are for their own health and benefit.

260. M. Let us proceed now to an exposition of the words. And, first; why is the name Father, in preference to any other, here attributed to God?

C. As the first requisite of prayer is to have a firm assurance of conscience, God assumes this name to himself, which signifies nothing but pure kindness, so that our minds being freed from all anxiety, he invites us, familiarly, to approach him in prayer.

261. M. May we then confidently use that freedom in approaching God, which children commonly use in addressing their parents?

C. Yes, entirely; and with a much surer confidence that we shall obtain what we ask. For, as our Lord teaches, if we, who are evil, cannot deny good things to our children; nor send them away empty; nor give them poison for bread; how much more beneficence is to be expected from our heavenly Father, who is not only the chief good, but goodness itself?[43]

262. M. May we not, from this name also, draw an argument, to prove that which was said in the beginning, that all prayers ought to be founded on the intercession of Christ.

C. It does most assuredly. For God holds us in the place of children, only as we are the members of Christ.[44]

---

43 Matt. 7:11.
44 John 15:17; Rom. 8:15.

263. M. Why do you call him *our Father* in common, rather than *your own*, as an individual?

C. Every believer is able to call him his own, but our Lord used this common appellation, that he might accustom us to the exercise of charity in our prayers; that no one should so much regard himself as to forget others.

264. M. What do you mean by that clause, *Who art in heaven*?

C. It is the same, as if I should call him, exalted, powerful, and incomprehensible.

265. M. Wherefore is it, and in what manner?

C. Truly, in this manner we are taught to raise our minds on high, when we pray to him, that our thoughts may not be occupied by earthly and carnal things; that we may neither limit him by the measure of our understanding, nor by judging too meanly of him, be disposed to bring him into subjection to our wills; but that we may rather be taught to adore his glorious Majesty with fear and reverence. It tends also to awaken and confirm our confidence in him, while he is declared to be the Lord and ruler of heaven, ordering all things after the counsel of his own will.

266. M. What is the sum of the first petition?

C. By the name of God, the scriptures understand, that knowledge and glory of his which is celebrated among men. We pray therefore that his glory may be advanced every where and by all people.

267. M. But can any thing be added to, or taken from his glory?

C. In himself he is neither increased nor diminished. But we desire him to be made manifest according to his excellency among all people; that whatever God does, that all his works, as they are, so they may appear to be, glorious; and that he may be glorified by all means.

268. M. What do you understand by *the kingdom of God*, in the second petition?

C. It consists chiefly in two things; that he governs his elect, by his Spirit; and that he destroys the reprobate, who obstinately refuse to give up themselves in obedience to him; that it may be manifest to all, that there is nothing, that is able to resist his power.

269. M. How do you pray, that *this kingdom may come*?

C. That the Lord would daily increase the number of believers; that he would enrich them constantly with fresh gifts of his Spirit, until they shall be perfected. Moreover, that he would render his truth more luminous, and his righteousness more manifest, by scattering the darkness of Satan, and abolishing all iniquity.

270. M. Do not all these things daily come to pass?

C. They so come to pass, that the kingdom of God may be said to be begun. We pray, therefore, that it may be continually increased and enlarged, until it shall be advanced to its highest glory; which we trust will be accomplished at the last day, when all creatures being reduced to subjection, God shall be exalted and shine forth; and thus he shall be all in all.[45]

271. M. What is the meaning of this petition, *Thy will be done*?

C. That all creatures may be in submission to him; and so depend on his pleasure, that nothing may be done but by his will.

272. M. Do you suppose then that any thing can be done contrary to his will?

C. We not only pray that what he has determined with himself may come to pass; but also that all obstinacy being subdued and subjected, he would bring the wills of all creatures into an harmonious obedience to his own.

273. M. By praying in this manner do we not give up our own wills?

C. Entirely. And not merely to this end that he would destroy in us, whatever desires are opposed to his will; but also that he would form our understandings and hearts anew, govern us by his Spirit, and direct our prayers, so that our wills may be in perfect agreement with his.

---

45 1 Cor. 15:28.

274. M. Why do you pray that *his will may be done on earth as it is in heaven*?

C. As the holy angels, who are his heavenly creatures, have but one purpose, to hear and obey his commands; so I pray that men may have the same disposition of obedience, and that each one may devote himself to him in a willing subjection.

275. M. Let us now proceed to the second division: What do you understand by the *daily bread* which you ask?

C. In general, whatever conduces to the preservation of this present life; not only food and raiment, but all those supports, by which the necessities of the body are supplied: and that we may eat our daily bread in quietness, as far as God shall judge to be expedient.

276. M. Why do you ask this to be given you of God, since he commands you to provide it by your own labour?

C. Although we must labour and sweat, for the purpose of preparing our daily food, yet we are not sustained by our labour, industry, and care; but by the blessing of God alone, by which the labour of our hands is prospered, which otherwise would be in vain. Besides, it is to be considered that although he supplies abundance of food to our hands, and we feed upon it, yet we are not supported by its substance, but by the power of God alone. For these things have originally no virtue of this kind in themselves, but their efficacy is of God, who from heaven administers it, through these as the organs of his bounty.[46]

277. M. But by what rule do you call it *your bread*, since you request it to be given you of God?

C. Truly, because it is made ours by the kindness of God, as it is by no means due to us. We are also admonished by this word, to refrain from seeking for ourselves, the bread of any other person; and to be contented with whatever comes to us, in a lawful way, as though it came to us immediately from the hand of God.

---

46 Deut. 8:3; Matt. 4:4.

278. M. Why do you add, *daily and this day*?

C. By these two particulars, we are instructed to use moderation and temperance; lest our desires exceed the measure of our necessity.

279. M. But as this prayer is for the use of all persons, how can the rich, who abound in provisions laid up in their houses for a long time, ask their bread to be given them daily?

C. It is the duty of the rich and the poor alike, to hold this as settled; that none of the things, which they possess, will profit only so far as God, by his favour, shall grant them the use, and make the use itself fruitful and effectual. Therefore, in possessing all things, we have nothing, only as we hourly receive from the hand of God, what is needful and enough.

280. M. What do you pray for in the fifth petition?

C. *That the Lord would pardon our sins.*

281. M. Is there no one to be found, of all men, who is so just, as not to need this forgiveness?

C. No, not one. For when Christ gave this form of prayer to his disciples, he appointed it for the whole Church. And therefore, he who would exempt himself from this petition, ought to depart from the society of believers. And we have the sure testimony of the scriptures, that he who would contend to justify himself in one point, before God, would be found guilty of a thousand others. This one thing therefore alone remains for all, to take refuge in his mercy.[47]

282. M. In what manner do you consider our sins to be forgiven us?

C. According to the meaning of the words of Christ; that they are debts, which hold us bound by the condemnation of eternal death, until God shall deliver us by his pure munificence.

283. M. You say then that we obtain the forgiveness of our sins by the abounding grace of God?

C. Entirely—For if the punishment of one sin, even the least, was to be redeemed, we could, by no means, make the satisfaction. It is necessary therefore, that all sins be gratuitously remitted and forgiven.

---

47 Job 9:3.

284. M. What benefit do we obtain by this remission?

C. Even this; as we are made acceptable to him, as though we were innocent and righteous; and at the same time, the confidence of his paternal benevolence is confirmed in our consciences, whence salvation is made sure to us.

285. M. What is the condition appointed, *That he would forgive us, as we forgive our debtors?* Does it mean, that by pardoning men their offences against us, we ourselves merit pardon of God?

C. By no means; for then it would not be a gratuitous remission; nor would it be founded, as it ought, solely on the satisfaction of Christ, which he made for us on the cross. But by forgiving the injuries committed against us, we shall imitate the clemency and goodness of God, and prove by this that we are the children of God. By this rule, he would confirm us; and at the same time, on the other hand, shew us that unless we are ready and willing to forgive others, we can expect nothing else from him, but the highest and most inexorable rigour and severity.

286. M. This then you say, that all those, who will not, from the heart, forgive offences, are rejected of God, and excluded from the adoption of children; nor can they hope that there will be, in heaven, any forgiveness with God.

C. So I think; that the saying may be fulfilled: The same measure which any one has meeted out to others, shall be measured back to him again.

287. M. What is the next petition?

C. *That the Lord would not lead us into temptation, but deliver us from evil.*

288. M. Do you include the whole of this, in one petition?

C. It must be one petition; as the last clause is an explanation of the first.

289. M. What does it summarily contain?

C. That the Lord would not permit us to fall into sin; nor leave us to be overcome by the devil, nor by the lusts of our flesh, which carry on an unceasing war with us; but that he would rather provide us with his power for resisting; sustain us by his hand, and defend and cover us with his shield; that so, under the confidence of his guardianship, we may dwell in safety.

290. M. But how is that done?

C. When, by the influence of his Spirit, we are imbued, with such a love and desire of righteousness, that we overcome sin, the flesh, and the devil; and on the other hand, with such a hatred of sin, as separates us from the world, and retains us in holiness. For our victory is effected by the power of the Spirit.

291. M. Have all persons need of this assistance?

C. Yes; for the devil continually watches us; and as a roaring lion goes about seeking whom he may devour. And we should at once consider how weak we are; nay, that we should be overcome at each moment, unless God prepared us for the warfare with his armour, and strengthened us by his hand.

292. M. What is the meaning of the word *temptation*?

C. The cunning and deceitfulness of Satan, with which he constantly attacks us, and would with ease entirely circumvent us, unless we were assisted by the help of God. For our understandings, from their native vanity, are exposed to his wiles; and our wills, from their depraved propensity to evil, would wholly yield to him.

293. M. But why do you pray, that God would not *lead you into temptation*, since it appears to be the work of Satan, and not of God?

C. As God defends believers by his protection, that they may neither be ensnared with the wiles of Satan, nor overcome by sin; so those, whom he accounts worthy of punishment, he not only deprives of his grace, but also strikes with blindness; gives up to a reprobate mind; and delivers over to the power of Satan, that they may be entirely the servants of sin, and exposed to all the assaults of temptation.

294. M. What is the meaning of this conclusion, *For thine is the kingdom, the power, and the glory forever*?

C. By this we are again reminded, that our prayers are more strengthened, by his power and goodness, than by any confidence of our own. Besides, we are taught to close all our prayers with the praises of God.

295. M. Is it lawful to ask nothing of God, but what is comprehended in this formulary?

C. Although we have liberty to pray in other words, and in another manner, still however, it is to be considered, that no prayer can be pleasing to God, which is not referred to this, as the correct standard of the nature of prayer.

IV. OF THE WORD OF GOD

296. M. Now the proposed method of instruction requires of us, to treat of the fourth part, of the honour due to God.

C. We said that it consisted in this, that we acknowledge God to be the author of all good, and that we confess his goodness, justice, wisdom, and power, with praise and thanksgiving; that the fulness and glory of all blessings may abide in him.

297. M. What rule has he prescribed for this duty?

C. Those praises of him, which are published in the scriptures, should be received as a rule for us.

298. M. Does not the Lord's prayer contain something which applies to this duty?

C. Yes, when we pray that his name may be sanctified, we desire that his glory may be manifested in all his works; that his mercy may appear in pardoning sinners, or his justice in punishing them; and his faithfulness in fulfilling his promises to his people; finally, that whatever of his works we behold, it may excite us to glorify him. This is truly to ascribe to him the praise of all blessings.

299. M. What shall we conclude from those things, about which we have already treated?

C. That which the truth itself teaches; and the same which I proposed at first; that this is eternal life, to know the only true God, the Father, and Jesus Christ, whom he hath sent. To know him, I say, that we may render to him due honour and worship; not only as he is our Lord, but also our Father and Saviour; and in our turn that we are his sons and servants; and therefore that we devote our life to the celebration of his glory.[48]

---

48 John 17:3.

300. M. In what way shall we arrive at so great a good?

C. For this end God has left us his holy word. For his spiritual doctrine is as the door by which we enter his celestial kingdom.

301. M. Where must we seek this word?

C. In the holy scriptures, in which it is contained.

302. M. How must the word be used, that we may receive fruit from it?

C. We must embrace it with a firm persuasion of heart, as the very truth delivered to us from heaven: we must yield ourselves teachable, and submit our understandings and wills, in obedience to it: we must love it from the heart, that being engraven on our souls, it may take deep root and produce its fruits in our lives: and when we are conformed to this rule, it will become our salvation, as it is appointed.

303. M. Are all these things put in our power?

C. Not one of them indeed. But it is of God alone, by the grace of his Holy Spirit, to effect in us all that I have mentioned.

304. M. But must we not give diligence, and strive with all earnestness, by reading, hearing, and meditating, that we may profit therein?

C. Yes, truly; and each one should not only daily exercise himself in private reading; but also at the same time, with special attention, frequently hear sermons in public meetings, where the doctrine of salvation is explained.

305. M. You say then that it is not sufficient for any one to read by himself at home; but that all must assemble together, to hear the same doctrine.

C. It is a duty to assemble together, when the opportunity is given.

306. M. Can you prove this to me?

C. The will of God alone ought to satisfy us, abundantly, for proof. He commended this order to his Church, not that two or three only should observe it; but that all should unitedly be subject to it. Besides, he declares this to be the only method for the edification and preservation of his Church. This therefore should be to us a holy and inviolable rule, that it is not lawful for any one to assume to himself, to be wise above his master.

307. M. Is it then necessary that there should be pastors in the Churches?

C. Yes; and it is our duty to hear them, and to receive from their mouths, with fear and reverence, the doctrines of Christ which they publish. Those then who contemn them, or withdraw from hearing them, despise Christ, and make a division in the society of believers.[49]

308. M. Is it enough for a man, to have been once instructed by his pastor; or ought this course to be pursued through life?

C. It is useless to begin, unless you persevere. For it becomes us to be the disciples of Christ even unto the end, or rather without end. And he hath committed this office to the ministers of the Church, that they should teach us in his name and stead.

V. OF THE SACRAMENTS

309. M. Are there not other means, besides the word, by which God communicates himself to us?

C. Yes, to the preaching of the word, he has added the sacraments.

310. M. What is a sacrament?

C. It is an outward testimony of the divine benevolence towards us, which, by a visible sign, shadows forth spiritual graces, by which the promises of God are sealed in our hearts, that the truth of them may be more firmly established.

311. M. Is there such great power in the visible sign, as to confirm our consciences in the confidence of salvation?

C. It has not indeed that efficacy of itself, but from the will of God, as it is instituted for this end.

---

49 Matt. 10:40.

312. M. Since it is the peculiar office of the Holy Spirit, to seal in our minds the promises of God, how do you attribute this to the sacraments?

C. The difference between the Spirit and these is very great. For it is truly the work of the Spirit alone to move and affect the heart, to illuminate the understanding, and to render the conscience stable and tranquil; and that work ought to be accounted wholly his own, and acceptance should be referred to him, lest the praise be transferred elsewhere. But this by no means prevents, but that God uses the sacraments as secondary organs, and applies those things in their use as seemeth him good; and he so does it, that nothing is derogated from the power of the Spirit.

313. M. You believe then, that the power and efficacy of the sacrament, do not consist in the external element, but that they proceed solely from the Spirit of God?

C. So I think. And truly it pleases the Lord to put forth his power, through his own institutions, for that end, for which he appointed them; and he does this in a manner, which detracts nothing from the power of his Spirit.

314. M. Can you give me a reason why he operates in this way?

C. Truly, in this manner, he consults our infirmity. If we were wholly spiritual, like the angels, then we should be able spiritually to discern both him and his graces: but as we are enclosed in this earthly body, we need figures or glasses, which, in some sensible manner, may exhibit the spiritual aspect of heavenly things; which otherwise we should not be able to discern. At the same time, it is for our benefit that all our senses be exercised on the promises of God, that they may be more strongly confirmed to us.

315. M. If it is true, that the sacraments were instituted of God, to be helps of our infirmities, must not those be justly condemned of arrogance, who judge themselves to be sufficient without them, or who account them useless?

C. Most certainly. And therefore, if any one abstain willfully from the use of them, as if he had no need of them, he despises Christ, spurns at his grace, and extinguishes the Spirit.

316. M. But what confidence or real security, for confirming our consciences, can be derived from the sacraments, which are used promiscuously by the good and the bad?

C. Although the gifts of God are, in the sacraments, offered to the wicked, yet they reduce them to nothing, as I may say, in so far as it respects themselves; still however, they do not destroy the nature and power which the sacraments have in themselves.

317. M. How and when does the effect follow the use of the sacraments?

C. When we receive them by faith, seeking, in them, only Christ and his grace.

318. M. Why do you say that Christ is to be sought in them?

C. I do not understand, that he is inherent in the visible signs, so that we should seek salvation from them, or imagine any power of conferring grace to be affixed to them, or shut up in them. But the sign is rather to be considered as a help, by which we are directly conducted to Christ, seeking from him salvation and every durable blessing.

319. M. As faith is required, for the right use of the sacraments, how do you say, that they are given to us for the confirmation of faith, that they may render us more certain of the promises of God?

C. It is by no means sufficient, that faith be once begun in us, unless it be continually nourished and increased daily, more and more. For this end the Lord instituted the sacraments, to nourish, strengthen, and increase our faith. And this Paul teaches, when he says that these avail for sealing the promises of God.[50]

320. M. But is it not a proof of unbelief, if we have not an established faith in the promises of God, unless they are confirmed to us by other means?

C. This surely argues the weakness of faith, under which the children of God labour; who still, on that account, do not cease to be believers, although as yet they are endowed with small and imperfect faith. For as long as we are

---

50 Rom. 4:11, etc.

conversant in this world, the remains of distrust always adhere to our flesh, which we are no otherwise able to shake off, than by continually making progress to the end of life. It is the duty of every one therefore to make farther progress in faith.

321. M. How many sacraments are there in the Christian Church?

C. Two only; the use of which is common among all believers.

322. M. Which are they?

C. Baptism and the Holy Supper.

323. M. What is the resemblance or difference between them?

C. Baptism is the appropriate way of entrance into the Church. For in this we have the testimony, that we who were before strangers and foreigners are received into the family of God, and numbered among his household. But the Supper witnesses that God, by nourishing our souls, shews himself a Father to us.

324. M. That the nature of each may more distinctly appear, let us treat them separately. First, what is the signification of Baptism?

C. It has two parts: First, it represents the forgiveness of sins: Secondly, the regeneration of the soul.[51]

325. M. What resemblance has water with these things, that it should represent them?

C. Forgiveness of sins is indeed a species of washing, by which souls are cleansed from their defilement, even as the filth of the body is washed off with water.

326. M. But how does water represent regeneration?

C. In as much as the beginning of regeneration is the mortification of our nature, and its end, our becoming new creatures; so, by putting water on the head, the figure of death is represented; and as we do not remain buried in the

---

51 Eph. 5:26; Rom. 6:4.

water, but enter it only for a moment, and come forth immediately as from a sepulchre, a resurrection to newness of life is typified.

327. M. Do you suppose the water is the laver of the soul?

C. By no means. It is unlawful to wrest this honour from the blood of Christ, which was shed for this end, that we being cleansed from all our spots, he might present us pure and undefiled before God. And we indeed receive the fruit of this cleansing, when the Holy Spirit sprinkles our consciences with his sacred blood. But we have the seal of this cleansing in the sacrament.[52]

328. M. Do you attribute any thing to the water, only as it is a figure of cleansing?

C. I consider it to be a figure, but at the same time, it has the substance connected with it. For God, in promising us his gifts, does not deceive us. Therefore, as forgiveness of sins and newness of life are offered to us in baptism, so it is certain that they are received by us.

329. M. Has this grace its effect, promiscuously upon all?

C. Many indeed close up the way to it, by their corruption, and make it a vain thing to themselves; so that believers only are partakers of this fruit; but that diminishes nothing from the nature of the sacrament.

330. M. Whence have we regeneration?

C. Both from the death and resurrection of Christ. For this power is in his death, that by it our old man is crucified, and the corruption of our nature is, in a manner, buried, so that it no more prevails in us; but it is the benefit of the resurrection, that we are begotten unto a new life, to the obedience of the righteousness of God.

331. M. How are these benefits conferred on us by baptism?

C. As by this we are clothed with Christ, and endowed with his Spirit, unless by rejecting the promises, we render the benefits offered therein to us unfruitful.

---

52 1 Peter 1:19; 1 John 1:7.

332. M. What must we do, in order to use baptism in a right manner?

C. The right use of baptism is placed in faith and repentance; that is, that we first determine, by a sure confidence of soul, that we are cleansed from all spots by the blood of Christ, and are acceptable to God; then that we believe that his Spirit dwells in us; and that we make this manifest by our works among others; and also that we assiduously exercise ourselves in striving for the mortification of the flesh, and obedience to the will of God.

333. M. If these things are required for the legitimate use of baptism, how comes it to pass that we baptize infants?

C. It is not necessary, that faith and repentance always precede baptism. These are required only of those who from age are capable of both. It is sufficient, if infants, after they come of age, produce the fruits of their baptism.

334. M. Can you prove to me that there is nothing unreasonable in this?

C. Truly, I can, if it is conceded to me, that our Lord instituted nothing which is unreasonable. For although Moses and all the prophets teach, that circumcision was the sign of repentance, and Paul that it was the seal of the righteousness of faith; yet, we see, that infants were not excluded from it.[53]

335. M. But are infants admitted to baptism now, for the same reason that they were then admitted to circumcision?

C. Entirely the same. For the promises, which God gave to the people of Israel, are now published through the whole world.

336. M. Do you conclude from this that the sign is also to be used?

C. He who well examines the subject on both sides, will observe that this is the consequence. For Christ has not made us partakers of his grace, which was before given to Israel, by a measure, which should be to us either more obscure, or in any part diminished; but he has rather poured forth his grace upon us, in a more clear and abundant manner.

---

53 Deut. 30:6; Jer. 4:4; Rom. 4:11.

337. M. Do you think, that if infants were excluded from baptism, they would, on that account, so lose any of the favour of God, as that it might be said, that their privileges were diminished by the coming of Christ?

C. That is indeed evidently manifest. For the sign being taken away, which availed so much in testifying the mercy, and confirming the promises of God; we should be deprived of that most excellent consolation, which the Church from the beginning enjoyed.

338. M. This is your opinion then; for as much as God, under the Old Testament, that he might shew himself to be the Father of little children, commanded the promise of salvation to be engraven on their bodies, by a visible sign; that it would be a reproach, if believers, after the coming of Christ, should have a less confirmation; when the same promise, which was formerly given to the Fathers, is ordained for us in these days, when God exhibits to us in Christ a clearer manifestation of his goodness?

C. So I think. Besides, as it is sufficiently evident, that the power and substance (so to speak) of baptism, are common to infants, then if the sign is denied them, which is inferiour to the substance, a manifest injury will be done them.

339. M. For what purpose then are infants baptized?

C. That they may have the visible seal, that they are the heirs of the blessings promised to the seed of believers; and that after they come to years of discretion, the substance of their baptism being acknowledged, they may, from it, receive and bring forth fruit.

340. M. Let us proceed to the Supper; and in the first place, I would know of you what is its signification.

C. It was instituted by Christ, that by the communion of his body and blood, he might nourish our souls in the hope, and give us assurance of eternal life.

341. M. Why is the body of our Lord represented by bread and the blood by wine?

C. We are taught by this, that as bread has the power of nourishing our bodies, and of sustaining the present life; so the same power is in the body of our Lord for the spiritual nourishment of our souls: and as with wine the hearts of men are cheered, their powers renewed, and the whole body strengthened, so from the blood of Christ, the same benefits are to be received by our souls.

342. M. Are we then fed by the body and blood of the Lord?

C. So I think. For as in this is placed our whole confidence of salvation, that the obedience which he has rendered to the Father should be imputed to us, and accounted as ours, so it is necessary that he should be received by us: for we are not otherwise made partakers of his benefits, but only as he makes himself ours.

343. M. But did he not then give himself to us, when he offered himself to death, that he might reconcile us, redeemed from the sentence of death, to the Father?

C. That is indeed true; but it is not sufficient for us, unless we now receive him, that we may partake of the fruit and efficacy of his death.

344. M. Does not the manner of our receiving Christ consist then in faith?

C. Yes, but I add this, that it be done, while we not only believe that he died to deliver us from death, and rose again to procure life for us; but also that we acknowledge that he dwells in us; and that we are united to him, by that kind of union, by which the members are united to the head, so that, by the privilege of this union, we may be made partakers of all his benefits.

345. M. Do we obtain this communion through the Supper only?

C. By no means. For by the gospel, as Paul testifies, Christ is communicated to us, as we are therein taught, that we are flesh of his flesh, and bone of his bone; that he is the living bread, which came down from heaven to nourish our souls; that we are one with him, even as he is one with the Father: and such like things.[54]

346. M. What other benefit does the sacrament confer on us?

C. This—That the communion which I mentioned is strengthened and confirmed to us. For although both in baptism and the gospel, Christ is offered to us; yet in these we receive him, only in part.

---

54 1 Cor. 1:6; Eph. 5:30; John 6:51; 17:21.

347. M. What have we then in the symbol of the bread?

C. The body of Christ: that as he was once offered a sacrifice for us, to reconcile us to God, so now he is to be given to us, that we may assuredly know that reconciliation belongs to us.

348. M. What have we in the symbol of the wine?

C. As Christ poured out his blood once, in satisfaction for sins, and as the price of our redemption; so we believe, that it is now reached out to be drank by us, that we may receive its benefits.

349. M. According to these two answers, the Holy Supper of the Lord calls us back to his death, that we may partake of its efficacy?

C. Yes, wholly. For at that time, one only and perpetual sacrifice was perfected; which might suffice for our salvation. Therefore nothing more remains for us, but to receive its fruits.

350. M. Was not the Supper then instituted for this end, that we should offer to God, the body of his Son?

C. By no means. For the prerogative of offering for sins belongs to Christ alone, as he is the eternal Priest. And this is the meaning of his word when he says, Take and eat. He does not here command us to offer his body but only that we should feed upon it.[55]

351. M. Why do we use two signs?

C. In this the Lord consults our infirmity, as he would teach us more familiarly, that he is not only the food for our souls, but also the drink; that we may seek our spiritual life wholly in him alone.

352. M. Should all persons without exception equally use both?

C. So Christ commands; and it is the highest impiety for any one to derogate in any manner from that, by attempting any thing different.

---

55 Heb. 5:10; Matt. 26:29.

353. M. Have we in the Supper the sign only of those benefits, you mentioned or are they therein, in very deed, given to us?

C. As Christ our Lord is truth itself, it is not to be doubted at all, but that he fulfils to us, at the same time, those promises which he gives to us therein, and adds its substance to the figure. Wherefore I do not doubt, but that as he is witnessed by words and signs, so he will make us partakers of his substance, that we may be united with him in one life.

354. M. But how can this be done, since the body of Christ is in heaven, and we are still sojourners on earth?

C. He effects this by the marvellous and secret influence of his Spirit; with whom it is easy to unite those things which are otherwise separated by a great distance of places.

355. M. You do not suppose then that the body of Christ is enclosed in the bread, or his blood in the cup?

C. By no means; but I think this, that in order to possess the substance of the signs, our minds must be raised to heaven, where Christ is, and from whence we look for him, the Judge and Redeemer. But it is wicked and useless to look for him in these earthly elements.

356. M. That we may sum up in one head the things which you have said: You assert that there are two things in the Supper, viz. *Bread and wine*, which are seen with the eyes, handled with the hands, and perceived by the taste; and finally that our souls spiritually feed upon Christ, as their own proper aliment.

C. Yes, truly; and therein is the resurrection of our bodies also confirmed to us, as by a given pledge, as they are made partakers of the symbol of life.

357. M. But what is the true and lawful use of this sacrament?

C. Such as Paul defines it to be: Let a man examine himself, and so let him eat of that bread and drink of that cup.[56]

---

56 1 Cor. 11:28.

358. M. What should be the object of this examination?

C. Whether he is a true member of Christ.

359. M. By what evidence shall he know that he is a true member of Christ?

C. If he possesses true faith and repentance; if he exercises sincere love towards his neighbours; if his mind is free from all hatred and malice.

360. M. But do you require in man perfect faith and charity?

C. Truly, it is necessary that both faith and charity be free from all hypocrisy. But among men no one will ever be found absolutely perfect. Therefore the Holy Supper would have been instituted in vain, if no one might partake of it who is not wholly perfect.

361. M. Should not the imperfection then, under which we here labour, prevent our coming to the Supper?

C. By no means, for if we were perfect, the Supper would have no further use among us, as it is appointed to be a help for relieving our weakness, and a refuge for our imperfection.

362. M. Have not these two sacraments some other proposed end?

C. They are also marks, and as it were tokens of our profession. For in the use of them we profess our faith among men, and testify, that we have one mind in the religion of Christ.

363. M. If any one should despise the use of these, in what estimation is he to be held?

C. This certainly would be judged to be an indirect denial of Christ; and certainly such an one, since he disdains to profess himself a Christian, is unworthy to be numbered among Christians.

364. M. Is it sufficient to have received each sacrament once in a whole life?

C. One baptism is indeed sufficient, and this cannot lawfully be repeated: But with regard to the Supper it is different.

365. M. What is that difference?

C. By baptism the Lord introduces and adopts us into his Church, and thenceforward considers us, as of his family: after he has written us in the number of his people, he testifies by the Supper, that he takes care of us, and nourishes us as his members.

366. M. Does the administration of baptism and the Supper alike appertain to all.

C. By no means: for these are the peculiar duties of those to whom is committed the public office of teaching: for to feed the Church with the doctrine of salvation and to administer the sacraments are things united in a perpetual connection among themselves.

367. M. Are you able to prove that to me by the testimony of scripture?

C. Christ, indeed, gave the commission of baptizing expressly to the apostles; but in the celebration of the Supper, he commanded us to follow his example: and the Evangelists inform us, that he performed in that distribution the office of a public minister.[57]

368. M. But ought those pastors, to whom the dispensation of the sacraments is committed, generally to admit all persons without distinction?

C. As it respects baptism, since it is administered at the present day only to infants, all are to be admitted without distinction: but at the Supper, the minister ought to take care not to communicate it to any one who is publicly known to be unworthy.

369. M. Why not?

C. Because it cannot be done without a contempt and profanation of the sacrament.

370. M. But did not Christ honour Judas, however impious, with the sacrament?

---

57 Matt. 28:19; Luke 22:19.

C. Yes, but his impiety was at that time secret; for although Christ himself knew it, still it was not as yet known to man.

371. M. What then shall be done with hypocrites?

C. The pastor has no power to reject them as unworthy; but he ought to wait till God so far reveals their iniquity, as that it becomes known to men.

372. M. What if he should know or be informed, that some one was unworthy?

C. That would by no means be sufficient for rejecting him from the communion, unless there be first had a legitimate trial and judgment of the Church.

373. M. It is important then to have a certain order of government established in the Churches?

C. It is true; for otherwise they can neither be well established nor correctly governed. And this is the order; that Elders be chosen who may preside in the *Censura morum*, or superintend the discipline of morals, and watch to correct small offences; and who shall reject from the communion, those whom they know to be without a capacity for receiving the Supper; and those who cannot be admitted without dishonouring God, and giving offence to the brethren.

9

French Confession of Faith

(1559)

While the Reformation achieved success in many European nations, in others the Roman Catholic Church maintained hegemony. An example of the latter is France. A staunchly Roman Catholic crown suppressed the Protestant movement, causing leaders such as John Calvin, Theodore Beza, William Farel, and Pierre Viret to flee.

The Reformation continued to seep into France, however. In 1559, a national synod of Protestants—known as Huguenots—adopted the French Confession of Faith. The confession was likely written in large part by Calvin, perhaps with contributions from Beza and Viret. The French Protestants, in an attempt to secure their acceptance by the monarch as upright citizens and obedient servants of the crown, submitted the confession in 1560 to King Francis II (who refused to receive it) and in 1561 to King Charles IX (who received it).

Unfortunately, tensions between the Huguenots and Roman Catholics continued through the French Wars of Religion (1562–98). The violence reached a climax in a brutal mob uprising known as the St. Bartholomew's Day Massacre in 1572.

French Confession of Faith

The French Subjects Who Wish to Live in the Purity of the Gospel of Our Lord Jesus Christ.

To the King.

Sire, we thank God that hitherto having had no access to your Majesty to make known the rigor of the persecutions that we have suffered, and suffer daily, for wishing to live in the purity of the Gospel and in peace with our own consciences, he now permits us to see that you wish to know the worthiness of our cause, as is shown by the last Edict given at Amboise in the month of March of this present year, 1559, which it has pleased your Majesty to cause to be published. This emboldens us to speak, which we have been prevented from doing hitherto through the injustice and violence of some of your officers, incited rather by hatred of us than by love of your service. And to the end, Sire, that we may fully inform your Majesty of what concerns this cause, we humbly beseech that you will see and hear our Confession of Faith, which we present to you, hoping that it will prove a sufficient answer to the blame and opprobrium unjustly laid upon us by those who have always made a point of condemning us without having any knowledge of our cause. In the which, Sire, we can affirm that there is nothing contrary to the Word of God, or to the homage which we owe to you.

For the articles of our faith, which are all declared at some length in our Confession, all come to this: that since God has sufficiently declared his will to us through his Prophets and Apostles, and even by the mouth of his Son, our Lord Jesus Christ, we owe such respect and reverence to the Word of God as shall prevent us from adding to it any thing of our own, but shall make us conform entirely to the rules it prescribes. And inasmuch as the Roman Church, forsaking the use and customs of the primitive Church, has introduced new commandments and a new form of worship of God, we esteem it but reasonable to prefer the commandments of God, who is himself truth, to the commandments of men, who by their nature are inclined to deceit and vanity. And whatever our enemies may say against us, we can declare this before God and men, that we suffer for no other reason than for maintaining our Lord Jesus Christ to be our only Saviour and Redeemer, and his doctrine to be the only doctrine of life and salvation.

And this is the only reason, Sire, why the executioners' hands have been stained so often with the blood of your poor subjects, who, sparing not their lives to maintain this same Confession of Faith, have shown to all that they were moved by some other spirit than that of men, who naturally care more for their own peace and comfort than for the honor and glory of God.

And therefore, Sire, in accordance with your promises of goodness and mercy toward your poor subjects, we humbly beseech your Majesty graciously to examine the cause for which, being threatened at all times with death or exile, we thus lose the power of rendering the humble service that we owe you. May it please your Majesty, then instead of the fire and sword which have been used hitherto, so have our confession of Faith decided by the Word of God: giving permission and security for this. And we hope that you yourself will be the judge of our innocence, knowing that there is in us no rebellion or heresy whatsoever, but that our only endeavor is to live in peace of conscience, serving God according to his commandments, and honoring your Majesty by all obedience and submission.

And because we have great need, by the preaching of the Word of God, to be kept in our duty to him, as well as to yourself, we humbly beg, sire, that we may sometimes be permitted to gather together, to be exhorted to the fear of God by his Word, as well as to be confirmed by the administration of the Sacraments which the Lord Jesus Christ instituted in his Church. And if it should please your Majesty to give us a place where any one may see what passes in our assemblies, we shall thereby be absolved from the charge of the enormous crimes with which these same assemblies have been defamed. For nothing will be seen but what is decent and well-ordered, and nothing will be heard but the praise of God, exhortations to his service, and prayers for the preservation of your Majesty and of your kingdom. And if it do not please you to grant us this favor, at least let it be permitted us to follow the established order in private among ourselves.

We beseech you most humbly, Sire, to believe that in listening to this application which is now presented to you, listen to the cries and groans of an infinite number of your poor subjects, who implore of your mercy that you extinguish the fires which the cruelty of your judges has lighted in your kingdom. And that we may thus be permitted, in serving your Majesty, to serve him who has raised you to your power and dignity.

And if it should not please you, Sire, to listen to our voice, may it please you to listen to that of the Son of God, who, having given you power over our property, our bodies, and even our lives, demands that the control and dominion of our souls and consciences, which he purchased with his own blood, be reserved to him.

We beseech him, Sire, that he may lead you always by his Spirit, increasing with your age, your greatness and power, giving you victory over all your enemies, and establishing for ever, in all equity and justice, the throne of your Majesty: before whom, may it please him that we find grace, and some fruit of this our present supplication, so that having exchanged our pains and afflictions for some peace and liberty, we may also change our tears and lamentations into a perpetual thanksgiving to God, and to your Majesty for having done that which is most agreeable to him, most worthy, of your goodness and mercy, and most necessary for the preservation of your most humble and obedient subjects and servants.

CONFESSION OF FAITH

Made in one accord by the French people, who desire to live according to the purity of the Gospel of our Lord Jesus Christ. A.D. 1559.

I. We believe and confess that there is but one God, who is one sole and simple essence, spiritual, eternal, invisible, immutable, infinite, incomprehensible, ineffable, omnipotent; who is all-wise, all-good, all-just, and all-merciful.

II. As such this God reveals himself to men; firstly, in his works, in their creation, as well as in their preservation and control. Secondly, and more clearly, in his Word, which was in the beginning revealed through oracles, and which was afterward committed to writing in the books which we call the Holy Scriptures.

III. These Holy Scriptures are comprised in the canonical books of the Old and New Testaments, as follows: the five books of Moses, namely: Genesis,

Exodus, Leviticus, Numbers, Deuteronomy; Then Joshua, Judges, Ruth, the first and second books of Samuel, the first and second books of the Kings, the first and second books of the Chronicles, otherwise called Paralipomenon, the first book of Ezra; then Nehemiah, the book of Esther, Job, the Psalms of David, the Proverbs or Maxims of Solomon; the book of Ecclesiastes, called the Preacher, the Song of Solomon; then the book of Isaiah, Jeremiah, Lamentations of Jeremiah, Ezekiel, Daniel, Hosea, Joel, Amos, Obadiah, Jonah, Micah, Nahum, Habakkuk, Zephaniah, Haggai, Zechariah, Malachi; then the Holy Gospel according to St. Matthew, according to St. Mark, according to St. Luke, and according to St. John; then the second book of St. Luke, otherwise called the Acts of the Apostles; then the Epistles of St. Paul: one to the Romans, two to the Corinthians, one to the Galatians, one to the Ephesians, one to the Philippians, one to the Colossians, two to the Thessalonians, two to Timothy, one to Titus, one to Philemon; then the Epistle to the Hebrews, the Epistle of St. James, the first and second Epistles of St. Peter, the first, second, and third Epistles of St. John, the Epistle of St. Jude; and then the Apocalypse, or Revelation of St. John.

IV. We know these books to be canonical, and the sure rule of our faith, not so much by the common accord and consent of the Church, as by the testimony and inward illumination of the Holy Spirit, which enables us to distinguish them from other ecclesiastical books upon which, however useful, we can not found any articles of faith.

V. We believe that the Word contained in these books has proceeded from God, and receives its authority from him alone, and not from men. And inasmuch as it is the rule of all truth, containing all that is necessary for the service of God and for our salvation, it is not lawful for men, nor even for angels, to add to it, to take away from it, or to change it. Whence it follows that no authority, whether of antiquity, or custom, or numbers, or human wisdom, or judgments, or proclamations, or edicts, or decrees, or councils, or visions, or miracles, should be opposed to these Holy Scriptures, but, on the contrary, all things should be examined, regulated, and reformed according to them. And therefore we confess the three creeds, to wit: the Apostles', the Nicene, and the Athanasian, because they are in accordance with the Word of God.

VI. These Holy Scriptures teach us that in this one sole and simple divine essence, whom we have confessed, there are three persons: the Father, the Son, and the Holy Spirit. The Father, first cause, principle, and origin of all things. The Son, his Word and eternal wisdom. The Holy Spirit, his virtue, power, and efficacy. The Son begotten from eternity by the Father. The Holy Spirit proceeding eternally from them both; the three persons not confused, but distinct, and yet not separate, but of the same essence, equal in eternity and power. And in this we confess that which hath been established by the ancient councils, and we detest all sects and heresies which were rejected by the holy doctors, such as St. Hilary, St. Athanasius, St. Ambrose, and St. Cyril.

VII. We believe that God, in three co-working persons, by his power, wisdom, and incomprehensible goodness, created all things, not only the heavens and the earth and all that in them is, but also invisible spirits, some of whom have fallen away and gone into perdition, while others have continued in obedience. That the first, being corrupted by evil, are enemies of all good, consequently of the whole Church. The second, having been preserved by the grace of God, are ministers to glorify God's name, and to promote the salvation of his elect.

VIII. We believe that he not only created all things, but that he governs and directs them, disposing and ordaining by his sovereign will all that happens in the world; not that he is the author of evil, or that the guilt of it can be imputed to him, as his will is the sovereign and infallible rule of all right and justice; but he hath wonderful means of so making use of devils and sinners that he can turn to good the evil which they do, and of which they are guilty. And thus, confessing that the providence of God orders all things, we humbly bow before the secrets which are hidden to us, without questioning what is above our understanding; but rather making use of what is revealed to us in Holy Scripture for our peace and safety, inasmuch as God, who has all things in subjection to him, watches over us with a Father's care, so that not a hair of our heads shall fall without his will. And yet he restrains the devils and all our enemies, so that they can not harm us without his leave.

IX. We believe that man was created pure and perfect in the image of God, and that by his own guilt he fell from the grace which he received, and is thus alienated from God, the fountain of justice and of all good, so that his nature is totally corrupt. And being blinded in mind, and depraved in heart, he has lost all integrity, and there is no good in him. And although he can still discern good and evil, we say, notwithstanding, that the light he has becomes darkness when he seeks for God, so that he can in nowise approach him by his intelligence and reason. And although he has a will that incites him to do this or that, yet it is altogether captive to sin, so that he has no other liberty to do right than that which God gives him.

X. We believe that all the posterity of Adam is in bondage to original sin, which is an hereditary evil, and not an imitation merely, as was declared by the Pelagians, whom we detest in their errors. And we consider that it is not necessary to inquire how sin was conveyed from one man to another, for what God had given Adam was not for him alone, but for all his posterity; and thus in his person we have been deprived of all good things, and have fallen with him into a state of sin and misery.

XI. We believe, also, that this evil is truly sin, sufficient for the condemnation of the whole human race, even of little children in the mother's womb, and that God considers it as such; even after baptism it is still of the nature of sin, but the condemnation of it is abolished for the children of God, out of his mere free grace and love. And further, that it is a perversity always producing fruits of malice and of rebellion, so that the most holy men, although they resist it, are still stained with many weaknesses and imperfections while they are in this life.

XII. We believe that from this corruption and general condemnation in which all men are plunged, God, according to his eternal and immutable counsel, calleth those whom he hath chosen by his goodness and mercy alone in our Lord Jesus Christ, without consideration of their works, to display in them the riches of his mercy; leaving the rest in this same corruption and condemnation to show in them his justice. For the ones are no better than the others, until God discerns them according to his immutable purpose which he has determined in Jesus Christ before the creation of the world. Neither can any man gain such a reward by his own virtue, as by nature we can not have a single good feeling, affection, or thought, except God has first put it into our hearts.

XIII. We believe that all that is necessary for our salvation was offered and communicated to us in Jesus Christ. He is given to us for our salvation, and "is made unto us wisdom, and righteousness, and sanctification, and redemption:" so that if we refuse him, we renounce the mercy of the Father, in which alone we can find a refuge.

XIV. We believe that Jesus Christ, being the wisdom of God and his eternal Son, has put on our flesh, so as to be God and man in one person; man, like unto us, capable of suffering in body and soul, yet free from all stain of sin. And as to his humanity, he was the true seed of Abraham and of David, although he was conceived by the secret power of the Holy Spirit. In this we detest all the heresies that have of old troubled the Church, and especially the diabolical conceits of Servetus, which attribute a fantastical divinity to the Lord Jesus, calling him the idea and pattern of all things, and the personal or figurative Son of God, and, finally, attribute to him a body of three uncreated elements, thus confusing and destroying the two natures.

XV. We believe that in one person, that is, Jesus Christ, the two natures are actually and inseparably joined and united, and yet each remains in its proper character: so that in this union the divine nature, retaining its attributes, remained uncreated, infinite, and all-pervading; and the human nature remained finite, having its form, measure, and attributes; and although Jesus Christ, in rising from the dead, bestowed immortality upon his body, yet he did not take from it the truth of its nature, and we so consider him in his divinity that we do not despoil him of his humanity.

XVI. We believe that God, in sending his Son, intended to show his love and inestimable goodness towards us, giving him up to die to accomplish all righteousness, and raising him from the dead to secure for us the heavenly life.

XVII. We believe that by the perfect sacrifice that the Lord Jesus offered on the cross, we are reconciled to God, and justified before him; for we can not be acceptable to him, nor become partakers of the grace of adoption, except as he pardons [all] our sins, and blots them out. Thus we declare that through Jesus Christ we are cleansed and made perfect; by his death we are fully justified, and through him only can we be delivered from our iniquities and transgressions.

XVIII. We believe that all our justification rests upon the remission of our sins, in which also is our only blessedness, as saith the Psalmist (Ps. 32:2). We therefore reject all other means of justification before God, and without claiming any virtue or merit, we rest simply in the obedience of Jesus Christ, which is imputed to us as much to blot out all our sins as to make us find grace and favor in the sight of God. And, in fact, we believe that in falling away from this foundation, however slightly, we could not find rest elsewhere, but should always be troubled. Forasmuch as we are never at peace with God till we resolve to be loved in Jesus Christ, for of ourselves we are worthy of hatred.

XIX. We believe that by this means we have the liberty and privilege of calling upon God, in full confidence that he will show himself a Father to us. For we should have no access to the Father except through this Mediator. And to be heard in his name, we must hold our life from him as from our chief.

XX. We believe that we are made partakers of this justification by faith alone, as it is written: "He suffered for our salvation, that whosoever believeth on him should not perish." And this is done inasmuch as we appropriate to our use the promises of life which are given to us through him, and feel their effect when we accept them, being assured that we are established by the Word of God and shall not be deceived. Thus our justification through faith depends upon the free promises by which God declares and testifies his love to us.

XXI. We believe that we are enlightened in faith by the secret power of the Holy Spirit, that it is a gratuitous and special gift which God grants to whom he will, so that the elect have no cause to glory, but are bound to be doubly thankful that they have been preferred to others. We believe also that faith is not given to the elect only to introduce them into the right way, but also to make them continue in it to the end. For as it is God who hath begun the work, he will also perfect it.

XXII. We believe that by this faith we are regenerated in newness of life, being by nature subject to sin. Now we receive by faith grace to live holily and in the fear of God, in accepting the promise which is given to us by the Gospel, namely: that God will give us his Holy Spirit. This faith not only doth not hinder us from holy living, or turn us from the love of righteousness, but of necessity begetteth in us all good works. Moreover, although God worketh in us for our salvation, and reneweth our hearts, determining us to that which is good, yet we confess that the good works which we do proceed from his Spirit, and can not be accounted to us for justification, neither do they entitle us to the adoption of sons, for we should always be doubting and restless in our hearts, if we did not rest upon the atonement by which Jesus Christ hath acquitted us.

XXIII. We believe that the ordinances of the law came to an end at the advent of Jesus Christ; but, although the ceremonies are no more in use, yet their substance and truth remain in the person of him in whom they are fulfilled. And, moreover, we must seek aid from the law and the prophets for the ruling of our lives, as well as for our confirmation in the promises of the gospel.

XXIV. We believe, as Jesus Christ is our only advocate, and as he commands us to ask of the Father in his name, and as it is not lawful for us to pray except in accordance with the model God hath taught us by his Word, that all imaginations of men concerning the intercession of dead saints are an abuse and a device of Satan to lead men from the right way of worship. We reject, also, all other means by which men hope to redeem themselves before God, as derogating from the sacrifice and passion of Jesus Christ.

Finally, we consider purgatory as an illusion proceeding from the same source, from which have also sprung monastic vows, pilgrimages, the prohibition of marriage, and of eating meat, the ceremonial observance of days, auricular confession, indulgences, and all such things by which they hope to merit forgiveness and salvation. These things we reject, not only for the false idea of merit which is attached to them, but also because they are human inventions imposing a yoke upon the conscience.

XXV. Now as we enjoy Christ only through the gospel, we believe that the order of the Church, established by his authority, ought to be sacred and inviolable, and that, therefore, the Church can not exist without pastors for instruction, whom we should respect and reverently listen to, when they are properly called and exercise their office faithfully. Not that God doth require such aid and subordinate means, but because it pleaseth him to govern us by such restraints. In this we detest all visionaries who would like, so far as lies in their power, to destroy the ministry and preaching of the Word and sacraments.

XXVI. We believe that no one ought to seclude himself and be contented to be alone; but that all jointly should keep and maintain the union of the Church, and submit to the public teaching, and to the yoke of Jesus Christ, wherever God shall have established a true order of the Church, even if the magistrates and their edicts are contrary to it. For if they do not take part in it, or if they separate themselves from it, they do contrary to the Word of God.

XXVII. Nevertheless we believe that it is important to discern with care and prudence which is the true Church, for this title has been much abused. We say, then, according to the Word of God, that it is the company of the faithful who agree to follow his Word, and the pure religion which it teaches; who grow in grace all their lives, believing and becoming more confirmed in the fear of God according as they feel the want of growing and pressing onward. Even although they strive continually, they can have no hope save in the remission of their sins. Nevertheless we do not deny that among the faithful there may be hypocrites and reprobates, but their wickedness can not destroy the title of the Church.

XXVIII. In this belief we declare that, properly speaking, there can be no Church where the Word of God is not received, nor profession made of subjection to it, nor use of the sacraments. Therefore we condemn the papal assemblies, as the pure Word of God is banished from them, their sacraments are corrupted, or falsified, or destroyed, and all superstitions and idolatries are in them. We hold, then, that all who take part in these acts, and commune in that Church, separate and cut themselves off from the body of Christ. Nevertheless, as some trace of the Church is left in the papacy, and the virtue and substance of baptism remain, and as the efficacy of baptism does not depend upon the person who administers it, we confess that those baptized in it do not need a second baptism. But, on account of its corruptions, we can not present children to be baptized in it without incurring pollution.

XXIX. As to the true Church, we believe that it should be governed, according to the order established by our Lord Jesus Christ. That there should be pastors, overseers, and deacons, so that true doctrine may have its course, that errors may be corrected and suppressed, and the poor and all who are in affliction may be helped in their necessities; and that assemblies may be held in the name of God, so that great and small may be edified.

XXX. We believe that all true pastors, wherever they may be, have the same authority and equal power under one head, one only sovereign and universal bishop, Jesus Christ; and that consequently no Church shall claim any authority or dominion over any other.

XXXI. We believe that no person should undertake to govern the Church upon his own authority, but that this should be derived from election, as far as it is possible, and as God will permit. And we make this exception especially, because sometimes, and even in our own days, when the state of the Church has been interrupted, it has been necessary for God to raise men in an extraordinary manner to restore the Church which was in ruin and desolation. But, notwithstanding, we believe that this rule must always be binding: that all pastors, overseers, and deacons should have evidence of being called to their office.

XXXII. We believe, also, that it is desirable and useful that those elected to be superintendents devise among themselves what means should be adopted for the government of the whole body, and yet that they should never depart from that which was ordained by our Lord Jesus Christ. Which does not prevent there being some special ordinances in each place, as convenience may require.

XXXIII. However, we reject all human inventions, and all laws which men may introduce under the pretense of serving God, by which they wish to bind consciences; and we receive only that which conduces to concord and holds all in obedience, from the greatest to the least. In this we must follow that which the Lord Jesus Christ declared as to excommunication, which we approve and confess to be necessary with all its antecedents and consequences.

XXXIV. We believe that the sacraments are added to the Word for more ample confirmation, that they may be to us pledges and seals of the grace of God, and by this means aid and comfort our faith, because of the infirmity which is in us, and that they are outward signs through which God operates by his Spirit, so that he may not signify any thing to us in vain. Yet we hold that their substance and truth is in Jesus Christ, and that of themselves they are only smoke and shadow.

XXXV. We confess only two sacraments common to the whole Church, of which the first, baptism, is given as a pledge of our adoption; for by it we are grafted into the body of Christ, so as to be washed and cleansed by his blood, and then renewed in purity of life by his Holy Spirit. We hold, also, that although we are baptized only once, yet the gain that it symbolizes to us reaches over our whole lives and to our death, so that we have a lasting witness that Jesus Christ will always be our justification and sanctification. Nevertheless, although it is a sacrament of faith and penitence, yet as God receives little children into the Church with their fathers, we say, upon the authority of Jesus Christ, that the children of believing parents should be baptized.

XXXVI. We confess that the Lord's Supper, which is the second sacrament, is a witness of the union which we have with Christ, inasmuch as he not only died and rose again for us once, but also feeds and nourishes us truly with his flesh and blood, so that we may be one in him, and that our life may be in common. Although he be in heaven until he come to judge all the earth, still we believe that by the secret and incomprehensible power of his Spirit he feeds and strengthens us with the substance of his body and of his blood. We hold that this is done spiritually, not because we put imagination and fancy in the place of fact and truth, but because the greatness of this mystery exceeds the measure of our senses and the laws of nature. In short, because it is heavenly, it can only be apprehended by faith.

XXXVII. We believe, as has been said, that in the Lord's Supper, as well as in baptism, God gives us really and in fact that which he there sets forth to us; and that consequently with these signs is given the true possession and enjoyment of that which they present to us. And thus all who bring a pure faith, like a vessel, to the sacred table of Christ, receive truly that of which it is a sign; for the body and the blood of Jesus Christ give food and drink to the soul, no less than bread and wine nourish the body.

XXXVIII. Thus we hold that water, being a feeble element, still testifies to us in truth the inward cleansing of our souls in the blood of Jesus Christ by the efficacy of his Spirit, and that the bread and wine given to us in the sacrament serve to our spiritual nourishment, inasmuch as they show, as to our sight, that the body of Christ is our meat, and his blood our drink. And we reject the Enthusiasts and Sacramentarians who will not receive such signs and marks, although our Saviour said: "This is my body, and this cup is my blood."

XXXIX. We believe that God wishes to have the world governed by laws and magistrates, so that some restraint may be put upon its disordered appetites. And as he has established kingdoms, republics, and all sorts of principalities, either hereditary or otherwise, and all that belongs to a just government, and wishes to be considered as their Author, so he has put the sword into the hands of magistrates to suppress crimes against the first as well as against the second table of the Commandments of God. We must therefore, on his account, not only submit to them as superiors, but honor and hold them in all reverence as his lieutenants and officers, whom he has commissioned to exercise a legitimate and holy authority.

XL. We hold, then, that we must obey their laws and statutes, pay customs, taxes, and other dues, and bear the yoke of subjection with a good and free will, even if they are unbelievers, provided that the sovereign empire of God remain intact. Therefore we detest all those who would like to reject authority, to establish community and confusion of property, and overthrow the order of justice.

10

Scots Confession

(1560)

The theology of the Reformation had a difficult time making inroads into Scotland. In 1528, the cause claimed its first martyr, Patrick Hamilton, who had encountered the writings of Martin Luther while in France and was converted. Upon returning to Scotland, he encountered resistance from the local archbishop and fled to Germany. But he soon returned, knowing the danger he faced. He preached the gospel boldly, leading to many conversions, before he was arrested and burned at the stake.

Reformation theology continued to make its way into Scotland from England, however, and the execution of another martyr, George Wishart, in 1546 moved the Protestants to act. They stormed St. Andrews Castle and executed the archbishop. But the Reformation would not triumph just yet. The queen of Scotland, Mary of Guise, enlisted the aid of the French to expel the rebels. One of their leaders, John Knox, would spend the next two years as a galley slave, before being exiled to England and fleeing to Geneva.

Finally, in 1559, the time was ripe for change. Knox returned to Scotland and inspired an uprising that ended with the Protestants ascendant. A new Parliament met in 1560 and approved the Scots Confession and the First Book of Discipline, thus formalizing the Reformation's triumph in Scotland.

Scots Confession

Professed and believed by the Protestants within the realm of Scotland. Published by them in Parliament and by the estates thereof. Ratified and approved, as wholesome and sound doctrine grounded upon the infallible truth of God's Word.

MATTHEW 24

And these glad tidings of the kingdom will be preached through the whole world for a witness unto all nations: And then will the end come.

The Estates of Scotland, with the inhabitants of the same, professing Christ Jesus, His holy gospel, to their natural countrymen and to all other realms and nations professing the same Lord Jesus with them, wish grace, mercy, and peace from God the Father of our Lord Jesus Christ, with the spirit of righteous judgment, for salvation.

Long have we thirsted, dear brethren, to have notified unto the world the sum of that doctrine which we profess and for which we have sustained infamy and danger. But such has been the rage of Satan against us and against Christ Jesus His eternal verity, lately borne among us that to this day no time has been granted unto us to clear our consciences, as most gladly we would have done. For how we have been tossed heretofore, the most part of Europe (as we suppose) does understand. But seeing that of the infinite goodness of our God (which never suffers His afflicted utterly to be confounded) above expectation, we have obtained some rest and liberty, [and] we could not but set forth this brief and plain confession of such doctrine as is propounded unto us, and as we believe and profess, partly for satisfaction of our brethren, whose hearts we doubt not have been and yet are wounded by the despiteful railing of such as yet have not learned to speak well: and partly for stopping the mouths of the impudent blasphemers, which boldly damn that which they have neither heard nor yet understood. Not that we judge that the cankered malice of such is able to be cured by this our simple confession. No, we know that the sweet savor of the gospel is and will be death to the sons of perdition. But we have chief respect to our weak and infirm brethren, to whom we would communicate the bottom of our hearts, lest they be troubled or carried away by [the] diversity of rumors which Satan spreads contrary to us, to the defacing of this our most godly enterprise. Protesting that if any man will note in this our confession any article or sentence repugnant to God's holy Word, that it would please him, of his gentleness and for Christian charity's sake, to admonish us of the same in writing. And we on our honor and fidelity do promise unto him satisfaction from the mouth of God (that is, from His Holy Scriptures) or else reformation of that which he will prove to be amiss. For God we take to record in our conscience, that from our hearts we abhor all sects of heresy and all teachers of erroneous doctrine, and that with all humility we embrace the purity of Christ's gospel, which is the only food of our souls—and, therefore, so precious unto us, that we are determined to suffer the extremity of worldly danger, rather than that we will suffer our selves to be defrauded of the same. For hereof we are most certainly persuaded, that whosoever denies Christ Jesus or is ashamed of Him in the presence of men, will be denied before the Father, and before His holy angels. And, therefore, by the assistance of the mighty Spirit of the same our Lord Jesus, we firmly purpose to abide to the end in the confession of this our faith, as by the following articles.

I. Of God

We confess and acknowledge one only God, to whom only we must cleave, whom only we must serve (Deut. 6), whom only we must worship (Isa. 44), and in whom only we put our trust (Deut. 4). Who is eternal, infinite, immeasurable, incomprehensible, omnipotent, invisible, one in substance and yet distinct in three persons, the Father, the Son, and the Holy Ghost (Matt. 28). By whom we confess and believe, all things in heaven and earth (Gen. 1), as well visible as invisible, to have been created, to be retained in their being, and to be ruled and guided by His inscrutable providence, to such end as His eternal wisdom (Prov. 16), goodness, and justice has appointed them to the manifestation of His own glory.

II. Of the Creation of Man

We confess and acknowledge this our God to have created man (to wit, our first father Adam) to His own image and similitude (Gen. 1–2). To whom He gave wisdom, lordship, justice, free will, and clear knowledge of Himself. So that in the whole nature of man, there could be noted no imperfection. From which honor and perfection, man and woman did both fall (Gen. 3), the woman being deceived by the Serpent, and man obeying the voice of the woman: both conspiring against the sovereign majesty of God, who in express words had before threatened death, if they presumed to eat of the forbidden tree.

III. Of Original Sin

By which transgression, commonly called original sin, was the image of God utterly defaced in man. And he and his posterity of nature became enemies to God, slaves to Satan, and servants to sin (Eph. 2; Rom. 5), that death everlasting has had, and insofar will have, power and domination over all that have not been, are not, or will not be regenerated from above (John 3). Which regeneration is wrought by the power of the Holy Ghost (Rom. 5–6) working in the hearts of the elect of God, an assured faith in the promises of God revealed to us in His Word, by which faith they apprehend Christ Jesus with the graces and benefits promised in Him.

IV. Of the Revelation of the Promise

For this we constantly believe that God, after the fearful and horrible defection of man from His obedience, did seek Adam again, call upon him, rebuke his sin (Gen. 3), convict him of the same, and in the end made unto him a most joyful promise: to wit, that the seed of the woman should break down the Serpent's head, that is, He should destroy the works of the devil. Which promise, as it was repeated and made more clear from time to time (Gen. 12, 15, etc.; Isa. 7–8, etc.), so was it embraced with joy and most constantly retained of all the faithful from Adam to Noah, from Noah to Abraham, from Abraham to David, and so forth to the incarnation of Christ Jesus. Who all (we mean the faithful fathers) under the Law did see the joyful days of Christ Jesus and did rejoice.

V. The Continuance, Increase, and Preservation of the Kirk

We most constantly believe that God preserved, instructed, multiplied, honored, adorned (Ezek. 16), and from death called to life His kirk in all ages from Adam till the coming of Christ Jesus in the flesh. For Abraham, He called from his father's country (Gen. 12), him He instructed, his seed He multiplied (Ex. 1–2, 13), the same He marvelously preserved and more marvelously delivered from the bondage and tyranny of Pharaoh. To them He gave His laws (Ex. 20), constitutions, and ceremonies. Them He possessed in the land of Canaan (Josh. 1–3, etc.): to them, after judges and after Saul, He gave David to be king (1 Sam. 16), to whom He made promise that of the fruit of his loins should one sit forever upon His regal seat. To this same people, from time to time, He sent prophets to reduce them to the right way of their God (2 Kings 17), from which oftentimes they declined by idolatry (2 Kings 7, 24–25). And albeit that for their stubborn contempt of justice, He was compelled to give them into the hands of their enemies, as before was threatened by the mouth of Moses (Deut. 29), in so much that the holy city was destroyed, the temple burnt with fire, and the whole land left desolate the space of 70 years (Jer. 39; Ezra 1; Hag. 1–2; Zech. 3), yet of mercy did He lead them again to Jerusalem. Where the city and temple were rebuilt and they against all temptations and assaults of Satan did abide, till the Messiah came according to the promise.

VI. Of the Incarnation of Christ Jesus

When the fullness of time came (Gal. 4), God sent His Son, His eternal wisdom, the substance of His own glory, into this world, who took the nature of manhood of the substance of a woman, to wit, of a virgin, and that by operation of the Holy Ghost (Luke 1–2), and so was born the just seed of David, the angel of the great counsel of God, the very Messiah promised (Isa. 7). Whom we acknowledge and confess, Immanuel, very God and very man, two perfect natures united and joined in one person. By which our confession, we condemn the damnable and pestilent heresies of Arius, Marcion, Eutyches, Nestorius, and such others, as either deny the eternity of His Godhead, or the verity of His human nature, or confounded them, or yet denied them.

VII. Why It Behooved the Mediator to Be Very God and Very Man

We acknowledge and confess that this most wondrous conjunction between the Godhead and the manhood in Christ Jesus did proceed from the eternal and immutable decree of God, whence also our salvation springs and depends.

VIII. Election

For that same eternal God and Father, who of mere grace elected us in Christ Jesus His Son before the foundation of the world was laid (Eph. 1), appointed Him to be our Head, our brother (Heb. 2), our pastor, and great bishop of our souls (John 10). But because the enmity betwixt the justice of God and our sins was such that no flesh by itself could or might have attained unto God, it behooved that the Son of God should descend unto us and take Himself a body of our body, flesh of our flesh, and bones of our bones: and so become the perfect mediator betwixt God and man, giving power to so many as believe in Him to be the sons of God (John 1). As He Himself does witness, "I pass up to my Father and unto your Father, to my God and unto your God" (John 20). By which most holy fraternity, whatsoever we have lost in Adam is restored to us again. And for this cause are we not afraid to call God our Father, not so much that He has created us (which we have common with the reprobate) as for that, that He has given to us His only Son, to be our brother, and given unto us grace to acknowledge and embrace Him for our only mediator, as before was said. It behooved further the Messiah and Redeemer to be very God and very man because He was to undergo the punishment due for our transgressions (Isa. 53), and to present Himself in the presence of His Father's judgment as in our person to suffer for our transgression and disobedience by death, to overcome him that was author of death. But because the only Godhead could not suffer death, neither yet could the only manhood overcome the same, He joined both together in one person that the weakness of the one should suffer and be subject to death (which we had deserved), and the infinite and invincible power of the other, to wit, of the Godhead, should triumph and purchase to us life, liberty, and perpetual victory. And so we confess and most undoubtedly believe.

IX. Christ's Death, Passion, Burial, Etc.

That our Lord Jesus offered Himself a voluntary sacrifice unto His Father for us (Heb. 10), that He suffered contradiction of sinners, that He was wounded and plagued for our transgressions (Isa. 53), that He being the clean and innocent Lamb of God was damned in the presence of an earthly judge, that we should be absolved before the tribunal seat of our God. That He suffered not only the cruel death of the cross (which was accursed by the sentence of God [Deut. 21; Gal. 3]), but also that He suffered for a season the wrath of His Father, which sinners had deserved. But yet we avow that He remained the only well beloved and blessed Son of His Father, even in the midst of His anguish and torment which He suffered in body and soul to make that full satisfaction for the sins of His people (Heb. 10). After which we confess and avow that there remains no other sacrifice for sin, which if any affirm, we nothing doubt to avow that they are blasphemous against Christ's death and the everlasting purgation and satisfaction purchased to us by the same.

X. Resurrection

We undoubtedly believe that in as much as it was impossible that the sorrows of death should retain in bondage the author of life (Acts 2–3), that our Lord Jesus, crucified, died, and buried (Rom. 6), who descended into hell, did rise again for our justification, and destroying him who was author of death brought life again unto us that were subject to death and to the bondage of the same. We know that His resurrection was confirmed by the testimony of His very enemies (Matt. 28), by the resurrection of the dead whose sepulchers did open and they did arise and appeared to many within the city of Jerusalem (Matt. 27). It was also confirmed by the testimony of angels and by the senses and judgments of His apostles and of others (John 20–21), who had conversation and did eat and drink with Him after His resurrection.

XI. Ascension

We nothing doubt but that the selfsame body which was born of the virgin, was crucified, and buried, and which did rise again, did ascend into the heavens (Acts 1), for the accomplishment of all things where in our names and for our comfort, He has received all power in heaven and earth (Matt. 28), where He sits at the right hand of the Father (1 John 2), inaugurating His kingdom, advocate and only mediator for us (1 Tim. 2; Ps. 110). Which glory, honor, and prerogative, He alone amongst the brethren will possess till all His enemies are made His footstool, as that we undoubtedly believe they will be in the final judgment: to the execution whereof we certainly believe that the same Lord Jesus will visibly return as He was seen to ascend (Acts 1). And then we firmly believe that the time of refreshing and restitution of all things will come (John 19; Acts 3), in so much that those who from the beginning have suffered violence, injury, and wrong for righteousness' sake will inherit that blessed immortality promised from the beginning. But contrariwise the stubborn, disobedient, cruel oppressors, filthy persons, idolaters, and all sorts of unfaithful (Rev. 20; Isa. 66) will be cast in the dungeon of utter darkness, where their worm will not die, neither yet their fire be extinguished. The remembrance of which day and of the judgment to be executed in the same is not only to us a bridle whereby our carnal lusts are restrained, but also such inestimable comfort that neither may the threatening of worldly princes, neither yet the fear of temporal death and present danger move us to renounce and forsake that blessed society which we the members have with our Head and only Mediator, Christ Jesus. Whom we confess and avow to be the Messiah promised, the only Head of His kirk, our just Lawgiver, our only High Priest, Advocate and Mediator (Isa. 7; Col. 1; Heb. 6, 10). In which honors and offices, if man or angel presumes to intrude themselves, we utterly detest and abhor them as blasphemous to our sovereign and supreme governor Christ Jesus.

XII. Faith in the Holy Ghost

This our faith and the assurance of the same proceeds not from flesh and blood (Matt. 16), that is to say, from no natural powers within us, but is the inspiration of the Holy Ghost (John 14–16), whom we confess God equal with the Father and with the Son, who sanctifies us and brings us in all verity by His own operation, without whom we should remain forever enemies to God and ignorant of His Son, Christ Jesus. For by nature we are so dead, so blind, and so perverse that neither can we feel when we are pricked, see the light when it shines, nor assent to the will of God when it is revealed, unless the Spirit of the Lord Jesus quicken that which is dead, remove the darkness from our minds, and bow our stubborn hearts to the obedience of His blessed will. And so as we confess that God the Father created us when we were not; as His Son our Lord Jesus redeemed us when we were enemies to Him (Rom. 5); so also do we confess that the Holy Ghost does sanctify and regenerate us without all respect of any merit proceeding from us, be it before or be it after our regeneration. To speak this one thing, yet in more plain words, as we willingly spoil our selves of all honor and glory of our own creation and redemption, so do we also of our regeneration and sanctification, for of our selves we are not sufficient to think any good thought (2 Cor. 7). But He who has begun the good work in us is only He that continues us in the same to the praise and glory of His undeserved grace.

XIII. The Cause of Good Works

So that the cause of good works we confess to be not our free will, but the Spirit of the Lord Jesus (John 15; Eph. 2), who dwelling in our hearts by true faith brings forth such good works as God has prepared for us to walk in. For this we most boldly affirm, that it is blasphemy to say that Christ Jesus abides in the heart of those in whom is no spirit of sanctification. And, therefore, we fear not to affirm that murderers, oppressors, cruel persecutors, adulterers, whoremongers, filthy persons, idolaters, drunkards, thieves, and all workers of iniquity have neither true faith nor any portion of the Spirit of the Lord Jesus so long as they obstinately continue in their wickedness. For how soon that ever the Spirit of the Lord Jesus (which God's elect children receive by true faith) takes possession in the heart of any man, so soon does He regenerate and renew the same man so that he begins to hate that which before he loved and begins to love that which before he hated. And from thence comes that continual battle which is betwixt the flesh and the spirit in God's children. While flesh and the natural man (according to their own corruption) lusts for things pleasing and delectable unto the self (Gal. 3), grudges in adversity, is lifted up in prosperity, and at every moment is prone and ready to offend the majesty of God. But the Spirit of God, who gives witness to our spirit that we are the sons of God (Rom. 8), makes us to resist the devil, to abhor filthy pleasures, to groan in God's presence for deliverance from this bondage of corruption, and finally to triumph over sin that it reign not in our mortal bodies. This battle has not the carnal man being destitute of God's Spirit: but do follow and obey sin with greediness and without repentance, even as the devil and their corrupt lusts do prick them. But the sons of God (as before was said), do fight against sin, do sob and mourn when they perceive themselves tempted to iniquity; and if they fall, they rise again with earnest and unfeigned repentance, and these things they do not by their own power, but by the power of the Lord Jesus without whom they were able to do nothing (John 15).

XIV. What Works Are Reputed Good before God

We confess and acknowledge that God has given to man His holy law (Ex. 20; Deut. 4–5) in which not only are forbidden all such works as displease and offend His godly majesty, but also are commanded all such as please Him and as He has promised to reward. And these works be of two sorts. The one are done to the honor of God; the other to the profit of our neighbors; and both have the revealed will of God for their assurance. To have one God, to worship and honor Him, to call upon Him in all our troubles, reverence His holy name, to hear His Word, to believe the same, to communicate with His holy sacraments are the works of the first table. To honor father and mother (Eph. 6), princes, rulers and superior powers (Rom. 13; 1 Tim. 2, 6), to love them, to support them, yes to obey their charges (not repugnant to the commandments of God), to save the lives of innocents (Ezek. 22), to repress tyranny (Jer. 22), to defend the oppressed (Isa. 58), to keep our bodies clean and holy (1 Thess. 4), to live in sobriety and temperance (Luke 2), to deal justly with all men both in word and deed, and finally to repress all appetite of our neighbor's hurt, are the good works of the second table which are most pleasing and acceptable unto God as those works that are commanded by Himself. The contrary of which is sin most odious which always displeases Him and provokes Him to anger (Eph. 5). As not to call upon Him alone when we have need, not to hear His Word with reverence, to condemn and despise it, to have or to worship idols, to maintain and defend idolatry, lightly to esteem the revered name of God, to profane, abuse, or condemn the sacraments of Christ Jesus, to disobey or resist any that God has placed in authority (while they pass not over the bounds of their office) (Rom. 13), to murder, to consent thereto, to bear hatred or to suffer innocent blood to be shed, if we may withstand it (Ezek. 22), and finally the transgression of any other commandment in the first or second table, we confess and affirm to be sin by which God's hot displeasure is kindled against the proud and unthankful world.

So that good works we affirm to be these only that are done in faith, at God's commandment, who in His law has expressed what are the things that please Him. And evil works we affirm [are] not only those that expressly are done against God's commandment, but those also that in matters of religion and worshipping of God have no other assurance but the invention and opinion of man, which God from the beginning has ever rejected. As by the prophet Isaiah and by our master Christ Jesus, we are taught in these words, "In vain do they worship Me, teaching the doctrines and precepts of men" (Isa. 29; Matt. 13).

XV. The Perfection of the Law and Imperfection of Man

The Law of God we confess and acknowledge most just, most equal, most holy, and most perfect (Rom. 7; Ps. 19), commanding those things which being wrought in perfection were able to give life and to bring man to eternal felicity (Deut. 5). But our nature is so corrupt, so weak, and so imperfect (Rom. 10) that we are never able to fulfill the works of the Law in perfection. Yes, if we say we have no sin (even after we are regenerate, 1 John 1), we deceive ourselves and the verity of God is not in us. And, therefore, it behooves us to apprehend Christ Jesus with His justice and satisfaction, who is the end and accomplishment of the Law (Rom. 10), by whom we are set at this liberty (Gal. 3) that the curse and malediction of the Law (Deut. 26) fall not upon us, albeit we fulfill not the same in all points (Eph. 1; Rom. 4). For God the Father beholding us in the body of His Son Christ Jesus, accepts our imperfect obedience as it were perfect, and covers our works, which are defiled with many spots, with the justice of His Son. We do not mean that we are set so at liberty that we owe no obedience to the Law (for that before we have plainly confessed). But this we affirm that no man in earth (Christ Jesus only excepted) has given, gives, or will give in work that obedience to the Law which the Law requires (Luke 10). But when we have done all things, we must fall down and unfeignedly confess that we are unprofitable servants. And, therefore, whosoever boast themselves of the merits of their own works or put their trust in the works of supererogation boast themselves of that which is not, and put their trust in damnable idolatry.

XVI. Of the Kirk

As we believe in one God, Father, Son and Holy Ghost, so we must constantly believe that from the beginning there has been, now is and to the end of the world will be (Matt. 28), a kirk, that is to say, one company and multitude of men chosen of God (Eph. 1), who rightly worship and embrace Him by true faith in Christ Jesus, who is the only head of the same kirk, which also is the body and spouse of Christ Jesus (Col. 1; Eph. 5). Which kirk is catholic, that is universal, because it contains the elect of all ages, all realms, nations, and tongues (Rev. 7) be they of the Jews or be they of the Gentiles; who have communion and society with God the Father and with His Son Christ Jesus, through the sanctification of His Holy Spirit, and, therefore, is it called the communion (not of profane persons) but of saints, who as citizens of the heavenly Jerusalem (Eph. 2) have the fruition of the most inestimable benefits, to wit, of one God, one Lord Jesus, one faith, and of one baptism, out of which kirk there is neither life nor eternal felicity. And, therefore, we utterly abhor the blasphemy of those that affirm that men, who live according to equity and justice, will be saved whatsoever religion they have professed. For as without Christ Jesus there is neither life nor salvation, so will none be participant thereof, but such as the Father has given unto His Son Christ Jesus (John 5–6), and those in time come unto Him, avow His doctrine and believe in Him (we comprehend the children with the faithful parents). This kirk is invisible, known only to God who alone knows it, whom He has chosen, and comprehends as well (as is said) the elect that be departed (commonly called the kirk triumphant) as those that yet live and fight against sin and Satan as will live hereafter.

XVII. The Immortality of the Soul

The elect departed are in peace and rest from their labors (Rev. 14), not that they will sleep and come to any certain oblivion (as some fanatics do affirm), but they are delivered from all fear, all torment, and all temptation to which we and all God's elect are subject in this life (Rev. 7), and, therefore, do bear the name of the kirk militant. As contrariwise the reprobate and unfaithful departed have anguish, torment, and pain that cannot be expressed. So that neither are the one nor the other in such sleep that they feel not joy or torment as the parable of Christ in the sixteenth of Luke, His words to the thief and these words of the souls crying under the altar, "O Lord thou that are righteous and just, how long will thou not revenge our blood upon those that dwell on the earth?" doth plainly testify.

XVIII. Of the Notes by Which the True Kirk Is Discerned from the False and Who Will Be Judge of the Doctrine

Because that Satan from the beginning has labored to deck his pestilent synagogue with the title of the kirk of God and has inflamed the hearts of cruel murderers to persecute, trouble and molest the true kirk and members thereof, as Cain did Abel, Ishmael Isaac, Esau Jacob (Gen. 4, 21, 27), and the whole priesthood of the Jews, Christ Jesus Himself and His apostles after Him (Matt. 23; John 11; Acts 3), it is one thing most requisite that the true kirk be discerned from the filthy synagogue by clear and perfect notes, lest we being deceived receive and embrace to our own condemnation the one for the other. The notes, signs, and assured tokens by which the immaculate spouse of Christ Jesus is known from that horrible harlot, the kirk malignant, we affirm are neither antiquity, title usurped, lineal descent, place appointed, nor multitude of men approving any error. For Cain in age and title was preferred to Abel and Seth. Jerusalem had prerogative above all places of the earth, where also were the priests lineally descended from Aaron, and a greater multitude followed the scribes and Pharisees and priests than unfeignedly believed and approved Christ Jesus and His doctrine. And yet as we suppose no man (of whole judgment) will grant that any of the forenamed were the kirk of God. The notes, therefore, of the true kirk of God, we believe, confess and avow to be first, the true preaching of the Word of God, in which God has revealed Himself to us (John 1, 10) as the writings of the prophets and apostles do declare. Secondly, the right administration of the sacraments of Christ Jesus must be annexed unto the Word and promises of God to seal and confirm the same in our hearts. Last, ecclesiastical discipline (Rom. 4), uprightly ministered as God's Word prescribes whereby vice is reproved and virtue nourished (1 Cor. 5). Wheresoever then these former notes are seen and of any time continue (be the number never so few, about two or three), there without all doubt is the true kirk of Christ, who according to His promise is in the midst of them: not that universal (of which we have before spoken) but particular, such as was in Corinth, Galatia, Ephesus, and other places (Acts 16, 18, etc.; 1 Cor. 1; Acts 20) in which the ministry was planted by Paul and were of himself named the kirks of God. And such kirks we the inhabitants of the realm of Scotland, professors of Christ Jesus, confess ourselves to have in our cities, towns, and places reformed. For the doctrine taught in our kirks is contained in the written Word of God, to wit, in the books of the New and Old Testaments. In those books we mean which of the ancient have been reputed canonical in the which we affirm that all things necessary to be believed for the salvation of mankind is sufficiently expressed (John 21), the interpretation whereof we confess neither appertains to private nor public persons, neither yet to any kirk for any preeminence or prerogative personal or local which one has above another, but appertains to the Spirit of God by which also the Scripture was written.

When controversy then happens, for the right understanding of any place or sentence of Scripture or for the reformation of any abuse within the kirk of God, we ought not so much to look at what men before us have said or done, as unto that which the Holy Ghost uniformly speaks within the body of the Scriptures, and unto that which Christ Jesus Himself did and commanded to be done (1 Cor. 11). For this is a thing universally granted, that the Spirit of God (which is the spirit of unity) is in nothing contrary unto Himself. If then the interpretation, determination or sentence of any doctor, kirk or council, repugnant to the plain Word of God written in any other place of Scripture, it is a thing most certain that there is not the true understanding and meaning of the Holy Ghost, supposing that councils, realms, and nations have approved and received the same. For we dare not receive nor admit any interpretation which is directly repugnant to any principal point of our faith, to any other plain text of Scripture or yet unto the rule of charity.

XIX. The Authority of the Scriptures

As we believe and confess the Scriptures of God sufficient to instruct and make the man of God perfect (2 Tim. 3), so do we affirm and avow the authority of the same to be of God and neither to depend on men nor angels. We affirm, therefore, that such as allege the Scripture to have no authority but that which it receives from the kirk, to be blasphemous against God and injurious to the true kirk which always hears and obeys the voice of her own spouse and pastor (John 10), but takes not upon her to be mistress over the same.

XX. Of General Councils. Of Their Power, Authority, and Cause of Their Convention

As we do not rashly damn that which godly men assembled together in general councils lawfully gathered have propounded unto us, so without just examination dare we not receive whatsoever is forced upon men under the name of general councils. For plain it is that as they were men so have some of them manifestly erred and that in matters of great weight and importance. So far then as the council proves the determination and commandment that it gives by the plain Word of God, so far do we reverence and embrace the same. But if men under the name of a council pretend to forge unto us new articles of our faith or to make constitutions repugnant to the Word of God, then utterly we must refuse the same as the doctrine of devils which draw our souls from the voice of our only God to follow the doctrines and constitutions of men (1 Tim. 4). The cause then why general councils convened was neither to make any perpetual law (which God before had not made) neither yet to forge new articles of our belief, neither to give the Word of God authority, much less to make that to be His Word or yet the true interpretation of the same which was not before by His holy will expressed in His Word. But the cause of councils (we mean of such as merit the name of councils) was partly for confutation of heresies and for giving public confession of their faith to the posterity following which both they did by the authority of God's written Word and not by any opinion or prerogative that they could not err by reason of their general assembly. And this we judge to have been the chief cause of general councils. The other was for good policy and order to be constituted and observed in the kirk, in which (as in the house of God) it becomes all things to be done decently and in order (1 Cor. 14). Not that we think that one policy and one order in ceremonies can be appointed for all ages, times, and places: for as ceremonies (such as man has devised) are but temporal so may and ought they to be changed when they rather foster superstition than that they edify the kirk using the same.

XXI. Of the Sacraments

As the fathers under the Law (besides the verity of the sacrifices) had two chief sacraments, to wit, circumcision and the Passover, the despisers and contemners whereof were not reputed for God's people (Gen. 17), so we do acknowledge and confess that we now in the time of the gospel have two sacraments only, instituted by the Lord Jesus and commanded to be used of all those that will be reputed members of His body (Matt. 26, 28), to wit, baptism and the Supper or table of the Lord Jesus called the communion of His body and blood. And these sacraments (as well of the Old as of the New Testament) were instituted of God, not only to make a visible difference betwixt His people and those that were without His league, but also to exercise the faith of His children and by participation of the same sacraments to seal in their hearts the assurance of His promises and of that most blessed conjunction, union and society which the elect have with their head, Christ Jesus.

And thus we utterly damn the vanity of those that affirm sacraments to be nothing else but naked and bare signs (Rom. 8). No, we assuredly believe that by baptism we are engrafted in Christ Jesus to be made partakers of His justice by which our sins are covered and remitted (1 Cor. 10). And also that in the Supper rightly used, Christ Jesus is so joined with us (John 6) that He becomes the very nourishment and food of our souls. Not that we imagine any transubstantiation of bread in Christ's natural body and of wine in His natural blood (as the papists have perniciously taught and damnably believe), but this union and conjunction which we have with the body and blood of Christ Jesus in the right use of the sacraments is wrought by operation of the Holy Ghost, who by true faith carries us above all things that are visible, carnal, and earthly, and makes us to feed upon the body and blood of Christ Jesus which was once broken and shed for us which now is in heaven (Heb. 6, 10) and appears in the presence of His Father for us; and yet notwithstanding the far distance of the place which is betwixt His body now glorified in heaven and us now mortal in this earth, yet we most assuredly believe that the bread that we break is the communion of Christ's body (1 Cor. 10), and the cup which we bless is the communion of His blood. So that we confess and undoubtedly believe that the faithful, in the right use of the Lord's table do so eat the body and drink the blood of the Lord Jesus (John 6) that He remains in them and they in Him, yes that they are so made flesh of His flesh and bone of His bones that as the eternal Godhead has given to the flesh of Christ Jesus (which of its own condition and nature was mortal and corruptible) life and immortality (Eph. 5), so does Christ Jesus, His flesh and blood eaten and drunk by us, give to us the same prerogatives (John 6). Which albeit we confess are neither given unto us at that only time neither yet by the proper power and virtue of the sacrament only, yet we affirm that the faithful in the right use of the Lord's table have such conjunction with Christ Jesus as the natural man can not apprehend. Yes and farther we affirm that albeit the faithful oppressed by negligence and manly infirmity do not profit so much as they would in the very instant action of the Supper, yet will it after bring forth fruit as lively seed sown in good ground. For the Holy Spirit (which can never be divided from the right institution of the Lord Jesus) will not frustrate the faithful of the fruit of that mystical action, but all this we say comes by true faith which apprehends Christ Jesus who only makes His sacrament effectual unto us. And, therefore, whosoever slanders us, as that we affirmed or believed sacraments to be only naked and bare signs, do injury unto us and speak against a manifest truth. But this liberally and frankly we must confess, that we make a distinction betwixt Christ Jesus in His natural substance and betwixt the elements in the sacramental signs. So that we will neither worship the signs in place of that which is signified by them, neither yet do we despise and interpret them as unprofitable and vain, but do use them with all reverence, examining ourselves diligently before, that so we do because we are assured by the mouth of the apostle that such as eat of the bread and drink of that cup unworthily are guilty of the body and blood of the Lord Jesus (1 Cor. 11).

XXII. Of the Right Administration of the Sacraments

That sacraments be rightly ministered, we judge two things requisite: the one, that they be ministered by lawful ministers whom we affirm to be only they that are appointed to the preaching of the Word or unto whose mouths God has put some sermon of exhortation, they being men lawfully chosen thereto by some kirk. The other, that they be ministered in such elements and in such sort as God has appointed. Else we affirm that they cease to be right sacraments of Christ Jesus. And therefore it is that we flee the society with the papistical kirk in participation of their sacraments. First, because their ministers are not ministers of Christ Jesus (1 Tim. 6); (yes, which is more horrible) they suffer women, whom the Holy Ghost will not suffer, to teach in the congregation [and] to baptize. And secondly, because they have so adulterated both the one sacrament and the other with their own inventions that no part of Christ's action abides in the original purity. For oil, salt, spittle, and such like in baptism are but men's inventions, adoration, veneration, bearing through streets and towns and keeping of bread in boxes or buists [small boxes] are profanation of Christ's sacraments and no use of the same. For Christ Jesus said, "Take and eat. Do ye this in remembrance of me"

(Matt. 26, etc.). By which words and charge He sanctified bread and wine to be the sacrament of His body and blood to the end that the one should be eaten and that all should drink of the other; and not that they should be kept to be worshipped and honored as God, as the papists have done heretofore, who also have committed sacrilege, stealing from the people the one part of the sacrament, to wit, the blessed cup. Moreover that the sacraments are rightly used, it is requisite that the end and cause why the sacraments were instituted be understood and observed, as well of the minister as the receivers. For if the opinion be changed in the receiver, the right use ceases which is most evident by the rejection of the sacrifices as also if the teacher plainly teaches false doctrine (Isa. 1), which were odious and abominable unto God (albeit they were His own ordinance) because that wicked men used them to one other end than God had ordained. The same affirm we of the sacraments (Jer. 7; Isa. 66) in the papistical kirk in which we affirm the whole action of the Lord Jesus to be adulterated, as well in the external form as in the end and opinion. What Christ Jesus did and commanded to be done is evident by three evangelists (Matt. 26) and by St. Paul (1 Cor. 11, etc.). What the priest does at his altar we need not rehearse. The end and cause of Christ's institution and why the selfsame should be used is expressed in these words: "Do ye this in remembrance of Me. As often as ever ye will eat of this bread and drink of this cup, ye will show forth (that is, extol, preach, magnify, and praise) the Lord's death till He come." But to what end and in what opinion the priests say their Masses, let the words of the same, their own doctors and writings witness. To wit, that they as mediators betwixt Christ and His kirk do offer unto God the Father a sacrifice propitiatory for the sins of the quick and the dead. Which doctrine as blasphemous to Christ Jesus and making derogation to the sufficiency of His only sacrifice once offered for purgation of all those that will be sanctified, we utterly abhor, detest, and renounce.

XXIII. To Whom Sacraments Appertain

We confess and acknowledge that baptism appertains as well to the infants of the faithful as unto those that be of age and discretion. And so we damn the error of Anabaptists who deny baptism to appertain to children before they have faith and understanding. But the Supper of the Lord, we confess to appertain to such only as be of the household of faith, can try and examine themselves as well in their faith as in their duty towards their neighbors. Such as eat and drink at that holy table without faith or being at dissension and disunion with their brethren do eat unworthily. And, therefore, it is that in our kirks our ministers take public and particular examination of the knowledge and conversation of such as are to be admitted to the table of the Lord Jesus.

XXIV. Of the Civil Magistrate

We confess and acknowledge empires, kingdoms, dominions, and cities to be distinguished and ordered by God (Dan. 1–2, etc.; Ezra 1, etc.), the powers and authority in the same (be it of emperors in their empires, of kings in their realms, dukes, and princes in their dominions or of other magistrates in free cities) to be God's holy ordinance (Rom. 13) ordained for manifestation of His own glory and for the singular profit and commodity of mankind. So that whosoever goes about to take away or to confound the whole state of civil policies now long established, we affirm the same men not only to be enemies to mankind, but also wickedly to fight against God's expressed will.

We further confess and acknowledge that such persons as are placed in authority are to be loved, honored, feared and held in most reverent estimation (Rom. 13; 1 Peter 2; Ps. 81) because they are the lieutenants of God, in whose sessions God Himself does sit and judge (yes, even the judges and princes themselves), to whom by God is given the sword to the praise and defense of good men, and to revenge and punish all open malefactors. To kings moreover, princes, rulers, and magistrates, we affirm that chiefly and most principally the conversation and purgation of religion appertains. So that not only are they appointed for civil policy, but also for maintenance of the true religion and for suppressing of idolatry and superstition whatsoever, as in David, Jehoshaphat, Hezekiah, Josiah, and others highly commended for their zeal in that case may be espied.

And, therefore, we confess and avow that such as resist the supreme power (doing that thing which appertains to His charge) do resist God's ordinance (Rom. 13) and, therefore, cannot be guiltless. And further we affirm that whosoever deny unto them their aid, counsel and comfort while the princes and rulers vigilantly travel in execution of their office, that the same deny their help, support and counsel to God, who by the presence of His lieutenant craves it of them.

XXV. The Gifts Freely Given to the Church

Albeit that the Word of God truly preached, the sacraments rightly minis-tered and discipline executed according to the Word of God, be the certain and infallible signs of the true kirk, yet do we not so mean that every partic-ular person joined with such a company is an elect member of Christ Jesus. For we acknowledge and confess that darnel, cockle, and chaff may be sown, grow and in great abundance lie in the midst of the wheat (Matt. 3, 13), that is, the reprobate may be joined in the society of the elect and may externally use with them the benefits of the Word and sacraments; but such being but temporal professors in mouth, but not in heart, do fall back and continue not to the end. And, therefore, have they no fruit of Christ's death, resurrec-tion, nor ascension; but such as whose heart unfeignedly believe (Rom. 10) and whose mouth boldly confess the Lord Jesus (as before we have said) will most assuredly receive these gifts first in this life, remission of sins, and that by only faith in Christ's blood (John 3; Rom. 3–5, 8), in so much that albeit sin remains and continually abides in these our mortal bodies, yet is it not imputed unto us, but is remitted and covered with Christ's justice. Second-arily, in the general judgment there will be given to every man and woman resurrection of the flesh (Isa. 66; Dan. 12; 1 Cor. 15; Job 19); for the sea will give up her dead, the earth those that therein be enclosed: yes, our eternal God will stretch out His hand upon the dust and the dead will arise incor-ruptible and that in the substance of the selfsame flesh that every man now bears, to receive according to their works, glory, or punishment (Rom. 2). For such as now dealt in vanity, cruelty, filthiness, superstition, or idolatry will be adjudged to that fire inextinguishable in which they will be commit-ted for ever (Rev. 20–21), as well in their own bodies as in their souls which now they give to serve the devil in all abomination. But such as continue in well doing to the end, boldly professing the Lord Jesus, who constantly believe that they will receive glory, honor, and immortality to reign forever in life everlasting with Christ Jesus, to whose glorified body all His elect will be made like (1 John 5), when He will appear again to judgment and will render up the kingdom to God His Father, who then will be and ever will remain all in all things (1 Cor. 15), God blessed forever. To whom with the Son and with the Holy Ghost be all honor and glory, now and ever.

Finis

Arise, O Lord, and let Thy enemies be confounded, let them flee from Thy presence that hate Thy godly name. Give Thy servants strength to speak Thy word in boldness, and let all nations attain to Thy true knowledge. So be it.

11

Belgic Confession

(1561)

G uido de Brès, a French-speaking Reformed Protestant, penned the Belgic Confession to provide the Low Countries—or Netherlands—with
its own confession. De Brès had been a student of John Calvin in Geneva, and
he sent his confession to other Reformed churches for approval.

At the time, the Low Countries were ruled by King Philip II of Spain,
a fiercely devout Roman Catholic who saw himself as defender of the faith
against the Muslim Ottoman Empire and the Protestant Reformation. De
Brès sought to secure toleration for the Reformed along similar lines as the
French Confession: by portraying them as loyal and peaceful subjects and
adherents to the historic Christian faith. Persecution of Protestantism continued, however, and de Brès himself was even tried by the Spanish Inquisition
and martyred in 1567.

The confession is one of the three standards of Dutch Reformed churches,
the Three Forms of Unity, which also include the Canons of Dort and the
Heidelberg Catechism. The Belgic Confession has been revised numerous
times and is among the most widely accepted Reformed confessions in the
world.

Belgic Confession

Article 1: The Only God

We all believe in our hearts and confess with our mouths that there is a single and simple spiritual being, whom we call God—eternal, incomprehensible, invisible, unchangeable, infinite, almighty; completely wise, just, and good, and the overflowing source of all good.

Article 2: The Means by Which We Know God

We know him by two means: First, by the creation, preservation, and government of the universe, since that universe is before our eyes like a beautiful book in which all creatures, great and small, are as letters to make us ponder the invisible things of God: his eternal power and his divinity, as the apostle Paul says in Romans 1:20. All these things are enough to convict men and to leave them without excuse.

Second, he makes himself known to us more openly by his holy and divine Word, as much as we need in this life, for his glory and for the salvation of his own.

Article 3: The Written Word of God

We confess that this Word of God was not sent nor delivered by the will of men, but that holy men of God spoke, being moved by the Holy Spirit, as Peter says.[1] Afterwards our God—because of the special care he has for us and our salvation—commanded his servants, the prophets and apostles, to commit this revealed Word to writing. He himself wrote with his own finger the two tables of the law. Therefore we call such writings holy and divine Scriptures.

---

1 2 Peter 1:21.

Article 4: The Canonical Books

We include in the Holy Scripture the two volumes of the Old and New Testaments. They are canonical books with which there can be no quarrel at all. In the church of God the list is as follows:

In the Old Testament, the five books of Moses—Genesis, Exodus, Leviticus, Numbers, Deuteronomy; the books of Joshua, Judges, Ruth; the two books of Samuel, the two books of Kings, the two books of Chronicles; the books of Ezra, Nehemiah, Esther; the book of Job, the Psalms, the three books of Solomon—Proverbs, Ecclesiastes, the Song of Songs; the five books of the four major prophets—Isaiah, Jeremiah, Lamentations, Ezekiel, Daniel; the books of the twelve minor prophets—Hosea, Joel, Amos, Obadiah, Jonah, Micah, Nahum, Habakkuk, Zephaniah, Haggai, Zechariah, Malachi.

In the New Testament, the four Gospels—Matthew, Mark, Luke, John; the Acts of the Apostles; the thirteen letters of Paul—to the Romans; the two letters to the Corinthians; to the Galatians, Ephesians, Philippians, Colossians; the two letters to the Thessalonians; the two letters to Timothy; to Titus, Philemon; the letter to the Hebrews; the seven letters of the other apostles—one of James; two of Peter; three of John; one of Jude; and the Revelation of the apostle John.

Article 5: The Authority of Scripture

We receive all these books and these only as holy and canonical, for the regulating, founding, and establishing of our faith. And we believe without a doubt all things contained in them—not so much because the church receives and approves them as such but above all because the Holy Spirit testifies in our hearts that they are from God, and also because they prove themselves to be from God. For even the blind themselves are able to see that the things predicted in them do happen.

Article 6: The Difference between Canonical and Apocryphal Books

We distinguish between these holy books and the apocryphal ones, which are: the third and fourth books of Esdras; the books of Tobit, Judith, Wisdom, Jesus Sirach, Baruch; what was added to the Story of Esther; the Song of the Three Children in the Furnace; the Story of Susannah; the Story of Bel and the Dragon; the Prayer of Manasseh; and the two books of Maccabees. The church may certainly read these books and learn from them as far as they agree with the canonical books. But they do not have such power and virtue that one could confirm from their testimony any point of faith or of the Christian religion. Much less can they detract from the authority of the other holy books.

Article 7: The Sufficiency of Scripture

We believe that this Holy Scripture contains the will of God completely and that everything one must believe to be saved is sufficiently taught in it. For since the entire manner of service which God requires of us is described in it at great length, no one—even an apostle or an angel from heaven, as Paul says[2]—ought to teach other than what the Holy Scriptures have already taught us. For since it is forbidden to add to or subtract from the Word of God,[3] this plainly demonstrates that the teaching is perfect and complete in all respects. Therefore we must not consider human writings—no matter how holy their authors may have been—equal to the divine writings; nor may we put custom, nor the majority, nor age, nor the passage of time or persons, nor councils, decrees, or official decisions above the truth of God, for truth is above everything else. For all human beings are liars by nature and more vain than vanity itself. Therefore we reject with all our hearts everything that does not agree with this infallible rule, as we are taught to do by the apostles when they say, "Test the spirits to see if they are of God,"[4] and also, "If anyone comes to you and does not bring this teaching, do not receive him into your house."[5]

Article 8: The Trinity

In keeping with this truth and Word of God we believe in one God, who is one single essence, in whom there are three persons, really, truly, and eternally distinct according to their incommunicable properties—namely, Father, Son, and Holy Spirit. The Father is the cause, origin, and source of all things, visible as well as invisible. The Son is the Word, the Wisdom, and the image of the Father. The Holy Spirit is the eternal power and might, proceeding from

2 Gal. 1:8.
3 Deut. 12:32; Rev. 22:18–19.
4 1 John 4:1.
5 2 John 10.

the Father and the Son. Nevertheless, this distinction does not divide God into three, since Scripture teaches us that the Father, the Son, and the Holy Spirit each has his own subsistence distinguished by characteristics—yet in such a way that these three persons are only one God. It is evident then that the Father is not the Son and that the Son is not the Father, and that likewise the Holy Spirit is neither the Father nor the Son. Nevertheless, these persons, thus distinct, are neither divided nor fused or mixed together. For the Father did not take on flesh, nor did the Spirit, but only the Son. The Father was never without his Son, nor without his Holy Spirit, since all these are equal from eternity, in one and the same essence. There is neither a first nor a last, for all three are one in truth and power, in goodness and mercy.

Article 9: The Scriptural Witness on the Trinity

All these things we know from the testimonies of Holy Scripture as well as from the effects of the persons, especially from those we feel within ourselves. The testimonies of the Holy Scriptures, which teach us to believe in this Holy Trinity, are written in many places of the Old Testament, which need not be enumerated but only chosen with discretion. In the book of Genesis God says, "Let us make man in our image, according to our likeness." So "God created man in his own image"—indeed, "male and female he created them."[6] "Behold, man has become like one of us."[7] It appears from this that there is a plurality of persons within the Deity, when he says, "Let us make man in our image"—and afterwards he indicates the unity when he says, "God created." It is true that he does not say here how many persons there are—but what is somewhat obscure to us in the Old Testament is very clear in the New.

For when our Lord was baptized in the Jordan, the voice of the Father was heard saying, "This is my dear Son";[8] the Son was seen in the water; and the Holy Spirit appeared in the form of a dove. So, in the baptism of all believers this form was prescribed by Christ: "Baptize all people in the name of the Father, and of the Son, and of the Holy Spirit."[9] In the Gospel according to Luke the angel Gabriel says to Mary, the mother of our Lord: "The Holy Spirit

---

6 Gen. 1:26–27.
7 Gen. 3:22.
8 Matt. 3:17.
9 Matt. 28:19.

will come upon you, and the power of the Most High will overshadow you; and therefore that holy one to be born of you shall be called the Son of God."[10] And in another place it says: "The grace of our Lord Jesus Christ, and the love of God, and the fellowship of the Holy Spirit be with you."[11] "There are three who bear witness in heaven—the Father, the Word, and the Holy Spirit—and these three are one."[12] In all these passages we are fully taught that there are three persons in the one and only divine essence. And although this doctrine surpasses human understanding, we nevertheless believe it now, through the Word, waiting to know and enjoy it fully in heaven.

Furthermore, we must note the particular works and activities of these three persons in relation to us. The Father is called our Creator, by reason of his power. The Son is our Savior and Redeemer, by his blood. The Holy Spirit is our Sanctifier, by his living in our hearts.

This doctrine of the holy Trinity has always been maintained in the true church, from the time of the apostles until the present, against Jews, Muslims, and certain false Christians and heretics, such as Marcion, Mani, Praxeas, Sabellius, Paul of Samosata, Arius, and others like them, who were rightly condemned by the holy fathers.

And so, in this matter we willingly accept the three ecumenical creeds—the Apostles', Nicene, and Athanasian—as well as what the ancient fathers decided in agreement with them.

Article 10: The Deity of Christ

We believe that Jesus Christ, according to his divine nature, is the only Son of God—eternally begotten, not made nor created, for then he would be a creature. He is one in essence with the Father; coeternal; the exact image of the person of the Father and the "reflection of his glory,"[13] being in all things like him. He is the Son of God not only from the time he assumed our nature but from all eternity, as the following testimonies teach us when they are taken together. Moses says that God "created the world";[14] and John says

---

10 Luke 1:35.
11 2 Cor. 13:14.
12 1 John 5:7, KJV.
13 Col. 1:15; Heb. 1:3.
14 Gen. 1:1.

that "all things were created by the Word,"[15] which he calls God. The letter to the Hebrews says that "God made the world by his Son."[16] Paul says that "God created all things by Jesus Christ."[17] And so it must follow that he who is called God, the Word, the Son, and Jesus Christ already existed when all things were created by him. Therefore the prophet Micah says that his origin is "from ancient times, from eternity."[18] And Hebrews says that he has "neither beginning of days nor end of life."[19] So then, he is the true eternal God, the Almighty, whom we invoke, worship, and serve.

Article 11: The Deity of the Holy Spirit

We believe and confess also that the Holy Spirit proceeds eternally from the Father and the Son—neither made, nor created, nor begotten, but only proceeding from the two of them. In regard to order, he is the third person of the Trinity—of one and the same essence, and majesty, and glory, with the Father and the Son. He is true and eternal God, as the Holy Scriptures teach us.

Article 12: The Creation of All Things

We believe that the Father created heaven and earth and all other creatures from nothing, when it seemed good to him, by his Word—that is to say, by his Son. He has given all creatures their being, form, and appearance, and their various functions for serving their Creator. Even now he also sustains and governs them all, according to his eternal providence, and by his infinite power, that they may serve man, in order that man may serve God.

He has also created the angels good, that they might be his messengers and serve his elect. Some of them have fallen from the excellence in which God created them into eternal perdition; and the others have persisted and remained in their original state, by the grace of God. The devils and evil spirits are so corrupt that they are enemies of God and of everything good. They lie in wait for the church and every member of it like thieves, with all their power, to destroy and spoil everything by their deceptions. So then, by their

---

15 John 1:3.
16 Heb. 1:2.
17 Col. 1:16.
18 Mic. 5:2.
19 Heb. 7:3.

own wickedness they are condemned to everlasting damnation, daily awaiting their torments. For that reason we detest the error of the Sadducees, who deny that there are spirits and angels, and also the error of the Manicheans, who say that the devils originated by themselves, being evil by nature, without having been corrupted.

Article 13: The Doctrine of God's Providence

We believe that this good God, after he created all things, did not abandon them to chance or fortune but leads and governs them according to his holy will, in such a way that nothing happens in this world without his orderly arrangement. Yet God is not the author of, nor can he be charged with, the sin that occurs. For his power and goodness are so great and incomprehensible that he arranges and does his work very well and justly even when the devils and wicked men act unjustly. We do not wish to inquire with undue curiosity into what he does that surpasses human understanding and is beyond our ability to comprehend. But in all humility and reverence we adore the just judgments of God, which are hidden from us, being content to be Christ's disciples, so as to learn only what he shows us in his Word, without going beyond those limits.

This doctrine gives us unspeakable comfort since it teaches us that nothing can happen to us by chance but only by the arrangement of our gracious heavenly Father. He watches over us with fatherly care, keeping all creatures under his control, so that not one of the hairs on our heads (for they are all numbered) nor even a little bird can fall to the ground without the will of our Father.[20] In this thought we rest, knowing that he holds in check the devils and all our enemies, who cannot hurt us without his permission and will. For that reason we reject the damnable error of the Epicureans, who say that God involves himself in nothing and leaves everything to chance.

Article 14: The Creation and Fall of Man

We believe that God created man from the dust of the earth and made and formed him in his image and likeness—good, just, and holy; able by his own will to conform in all things to the will of God. But when he was in honor he

---

20 Matt. 10:29–30.

did not understand it and did not recognize his excellence.[21] But he subjected himself willingly to sin and consequently to death and the curse, lending his ear to the word of the devil. For he transgressed the commandment of life, which he had received, and by his sin he separated himself from God, who was his true life, having corrupted his entire nature. So he made himself guilty and subject to physical and spiritual death, having become wicked, perverse, and corrupt in all his ways. He lost all his excellent gifts which he had received from God, and he retained none of them except for small traces which are enough to make him inexcusable. Moreover, all the light in us is turned to darkness, as the Scripture teaches us: "The light shone in the darkness, and the darkness did not receive it."[22] Here John calls men "darkness."

Therefore we reject everything taught to the contrary concerning man's free will, since man is nothing but the slave of sin and cannot do a thing unless it is "given him from heaven."[23] For who can boast of being able to do anything good by himself, since Christ says, "No one can come to me unless my Father who sent me draws him"?[24] Who can glory in his own will when he understands that "the mind of the flesh is enmity against God"?[25] Who can speak of his own knowledge in view of the fact that "the natural man does not understand the things of the Spirit of God"?[26] In short, who can produce a single thought, since he knows that we are "not able to think a thing" about ourselves, by ourselves, but that "our ability is from God"?[27] And therefore, what the apostle says ought rightly to stand fixed and firm: "God works within us both to will and to do according to his good pleasure."[28] For there is no understanding nor will conforming to God's understanding and will apart from Christ's work, as he teaches us when he says, "Without me you can do nothing."[29]

---

21 Ps. 49:20.
22 John 1:5.
23 John 3:27.
24 John 6:44.
25 Rom. 8:7.
26 1 Cor. 2:14.
27 2 Cor. 3:5.
28 Phil. 2:13.
29 John 15:5.

Article 15: The Doctrine of Original Sin

We believe that by the disobedience of Adam original sin has been spread through the whole human race.[30] It is a corruption of all nature—an inherited depravity which even infects small infants in their mother's womb, and the root which produces in man every sort of sin. It is therefore so vile and enormous in God's sight that it is enough to condemn the human race, and it is not abolished or wholly uprooted even by baptism, seeing that sin constantly boils forth as though from a contaminated spring. Nevertheless, it is not imputed to God's children for their condemnation but is forgiven by his grace and mercy—not to put them to sleep but so that the awareness of this corruption might often make believers groan as they long to be set free from the "body of this death."[31] Therefore we reject the error of the Pelagians who say that this sin is nothing else than a matter of imitation.

Article 16: The Doctrine of Election

We believe that—all Adam's descendants having thus fallen into perdition and ruin by the sin of the first man—God showed himself to be as he is: merciful and just. He is merciful in withdrawing and saving from this perdition those whom he, in his eternal and unchangeable counsel, has elected and chosen in Jesus Christ our Lord by his pure goodness, without any consideration of their works. He is just in leaving the others in their ruin and fall into which they plunged themselves.

Article 17: The Recovery of Fallen Man

We believe that our good God, by his marvelous wisdom and goodness, seeing that man had plunged himself in this manner into both physical and spiritual death and made himself completely miserable, set out to find him, though man, trembling all over, was fleeing from him. And he comforted him, promising to give him his Son, "born of a woman,"[32] to crush the head of the serpent,[33] and to make him blessed.

---

30 Rom. 5:12–13.
31 Rom. 7:24.
32 Gal. 4:4.
33 Gen. 3:15.

Article 18: The Incarnation

So then we confess that God fulfilled the promise which he had made to the early fathers by the mouth of his holy prophets when he sent his only and eternal Son into the world at the time set by him. The Son took the "form of a servant" and was made in the "likeness of man,"[34] truly assuming a real human nature, with all its weaknesses, except for sin; being conceived in the womb of the blessed virgin Mary by the power of the Holy Spirit, without male participation. And he not only assumed human nature as far as the body is concerned but also a real human soul, in order that he might be a real human being. For since the soul had been lost as well as the body he had to assume them both to save them both together. Therefore we confess, against the heresy of the Anabaptists who deny that Christ assumed human flesh from his mother, that he "shared the very flesh and blood of children";[35] that he is "fruit of the loins of David" according to the flesh;[36] "born of the seed of David" according to the flesh;[37] "fruit of the womb of the virgin Mary";[38] "born of a woman";[39] "the seed of David";[40] "a shoot from the root of Jesse";[41] "the offspring of Judah,"[42] having descended from the Jews according to the flesh; "from the seed of Abraham"—for he "assumed Abraham's seed" and was "made like his brothers except for sin."[43] In this way he is truly our Immanuel—that is: "God with us."[44]

Article 19: The Two Natures of Christ

We believe that by being thus conceived the person of the Son has been inseparably united and joined together with human nature, in such a way that there are not two Sons of God, nor two persons, but two natures united in a single person, with each nature retaining its own distinct properties. Thus his divine

---

34 Phil. 2:7.
35 Heb. 2:14.
36 Acts 2:30.
37 Rom. 1:3.
38 Luke 1:42.
39 Gal. 4:4.
40 2 Tim. 2:8.
41 Rom. 15:12.
42 Heb. 7:14.
43 Heb. 2:17; 4:15.
44 Matt. 1:23.

nature has always remained uncreated, "without beginning of days or end of life,"[45] filling heaven and earth. His human nature has not lost its properties but continues to have those of a creature—it has a beginning of days; it is of a finite nature and retains all that belongs to a real body. And even though he, by his resurrection, gave it immortality, that nonetheless did not change the reality of his human nature; for our salvation and resurrection depend also on the reality of his body.

But these two natures are so united together in one person that they are not even separated by his death. So then, what he committed to his Father when he died was a real human spirit which left his body. But meanwhile his divine nature remained united with his human nature even when he was lying in the grave; and his deity never ceased to be in him, just as it was in him when he was a little child, though for a while it did not show itself as such. These are the reasons why we confess him to be true God and true man—true God in order to conquer death by his power, and true man that he might die for us in the weakness of his flesh.

Article 20: The Justice and Mercy of God in Christ

We believe that God—who is perfectly merciful and also very just—sent his Son to assume the nature in which the disobedience had been committed, in order to bear in it the punishment of sin by his most bitter passion and death. So God made known his justice toward his Son, who was charged with our sin, and he poured out his goodness and mercy on us, who are guilty and worthy of damnation, giving to us his Son to die, by a most perfect love, and raising him to life for our justification, in order that by him we might have immortality and eternal life.

Article 21: The Atonement

We believe that Jesus Christ is a high priest forever according to the order of Melchizedek—made such by an oath—and that he presented himself in our name before his Father, to appease his wrath with full satisfaction by offering himself on the tree of the cross and pouring out his precious blood for the cleansing of our sins, as the prophets had predicted. For it is written that "the

---

45 Heb. 7:3.

chastisement of our peace" was placed on the Son of God and that "we are healed by his wounds." He was "led to death as a lamb"; he was "numbered among sinners"[46] and condemned as a criminal by Pontius Pilate, though Pilate had declared that he was innocent. So he paid back what he had not stolen,[47] and he suffered—the "just for the unjust,"[48] in both his body and his soul—in such a way that when he sensed the horrible punishment required by our sins his sweat became like "big drops of blood falling on the ground."[49] He cried, "My God, my God, why have you abandoned me?"[50] And he endured all this for the forgiveness of our sins.

Therefore we rightly say with Paul that we "know nothing but Jesus and him crucified";[51] we consider all things as "dung for the excellence of the knowledge of our Lord Jesus Christ."[52] We find all comforts in his wounds and have no need to seek or invent any other means to reconcile ourselves with God than this one and only sacrifice, once made, which renders believers perfect forever. This is also why the angel of God called him Jesus—that is, "Savior"—because he would save his people from their sins.[53]

Article 22: The Righteousness of Faith

We believe that for us to acquire the true knowledge of this great mystery the Holy Spirit kindles in our hearts a true faith that embraces Jesus Christ, with all his merits, and makes him its own, and no longer looks for anything apart from him. For it must necessarily follow that either all that is required for our salvation is not in Christ or, if all is in him, then he who has Christ by faith has his salvation entirely. Therefore, to say that Christ is not enough but that something else is needed as well is a most enormous blasphemy against God—for it then would follow that Jesus Christ is only half a Savior.

And therefore we justly say with Paul that we are justified "by faith alone" or by faith "apart from works."[54] However, we do not mean, properly speaking,

---

46 Isa. 53:4–12.
47 Ps. 69:4.
48 1 Peter 3:18.
49 Luke 22:44.
50 Matt. 27:46.
51 1 Cor. 2:2.
52 Phil. 3:8.
53 Matt. 1:21.
54 Rom. 3:28.

that it is faith itself that justifies us—for faith is only the instrument by which we embrace Christ, our righteousness. But Jesus Christ is our righteousness crediting to us all his merits and all the holy works he has done for us and in our place. And faith is the instrument that keeps us in communion with him and with all his benefits. When those benefits are made ours they are more than enough to absolve us of our sins.

Article 23: The Justification of Sinners

We believe that our blessedness lies in the forgiveness of our sins because of Jesus Christ, and that in it our righteousness before God is contained, as David and Paul teach us when they declare that man blessed to whom God grants righteousness apart from works.[55] And the same apostle says that we are justified "freely" or "by grace" through redemption in Jesus Christ.[56]

And therefore we cling to this foundation, which is firm forever, giving all glory to God, humbling ourselves, and recognizing ourselves as we are; not claiming a thing for ourselves or our merits and leaning and resting only on the obedience of Christ crucified, which is ours when we believe in him. That is enough to cover all our sins and to make us confident, freeing the conscience from the fear, dread, and terror of God's approach, without doing what our first father, Adam, did, who trembled as he tried to cover himself with fig leaves. In fact, if we had to appear before God relying—no matter how little— on ourselves or some other creature, then, alas, we would be swallowed up. Therefore everyone must say with David: "Lord, do not enter into judgment with your servants, for before you no living person shall be justified."[57]

Article 24: The Sanctification of Sinners

We believe that this true faith, produced in man by the hearing of God's Word and by the work of the Holy Spirit, regenerates him and makes him a "new man,"[58] causing him to live the "new life"[59] and freeing him from the slavery of sin. Therefore, far from making people cold toward living in a pious and

---

55 Ps. 32:1; Rom. 4:6.
56 Rom. 3:24.
57 Ps. 143:2.
58 2 Cor. 5:17.
59 Rom. 6:4.

holy way, this justifying faith, quite to the contrary, so works within them that apart from it they will never do a thing out of love for God but only out of love for themselves and fear of being condemned. So then, it is impossible for this holy faith to be unfruitful in a human being, seeing that we do not speak of an empty faith but of what Scripture calls "faith working through love,"[60] which leads a man to do of himself the works that God has commanded in his Word. These works, proceeding from the good root of faith, are good and acceptable to God, since they are all sanctified by his grace. Yet they do not count toward our justification—for by faith in Christ we are justified, even before we do good works. Otherwise they could not be good, any more than the fruit of a tree could be good if the tree is not good in the first place.

So then, we do good works, but not for merit—for what would we merit? Rather, we are indebted to God for the good works we do, and not he to us, since it is he who "works in us both to will and do according to his good pleasure"[61]—thus keeping in mind what is written: "When you have done all that is commanded you, then you shall say, 'We are unworthy servants; we have done what it was our duty to do.'"[62]

Yet we do not wish to deny that God rewards good works—but it is by his grace that he crowns his gifts. Moreover, although we do good works we do not base our salvation on them; for we cannot do any work that is not defiled by our flesh and also worthy of punishment. And even if we could point to one, memory of a single sin is enough for God to reject that work. So we would always be in doubt, tossed back and forth without any certainty, and our poor consciences would be tormented constantly if they did not rest on the merit of the suffering and death of our Savior.

Article 25: The Fulfillment of the Law

We believe that the ceremonies and symbols of the law have ended with the coming of Christ, and that all foreshadowings have come to an end, so that the use of them ought to be abolished among Christians. Yet the truth and substance of these things remain for us in Jesus Christ, in whom they have been fulfilled. Nevertheless, we continue to use the witnesses drawn from the

---

60 Gal. 5:6.
61 Phil. 2:13.
62 Luke 17:10.

law and prophets to confirm us in the gospel and to regulate our lives with full integrity for the glory of God, according to his will.

Article 26: The Intercession of Christ

We believe that we have no access to God except through the one and only Mediator and Intercessor: Jesus Christ the Righteous.[63] He therefore was made man, uniting together the divine and human natures, so that we human beings might have access to the divine Majesty. Otherwise we would have no access. But this Mediator, whom the Father has appointed between himself and us, ought not terrify us by his greatness, so that we have to look for another one, according to our fancy. For neither in heaven nor among the creatures on earth is there anyone who loves us more than Jesus Christ does. Although he was "in the form of God," he nevertheless "emptied himself," taking the form of "a man" and "a servant" for us;[64] and he made himself "completely like his brothers."[65] Suppose we had to find another intercessor. Who would love us more than he who gave his life for us, even though "we were his enemies"?[66] And suppose we had to find one who has prestige and power. Who has as much of these as he who is seated "at the right hand of the Father,"[67] and who has all power "in heaven and on earth"?[68] And who will be heard more readily than God's own dearly beloved Son?

So then, sheer unbelief has led to the practice of dishonoring the saints, instead of honoring them. That was something the saints never did nor asked for, but which in keeping with their duty, as appears from their writings, they consistently refused. We should not plead here that we are unworthy—for it is not a question of offering our prayers on the basis of our own dignity but only on the basis of the excellence and dignity of Jesus Christ, whose righteousness is ours by faith.

Since the apostle for good reason wants us to get rid of this foolish fear—or rather, this unbelief—he says to us that Jesus Christ was "made like his brothers in all things," that he might be a high priest who is merciful and

---

63 1 John 2:1.
64 Phil. 2:6–8.
65 Heb. 2:17.
66 Rom. 5:10.
67 Rom. 8:34; Heb. 1:3.
68 Matt. 28:18.

faithful to purify the sins of the people.[69] For since he suffered, being tempted, he is also able to help those who are tempted.[70] And further, to encourage us more to approach him he says, "Since we have a high priest, Jesus the Son of God, who has entered into heaven, we maintain our confession. For we do not have a high priest who is unable to have compassion for our weaknesses, but one who was tempted in all things, just as we are, except for sin. Let us go then with confidence to the throne of grace that we may obtain mercy and find grace, in order to be helped."[71]

The same apostle says that we "have liberty to enter into the holy place by the blood of Jesus. Let us go, then, in the assurance of faith. . . ."[72] Likewise, "Christ's priesthood is forever. By this he is able to save completely those who draw near to God through him who always lives to intercede for them."[73] What more do we need? For Christ himself declares: "I am the way, the truth, and the life; no one comes to my Father but by me."[74] Why should we seek another intercessor? Since it has pleased God to give us his Son as our Intercessor, let us not leave him for another—or rather seek, without ever finding. For when God gave him to us he knew well that we were sinners.

Therefore, in following the command of Christ we call on the heavenly Father through Christ, our only Mediator, as we are taught by the Lord's Prayer, being assured that we shall obtain all we ask of the Father in his name.

Article 27: The Holy Catholic Church

We believe and confess One single catholic or universal church—a holy congregation and gathering of true Christian believers, awaiting their entire salvation in Jesus Christ being washed by his blood, and sanctified and sealed by the Holy Spirit. This church has existed from the beginning of the world and will last until the end, as appears from the fact that Christ is eternal King who cannot be without subjects. And this holy church is preserved by God against the rage of the whole world, even though for a time it may appear very small in the eyes of men—as though it were snuffed out. For example, during

69 Heb. 2:17.
70 Heb. 2:18.
71 Heb. 4:14–16.
72 Heb. 10:19, 22.
73 Heb. 7:24–25.
74 John 14:6.

the very dangerous time of Ahab the Lord preserved for himself seven thousand men who did not bend their knees to Baal.[75]

And so this holy church is not confined, bound, or limited to a certain place or certain persons. But it is spread and dispersed throughout the entire world, though still joined and united in heart and will, in one and the same Spirit, by the power of faith.

Article 28: The Obligations of Church Members

We believe that since this holy assembly and congregation is the gathering of those who are saved and there is no salvation apart from it, no one ought to withdraw from it, content to be by himself, regardless of his status or condition. But all people are obliged to join and unite with it, keeping the unity of the church by submitting to its instruction and discipline, by bending their necks under the yoke of Jesus Christ, and by serving to build up one another, according to the gifts God has given them as members of each other in the same body.

And to preserve this unity more effectively, it is the duty of all believers, according to God's Word, to separate themselves from those who do not belong to the church, in order to join this assembly wherever God has established it, even if civil authorities and royal decrees forbid and death and physical punishment result. And so, all who withdraw from the church or do not join it act contrary to God's ordinance.

Article 29: The Marks of the True Church

We believe that we ought to discern diligently and very carefully, by the Word of God, what is the true church—for all sects in the world today claim for themselves the name of "the church." We are not speaking here of the company of hypocrites who are mixed among the good in the church and who nonetheless are not part of it, even though they are physically there. But we are speaking of distinguishing the body and fellowship of the true church from all sects that call themselves "the church."

The true church can be recognized if it has the following marks: The church engages in the pure preaching of the gospel; it makes use of the pure

---

75 1 Kings 19:18.

administration of the sacraments as Christ instituted them; it practices church discipline for correcting faults. In short, it governs itself according to the pure Word of God, rejecting all things contrary to it and holding Jesus Christ as the only Head. By these marks one can be assured of recognizing the true church—and no one ought to be separated from it.

As for those who are of the church, we can recognize them by the distinguishing marks of Christians: namely by faith, and by their fleeing from sin and pursuing righteousness, once they have received the one and only Savior, Jesus Christ. They love the true God and their neighbors, without turning to the right or left, and they crucify the flesh and its works. Though great weakness remains in them, they fight against it by the Spirit all the days of their lives, appealing constantly to the blood, suffering, death, and obedience of the Lord Jesus, in whom they have forgiveness of their sins, through faith in him.

As for the false church, it assigns more authority to itself and its ordinances than to the Word of God; it does not want to subject itself to the yoke of Christ; it does not administer the sacraments as Christ commanded in his Word; it rather adds to them or subtracts from them as it pleases; it bases itself on men, more than on Jesus Christ; it persecutes those who live holy lives according to the Word of God and who rebuke it for its faults, greed, and idolatry. These two churches are easy to recognize and thus to distinguish from each other.

Article 30: The Government of the Church

We believe that this true church ought to be governed according to the spiritual order that our Lord has taught us in his Word. There should be ministers or pastors to preach the Word of God and administer the sacraments. There should also be elders and deacons, along with the pastors, to make up the council of the church. By this means true religion is preserved; true doctrine is able to take its course; and evil men are corrected spiritually and held in check, so that also the poor and all the afflicted may be helped and comforted according to their need. By this means everything will be done well and in good order in the church, when such men are elected who are faithful and are chosen according to the rule that Paul gave to Timothy.[76]

---

76 1 Tim. 3.

Article 31: The Officers of the Church

We believe that ministers of the Word of God, elders, and deacons ought to be chosen to their offices by a legitimate election of the church, with prayer in the name of the Lord, and in good order, as the Word of God teaches. So everyone must be careful not to push himself forward improperly, but he must wait for God's call, so that he may be assured of his calling and be certain and sure that he is chosen by the Lord.

As for the ministers of the Word, they all have the same power and authority, no matter where they may be, since they are all servants of Jesus Christ, the only universal bishop, and the only head of the church. Moreover, to keep God's holy order from being violated or despised, we say that everyone ought, as much as possible, to hold the ministers of the Word and elders of the church in special esteem, because of the work they do, and be at peace with them, without grumbling, quarreling, or fighting.

Article 32: The Order and Discipline of the Church

We also believe that although it is useful and good for those who govern the churches to establish and set up a certain order among themselves for maintaining the body of the church, they ought always to guard against deviating from what Christ, our only Master, has ordained for us.

Therefore we reject all human innovations and all laws imposed on us, in our worship of God, which bind and force our consciences in any way. So we accept only what is proper to maintain harmony and unity and to keep all in obedience to God. To that end excommunication, with all it involves, according to the Word of God, is required.

Article 33: The Sacraments

We believe that our good God, mindful of our crudeness and weakness, has ordained sacraments for us to seal his promises in us, to pledge his good will and grace toward us, and also to nourish and sustain our faith. He has added these to the Word of the gospel to represent better to our external senses both what he enables us to understand by his Word and what he does inwardly in our hearts, confirming in us the salvation he imparts to us. For they are visible signs and seals of something internal and invisible, by means of which God works in us through the power of the Holy Spirit. So they are not empty and hollow signs to fool and deceive us, for their truth is Jesus Christ, without whom they would be nothing.

Moreover, we are satisfied with the number of sacraments that Christ our Master has ordained for us. There are only two: the sacrament of baptism and the Holy Supper of Jesus Christ.

Article 34: The Sacrament of Baptism

We believe and confess that Jesus Christ, in whom the law is fulfilled, has by his shed blood put an end to every other shedding of blood, which anyone might do or wish to do in order to atone or satisfy for sins. Having abolished circumcision, which was done with blood, he established in its place the sacrament of baptism. By it we are received into God's church and set apart from all other people and alien religions, that we may be dedicated entirely to him, bearing his mark and sign. It also witnesses to us that he will be our God forever, since he is our gracious Father.

Therefore he has commanded that all those who belong to him be baptized with pure water "in the name of the Father, and the Son, and the Holy Spirit."[77] In this way he signifies to us that just as water washes away the dirt of the body when it is poured on us and also is seen on the body of the baptized when it is sprinkled on him, so too the blood of Christ does the same thing internally, in the soul, by the Holy Spirit. It washes and cleanses it from its sins and transforms us from being the children of wrath into the children of God. This does not happen by the physical water but by the sprinkling of the precious blood of the Son of God, who is our Red Sea, through which we must pass to escape the tyranny of Pharaoh, who is the devil, and to enter the spiritual land of Canaan.

So ministers, as far as their work is concerned, give us the sacrament and what is visible, but our Lord gives what the sacrament signifies—namely the invisible gifts and graces; washing, purifying, and cleansing our souls of all filth and unrighteousness; renewing our hearts and filling them with all comfort; giving us true assurance of his fatherly goodness; clothing us with the "new man" and stripping off the "old," with all its works.[78]

For this reason we believe that anyone who aspires to reach eternal life

---

77 Matt. 28:19.
78 Col. 3:9–10.

ought to be baptized only once without ever repeating it—for we cannot be born twice. Yet this baptism is profitable not only when the water is on us and when we receive it but throughout our entire lives.

For that reason we detest the error of the Anabaptists who are not content with a single baptism once received and also condemn the baptism of the children of believers. We believe our children ought to be baptized and sealed with the sign of the covenant, as little children were circumcised in Israel on the basis of the same promises made to our children. And truly, Christ has shed his blood no less for washing the little children of believers than he did for adults. Therefore they ought to receive the sign and sacrament of what Christ has done for them, just as the Lord commanded in the law that by offering a lamb for them the sacrament of the suffering and death of Christ would be granted them shortly after their birth. This was the sacrament of Jesus Christ. Furthermore, baptism does for our children what circumcision did for the Jewish people. That is why Paul calls baptism the "circumcision of Christ."[79]

Article 35: The Sacrament of the Lord's Supper

We believe and confess that our Savior Jesus Christ has ordained and instituted the sacrament of the Holy Supper to nourish and sustain those who are already born again and ingrafted into his family: his church.

Now those who are born again have two lives in them. The one is physical and temporal—they have it from the moment of their first birth, and it is common to all. The other is spiritual and heavenly, and is given them in their second birth; it comes through the Word of the gospel in the communion of the body of Christ; and this life is common to God's elect only. Thus, to support the physical and earthly life God has prescribed for us an appropriate earthly and material bread, which is as common to all as life itself also is. But to maintain the spiritual and heavenly life that belongs to believers he has sent a living bread that came down from heaven: namely Jesus Christ, who nourishes and maintains the spiritual life of believers when eaten—that is, when appropriated and received spiritually by faith.

To represent to us this spiritual and heavenly bread Christ has instituted an earthly and visible bread as the sacrament of his body and wine as the

---

79 Col. 2:11.

sacrament of his blood. He did this to testify to us that just as truly as we take and hold the sacraments in our hands and eat and drink it in our mouths, by which our life is then sustained, so truly we receive into our souls, for our spiritual life, the true body and true blood of Christ, our only Savior. We receive these by faith, which is the hand and mouth of our souls.

Now it is certain that Jesus Christ did not prescribe his sacraments for us in vain, since he works in us all he represents by these holy signs, although the manner in which he does it goes beyond our understanding and is incomprehensible to us, just as the operation of God's Spirit is hidden and incomprehensible. Yet we do not go wrong when we say that what is eaten is Christ's own natural body and what is drunk is his own blood—but the manner in which we eat it is not by the mouth but by the Spirit, through faith. In that way Jesus Christ remains always seated at the right hand of God the Father in heaven—but he never refrains on that account to communicate himself to us through faith. This banquet is a spiritual table at which Christ communicates himself to us with all his benefits. At that table he makes us enjoy himself as much as the merits of his suffering and death, as he nourishes, strengthens, and comforts our poor, desolate souls by the eating of his flesh, and relieves and renews them by the drinking of his blood.

Moreover, though the sacraments and the thing signified are joined together, not all receive both of them. The wicked person certainly takes the sacrament, to his condemnation, but does not receive the truth of the sacrament, just as Judas and Simon the Sorcerer both indeed received the sacrament, but not Christ, who was signified by it. He is communicated only to believers.

Finally, with humility and reverence we receive the holy sacrament in the gathering of God's people, as we engage together, with thanksgiving, in a holy remembrance of the death of Christ our Savior, and as we thus confess our faith and Christian religion. Therefore no one should come to this table without examining himself carefully, lest "by eating this bread and drinking this cup he eat and drink to his own judgment."[80] In short, by the use of this holy sacrament we are moved to a fervent love of God and our neighbors.

Therefore we reject as desecrations of the sacraments all the muddled ideas and damnable inventions that men have added and mixed in with them.

---

80 1 Cor. 11:27.

And we say that we should be content with the procedure that Christ and the apostles have taught us and speak of these things as they have spoken of them.

Article 36: The Civil Government

We believe that because of the depravity of the human race our good God has ordained kings, princes, and civil officers. He wants the world to be governed by laws and policies so that human lawlessness may be restrained and that everything may be conducted in good order among human beings.

For that purpose he has placed the sword in the hands of the government, to punish evil people and protect the good.

And being called in this manner to contribute to the advancement of a society that is pleasing to God, the civil rulers have the task, subject to God's law, of removing every obstacle to the preaching of the gospel and to every aspect of divine worship.

They should do this while completely refraining from every tendency toward exercising absolute authority, and while functioning in the sphere entrusted to them, with the means belonging to them. They should do it in order that the Word of God may have free course; the kingdom of Jesus Christ may make progress; and every anti-Christian power may be resisted.*

Moreover everyone, regardless of status, condition, or rank, must be subject to the government, and pay taxes, and hold its representatives in honor and respect, and obey them in all things that are not in conflict with God's Word, praying for them that the Lord may be willing to lead them in all their ways and that we may live a peaceful and quiet life in all piety and decency.

And on this matter we denounce the Anabaptists, other anarchists, and in general all those who want to reject the authorities and civil officers and to subvert justice by introducing common ownership of goods and corrupting the moral order that God has established among human beings.

* The preceding three paragraphs are a substitution for the original paragraph below, which various Reformed Synods have judged to be unbiblical:

"And the government's task is not limited to caring for and watching over the public domain but extends also to upholding the sacred ministry, with a view to removing and destroying all idolatry and false worship of the Antichrist; to promoting the kingdom of Jesus Christ; and to furthering the preaching of the gospel everywhere; to the end that God may be honored and served by everyone, as he requires in his Word."

Article 37: The Last Judgment

Finally, we believe, according to God's Word, that when the time appointed by the Lord is come (which is unknown to all creatures) and the number of the elect is complete, our Lord Jesus Christ will come from heaven, bodily and visibly, as he ascended, with great glory and majesty, to declare himself the judge of the living and the dead. He will burn this old world, in fire and flame, in order to cleanse it.

Then all human creatures will appear in person before that great judge—men, women, and children, who have lived from the beginning until the end of the world. They will be summoned there by the voice of the archangel and by the sound of the divine trumpet.[81]

For all those who died before that time will be raised from the earth, their spirits being joined and united with their own bodies in which they lived. And as for those who are still alive, they will not die like the others but will be changed "in the twinkling of an eye" from "corruptible to incorruptible."[82] Then "the books" (that is, the consciences) will be opened, and the dead will be judged according to the things they did in the world,[83] whether good or evil.

Indeed, all people will give account of all the idle words they have spoken,[84] which the world regards as only playing games. And then the secrets and hypocrisies of men will be publicly uncovered in the sight of all.

Therefore, with good reason the thought of this judgment is horrible and dreadful to wicked and evil people.

But it is very pleasant and a great comfort to the righteous and elect, since their total redemption will then be accomplished. They will then receive the fruits of their labor and of the trouble they have suffered; their innocence will be openly recognized by all; and they will see the terrible vengeance that God will bring on the evil ones who tyrannized, oppressed, and tormented them in this world.

---

81 1 Thess. 4:16.
82 1 Cor. 15:51–53.
83 Rev. 20:12.
84 Matt. 12:36.

The evil ones will be convicted by the witness of their own consciences, and shall be made immortal—but only to be tormented in the everlasting fire prepared for the devil and his angels.[85]

In contrast, the faithful and elect will be crowned with glory and honor. The Son of God will "confess their names"[86] before God his Father and the holy and elect angels; all tears will be "wiped from their eyes";[87] and their cause—at present condemned as heretical and evil by many judges and civil officers—will be acknowledged as the "cause of the Son of God." And as a gracious reward the Lord will make them possess a glory such as the heart of man could never imagine.

So we look forward to that great day with longing in order to enjoy fully the promises of God in Christ Jesus, our Lord.

---

85 Matt. 25:14.
86 Matt. 10:32.
87 Rev. 7:17.

12

Thirty-Nine Articles

(1563)

The theology of the Reformation made its way to England early on, as Martin Luther's ideas were known and discussed in the kingdom by the 1520s. William Tyndale's highly influential English translation of the Bible, which began to be published in 1526, helped make Scripture accessible to the masses and aided the spread of Protestant ideas. But Roman Catholicism had a strong hold on the country, and many Protestants—including Tyndale—were martyred for their faith.

Things changed dramatically in the 1530s thanks to political considerations. King Henry VIII, concerned that his wife, Catherine of Aragon, had failed to produce a male heir, sought an annulment from Pope Clement VII but was refused. In response, Henry broke with Rome and pronounced himself supreme head of the Church of England. Christianity in England lurched violently between periods of greater and lesser reform—and even between Protestantism and Roman Catholicism—depending on who sat on the throne until a rough equilibrium was finally reached in 1660. Beginning in seed form with Thomas Cranmer (Archbishop of Canterbury) in 1538, these articles of the Anglican church were penned to distinguish it from Roman Catholicism on the one hand and from Protestant non-conformists (those who did not conform to the Church of England) on the other hand.

Based on earlier statements of belief, the Thirty-Nine Articles were adopted in 1563 and reached their final form in 1571. They represent the distinctive Anglican form of Protestantism.

Thirty-Nine Articles

Article 1

Of Faith in the Holy Trinity

There is but one living and true God, everlasting, without body, parts, or passions; of infinite power, wisdom, and goodness; the maker and preserver of all things both visible and invisible. And in unity of this Godhead there be three Persons, of one substance, power, and eternity; the Father, the Son, and the Holy Ghost.

Article 2

Of the Word, or Son of God, Which Was Made Very Man

The Son, which is the Word of the Father, begotten from everlasting of the Father, the very and eternal God, and of one substance with the Father, took man's nature in the womb of the blessed Virgin, of her substance: so that two whole and perfect natures, that is to say, the Godhead and manhood, were joined together in one person, never to be divided, whereof is one Christ, very God and very man, who truly suffered, was crucified, dead, and buried, to reconcile His Father to us, and to be a sacrifice, not only for original guilt, but also for all actual sins of men.

Article 3

Of the Going Down of Christ into Hell

As Christ died for us, and was buried, so also is it to be believed that He went down into Hell.

Article 4

Of the Resurrection of Christ

Christ did truly rise again from death, and took again His body, with flesh, bones, and all things appertaining to the perfection of man's nature, wherewith

He ascended into heaven, and there sitteth until He return to judge all men at the last day.

Article 5

Of the Holy Ghost

The Holy Ghost, proceeding from the Father and the Son, is of one substance, majesty, and glory with the Father and the Son, very and eternal God.

Article 6

Of the Sufficiency of the Holy Scripture for Salvation

Holy Scripture containeth all things necessary to salvation: so that whatsoever is not read therein, nor may be proved thereby, is not to be required of any man, that it should be believed as an article of the faith, or be thought requisite or necessary to salvation.

In the name of Holy Scripture, we do understand those Canonical books of the Old and New Testament, of whose authority was never any doubt in the Church.

Of the Names and Number of the Canonical Books

Genesis.
Exodus.
Leviticus.
Numbers.
Deuteronomy.
Joshua.
Judges.
Ruth.
The First Book of Samuel.
The Second Book of Samuel.
The First Book of Kings.
The Second Book of Kings.
The First Book of Chronicles.
The Second Book of Chronicles.
The First Book of Esdras.
The Second Book of Esdras.

The Book of Esther.

The Book of Job.

The Psalms.

The Proverbs.

Ecclesiastes, or the Preacher.

Cantica, or Songs of Solomon.

Four Prophets the Greater.

Twelve Prophets the Less.

All the books of the New Testament, as they are commonly received, we do receive, and account them Canonical.

And the other books (as Hierome saith) the Church doth read for example of life and instruction of manners; but yet doth it not apply them to establish any doctrine. Such are these following:

The Third Book of Esdras.

The Fourth Book of Esdras.

The Book of Tobias.

The Book of Judith.

The rest of the Book of Esther.

The Book of Wisdom.

Jesus the Son of Sirach.

Baruch the Prophet.

The Song of the Three Children.

The Story of Susanna.

Of Bel and the Dragon.

The Prayer of Manasses.

The First Book of Maccabees.

The Second Book of Maccabees.

Article 7

Of the Old Testament

The Old Testament is not contrary to the New; for both in the Old and New Testament everlasting life is offered to mankind by Christ, who is the only Mediator between God and man, being both God and man. Wherefore they are not to be heard which feign that the old fathers did look only for transitory promises. Although the law given from God by Moses, as touching ceremonies and rites, do not bind Christian men, nor the civil precepts thereof ought of necessity to be received in any commonwealth; yet, notwithstanding, no Christian man whatsoever is free from the obedience of the commandments which are called moral.

Article 8

Of the Three Creeds

The three Creeds, Nicene Creed, Athanasius' Creed, and that which is commonly called the Apostles' Creed, ought thoroughly to be received and believed; for they may be proved by most certain warrants of Holy Scripture.

Article 9

Of Original or Birth Sin

Original sin standeth not in the following of Adam (as the Pelagians do vainly talk), but it is the fault and corruption of the nature of every man that naturally is engendered of the offspring of Adam, whereby man is very far gone from original righteousness, and is of his own nature inclined to evil, so that the flesh lusteth always contrary to the spirit; and therefore in every person born into this world, it deserveth God's wrath and damnation. And this infection of nature doth remain, yea, in them that are regenerated, whereby the lust of the flesh, called in Greek *phronōema sarkos* (which some do expound the wisdom, some sensuality, some the affection, some the desire of the flesh), is not subject to the law of God. And although there is no condemnation for them that believe and are baptized, yet the Apostle doth confess that concupiscence and lust hath itself the nature of sin.

Article 10

Of Free Will

The condition of man after the fall of Adam is such, that he cannot turn and prepare himself, by his own natural strength and good works, to faith and calling upon God. Wherefore we have no power to do good works pleasant and acceptable to God, without the grace of God by Christ preventing us that we may have a good will, and working with us when we have that good will.

Article 11

Of the Justification of Man

We are accounted righteous before God, only for the merit of our Lord and Saviour Jesus Christ by faith, and not for our own works or deservings. Wherefore that we are justified by faith only is a most wholesome doctrine, and very full of comfort; as more largely is expressed in the Homily of Justification.

Article 12

Of Good Works

Albeit that good works, which are the fruits of faith and follow after justification, cannot put away our sins and endure the severity of God's judgment, yet are they pleasing and acceptable to God in Christ, and do spring out necessarily of a true and lively faith, insomuch that by them a lively faith may be as evidently known as a tree discerned by the fruit.

Article 13

Of Works before Justification

Works done before the grace of Christ and the inspiration of His Spirit, are not pleasant to God, forasmuch as they spring not of faith in Jesus Christ, neither do they make men meet to receive grace, or (as the School authors say) deserve grace of congruity: yea, rather for that they are not done as God hath willed and commanded them to be done, we doubt not but they have the nature of sin.

Article 14

Of Works of Supererogation

Voluntary works besides, over and above, God's commandments which they call Works of Supererogation, cannot be taught without arrogancy and impiety. For by them men do declare that they do not only render unto God as much as they are bound to do, but that they do more for His sake than of bounden duty is required: Whereas Christ saith plainly, When ye have done all that are commanded to you, say, We be unprofitable servants.

Article 15

Of Christ Alone without Sin

Christ in the truth of our nature was made like unto us in all things, sin only except, from which He was clearly void, both in His flesh and in His spirit. He came to be the lamb without spot, Who by sacrifice of Himself once made, should take away the sins of the world: and sin, as S. John saith, was not in Him. But all we the rest, although baptized and born again in Christ, yet offend in many things: and if we say we have no sin, we deceive ourselves, and the truth is not in us.

Article 16

Of Sin after Baptism

Not every deadly sin willingly committed after Baptism is sin against the Holy Ghost, and unpardonable. Wherefore the grant of repentance is not to be denied to such as fall into sin after Baptism. After we have received the Holy Ghost, we may depart from grace given and fall into sin, and by the grace of God we may arise again and amend our lives. And therefore they are to be condemned, which say they can no more sin as long as they live here, or deny the place of forgiveness to such as truly repent.

Article 17

Of Predestination and Election

Predestination to life is the everlasting purpose of God, whereby, before the foundations of the world were laid, He hath constantly decreed by His counsel secret to us, to deliver from curse and damnation those whom He hath chosen in Christ out of mankind, and to bring them by Christ to everlasting salvation as vessels made to honour. Wherefore they which be endued with so excellent a benefit of God be called according to God's purpose by His Spirit working in due season; they through grace obey the calling; they be justified freely; they be made sons of God by adoption; they be made like the image of His only-begotten Son Jesus Christ; they walk religiously in good works; and at length by God's mercy they attain to everlasting felicity.

As the godly consideration of Predestination and our Election in Christ is full of sweet, pleasant, and unspeakable comfort to godly persons and such as feel in themselves the working of the Spirit of Christ, mortifying the works of the flesh and their earthly members and drawing up their mind to high and heavenly things, as well because it doth greatly establish and confirm their faith of eternal salvation to be enjoyed through Christ, as because it doth fervently kindle their love towards God: so for curious and carnal persons, lacking the Spirit of Christ, to have continually before their eyes the sentence of God's Predestination is a most dangerous downfall, whereby the devil doth thrust them either into desperation or into wretchlessness of most unclean living no less perilous than desperation.

Furthermore, we must receive God's promises in such wise as they be generally set forth in Holy Scripture; and in our doings that will of God is to be followed which we have expressly declared unto us in the word of God.

Article 18

Of Obtaining Eternal Salvation Only by the Name of Christ

They also are to be had accursed that presume to say that every man shall be saved by the law or sect which he professeth, so that he be diligent to frame his life according to that law and the light of nature. For Holy Scripture doth set out to us only the name of Jesus Christ, whereby men must be saved.

Article 19

Of the Church

The visible Church of Christ is a congregation of faithful men, in the which the pure word of God is preached and the sacraments be duly ministered according to Christ's ordinance in all those things that of necessity are requisite to the same. As the Church of Jerusalem, Alexandria, and Antioch have erred: so also the Church of Rome hath erred, not only in their living and manner of ceremonies, but also in matters of faith.

Article 20

Of the Authority of the Church

The Church hath power to decree rites or ceremonies and authority in controversies of faith; and yet it is not lawful for the Church to ordain anything contrary to God's word written, neither may it so expound one place of Scripture, that it be repugnant to another. Wherefore, although the Church be a witness and a keeper of Holy Writ: yet, as it ought not to decree anything against the same, so besides the same ought it not to enforce anything to be believed for necessity of salvation.

Article 21

Of the Authority of General Councils

General Councils may not be gathered together without the commandment and will of princes. And when they be gathered together, forasmuch as they be an assembly of men, whereof all be not governed with the Spirit and word of God, they may err and sometime have erred, even in things pertaining unto God. Wherefore things ordained by them as necessary to salvation have neither strength nor authority, unless it may be declared that they be taken out of Holy Scripture.

Article 22

Of Purgatory

The Romish doctrine concerning Purgatory, Pardons, worshipping and adoration as well of Images as of Relics, and also Invocation of Saints, is a fond thing vainly invented, and grounded upon no warranty of Scripture; but rather repugnant to the word of God.

Article 23

Of Ministering in the Congregation

It is not lawful for any man to take upon him the office of public preaching or ministering the sacraments in the congregation, before he be lawfully called and sent to execute the same. And those we ought to judge lawfully called and sent, which be chosen and called to this work by men who have public authority given unto them in the congregation to call and send ministers into the Lord's vineyard.

Article 24

Of Speaking in the Congregation in Such a Tongue as the People Understandeth

It is a thing plainly repugnant to the word of God and the custom of the primitive Church, to have public prayer in the Church, or to minister the sacraments in a tongue not understood of the people.

Article 25

Of the Sacraments

Sacraments ordained of Christ be not only badges or tokens of Christian men's profession, but rather they be certain sure witnesses and effectual signs of grace and God's good will towards us, by the which He doth work invisibly in us, and doth not only quicken, but also strengthen and confirm, our faith in Him. There are two Sacraments ordained of Christ our Lord in the Gospel, that is to say, Baptism and the Supper of the Lord.

Those five, commonly called Sacraments, that is to say, Confirmation, Penance, Orders, Matrimony, and Extreme Unction, are not to be counted for Sacraments of the Gospel, being such as have grown partly of the corrupt following of the Apostles, partly are states of life allowed in the Scriptures; but yet have not the like nature of Sacraments with Baptism and the Lord's Supper, for that they have not any visible sign or ceremony ordained of God.

The Sacraments were not ordained of Christ to be gazed upon or to be carried about, but that we should duly use them. And in such only as worthily receive the same, have they a wholesome effect or operation: but they that receive them unworthily, purchase to themselves damnation, as S. Paul saith.

Article 26

Of the Unworthiness of the Ministers, Which Hinders Not the Effect of the Sacraments

Although in the visible Church the evil be ever mingled with the good, and sometime the evil have chief authority in the ministration of the word and sacraments; yet forasmuch as they do not the same in their own name, but in Christ's, and do minister by His commission and authority, we may use their ministry both in hearing the word of God and in the receiving of the sacraments. Neither is the effect of Christ's ordinance taken away by their wickedness, nor the grace of God's gifts diminished from such as by faith and rightly do receive the sacraments ministered unto them, which be effectual because of Christ's institution and promise, although they be ministered by evil men.

Nevertheless it appertaineth to the discipline of the Church that inquiry be made of evil ministers, and that they be accused by those that have knowledge of their offences; and finally, being found guilty by just judgment, be deposed.

Article 27

Of Baptism

Baptism is not only a sign of profession and mark of difference whereby Christian men are discerned from other that be not christened, but is also a sign of regeneration or new birth, whereby, as by an instrument, they that receive baptism rightly are grafted into the Church; the promises of the forgiveness of sin, and of our adoption to be the sons of God, by the Holy Ghost are visibly signed and sealed; faith is confirmed, and grace increased by virtue of prayer unto God. The baptism of young children is in any wise to be retained in the Church as most agreeable with the institution of Christ.

Article 28

Of the Lord's Supper

The Supper of the Lord is not only a sign of the love that Christians ought to have among themselves, one to another, but rather it is a sacrament of our redemption by Christ's death: insomuch that to such as rightly, worthily, and with faith receive the same, the bread which we break is a partaking of the body of Christ, and likewise the cup of blessing is a partaking of the blood of Christ.

Transubstantiation (or the change of the substance of bread and wine) in the Supper of the Lord, cannot be proved by Holy Writ, but is repugnant to the plain words of Scripture, overthroweth the nature of a Sacrament, and hath given occasion to many superstitions.

The body of Christ is given, taken, and eaten in the Supper, only after an heavenly and spiritual manner. And the mean whereby the body of Christ is received and eaten in the Supper is faith.

The Sacrament of the Lord's Supper was not by Christ's ordinance reserved, carried about, lifted up, or worshipped.

Article 29

Of the Wicked Which Do Not Eat the Body of Christ, in the Use of the Lord's Supper

The wicked and such as be void of a lively faith, although they do carnally and visibly press with their teeth (as S. Augustine saith) the sacrament of the body and blood of Christ, yet in no wise are they partakers of Christ, but rather to their condemnation do eat and drink the sign or sacrament of so great a thing.

Article 30

Of Both Kinds

The Cup of the Lord is not to be denied to the lay people; for both parts of the Lord's sacrament, by Christ's ordinance and commandment, ought to be ministered to all Christian men alike.

Article 31

Of the One Oblation of Christ Finished upon the Cross

The offering of Christ once made is the perfect redemption, propitiation, and satisfaction for all the sins of the whole world, both original and actual, and there is none other satisfaction for sin but that alone. Wherefore the sacrifices of Masses, in the which it was commonly said that the priests did offer Christ for the quick and the dead to have remission of pain or guilt, were blasphemous fables and dangerous deceits.

Article 32

Of the Marriage of Priests

Bishops, Priests, and Deacons are not commanded by God's laws either to vow the estate of single life or to abstain from marriage. Therefore it is lawful also for them, as for all other Christian men, to marry at their own discretion, as they shall judge the same to serve better to godliness.

Article 33

Of Excommunicated Persons, How They Are to Be Avoided

That person which by open denunciation of the Church is rightly cut off from the unity of the Church and excommunicated, ought to be taken of the whole multitude of the faithful as an heathen and publican, until he be openly reconciled by penance and received into the Church by a judge that hath authority thereto.

Article 34

Of the Traditions of the Church

It is not necessary that traditions and ceremonies be in all places one or utterly alike; for at all times they have been diverse, and may be changed according to the diversity of countries, times, and men's manners, so that nothing be ordained against God's word.

Whosoever through his private judgment willingly and purposely doth openly break the traditions and ceremonies of the Church which be not repugnant to the word of God, and be ordained and approved by common authority, ought to be rebuked openly that other may fear to do the like, as he that offendeth against common order of the Church, and hurteth the authority of the magistrate, and woundeth the conscience of the weak brethren.

Every particular or national Church hath authority to ordain, change, and abolish ceremonies or rites of the Church ordained only by man's authority, so that all things be done to edifying.

Article 35

Of Homilies

The second Book of Homilies, the several titles whereof we have joined under this Article, doth contain a godly and wholesome doctrine and necessary for these times, as doth the former Book of Homilies which were set forth in the time of Edward the Sixth: and therefore we judge them to be read in Churches by the ministers diligently and distinctly, that they may be understood of the people.

Of the Names of the Homilies

1. Of the Right Use of the Church.
2. Against Peril of Idolatry.
3. Of the Repairing and Keeping Clean of Churches.
4. Of Good Works: First of Fasting.
5. Against Gluttony and Drunkenness.
6. Against Excess of Apparel.
7. Of Prayer.

8. Of the Place and Time of Prayer.
9. That Common Prayers and Sacraments ought to Be Ministered in a Known Tongue.
10. Of the Reverend Estimation of God's Word.
11. Of Alms-doing.
12. Of the Nativity of Christ.
13. Of the Passion of Christ.
14. Of the Resurrection of Christ.
15. Of the Worthy Receiving of the Sacrament of the Body and Blood of Christ.
16. Of the Gifts of the Holy Ghost.
17. For the Rogation-days.
18. Of the State of Matrimony.
19. Of Repentance.
20. Against Idleness.
21. Against Rebellion.

Article 36

Of Consecration of Bishops and Ministers

The Book of Consecration of Archbishops and Bishops and ordering of Priests and Deacons, lately set forth in the time of Edward the Sixth and confirmed at the same time by authority of Parliament, doth contain all things necessary to such consecration and ordering; neither hath it anything that of itself is superstitious or ungodly.

And therefore whosoever are consecrate or ordered according to the rites of that book, since the second year of the aforenamed King Edward unto this time, or hereafter shall be consecrated or ordered according to the same rites, we decree all such to be rightly, orderly, and lawfully consecrated or ordered.

Article 37

Of the Civil Magistrates

The Queen's Majesty hath the chief power in this realm of England and other her dominions, unto whom the chief government of all estates of this realm, whether they be ecclesiastical or civil, in all causes doth appertain, and is not nor ought to be subject to any foreign jurisdiction.

Where we attribute to the Queen's Majesty the chief government, by which titles we understand the minds of some slanderous folks to be offended, we give not to our princes the ministering either of God's word or of sacraments, the which thing the Injunctions also lately set forth by Elizabeth our Queen doth most plainly testify: but only that prerogative which we see to have been given always to all godly princes in Holy Scriptures by God himself, that is, that they should rule all estates and degrees committed to their charge by God, whether they be ecclesiastical or temporal, and restrain with the civil sword the stubborn and evil-doers.

The Bishop of Rome hath no jurisdiction in this realm of England.

The laws of the realm may punish Christian men with death for heinous and grievous offences.

It is lawful for Christian men at the commandment of the Magistrate to wear weapons and serve in the wars.

Article 38

Of Christian Men's Good Which Are Not Common

The riches and goods of Christians are not common, as touching the right, title, and possession of the same, as certain Anabaptists do falsely boast; notwithstanding every man ought of such things as he possesseth liberally to give alms to the poor, according to his ability.

Article 39

Of a Christian Man's Oath

As we confess that vain and rash swearing is forbidden Christian men by our Lord Jesus Christ, so we judge that Christian religion doth not prohibit but that a man may swear when the magistrate requireth in a cause of faith and charity, so it be done according to the Prophet's teaching in justice, judgment, and truth.

13

Heidelberg Catechism

(1563)

After the imperial Diet of Augsburg in 1530, Lutheranism was the only legal form of Protestantism in the Holy Roman Empire. But in one imperial state, the Electoral Palatinate, centered on the city of Heidelberg, Protestants of different stripes were welcome. And despite Lutheranism's legal monopoly, Reformed ideas began to seep into Heidelberg, especially through its famed university.

A disputation on the Lord's Supper at the University of Heidelberg was pivotal. The Reformed vigorously disputed the physical presence of Christ in the supper, contra Lutheranism. Elector Frederick III was increasingly convinced of Reformed ideas and—alarmed at the state of instruction in the faith within his realm—commissioned a catechism that would present a broadly "Christian" summary of the faith aimed at achieving religious consensus.

Drafting the Heidelberg Catechism was assigned to a group of Heidelberg ministers and professors. It is believed that two men in particular, Zacharias Ursinus and Caspar Olevanius, were largely responsible for its writing, with Ursinus being the primary author. The catechism is one of the Three Forms of Unity of the Dutch Reformed churches and is beloved for its pastoral tone.

Heidelberg Catechism

1. Q. What is your only comfort in life and in death?

A. That I am not my own,[1]
but belong—body and soul, in life and in death[2]—
to my faithful Savior, Jesus Christ.[3]
He has fully paid for all my sins with his precious blood,[4]
and has delivered me from the tyranny of the devil.[5]
He also watches over me in such a way[6]
that not a hair can fall from my head
without the will of my Father in heaven;[7]
in fact, all things must work together for my salvation.[8]
Because I belong to him,
Christ, by his Holy Spirit,
also assures me of eternal life[9]
and makes me wholeheartedly willing and ready
from now on to live for him.[10]

1. 1 Cor. 6:19–20. **2.** Rom. 14:7–9. **3.** 1 Cor. 3:23; Titus 2:14. **4.** 1 Peter 1:18–19; 1 John 1:7–9; 2:2. **5.** John 8:34–36; Heb. 2:14–15; 1 John 3:1–11. **6.** John 6:39–40; 10:27–30; 2 Thess. 3:3; 1 Peter 1:5. **7.** Matt. 10:29–31; Luke 21:16–18. **8.** Rom. 8:28. **9.** Rom. 8:15–16; 2 Cor. 1:21–22; 5:5; Eph. 1:13–14. **10.** Rom. 8:1–17.

2. Q. How many things must you know to live and die in the joy of this comfort?

A. Three:
first, how great my sin and misery are;[1]
second, how I am delivered from all my sins and misery;[2]
third, how I am to thank God for such deliverance.[3]

1. Rom. 3:9–10; 1 John 1:10. **2.** John 17:3; Acts 4:12; 10:43. **3.** Matt. 5:16; Rom. 6:13; Eph. 5:8–10; 2 Tim. 2:15; 1 Peter 2:9–10.

PART I: MISERY

LORD'S DAY 2

3. Q. How do you come to know your misery?

A. The law of God tells me.[1]

1. Rom. 3:20; 7:7–25.

4. Q. What does God's law require of us?

A. Christ teaches us this in summary in Matthew 22:37–40:
"You shall love the Lord your God
with all your heart
and with all your soul
and with all your mind,
and with all your strength."[1]
This is the greatest and first commandment.
And a second is like it:
"You shall love your neighbor as yourself."[2]
On these two commandments hang all the Law and the Prophets.

1. Deut. 6:5. 2. Lev. 19:18.

5. Q. Can you live up to all this perfectly?

A. No.[1]
I am inclined by nature
to hate God and my neighbor.[2]

1. Rom. 3:9–20, 23; 1 John 1:8, 10. 2. Gen. 6:5; Jer. 17:9; Rom. 7:23–24; 8:7; Eph. 2:1–3; Titus 3:3.

LORD'S DAY 3

6. Q. Did God create man so wicked and perverse?

A. No.
God created man good[1] and in his own image,[2]
that is, in true righteousness and holiness,[3]
so that he might
truly know God his creator,[4]

231

love him with all his heart,
and live with God in eternal happiness,
for his praise and glory.[5]

1. Gen. 1:31. 2. Gen. 1:26–27. 3. Eph. 4:24. 4. Col. 3:10. 5. Ps. 8.

7. Q. Then where does man's corrupt nature come from?

A. From the fall and disobedience of our first parents,
Adam and Eve, in Paradise.[1]
This fall has so poisoned our nature[2]
that we are all conceived and born in sin.[3]

1. Gen. 3. 2. Rom. 5:12, 18–19. 3. Ps. 51:5.

8. Q. But are we so corrupt that we are totally unable to do any good and inclined toward all evil?

A. Yes,[1]
unless we are born again
by the Spirit of God.[2]

1. Gen. 6:5; 8:21; Job 14:4; Isa. 53:6. 2. John 3:3–5.

LORD'S DAY 4

9. Q. But doesn't God do man an injustice by requiring in his law what man is unable to do?

A. No, God created man with the ability to keep the law.[1]
Man, however, at the instigation of the devil,[2]
in willful disobedience,[3]
robbed himself and all his descendants of these gifts.[4]

1. Gen. 1:31; Eph. 4:24. 2. Gen. 3:13; John 8:44. 3. Gen. 3:6. 4. Rom. 5:12, 18–19.

10. Q. Will God permit such disobedience and rebellion to go unpunished?

A. Certainly not.
He is terribly angry
with the sin we are born with

as well as our actual sins.

God will punish them by a just judgment

both now and in eternity,[1]

having declared:

"Cursed is everyone who does not observe and obey

all the things written in the book of the law."[2]

1. Ex. 34:7; Ps. 5:4–6; Nah. 1:2; Rom. 1:18; Eph. 5:6; Heb. 9:27. 2. Gal. 3:10; Deut. 27:26.

11. Q. But isn't God also merciful?

A. God is certainly merciful,[1]

but he is also just.[2]

His justice demands

that sin, committed against his supreme majesty,

be punished with the supreme penalty—

eternal punishment of body and soul.[3]

1. Ex. 34:6–7; Ps. 103:8–9. 2. Ex. 34:7; Deut. 7:9–11; Ps. 5:4–6; Heb. 10:30–31. 3. Matt. 25:35–46.

PART II: DELIVERANCE

LORD'S DAY 5

12. Q. According to God's righteous judgment we deserve punishment both now and in eternity: how then can we escape this punishment and return to God's favor?

A. God requires that his justice be satisfied.[1]

Therefore the claims of this justice

must be paid in full,

either by ourselves or by another.[2]

1. Ex. 23:7; Rom. 2:1–11. 2. Isa. 53:11; Rom. 8:3–4.

13. Q. Can we make this payment ourselves?

A. Certainly not.

Actually, we increase our debt every day.[1]

1. Matt. 6:12; Rom. 2:4–5.

14. Q. Can another creature—any at all—pay this debt for us?

A. No.
To begin with,
God will not punish any other creature
for what a human is guilty of.[1]
Furthermore,
no mere creature can bear the weight
of God's eternal wrath against sin
and deliver others from it.[2]

1. Ezek. 18:4, 20; Heb. 2:14–18. 2. Pss. 49:7–9; 130:3.

15. Q. What kind of mediator and deliverer should we look for then?

A. One who is a true[1] and righteous[2] man,
yet more powerful than all creatures,
that is, one who is also true God.[3]

1. Rom. 1:3; 1 Cor. 15:21; Heb. 2:17. 2. Isa. 53:9; 2 Cor. 5:21; Heb. 7:26. 3. Isa. 7:14; 9:6; Jer. 23:6; John 1:1.

LORD'S DAY 6

16. Q. Why must the mediator be a true and righteous man?

A. Because God's justice requires
that human nature, which has sinned,
must pay for its sin;[1]
but a sinner could never pay for others.[2]

1. Rom. 5:12, 15; 1 Cor. 15:21; Heb. 2:14–16. 2. Heb. 7:26–27; 1 Peter 3:18.

17. Q. Why must he also be true God?

A. So that,
by the power of his divinity,
he might bear in his humanity
the weight of God's wrath,
and earn for us

and restore to us
righteousness and life.[1]

1. Isa. 53; John 3:16; 2 Cor. 5:21.

18. Q. Then who is this mediator—true God and at the same time a true and righteous man?

A. Our Lord Jesus Christ,[1]
who was given to us
for our complete deliverance
and righteousness.[2]

1. Matt. 1:21–23; Luke 2:11; 1 Tim. 2:5. 2. 1 Cor. 1:30.

19. Q. How do you come to know this?

A. The holy gospel tells me.
God himself began to reveal the gospel already in Paradise;[1]
later, he proclaimed it
by the holy patriarchs[2] and prophets[3]
and foreshadowed it
by the sacrifices and other ceremonies of the law;[4]
and finally he fulfilled it
through his own beloved Son.[5]

1. Gen. 3:15. 2. Gen. 22:18; 49:10. 3. Isa. 53; Jer. 23:5–6; Mic. 7:18–20; Acts 10:43; Heb. 1:1–2. 4. Lev. 1–7; John 5:46; Heb. 10:1–10. 5. Rom. 10:4; Gal. 4:4–5; Col. 2:17.

LORD'S DAY 7

20. Q. Are all people then saved through Christ just as they were lost through Adam?

A. No.
Only those are saved
who through true faith
are grafted into Christ
and accept all his benefits.[1]

1. Matt. 7:14; John 3:16, 18, 36; Rom. 11:16–21.

21. Q. What is true faith?

A. True faith is
not only a sure knowledge by which I hold as true
all that God has revealed to us in his Word;[1]
it is also a wholehearted trust,[2]
which the Holy Spirit works in me[3] by the gospel,[4]
that God has freely granted, not only to others but to me also,[5]
forgiveness of sins,
eternal righteousness,
and salvation.[6]
These gifts are purely of grace,
only because of Christ's merit.[7]

1. John 17:3, 17; Heb. 11:1–3; James 2:19. **2.** Rom. 4:18–21; 5:1; 10:10; Heb. 4:14–16.
3. Matt. 16:15–17; John 3:5; Acts 16:14. **4.** Rom. 1:16; 10:17; 1 Cor. 1:21. **5.** Gal. 2:20.
6. Rom. 1:17; Heb. 10:10. **7.** Rom. 3:21–26; Gal. 2:16; Eph. 2:8–10.

22. Q. What then must a Christian believe?

A. All that is promised us in the gospel,[1]
a summary of which is taught us
in the articles of our catholic and undoubted Christian faith.

1. Matt. 28:18–20; John 20:30–31.

23. Q. What are these articles?

A. I believe in God, the Father Almighty,
Creator of heaven and earth.
I believe in Jesus Christ, his only begotten Son, our Lord,
who was conceived by the Holy Spirit,
born of the virgin Mary;
suffered under Pontius Pilate,
was crucified, dead, and buried;
he descended into hell;
the third day he rose again from the dead;
he ascended to heaven,
and sits at the right hand of God the Father Almighty;

from there he will come
to judge the living and the dead.
I believe in the Holy Spirit;
the holy catholic church;
the communion of saints;
the forgiveness of sins;
the resurrection of the body;
and the life everlasting. Amen.

LORD'S DAY 8

24. Q. How are these articles divided?

A. Into three parts:
God the Father and our creation;
God the Son and our deliverance;
and God the Holy Spirit and our sanctification.

25. Q. Since there is only one divine being,[1] why do you speak of three: Father, Son, and Holy Spirit?

A. Because that is how
God has revealed himself in his Word:[2]
these three distinct persons
are one, true, eternal God.

1. Deut. 6:4; 1 Cor. 8:4, 6. 2. Matt. 3:16–17; 28:18–19; Luke 4:18 (Isa. 61:1); John 14:26; 15:26; 2 Cor. 13:14; Gal. 4:6; Titus 3:5–6.

LORD'S DAY 9

26. Q. What do you believe when you say, "I believe in God, the Father Almighty, Creator of heaven and earth"?

A. That the eternal Father of our Lord Jesus Christ,
who out of nothing created heaven and earth
and everything in them,[1]
who still upholds and rules them
by his eternal counsel and providence,[2]
is my God and Father

for the sake of Christ his Son.[3]
I trust God so much that I do not doubt
he will provide
whatever I need
for body and soul,[4]
and will turn to my good
whatever adversity he sends upon me
in this vale of tears.[5]
He is able to do this because he is almighty God;[6]
he desires to do this because he is a faithful Father.[7]

1. Gen. 1–2; Ex. 20:11; Ps. 33:6; Isa. 44:24; Acts 4:24; 14:15. 2. Ps. 104; Matt. 6:30; 10:29; Eph. 1:11. 3. John 1:12–13; Rom. 8:15–16. 4. Ps. 55:22; Matt. 6:25–26; Luke 12:22–31. 5. Rom. 8:28. 6. Gen. 18:14; Rom. 8:31–39. 7. Matt. 7:9–11.

LORD'S DAY 10

27. Q. What do you understand by the providence of God?

A. Providence is
the almighty and ever present power of God[1]
by which God upholds, as with his hand,
heaven
and earth
and all creatures,[2]
and so rules them that
leaf and blade,
rain and drought,
fruitful and lean years,
food and drink,
health and sickness,
prosperity and poverty—[3]
all things, in fact, come to us
not by chance[4]
but by his fatherly hand.[5]

1. Jer. 23:23–24; Acts 17:24–28. 2. Heb. 1:3. 3. Jer. 5:24; Acts 14:15–17; John 9:3; Prov. 22:2. 4. Prov. 16:33. 5. Matt. 10:29.

28. Q. How does the knowledge of God's creation and providence help us?

A. We can be patient in adversity,[1]

thankful in prosperity,[2]

and for the future we can have

good confidence in our faithful God and Father

that no creature will separate us from his love.[3]

For all creatures are so completely in his hand

that without his will

they can neither move nor be moved.[4]

1. Job 1:21–22; James 1:3. 2. Deut. 8:10; 1 Thess. 5:18. 3. Ps. 55:22; Rom. 5:3–5; 8:38–39. 4. Job 1:12; 2:6; Prov. 21:1; Acts 17:24–28.

LORD'S DAY 11

29. Q. Why is the Son of God called "Jesus," meaning "savior"?

A. Because he saves us from our sins;[1]

and because salvation is not to be sought

or found in anyone else.[2]

1. Matt. 1:21; Heb. 7:25. 2. Isa. 43:11; John 15:5; Acts 4:11–12; 1 Tim. 2:5.

30. Q. Do those who look for their salvation and security in saints, in themselves, or elsewhere really believe in the only savior Jesus?

A. No.

Although they boast of being his,

by their actions they deny

the only savior, Jesus.[1]

Either Jesus is not a perfect savior,

or those who in true faith accept this savior

have in him all they need for their salvation.[2]

1. 1 Cor. 1:12–13; Gal. 5:4. 2. Col. 1:19–20; 2:10; 1 John 1:7.

LORD'S DAY 12

31. Q. Why is he called "Christ," meaning "anointed"?

A. Because he has been ordained by God the Father and has been anointed with the Holy Spirit[1] to be

our chief prophet and teacher[2]

who fully reveals to us

the secret counsel and will of God concerning our deliverance;[3]

our only high priest[4]

who has delivered us by the one sacrifice of his body,[5]

and who continually intercedes for us before the Father;[6]

and our eternal king[7]

who governs us by his Word and Spirit,

and who guards us and keeps us

in the deliverance he has won for us.[8]

1. Luke 3:21–22; 4:14–19 (Isa. 61:1); Heb. 1:9 (Ps. 45:7). 2. Acts 3:22 (Deut. 18:15). 3. John 1:18; 15:15. 4. Heb. 7:17 (Ps. 110:4). 5. Heb. 9:12; 10:11–14. 6. Rom. 8:34; Heb. 9:24. 7. Matt. 21:5 (Zech. 9:9). 8. Matt. 28:18–20; John 10:28; Rev. 12:10–11.

32. Q. But why are you called a Christian?

A. Because by faith I am a member of Christ[1]

and so I share in his anointing.[2]

I am anointed

to confess his name,[3]

to present myself to him as a living sacrifice of thanks,[4]

to strive with a free conscience against sin and the devil

in this life,[5]

and afterward to reign with Christ

over all creation

for eternity.[6]

1. 1 Cor. 12:12–27. 2. Acts 2:17 (Joel 2:28); 1 John 2:27. 3. Matt. 10:32; Rom. 10:9–10; Heb. 13:15. 4. Rom. 12:1; 1 Peter 2:5, 9. 5. Gal. 5:16–17; Eph. 6:11; 1 Tim. 1:18–19. 6. Matt. 25:34; 2 Tim. 2:12.

LORD'S DAY 13

33. Q. Why is he called God's "only begotten Son" when we also are God's children?

A. Because Christ alone is the eternal, natural Son of God.[1]

We, however, are adopted children of God—
adopted by grace for the sake of Christ.[2]

1. John 1:1–3, 14, 18; Heb. 1. 2. John 1:12; Rom. 8:14–17; Eph. 1:5–6.

34. Q. Why do you call him "our Lord"?

A. Because—
not with gold or silver,
but with his precious blood[1]—
he has delivered and purchased us
body and soul
from sin and from the tyranny of the devil,[2]
to be his very own.[3]

1. 1 Peter 1:18–19. 2. Col. 1:13–14; Heb. 2:14–15. 3. 1 Cor. 6:20; 1 Tim. 2:5–6.

LORD'S DAY 14

35. Q. What does it mean that he "was conceived by the Holy Spirit, born of the virgin Mary"?

A. That the eternal Son of God,
who is and remains
true and eternal God,[1]
took to himself,
through the working of the Holy Spirit,[2]
from the flesh and blood of the virgin Mary,[3]
a true human nature
so that he might also become David's true descendant,[4]
like his brothers in all things[5]
except for sin.[6]

1. John 1:1; 10:30–36; Acts 13:33 (Ps. 2:7); Col. 1:15–17; 1 John 5:20. 2. Luke 1:35. 3. Matt. 1:18–23; John 1:14; Gal. 4:4; Heb. 2:14. 4. 2 Sam. 7:12–16; Ps. 132:11; Matt. 1:1; Rom. 1:3. 5. Phil. 2:7; Heb. 2:17. 6. Heb. 4:15; 7:26–27.

36. Q. How does the holy conception and birth of Christ benefit you?

A. He is our mediator[1]
and, in God's sight,

he covers with his innocence and perfect holiness
my sin, in which I was conceived.[2]

1. 1 Tim. 2:5–6; Heb. 9:13–15. **2.** Rom. 8:3–4; 2 Cor. 5:21; Gal. 4:4–5; 1 Peter 1:18–19.

LORD'S DAY 15

37. Q. What do you understand by the word "suffered"?

A. That during his whole life on earth,
but especially at the end,
Christ sustained
in body and soul
the wrath of God against the sin of the whole human race.[1]
This he did in order that,
by his suffering as the only atoning sacrifice,[2]
he might deliver us, body and soul,
from eternal condemnation,[3]
and gain for us
God's grace,
righteousness,
and eternal life.[4]

1. Isa. 53; 1 Peter 2:24; 3:18. **2.** Rom. 3:25; Heb. 10:14; 1 John 2:2; 4:10. **3.** Rom. 8:1–4; Gal. 3:13. **4.** John 3:16; Rom. 3:24–26.

38. Q. Why did he suffer "under Pontius Pilate" as judge?

A. So that he,
though innocent,
might be condemned by an earthly judge,[1]
and so free us from the severe judgment of God
that was to fall on us.[2]

1. Luke 23:13–24; John 19:4, 12–16. **2.** Isa. 53:4–5; 2 Cor. 5:21; Gal. 3:13.

39. Q. Is it significant that he was "crucified" instead of dying some other way?

A. Yes.
By this death I am convinced

that he shouldered the curse
which lay on me,
since death by crucifixion was cursed by God.[1]

1. Gal. 3:10–13 (Deut. 21:23).

LORD'S DAY 16

40. Q. Why did Christ have to suffer death?

A. Because God's justice and truth require it:[1]
nothing else could pay for our sins
except the death of the Son of God.[2]

1. Gen. 2:17. 2. Rom. 8:3–4; Phil. 2:8; Heb. 2:9.

41. Q. Why was he "buried"?

A. His burial testifies
that he really died.[1]

1. Isa. 53:9; John 19:38–42; Acts 13:29; 1 Cor. 15:3–4.

42. Q. Since Christ has died for us, why do we still have to die?

A. Our death is not a payment for our sins,[1]
but only a dying to sins
and an entering into eternal life.[2]

1. Ps. 49:7. 2. John 5:24; Phil. 1:21–23; 1 Thess. 5:9–10.

43. Q. What further benefit do we receive from Christ's sacrifice and death on the cross?

A. By his power
our old man is crucified, put to death, and buried with him,[1]
so that the evil desires of the flesh
may no longer rule us,[2]
but that instead we may offer ourselves
as a sacrifice of thanksgiving to him.[3]

1. Rom. 6:5–11; Col. 2:11–12. 2. Rom. 6:12–14. 3. Rom. 12:1; Eph. 5:1–2.

44. Q. Why does the creed add, "He descended into hell"?

A. To assure me during attacks of deepest dread and temptation
that Christ my Lord,
by suffering unspeakable anguish, pain, and terror of soul,
on the cross but also earlier,
has delivered me from hellish anguish and torment.[1]

1. Isa. 53; Matt. 26:36–46; 27:45–46; Luke 22:44; Heb. 5:7–10.

LORD'S DAY 17

45. Q. How does Christ's resurrection benefit us?

A. First, by his resurrection he has overcome death,
so that he might make us share in the righteousness
he obtained for us by his death.[1]
Second, by his power we too
are already raised to a new life.[2]
Third, Christ's resurrection
is a sure pledge to us of our blessed resurrection.[3]

1. Rom. 4:25; 1 Cor. 15:16–20; 1 Peter 1:3–5. 2. Rom. 6:5–11; Eph. 2:4–6; Col. 3:1–4.
3. Rom. 8:11; 1 Cor. 15:12–23; Phil. 3:20–21.

LORD'S DAY 18

46. Q. What do you mean by saying, "He ascended to heaven"?

A. That Christ,
while his disciples watched,
was taken up from the earth into heaven[1]
and remains there on our behalf[2]
until he comes again
to judge the living and the dead.[3]

1. Luke 24:50–51; Acts 1:9–11. 2. Rom. 8:34; Eph. 4:8–10; Heb. 7:23–25; 9:24.
3. Acts 1:11.

47. Q. But isn't Christ with us until the end of the world as he promised us?[1]

A. Christ is true man and true God.
In his human nature Christ is not now on earth;[2]

but in his divinity, majesty, grace, and Spirit
he is never absent from us.[3]

1. Matt. 28:20. 2. Acts 1:9–11; 3:19–21. 3. Matt. 28:18–20; John 14:16–19.

48. Q. If his humanity is not present wherever his divinity is, then aren't the two natures of Christ separated from each other?

A. Certainly not.
Since divinity
is not limited
and is present everywhere,[1]
it is evident that
Christ's divinity is surely beyond the bounds of
the humanity that has been taken on,
but at the same time his divinity is in
and remains personally united to
his humanity.[2]

1. Jer. 23:23–24; Acts 7:48–49 (Isa. 66:1). 2. John 1:14; 3:13; Col. 2:9.

49. Q. How does Christ's ascension to heaven benefit us?

A. First, he is our advocate
in heaven
in the presence of his Father.[1]
Second, we have our own flesh in heaven
as a sure pledge that Christ our head
will also take us, his members,
up to himself.[2]
Third, he sends his Spirit to us on earth
as a corresponding pledge.[3]
By the Spirit's power
we seek not earthly things
but the things above, where Christ is,
sitting at God's right hand.[4]

1. Rom. 8:34; 1 John 2:1. 2. John 14:2; 17:24; Eph. 2:4–6. 3. John 14:16; 2 Cor. 1:21–22; 5:5. 4. Col. 3:1–4.

50. Q. Why the next words: "and sits at the right hand of God"?

A. Christ ascended to heaven,
there to show that he is head of his church,[1]
the one through whom the Father governs all things.[2]

1. Eph. 1:20–23; Col. 1:18. 2. Matt. 28:18; John 5:22–23.

51. Q. How does this glory of Christ our head benefit us?

A. First, through his Holy Spirit
he pours out gifts from heaven
upon us his members.[1]
Second, by his power
he defends us and preserves us
from all enemies.[2]

1. Acts 2:33; Eph. 4:7–12. 2. Ps. 110:1–2; John 10:27–30; Rev. 19:11–16.

52. Q. How does Christ's return "to judge the living and the dead" comfort you?

A. In all distress and persecution,
with uplifted head,
I confidently await the very judge
who has already offered himself to the judgment of God
in my place and removed the whole curse from me.[1]
Christ will cast all his enemies and mine
into everlasting condemnation,
but will take me and all his chosen ones
to himself
into the joy and glory of heaven.[2]

1. Luke 21:28; Rom. 8:22–25; Phil. 3:20–21; Titus 2:13–14. 2. Matt. 25:31–46; 2 Thess. 1:6–10.

53. Q. What do you believe concerning "the Holy Spirit"?

A. First, that the Spirit, with the Father and the Son,

is eternal God.[1]
Second, that he is given also to me,[2]
so that, through true faith,
he makes me share in Christ and all his benefits,[3]
comforts me,[4]
and will remain with me forever.[5]

1. Gen. 1:1–2; Matt. 28:19; Acts 5:3–4. 2. 1 Cor. 6:19; 2 Cor. 1:21–22; Gal. 4:6. 3. Gal. 3:14. 4. John 15:26; Acts 9:31. 5. John 14:16–17; 1 Peter 4:14.

LORD'S DAY 21

54. Q. What do you believe concerning "the holy catholic church"?

A. I believe that the Son of God
through his Spirit and Word,[1]
out of the entire human race,[2]
from the beginning of the world to its end,[3]
gathers, protects, and preserves for himself
a community chosen for eternal life[4]
and united in true faith.[5]
And of this community I am[6] and always will be[7]
a living member.

1. John 10:14–16; Acts 20:28; Rom. 10:14–17; Col. 1:18. 2. Gen. 26:3b–4; Rev. 5:9. 3. Isa. 59:21; 1 Cor. 11:26. 4. Matt. 16:18; John 10:28–30; Rom. 8:28–30; Eph. 1:3–14. 5. Acts 2:42–47; Eph. 4:1–6. 6. 1 John 3:14, 19–21. 7. John 10:27–28; 1 Cor. 1:4–9; 1 Peter 1:3–5.

55. Q. What do you understand by "the communion of saints"?

A. First, that believers one and all,
as members of Christ the Lord,
have communion with him
and share in all his treasures and gifts.[1]
Second, that each member
should consider it a duty
to use these gifts
readily and joyfully

for the service and enrichment
of the other members.[2]

1. Rom. 8:32; 1 Cor. 6:17; 12:4–7, 12–13; 1 John 1:3. 2. Rom. 12:4–8; 1 Cor. 12:20–27; 13:1–7; Phil. 2:4–8.

56. Q. What do you believe concerning "the forgiveness of sins"?

A. I believe that God,
because of Christ's satisfaction,
will no longer remember
any of my sins[1]
or my sinful nature
which I need to struggle against all my life.[2]
Rather, by his grace
God grants me the righteousness of Christ
that I may never come into judgment.[3]

1. Ps. 103:3–4, 10, 12; Mic. 7:18–19; 2 Cor. 5:18–21; 1 John 1:7; 2:2. 2. Rom. 7:21–25. 3. John 3:17–18; Rom. 8:1–2.

LORD'S DAY 22

57. Q. How does "the resurrection of the body" comfort you?

A. Not only will my soul
be taken immediately after this life
to Christ its head,[1]
but also my very flesh, raised by the power of Christ,
will be reunited with my soul,
and made like Christ's glorious body.[2]

1. Luke 23:43; Phil. 1:21–23. 2. 1 Cor. 15:20, 42–46, 54; Phil. 3:21; 1 John 3:2.

58. Q. How does the article concerning "life everlasting" comfort you?

A. Even as I already now
experience in my heart
the beginning of eternal joy,[1]
so after this life I will have
perfect blessedness such as

no eye has seen,

no ear has heard,

no heart has ever imagined:

a blessedness in which to praise God eternally.[2]

1. Rom. 14:17. 2. John 17:3; 1 Cor. 2:9.

LORD'S DAY 23

59. Q. But how does it help you now that you believe all this?

A. That I am righteous in Christ before God

and an heir to life everlasting.[1]

1. John 3:36; Rom. 1:17 (Hab. 2:4); Rom. 5:1–2.

60. Q. How are you righteous before God?

A. Only by true faith in Jesus Christ.[1]

Even though my conscience accuses me

of having grievously sinned against all God's commandments,

of never having kept any of them,[2]

and of still being inclined toward all evil,[3]

nevertheless,

without any merit of my own,[4]

out of sheer grace,[5]

God grants and credits to me

the perfect satisfaction, righteousness, and holiness of Christ,[6]

as if I had never sinned nor been a sinner,

and as if I had been as perfectly obedient

as Christ was obedient for me—[7]

if only I accept this gift with a believing heart.[8]

1. Rom. 3:21–28; Gal. 2:16; Eph. 2:8–9; Phil 3:8–11. 2. Rom. 3:9–10. 3. Rom. 7:23.
4. Titus 3:4–5. 5. Rom. 3:24; Eph. 2:8. 6. Rom. 4:3–5 (Gen. 15:6); 2 Cor. 5:17–19;
1 John 2:1–2. 7. Rom. 4:24–25; 2 Cor. 5:21. 8. John 3:18; Acts 16:30–31.

61. Q. Why do you say that through faith alone you are righteous?

A. Not because I please God

by the worthiness of my faith,

for only Christ's satisfaction, righteousness, and holiness
are my righteousness before God,[1]
and I can receive this righteousness and make it mine
in no other way
than by faith alone.[2]

1. 1 Cor. 1:30–31. **2.** Rom. 10:10; 1 John 5:10–12.

LORD'S DAY 24

62. Q. Why can't our good works be our righteousness before God, or at least a part of our righteousness?

A. Because the righteousness
which can pass God's judgment
must be entirely perfect
and must in every way measure up to the divine law.[1]
But even our best works in this life
are all imperfect
and stained with sin.[2]

1. Rom. 3:20; Gal. 3:10 (Deut. 27:26). **2.** Isa. 64:6.

63. Q. How can our good works be said to merit nothing when God promises to reward them in this life and the next?[1]

A. This reward is not merited;
it is a gift of grace.[2]

1. Matt. 5:12; Heb. 11:6. **2.** Luke 17:10; 2 Tim. 4:7–8.

64. Q. But doesn't this teaching make people indifferent and wicked?

A. No.
It is impossible
for those grafted into Christ by true faith
not to produce fruits of gratitude.[1]

1. Luke 6:43–45; John 15:5.

LORD'S DAY 25

65. Q. It is by faith alone that we share in Christ and all his benefits: where then does that faith come from?

A. The Holy Spirit works it in our hearts[1]
by the preaching of the holy gospel,[2]
and confirms it
by the use of the holy sacraments.[3]

1. John 3:5; 1 Cor. 2:10–14; Eph. 2:8. 2. Rom. 10:17; 1 Peter 1:23–25. 3. Matt. 28:19–20; 1 Cor. 10:16.

66. Q. What are sacraments?

A. Sacraments are visible, holy signs and seals.
They were instituted by God so that
by our use of them
he might make us understand more clearly
the promise of the gospel,
and seal that promise.[1]
And this is God's gospel promise:
he grants us forgiveness of sins and eternal life
by grace
because of Christ's one sacrifice
accomplished on the cross.[2]

1. Gen. 17:11; Deut. 30:6; Rom. 4:11. 2. Matt. 26:27–28; Acts 2:38; Heb. 10:10.

67. Q. Are both the word and the sacraments then intended to focus our faith on the sacrifice of Jesus Christ on the cross as the only ground of our salvation?

A. Yes indeed!
The Holy Spirit teaches us in the gospel
and confirms by the holy sacraments
that our entire salvation
rests on Christ's one sacrifice for us on the cross.[1]

1. Rom. 6:3; 1 Cor. 11:26; Gal. 3:27.

68. Q. How many sacraments did Christ institute in the New Testament?

A. Two: holy baptism and the holy supper.[1]

1. Matt. 28:19–20; 1 Cor. 11:23–26.

LORD'S DAY 26

69. Q. How does holy baptism remind and assure you that Christ's one sacrifice on the cross benefits you personally?

A. In this way:
Christ instituted this outward washing[1]
and with it promised that,
as surely as water washes away the dirt from the body,
so certainly his blood and his Spirit
wash away my soul's impurity,
that is, all my sins.[2]

1. Acts 2:38. 2. Matt. 3:11; Rom. 6:3–10; 1 Peter 3:21.

70. Q. What does it mean to be washed with Christ's blood and Spirit?

A. To be washed with Christ's blood means
that God, by grace, has forgiven our sins
because of Christ's blood
poured out for us in his sacrifice on the cross.[1]
To be washed with Christ's Spirit means
that the Holy Spirit has renewed
and sanctified us to be members of Christ,
so that more and more
we die to sin
and live holy and blameless lives.[2]

1. Zech. 13:1; Eph. 1:7–8; Heb. 12:24; 1 Peter 1:2; Rev. 1:5. 2. Ezek. 36:25–27; John 3:5–8; Rom. 6:4; 1 Cor. 6:11; Col. 2:11–12.

71. Q. Where does Christ promise that we are washed with his blood and Spirit as surely as we are washed with the water of baptism?

A. In the institution of baptism, where he says:

"Go therefore and make disciples of all nations,
baptizing them in the name of the Father
and of the Son
and of the Holy Spirit."[1]
"Whoever believes and is baptized will be saved;
but whoever does not believe will be condemned."[2]
This promise is repeated when Scripture calls baptism
"the washing of regeneration"[3] and
the washing away of sins.[4]

1. Matt. 28:19. 2. Mark 16:16. 3. Titus 3:5. 4. Acts 22:16.

LORD'S DAY 27

72. Q. Does this outward washing with water itself wash away sins?

A. No, only Jesus Christ's blood and the Holy Spirit
cleanse us from all sins.[1]

1. Matt. 3:11; 1 Peter 3:21; 1 John 1:7.

73. Q. Why then does the Holy Spirit call baptism the water of rebirth and the washing away of sins?

A. God has good reason for these words.
To begin with, he wants to teach us that
the blood and Spirit of Christ take away our sins
just as water removes dirt from the body.[1]
But more importantly,
he wants to assure us, by this divine pledge and sign,
that we are as truly washed of our sins spiritually
as our bodies are washed with water physically.[2]

1. 1 Cor. 6:11; Rev. 1:5; 7:14. 2. Acts 2:38; Rom. 6:3–4; Gal. 3:27.

74. Q. Should infants also be baptized?

A. Yes.
Infants as well as adults
are included in God's covenant and people,[1]

and they, no less than adults, are promised
deliverance from sin through Christ's blood
and the Holy Spirit who works faith.[2]
Therefore, by baptism, the sign of the covenant,
they too should be incorporated into the Christian church
and distinguished from the children of unbelievers.[3]
This was done in the Old Testament by circumcision,[4]
which was replaced in the New Testament by baptism.[5]

1. Gen. 17:7; Matt. 19:14. **2.** Isa. 44:1–3; Acts 2:38–39; 16:31. **3.** Acts 10:47; 1 Cor. 7:14. **4.** Gen. 17:9–14. **5.** Col. 2:11–13.

LORD'S DAY 28

75. Q. How does the holy supper remind and assure you that you share in Christ's one sacrifice on the cross and in all his benefits?

A. In this way:
Christ has commanded me and all believers
to eat this broken bread and to drink this cup
in remembrance of him.
With this command come these promises:[1]
First,
as surely as I see with my eyes
the bread of the Lord broken for me
and the cup shared with me,
so surely
his body was offered and broken for me
and his blood poured out for me
on the cross.
Second,
as surely as
I receive from the hand of him who serves,
and taste with my mouth
the bread and cup of the Lord,
given me as sure signs of Christ's body and blood,
so surely

he nourishes and refreshes my soul for eternal life
with his crucified body and poured-out blood.

1. Matt. 26:26–28; Mark 14:22–24; Luke 22:19–20; 1 Cor. 11:23–25.

76. Q. What does it mean to eat the crucified body of Christ and to drink his poured-out blood?

A. It means
to accept with a believing heart
the entire suffering and death of Christ
and in this way
to receive forgiveness of sins and eternal life.[1]
But it means more.
Through the Holy Spirit, who lives both in Christ and in us,
we are united more and more to Christ's blessed body.[2]
And so, although he is in heaven[3] and we are on earth,
we are flesh of his flesh and bone of his bone.[4]
And we forever live on and are governed by one Spirit,
as the members of our body are by one soul.[5]

1. John 6:35, 40, 50–54. 2. John 6:55–56; 1 Cor. 12:13. 3. Acts 1:9–11; 1 Cor. 11:26; Col. 3:1. 4. 1 Cor. 6:15–17; Eph. 5:29–30; 1 John 4:13. 5. John 6:56–58; 15:1–6; Eph. 4:15–16; 1 John 3:24.

77. Q. Where does Christ promise to nourish and refresh believers with his body and blood as surely as they eat this broken bread and drink this cup?

A. In the institution of the Lord's Supper:
"The Lord Jesus on the night when he was betrayed
took bread, and when he had given thanks,
he broke it, and said,
'Take, eat, this is my body which is broken for you.
Do this in remembrance of me.'
In the same way also he took the cup, after supper, saying,
'This cup is the new covenant in my blood.
Do this, as often as you drink it,

in remembrance of me.'
For as often as you eat this bread and drink the cup,
you proclaim the Lord's death
until he comes."[1]
This promise is repeated by Paul in these words:
"The cup of blessing that we bless,
is it not a participation in the blood of Christ?
The bread that we break,
is it not a participation in the body of Christ?
Because there is one bread, we who are many are one body,
for we all partake of the one bread."[2]

1. 1 Cor. 11:23–26. 2. 1 Cor. 10:16–17.

LORD'S DAY 29

78. Q. Do the bread and wine become the real body and blood of Christ?
A. No.
Just as the water of baptism
is not changed into Christ's blood
and does not itself wash away sins
but is simply a divine sign and assurance[1] of these things,
so too the holy bread of the Lord's Supper
does not become the body of Christ itself,[2]
even though it is called the body of Christ[3]
in keeping with the nature and language of sacraments.[4]

1. Eph. 5:26; Titus 3:5. 2. Matt. 26:26–29. 3. 1 Cor. 10:16–17; 11:26–28. 4. Gen. 17:10–11; Ex. 12:11, 13; 1 Cor. 10:1–4.

79. Q. Why then does Christ call the bread his body and the cup his blood, or the new covenant in his blood, and Paul use the words, a participation in Christ's body and blood?

A. Christ has good reason for these words.
He wants to teach us that
just as bread and wine nourish the temporal life,
so too his crucified body and poured-out blood

are the true food and drink of our souls for eternal life.[1]
But more important,
he wants to assure us, by this visible sign and pledge,
that we, through the Holy Spirit's work,
share in his true body and blood
as surely as our mouths
receive these holy signs in his remembrance,[2]
and that all of his suffering and obedience
are as definitely ours
as if we personally
had suffered and made satisfaction for our sins.[3]

1. John 6:51, 55. 2. 1 Cor. 10:16–17; 11:26. 3. Rom. 6:5–11.

LORD'S DAY 30

80. Q. How does the Lord's Supper differ from the Roman Catholic Mass?

A. The Lord's Supper declares to us
that all our sins are completely forgiven
through the one sacrifice of Jesus Christ,
which he himself accomplished on the cross once for all.[1]
It also declares to us
that the Holy Spirit grafts us into Christ,[2]
who with his true body
is now in heaven at the right hand of the Father[3]
where he wants us to worship him.[4]
But the Mass teaches
that the living and the dead
do not have their sins forgiven
through the suffering of Christ
unless Christ is still offered for them daily by the priests.
It also teaches
that Christ is bodily present
under the form of bread and wine
where Christ is therefore to be worshiped.

Thus the Mass is basically
nothing but a denial
of the one sacrifice and suffering of Jesus Christ
and a condemnable idolatry.

1. John 19:30; Heb. 7:27; 9:12, 25–26; 10:10–18. 2. 1 Cor. 6:17; 10:16–17. 3. Acts 7:55–56; Heb. 1:3; 8:1. 4. Matt. 6:20–21; John 4:21–24; Phil. 3:20; Col. 3:1–3.

81. Q. Who should come to the Lord's table?

A. Those who are displeased with themselves
because of their sins,
but who nevertheless trust
that their sins are pardoned
and that their remaining weakness is covered
by the suffering and death of Christ,
and who also desire more and more
to strengthen their faith
and to lead a better life.
Hypocrites and those who are unrepentant, however,
eat and drink judgment on themselves.[1]

1. 1 Cor. 10:19–22; 11:26–32.

82. Q. Should those be admitted to the Lord's Supper who show by what they profess and how they live that they are unbelieving and ungodly?

A. No, that would dishonor God's covenant
and bring down God's wrath upon the entire congregation.[1]
Therefore, according to the instruction of Christ
and his apostles,
the Christian church is duty-bound to
exclude such people,
by the official use of the keys of the kingdom,
until they reform their lives.

1. 1 Cor. 11:17–32; Ps. 50:14–16; Isa. 1:11–17.

83. Q. What are the keys of the kingdom?

A. The preaching of the holy gospel
and Christian discipline toward repentance.
Both of them
open the kingdom of heaven to believers
and close it to unbelievers.[1]

1. Matt. 16:19; John 20:22–23.

84. Q. How does preaching the holy gospel open and close the kingdom of heaven?

A. According to the command of Christ:
The kingdom of heaven is opened
by proclaiming and publicly declaring
to all believers, each and every one, that,
as often as they accept the gospel promise in true faith,
God, because of Christ's merit,
truly forgives all their sins.
The kingdom of heaven is closed, however,
by proclaiming and publicly declaring
to unbelievers and hypocrites that,
as long as they do not repent,
the wrath of God and eternal condemnation
rest on them.
God's judgment, both in this life and in the life to come,
is based on this gospel testimony.[1]

1. Matt. 16:19; John 3:31–36; 20:21–23.

85. Q. How is the kingdom of heaven closed and opened by Christian discipline?

A. According to the command of Christ:
Those who, though called Christians,
profess unchristian teachings

or live unchristian lives,

and who, after repeated personal and loving admonitions,

refuse to abandon their errors and evil ways,

and who, after being reported to the church,

that is, to those ordained by the church for that purpose,

fail to respond also to the church's admonitions—

such persons the church excludes

from the Christian community

by withholding the sacraments from them,

and God also excludes them

from the kingdom of Christ.[1]

Such persons,

when promising and demonstrating genuine reform,

are received again

as members of Christ

and of his church.[2]

1. Matt. 18:15–20; 1 Cor. 5:3–5, 11–13; 2 Thess. 3:14–15. 2. Luke 15:20–24; 2 Cor. 2:6–11.

PART III: GRATITUDE

LORD'S DAY 32

86. Q. Since we have been delivered from our misery by grace through Christ without any merit of our own, why then should we do good works?

A. Because Christ, having redeemed us by his blood,

is also renewing us by his Spirit into his image,

so that with our whole lives

we may show that we are thankful to God

for his benefits,[1]

and that he may be praised through us,[2]

and further,

so that we may be assured of our faith by its fruits,[3]

and by our godly living

our neighbors may be won over to Christ.[4]

1. Rom. 6:13; 12:1–2; 1 Peter 2:5–10. 2. Matt. 5:16; 1 Cor. 6:19–20. 3. Matt. 7:17–18; Gal. 5:22–24; 2 Peter 1:10–11. 4. Matt. 5:14–16; Rom. 14:17–19; 1 Peter 2:12; 3:1–2.

87. Q. Can those be saved who do not turn to God from their ungrateful and unrepentant ways?

A. By no means.
Scripture tells us that
no unchaste person,
no idolater, adulterer, thief,
no covetous person,
no drunkard, slanderer, robber,
or the like
will inherit the kingdom of God.[1]

1. 1 Cor. 6:9–10; Gal. 5:19–21; Eph. 5:1–20; 1 John 3:14.

LORD'S DAY 33

88. Q. What is involved in genuine repentance or conversion?

A. Two things:
the dying-away of the old self,
and the rising-to-life of the new.[1]

1. Rom. 6:1–11; 2 Cor. 5:17; Eph. 4:22–24; Col. 3:5–10.

89. Q. What is the dying-away of the old self?

A. To be genuinely sorry for sin
and more and more to hate
and run away from it.[1]

1. Ps. 51:3–4, 17; Joel 2:12–13; Rom. 8:12–13; 2 Cor. 7:10.

90. Q. What is the rising-to-life of the new self?

A. Wholehearted joy in God through Christ[1]
and a love and delight to live
according to the will of God
by doing every kind of good work.[2]

1. Ps. 51:8, 12; Isa. 57:15; Rom. 5:1; 14:17. 2. Rom. 6:10–11; Gal. 2:20.

91. Q. But what are good works?

A. Only those which
are done out of true faith,[1]
conform to God's law,[2]
and are done for his glory;[3]
and not those based
on our own opinion
or human tradition.[4]

1. John 15:5; Heb. 11:6. **2.** Lev. 18:4; 1 Sam. 15:22; Eph. 2:10. **3.** 1 Cor. 10:31. **4.** Deut. 12:32; Isa. 29:13; Ezek. 20:18–19; Matt. 15:7–9.

LORD'S DAY 34

92. Q. What is God's law?

A. God spoke all these words:
I am the Lord your God,
who brought you out of the land of Egypt,
out of the house of slavery.

    I.   You shall have no other gods before me.

    II.   You shall not make for yourself an idol,
        whether in the form of anything that is in heaven above,
        or that is on the earth beneath,
        or that is in the water under the earth.
        You shall not bow down to them or worship them;
        for I the Lord your God am a jealous God,
        punishing children for the iniquity of parents,
        to the third and fourth generation
        of those who reject me,
        but showing love to the thousandth generation of those
        who love me and keep my commandments.

    III. You shall not make wrongful use of the name of the Lord your God,
        for the Lord will not acquit anyone who misuses his name.

    IV. Remember the Sabbath day and keep it holy.
        Six days you shall labor and do all your work.

But the seventh day is a Sabbath to the Lord your God;
you shall not do any work—
you, your son or your daughter,
your male or female servant,
your livestock,
or the alien resident in your towns.
For in six days the Lord made
the heaven and earth, the sea,
and all that is in them,
but rested the seventh day;
therefore the Lord blessed the Sabbath day
and consecrated it.

V.   Honor your father and your mother,
so that your days may be long
in the land that the Lord your God is giving to you.

VI. You shall not murder.

VII. You shall not commit adultery.

VIII. You shall not steal.

IX. You shall not bear false witness
against your neighbor.

X.   You shall not covet your neighbor's house;
you shall not covet your neighbor's wife,
or male or female servant,
or ox, or donkey,
or anything that belongs to your neighbor.[1]

1. Ex. 20:1–17; Deut. 5:6–21.

93. Q. How are these commandments divided?

A. Into two tables.
The first has four commandments,
teaching us how we should live in relation to God.
The second has six commandments,
teaching us what we owe our neighbor.[1]

1. Matt. 22:37–39.

94. Q. What does the Lord require in the first commandment?

A. That I, not wanting to endanger my own salvation,
avoid and shun
all idolatry,[1] sorcery,[2] superstitious rites,
and prayer to saints or to other creatures.[3]
That I rightly know the only true God,[4]
trust him alone,[5]
and look to God for every good thing[6]
humbly[7] and patiently,[8]
and love,[9] fear,[10] and honor[11] him
with all my heart.
In short,
that I renounce all created things
rather than go against God's will in any way.[12]

[1]. 1 Cor. 6:9–10; 10:5–14; 1 John 5:21. [2]. Lev. 19:31; Deut. 18:9–12. [3]. Matt. 4:10; Rev. 19:10; 22:8–9. [4]. John 17:3. [5]. Jer. 17:5, 7. [6]. Ps. 104:27–28; James 1:17. [7]. 1 Peter 5:5–6. [8]. Col. 1:11; Heb. 10:36. [9]. Matt. 22:37 (Deut. 6:5). [10]. Prov. 9:10; 1 Peter 1:17. [11]. Matt. 4:10 (Deut. 6:13). [12]. Matt. 5:29–30; 10:37–39.

95. Q. What is idolatry?

A. Idolatry is
having or inventing something in which one trusts
in place of or alongside of the only true God,
who has revealed himself in his Word.[1]

[1]. 1 Chron. 16:26; Gal. 4:8–9; Eph. 5:5; Phil. 3:19.

LORD'S DAY 35

96. Q. What is God's will for us in the second commandment?

A. That we in no way make any image of God[1]
nor worship him in any other way
than has been commanded in God's Word.[2]

[1]. Deut. 4:15–19; Isa. 40:18–25; Acts 17:29; Rom. 1:22–23. [2]. Lev. 10:1–7; 1 Sam. 15:22–23; John 4:23–24.

97. Q. May we then not make any image at all?

A. God cannot and may not
be visibly portrayed in any way.
Although creatures may be portrayed,
yet God forbids making or having such images
in order to worship them
or serve God through them.[1]

1. Ex. 34:13–14, 17; 2 Kings 18:4–5.

98. Q. But may not images, as books for the unlearned, be permitted in churches?

A. No, we should not try to be wiser than God.
He wants the Christian community instructed
by the living preaching of his Word[1]—
not by idols that cannot even talk.[2]

1. Rom. 10:14–15, 17; 2 Tim. 3:16–17; 2 Peter 1:19. 2. Jer. 10:8; Hab. 2:18–20.

LORD'S DAY 36

99. Q. What is God's will for us in the third commandment?

A. That we neither blaspheme
nor misuse the name of God
by cursing,[1] perjury,[2] or unnecessary oaths,[3]
nor share in such horrible sins
by being silent bystanders.[4]
In summary,
we must use the holy name of God
only with reverence and awe,[5]
so that we may properly
confess him,[6]
call upon him,[7]
and praise him in everything we do and say.[8]

1. Lev. 24:10–17. 2. Lev. 19:12. 3. Matt. 5:37; James 5:12. 4. Lev. 5:1; Prov. 29:24. 5. Ps. 99:1–5; Jer. 4:2. 6. Matt. 10:32–33; Rom. 10:9–10. 7. Ps. 50:14–15; 1 Tim. 2:8. 8. Col. 3:17.

100 Q. Is blasphemy of God's name by swearing and cursing really such serious sin that God is angry also with those who do not do all they can to help prevent and forbid it?

A. Yes, indeed.[1]
No sin is greater
or provokes God's wrath more
than blaspheming his name.
That is why he commanded it to be punished with death.[2]

1. Lev. 5:1. **2.** Lev. 24:10–17.

LORD'S DAY 37

101. Q. But may we swear an oath in God's name if we do it reverently?

A. Yes, when the government demands it,
or when necessity requires it,
in order to maintain and promote truth and trustworthiness
for God's glory and our neighbor's good.
Such oath-taking is grounded in God's Word[1]
and was rightly used by the saints
in the Old and New Testaments.[2]

1. Deut. 6:13; 10:20; Jer. 4:1–2; Heb. 6:16. **2.** Gen. 21:24; Josh. 9:15; 1 Kings 1:29–30; Rom. 1:9; 2 Cor. 1:23.

102. Q. May we also swear by saints or other created things?

A. No.
A legitimate oath is calling upon God
as the one who knows my heart
to witness to the truth
and to punish me if I swear falsely.[1]
No created thing is worthy of such honor.[2]

1. Rom. 9:1; 2 Cor. 1:23. **2.** Matt. 5:34–37; 23:16–22; James 5:12.

LORD'S DAY 38

103. Q. What is God's will for you in the fourth commandment?

A. First,

266

that the gospel ministry and schools for it be maintained,[1]
and that, especially on the festive day of rest,
I diligently attend the assembly of God's people[2]
to learn what God's Word teaches,[3]
to participate in the sacraments,[4]
to pray to the Lord publicly,[5]
and to bring Christian offerings for the poor.[6]
Second,
that every day of my life
I rest from my evil ways,
let the Lord work in me through his Spirit,
and so begin in this life
the eternal Sabbath.[7]

1. Deut. 6:4–9, 20–25; 1 Cor. 9:13–14; 2 Tim. 2:2; 3:13–17; Titus 1:5. 2. Deut. 12:5–12; Pss. 40:9–10; 68:26; Acts 2:42–47; Heb. 10:23–25. 3. Rom. 10:14–17; 1 Cor. 14:31–32; 1 Tim. 4:13. 4. 1 Cor. 11:23–25. 5. Col. 3:16; 1 Tim. 2:1. 6. Ps. 50:14; 1 Cor. 16:2; 2 Cor. 8–9. 7. Isa. 66:23; Heb. 4:9–11.

LORD'S DAY 39

104. Q. What is God's will for you in the fifth commandment?

A. That I show honor, love, and faithfulness to
my father and mother
and all those in authority over me;
submit myself with proper obedience
to all their good teaching and discipline;[1]
and also that I be patient with their failings[2]—
for by their hand God wills to rule us.[3]

1. Ex. 21:17; Prov. 1:8; 4:1; Rom. 13:1–2; Eph. 5:21–22; 6:1–9; Col. 3:18–4:1. 2. Prov. 20:20; 23:22; 1 Peter 2:18. 3. Matt. 22:21; Rom. 13:1–8; Eph. 6:1–9; Col. 3:18–21.

LORD'S DAY 40

105. Q. What is God's will for you in the sixth commandment?

A. I am not to belittle, hate, insult, or kill my neighbor—
not by my thoughts, my words, my look or gesture,

and certainly not by actual deeds—
and I am not to be party to this in others;[1]
rather, I am to put away all desire for revenge.[2]
I am not to harm or recklessly endanger myself either.[3]
Prevention of murder is also why
government is armed with the sword.[4]

1. Gen. 9:6; Lev. 19:17–18; Matt. 5:21–22; 26:52. 2. Prov. 25:21–22; Matt. 18:35; Rom. 12:19; Eph. 4:26. 3. Matt. 4:7; 26:52; Rom. 13:11–14. 4. Gen. 9:6; Ex. 21:14; Rom. 13:4.

106. Q. Does this commandment refer only to murder?

A. By forbidding murder God teaches us
that he hates the root of murder:
envy, hatred, anger, vengefulness.[1]
In God's sight all such are disguised forms of murder.[2]

1. Prov. 14:30; Rom. 1:29; 12:19; Gal. 5:19–21; 1 John 2:9–11. 2. 1 John 3:15.

107. Q. Is it enough then that we do not murder our neighbor in any such way?

A. No.
By condemning envy, hatred, and anger
God wants us
to love our neighbors as ourselves,[1]
to be patient, peace-loving, gentle,
merciful, and friendly toward them,[2]
to protect them from harm as much as we can,
and to do good even to our enemies.[3]

1. Matt. 7:12; 22:39; Rom. 12:10. 2. Matt. 5:3–12; Luke 6:36; Rom. 12:10, 18; Gal. 6:1–2; Eph. 4:2; Col. 3:12; 1 Peter 3:8. 3. Ex. 23:4–5; Matt. 5:44–45; Rom. 12:20–21 (Prov. 25:21–22).

LORD'S DAY 41

108. Q. What is God's will for us in the seventh commandment?

A. That God condemns all unchastity,[1]

and that we should therefore detest it wholeheartedly[2]
and live decent and chaste lives,[3]
within or outside of the holy state of marriage.

1. Lev. 18:30; Eph. 5:3–5. 2. Jude 22–23. 3. 1 Cor. 7:1–9; 1 Thess. 4:3–8; Heb. 13:4.

109. Q. Does God, in this commandment, forbid only such scandalous sins as adultery?

A. We are temples of the Holy Spirit, body and soul,
and God wants both to be kept clean and holy.
That is why God forbids
all unchaste actions, looks, talk, thoughts, or desires,[1]
and whatever may incite someone to them.[2]

1. Matt. 5:27–29; 1 Cor. 6:18–20; Eph. 5:3–4. 2. 1 Cor. 15:33; Eph. 5:18.

LORD'S DAY 42

110. Q. What does God forbid in the eighth commandment?

A. He forbids not only outright theft and robbery,
which governing authorities punish,[1]
but in God's sight theft also includes
all evil tricks and schemes
designed to get our neighbor's goods for ourselves,
whether by force or means that appear legitimate,[2]
such as
inaccurate measurements of weight, size, or volume;
fraudulent merchandising;
counterfeit money;
excessive interest;
or any other means forbidden by God.[3]
In addition God forbids all greed[4]
and pointless squandering of his gifts.[5]

1. Ex. 22:1; 1 Cor. 5:9–10; 6:9–10. 2. Mic. 6:9–11; Luke 3:14; James 5:1–6. 3. Deut. 25:13–16; Ps. 15:5; Prov. 11:1; 12:22; Ezek. 45:9–12; Luke 6:35. 4. Luke 12:15; Eph. 5:5. 5. Prov. 21:20; 23:20–21; Luke 16:10–13.

111. Q. What does God require of you in this commandment?

A. That I do whatever I can and may
for my neighbor's good,
that I treat others
as I would like them to treat me,
and that I work faithfully
so that I may help the needy in their hardship.[1]

1. Isa. 58:5–10; Matt. 7:12; Gal. 6:9–10; Eph. 4:28.

LORD'S DAY 43

112. Q. What is God's will for you in the ninth commandment?

A. That I
never give false testimony against anyone,
twist no one's words,
not gossip or slander,
nor join in condemning anyone
rashly or without a hearing.[1]
Rather, I should avoid, under penalty of God's wrath,[2]
every kind of lying and deceit
as the very works of the devil;
and, in court and everywhere else,
I should love the truth,
speak it candidly,
and openly acknowledge it.[3]
And I should do what I can
to defend and advance my neighbor's honor and reputation.[4]

1. Ps. 15; Prov. 19:5; Matt. 7:1; Luke 6:37; Rom. 1:28–32. 2. Lev. 19:11–12; Prov. 12:22;
13:5; John 8:44; Rev. 21:8a. 3. 1 Cor. 13:6; Eph. 4:25. 4. 1 Peter 3:8–9; 4:8.

LORD'S DAY 44

113. Q. What is God's will for you in the tenth commandment?

A. That not even the slightest desire or thought
contrary to any one of God's commandments
should ever arise in our hearts.

270

Rather, with all our hearts
we should always hate sin
and delight in all righteousness.[1]

1. Pss. 19:7–14; 139:23–24; Rom. 7:7–8.

114. Q. But can those converted to God keep these commandments perfectly?

A. No.
In this life even the holiest
have only a small beginning of this obedience.[1]
Nevertheless, with all seriousness of purpose,
they do begin to live
according to all, not only some,
of God's commandments.[2]

1. Eccl. 7:20; Rom. 7:14–15; 1 Cor. 13:9; 1 John 1:8–10. 2. Ps. 1:1–2; Rom. 7:22–25; Phil. 3:12–16.

115. Q. Since no one in this life can keep the Ten Commandments perfectly, why does God want them preached so pointedly?

A. First, so that all our life long
we may more and more come to know our sinful nature
and thus more eagerly seek the forgiveness of sins
and righteousness in Christ.[1]
Second, so that
we may never stop striving
and never stop praying to God for the grace of the Holy Spirit,
so that we may be renewed more and more after God's image,
until after this life we reach our goal:
perfection.[2]

1. Ps. 32:5; Rom. 3:19–26; 7:7, 24–25; 1 John 1:9. 2. 1 Cor. 9:24; Phil. 3:12–14; 1 John 3:1–3.

LORD'S DAY 45

116. Q. Why do Christians need to pray?

A. Because prayer is the most important part

of the thankfulness God requires of us.[1]
And also because God will give his grace and Holy Spirit
only to those who continually and with heartfelt longing
ask God for these gifts
and thank him for them.[2]

1. Pss. 50:14–15; 116:12–19; 1 Thess. 5:16–18. 2. Matt. 7:7–8; Luke 11:9–13.

117. Q. How does God want us to pray so that he will listen to us?

A. First, we must pray from the heart
to no other than the one true God,
who has revealed himself to us in his Word,
asking for everything he has commanded us to ask of him.[1]
Second, we must fully recognize our need and misery,
so that we humble ourselves in God's majestic presence.[2]
Third, we must rest on this unshakable foundation:
even though we do not deserve it,
God will surely listen to our prayer
because of Christ our Lord,
as he has promised us in his Word.[3]

1. Ps. 145:18–20; John 4:22–24; Rom. 8:26–27; James 1:5; 1 John 5:14–15. 2. 2 Chron. 7:14; Pss. 2:11; 34:18; 62:8; Isa. 66:2; Rev. 4. 3. Dan. 9:17–19; Matt. 7:8; John 14:13–14; 16:23; Rom. 10:13; James 1:6.

118. Q. What has God commanded us to ask of him?

A. Everything we need, spiritually and physically,[1]
as embraced in the prayer
Christ our Lord himself taught us.

1. James 1:17; Matt. 6:33.

119. Q. What is this prayer?

A. Our Father who is in heaven,
hallowed be your name.
Your kingdom come.

Your will be done,
on earth as it is in heaven.
Give us this day our daily bread,
and forgive us our debts,
as we forgive our debtors.
And lead us not into temptation,
but deliver us from evil.
For yours is the kingdom
and the power
and the glory, forever.
Amen.[1]

1. Matt. 6:9–13; Luke 11:2–4.

LORD'S DAY 46

120. Q. Why has Christ commanded us to address God as "our Father"?

A. To awaken in us
at the very beginning of our prayer
what should be basic to our prayer—
a childlike reverence and trust
that through Christ God has become our Father,
and will much less refuse to give us
what we ask in faith
than will our parents refuse us
the things of this life.[1]

1. Matt. 7:9–11; Luke 11:11–13.

121. Q. Why the words "who is in heaven"?

A. These words teach us
not to think of God's heavenly majesty
in an earthly way,[1]
and to expect from his almighty power
everything needed for body and soul.[2]

1. Jer. 23:23–24; Acts 17:24–25. 2. Matt. 6:25–34; Rom. 8:31–32.

122. Q. What does the first petition mean?

A. "Hallowed be your name" means:
Help us to truly know you,[1]
to honor, glorify, and praise you
for all your works
and for all that shines forth from them:
your almighty power, wisdom, kindness,
justice, mercy, and truth.[2]
And it means,
Help us to direct all our living—
what we think, say, and do—
so that your name will never be blasphemed because of us
but always honored and praised.[3]

1. Jer. 9:23–24; 31:33–34; Matt. 16:17; John 17:3. 2. Ex. 34:5–8; Ps. 145; Jer. 32:16–20; Luke 1:46–55, 68–75; Rom. 11:33–36. 3. Ps. 115:1; Matt. 5:16.

123. Q. What does the second petition mean?

A. "Your kingdom come" means:
Rule us by your Word and Spirit in such a way
that more and more we submit to you.[1]
Preserve and increase your church.[2]
Destroy the devil's work;
destroy every force which revolts against you
and every conspiracy against your holy Word.[3]
Do all this until your kingdom fully comes,
when you will be
all in all.[4]

1. Pss. 119:5, 105; 143:10; Matt. 6:33. 2. Ps. 122:6–9; Matt. 16:18; Acts 2:42–47. 3. Rom. 16:20; 1 John 3:8. 4. Rom. 8:22–23; 1 Cor. 15:28; Rev. 22:17, 20.

124. Q. What does the third petition mean?

A. "Your will be done on earth as it is in heaven" means:
Help us and all people
to renounce our own wills
and without any back talk to obey your will,
for it alone is good.[1]
Help everyone carry out his office and calling,[2]
as willingly and faithfully as the angels in heaven.[3]

1. Matt. 7:21; 16:24–26; Luke 22:42; Rom. 12:1–2; Titus 2:11–12. **2.** 1 Cor. 7:17–24; Eph. 6:5–9. **3.** Ps. 103:20–21.

125. Q. What does the fourth petition mean?

A. "Give us this day our daily bread" means:
Provide for all our physical needs[1]
so that we may recognize
that you are the only source of everything good,[2]
and that neither our care and work
nor your gifts
can do us any good without your blessing.[3]
Therefore may we withdraw our trust from all creatures
and place it in you alone.[4]

1. Pss. 104:27–30; 145:15–16; Matt. 6:25–34. **2.** Acts 14:17; 17:25; James 1:17. **3.** Deut. 8:3; Pss. 37:16; 127:1–2; 1 Cor. 15:58. **4.** Pss. 55:22; 62; 146; Jer. 17:5–8; Heb. 13:5–6.

126. Q. What does the fifth petition mean?

A. "Forgive us our debts,
as we forgive our debtors" means:

Because of Christ's blood,
do not impute to us, poor sinners that we are,
any of the transgressions we do
or the evil that constantly clings to us.[1]
Forgive us just as we are fully determined,
as evidence of your grace in us,
wholeheartedly to forgive our neighbors.[2]

1. Pss. 51:1–7; 143:2; Rom. 8:1; 1 John 2:1–2. 2. Matt. 6:14–15; 18:21–35.

LORD'S DAY 52

127. Q. What does the sixth petition mean?

A. "And lead us not into temptation,
but deliver us from evil" means:
We are so weak that we cannot stand
on our own for a moment,[1]
and our sworn enemies—
the devil,[2] the world,[3] and our own flesh[4]—
never stop attacking us.
And so, Lord,
uphold us and make us strong
by the power of your Holy Spirit,
so that we may not be defeated
in this spiritual fight,[5]
but may firmly resist our enemies
until we finally win the complete victory.[6]

1. Ps. 103:14–16; John 15:1–5. 2. 2 Cor. 11:14; Eph. 6:10–13; 1 Peter 5:8. 3. John 15:18–21. 4. Rom. 7:23; Gal. 5:17. 5. Matt. 10:19–20; 26:41; Mark 13:33; Rom. 5:3–5. 6. 1 Cor. 10:13; 1 Thess. 3:13; 5:23.

128. Q. How do you conclude this prayer?

A. "For yours is the kingdom
and the power
and the glory forever."
This means

we have made all these petitions of you
because, as our all-powerful king,
you are both willing and able
to give us all that is good;[1]
and because your holy name,
and not we ourselves,
should receive all the praise, forever.[2]

1. Rom. 10:11–13; 2 Peter 2:9. 2. Ps. 115:1; John 14:13.

129. Q. What does that little word "Amen" express?

A. "Amen" means:
This shall truly and surely be!
For it is much more certain
that God has heard my prayer
than I feel in my heart
that I desire such things from him.[1]

1. Isa. 65:24; 2 Cor. 1:20; 2 Tim. 2:13.

14

Second Helvetic Confession

(1566)

H einrich Bullinger had earlier written the First Helvetic Confession in 1536, and in 1562 he drafted a successor document. He did so at the request of Frederick III, elector of the Palatinate in Germany. Frederick, who had converted to the Reformed faith and had earlier commissioned the Heidelberg Catechism, wanted a summary of the faith to present to the Holy Roman emperor, Maximillian II.

Bullinger wrote the confession in 1562 and revised it in 1564. He presented it to Frederick in 1564, and Frederick in turn presented it to the imperial Diet of Augsburg in 1566. The Swiss churches, with the exception of Basel, adopted the confession as their own. The church in Basel preferred its own earlier confession.

The confession, in its robust and thorough approach, attests to the decades of study that Bullinger devoted to Reformed theology. It has been widely translated and adopted by Reformed churches well beyond Switzerland.

Second Helvetic Confession

Chapter 1. Of the Holy Scripture Being the True Word of God

We believe and confess the canonical Scriptures of the holy prophets and apostles of both Testaments to be the very true Word of God, and to have sufficient authority of themselves, not of men. For God Himself spoke to the fathers, prophets, apostles, and speaks yet unto us by the Holy Scriptures.

And in this Holy Scripture, the universal church of Christ has all things fully expounded, whatsoever belong both to a saving faith, and also to the framing of a life acceptable to God: in which respect it is expressly commanded of God that nothing be either put to or taken from the same (Deut. 4:2; Rev. 22:18–19).

We judge, therefore, that from these Scriptures is to be taken true wisdom and godliness, the reformation and government of churches; as also instruction in all duties of piety: and to be short, the confirmation of opinions, and the confutation of errors, with all exhortations; according to that of the apostle: "All Scripture inspired of God is profitable for doctrine, for reproof" (2 Tim. 3:16–17). Again, "These things I write unto thee," says the apostle to Timothy, "that thou mayest know how it behoveth thee to be conversant in the house of God" (1 Tim. 3:14–15). Again, the self-same apostle to the Thessalonians: "When," says he, "ye received the word from us, ye received not the word of men, but, as it was indeed, the Word of God" (1 Thess. 2:13). For the Lord Himself has said in the gospel, "It is not ye that speak, but the Spirit of my Father speaketh in you" (Matt. 10:20); therefore, "he that heareth you, heareth Me; and he that despiseth you, despiseth Me" (Luke 10:16).

Wherefore when this Word of God is now preached in the church by preachers and received of the faithful; and that neither any other Word of God is to be feigned nor to be expected from heaven: and that now the Word of God which is preached is to be regarded, not the minister that preaches; who although he may be evil and a sinner, nevertheless the Word of God abides true and good.

Neither do we think that, therefore, the outward preaching is to be thought as fruitless because the instruction in true religion depends on the inward illumination of the Spirit; or because it is written, "No man shall teach his neighbor; for all men shall know Me" (Jer. 31:34) and "He that watereth or he that planteth is nothing but God who giveth the increase" (1 Cor. 3:7). For albeit, "No man can come to Christ unless he is drawn by the Heavenly Father" (John 6:44) and is inwardly lightened by the Holy Ghost, yet we know undoubtedly that it is the will of God that His Word should be preached even outwardly. God could indeed by His Holy Spirit or by the ministry of an angel without the ministry of St. Peter have taught Cornelius in the Acts; but nevertheless, He refers him to Peter of whom the angel speaking says, "He shall tell thee what thou must do" (Acts 10:6).

For he that illumines inwardly by giving men the Holy Ghost, the self-same, by way of commandment, said unto His disciples. "Go ye into the whole world, and preach the gospel to every creature" (Mark 16:15). And so Paul preached the Word outwardly to Lydia, a purple-seller among the Philippians: but the Lord inwardly opened the woman's heart (Acts 16:14). And the same Paul, upon an elegant gradation, fitly placed in the tenth chapter to the Romans, at last infers, "Therefore, faith is by hearing, and hearing by the Word of God" (Rom. 10:14–17). We know in the meantime that God can illumine whom and when He will, even without the external ministry, which is a thing pertaining to His power: but we speak of the usual way of instructing men, delivered unto us of God, both in commandment and examples.

We, therefore, detest all the heresies of Artemon, the Manichees, the Valentinians, of Cerdon, and the Marcionites, who denied that the Scriptures proceeded from the Holy Ghost; or else received not, or polished and corrupted some of them.

And yet we do not deny that certain books of the Old Testament were of the ancient authors called apocryphal; and of others, ecclesiastical; to wit, such as they would have to be read in the churches, but not alleged to avouch or confirm the authority of faith by them. As also, Augustine in his *De Civitate Dei* (Book 18, chapter 38) makes mention that "in the books of the Kings, the names and books of certain prophets are reckoned," but he adds that "they are not in the Canon;" and that "those books which we have, suffice unto godliness."

Chapter 2. Of Interpreting the Holy Scriptures; Of Fathers, Councils, and Traditions

The apostle Peter has said that "The Holy Scriptures are not of any private interpretation" (2 Peter 1:20); therefore, we do not allow all expositions. Whereupon, we do not acknowledge that which they call the meaning of the Church of Rome for the true and natural interpretation of the Scriptures; which the defenders of the Roman Church strive to force all men simply to receive: but we acknowledge that interpretation of Scriptures to be authentic and proper, which being taken from the Scriptures themselves (that is, from the phrase of that tongue in which they were written, they being also weighed according to the circumstances, and expounded according to the proportion of places, either of like or of unlike, also of more and plainer) accords with the rule of faith and charity, and makes notably for God's glory and man's salvation.

Wherefore we do not condemn the holy treatises of the fathers, agreeing with the Scriptures; from whom, notwithstanding, we do modestly dissent, as they are deprehended to set down things merely strange, or altogether contrary to the same. Neither do we think that we do them any wrong in this matter; seeing that they all, with one consent, will not have their writings matched with the canonical Scriptures; but bid us allow of them so far forth as they either agree with them, or disagree, and bid us take those things that agree, and leave those that disagree.

And according to this order we do account of the decrees or canons of councils. Wherefore we suffer not ourselves in controversies about religion or matters of faith, to be pressed with the bare testimonies of fathers, or decrees of councils; much less with received customs, or with the multitude of men being of one judgment, or with prescription of long time. Therefore, in controversies of religion, or matters of faith, we cannot admit any other judge than God Himself, pronouncing by the Holy Scriptures, what is true, what is false, what is to be followed, or what is to be avoided. So we do not rest but in the judgments of spiritual men, drawn from the Word of God. Certainly Jeremiah and other prophets vehemently condemned the assemblies of priests, gathered against the law of God: and diligently forewarned us that we should not hear the fathers, or tread in their path, who, walking in their own inventions swerved from the law of God (Ezek. 20:18).

Likewise we reject human traditions which, although they are set out with goodly titles, as though they were divine and apostolic, delivered to the church by the lively voice of the apostles, and as it were, by the hands of apostolic men by means of bishops succeeding in their places yet being compared with the Scriptures, disagree with them and by that disagreement betray themselves in no wise to be apostolic. For as the apostles did not disagree among themselves in doctrine, so the apostles' scholars did not set forth things contrary to the apostles. Nay, it is blasphemous to avow that the apostles by lively voice delivered things contrary to their writings. Paul affirms expressly that he "taught the same things in all churches" (1 Cor. 4:17). And again, "We," says he, "write no other things unto you, than which ye read, or also acknowledge" (2 Cor. 1:13). Also, in another place, he witnesses that he and His disciples, to wit apostolic men, "walked in the same way, and jointly by the same Spirit did all things" (2 Cor. 12:18). The Jews also, in time past, had their traditions of elders; but these traditions were severely confuted by the Lord, showing that the keeping of them hinders God's law, and that "God is in vain worshipped of such" (Matt. 15:9; Mark 7:6–7).

Chapter 3. Of God; The Unity and the Trinity

We believe and teach that God is one in essence or nature, subsisting by Himself, all sufficient in Himself, invisible, without a body, infinite, eternal, the Creator of all things both visible and invisible, the chief good, living, quickening and preserving all things, Almighty, and exceeding wise, gentle or merciful, just and true. And we detest the multitude of gods, because it is expressly written, "The Lord thy God is one God" (Deut. 6:4). "I am the Lord thy God, thou shalt have no strange gods before My face" (Ex. 20:2–3). "I am the Lord, and there is none other; beside Me there is no god. Am not I the Lord, and there is none other beside Me alone? a just God, and a Savior, there is none beside Me" (Isa. 45:5, 21). "I the Lord, Jehovah, the merciful God, gracious, and long-suffering, and abundant in goodness and truth" (Ex. 34:6).

We nevertheless believe and teach that the same infinite, one, and indivisible God, is in persons inseparably and without confusion distinguished into the Father, the Son, and the Holy Ghost: so as the Father has begotten the Son from everlasting; the Son is begotten by an unspeakable manner; and the Holy Ghost proceeds from them both, and that from everlasting, and is to be worshipped with them both. There are not three Gods, but three persons, consubstantial, co-eternal, and co-equal; distinct, as touching their persons; and, in order, one going before another, yet without any inequality. For as touching their nature or essence, they are so joined together that they are but one God; and the divine essence is common to the Father, the Son, and the Holy Ghost.

For the Scripture has delivered unto us a manifest distinction of persons: the angel, among other things, saying thus to the blessed virgin, "The Holy Ghost shall come upon thee, and the power of the Highest shall overshadow thee, and that holy thing which shall be born, shall be called the Son of God" (Luke 1:35). Also in the baptism of Christ, a voice was heard from heaven, saying, "This is My beloved Son" (Matt. 3:17). The Holy Ghost also appeared "in the likeness of a dove" (John 1:32). And when the Lord Himself commanded to baptize, He commanded to baptize "in the name of the Father and of the Son and of the Holy Ghost" (Matt. 28:19). In like sort elsewhere in the gospel He said, "The Father will send the Holy Ghost in My name" (John 14:26). Again He says, "When the Comforter shall come, whom I will send unto you from the Father, the Spirit of Truth, who proceedeth from the Father, He shall bear witness of Me" (John 15:26). To be short, we receive the Apostles' Creed because it delivers unto us the true faith.

We, therefore, condemn the Jews and the Mohammedans, and all those that blaspheme the Trinity, which is sacred, and only to be adored. We also condemn all heresies and heretics, which teach that the Son and the Holy Ghost are God only in name; also, that there is in the Trinity something created, and that serves and ministers unto another; finally, that there is in it something unequal, greater or less, corporal or corporally fashioned, in manners or in will divers, either confounded or sole by itself: as if the Son and Holy Ghost were the affections and qualities of one God the Father; as the Monarchists, the Novatians, Praxeas, the Patripassians, Sabellius, Samosatenus, Aetius, Macedonius, Arius, and such like have thought.

Chapter 4. Of Idols or Images of God, of Christ, and of Saints

And because God is an invisible Spirit, and an incomprehensible essence, He cannot, therefore, by any art or image be expressed. For which cause we fear not, with the Scripture, to term the images of God mere lies. We do, therefore, reject not only the idols of the Gentiles, but also the images of Christians. For although Christ took upon Him man's nature, yet He did not, therefore, take it that He might set forth a pattern for carvers and painters. He denied that He came "to destroy the Law and the prophets" (Matt. 5:17), but images are forbidden in the Law and the prophets. He denied that His bodily presence would any way profit the church (Deut. 4:15; Isa. 40:18). He promises that "He would by His Spirit be present with us for ever" (John 16:7; 2 Cor. 5:5); who would then believe that the shadow or picture of His body in any way benefits the godly? And seeing that He abides in us by His Spirit, "We are therefore the temples of God" (1 Cor. 3:16), but "what agreement hath the temple of God with images?" (2 Cor. 6:16). And seeing that the blessed spirits and saints in heaven, while they lived here abhorred all worship done unto themselves (Acts 14:15; Rev. 14:7; 19:10; 22:8–9) and spoke against images, who can think it likely that the saints in heaven and the angels are delighted with their own images, to whom men bow their knees, uncover their heads and give such other like honor?

But that men might be instructed in religion, and put in mind of heavenly things and of their own salvation, the Lord commanded "preach the gospel" (Mark 16:15), not to paint and instruct the laity by pictures: He also instituted sacraments, but nowhere did He appoint images. Furthermore, in every place, in whatever way we turn our eyes, we see the lively and true creatures of God, which if they are marked, as is meet, they much more effectually move the beholder than all the images; or vain, unmovable, rotten, and dead pictures of men whatsoever; of which the prophet spoke truly, "They have eyes, and see not" (Ps. 115:5).

Therefore, we approve the judgment of Lactantius, an ancient writer, who says, "Undoubtedly there is no religion, wheresoever there is a picture." And we affirm that the blessed bishop Epiphanius did well, who, finding on the church doors a veil, that had painted on it the picture as it might be of Christ or of some saint or other, he cut and took it away; for, contrary to the authority of the Scriptures, he had seen the picture of a man hanging in the church of Christ: and, therefore, he charged that from thenceforth no such veils, which were contrary to our religion, should be hung up in the church of Christ, but that rather such scruple should be taken away which was unworthy the church of Christ and all faithful people. Moreover we approve this sentence of St. Augustine, "Let not the worship of men's works be a religion unto us. For the workmen themselves that make such things are better; whom yet we ought not to worship" *(De Vera Religion,* Chap. 55*).*

Chapter 5. Of the Adoring, Worshipping, and Invocating of God, through the Only Mediator, Jesus Christ

We teach men to adore and worship the true God alone. This honor we impart to none, according to the commandment of the Lord, "Thou shalt adore the Lord thy God, and Him alone shalt thou worship" or "Him only shalt thou serve" (Matt. 4:10). Surely all the prophets inveighed earnestly against the people of Israel, whenever they adored and worshipped strange gods, and not the one only true God. But we teach that "God is to be adored and worshipped" as He Himself has taught us to worship Him, to wit, "in spirit and truth" (John 4:24); not with any superstition, but with sincerity, according to His Word, lest at any time He also say unto us, "Who hath required these things at your hands?" (Isa. 1:12). For Paul also says, "God is not worshipped with men's hands, as though He needed any thing" (Acts 17:25).

We, in all dangers and casualties of life, call on Him alone, and that by the mediation of the only mediator, and our intercessor, Jesus Christ. For it is expressly commanded us, "Call upon Me in the day of trouble, and I will deliver thee, and thou shalt glorify Me" (Ps. 50:15). Moreover, the Lord has made a very large promise saying, "Whatsoever ye shall ask of My Father, He shall give it you" (John 16:23). And again, "Come unto me, all ye that labor and are heavy laden, and I will refresh you" (Matt. 11:28). And seeing it is written, "How shall they call upon Him in whom they have not believed?" (Rom. 10:14) and we believe in God alone, therefore, we call upon Him only and that through Christ. "There is one God," says the apostle, "and one mediator between God and men, Christ Jesus" (1 Tim. 2:5). Again, "If any man sin, we have an advocate with the Father, Jesus Christ the righteous" (1 John 2:1).

Therefore, we do neither adore, worship, nor pray unto the saints in heaven, or to other gods; neither do we acknowledge them for our intercessors or mediators before the Father in heaven. For God and the mediator Christ are sufficient for us, neither do we impart unto others the honor due to God alone and to His Son: because He has plainly said, "I will not give my glory to another" (Isa. 42:8); and because Peter has said, "There is no other name given unto men whereby they must be saved, but the name of Christ" (Acts

4:12). In which, doubtless, they that rest by faith, do not seek anything outside of Christ.

Yet for all that, we do neither despise the saints, nor think basely of them. For we acknowledge them to be the lively members of Christ, the friends of God, who have gloriously overcome the flesh and the world. We, therefore, love them as brethren and honor them also; yet not with any worship, but with an honorable opinion of them; and, to conclude, with just praises of them. We also imitate them. For we desire with most earnest affections and prayers, to be followers of their faith and virtues; to be partakers also with them of everlasting salvation; to dwell together with them everlastingly with God, and to rejoice with them in Christ. And in this point, we approve that saying of St. Augustine, in his book, *De Vera Religione*, "Let not the worship of men departed be any religion unto us. For if they have lived holily, they are not so to be esteemed, as that they seek such honors, but they will have us to worship Him, by whose illumination they rejoice that we are fellow servants, as touching the reward. They are, therefore, to be honored for imitation, not to be worshipped for religion's sake."

And we much less believe that the relics of the saints are to be adored and worshipped. Those ancient men seemed sufficiently to have honored their dead, if they had honestly committed their bodies to the earth, after the soul was gone up into heaven: and they thought that the most noble relics of their ancestors were their virtues, doctrine, and faith; which as they commended with the praise of the dead, so they did endeavor to express the same so long as they lived upon earth. Those ancient men did not swear but by the name of the Jehovah only, as it is commanded by the law of God. Therefore, as we are forbidden to "swear by the name of strange gods" (Ex. 23:13; Josh. 23:7), so we do not swear by saints, although we are requested to. Therefore, in all these things we reject that doctrine which gives too much unto the saints in heaven.

Chapter 6. Of the Providence of God

We believe that all things, both in heaven and in earth and in all creatures, are sustained and governed by the providence of this wise, eternal, and omnipotent God. For David witnesses and says, "The Lord is high above all nations, and His glory above the heavens. Who is as our God, who dwelleth on high, and yet humbleth Himself to behold the things that are in heaven and earth?"

(Ps. 113:4–6). Again, he says, "Thou hast foreseen all my ways; for there is not a word in my tongue, which thou knowest not wholly, O Lord" (Ps. 139:3–4). Paul also witnesses and says, "By Him we live, move, and have our being" (Acts 17:28). And "Of Him and through Him, and from Him are all things" (Rom. 11:36). Therefore, Augustine both truly, and according to the Scripture, said in his book, *De Agone Christi*, Chap. 8: "The Lord said, 'Are not two sparrows sold for a farthing? And one of them shall not fall on the ground without the will of your Father.' By speaking thus He wanted us to understand that whatever men count most vile, that also is governed by the almighty power of God. For the truth which said that all the hairs of our heads are numbered, saith also that the birds of the air are fed by Him, and the lilies of the field are clothed by Him."

We, therefore, condemn the Epicureans who deny the providence of God, and all those who blasphemously affirm that God is occupied about the poles of heaven, and that He neither sees nor regards us nor our affairs. The princely prophet David also condemned these men, when he said, "O Lord, How long, how long shall the wicked triumph? They say the Lord doth not see, neither doth the God of Jacob regard it. Understand, ye unwise among the people; and ye fools, when will ye be wise? He that hath planted the ear, shall He not hear? and He that hath formed the eye, how should He not see?" (Ps. 94:3, 7–9).

Notwithstanding we do not condemn the means whereby the providence of God works, as though they were unprofitable; but we teach that we must apply ourselves unto them, as far as they are commended to us in the Word of God. Wherefore we dislike the rash speeches of such as say, that if by the providence of God all things are governed, then all our studies and endeavors are unprofitable. It shall be sufficient if we leave or permit all things to be governed by the providence of God, and we shall not need hereafter to behave or act with carefulness in any matter. For though Paul did confess that he did sail by the providence of God, who had said to him, "Thou must testify of Me also at Rome" (Acts 23:11), who moreover promised and said, "There shall not so much as one soul perish, neither shall an hair fall from your heads" (Acts 27:22, 34), yet the mariners devising how they might find a way to escape, the same Paul says to the centurion and to the soldiers, "Unless these remain in the ship, ye cannot be safe" (Acts 27:31). For God, who has appointed everything to its end, has also ordained the beginning and the means by which we must attain unto the end. The heathens ascribe things to blind fortune and uncertain chance; but St. James would not have us say, "Today or tomorrow we will go into such a city, and there buy and sell," but he adds, "For that which ye should say, If the Lord will, and if we live, we will do this or that" (James 4:13, 15). And Augustine says, "All those things which seem to vain men to be done by chance in the world, they do but accomplish His word, because they are done by His commandment" (in his exposition on the 148th Psalm). It seemed to be done by chance that Saul seeking his father's asses should light on the prophet Samuel; but the Lord had before said to the prophet, "Tomorrow I will send unto thee a man of the tribe of Benjamin" (1 Sam. 9:16).

Chapter 7. Of the Creation of All Things: Of Angels, the Devil, and Man

This good and almighty God created all things, both visible and invisible, by His eternal Word, and preserves the same also by His eternal Spirit: as David witnesses, saying, "By the word of the Lord were the heavens made, and all the host of them by the breath of His mouth" (Ps. 33:6). And as the Scripture says: "All things that the Lord created were very good" (Gen. 1:31) and made for the use and profit of man. Now we say that all those things proceed from one beginning: and, therefore, we detest the Manichees and Marcionites, who did wickedly imagine two substances and natures, the one of good, the other of evil; and also two beginnings, and two gods, one contrary to the other, a good and an evil.

Among all the creatures, the angels and men are most excellent. Touching angels, the Holy Scripture says, "Who maketh His angels spirits, and His ministers a flame of fire" (Ps. 104:4). Also, "Are they not ministering spirits sent forth to minister for their sakes, which shall be the heirs of salvation?" (Heb. 1:14). And the Lord Jesus Himself testifies of the devil, saying, "He hath been a murderer from the beginning, and abode not in the truth, because there is no truth in him. When he speaketh a lie, he speaketh of his own; for he is a liar, and the father thereof" (John 8:44). We teach, therefore, that some angels persisted in obedience and were appointed unto the faithful service of God and men; and that others fell of their own accord and ran headlong into destruction, and so became enemies to all good, and to all the faithful.

Now, touching man, the Spirit says that in the beginning he was "created good according to the image and likeness of God" (Gen. 1:27); that God placed him in Paradise, and made all things subject unto him; which David most nobly sets forth in the eighth Psalm. Moreover God gave unto him a wife and blessed them. We say also that man consists of two, and those divers substances in one person; of a soul immortal (as that which being separated from his body, neither sleeps nor dies) and a body mortal, which notwithstanding at the last judgment shall be raised again from the dead, that from henceforth the whole man may continue for ever, in life or in death.

We condemn all those who mock, or by subtle disputations call into doubt, the immortality of the soul, or say that the soul sleeps, or that it is a part of God. In short, we condemn all opinions of all men whatsoever, who think otherwise of the creation of angels, devils, and men than is delivered unto us by the Scriptures in the apostolic church of Christ.

Chapter 8. Of Man's Fall, Sin, and the Cause of Sin

Man was from the beginning created of God after the image of God, in righteousness and true holiness, good and upright; but by the instigation of the serpent and his own fault, falling from goodness and uprightness, he became subject to sin, death, and divers calamities; and such a one as he became by his fall, such are all his offspring, even subject to sin, death, and sundry calamities.

And we take sin to be that natural corruption of man, derived or spread from our first parents unto us all, through which we, being drowned in evil concupiscence, and clean turned away from God, but prone to all evil, full of all wickedness, distrust, contempt, and hatred of God, can do no good of ourselves, no not so much as think any (Matt. 12:33–35). And, what is more, even as we grow in years, so by wicked thoughts, words, and deeds, committed against the law of God, we bring forth corrupt fruits, worthy of an evil tree: in which respect, we, through our own desert, being subject to the wrath of God, are in danger of just punishment; so that we had all been cast away from God, had not Christ, the deliverer, brought us back again.

By death, therefore, we understand not only bodily death, which is once to be suffered of us all for sins, but also everlasting punishments due to our corruption and to our sins. For the apostle says, "We were dead in trespasses and sins, and were by nature the children of wrath, as well as others; but God who is rich in mercy, even when we were dead by sins, quickened us together in Christ" (Eph. 2:1–5). Again, "As by one man sin entered into the world, and by sin, death, and so death went over all men, forasmuch as all men have sinned" (Rom. 5:12).

We, therefore, acknowledge that original sin is in all men; we acknowledge that all other sins which spring therefrom, are both called and are indeed sins, by what name soever they are termed, whether mortal or venial, or also that which is called sin against the Holy Ghost, which is never forgiven (Mark 3:29; 1 John 5:16–17). We also confess that sins are not equal, although they spring from the same fountain of corruption and unbelief, but that some are more grievous than others; even as the Lord has said, "It shall be easier for Sodom, than for the city that despiseth the word of the gospel" (Matt. 10:15).

We, therefore, condemn all those that have taught things contrary to these; but especially Pelagius, and all the Pelagians, together with the Jovinians who, with the Stoics, count all sins equal. In this matter we agree fully with St. Augustine, who produced and maintained his sayings out of the Holy Scriptures. Moreover we condemn Florinus Blastus (against whom also Irenaeus wrote) and all those that make God the author of sin; seeing it is expressly written, "Thou art not a God that loveth wickedness; thou hatest all them that work iniquity, and wilt destroy all that speak lies" (Ps. 5:4–6). And again, "When the devil speaketh a lie, he speaketh of his own; because he is a liar, and the father of lying" (John 8:44). Yes, there is even in ourselves sin and corruption enough, so that there is no need that God should infuse into us either a new or greater measure of wickedness. Therefore, when God is said in the Scripture to harden (Ex. 7:13), to blind (John 12:40) and to deliver us up into a reprobate sense (Rom. 1:28), it is to be understood that God does it by just judgment, as a just judge and avenger. To conclude, as often as God in the Scripture is said and seems to do some evil, it is not thereby meant that man does not commit evil, but that God suffers it to be done, and does not hinder it; and by His just judgment, who could hinder it, if He would: or because He makes good use of the evil of men, as He did in the sins of Joseph's brethren; or because He Himself rules sins that they do not break out and rage more violently than is meet. St. Augustine, in his *Enchiridion*, says, "After a wonderful and unspeakable manner, that is not done beside His will which is done contrary to His will; because it could not be done, if He should not suffer it to be done; and yet He does not suffer it to be done unwillingly, but willingly; neither would He, being God, suffer

any evil to be done, unless, being also Almighty, He could make good of evil."
Thus far Augustine.

Other questions, as, whether God would have Adam fall, or whether He forced him to fall, or why He did not hinder his fall, and such like, we count among curious questions (unless perchance the forwardness of heretics or of men otherwise importunate compels us to open these points also out of the Word of God, as the godly doctors of the church have often done), knowing that the Lord did forbid that man should eat of the forbidden fruit and punished his transgression; and also that the things done are not evil in respect of the providence, will, and power of God, but in respect of Satan and our will resisting the will of God.

Chapter 9. Of Free Will, and So of Man's Power and Ability

We teach in this matter, which at all times has been the cause of many conflicts in the church, that there is a triple condition or estate of man to be considered. First, what man was before his fall; to wit, upright and free, who might both continue in goodness and decline to evil; but he declined to evil and has wrapped both himself and all mankind in sin and death, as has been shown before. Secondly, we are to consider what man was after his fall. His understanding indeed was not taken from him, neither was he deprived of will and altogether changed into a stone or stock. Nevertheless, these things are so altered in man that they are not able to do that now which they could do before his fall. For his understanding is darkened, and his will, which before was free, is now become a servile will; for it serves sin, not nilling, but willing; for it is called a will, and not a nill.

Therefore, as touching evil or sin, man does evil, not compelled either by God or the devil, but of his own accord; and in this respect he has a most free will: but whereas we see that oftentimes the most evil deeds and counsels of man are hindered by God, that they cannot attain to their end, this does not take from man liberty in evil, but God by His power prevents that which man otherwise purposed freely: as Joseph's brethren did freely purpose to slay Joseph; but they were not able to do it because it seemed otherwise good to God in His secret counsel.

But as touching goodness and virtues, man's understanding does not of itself judge aright of heavenly things. For the evangelical and apostolic Scripture requires regeneration of every one of us that will be saved. Wherefore our first birth by Adam profits nothing to salvation. Paul says, "The natural man perceiveth not the things which are of the Spirit" (1 Cor. 2:14). The same Paul elsewhere denies that we are "fit of ourselves, to think any good" (2 Cor. 3:5). Now it is evident that the mind or understanding is the guide of the will; and seeing the guide is blind, it is easy to be seen how far the will can reach. Therefore, man, not as yet regenerate, has no free will to good, no strength to perform that which is good. The Lord says in the gospel, "Verily, verily, I say unto you, that every one that commits sin, is the servant of sin" (John 8:34). And Paul the apostle says, "The wisdom of the flesh is enmity against God: for it is not subject to the law of God, neither indeed can be" (Rom. 8:7). Furthermore, there is some understanding of earthly things remaining in man after his fall.

For God has of mercy left him wit, though much differing from that which was in him before his fall; God commands us to cultivate our wit, and therewithal He gives gifts and also the increase thereof. And it is a clear case that we can profit very little in all arts without the blessing of God. The Scripture, doubtless, refers all arts to God: yes and the Ethnicks also did ascribe the beginnings of arts to the gods, as to the authors thereof.

Lastly, we are to consider whether the regenerate have free will and how far forth they have it. In regeneration, the understanding is illuminated by the Holy Ghost that it may understand both the mysteries and will of God. And the will itself is not only changed by the Spirit, but is also endued with faculties, that, of its own accord, it may both will and do good (Rom. 8:4–6). Unless we grant this, we shall deny Christian liberty and bring in the bondage of the Law. Besides, the prophet brings in God speaking thus: "I will put My laws in their minds, and write them in their hearts" (Jer. 31:33; Ezek. 36:27). The Lord also says in the gospel, "If the Son make you free, then are you free indeed" (John 8:36). Paul also to the Philippians: "Unto you it is given, for Christ, not only to believe in Him, but also to suffer for His sake" (1:29). And again, "I am persuaded that He that began this good work in you will perform it until the day of the Lord Jesus" (v. 6). Also, "It is God that worketh in you the will and the deed" (Phil. 2:13).

Where, nevertheless, we teach that there are two things to be observed: first, that the regenerate, in the choice and working of that which is good, do not only work passively, but actively. For they are moved of God, that themselves may do that which they do. And Augustine truly alleges that saying that "God is said to be our helper: but no man can be helped, but he that does somewhat." The Manichees robbed man of all action and made him like a stone and a block.

Secondly, that in the regenerate there remains infirmity. For seeing that sin dwells in us and that the flesh in the regenerate strives against the spirit, even to the end of our lives, they do not readily perform in every point that which they had purposed. These things are confirmed by the apostle (Rom. 7:13–25; Gal. 5:17). Therefore, our free will is weak by reason of the relics of the old Adam remaining in us so long as we live, and of the human corruption which so nearly cleaves to us. In the meantime, because the strength of the flesh and relics of the old man are not of such great force that they can wholly quench the work of the Spirit, therefore, the faithful are called free; yet so that they acknowledge their infirmity and glory not at all in their free will. For that which St. Augustine repeats so often out of the apostle ought always to be kept in mind by the faithful: "What hast thou, that thou hast not received? and if thou hast received it, why dost thou boast, as though thou hadst not received it?" (1 Cor. 4:7). Hitherto may be added that that comes not straightway to pass which we have purposed: for the events of things are in the hand of God. For which cause, Paul besought the Lord that He would prosper his journey (Rom. 1:10). Wherefore, in this respect also, free will is very weak.

But in outward things, no man denies but that both the regenerate and unregenerate have their free will. For man has this constitution common with other creatures (to whom he is not inferior) to will some things and to nill other things. So he may speak or keep silence; go out of his house or abide within. Although herein also God's power is evermore to be marked which brought to pass that Balaam could not go as far as he would (Num. 24:13) and that Zacharias, coming out of the Temple, could not speak as he would have done (Luke 1:22).

In this matter we condemn the Manichees, who deny that the beginning of evil unto man, being good, came from his free will. We condemn also the Pelagians who affirm that an evil man has free will sufficiently to perform a good precept. Both these are confuted by the Scripture, which says to the former, "God made man upright" (Eccl. 7:29) and to the latter, "If the Son make you free, then are you free indeed" (John 8:36).

Chapter 10. Of the Predestination of God, and the Election of the Saints

God has from the beginning freely, and of His mere grace, without any respect of men, predestinated or elected the saints, whom He will save in Christ, according to the saying of the apostle, "And He hath chosen us in Him before the foundation of the world" (Eph. 1:4); and again, "Who hath saved us, and called us with an holy calling, not according to our works, but according to His own purpose and grace, which was given unto us, through Jesus Christ, before the world was, but is now made manifest by the appearance of our Savior Jesus Christ" (2 Tim. 1:9–10).

Therefore, though not for any merit of ours, yet not without a means, but in Christ, and for Christ, did God choose us; and they who are now engrafted into Christ by faith, the same also were elected. But such as are without Christ were rejected, according to that saying of the apostle, "Prove yourselves, whether ye be in the faith. Know ye not your own selves, how that Jesus Christ is in you, except ye be reprobates?" (2 Cor. 13:5).

To conclude, the saints are chosen in Christ by God unto a sure end, which end the apostle declares, when he says, "He hath chosen us in Him, that we should be holy and without blame before Him through love; who hath predestinated as to be adopted through Jesus Christ unto Himself, for the praise of His glorious grace" (Eph. 1:4–6).

And although God knows who are His, and now and then mention is made of the small number of the elect, yet we must hope well of all and not rashly judge any man to be a reprobate: for Paul says to the Philippians, "I thank my God for you all" (now he speaks of the whole church of the Philippians) "that ye are come into the fellowship of the gospel; and I am persuaded, that He that hath begun this work in you, will perform it, as it becometh me to judge of you all" (Phil. 1:3–7).

And when the Lord was asked whether there were few that should be saved, He does not answer and tell them that few or more should be saved or damned; but rather He exhorts every man to "strive to enter in at the strait gate" (Luke 13:24), as if He should say, It is not for you to rashly inquire of these matters, but rather to endeavor that you may enter into heaven by the straight way.

Wherefore we do not allow of the wicked speeches of some who say, Few are chosen, and seeing I know not whether I am in the number of those few,

I will not defraud my nature of her desires. Others there are which say, If I am predestinated and chosen of God, nothing can hinder me from salvation, which is already certainly appointed for me, whatever I do at any time; but if I am in the number of the reprobate, no faith or repentance will help me, seeing the decree of God cannot be changed: therefore, all teachings and admonitions are to no purpose. Now against these men the saying of the apostle makes much, "The servants of God must be apt to teach, instructing them that are contrary minded, proving if God at any time will give them repentance, that they may come to amendment out of the snare of the devil, which are taken of him at his pleasure" (2 Tim. 2:24–26). Beside, Augustine also teaches that "Both the grace of free election and predestination, and also wholesome admonitions and doctrines, are to be preached" (*Lib. De Bono Perseverantiae.* Chap. 14).

We, therefore, condemn those who seek other than in Christ, whether they are chosen from all eternity, and what God has decreed of them before all beginning. For men must hear the gospel preached and believe it. If you believe and are in Christ, you may undoubtedly reckon that you are elected. For the Father has revealed unto us in Christ His eternal sentence of predestination, as we even now showed out of the apostle in 2 Timothy 1:9–10. This is, therefore, above all to be taught and well weighed, what great love of the Father towards us in Christ is revealed. We must hear what the Lord daily preaches unto us in His gospel, how He calls and says, "Come unto me all ye that labor and are burdened, and I will refresh you" (Matt. 11:28). And, "So God loved the world that He gave His only-begotten Son for it, that all which believe in Him should not perish but have life everlasting" (John 3:16). Also, "It is not the will of the Father, that any of these little ones should perish" (Matt. 18:14). Let Christ, therefore, be our looking glass, in whom we may behold our predestination. We shall have a most evident and sure testimony that we are written in the book of life, if we communicate with Christ; and He is ours and we His by a true faith.

Let this comfort us in the temptation touching predestination, than which there is none more dangerous: that the promises of God are general to the faithful, in that He says, "Ask, and ye shall receive; every one that asketh, receiveth" (Luke 11:9–10); and to conclude, in that we pray, with all the church of God, "Our Father which art in heaven" (Matt. 6:9); and for that in baptism we are ingrafted into the body of Christ and are fed in His church, oftentimes with His flesh and blood unto everlasting life. Thereby being strengthened, we are commanded to "work out our salvation with fear and trembling" according to that precept of Paul in Philippians 2:12.

Chapter 11. Of Jesus Christ, Being True God and Man, and the Only Savior of the World

Moreover, we believe and teach that the Son of God, our Lord Jesus Christ, was from all eternity predestinated and foreordained of the Father to be the Savior of the world. And we believe that He was begotten, not only then, when He took flesh of the virgin Mary, nor yet a little before the foundations of the world were laid, but before all eternity; and that of the Father, after an unspeakable manner. For Isaiah says, "Who can tell His generation?" (53:8). And Micah says, "Whose egress hath been from everlasting" (5:2). And John says, "In the beginning was the Word, and the Word was with God, and God was the Word" (1:1). Therefore, the Son is co-equal and consubstantial with the Father, as touching His divinity: true God, not by name only, or by adoption, or by special favor, but in substance and nature (Phil. 2:6). Even as the apostle says elsewhere, "This is the true God, and life everlasting" (1 John 5:20). Paul also says, "He hath made His Son the heir of all things, by whom also He made the world: the same is the brightness of His glory, and the engraved form of His person, bearing up all things by His mighty word" (Heb. 1:2–3). "Likewise in the gospel the Lord Himself says, "Father, glorify thou Me with Thyself, with the glory which I had with Thee before the world was" (John 17:5). Also elsewhere it is written in the gospel, "The Jews sought how to kill Jesus, because He said that God was His Father, making Himself equal with God" (John 5:18).

We, therefore, abhor the blasphemous doctrine of Arius, and all the Arians, uttered against the Son of God; and especially the blasphemies of Michael Servetus the Spaniard, and of his accomplices, which Satan by them has, as it were, drawn out of hell, and most boldly and impiously spread abroad throughout the world against the Son of God.

We teach also and believe that the eternal Son of the eternal God was made the Son of man, of the seed of Abraham and David (Matt. 1:1–25), not by the means of any man, as Ebion affirmed; but that He was most purely conceived by the Holy Ghost, and was born of Mary, who was always a virgin, even as the history of the gospel declares. And Paul says, "He took in no sort the angels, but the seed of Abraham" (Heb. 2:16). And John the apostle says, "He that believeth not that Jesus Christ is come in the flesh, is not of God" (1 John 4:3). The flesh of Christ, therefore, was neither flesh in show only, nor yet flesh brought from heaven, as Valentinus and Marcion dreamed.

Moreover, our Lord Jesus Christ did not have a soul without sense and reason, as Apollinaris thought; nor flesh without a soul, as Eunomius taught: but a soul with its reason and flesh with its senses, by which senses He felt true grief in the time of His passion, even as He Himself witnessed when He said, "My soul is heavy even to death" (Matt. 26:38) and "My soul is troubled" (John 12:27).

We acknowledge, therefore, that there are in one and the same Jesus Christ our Lord two natures, the divine and the human nature; and we say that these two are so conjoined or united that they are not swallowed up, confounded, or mingled together, but rather united or joined together in one person, the properties of each nature being safe and remaining still: so that we worship one Christ our Lord, and not two; I say, one true God and man; as touching His divine nature of the same substance with the Father, and as touching His human nature of the same substance with us and "like unto us in all things, sin only excepted" (Heb. 4:15).

As, therefore, we detest the heresy of Nestorius, which makes two Christs of one, and dissolves the union of the person; so do we curse the madness of Eutyches and of the Monothelites or Monophysites who overthrow the propriety of the human nature.

Therefore, we do not teach that the divine nature in Christ suffered or that Christ according to His human nature is yet in the world, and so in every place. For we do neither think nor teach that the body of Christ ceased to be a true body after His glorification, or that it was deified, and so deified that it put off its properties, as touching body and soul, and became altogether a divine nature and began to be one substance alone: and, therefore, we do not allow or receive the unwitty subtleties, and the intricate, obscure, and inconstant disputations of Schwenkfeld and such other vain janglers about this matter; neither are we Schwenkfeldians.

Moreover, we believe that our Lord Jesus Christ did truly suffer and die for us in the flesh as Peter says (1 Peter 4:1). We abhor the most horrible madness of the Jacobites and all the Turks, which abandon the passion of our Lord. Yet we deny not but that "the Lord of glory (according to the saying of Paul) was crucified for us" (1 Cor. 2:8). For we reverently and religiously receive and use the communication of expressions drawn from Scripture, and used of all antiquity in expounding and reconciling places of Scripture which at first sight seem to disagree one from another.

We believe and teach that the same Lord Jesus Christ, in that true flesh in which He was crucified and died, rose again from the dead; and that He did not rise up another flesh instead of that which was buried, nor took a spirit instead of flesh, but retained a true body: therefore, while His disciples thought that they saw the spirit of their Lord Christ, He showed them His hands and feet, which were marked with the prints of the nails and wounds, saying, "Behold my hands and my feet, for I am He indeed: handle me and see, for a spirit hath not flesh and bones, as ye see me have" (Luke 24:39).

We believe that our Lord Jesus Christ, in the same flesh, did ascend above all the visible heavens into the very highest heaven, that is to say, the seat of God and of the blessed spirits, unto the right hand of God the Father. Which, although it signifies an equal participation of glory and majesty, yet it is also taken for a certain place of which the Lord, speaking in the gospel, says that "He will go and prepare a place for His" (John 14:2). Also the apostle Peter says, "The heavens must contain Christ, until the time of restoring of all things" (Acts 3:21). And out of heaven the same Christ will return unto judgment, even then, when wickedness shall chiefly reign in the world, and when Antichrist, having corrupted true religion, shall fill all things with superstition and impiety, and shall most cruelly destroy the church with fire and bloodshed. Now Christ shall return to redeem His, and to abolish Antichrist by His coming and to judge the quick and the dead (Acts 17:31). For the dead shall arise and "those which shall be found alive in that day" (which is unknown unto all creatures) "shall be changed in the twinkling of an eye" (1 Cor. 15:51–52). And all the faithful shall be taken up to meet Christ in the air (1 Thess. 4:17) that thenceforth they may enter with Him into heaven, there to live forever (2 Tim. 2:11), but the unbelievers, or ungodly, shall descend with the devils into hell, there to burn forever, and never to be delivered out of torments (Matt. 25:41).

We, therefore, condemn all those which deny the true resurrection of the flesh, and those which think amiss of the glorified bodies; as did John of

Jerusalem, against whom Jerome wrote. We also condemn those which have thought that both the devils and all the wicked shall at length be saved and have an end of their torments: for the Lord Himself has absolutely set it down that, "Their fire is never quenched, and their worm never dieth" (Mark 9:44). Moreover we condemn the Jewish dreams that before the day of judgment there shall be a golden world in the earth; and that the godly shall possess the kingdoms of the world, their wicked enemies being trodden under foot: for the evangelical truth, Matthew 24 and 25, and Luke 21, and the apostolic doctrine in the second epistle to the Thessalonians 2, and in the second epistle to Timothy 3 and 4, are found to teach far otherwise.

Furthermore, by His passion or death, and by all those things which He did and suffered for our sakes from the time of His coming in the flesh, our Lord reconciled His heavenly Father unto all the faithful (Rom. 5:10), purged their sin (Heb. 1:3), spoiled death, broke asunder condemnation and hell, and by His resurrection from the dead, brought again and restored life and immortality (2 Tim. 1:10). For He is our righteousness, life, and resurrection (John 6:44); and, to be short, He is the fullness and perfection, the salvation and most abundant sufficiency of all the faithful. For the apostle says, "So it pleaseth the Father that all fullness should dwell in Him" (Col. 1:19); and "In Him ye are complete" (Col. 2:10).

For we teach and believe that this Jesus Christ our Lord is the only and eternal Savior of mankind, yes, and of the whole world; in whom are saved by faith all that ever were saved before the Law, under the Law, and in the time of the gospel, and so many as shall yet be saved to the end of the world. For the Lord Himself in the gospel says, "He that entereth not in by the door into the sheepfold, but climbeth up another way, he is a thief and a robber" (John 10:1). "I am the door of the sheep" (v. 7). And also in another place of the same gospel He says, "Abraham saw my day, and rejoiced" (John 8:56). And the apostle Peter says, "Neither is there salvation in any other, but in Christ; for among men there is given no other name under heaven whereby they might be saved" (Acts 4:12). We believe, therefore, that through the grace of our Lord Christ we shall be saved, even as our fathers were. For Paul says that "All our fathers did eat the same spiritual meat and drink the same spiritual drink, for they drank of the spiritual rock that followed them, and that rock was Christ" (1 Cor. 10:3–4). And, therefore, we read that John said that "Christ was that

Lamb which was slain from the beginning of the world" (Rev. 13:8) and that John the Baptist witnesses that "Christ is that Lamb of God that taketh away the sins of the world" (John 1:29). Wherefore we do plainly and openly profess and preach that Jesus Christ the only Redeemer and Savior of the world, the King and High Priest, the true and looked for Messiah, that holy and blessed one (I say) whom all the shadows of the Law, and the prophecies of the prophets, did prefigure and promise; and that God supplied and sent Him unto us so that now we are not to look for any other. And now there remains nothing but that we all should give all glory to Him, believe in Him, and rest in Him only, condemning and rejecting all other aids of our life. For they are fallen from the grace of God, and make Christ of no value unto themselves, whosoever they be that seek salvation in any other things besides Christ alone (Gal. 5:4).

And to speak many things in few words, with a sincere heart we believe, and with liberty of speech we freely profess, whatsoever things are defined out of the Holy Scriptures, and comprehended in the creeds, and in the decrees of those four first and most excellent Councils held at Nicaea, Constantinople, Ephesus, and Chalcedon, together with blessed Athanasius' Creed, and all other creeds like to these, touching the mystery of the incarnation of our Lord Jesus Christ; and we condemn all things contrary to the same. And thus do we retain the Christian, sound, and catholic faith, whole and inviolable, knowing that nothing is contained in the foresaid creeds which is not agreeable to the Word of God, and makes wholly for the sincere declaration of the faith.

Chapter 12. Of the Law of God

We teach that the will of God is set down unto us in the Law of God; to wit, what He would have us to do or not to do, what is good and just, or what is evil and unjust. We, therefore, confess that "The law is good and holy" (Rom. 7:12) and that this Law is by the finger of God, either "written in the hearts of men" (Rom. 2:15) and so is called the law of nature, or engraven in the two tables of stone and more largely expounded in the books of Moses (Ex. 20:1–17; Deut. 5:6–21). For plainness' sake, we divide it into the moral law, which is contained in the commandments, or the two tables expounded in the books of Moses; into the ceremonial, which appoints ceremonies and the worship of God; and into the judicial law, which is occupied about political and domestic affairs.

We believe that the whole will of God, and all necessary precepts for every part of this life, are fully delivered in this Law. For otherwise the Lord would not have forbidden that "any thing should be either added to or taken away from this law" (Deut. 4:2; 12:32); neither would He have commanded us to go straight forward in this and "not to decline out of the way, either to the right hand or to the left" (Josh. 1:7).

We teach that this Law was not given to men that we should be justified by keeping it; but that by the knowledge thereof we might rather acknowledge our infirmity, sin, and condemnation; and so despairing of our own strength, might turn unto Christ by faith. For the apostle says plainly, "The law worketh wrath" (Rom. 4:15) and "By the law cometh the knowledge of sin" (Rom. 3:20) and "If there had been a law given, which could have justified and given us life, surely righteousness should have been by the law: but the scripture (to wit, of the law) hath concluded all under sin, that the promise by the faith of Jesus Christ should be given to them which believe" (Gal. 3:21–22). "Therefore, the law was our schoolmaster to bring us to Christ, that we might be justified by faith" (v. 24).

For neither could there ever, nor at this day can any flesh satisfy the law of God, and fulfill it, by reason of the weakness in our flesh, which remains and sticks fast in us, even to our last breath. For the apostle says again, "That which the law could not perform, inasmuch as it was weak through the flesh, that did God perform, sending His own Son in similitude of flesh subject to sin" (Rom. 8:3). Therefore, Christ is the perfecting of the Law, and our fulfilling of it (Rom. 10:4); who as He took away the curse of the Law, when He was made a curse for us (Gal. 3:13) so He communicates unto us by faith His fulfilling thereof, and His righteousness and obedience are imputed unto us.

The law of God, therefore, is thus far abrogated; that is, it does not henceforth condemn neither work wrath in us. "For we are under grace, and not under the law" (Rom. 6:14). Moreover, Christ did fulfill all the figures of the Law. Wherefore, the shadow ceased, when the body came; so that, in Christ, we have now all truth and fullness. Yet we do not therefore disdain or reject the Law. We remember the words of the Lord saying, "I came not to destroy the Law and the prophets, but to fulfill them" (Matt. 5:17). We know that in the Law are described unto us the kinds of virtues and vices. We know that the Scripture of the Law if it is expounded by the gospel is very profitable to the church, and that, therefore, the reading of it is not to be banished out of the church. For although the countenance of Moses was covered with a veil, yet the apostle affirms that the veil is taken away and abolished by Christ (2 Cor. 3:14). We condemn all things which the old or new heretics have taught against the Law of God.

Chapter 13. Of the Gospel of Jesus Christ: Also of Promises; of the Spirit and of the Letter

The gospel indeed is opposed to the Law: for the Law works wrath and denounces a curse; but the gospel preaches grace and blessing. John also says, "The law was given by Moses, but grace and truth came by Jesus Christ" (John 1:17). Yet notwithstanding, it is most certain that they which were before the Law and under the Law were not altogether destitute of the gospel. For they had notable evangelical promises, such as these: "The seed of the woman shall bruise the serpent's head" (Gen. 3:15). "In thy seed shall all the nations of the earth be blessed" (Gen. 22:18). "The scepter shall not be taken from Judah until Shiloh come" (Gen. 49:10). "The Lord shall raise up a prophet from His own brethren" (Deut. 18:15; Acts 3:22; 7:37).

And we acknowledge that the fathers had two kinds of promises revealed unto them, even as we have. For some of them were of present and transitory things: such as were the promises of the land of Canaan, and of victories; and such as are now-a-days, concerning our daily bread. Some others there were then, and also are now, of heavenly and everlasting things; as of God's favor, remission of sins, and life everlasting through faith in Jesus Christ.

Now the fathers had not only outward or earthly, but spiritual and heavenly promises in Christ. For the apostle Peter says that "The prophets, which prophesied of the grace that should come to us, have searched and inquired of this salvation" (1 Peter 1:10). Whereupon the apostle Paul also says that "The gospel of God, was promised before by the prophets of God in the Holy Scripture" (Rom. 1:1–2). Hereby then it appears evidently that the fathers were not altogether destitute of all the gospel.

And although, after this manner, our fathers had the gospel in the writings of the prophets, by which they attained salvation in Christ through faith, yet the gospel is properly called "glad and happy tidings": wherein, first by

John Baptist, then by Christ the Lord Himself, and afterwards by the apostles and their successors, is preached to us in the world, that God has now performed that which He promised from the beginning of the world, and has sent, yes and given unto us, His only Son, and, in Him, reconciliation with the Father, remission of sins, all fullness and everlasting life. The history, therefore, set down by the four evangelists, declaring how these things were done or fulfilled in Christ, and what He taught and did, and that they which believe in Him have all fullness; this, I say, is truly called the gospel. Also the preaching and writings of the apostles, in which they expound unto us how the Son was given us of the Father, and in Him, all things pertaining to life and salvation, is truly called the doctrine of the gospel, so as even at this day it loses not that worthy name, if it is sincere.

The same preaching of the gospel is by the apostle termed the Spirit and "the ministry of the Spirit" (2 Cor. 3:8) because it lives, and works through faith in the ears, yes in the hearts of the faithful, through the illumination of the Holy Spirit. For the letter, which is opposed unto the Spirit, indeed signifies every outward thing, but more especially the doctrine of the Law, which without the Spirit and faith, works wrath, and stirs up sin in the minds of them that do not truly believe. For which cause, it is called by the apostle, "the ministry of death" (2 Cor. 3:7). For hitherto pertains that saying of the apostle, "The letter killeth, but the Spirit giveth life" (v. 6). The false apostles preached the gospel, corrupted by mingling of the Law therewith, as though Christ could not save without the Law. Such also were the Ebionites said to be, which came of Ebion the heretic; and the Nazarites, who formerly were called Mineans. All which we condemn, sincerely preaching the Word, and teaching that believers are justified through the Spirit only, and not through the Law. But of this matter there shall follow a more large discourse under the title of justification.

And although the doctrine of the gospel, compared with the Pharisee's doctrine of the Law, might seem (when it was first preached by Christ) to be a new doctrine (which Jeremiah also prophesied of the New Testament), yet indeed it not only was and as yet is (though the papists call it new, in regard of popish doctrine, which has been received for a long time) an ancient doctrine but also the most ancient in the world. For God from all eternity foreordained to save the world by Christ; and this His predestination and eternal counsel has He opened to the world by the gospel (2 Tim. 1:9–10). Whereby it appears that the evangelical doctrine and religion was the most ancient of all that ever were, are, or ever shall be; wherefore we say that all they err foully, and speak things unworthy of the eternal counsel of God, who term the evangelical doctrine and religion a new startup faith, scarce thirty years old: to whom that saying of Isaiah very well agrees: "Woe unto them that speak good of evil, and evil of good, which put darkness for light, and light for darkness, that put bitter for sweet, and sweet for sour" (5:20).

Chapter 14. Of Repentance, and the Conversion of Man

The gospel has the doctrine of repentance joined with it: for so said the Lord in the gospel, "In my name must repentance and remission of sins be preached among all nations" (Luke 24:47). By repentance we understand the change of the mind in a sinful man, stirred up by the preaching of the gospel through the Holy Spirit and received by a true faith; by which a sinful man acknowledges his natural corruption and all his sins, convinced of them by the Word of God, and is heartily grieved for them, and not only bewails and freely confesses them before God with shame, but also loathes and abhors them with indignation, thinking seriously of present amendment and of a continual concern for innocence and virtue, wherein to exercise himself in a holy manner all the rest of his life.

And surely this is true repentance, namely, an unfeigned turning unto God and to all goodness, and a serious return from the devil and from all evil. Now we expressly say that this repentance is the mere gift of God, and not the work of our own strength. For the apostle wishes the faithful minister diligently to "instruct those which withstand the truth, if so be at any time the Lord may give them repentance, that they may acknowledge the truth" (2 Tim. 2:25). Also, the sinful woman in the gospel, which washed Christ's feet with her tears; and Peter, which bitterly wept and bewailed his denial of his Master; manifestly show what mind the penitent man should have, to wit, very earnestly lamenting his sins committed. Moreover, the prodigal son, and the publican in the gospel, that are compared with the Pharisee, set forth unto us a most fit pattern of confessing our sins to God. The prodigal son said, "Father, I have sinned against heaven, and against thee: I am not worthy to be called thy son, make me as one of thy hired servants" (Luke 15:18–19). The publican also, not daring to lift up his eyes to heaven, but knocking his breast, cried, "God, be merciful unto me a sinner" (Luke 18:13). And we doubt not but the Lord received them to mercy. For John the apostle says, "If we confess our sins, He is faithful and just to forgive us our sins, and to purge us from all iniquity. If we say we have not sinned, we make Him a liar, and His word is not in us" (1 John 1:9–10).

We believe that this sincere confession which is made to God alone, either privately between God and the sinner, or openly in the church, where that general confession of sins is rehearsed, is sufficient, and that it is not necessary for the obtaining of remission of sins that any man should confess his sins unto the priest, whispering them into his ears, that, the priest laying his hands on his head, he might receive absolution; because we find no commandment nor example thereof in the Holy Scripture. David protests and says, "I made my fault known to thee, and my unrighteousness did I not hide from thee. I said, I will confess my wickedness to the Lord against myself, and thou hast forgiven the heinousness of my sin" (Ps. 32:5). Yes, and the Lord teaching us to pray, and also to confess our sins, said, "So shall ye pray; Our Father, which art in heaven, forgive us our debts, even as we forgive our debtors" (Matt. 6:9, 12). It is requisite, therefore that we should confess our sins unto God, and be reconciled with our neighbor, if we have offended him. And the apostle James speaking generally of confession says, "Confess each of you your sins one to another" (James 5:16). If any man, being overwhelmed with the burden of his sins and troublesome temptations, will privately ask counsel, instruction, or comfort, either of a minister of the church, or of any other brother that is learned in the law of God, we do not dislike it. Also we fully allow that general and public confession, which is wont to be rehearsed in the church, and in holy meetings (whereof we spoke before) being, as it is, agreeable with the Scripture.

Concerning the keys of the kingdom of heaven which the Lord committed to His apostles, they prate many strange things: and of these keys they make swords, spears, scepters, and crowns, and full power over mighty kingdoms, yes, and over men's souls and bodies. But we, judging uprightly according to the Word of God, say that all ministers, truly called, have and exercise the keys or the use of them, when they preach the gospel, that is to say, when they teach, exhort, reprove, and keep in order the people committed to their charge. For so do they open the kingdom of God to the obedient, and shut it against the disobedient. These keys did the Lord promise to the apostles in Matthew 16:19; and delivered them in John 20:23, Mark 16:15–16 and Luke 24:47 when He sent forth His disciples, and commanded them to preach the gospel in all the world, and to remit sins.

The apostle in the epistle to the Corinthians says that the Lord "gave to His ministers the ministry of reconciliation" (2 Cor. 5:18). And what this was, he straightway makes plain and says, "The word or doctrine of reconciliation" (v. 19). And yet more plainly expounding his words, he adds that the ministers of Christ, as it were, "go an embassage in Christ's name, as if God Himself should by His ministers exhort the people to be reconciled to God" (v. 20); to wit, by faithful obedience. They use the keys, therefore, when they persuade to faith and repentance. Thus do they reconcile men to God; thus they forgive sins; thus they open the kingdom of heaven, and bring in believers; much differing herein from those of whom the Lord spoke in the gospel, "Woe unto you lawyers, for ye have taken away the key of knowledge: ye have not entered in yourselves, and those that would have entered ye forbade" (Luke 11:52).

Rightly, therefore, and effectually do ministers absolve, when they preach the gospel of Christ, and thereby remission of sins; which is promised to every one that believes, even as every one is baptized; and testify of it that it particularly appertains to all. Neither do we imagine that this absolution is made any whit more effectual for that which is mumbled into some priest's ear, or upon some man's head particularly; yet we judge that men must be taught diligently to seek remission of sins in the blood of Christ, and that everyone is to be put in mind that forgiveness of sins belongs unto Him.

But how diligent and careful every penitent man ought to be in the endeavor of a new life, and in slaying the old man, and raising up the new man, the examples in the gospel teach us. For the Lord says to him whom He had healed of the palsy, "Behold thou art made whole, sin no more, lest a worse thing come unto thee" (John 5:14). Likewise to the adulterous woman which was delivered, He said, "Go thy way, and sin no more" (John 8:11). By which words He did not mean that any man could be free from sin, while he lived in this flesh; but He commends unto diligence and an earnest care, that we (I say) should endeavor by all means, and beg of God by prayer, that we may not fall again into sins, out of which we are risen after a manner, and that we may not be overcome of the flesh, the world, or the devil. Zacchaeus, the publican, being received into favor by the Lord, cries out in the gospel, "Behold, Lord, the half of my goods I give to the poor, and if I have taken from any man any thing by fraud, I restore him fourfold" (Luke 19:8). After the same manner, we preach that restitution and mercy, yes, and giving of alms, are necessary for them which truly repent. And generally out of the apostle's words, we exhort men, saying, "Let not sin reign in your mortal body, that ye should obey it through the lusts thereof. Neither give ye your members, as weapons of unrighteousness, to sin; but give yourselves unto God, as they that are alive from the dead; and give your members, as weapons of righteousness, unto God" (Rom. 6:12–13).

Wherefore, we condemn all the ungodly speeches of certain ones who abuse the preaching of the gospel and say, "To return unto God is very easy, for Christ has purged all our sins: forgiveness of sins is easily obtained: what, therefore, will it hurt to sin?" And, "We need not take any great care for repentance," etc. Notwithstanding, we always teach that an entrance unto God is open for all sinners, and that this God forgives all the sins of the faithful, only that one sin excepted which is committed against the Holy Ghost (Mark 3:28–29). And, therefore, we condemn the old and new Novatians and Catharists, and especially we condemn the pope's lucrative doctrine of penance; and against his simony, and simonaical indulgences, we use that sentence of Simon Peter, "Thy money perish with thee, because thou thoughtest that the gift of God might be bought with money. Thou hast no part or fellowship in this matter, for thy heart is not upright before God" (Acts 8:20–21).

We also disapprove of those who think that they themselves by their own satisfactions can make recompense for their sins committed. For we teach that Christ alone, by His death and passion, is the satisfaction, propitiation, and purging of all sins (Isa. 53:4). Nevertheless, we cease not to urge, as was before said, the mortification of the flesh; and yet we add further that it must not be proudly thrust upon God for a satisfaction for our sins (1 Cor. 8:8), but must humbly, as it becomes the sons of God, be performed as a new obedience to show thankful minds for the deliverance and full satisfaction obtained by the death and satisfaction of the Son of God."

Chapter 15. Of the True Justification of the Faithful

To justify, in the apostle's disputation touching justification, signifies to remit sin, to absolve from the fault and the punishment thereof, to receive into favor, to pronounce a man just. For the apostle says to the Romans, "God is He that justifieth; who is he that can condemn?" (Rom. 8:33–34) where to justify and to condemn are opposed. And in the Acts of the Apostles, the apostle says, "Through Christ is preached unto you forgiveness of sins; and from all things (from which ye could not be justified by the law of Moses) by Him, every one that believeth is justified" (Acts 13:38–39). For in the Law also and in the prophets, we read that "If a controversy were risen amongst any, and they came to judgment, the judge should judge them; that is, justify the righteous, and make wicked, or condemn, the wicked" (Deut. 25:1). And in Isaiah, "Woe to them which justify the wicked for rewards" (5:23).

Now it is most certain that we are all by nature sinners, and before the judgment seat of God convicted of ungodliness and guilty of death. But we are justified, that is, acquitted from sin and death by God the Judge through the grace of Christ alone, and not by any respect or merit of ours. For what is more plain than that which Paul says? "All have sinned, and are destitute of the glory of God, and are justified freely by His grace, through the redemption which is in Christ Jesus" (Rom. 3:23–24). For Christ took upon Himself and bare the sins of the world and satisfied the justice of God. God, therefore, is merciful unto our sins, for Christ alone, that suffered and rose again, and does not impute them unto us. But He imputes the righteousness of Christ unto us for our own: so that now we are not only cleansed from sin, and purged, and holy, but also endued with the righteousness of Christ; yes, and acquitted from sin, death, and condemnation (2 Cor. 5:19–21); finally, we are righteous and heirs of eternal life. To speak properly, then, it is God alone that justifies us, and that only for Christ by not imputing unto us our sins, but imputing Christ's righteousness unto us (Rom. 4:23–25).

But because we receive this justification, not by any works, but by faith in the mercy of God, and in Christ; therefore, we teach and believe with the apostle that sinful man is justified only by faith in Christ, not by the Law, or by any works. For the apostle says, "We conclude that man is justified by faith, without the works of the law" (Rom. 3:28). "If Abraham was justified by works, he hath whereof to boast; but not with God: for what saith the

Scripture? Abraham believed God, and it was imputed to him for righteousness, but to him that worketh not, but believeth in Him that justifieth the ungodly his faith is counted for righteousness" (Rom. 4:2–3, 5; Gen. 15:6). And again; "Ye are saved by grace through faith and that not of yourselves, it is the gift of God, not by works lest any might have cause to boast" (Eph. 2:8–9). Therefore, because faith apprehends Christ our righteousness and attributes all to the praise of God in Christ, in this respect justification is attributed to faith, chiefly because of Christ whom it receives, and not because it is a work of ours; for it is the gift of God.

Now that we do receive Christ by faith, the Lord shows at large (John 6:27, 33, 35, 48–58) where He puts eating for believing, and believing for eating. For as by eating we receive meat, so by believing we are made partakers of Christ. Therefore, we do not part the benefit of justification, giving part to the grace of God or to Christ, and part to ourselves, our charity, works or merit; but we attribute it wholly to the praise of God in Christ, and that through faith. Moreover, our charity and our works cannot please God, if they are done of such as are not just; wherefore, we must first be just before we can love or do any just works. We are made just (as we have said) through faith in Christ, by the mere grace of God; who does not impute unto us our sins, but imputes unto us the righteousness of Christ; yes, and our faith in Christ He imputes for righteousness unto us. Moreover, the apostle plainly derives love from faith, saying, "The end of the commandment is love, proceeding from a pure heart, a good conscience, and faith unfeigned" (1 Tim. 1:5).

Wherefore, in this matter we speak not of a feigned, vain, or dead faith, but of a lively and quickening faith; which, for Christ (who is life, and gives life) whom it apprehends, both is indeed, and is so called, a lively faith, and proves itself to be lively, by lively works. And, therefore, James does not speak contrary to our doctrine, for he speaks of a vain and dead faith, which certain bragged of but did not have Christ living within them by faith. And James also says that works do justify (2:14–16); yet he is not contrary to Paul (for then he would be rejected), but he shows that Abraham declared his lively and justifying faith by works. And so do all the godly, who yet trust in Christ alone, not to their own works. For the apostle said again, "I live, howbeit not I, but Christ liveth in me. But the life which now I live, in the flesh, I live through the faith of the Son of God, who loved me, and gave Himself for me. I do not despise the grace of God, for if righteousness is by the law, then Christ died in vain" (Gal. 2:20–21).

Chapter 16. Of Faith and Good Works: Of Their Reward and of Man's Merit

Christian faith is not an opinion or human persuasion, but a sure trust and an evident and steadfast assent of the mind; to be most brief, a most sure comprehension of the truth of God set forth in the Scriptures and in the Apostles' Creed; yes and of God Himself, the chief blessedness; and especially of God's promise, and of Christ, who is the consummation of all the promises. And this faith is the mere gift of God because God alone of His power gives it to His elect according to measure; and that when, to whom, and how much He will; and that by His Holy Spirit, through the means of preaching the gospel and of faithful prayer. This faith has also her increases; which unless they were likewise given of God, the apostles would never have said, "Lord, increase, our faith" (Luke 17:5).

Now all these things which we have said before of faith, the apostles taught them before us, even as we set them down. For Paul says, "Faith is the ground," or sure subsistence, "of things hoped for, and the evidence," or clear and certain comprehension, "of things which are not seen" (Heb. 11:1). And again he says that "All the promises of God in Christ are Yea, and in Christ are Amen" (2 Cor. 1:20). And the same apostle says to the Philippians that "it was given them to believe in Christ" (Phil. 1:29). And also, "God doth distribute unto every man a measure of faith" (Rom. 12:3). And again, "All men have not faith" (2 Thess. 3:2); and "All do not obey the gospel" (2 Thess. 1:8). Besides, Luke witnesses and says, "As many as were ordained to life, believed" (Acts 13:48). And, therefore, Paul also calls faith, "the faith of God's elect" (Titus 1:1). And again, "Faith cometh by hearing, and hearing by the word of God" (Rom. 10:17). And in other places he often wishes men to pray for faith. And the same also calls faith "powerful, and that showeth itself by love" (Gal. 5:6).

This faith pacifies the conscience and opens to us a free access unto God; that with confidence we may come unto Him and may obtain at His hands whatsoever is profitable and necessary. The same faith keeps us in our duty which we owe to God and to our neighbor and fortifies our patience in adversity: it frames and makes a true confession, and (in a word) it brings forth good fruit of all sorts; and good works (which are good indeed) proceed from a lively faith, by the Holy Ghost, and are done of the faithful according to the will or rule of God's Word. For Peter the apostle says, "Therefore, giving all diligence thereunto, join moreover virtue with your faith, and with virtue knowledge, and with knowledge temperance" (2 Peter 1:5–6).

It was said before that the law of God, which is the will of God, prescribes unto us the pattern of good works. And the apostle says, "This is the will of God, even your sanctification, that ye abstain from all uncleanness, and that no man oppress or deceive his brother in any matter" (1 Thess. 4:3, 6). But as for such works and worship of God as are taken up upon our own liking, which St. Paul calls "will-worship" (Col. 2:23), they are not allowed nor liked of God. Of such the Lord says in the gospel, "They worship Me in vain, teaching for doctrine the precepts of men" (Matt. 15:9).

We, therefore, disallow all such manner of works, and we approve and urge men unto such as are according to the will and commandment of God. Yes, and these same works that are agreeable to God's will must be done, not to the end to merit eternal life by them; for "life everlasting," as the apostle says, "is the gift of God" (Rom. 6:23), nor for ostentation's sake, which the Lord rejects (Matt. 6:1, 5, 16), nor for lucre, which also He dislikes (Matt. 23:23), but to the glory of God to commend and set forth our calling and to yield thankfulness unto God, and also for the profit of our neighbors. For the Lord says again in the gospel, "Let your light so shine before men, that they may see your good works, and glorify your Father which is in heaven" (Matt. 5:16). Likewise the apostle Paul says, "Walk worthy of your calling" (Eph. 4:1). Also, "Whatsoever ye do," he says, "either in word or in deed, do all in the name of the Lord Jesus, giving thanks to God the Father by Him" (Col. 3:17). "Let no man seek his own his own, but every man his brother's" (Phil. 2:4). And, "Let ours also learn to show forth good works for necessary uses; that they be not unprofitable" (Titus 3:14).

Notwithstanding, therefore, that we teach, with the apostle, that a man is justified by faith in Christ and not by any good works (Rom. 3:28), yet we do not lightly esteem or condemn good works: because we know that a man is not created or regenerated through faith that he should be idle, but rather that without ceasing he should do those things which are good and profitable. For in the gospel the Lord says, "A good tree bringeth forth good fruit"

(Matt. 12:33); and again, "Whosoever abideth in Me, bringeth forth much fruit" (John 15:5). And lastly, the apostle says, "We are the workmanship of God, created in Christ Jesus to good works, which God hath prepared that we should walk in them" (Eph. 2:10). And again, "Who gave Himself for us, that He might deliver us from all iniquity, and purge us to be a peculiar people to Himself, zealous of good works" (Titus 2:14). We, therefore, condemn all those which do condemn good works, and do babble that they are needless and not to be regarded. Nevertheless, as was said before, we do not think that we are saved by good works, or that they are so necessary to salvation that no man was ever saved without them. For we are saved by grace and by the benefit of Christ alone. Works do necessarily proceed from faith: but salvation is improperly attributed to them, which is most properly ascribed to grace. That sentence of the apostle is very notable: "If by grace, then not of works; for then grace were no more grace: but if of works, then is it not of grace; for then works were no more works" (Rom. 11:6).

Now the works which we do are accepted and allowed of God through faith because they which do them please God by faith in Christ, and also the works themselves are done by the grace of God through His Holy Spirit. For St. Peter says that "Of every nation, he that feareth God, and worketh righteousness, is accepted with Him" (Acts 10:35). And Paul also, "We cease not to pray for you, that ye may walk worthy of the Lord, and in all things please Him, being fruitful in very good work" (Col. 1:9–10).

Here, therefore, we diligently teach, not false and philosophical, but true virtues, true good works, and the true duties of a Christian man. And this we do with all the diligence and earnestness that we can inculcate and beat into men's minds; sharply reproving the slothfulness and hypocrisy of all those who with their mouths praise and profess the gospel, and yet with their shameful life do dishonor the same; setting before their eyes, in this case, God's horrible threatening, large promises, and bountiful rewards, and that by exhorting, comforting, and rebuking.

For we teach that God bestows great rewards on them that do good, according to that saying of the prophet, "Refrain thy voice from weeping, because thy work shall have a reward" (Jer. 31:16). In the gospel also the Lord said, "Rejoice, and be glad, because your reward is great in the heavens" (Matt. 5:12). And, "He that shall give to one of these little ones a cup of cold water, verily I say unto you, he shall not lose his reward" (Matt. 10:42). Yet we do not attribute this reward, which God gives, to the merit of the man that receives it, but to the goodness, or liberality, and truth of God, which promises and gives it: who although He owes nothing unto any, yet He has promised to give a reward to those that faithfully worship Him, notwithstanding that He also gives them grace to worship Him. Besides, there are many things unworthy of the majesty of God, and many imperfect things are found in the works even of the saints; and yet because God receives into favor and embraces those who work them for Christ's sake, therefore, He performs unto them the promised reward. For otherwise, our righteousnesses are compared to a menstruous cloth (Isa. 64:6); yes, and the Lord in the gospel says, "When ye have done all things that are commanded you, say, We are unprofitable servants; that which we ought to do, we have done" (Luke 17:10).

So that though we teach that God gives a reward to our good deeds, yet withal we teach with Augustine that "God doth crown in us, not our deserts, but His own gifts." And, therefore, whatsoever reward we receive, we say that it is a grace, and rather a grace than a reward: because those good things which we do, we do them rather by God than by ourselves; and because Paul says, "What hast thou that thou hast not received? but if thou hast received it, why dost thou boast, as though thou hadst not received it?" (1 Cor. 4:7). Which thing also the blessed martyr Cyprian gathers out of this place, that "we must not boast of anything, seeing nothing is our own." We, therefore, condemn those who defend the merits of men that they may frustrate the grace of God.

Chapter 17. Of the Catholic and Holy Church of God, and of the One Only Head of the Church

Forasmuch as God from the beginning would have men to be saved and to come to the knowledge of the truth (1 Tim. 2:4), therefore, it is necessary that there always should have been, and should be at this day, and to the end of the world, a church: that is, a company of the faithful, called and gathered out of the world; that is, a company (I say) of all saints, that is, of them who do truly know, and rightly worship and serve, the true God, in Jesus Christ the Savior by the Word and the Holy Spirit, and who by faith are partakers of all those good graces which are freely offered through Christ. These all are citizens of one and the same city living under one Lord, under the same laws, and in the same fellowship of all good things: for so the apostle calls them "fellow citizens with the saints, and of the household of God" (Eph. 2:19), terming the faithful upon the earth saints (1 Cor. 6:11) who are sanctified by the blood of the Son of God. Of these is that article of our Creed wholly to be understood: "I believe the catholic church, the communion of saints."

And seeing that there is always but "one God, and one mediator between God and man, Jesus Christ" (1 Tim. 2:5); also, one shepherd of the whole flock, one head of this body, and to conclude one Spirit, one salvation, one faith, one testament or covenant, it follows necessarily that there is but one church: which we, therefore, call catholic because it is universal, spread abroad through all the parts and quarters of the world, and reaches unto all times, and is not limited within the compass either of time or place. Here, therefore, we must condemn the Donatists who pinned up the church within the corners of Africa; neither do we allow of the Roman clergy, who vaunt that the Church of Rome alone is in a manner catholic.

The church is divided by some into divers parts or sorts: not that it is rent and divided from itself, but rather distinguished in respect of the diversity of the members that are in it. One part thereof they make to be the church militant, the other the church triumphant. The militant wars still on the earth and fights against the flesh, the world, the prince of the world, the devil, against sin, and against death. The other, being already set at liberty, is now in heaven and triumphs over all those things overcome, and continually rejoices before the Lord. Yet these two churches have notwithstanding a communion and fellowship among themselves.

Moreover, the church militant upon the earth has evermore had in it many particular churches, which must all notwithstanding be referred to the unity of the catholic church. This militant church was otherwise ordered and governed before the Law, among the patriarchs; otherwise under Moses, by the Law; and otherwise of Christ, by the gospel. There are but two sorts of people for the most part mentioned, to wit, the Israelites and the Gentiles; or they which, of the Jews and Gentiles, were gathered to make a church. There are also two testaments, the old and the new. Yet both these sorts of people have had, and still have, one fellowship, one salvation, in one and the same Messiah; in whom, as members of one body, they are all joined together under one head, and by one faith are all partakers of one and the same spiritual meat and drink. Yet here we do acknowledge a diversity of times, and a diversity in the pledges and signs of Christ promised and exhibited; and that now the ceremonies being abolished, the light shines unto us more clearly, our gifts and graces are more abundant and our liberty is more full and ample.

This holy church of God is called "the house of the living God" (2 Cor. 6:16), "builded of living and spiritual stones" (1 Peter 2:5) "founded upon a rock" (Matt. 16:18) "that cannot be removed" (Heb. 12:28) "upon a foundation, besides which none can be laid" (1 Cor. 3:11). Whereupon it is called "the pillar and foundation of the truth" (1 Tim. 3:15) that does not err, so long as it relies upon the rock Christ, and upon the foundation of the prophets and apostles. And no marvel if it does err, as often as it forsakes Him who alone is the truth. This church is also called "a virgin" (2 Cor. 11:2) and "the spouse of Christ" (Song 4:8) and "his only beloved" (Song 5:16). For the apostle says, "I have joined you unto one husband, that I might present you a chaste virgin unto Christ" (2 Cor. 11:2). The church is called "a flock of sheep under one shepherd" even Christ (Ezek. 34:22–23 and John 10:16) also, "the body of Christ" (Col. 1:24) because the faithful are the lively members of Christ, having Him for their head.

It is the head which has the preeminence in the body, and from whence the whole body receives life; by whose spirit it is governed in all things, of whom also it receives increase that it may grow up. Also there is but one head of the body which has agreement with the body; and, therefore, the church cannot have any other head beside Christ. For as the church is a spiritual body, so must it have a spiritual head like unto itself. Neither can it be governed by any other spirit than by the Spirit of Christ. Wherefore Paul says, "And He is the head of His body the church, who is the beginning, the first born of the dead, that in all things He might have the preeminence" (Col. 1:18). And in another place, "Christ (he says) is the head of the church, and the same is the Savior of His body" (Eph. 5:23). And again, "Who is the head of the church, which is His body, even the fullness of Him, which filleth all in all things" (Eph. 1:22–23). Again, "Let us in all things grow up into Him which is the head, that is Christ; by whom all the body being knit together, receiveth increase" (Eph. 4:15–16). And, therefore, we do not allow of the doctrine of the Roman prelates, who would make the pope the general pastor and supreme head of the church of Christ militant here on earth, and the very vicar of Christ, who has (as they say) all fullness of power and sovereign authority in the church. For we hold and teach, that Christ our Lord is, and remains still the only universal pastor, and highest bishop, before God His Father; and that in the church He performs all the duties of a pastor or bishop, even to the world's end: and, therefore, does not stand in need of any other to supply His place. For he is said to have a substitute, who is absent: but Christ is present in His church, and is the head that gives life thereunto. He did straitly forbid His apostles and their successors all superiority or dominion in the church. They, therefore, that by gainsaying set themselves against so manifest a truth and bring another kind of government into the church; see not that they are to be counted in the number of them of whom the apostles of Christ prophesied as Peter (2 Peter 2:1) and Paul (Acts 20:29; 2 Cor. 11:13; 2 Thess. 2:8–9) and in many other places.

Now by taking away the Roman head, we do not bring any confusion or disorder into the church. For we teach that the government of the church which the apostles set down, is sufficient to keep the church in due order; which, from the beginning, while as yet it wanted such a Roman head as is now pretended to keep it in order, was not disordered or full of confusion. The Roman head indeed maintains his tyranny and corruption which have been brought into the church: but in the meantime he hinders, resists, and, with all the might he can make, cuts off the right and lawful reformation of the church.

They object to us that there have been great strifes and dissensions in our churches, since they did sever themselves from the Church of Rome; and that, therefore, they cannot be true churches. As though there were never in the Church of Rome any sects, any contentions and quarrels; and that in matters of religion, maintained not so much in the schools as in the holy chairs, even in the audience of the people. We know that the apostle said, "God is not the author of dissension, but of peace" (1 Cor. 14:33); and, "Seeing there is amongst you emulation and contention, are ye not carnal?" (1 Cor. 3:3–4). Yet may we not deny but that God was in that church planted by the apostle, and that the apostolic church was a true church, howsoever there were strifes and dissensions in it. The apostle Paul reprehended Peter, an apostle (Gal. 2:11), and Barnabas fell at variance with Paul (Acts 15:39). Great contention arose in the church of Antioch, between them that preached one and the same

Christ, as Luke records in the Acts of the Apostles (15:2). And there have at all times been great contentions in the church, and the most excellent doctors of the church have about no small matters differed in opinion: yet so as in the meantime the church ceased not to be the church for all these contentions. For thus it pleases God to use the dissensions that arise in the church to the glory of His name, to the setting forth of the truth, and to the end that such as are not approved might be manifest (1 Cor. 11:19).

Now, as we acknowledge no other head of the church than Christ, so we do not acknowledge every church to be the true church which vaunts herself so to be: but we teach that to be the true church indeed in which the marks and tokens of the true church are to be found. First and chiefly, the lawful or sincere preaching of the Word of God, as it is left unto us in the writings of the prophets and apostles, which all seem to lead us unto Christ, who in the gospel has said, "My sheep hear My voice, and I know them, and they follow Me; and I give unto them eternal life. A stranger they do not hear, but flee from him, because they know not his voice" (John 10:5, 27–28). And they that are such in the church of God have all but one faith and one Spirit; and, therefore, they worship but one God: and Him alone they serve in spirit and in truth, loving Him with all their hearts and with all their strength, praying unto Him alone through Jesus Christ the only mediator and intercessor; and they seek not life or justice but only in Christ, and by faith in Him: because they acknowledge Christ the only head and foundation of His church, and, being surely founded on Him, daily repair themselves by repentance and with patience bear the cross laid upon them; and besides, by unfeigned love joining themselves to all the members of Christ, they declare themselves to be the disciples of Christ, by continuing in the bond of peace and holy unity. They do withal communicate in the sacraments ordained by Christ and delivered to us by His apostles, using them in no other manner than as they received them from the Lord Himself. That saying of the apostle Paul is well known to all, "I received from the Lord that which I delivered unto you" (1 Cor. 11:23). For which cause we condemn all such churches as strangers from the true church of Christ, who are not such as we have heard they ought to be; howsoever, in the meantime, they brag of the succession of bishops, of unity, and of antiquity. Moreover we have in charge from the apostles of Christ "to shun idolatry" (1 Cor. 10:14; 1 John 5:21) and "to come out of Babylon, and to have no fellowship with her, unless we mean to be partakers with her of all God's plagues laid upon her" (Rev. 18:4; 2 Cor. 6:17).

But as for communicating with the true church of Christ, we so highly esteem of it, that we say plainly that none can live before God which do not communicate with the true church of God, but separate themselves from the same. For as without the ark of Noah there was no escaping when the world perished in the flood; even so do we believe that without Christ, who in the church offers Himself to be enjoyed of the elect, there can be no certain salvation: and, therefore, we teach that such as would be saved must not separate themselves from the true church of Christ.

But yet we do not so strictly shut up the church within those marks before mentioned, as thereby to exclude all those out of the church which either do not communicate in the sacraments (not willingly, nor upon contempt, but who, being constrained by necessity, against their will abstain from them, or else do want them); or in whom faith sometimes fails, though not quite decay, nor altogether die: or in whom some slips and errors of infirmity may be found. For we know that God had some friends in the world that were not of the commonwealth of Israel. We know what befell the people of God in the captivity of Babylon, where they wanted their sacrifices seventy years. We know what happened to St. Peter, who denied his Master, and what is wont daily to fall out among the faithful and chosen of God, which go astray and are full of infirmities. We know moreover what manner of churches the churches at Galatia and Corinth were in the apostles' times: in which the apostle Paul condemns divers great and heinous crimes; yet he calls them the holy churches of Christ (1 Cor. 1:2; Gal. 1:2).

Yes, and it falls out sometimes that God in His just judgment suffers the truth of His Word and the catholic faith and His own true worship to be so obscured and defaced, that the church seems almost quite razed out, and not so much as a face of a church remains; as we see fell out in the days of Elijah (1 Kings 19:10, 14) and at other times. And yet, in the meantime, the Lord has in this world, even in this darkness, His true worshippers, and those not a few, but even seven thousand (v. 18) and more (Rev. 7:4). For the apostle cries, "The foundation of the Lord standeth sure, and hath this seal, The Lord knoweth who are His" (2 Tim. 2:19). Whereupon the church of God may be termed invisible: not that the men whereof it consists are invisible; but because, being hidden from our sight, and known only unto God, it cannot be discerned by the judgment of man.

Again not all that are reckoned in the number of the church are saints, and lively and true members of the church. For there are many hypocrites which outwardly hear the Word of God and publicly receive the sacraments, and seem to pray unto God alone through Christ, to confess Christ to be their only righteousness, and to worship God, and to exercise the duties of charity to the brethren, and for a while through patience to endure in troubles and calamities. And yet they are altogether destitute of the inward illumination of the Spirit of God, of faith and sincerity of heart, and of perseverance or continuance to the end. And these men are for the most part at the length laid open what they are. For the apostle John says, "They went out from among us, but they were not of us: for if they had been of us, they would have tarried with us" (1 John 2:19). Yet these men, while they pretend religion, are accounted to be in the church, however indeed they are not of the church. Even as traitors in a commonwealth, before they are detected are counted in the number of good citizens; and as the cockle and darnel and chaff are found among the wheat; and as tumors and swellings are in a perfect body, when they are rather diseases and deformities than true members of the body. And, therefore, the church is very well compared to a dragnet which draws up fish of all sorts, and to a field wherein is found both darnel and good corn (Matt. 13:25–26). We are to have a special regard that we judge not rashly before the time, nor go about to exclude and cast off or cut away those whom the Lord would not have excluded nor cut off, or whom, without some damage to the church, we cannot separate from it. Again, we must be very vigilant lest the godly falling fast asleep, the wicked grow stronger and do some mischief to the church.

Furthermore we teach, that it is carefully to be marked wherein especially the truth and unity of the church consists, lest we either rashly breed or nourish schisms in the church. It consists not in outward rites and ceremonies, but rather in the truth and unity of the catholic faith. This catholic faith is not taught us by the ordinances or laws of men, but by the Holy Scriptures, a compendious and short sum whereof is the Apostles' Creed. And, therefore, we read in the ancient writers that there were manifold diversities of ceremonies, but that those were always free; neither did any man think that the unity of the church was thereby broken or dissolved. We say then that the true unity of the church consists in several points of doctrine: in the true and uniform preaching of the gospel, and in such rites as the Lord Himself has expressly set down; and here we urge that saying of the apostle very earnestly, "As many of us, therefore, as are perfect, let us be thus minded. If any man think otherwise, the Lord shall reveal the same unto him. And yet in that whereunto we have attained, let us follow one direction, and all of us be like affected one towards another" (Phil. 3:15–16).

Chapter 18. Of the Ministers of the Church, Their Institution and Offices

God has always used His ministers, for the gathering or erecting of a church to Himself, and for the governing and preservation of the same; and still He does and always will use them, so long as the church remains on the earth. Therefore, the first beginning, institution, and office of the ministers, is a most ancient ordinance of God Himself, not a new device appointed by men. It is true that God can by His power, without any means, take unto Himself a church from among men, but He had rather deal with men by the ministry of men. Therefore, ministers are to be considered not as ministers by themselves alone, but as the ministers of God, even such as by whose means God works the salvation of mankind.

For which cause we give counsel to beware that we do not so attribute the things that appertain to our conversion and instruction unto the secret virtue of the Holy Ghost, that we frustrate the ecclesiastical ministry. For it behooves us always to have in mind the words of the apostle, "How shall they believe in Him, of whom they have not heard? and how shall they hear without a preacher? Therefore, faith is by hearing and hearing by the word of God" (Rom. 10:14, 17). And that also which the Lord says in the gospel, "Verily, verily, I say unto you, he that receiveth those that I shall send receiveth Me, and he that receiveth Me, receiveth Him who sent Me" (John 13:20). Likewise what a man of Macedonia, appearing in a vision to Paul, being then in Asia, said unto him: "Come into Macedonia, and help us" (Acts 16:9). And in another place the same apostle says, "We together are God's laborers; and ye are His husbandry, and His building" (1 Cor. 3:9).

Yet, on the other side, we must take heed that we do not attribute too much to the ministers and ministry, herein remembering also the words of our Lord in the gospel, "No man cometh to Me, except the Father, which hath sent Me, draw him" (John 6:44); and the words of the apostle, "Who then is Paul, and who is Apollos; but the ministers by whom ye believed; and as the Lord gave unto every one? Therefore, neither is he that planteth anything, nor he that watereth, but God that giveth the increase" (1 Cor. 3:5, 7). Therefore, let us believe that God teaches us by His Word outwardly through His ministers, and inwardly moves and persuades the hearts of His elect unto belief by His Holy Spirit: and that, therefore, we ought to render all the glory of this whole benefit unto God. But we have spoken of this matter in the first chapter of our declaration.

God has used for His ministers even from the beginning of the world, the best and most eminent men in the world (for divers of them were but simple for worldly wisdom or philosophy; yet surely in true divinity they were most excellent), namely, the patriarchs, to whom He spoke very often by His angels. For the patriarchs were the prophets or teachers of their age whom God for this purpose would have to live many years, that they might be as it were fathers and lights of the world. After them followed Moses, together with the prophets, that were most famous throughout the whole world. Then, after all these, our heavenly Father sent His only-begotten Son, the most absolute and perfect teacher of the world; in whom is hidden the wisdom of God, and from Him derived unto us by that most holy, perfect, and pure of all doctrine. For He chose unto Himself disciples whom He made apostles, and they going out into the whole world gathered together churches in all places by the preaching of the gospel. And afterward they ordained pastors and teachers in all churches by the commandment of Christ, who by such as succeeded them have taught and governed the church unto this day. Therefore, as God gave unto His ancient people the patriarchs, together with Moses and the prophets, so also to His people under the new covenant He has sent His only-begotten Son, and, with Him, the apostles and teachers of the church.

Furthermore, the ministers of the new covenant are termed by divers names; for they are called apostles, prophets, evangelists, bishops, elders, pastors, and teachers (1 Cor. 12:28; Eph. 4:11). The apostles remained in no certain place, but gathered together divers churches throughout the whole world: which churches when they were once established, there ceased to be any more apostles, and in their places were particular pastors appointed in every church. The prophets in old time did foresee and foretell things to come; and besides did interpret the Scriptures: and such are found some among us at this day. They were called evangelists, which were the authors of the history of the gospel, and were also preachers of the gospel of Christ; as the apostle Paul gives in charge unto Timothy "to fulfill the work of an evangelist" (2 Tim. 4:5). Bishops are the overseers and the watchmen of the church, which distribute food and other necessities to the church. The elders are the ancients, and as it were the senators and fathers of the church, governing it with wholesome counsel. The pastors both keep the Lord's flock and also provide things necessary for it. The teachers do instruct, and teach the true faith and godliness.

Therefore, the church ministers that now are may be called bishops, elders, pastors, and teachers. But in process of time there were many more names of ministers brought into the church. For some were created patriarchs, others archbishops, others suffragans: also metropolitans, archdeacons, deacons, subdeacons, acolytes, exorcists, choristers, porters, and I know not what a rabble besides; cardinals, provosts, and priors; abbots, greater and lesser; orders, higher and lower. But touching all these, we little heed what they have been in time past, or what they are now; it is sufficient for us that, so much as concerns ministers, we have the doctrine of the apostles.

We, therefore, knowing certainly that monks and the orders or sects of them are instituted neither of Christ nor of His apostles, teach that they are so far from being profitable, that they are pernicious and hurtful unto the church of God. For although in former times they were somewhat tolerable (when they lived solitarily, getting their livings with their own hands, and were burdensome to none, but did in all places obey their pastors, even as laymen), yet what kind of men they are now, all the world sees and perceives. They pretend I know not what vows; but they lead a life altogether disagreeing with their vows: so that the very best of them may justly be numbered among those of whom the apostle speaks; "We hear say that there be some among you which walk inordinately, and work not at all, but are busy bodies" (2 Thess. 3:11). Therefore, we have no such in our churches: and besides we teach that they should not be allowed in the churches of Christ.

Furthermore, no man ought to usurp the honor of the ecclesiastical ministry; that is to say, greedily to pluck it to himself by bribes or any evil shifts or of his own accord. But let the ministers of the church be called and chosen by a lawful and ecclesiastical election and vocation: that is to say, let them be chosen religiously of the church, or of those which are appointed thereunto by the church, and that in due order, without any tumult, seditions, or contention. But we must have an eye to this, that not every one that will should be elected, but such men as are fit and have sufficient learning, especially in the Scriptures, and godly eloquence and wise simplicity; to conclude, such men as are of good report for a moderation and honesty of life, according to that apostolic rule, which St. Paul gives in the first epistle to Timothy (3:2–7) and to Titus (1:7–9).

And those which are chosen, let them be ordained of the elders with public prayer and laying on of hands. We here, therefore, condemn all those which run of their own accord, being neither chosen, sent, nor ordained. We do also utterly disallow unfit ministers, and such as are not furnished with gifts requisite for a pastor. In the meantime, we are not ignorant that the innocent simplicity of certain pastors in the primitive church did sometimes more profit the church, than the manifold, exquisite, and nice learning of some others that were over-lofty and high minded. And for this cause we also at this day do not reject the honest simplicity of certain men who yet are not destitute of all knowledge and learning.

The apostles of Christ do term all those which believe in Christ priests, but not in regard of their ministry, but because all the faithful, being made kings and priests, may through Christ, offer up spiritual sacrifices unto God (Ex. 19:6; 1 Peter 2:5, 9; Rev. 1:6). The ministry, then, and the priesthood are things far different one from the other. For the priesthood, as we said even now, is common to all Christians; so is not the ministry. And we have not taken away the ministry of the church because we have thrust the popish priesthood out of the church of Christ. For surely in the new covenant of Christ, there is no longer any such priesthood, as was in the ancient church of the Jews; which had an external anointing, holy garments, and very many ceremonies which were figures and types of Christ: who by His coming fulfilled and abolished them (Heb. 9:10–11). And He Himself remains the only priest forever: and we do not communicate the name of priest to any of the ministers, lest we should detract any thing from Christ. For the Lord Himself has not appointed in the church any priests of the New Testament who, having received authority from the suffragan, may offer up the host every day, that is, the very flesh and the very blood of our Savior, for the quick and the dead; but ministers, which may teach and administer the sacraments.

Paul declares plainly and shortly what we are to think of the ministers of the New Testament, or of the church of Christ, and what we must attribute unto them; "Let a man," says he, "thus account of us, as of the ministers of Christ, and dispensers of the mysteries of God" (1 Cor. 4:1). So that the apostle's mind is that we should esteem ministers, as ministers. Now the apostle calls them υπηρετας, as it were, "under-rowers," which have an eye only to their pilot; that is to say, men that live not unto themselves, nor according to their own will, but for others; to wit, their masters, at whose beck and commandment they ought to be. For the minister of the church is commanded wholly, and in all parts of his duty not to please himself, but to execute that only which he has received in commandment from his Lord. And in this same place, it is expressly declared who is our master, even Christ; to whom the ministers are in subjection in all the functions of their ministry.

And to the end that he might the more fully declare their ministry, he adds further that the ministers of the church are "stewards, and dispensers of the mysteries of God" (1 Cor. 4:1). Now the mysteries of God, Paul in many places and especially in Eph. 3:4, calls "the gospel of Christ." And the sacraments of Christ are also called mysteries by the ancient writers. Therefore, for this purpose are the ministers called, namely to preach the gospel of Christ unto the faithful, and to administer the sacraments. We read also in another place in the gospel of "the faithful and wise servant" that "his Lord set him over his family, to give food unto it in due season" (Luke 12:42). Again, in another place of the gospel, a man goes into a strange country, and, leaving his house, gives unto his servants authority therein, commits to them his substance, and appoints every man his work (Matt. 25:14).

This is now a fit place to speak somewhat also of the power and office of the ministers of the church. And concerning their power some have disputed over busily, and would bring all things, even the very greatest, under their jurisdiction; and that against the commandment of God who forbade unto His disciples all dominion, and highly commended humility (Luke 22:26; Matt. 18:3). Indeed there is one kind of power, which is a mere and absolute power, called the power of right. According to this power, all things in the whole world are subject unto Christ, who is Lord of all: even as He Himself witnesses saying, "All power is given unto me in heaven and in earth" (Matt. 28:18); and again, "I am the first, and the last, and behold I live forever, and I have the keys of hell and of death" (Rev. 1:17–18); also "He hath the key of David, which openeth, and no man shutteth, and shutteth, and no man openeth" (Rev. 3:7).

This power the Lord reserves to Himself and does not transfer it to any other, that He might sit idly by and look on His ministers while they wrought. For Isaiah says, "I will put the key of the house of David upon His shoulder" (Isa. 22:22); and again, "Whose government shall be upon His shoulders" (Isa. 9:6). For He does not lay the government on other men's shoulders, but still keeps and uses His own power, thereby governing all things.

Furthermore, there is another power—that of office; or ministerial power, limited by Him, who has full and absolute power and authority. And this is more like a service than a dominion. For we see that a master gives unto the steward of his house authority and power over his house, and for that cause delivers to him his keys that he may admit or exclude such as his master will have admitted or excluded. According to this power the minister does, by his office, that which the Lord has commanded him to do: and the Lord ratifies and confirms that which he does, and will have the deeds of His ministers acknowledged and esteemed as His own deeds. Unto which end are those speeches in the gospel: "I will give unto thee the keys of the kingdom of heaven; and whatsoever thou bindest, or loosest in earth, shall be bound, or loosed in heaven" (Matt. 16:19). Again "Whose sins soever ye remit, they shall be remitted: and whose sins soever ye retain, they shall be retained" (John 20:23). But if the minister deals not in all things as his Lord has commanded him, but passes the limits and bounds of faith, then the Lord makes void that which he does. Wherefore the ecclesiastical power of the ministers of the church is that function whereby they do indeed govern the church of God; but yet so do all things in the church, as He has prescribed in His Word: which thing being so done, the faithful esteem them as done of the Lord Himself. But touching the keys, we have spoken somewhat before.

Now the power or function that is given to the ministers of the church is the same and alike in all. Certainly, in the beginning, the bishops or elders did, with a common consent and labor, govern the church; no man lifted up himself above another, none usurped greater power or authority over his fellow bishops. For they remembered the words of the Lord, "He which will be the chiefest among you, let him be your servant" (Luke 22:26); they kept in themselves by humility, and did mutually aid one another in the government and preservation of the church.

Notwithstanding, for order's sake, some one of the ministers called the assembly together, propounded unto the assembly the matters to be consulted, gathered together the voices or sentences of the rest, and, to be brief, as much as lay in him, provided that there might arise no confusion. So did St. Peter, as we read in the Acts of the Apostles (11:4–18), who yet, for all that, neither was above the rest nor had greater authority than the rest. Very true, therefore, is that saying of Cyprian the Martyr, in his book *De Simplicitate Clericorum*: "The same doubtless were the rest of the apostles that Peter was, having an equal fellowship with him both in honor and power: but the beginning hereof proceeds from unity, to signify unto us that there is but one church."

St. Jerome also, in his *Commentary upon the Epistle of Paul to Titus*, has a saying not much unlike this: "Before that, by the instinct of the devil, there arose parties in religion, the churches were governed by the common advice of the elders: but after that every one thought that those whom he had baptized were his own and not Christ's, it was decreed that one of the elders should be chosen and set over the rest, who should have the care of the whole church laid upon him, and by whose means all schisms should be removed." Yet Jerome does not avow this as an order set down of God: for straightway after he adds, "Even as the elders knew, by the continual custom of the church, that they were subject to him that is set over them: so the bishops must know that they are above the elders, rather by custom, than by the prescript rule of God's truth, and that they ought to have the government of the church in common with them." Thus far Jerome. Now, therefore, no man can forbid by any right that we may return to the old appointment of God; and rather receive that than the custom devised by men.

The offices of the ministers are divers: yet notwithstanding most men restrain them to two in which all the rest are comprehended; to the teaching of the gospel of Christ, and to the lawful administration of the sacraments. For it is the duty of the ministers to gather together a holy assembly, therein to expound the Word of God and also to apply the general doctrine to the state and use of the church; to the end that the doctrine which they teach may profit the hearers and may build up the faithful. The minister's duty I say is to teach the unlearned and to exhort, yes and to urge them to go forward in the way of the Lord, who stand still or linger and go slowly on; moreover, to comfort and to strengthen those which are fainthearted and to arm them against the manifold temptations of Satan; to rebuke offenders; to bring them home that go astray; to raise them up that are fallen; to convince the gainsayer; to chase away the wolf from the Lord's flock; to rebuke wickedness and wicked men, wisely and severely; not to wink at, nor to pass over great wickedness. And besides, to administer the sacraments, and to commend the right use of them, and to prepare all men by wholesome doctrine to receive them; to keep together all the faithful in an holy unity; and to encounter schisms. To conclude, to catechize the ignorant, to commend the necessity of the poor to the church, to visit and instruct those that are sick or entangled with divers temptations, and so to keep them in the way of life. Besides all this, to provide diligently that there be public prayers and supplications made in time of necessity, together with fasting, that is, a holy abstinence; and most carefully to look to those things which belong to the tranquility, peace, and safety of the church.

And to the end that the minister may perform all these things the better, and with more ease, it is required in him that he is one that fears God, prays diligently, gives himself much to the reading of the Scripture and in all things and at all times, is watchful and shows forth a good example unto all men of holiness of life. And seeing there must necessarily be discipline in the church, and that, among the ancient fathers excommunication was in use, and there were ecclesiastical judgments among the people of God, wherein this discipline was exercised by godly men; it belongs also to the minister's duty, for the edifying of the church, to moderate this discipline, according to the condition of the time and public estate, and according to necessity. Wherein this rule is always to be held, that "all things ought to be done to edification, decently, and honestly" (1 Cor. 14:40) without any oppression or tumult. For the apostle witnesses that "power was given to him of God, to edify and not to destroy" (2 Cor. 10:8). And the Lord Himself forbad the cockle to be plucked up in the Lord's field because there would be danger lest the wheat also should be plucked up with it (Matt. 13:29).

But as for the error of the Donatists, we do here utterly detest it; who esteem the doctrine and administration of the sacraments to be either effectual or not effectual according to the good or evil life of the ministers. For we know that the voice of Christ is to be heard, though it is out of the mouths of evil ministers; forasmuch as the Lord Himself said, "Do as they command you, but according to their works do ye not" (Matt. 23:3). We know that the sacraments are sanctified by the institution and through the word of Christ; and that they are effectual to the godly, although they are administered by ungodly ministers. Of which matter Augustine, that blessed servant of God, did reason diversely out of the Scriptures against the Donatists.

Yet notwithstanding there ought to be a straight discipline among the ministers: for there should be diligent inquiry in the synods touching the life and doctrine of the ministers: those that offend should be rebuked of the elders and be brought into the way, if they are not past recovery; or else be deposed, and, as wolves, be driven from the Lord's flock by the true pastors, if they are incurable. For if they are false teachers, they are not to be tolerated. Neither do we disapprove of general councils, if they are taken up according to the example of the apostles, to the salvation of the church, and not to the destruction thereof.

The faithful ministers also are worthy (as good workmen) of their reward; neither do they offend when they receive stipends, and all things that are necessary for themselves and their family. For the apostle shows that these things are for just cause offered by the church, and received of the ministers in 1 Cor. 9:14 and in 1 Tim. 5:17–18 and in other places also. The Anabaptists likewise are confuted by this apostolic doctrine, who condemn and rail upon those ministers which live upon the ministry.

Chapter 19. Of the Sacraments of the Church of Christ

God, even from the beginning, added unto the preaching of the Word His sacraments, or sacramental signs, in His church. And this the Holy Scripture plainly testifies. Sacraments are mystical symbols, or holy rites, or sacred actions, ordained of God Himself, consisting of His Word, of outward signs, and of things signified; whereby He keeps in continual memory, and recalls to mind in His church His great benefits bestowed upon man; and whereby He seals up His promises and outwardly represents, and, as it were, offers unto our sight, those things which inwardly He performs unto us, and therewith strengthens and increases our faith through the working of God's Spirit in our hearts; lastly, whereby He separates us from all other people and religions and consecrates and binds us wholly unto Himself, and gives us to understand what He requires of us.

These sacraments are either of the old church or of the new. The sacraments of the old were circumcision and the Pascal Lamb, which was offered up; under which name, reference is made to the sacrifices which were in use from the beginning of the world. The sacraments of the new church are baptism and the Supper of the Lord. Some there are which reckon seven sacraments of the new church, of which number we grant that repentance, matrimony, and the ordination of ministers (we mean not the popish, but the apostolic ordination) are very profitable ordinances of God, but not sacraments. As for confirmation and extreme unction, they are mere devices of men which the church may very well want, without any damage or discommodity at all: and, therefore, we do not have them in our churches because there are certain things in them which we can by no means permit. As for that merchandise which the Roman prelates use in ministering their sacraments, we utterly abhor it.

The author and institutor of all sacraments is not any man, but God alone: for men can by no means ordain sacraments because they belong to the worship of God, and it is not for man to appoint and prescribe a service of God, but to embrace and retain that which is taught unto him by the Lord. Besides the sacramental signs have God's promises annexed to them, which necessarily require faith: now faith rests itself only upon the Word of God; and the Word of God is resembled to writings or letters, the sacraments to seals which the Lord alone sets to His own letters.

And as the Lord is the author of the sacraments, so He continually works in that church, where they are rightly used; so that the faithful, when they receive them of the ministers, do know that the Lord works in His own ordinance, and, therefore, they receive them as from the hand of God: and the minister's faults (if there be any notorious in them) cannot hurt them, seeing they acknowledge the goodness of the sacraments to depend upon the ordinance of the Lord. For which cause they put a difference in the administration of the sacraments, between the Lord Himself and His minister; confessing that the substance of the sacraments is given them of the Lord, and the outward signs by the ministers of the Lord.

But the principal thing which in all the sacraments is offered of the Lord, and chiefly regarded of the godly of all ages (which some have called the substance and matter of the sacraments) is Christ our Savior: that only sacrifice (Heb. 10:12), and that Lamb of God slain from the beginning of the world (Rev. 13:8), that rock also, of which all our fathers drank (1 Cor. 10:4) by whom all the elect are circumcised with the circumcision made without hands through the Holy Spirit (Col. 2:11–12) and are washed from all their sins (Rev. 1:5), and are nourished with the very body and blood of Christ unto eternal life (John 6:54).

Now, in respect of that which is the chief thing, and the very matter and substance of the sacraments, the sacraments of both the Testaments are equal. For Christ, the only Mediator and Savior of the faithful, is the chief thing and substance in them both: one and the same God is author of them both: they were given unto both churches as signs and seals of the grace and promises of God; which should call to mind and renew the memory of God's great benefits to them, and should distinguish the faithful from all the religions in the world; lastly, which should be received spiritually by faith, and should bind the receivers unto the church and admonish them of their duty. In these, I say, and such like things, the sacraments of both churches are not unequal, although in the outward signs they are diverse.

And indeed we do yet put a greater difference between them: for ours are more firm and durable as those which are not to be changed to the end of the world. Again, ours testify that the substance and promise is already fulfilled and performed in Christ, whereas the other did only signify that they should be fulfilled. And again ours are more simple and not so painful, not so sumptuous, nor so full of ceremonies. Moreover they belong to a greater people that is dispersed through the face of the whole earth: and because they are more excellent and do by the Spirit of God stir up in us a greater measure of faith, therefore, a more plentiful measure of the Spirit follows them.

But now, since Christ the true Messiah is exhibited unto us and the abundance of grace is poured forth upon the people of the New Testament, the sacraments of the Old Law are surely abrogated and ceased; and in their stead the sacraments of the New Testament are placed: namely, for circumcision, baptism, and for the Pascal Lamb and sacrifices, the Supper of the Lord.

And as in the old church the sacraments consisted of the Word, the sign and the thing signified, so even at this day they are composed, as it were, of the same parts. For the Word of God makes them sacraments, which before were not: for they are consecrated by the Word and declared to be sanctified by Him who first ordained them. To sanctify or consecrate a thing is to dedicate it unto God and unto holy uses; that is, to take it from the common and ordinary use and to appoint it to some holy use. For the signs that are in the sacraments are drawn from common use; things external and visible. As in baptism, the outward sign is the element of water, and that visible washing which is done by the minister. But the thing signified is regeneration and the cleansing from sins. Likewise in the Lord's Supper, the outward sign is bread and wine, taken from things commonly used for meat and drink. But the thing signified is the body of Christ which was given, and His blood which was shed for us, and the communion of the body and blood of the Lord.

Wherefore the water, bread, and wine, considered in their own nature, and out of this holy use and institution of the Lord, are only that which they are called and which we find them to be. But let the Word of God be added to them together with invocation upon His holy name, and the renewing of their first institution and sanctification, and then these signs are consecrated and declared to be sanctified by Christ. For Christ's first institution and consecration of the sacraments stands yet in force in the church of God, in such sort that they which celebrate the sacraments no otherwise than the Lord Himself from the beginning has appointed, have still even to this day, the use and benefit of that first and most excellent consecration. And for this cause in the administration of the sacraments, the very words of Christ are repeated.

And forasmuch as we learn out of the Word of God that these signs were appointed unto another end and use than commonly they are used, therefore, we teach that they now, in this their holy use, take upon them the names of things signified, and are not still called bare water, bread, or wine: but that the water is called "regeneration, and washing of the new birth" (Titus 3:5), and the bread and wine "the body and blood of the Lord" (1 Cor. 10:16), or the pledges and sacraments of His body and blood. Not that the signs are turned into the things signified, or cease to be that which in their own nature they are (for then they could not be sacraments which should consist only of the thing signified and have no signs); but, therefore, do the signs bear the names of the things because they are mystical tokens of holy things, and because the signs and the things signified are sacramentally joined together: joined together I say, or united by a mystical signification, and by the purpose and will of Him who first instituted them. For the water, bread, and wine are not common, but holy signs. And He that instituted water in baptism did not institute it with that mind and purpose, that the faithful should only be dipped in the water of baptism; and He which commanded the bread to be eaten and the wine to be drunk in the Supper did not mean that the faithful should only receive bread and wine without any further mystery, as they eat bread at home in their own houses: but that they should spiritually be partakers of the things signified and by faith be truly purged from their sins and be partakers of Christ also.

And, therefore, we cannot allow of them which attribute the consecration of the sacraments to I know not what syllables; to the rehearsal of certain words pronounced by him that is consecrated, and that has an intent of consecrating; or to some other accidental things, which are not left unto us either by the word or by the example of Christ or His apostles. We also dislike the doctrine of those that speak no otherwise of the sacraments than of common signs, not sanctified, nor effectual. We condemn them also, who, because of the invisible things despise the visible and think the signs superfluous because they already enjoy the things themselves: such were the Messalians, as it is recorded. We disapprove their doctrine also who teach that grace and the things signified are to be so tied to and included in the signs, that whosoever outwardly receives the signs must necessarily inwardly participate in the grace and in the things signified, whatever manner of men they may be.

Notwithstanding, as we esteem not the goodness of the sacraments by the worthiness or unworthiness of the ministers, so likewise we do not weigh them by the condition of the recipients. For we know that the goodness of the sacraments depends upon the faithfulness or truth and the mere goodness of God. For even as God's Word remains the true Word of God, wherein not only bare words are uttered when it is preached, but there withal the things signified by the words are offered of God, although the wicked and unbelievers hear and understand the words, yet do not enjoy the things signified because they receive them not by a true faith: even so, the sacraments consisting of the Word, the signs, and the things signified, continue true and perfect sacraments not only because they are holy things, but also that God also offers the things signified; however unbelievers do not receive the things which are offered. This comes to pass not by any fault in God, the author and offerer of them; but by the fault of men, who receive them without faith and unlawfully: "whose unbelief cannot make the truth of God of none effect" (Rom. 3:3).

Now forasmuch as in the beginning, where we showed what the sacraments were, we did also by the way set down to what end they were ordained, it will not be necessary to trouble ourselves with repeating anything which has been already handled. Next, therefore, in order, it remains to speak severally of the sacraments of the new church.

Chapter 20. Of Holy Baptism

Baptism was instituted and consecrated by God; and the first that baptized was John who dipped Christ in the water in Jordan. From Him it came to the apostles, who also baptized with water. The Lord in plain words commanded them "to preach the gospel, and to baptize in the name of the Father, the Son, and the Holy Ghost" (Matt. 28:19). And Peter also, when divers demanded of him what they ought to do, said to them in the Acts, "Let every one of you be baptized in the name of Jesus Christ, for the remission of sins, and ye shall receive the gift of the Holy Ghost" (2:38). Whereupon baptism is called of some a sign of initiation for God's people, as that whereby the elected of God are consecrated unto God.

There is but one baptism in the church of God: for it is sufficient to be once baptized or consecrated unto God. For baptism once received continues all a man's life and is a perpetual sealing of our adoption unto us. For to be baptized in the name of Christ is to be enrolled, entered, and received into the covenant and family, and so into the inheritance of the sons of God; yes and in this life to be called after the name of God, that is to say, to be called a son of God; to be purged also from the filthiness of sins and to be endued with the manifold grace of God, to lead a new and innocent life. Baptism, therefore, calls to mind and keeps in remembrance the great benefit of God performed to mankind. For we are all born in the pollution of sin and are the sons of wrath. But God, who is rich in mercy, freely purges us from our sins by the blood of His Son, and in Him adopts us to be His sons, and by a holy covenant joins us to Himself, and enriches us with divers gifts, that we might live a new life. All these things are sealed unto us in baptism. For inwardly we are regenerated, purified, and renewed of God through the Holy Spirit: and outwardly we receive the sealing of most notable gifts by the water; by which also those great benefits are represented, and, as it were, set before our eyes to be looked upon. And, therefore, are we baptized, that is, washed and sprinkled with visible water. For the water makes clean that which is filthy, and refreshes and cools the bodies that are frail and faint. And the grace of God deals in like manner with the soul; and that invisibly and spiritually.

Moreover by the sacrament of baptism, God separates us from all other religions and nations, and consecrates us a peculiar people to Himself. We, therefore, by being baptized, confess our faith and are bound to give unto God obedience, mortification of the flesh, and newness of life; yes, and we are enlisted as soldiers for the holy warfare of Christ, that all our life long we should fight against the world, Satan, and our own flesh. Moreover, we are baptized into one body of the church that we may well agree with all the members of the church in the same religion and mutual duties.

We believe that is, of all others, the most perfect form of baptism, wherein Christ was baptized, and which the rest of the apostles used in baptism. Those things, therefore, which by man's device were added afterwards and used in the church, we think unnecessary to the perfection of baptism. Of which kind is exorcism and the use of lights, oil, salt, spittle and such other things; as namely, that baptism is twice every year consecrated with divers ceremonies. For we believe that the baptism of the church, which is but one, was sanctified in God's first institution of it, and is consecrated by the Word, and is now of full force, by and for the first blessing of God upon it.

We teach that baptism should not be ministered in the church by women or midwives. For Paul excludes women from ecclesiastical callings: but baptism belongs to ecclesiastical offices. We condemn the Anabaptists, who deny that young infants, born of faithful parents, are to be baptized. For according to the doctrine of the gospel "theirs is the kingdom of God" (Luke 18:16); and they are written in the covenant of God (Acts 3:25). Why then should not the sign of the covenant be given to them? Why should they not be consecrated by holy baptism who are God's peculiar people and in the church of God? We condemn also the Anabaptists in the rest of their opinions which they peculiarly hold against the Word of God. We, therefore, are not Anabaptists, neither do we agree with them in any point that is theirs.

Chapter 21. Of the Holy Supper of the Lord

The Supper of the Lord (which is also called the Lord's Table, and the Eucharist, that is, a thanksgiving) is, therefore, commonly called a Supper because it was instituted of Christ in His last Supper, and as yet represents the same, and in it the faithful are spiritually fed and nourished. For the author of the Supper of the Lord is not an angel or man, but the very Son of God, our Lord Jesus Christ, who first of all consecrated it to His church. And the same blessing and consecration still remains among all those who celebrate no other but that very Supper which the Lord instituted; and at that recite the words of the Supper of the Lord, and in all things look unto Christ only by a true faith; at whose hands, as it were, they receive that which they do receive by the ministry of the ministers of the church. The Lord by this sacred rite would have that great benefit to be kept in fresh remembrance which He performed for mankind; to wit, that by giving up His body to death and shedding His blood, He has forgiven us all our sins and redeemed us from eternal death and the power of the devil, and now feeds us with His flesh, and gives us His blood to drink: which things, being apprehended spiritually by a true faith, nourish us to life everlasting. And this so great a benefit is renewed so oft as the Supper is celebrated. For the Lord said, "Do this in remembrance of me" (Luke 22:19).

By this holy Supper also it is sealed unto us that the very body of Christ was truly given up for us and His blood shed for the remission of our sins, lest our faith might somewhat waver. And this is outwardly represented unto us by the minister in the sacrament after a visible manner, and, as it were, laid before our eyes to be seen, which is inwardly in the soul invisibly performed by the Holy Ghost. Outwardly bread is offered by the minister and the words of the Lord are heard: "Receive, eat, this is my body; take it, and divide it amongst you: drink ye all of this, this is my blood" (Matt. 26:26–28; Luke 22:17–20). Therefore, the faithful receive that which is given by the minister of the Lord and eat the bread of the Lord, and drink of the Lord's cup. But yet, by the working of Christ, through the Holy Ghost, they receive also the flesh and blood of the Lord and feed on them to life everlasting. For the flesh and blood of Christ is true meat and drink unto everlasting life: yes Christ Himself, in that He was delivered for us, and is our Savior, is that special thing and substance of the Supper; and, therefore, we suffer nothing to be put in His place.

But that it may the better and more plainly be understood how the flesh and blood of Christ are the meat and drink of the faithful, and are received by the faithful to life everlasting, we will add moreover these four things.

Eating is of divers sorts: for there is a corporal eating, whereby meat is taken into a man's mouth, chewed with the teeth, and swallowed down into the belly. After this manner did the Capernaites in times past think that they should eat the flesh of the Lord: but they are confuted by Him (John 6:30–63). For as the flesh of Christ cannot be eaten bodily without great wickedness and cruelty, so is it not meat for the belly, as all men do confess. We, therefore, disapprove that canon in the pope's decrees, *Ego Berengarius* (*De Consecrat.*, dist. 2). For neither did godly antiquity believe, neither yet do we believe that the body of Christ can be eaten corporally and essentially with a bodily mouth.

There is also a spiritual eating of Christ's body; not such a one whereby it may be thought that the very meat is changed into the spirit, but whereby (the Lord's body and blood remaining in their own essence and property) those things are spiritually communicated unto us, not after a corporal, but after a spiritual manner, through the Holy Ghost, who applies and bestows upon us those things (to wit, remission of sins, deliverance and life everlasting) which are prepared for us by the flesh and blood of our Lord, given for us: so that Christ now lives in us and we live in Him; and causes us to apprehend Him by true faith to this end, that He may become unto us such a spiritual meat and drink, that is to say, our life. For even as corporal meat and drink not only refresh and strengthen our bodies, but also keep them in life; even so the flesh of Christ delivered for us and His blood shed for us, do not only refresh and strengthen our souls, but also preserves them alive, not so far as they are corporally eaten and drunken, but so far as they are communicated unto us spiritually by the Spirit of God: the Lord saying, "The bread which I will give is my flesh, which I will give for the life of the world" (John 6:51); also "The flesh (to wit, corporally eaten) profiteth nothing, it is the Spirit which giveth life: and the words which I speak to you, are Spirit and life" (John 6:63).

And as we must by eating receive the meat into our bodies to the end that it may work in us and show its efficacy in us (because, while it is without us, it profits us not at all); even so it is necessary that we receive Christ by faith, that He may be made ours and that He may live in us and we in Him. For He says, "I am the bread of life; He that cometh to me shall not hunger, and He

337

that believeth in me, shall not thirst any more" (John 6:35); and also, "He that eateth me, shall live through me; and He abideth in me, and I in him" (John 6:56).

By all which it appears manifestly that by spiritual meat we do not mean any imaginary thing, but the very body of our Lord Jesus given to us; which yet is received of the faithful not corporally, but spiritually by faith: in which point we do wholly follow the doctrine of our Lord and Savior Christ in the 6th of John. And this eating of the flesh and drinking of the blood of the Lord is so necessary to salvation that without it no man can be saved. This spiritual eating and drinking is also without the Supper of the Lord; even so often as and where ever a man believes in Christ. To which purpose that sentence of St. Augustine happily belongs: "Why dost thou prepare thy teeth and belly? Believe, and thou hast eaten."

Besides that former spiritual eating, there is a sacramental eating of the body of the Lord; whereby the faithful man not only is partaker spiritually and internally of the true body and blood of the Lord; but also by coming to the Table of the Lord outwardly receives the visible sacraments of the body and blood of the Lord. It is true that the faithful man, by believing, before received the food that gives life, and still receives the same, but yet, when he receives the sacrament, he receives something more. For he goes on in continual communication of the body and blood of the Lord, and his faith is daily more and more kindled, more strengthened and refreshed by the spiritual nourishment. For while we live, faith has continual increasings: and he that outwardly receives the sacraments with a true faith, the same not only receives the sign, but also enjoys (as we have said) the thing itself. Moreover the same man obeys the Lord's institution and commandment, and with a joyful mind gives thanks for his and the redemption of all mankind; and makes a faithful remembrance of the Lord's death, and witnesses the same before the church, of which body he is a member. This also is sealed to those which receive the sacrament, that the body of the Lord was given and His blood shed, not only for men in general, but particularly for every faithful communicant whose meat and drink He is, to life everlasting.

But as for him that without faith comes to this holy Table of the Lord, he is made partaker of the sacrament only; but the matter of the sacrament from whence comes life and salvation, he receives not at all and such men do unworthily eat of the Lord's Table. "Now they which do unworthily eat of the Lord's bread and drink of the Lord's cup, they are guilty of the body and blood of the Lord, and they eat and drink it to their judgment" (1 Cor. 11:26–29). For as they do not approach with true faith, they do despite unto the death of Christ, and, therefore, eat and drink condemnation to themselves.

We do not, therefore, so join the body of the Lord and His blood with the bread and wine, as though we thought that the bread is the body of Christ more than after a sacramental manner; or that the body of Christ lies hidden corporally under the bread, so as it ought to be worshipped under the form of bread; or yet that whoever he is which receives the sign, he receives the thing itself. The body of Christ is in the heavens, at the right hand of His Father: and, therefore, our hearts are to be lifted up on high, and not to be fixed on the bread, neither is the Lord to be worshipped in the bread; though notwithstanding the Lord is not absent from His church when they celebrate the Supper. The sun, being absent from us in the heavens, is yet notwithstanding present among us effectually: how much more Christ, the Sun of Righteousness, though in body He is absent from us in the heavens, yet is present among us, not corporally, but spiritually, by His lively operation; and so as He Himself promised in His last Supper, to be present among us (John 14–16). Whereupon it follows that we have not the Supper without Christ, and yet that we have meanwhile an unbloody and mystical Supper, even as all antiquity called it.

Moreover, we are admonished in the celebration of the Supper of the Lord to be mindful of the body whereof we are made members; and that, therefore, we are at concord with all our brethren that we live holily and not pollute ourselves with wickedness and strange religions; but persevering in the true faith to the end of our life give diligence to excel in holiness of life.

It is, therefore, very requisite that, purposing to come to the Supper of the Lord, we do try ourselves according to the commandment of the apostle: first, with what faith we are endued, whether we believe that Christ is come to save sinners and to call them to repentance, and whether each man believes that he is in the number of them that, being delivered by Christ, are saved; and whether he has purposed to change his wicked life, to live holily, and persevere through God's assistance in true religion and in concord with his brethren, and to give worthy thanks to God for his delivery.

We think that rite, manner, or form of the Supper to be the most simple and excellent which comes nearest to the first institution of the Lord and to the apostles' doctrine: which consists in declaring the Word of God, in godly prayers, in the action itself that the Lord used, and the repeating of it; in the eating of the Lord's body and drinking of His blood; in the wholesome remembrance of the Lord's death and faithful giving of thanks; and in a holy fellowship in the union of the body of the church.

We, therefore, disapprove them which have taken from the faithful one part of the sacrament, to wit, the Lord's cup. For these do very grievously offend against the institution of the Lord, who says, "Drink all of you of this" (Matt. 26:27), which He did not so plainly say of the bread. What manner of mass it was that the fathers used, whether it were tolerable, or intolerable, we do not now dispute. But this we say freely, that the Mass which is now used throughout the Roman Church, which, for brevity's sake, we will not now particularly recite, for many and most just causes is quite abolished out of our churches. Truly we could not like it because of a most wholesome action, they have made a vain spectacle; also because it is made a meritorious matter and is said for money; likewise because in it the priest is said to make the very body of the Lord, and to offer the same really, even for the remission of the sins of the quick and the dead. Add this also; that they do it for the honor, worship, and reverence of the saints in heaven.

Chapter 22. Of Holy and Ecclesiastical Meetings

Although it is lawful for all men privately at home to read the Holy Scriptures and by instruction to edify one another in the true religion: yet that the Word of God may be lawfully preached to the people, and prayers and supplications publicly made; also that the sacraments may be lawfully ministered, and that collections may be made for the poor and to defray all necessary charges, or to supply the wants of the church; it is very needful there should be holy meetings and ecclesiastical assemblies. For it is manifest that in the apostolic church and primitive church, there were such assemblies frequented of godly men. So many then as do despise them and separate themselves from them are condemners of true religion and are to be compelled by the pastors and godly magistrates to cease stubbornly to separate and absent themselves from sacred assemblies.

Now ecclesiastical assemblies must not be hidden and secret, but public and common, unless persecution by the enemies of Christ and the church will not allow them to be public: for we know what manner of assemblies the primitive church had heretofore in secret corners, being under the tyranny of Roman emperors. But let those places where the faithful meet together be decent and in all respects fit for God's church. Therefore, let houses be chosen for that purpose, or churches that are large and fair, so that they may be purged from all such things as do not become the church. And let all things be ordered most meet for comeliness, necessity, and godly decency, that nothing may be wanting which is requisite for rites and orders and the necessary uses of the church.

And as we believe that God does not dwell in temples made with hands, so we know that by reason of the Word of God and holy exercises therein celebrated, places dedicated to God and His worship are not profane, but holy; and that, therefore, such as are conversant in them ought to behave themselves reverently and modestly as those who are in a sacred place in the presence of God and His holy angels. All excess of apparel, therefore, is to be abandoned from churches and places where Christians meet in prayer, together with all pride and whatever else does not become Christian humility, discipline, and modesty. For the true ornament of churches does not consist in ivory, gold, and precious stones; but in the sobriety, godliness, and virtues of those which are in the church. "Let all things be done comely and orderly" in the church (1 Cor. 14:26): to conclude "Let all things be done to edifying" (v. 40). Therefore, let all strange tongues keep silence in the holy assemblies, and let all things be uttered in the vulgar tongue which is understood of all men in the company.

Chapter 23. Of the Prayers of the Church, of Singing, and of Canonical Hours

It is true that a man may lawfully pray privately in any tongue that he understands, but public prayers ought in the holy assemblies to be made in the vulgar tongue or such a language as is known to all. Let all the prayers of the faithful be poured forth to God alone, through the mediation of Christ only, out of a true faith and pure love. As for invocation of saints or using them as intercessors to entreat for us, the priesthood of our Lord Christ, and true religion, will not permit us. Prayer must be made for magistracy, for kings and all that are placed in authority, for ministers of the church, and for all necessities of churches; and specially in any calamity of the church, prayer must be made, both privately and publicly, without ceasing.

Moreover we must pray willingly, and not by constraint, nor for any reward: neither must we superstitiously tie prayer to any place, as though it were not lawful to pray but in the church. There is no necessity that public prayers should be in form and in time the same or alike in all churches. Let all churches use their liberty. Socrates, in his *History*, says, "In any country or nation wheresoever, you shall not find two churches which do wholly agree in prayer." The authors of this difference I think were those which had the government of the churches in all ages. Thus, if any agrees, it deserves great commendation and is to be imitated of others.

Besides this, there must be a mean and measure, as in every other thing, so also in public prayers that they are not over long and tedious. Let, therefore, the most time be given to teaching the gospel in such holy assemblies: and let there be diligent heed taken that the people in the assemblies not be wearied with over long prayers so that, when the preaching of the gospel should be heard, they through wearisomeness either desire to go forth themselves or to have the assembly wholly dismissed. For unto such the sermons seem to be over long, which otherwise are brief enough. Yes, and the preachers ought to keep a mean.

Likewise the singing in sacred assemblies ought to be moderated where it is in use. That song which they call Gregory's has many gross things in it: wherefore it is upon good cause rejected of ours and of all other Reformed churches. If there are any churches which have faithful prayer in good manners and no singing at all, they are not, therefore, to be condemned: for all churches do not have the commodity and opportunity of singing. And it is certain by testimonies of antiquity that, as the custom of singing has been very ancient in the Eastern churches, so it was long ere it was received in the Western churches.

In ancient times, there were no such things as canonical hours; that is, known prayers framed for certain hours in the day and therein chanted or oft repeated, as the manner of the papists is: which may be proved by many of their lessons appointed in their hours, and divers other arguments. Moreover they have many absurd things (that I say no more) and, therefore, are well omitted by our churches, which have brought in their stead matters more wholesome for the whole church of God.

Chapter 24. Of Holy Days, Fasts, and the Choice of Meats

Although religion is not tied unto time, yet it cannot be planted and exercised without a due dividing and allotting out of time unto it. Every church, therefore, chooses unto itself a certain time for public prayers, and for preaching of the gospel, and for the celebration of the sacraments: and it is not lawful for everyone to overthrow this appointment of the church at his own pleasure. For except some due time and leisure were allotted to the outward exercise of religion, without doubt men would be quite drawn from it by their own affairs. In regard hereof, we see that in the ancient churches, there were not only certain set hours in the week appointed for meetings, but that also even for the Lord's Day itself, ever since the apostles' time, was consecrated to religious exercises and unto a holy rest; which also is now very well observed of our churches for the worship of God and increase of charity. Yet herein we give no place unto the Jewish observation of the day or to any superstitions. For we do not account one day to be holier than another, nor think that mere rest is of itself liked of God. Besides we do celebrate and keep the Lord's Day, and not the Sabbath, and that with a free observation.

Moreover, if the churches do religiously celebrate the memory of the Lord's nativity, circumcision, passion, resurrection, and of His ascension into heaven, and sending the Holy Ghost upon His disciples, according to Christian liberty, we do very well approve of it. But as for festival days ordained to men or departed saints, we cannot allow them. For indeed such feasts must be referred to the first table of the Law and belong peculiarly unto God. To conclude, these festival days, which are appointed to saints and abrogated of us, have in them many gross things, unprofitable and not to be tolerated. In the meantime, we confess that the remembrance of saints in due time and place may be to good use and profit commended unto the people in sermons, and the holy examples of holy men set before their eyes to be imitated of all.

Now, the more sharply that the church of Christ accuses surfeiting, drunkenness, and all kind of lusts and intemperance, so much the more earnestly does it commend unto us Christian fasting. For fasting is nothing else but the abstinence and temperance of the godly, and watching and chastising of our flesh taken up for the present necessity, whereby we are humbled before God and withdraw from the flesh those things whereby it is cherished, to the end it may the more willingly and easily obey the Spirit. Wherefore they do not fast at all that have no regard of those things, but do imagine that they fast if they stuff their bellies once a day, and for a set or prescribed time abstain from certain meats, thinking that by this very work wrought they please God and do a good work. Fasting is a help of the prayers of the saints and of all virtues: but the fasts wherein the Jews fasted from meat and not from wickedness, pleased God not at all, as we may see in the books of the prophets.

Now fasting is either public or private. In old time they celebrated public fasts in troublesome times and in the afflictions of the church: wherein they abstained altogether from meat unto the evening and bestowed all that time in holy prayers, the worship of God and repentance. These differed little from mournings and lamentations; and of these there is often mention made in the prophets, and especially in the second chapter of Joel. Such a fast should be kept at this day when the church is in distress. Private fasts are used of every one of us, according as every one feels the Spirit weakened in him: for so far forth he withdraws that which might cherish and strengthen the flesh. All fasts ought to proceed from a free and willing spirit and such a one as is truly humbled, and not framed to win applause and liking of men, much less to the end that a man might merit righteousness by them. But let everyone fast to this end that he may deprive the flesh of that which would cherish it and that he may the more zealously serve God.

The fast of Lent has testimony from antiquity but none out of the apostles' writings; and, therefore, ought not, nor cannot, be imposed on the faithful. It is certain that in old time there were divers manners and uses of this fast; whereupon Irenaeus, a most ancient writer, says, "Some think that this fast should be observed one day only, others two days, but others more, and some forty days. Which variety of keeping this fast began not now in our times, but long before us; by those as I suppose which, not simply holding that which was delivered to them from the beginning, fell shortly after into another custom, either through negligence or ignorance." Moreover, Socrates, the writer of the *History*, says, "Because no ancient record is found concerning this matter, I think the apostles left this to every man's own judgment, that every one might work that which is good without fear or constraint."

Now as concerning the choice of meats, we suppose that in fasting all that should be taken from the flesh whereby the flesh is made more lusty, wherein it most immoderately delights and whereby it is most of all pampered, whether they be fish, spices, dainties, or excellent wines. Otherwise we know that all the creatures of God were made for the use and service of men. All things which God made are good (Gen. 1:31) and are to be used in the fear of God and with due moderation, without putting any difference between them. For the apostle says, "To the pure, all things are pure" (Titus 1:15); and also, "Whatsoever is sold in the shambles, eat ye, and ask no question, for conscience' sake" (1 Cor. 10:25). The same apostle calls the doctrine of those which teach to abstain from meats, "the doctrine of devils" for "God created meats to be received of the faithful and such as know the truth with thanksgiving because whatsoever God has created, it is good, and is not to be refused, if it is received with giving of thanks" (1 Tim. 4:1, 3–4). The same apostle to the Colossians reproves those which by an overmuch abstinence will get into themselves an opinion of holiness (Col. 2:20–23). Therefore, we altogether dislike the Tatians, and the Encratites, and all the disciples of Eustathius, against whom the Synod of Gangra was assembled.

Chapter 25. Of Catechizing and of Comforting and Visiting the Sick

The Lord enjoined His ancient people to take great care and diligence in instructing the youth well, even from their infancy; and moreover commanded expressly in His law that they should teach them and declare the mystery of the sacraments unto them. Now, forasmuch as it is evident by the writings of the evangelists and apostles that God has no less care of the youth of His new people (seeing He says, "Suffer little children to come unto me, for of such is the kingdom of heaven," Matt. 19:14); therefore, the pastors act very wisely, which diligently and regularly catechize their youth, laying the first grounds of faith and faithfully teaching the rudiments of our religion by expounding the Ten Commandments, the Apostles' Creed, the Lord's Prayer, and the doctrine of the sacraments with other like principles and chief heads of our religion. And here let the church perform her faithfulness and diligence in bringing the children to be catechized, as being desirous and glad to have her children well instructed.

Seeing that men do never lie open to more grievous temptations than when they are exercised with infirmities or else are sick and brought low with diseases, it behooves the pastors of the churches to be never more vigilant and careful for the safety of the flock than in such diseases and infirmities. Therefore, let them visit the sick frequently and let them be quickly sent for by the sick, if the matter shall so require: let them comfort and confirm them in the true faith: finally, let them strengthen them against the dangerous suggestions of Satan. In like manner let them pray with the sick person at home in his house; and, if need be let them make prayers for the sick in the public meeting: and let them be careful that they may have a happy passage out of this life. As for popish visiting with the extreme unction, we have said before that we do not like it because it has many absurd things in it and such as are not approved by the canonical Scriptures.

Chapter 26. Of the Burial of the Faithful, and of the Care Which Is to Be Had for Such As Are Dead; of Purgatory, and the Appearing of Spirits

The Scripture wills that the bodies of the faithful, as being temples of the Holy Ghost, which we truly believe shall rise again at the last day, should be honestly, without any superstition, committed to the earth; and besides, that we should make honorable mention of the godly which have died in the Lord, and perform all duties of love to such as they leave behind them, as their widows and fatherless children. Other care to be taken for the dead, we teach none. Therefore, we do greatly dislike the Cynics, who neglected the bodies of the dead, or did very carelessly and disdainfully cast them into the earth, never speak so much as a good word of the deceased, nor any whit regarded those whom they left behind them. Again, we condemn those which are too much and preposterously officious toward the dead; who like Ethnics, do greatly lament and bewail their dead (we do not despise that moderate mourning which the apostle allows, 1 Thessalonians 4:13, but judge it an unnatural thing to be touched with no sorrow); and do sacrifice for the dead, and mumble certain prayers, not without their penny for their pains, thinking by these duties to deliver their friends from torments, wherein being wrapped by death, they suppose they may be rid of them again by such lamentable songs. For we believe that the faithful, after bodily death, go directly unto Christ, and, therefore, do not stand in need of helps or prayers for the dead or any other such duty of them which are alive. In like manner, we believe that the unbelievers are cast headlong directly into hell, from whence there is no return opened to the wicked by any duties of those which live.

But as touching that which some teach concerning the fire of purgatory, it is flat contrary to the Christian faith ("I believe the remission of sins, and life everlasting") and to the absolute purgation of sins made by Christ, and to these sayings of Christ our Lord: "Verily, verily I say unto you, he that heareth my word, and believeth in Him that sent me, hath everlasting life, and shall not come into condemnation; but hath passed from death unto life" (John 5:24). Again, "He that is washed, needeth not save to wash his feet, but is clean every whit: and ye are clean" (John 13:10).

Now that which is recorded of the spirits or souls of the dead sometimes appearing to them that are alive, and craving certain duties of them whereby they may be set free: we count those apparitions among the delusions, crafts, and deceits of the devil, who, as he can transform himself into an angel of light so he labors tooth and nail either to overthrow the true faith or else to call it into doubt. The Lord, in the Old Testament, forbade to enquire the truth of the dead and to have anything to do with spirits (Deut. 18:10–11). And to the glutton, being bound in torments, as the truth of the gospel declares, is denied any return to his brethren: the oracle of God pronouncing and saying, "They have Moses and the prophets, let them hear them. If they hear not Moses and the prophets, neither will they believe, if one shall arise from the dead" (Luke 16:29, 31).

Chapter 27. Of Rites, Ceremonies and Things Indifferent

Unto the ancient people were given in old time certain ceremonies, as a kind of schooling to those which were kept under the Law, as under a schoolmaster or tutor. But Christ the deliverer, being once come and the Law taken away, we which believe are no more under the Law (Rom. 6:14) and the ceremonies have vanished out of use. And the apostles were so far from retaining them or restoring them in the church of Christ that they witnessed plainly that they would not lay any burden upon the church (Acts 15:28). Wherefore we should seem to bring in and set up Judaism again, if we should multiply ceremonies or rites in the church according to the manner of the old church. And thus we are not of their judgment who would have the church of Christ kept in with many and divers rites as it were with a certain schooling. For if the apostles would not thrust upon the Christian people the ceremonies and rites which were appointed by God, who is there, I pray you, that is well in his wits, that will thrust upon it the inventions devised by man? The greater the heap of ceremonies is in the church, so much the more is taken not only from Christian liberty but also from Christ and from faith in Him; while the people seek those things in ceremonies which they should seek in the only Son of God, Jesus Christ, through faith. Wherefore a few moderate and simple rites that are not contrary to the Word of God are sufficient for the godly.

And in that there is found diversity of rites in the churches, let no man say, therefore, that the churches do not agree. Socrates says, "It is not possible to set down in writing all the ceremonies of the churches, which are throughout cities and countries. No religion doth keep everywhere the same ceremonies, although they admit and receive one and the selfsame doctrine touching them for even they which have one and the selfsame faith, do disagree among themselves about ceremonies." Thus much says Socrates; and we at this day having diversities in the celebration of the Lord's Supper, and in certain other things in our churches, yet we do not disagree in doctrine and faith, neither is the unity and society of our churches rent asunder. For the churches have always used their liberty in such rites as being things indifferent, which we also do at this day.

But yet, notwithstanding, we admonish men to take heed that they count not among things indifferent such as indeed are not indifferent; as some count the mass and the use of images in the church for things indifferent. "That is indifferent (said Jerome to Augustine) which is neither good nor evil, so that whether you do it, or do it not, you are never the more just, or unjust thereby." Therefore, when things indifferent are wrested to the confession of faith, they cease to be free: as Paul shows that it is lawful for a man to eat flesh, if no man admonishes him that it was offered to idols (1 Cor. 10:27–28), for then it is unlawful because he that eats it seems to approve idolatry by eating it.

Chapter 28. Of the Goods of the Church, and the Right Use of Them

The church of Christ has riches through the bountifulness of princes and the liberality of the faithful who have given their goods to the church. For the church has need of such goods; and has had goods from ancient times for the maintenance of things necessary for the church. Now the true use of church goods was and now is to maintain learning in schools, and in holy assemblies, with all the service, rites, and buildings of the church; finally, to maintain teachers, scholars, and ministers with other necessary things; and chiefly for the succor and relief of the poor. But for the lawful dispensing of these ecclesiastical goods, let men be chosen that fear God; wise men and such as are of good report for government of their families. But if the goods of the church by injury of the time, and the boldness, ignorance, or covetousness of some is turned to any abuse, let them be restored again by godly and wise men unto their holy use: for they must not wink at so impious an abuse. Therefore, we teach that schools and colleges, whereinto corruption is crept in doctrine in the service of God, and in manners, must be reformed: and that there must be order taken, godly, faithfully and wisely, for the relief of the poor.

Chapter 29. Of Single Life, Wedlock, and Household Government

Such as have the gift of chastity given unto them from above, so as they can with the heart or whole mind be pure and continent and not be grievously burned with lust, let them serve the Lord in that calling, as long as they shall feel themselves endued with that heavenly gift: and let them not lift up themselves above others, but let them serve the Lord daily in simplicity and humility. For such are more apt for doing of heavenly things than they which are distracted with the private affairs of a family. But if again the gift is taken away and they feel a continual burning, let them call to mind the words of the apostle, "It is better to marry, than to burn" (1 Cor. 7:9).

For wedlock (which is the medicine of incontinency and continency itself) was ordained by the Lord God Himself, who blessed it most bountifully, and willed man and woman to cleave one to the other inseparably and to live together in great love and concord (Gen. 2:24; Matt. 19:5–6). Whereupon we know the apostle said, "Marriage is honorable among all, and the bed undefiled" (Heb. 13:4). And again, "If a virgin marry, she sinneth not" (1 Cor. 7:28). We, therefore, condemn polygamy and those which condemn second marriages.

We teach that marriages ought to be made lawfully in the fear of the Lord and not against the laws which forbid certain degrees to join in matrimony, lest the marriages should be incestuous. Let marriages be made with consent of the parents or such as are in the place of parents; and for that end especially for which the Lord ordained marriages: and let them be confirmed publicly in the church with prayer and blessing. Moreover, let them be kept holy, with peace, faithfulness, dutifulness, love, and also purity of the persons coupled together. Therefore, let them take heed of brawlings, debates, lusts, and adulteries. Let lawful judgments and holy judges be established in the church, which may maintain marriages and may repress all dishonesty and shamefulness, and before whom controversies in matrimony may be decided and ended.

Let children also be brought up of the parents in the fear of the Lord; and let parents provide for their children, remembering the saying of the apostle, "He that provideth not for his own hath denied the faith, and is worse than an infidel" (1 Tim. 5:8). But specially let them teach their children honest sciences whereby they may maintain themselves: let them withdraw them from idleness and plant in them a true confidence in God in all these things; lest they, through distrust, or overmuch careless security or filthy covetousness, wax loose and in the end come to no good.

Now it is most certain that those works which parents do in a true faith, by the duties of marriage and government of their families, are, before God, holy and good works indeed, and please God no less than prayers, fasting, and alms deeds. For so the apostle has taught in his epistles, especially in those to Timothy and Titus. And with the same apostle we account the doctrine of such as forbid marriage, or do openly dispraise or secretly discredit it as not holy or clean, among the "doctrines of devils" (1 Tim. 4:1). And we do detest unclean single life, licentious lusts, and fornications, both open and close, and the continency of dissembling hypocrites, whenas they are of all men most incontinent. All that be such, God will judge. We do not disapprove of riches and rich men, if they are godly, and use their riches well; but we reprove the sect of the Apostolicals, etc.

Chapter 30. Of Magistracy

The magistracy, of whatever sort it is, is ordained of God Himself for the peace and quietness of mankind; and so he ought to have the chiefest place in the world. If he is an adversary to the church, he may hinder and disturb it very much, but if he is a friend and so a member of the church, he is a most useful and excellent member thereof, which may profit it very much, and finally may help and further it very excellently. His chief duty is to procure and maintain peace and public tranquility, which doubtless he shall never do more happily than when he shall be truly seasoned with the fear of God and true religion; namely, when he shall, after the example of the most holy kings and princes of the people of the Lord, advance the preaching of the truth and the pure and sincere faith, and shall root out lies and all superstition, with all impiety and idolatry, and shall defend the church of God. For indeed we teach that the care of religion chiefly pertains to the holy magistrate.

Let him, therefore, hold the Word of God in his hands and see to it that nothing is taught contrary thereunto. In like manner let him govern the people committed to him of God with good laws, made according to the Word of God. Let him hold them in discipline and in duty and in obedience: let him exercise judgment by judging uprightly: let him not accept any man's person or receive bribes: let him deliver widows, fatherless children, and those that are afflicted from wrong: let him repress, yes, and cut off such as are unjust, whether in deceit or by violence. "For he hath not received the sword of God in vain" (Rom. 13:4).

Therefore, let him draw forth this sword of God against all malefactors, seditious persons, thieves or murderers, oppressors, blasphemers, perjured persons, and all those whom God has commanded him to punish or even to execute. Let him suppress stubborn heretics (which are heretics indeed), who cease not to blaspheme the majesty of God, and to trouble the church, yes, and finally to destroy it. But if it is necessary to preserve the safety of the people by war, let him do it in the name of God, provided he has first sought peace by all means possible and can save his subjects in no way but by war. And while the magistrate does these things in faith, he serves God with those works, as with such as are good and shall receive a blessing from the Lord.

We condemn the Anabaptists, who, as they deny that a Christian man should bear the office of a magistrate, so also they deny that any man can justly be put to death by the magistrate, or that the magistrate may make war, or that oaths should be performed to the magistrate, and such like things. For as God will work the safety of His people by the magistrate, whom He has given to be, as it were, a father of the world; so all subjects are commanded to acknowledge this benefit of God in the magistrate. Therefore, let them honor and reverence the magistrate as the minister of God; let them love him, favor him, and pray for him as their father; and let them obey all his just and equal commandments. Finally, let them pay all customs and tributes and all other duties of the like sort, faithfully and willingly. And if the common safety of the country and justice require it, and the magistrate of necessity makes war, let them even lay down their life and spend their blood for the common safety and defense of the magistrate; and that in the name of God, willingly, valiantly and cheerfully. For he that opposes himself against the magistrate procures the wrath of God against him. We condemn, therefore, all condemners of magistrates, rebels, enemies of the commonwealth, seditious villains, and, in a word, all such as do either openly or closely refuse to perform those duties which they owe.

The Conclusion

We beseech God, our most merciful Father in heaven, that He will bless the princes of the people, and us, and His whole people, through Jesus Christ, our only Lord and Savior, to whom be praise and thanksgiving, both now and forever. Amen.

15

Canons of Dort

(1618–19)

The Netherlands in the late sixteenth and early seventeenth centuries was embroiled in controversy. The kingdom was thoroughly Reformed, with church leaders there having adopted the Belgic Confession and the Heidelberg Catechism in 1568. But a man named Jacob Arminius threatened to upset that consensus.

Arminius had studied under John Calvin's successor, Theodore Beza, in Geneva, but on returning to the Netherlands he soon raised suspicions regarding his Reformed commitments. Arminius' followers called for a synod to revise the church's standards, and after he died in 1609, they drafted a set of five objections to Reformed theology. These objections are known as the Remonstrance.

A synod was called in the city of Dort in 1618 to answer Arminius' followers. The answer, the Canons of Dort, addressed the five points of the Remonstrance with its own five points, which are often now called the five points of Calvinism. The Dutch Reformed church adopted the Canons of Dort as a doctrinal standard as part of the Three Forms of Unity alongside the Belgic Confession and the Heidelberg Catechism.

Canons of Dort

The Decision of the Synod of Dort on the Five Main Points of Doctrine in Dispute in the Netherlands

THE FIRST MAIN POINT OF DOCTRINE: DIVINE ELECTION AND REPROBATION

The Judgment concerning Divine Predestination Which the Synod Declares to Be in Agreement with the Word of God and Accepted Till Now in the Reformed Churches, Set Forth in Several Articles

Article 1: God's Right to Condemn All People

Since all people have sinned in Adam and have come under the sentence of the curse and eternal death, God would have done no one an injustice if it had been his will to leave the entire human race in sin and under the curse, and to condemn them on account of their sin. As the apostle says: "The whole world is liable to the condemnation of God" (Rom. 3:19), "All have sinned and are deprived of the glory of God" (Rom. 3:23), and "The wages of sin is death" (Rom. 6:23).

Article 2: The Manifestation of God's Love

But this is how God showed his love: he sent his only begotten Son into the world, so that whoever believes in him should not perish but have eternal life (1 John 4:9; John 3:16).

Article 3: The Preaching of the Gospel

In order that people may be brought to faith, God mercifully sends proclaimers of this very joyful message to the people he wishes and at the time he wishes. By this ministry people are called to repentance and faith in Christ crucified. For "how shall they believe in him of whom they have not heard? And how shall they hear without someone preaching? And how shall they preach unless they have been sent?" (Rom. 10:14–15).

Article 4: A Twofold Response to the Gospel

God's anger remains on those who do not believe this gospel. But those who do receive it and embrace Jesus the Savior with a true and living faith are delivered through him from God's anger and from destruction, and receive the gift of eternal life.

Article 5: The Sources of Unbelief and of Faith

The cause or blame for this unbelief, as well as for all other sins, is not at all in God, but in man. Faith in Jesus Christ, however, and salvation through him is a free gift of God. As Scripture says, "It is by grace you have been saved, through faith, and this not from yourselves; it is a gift of God" (Eph. 2:8). Likewise: "It has been freely given to you to believe in Christ" (Phil. 1:29).

Article 6: God's Eternal Decision

The fact that some receive from God the gift of faith within time, and that others do not, stems from his eternal decision. For "all his works are known to God from eternity" (Acts 15:18; Eph. 1:11). In accordance with this decision he graciously softens the hearts, however hard, of his chosen ones and inclines them to believe, but by his just judgment he leaves in their wickedness and hardness of heart those who have not been chosen. And in this especially is disclosed to us his act—unfathomable, and as merciful as it is just—of distinguishing between people equally lost. This is the well-known decision of election and reprobation revealed in God's Word. This decision the wicked, impure, and unstable distort to their own ruin, but it provides holy and godly souls with comfort beyond words.

Article 7: Election

Election [or choosing] is God's unchangeable purpose by which he did the following:

Before the foundation of the world, by sheer grace, according to the free good pleasure of his will, he chose in Christ to salvation a definite number of particular people out of the entire human race, which had fallen by its own fault from its original innocence into sin and ruin. Those chosen were neither better nor more deserving than the others, but lay with them in the common misery. He did this in Christ, whom he also appointed from eternity to be the mediator, the head of all those chosen, and the foundation of their salvation.

And so he decided to give the chosen ones to Christ to be saved, and to call and draw them effectively into Christ's fellowship through his Word and Spirit. In other words, he decided to grant them true faith in Christ, to justify them, to sanctify them, and finally, after powerfully preserving them in the fellowship of his Son, to glorify them.

God did all this in order to demonstrate his mercy, to the praise of the riches of his glorious grace.

As Scripture says, "God chose us in Christ, before the foundation of the world, so that we should be holy and blameless before him with love; he predestined us whom he adopted as his children through Jesus Christ, in himself, according to the good pleasure of his will, to the praise of his glorious grace, by which he freely made us pleasing to himself in his beloved" (Eph. 1:4–6). And elsewhere, "Those whom he predestined, he also called; and those whom he called, he also justified; and those whom he justified, he also glorified" (Rom. 8:30).

Article 8: A Single Decision of Election

This election is not of many kinds; it is one and the same election for all who were to be saved in the Old and the New Testament. For Scripture declares that there is a single good pleasure, purpose, and plan of God's will, by which he chose us from eternity both to grace and to glory, both to salvation and to the way of salvation, which he prepared in advance for us to walk in.

Article 9: Election Not Based on Foreseen Faith

This same election took place, not on the basis of foreseen faith, of the obedience of faith, of holiness, or of any other good quality and disposition, as though it were based on a prerequisite cause or condition in the person to be chosen, but rather for the purpose of faith, of the obedience of faith, of holiness, and so on. Accordingly, election is the source of each of the benefits of salvation. Faith, holiness, and the other saving gifts, and at last eternal life itself, flow forth from election as its fruits and effects. As the apostle says, "He chose us" (not because we were, but) "so that we should be holy and blameless before him in love" (Eph. 1:4).

Article 10: Election Based on God's Good Pleasure

But the cause of this undeserved election is exclusively the good pleasure of God. This does not involve his choosing certain human qualities or actions from among all those possible as a condition of salvation, but rather involves his adopting certain particular persons from among the common mass of sinners as his own possession. As Scripture says, "When the children were not yet born, and had done nothing either good or bad . . . , she [Rebecca] was told, 'The older will serve the younger.' As it is written, 'Jacob I loved, but Esau I hated'" (Rom. 9:11–13). Also, "All who were appointed for eternal life believed" (Acts 13:48).

Article 11: Election Unchangeable

Just as God himself is most wise, unchangeable, all-knowing, and almighty, so the election made by him can neither be suspended nor altered, revoked, or annulled; neither can his chosen ones be cast off, nor their number reduced.

Article 12: The Assurance of Election

Assurance of this their eternal and unchangeable election to salvation is given to the chosen in due time, though by various stages and in differing measure. Such assurance comes not by inquisitive searching into the hidden and deep things of God, but by noticing within themselves, with spiritual joy and holy delight, the unmistakable fruits of election pointed out in God's Word—such as a true faith in Christ, a childlike fear of God, a godly sorrow for their sins, a hunger and thirst for righteousness, and so on.

Article 13: The Fruit of This Assurance

In their awareness and assurance of this election God's children daily find greater cause to humble themselves before God, to adore the fathomless depth of his mercies, to cleanse themselves, and to give fervent love in return to him who first so greatly loved them. This is far from saying that this teaching concerning election, and reflection upon it, make God's children lax in observing his commandments or carnally self-assured. By God's just judgment this does usually happen to those who casually take for granted the grace of election or engage in idle and brazen talk about it but are unwilling to walk in the ways of the chosen.

Article 14: Teaching Election Properly

Just as, by God's wise plan, this teaching concerning divine election has been proclaimed through the prophets, Christ himself, and the apostles, in Old and New Testament times, and has subsequently been committed to writing in the Holy Scriptures, so also today in God's church, for which it was specifically intended, this teaching must be set forth—with a spirit of discretion, in a godly and holy manner, at the appropriate time and place, without inquisitive searching into the ways of the Most High. This must be done for the glory of God's most holy name, and for the lively comfort of his people.

Article 15: Reprobation

Moreover, Holy Scripture most especially highlights this eternal and undeserved grace of our election and brings it out more clearly for us, in that it further bears witness that not all people have been chosen but that some have not been chosen or have been passed by in God's eternal election—those, that is, concerning whom God, on the basis of his entirely free, most just, irreproachable, and unchangeable good pleasure, made the following decision: to leave them in the common misery into which, by their own fault, they have plunged themselves; not to grant them saving faith and the grace of conversion; but finally to condemn and eternally punish them (having been left in their own ways and under his just judgment), not only for their unbelief but also for all their other sins, in order to display his justice. And this is the decision of reprobation, which does not at all make God the author of sin (a blasphemous thought!) but rather its fearful, irreproachable, just judge and avenger.

Article 16: Responses to the Teaching of Reprobation

Those who do not yet actively experience within themselves a living faith in Christ or an assured confidence of heart, peace of conscience, a zeal for childlike obedience, and a glorying in God through Christ, but who nevertheless use the means by which God has promised to work these things in us—such people ought not to be alarmed at the mention of reprobation, nor to count themselves among the reprobate; rather they ought to continue diligently in the use of the means, to desire fervently a time of more abundant grace, and to wait for it in reverence and humility. On the other hand, those who seriously desire to turn to God, to be pleasing to him alone, and to be delivered from the body of death, but are not yet able to make such progress along the way of godliness and faith as they would like—such people ought much less to stand in fear of the teaching concerning reprobation, since our merciful God has promised that he will not snuff out a smoldering wick and that he will not break a bruised reed. However, those who have forgotten God and their Savior Jesus Christ and have abandoned themselves wholly to the cares of the world and the pleasures of the flesh—such people have every reason to stand in fear of this teaching, as long as they do not seriously turn to God.

Article 17: The Salvation of Deceased Infants of Believers

Since we must make judgments about God's will from his Word, which testifies that the children of believers are holy, not by nature but by virtue of the gracious covenant in which they together with their parents are included, godly parents ought not to doubt the election and salvation of their children whom God calls out of this life in infancy.

Article 18: The Proper Attitude toward Election and Reprobation

To those who complain about this grace of an undeserved election and about the severity of a just reprobation, we reply with the words of the apostle, "Who are you, O man, to talk back to God?" (Rom. 9:20), and with the words of our Savior, "Have I no right to do what I want with my own?" (Matt. 20:15). We, however, with reverent adoration of these secret things, cry out with the apostle: "Oh, the depths of the riches both of the wisdom and the knowledge of God! How unsearchable are his judgments, and his ways beyond tracing out! For who has known the mind of the Lord? Or who has been his counselor? Or who has first given to God, that God should repay him? For from him and through him and to him are all things. To him be the glory forever! Amen" (Rom. 11:33–36).

REJECTION OF THE ERRORS BY WHICH THE DUTCH CHURCHES HAVE FOR SOME TIME BEEN DISTURBED

Having set forth the orthodox teaching concerning election and reprobation, the Synod rejects the errors of those

I

Who teach that the will of God to save those who would believe and persevere in faith and in the obedience of faith is the whole and entire decision of election to salvation, and that nothing else concerning this decision has been revealed in God's Word.

For they deceive the simple and plainly contradict Holy Scripture in its testimony that God does not only wish to save those who would believe, but that he has also from eternity chosen certain particular people to whom, rather than to others, he would within time grant faith in Christ and perseverance. As Scripture says, "I have revealed your name to those whom you gave me" (John 17:6). Likewise, "All who were appointed for eternal life believed" (Acts 13:48), and "He chose us before the foundation of the world so that we should be holy" (Eph. 1:4).

II

Who teach that God's election to eternal life is of many kinds: one general and indefinite, the other particular and definite; and the latter in turn either incomplete, revocable, nonperemptory (or conditional), or else complete, irrevocable, and peremptory (or absolute). Likewise, who teach that there is one election to faith and another to salvation, so that there can be an election to justifying faith apart from a peremptory election to salvation.

For this is an invention of the human brain, devised apart from the Scriptures, which distorts the teaching concerning election and breaks up this golden chain of salvation: "Those whom he predestined, he also called; and those whom he called, he also justified; and those whom he justified, he also glorified" (Rom. 8:30).

III

Who teach that God's good pleasure and purpose, which Scripture mentions in its teaching of election, does not involve God's choosing certain particular people rather than others, but involves God's choosing, out of all possible conditions (including the works of the law) or out of the whole order of things, the intrinsically unworthy act of faith, as well as the imperfect obedience of faith, to be a condition of salvation; and it involves his graciously wishing to count this as perfect obedience and to look upon it as worthy of the reward of eternal life.

For by this pernicious error the good pleasure of God and the merit of Christ are robbed of their effectiveness and people are drawn away, by unprofitable inquiries, from the truth of undeserved justification and from the simplicity of the Scriptures. It also gives the lie to these words of the apostle: "God called us with a holy calling, not in virtue of works, but in virtue of his own purpose and the grace which was given to us in Christ Jesus before the beginning of time" (2 Tim. 1:9).

IV

Who teach that in election to faith a prerequisite condition is that man should rightly use the light of nature, be upright, unassuming, humble, and disposed to eternal life, as though election depended to some extent on these factors.

For this smacks of Pelagius, and it clearly calls into question the words of the apostle: "We lived at one time in the passions of our flesh, following the will of our flesh and thoughts, and we were by nature children of wrath, like everyone else. But God, who is rich in mercy, out of the great love with which he loved us, even when we were dead in transgressions, made us alive with Christ, by whose grace you have been saved. And God raised us up with him and seated us with him in heaven in Christ Jesus, in order that in the coming ages we might show the surpassing riches of his grace, according to his kindness toward us in Christ Jesus. For it is by grace you have been saved, through faith (and this not from yourselves; it is the gift of God) not by works, so that no one can boast" (Eph. 2:3–9).

V

Who teach that the incomplete and nonperemptory election of particular persons to salvation occurred on the basis of a foreseen faith, repentance, holiness, and godliness, which has just begun or continued for some time; but that complete and peremptory election occurred on the basis of a foreseen perseverance to the end in faith, repentance, holiness, and godliness. And that this is the gracious and evangelical worthiness, on account of which the one who is chosen is more worthy than the one who is not chosen. And therefore that faith, the obedience of faith, holiness, godliness, and perseverance are not fruits or effects of an unchangeable election to glory, but indispensable conditions and causes, which are prerequisite in those who are to be chosen in the complete election, and which are foreseen as achieved in them.

This runs counter to the entire Scripture, which throughout impresses upon our ears and hearts these sayings among others: "Election is not by works, but by him who calls" (Rom. 9:11–12); "All who were appointed for eternal life believed" (Acts 13:48); "He chose us in himself so that we should be holy" (Eph. 1:4); "You did not choose me, but I chose you" (John 15:16); "If by grace, not by works" (Rom. 11:6); "In this is love, not that we loved God, but that he loved us and sent his Son" (1 John 4:10).

VI

Who teach that not every election to salvation is unchangeable, but that some of the chosen can perish and do in fact perish eternally, with no decision of God to prevent it.

By this gross error they make God changeable, destroy the comfort of the godly concerning the steadfastness of their election, and contradict the Holy Scriptures, which teach that "the elect cannot be led astray" (Matt. 24:24), that "Christ does not lose those given to him by the Father" (John 6:39), and that "those whom God predestined, called, and justified, he also glorifies" (Rom. 8:30).

VII

Who teach that in this life there is no fruit, no awareness, and no assurance of one's unchangeable election to glory, except as conditional upon something changeable and contingent.

For not only is it absurd to speak of an uncertain assurance, but these things also militate against the experience of the saints, who with the apostle rejoice from an awareness of their election and sing the praises of this gift of God; who, as Christ urged, "rejoice" with his disciples "that their names have been written in heaven" (Luke 10:20); and finally who hold up against the flaming arrows of the devil's temptations the awareness of their election, with the question "Who will bring any charge against those whom God has chosen?" (Rom. 8:33).

VIII

Who teach that it was not on the basis of his just will alone that God decided to leave anyone in the fall of Adam and in the common state of sin and condemnation or to pass anyone by in the imparting of grace necessary for faith and conversion.

For these words stand fast: "He has mercy on whom he wishes, and he hardens whom he wishes" (Rom. 9:18). And also: "To you it has been given to know the secrets of the kingdom of heaven, but to them it has not been given" (Matt. 13:11). Likewise: "I give glory to you, Father, Lord of heaven and earth, that you have hidden these things from the wise and understanding, and have revealed them to little children; yes, Father, because that was your pleasure" (Matt. 11:25–26).

IX

Who teach that the cause for God's sending the gospel to one people rather than to another is not merely and solely God's good pleasure, but rather that one people is better and worthier than the other to whom the gospel is not communicated.

For Moses contradicts this when he addresses the people of Israel as follows: "Behold, to Jehovah your God belong the heavens and the highest heavens, the earth and whatever is in it. But Jehovah was inclined in his affection to love your ancestors alone, and chose out their descendants after them, you above all peoples, as at this day" (Deut. 10:14–15). And also Christ: "Woe to you, Korazin! Woe to you, Bethsaida! for if those mighty works done in you had been done in Tyre and Sidon, they would have repented long ago in sackcloth and ashes" (Matt. 11:21).

THE SECOND MAIN POINT OF DOCTRINE: CHRIST'S DEATH AND HUMAN REDEMPTION THROUGH IT

Article 1: The Punishment Which God's Justice Requires

God is not only supremely merciful, but also supremely just. His justice requires (as he has revealed himself in the Word) that the sins we have committed against his infinite majesty be punished with both temporal and eternal punishments, of soul as well as body. We cannot escape these punishments unless satisfaction is given to God's justice.

Article 2: The Satisfaction Made by Christ

Since, however, we ourselves cannot give this satisfaction or deliver ourselves from God's anger, God in his boundless mercy has given us as a guarantee his only begotten Son, who was made to be sin and a curse for us, in our place, on the cross, in order that he might give satisfaction for us.

Article 3: The Infinite Value of Christ's Death

This death of God's Son is the only and entirely complete sacrifice and satisfaction for sins; it is of infinite value and worth, more than sufficient to atone for the sins of the whole world.

Article 4: Reasons for This Infinite Value

This death is of such great value and worth for the reason that the person who suffered it is—as was necessary to be our Savior—not only a true and perfectly holy man, but also the only begotten Son of God, of the same eternal and infinite essence with the Father and the Holy Spirit. Another reason is that this death was accompanied by the experience of God's anger and curse, which we by our sins had fully deserved.

Article 5: The Mandate to Proclaim the Gospel to All

Moreover, it is the promise of the gospel that whoever believes in Christ crucified shall not perish but have eternal life. This promise, together with the command to repent and believe, ought to be announced and declared without differentiation or discrimination to all nations and people, to whom God in his good pleasure sends the gospel.

Article 6: Unbelief Man's Responsibility

However, that many who have been called through the gospel do not repent or believe in Christ but perish in unbelief is not because the sacrifice of Christ offered on the cross is deficient or insufficient, but because they themselves are at fault.

Article 7: Faith God's Gift

But all who genuinely believe and are delivered and saved by Christ's death from their sins and from destruction receive this favor solely from God's grace—which he owes to no one—given to them in Christ from eternity.

Article 8: The Saving Effectiveness of Christ's Death

For it was the entirely free plan and very gracious will and intention of God the Father that the enlivening and saving effectiveness of his Son's costly death should work itself out in all his chosen ones, in order that he might grant justifying faith to them only and thereby lead them without fail to salvation. In other words, it was God's will that Christ through the blood of the cross (by which he confirmed the new covenant) should effectively redeem from every people, tribe, nation, and language all those and only those who were chosen from eternity to salvation and given to him by the Father; that he should grant them faith (which, like the Holy Spirit's other saving gifts, he acquired for them by his death); that he should cleanse them by his blood from all their sins, both original and actual, whether committed before or after their coming to faith; that he should faithfully preserve them to the very end; and that he should finally present them to himself, a glorious people, without spot or wrinkle.

Article 9: The Fulfillment of God's Plan

This plan, arising out of God's eternal love for his chosen ones, from the beginning of the world to the present time has been powerfully carried out and will also be carried out in the future, the gates of hell seeking vainly to prevail against it. As a result the chosen are gathered into one, all in their own time, and there is always a church of believers founded on Christ's blood, a church which steadfastly loves, persistently worships, and—here and in all eternity—praises him as her Savior who laid down his life for her on the cross, as a bridegroom for his bride.

REJECTION OF THE ERRORS

Having set forth the orthodox teaching, the Synod rejects the errors of those

I

Who teach that God the Father appointed his Son to death on the cross without a fixed and definite plan to save anyone by name, so that the necessity, usefulness, and worth of what Christ's death obtained could have stood intact and altogether perfect, complete and whole, even if the redemption that was obtained had never in actual fact been applied to any individual.

For this assertion is an insult to the wisdom of God the Father and to the merit of Jesus Christ, and it is contrary to Scripture. For the Savior speaks as follows: "I lay down my life for the sheep, and I know them" (John 10:15, 27). And Isaiah the prophet says concerning the Savior: "When he shall make himself an offering for sin, he shall see his offspring, he shall prolong his days, and the will of Jehovah shall prosper in his hand" (Isa. 53:10). Finally, this undermines the article of the creed in which we confess what we believe concerning the church.

II

Who teach that the purpose of Christ's death was not to establish in actual fact a new covenant of grace by his blood, but only to acquire for the Father the mere right to enter once more into a covenant with men, whether of grace or of works.

For this conflicts with Scripture, which teaches that Christ "has become the guarantee and mediator" of a better—that is, "a new"—"covenant" (Heb. 7:22; 9:15), and that "a will is in force only when someone has died" (Heb. 9:17).

III

Who teach that Christ, by the satisfaction which he gave, did not certainly merit for anyone salvation itself and the faith by which this satisfaction of Christ is effectively applied to salvation, but only acquired for the Father the authority or plenary will to relate in a new way with men and to impose such new conditions as he chose, and that the satisfying of these conditions depends on the free choice of man; consequently, that it was possible that either all or none would fulfill them.

For they have too low an opinion of the death of Christ, do not at all acknowledge the foremost fruit or benefit which it brings forth, and summon back from hell the Pelagian error.

IV

Who teach that what is involved in the new covenant of grace which God the Father made with men through the intervening of Christ's death is not that we are justified before God and saved through faith, insofar as it accepts Christ's merit, but rather that God, having withdrawn his demand for perfect obedience to the law, counts faith itself, and the imperfect obedience of faith, as perfect obedience to the law, and graciously looks upon this as worthy of the reward of eternal life.

For they contradict Scripture: "They are justified freely by his grace through the redemption that came by Jesus Christ, whom God presented as a sacrifice of atonement, through faith in his blood" (Rom. 3:24–25). And along with the ungodly Socinus, they introduce a new and foreign justification of man before God, against the consensus of the whole church.

V

Who teach that all people have been received into the state of reconciliation and into the grace of the covenant, so that no one on account of original sin is liable to condemnation, or is to be condemned, but that all are free from the guilt of this sin.

For this opinion conflicts with Scripture which asserts that we are by nature children of wrath.

VI

Who make use of the distinction between obtaining and applying in order to instill in the unwary and inexperienced the opinion that God, as far as he is concerned, wished to bestow equally upon all people the benefits which are gained by Christ's death; but that the distinction by which some rather than others come to share in the forgiveness of sins and eternal life depends on their own free choice (which applies itself to the grace offered indiscriminately) but does not depend on the unique gift of mercy which effectively works in them, so that they, rather than others, apply that grace to themselves.

For, while pretending to set forth this distinction in an acceptable sense, they attempt to give the people the deadly poison of Pelagianism.

VII

Who teach that Christ neither could die, nor had to die, nor did die for those whom God so dearly loved and chose to eternal life, since such people do not need the death of Christ.

For they contradict the apostle, who says: "Christ loved me and gave himself up for me" (Gal. 2:20), and likewise: "Who will bring any charge against those whom God has chosen? It is God who justifies. Who is he that condemns? It is Christ who died," that is, for them (Rom. 8:33–34). They also contradict the Savior, who asserts: "I lay down my life for the sheep" (John 10:15), and "My command is this: Love one another as I have loved you. Greater love has no one than this, that one lay down his life for his friends" (John 15:12–13).

THE THIRD AND FOURTH MAIN POINTS OF DOCTRINE: HUMAN CORRUPTION, CONVERSION TO GOD, AND THE WAY IT OCCURS

Article 1: The Effect of the Fall on Human Nature

Man was originally created in the image of God and was furnished in his mind with a true and salutary knowledge of his Creator and things spiritual, in his will and heart with righteousness, and in all his emotions with purity; indeed, the whole man was holy. However, rebelling against God at the devil's instigation and by his own free will, he deprived himself of these outstanding gifts. Rather, in their place he brought upon himself blindness, terrible darkness, futility, and distortion of judgment in his mind; perversity, defiance, and hardness in his heart and will; and finally impurity in all his emotions.

Article 2: The Spread of Corruption

Man brought forth children of the same nature as himself after the fall. That is to say, being corrupt he brought forth corrupt children. The corruption spread, by God's just judgment, from Adam to all his descendants—except for Christ alone—not by way of imitation (as in former times the Pelagians would have it) but by way of the propagation of his perverted nature.

Article 3: Total Inability

Therefore, all people are conceived in sin and are born children of wrath, unfit for any saving good, inclined to evil, dead in their sins, and slaves to sin; without the grace of the regenerating Holy Spirit they are neither willing nor able to return to God, to reform their distorted nature, or even to dispose themselves to such reform.

Article 4: The Inadequacy of the Light of Nature

There is, to be sure, a certain light of nature remaining in man after the fall, by virtue of which he retains some notions about God, natural things, and the difference between what is moral and immoral, and demonstrates a certain eagerness for virtue and for good outward behavior. But this light of nature is far from enabling man to come to a saving knowledge of God and conversion to him—so far, in fact, that man does not use it rightly even in matters of nature and society. Instead, in various ways he completely distorts this light, whatever its precise character, and suppresses it in unrighteousness. In doing so he renders himself without excuse before God.

Article 5: The Inadequacy of the Law

In this respect, what is true of the light of nature is true also of the Ten Commandments given by God through Moses specifically to the Jews. For man cannot obtain saving grace through the Decalogue, because, although it does expose the magnitude of his sin and increasingly convict him of his guilt, yet it does not offer a remedy or enable him to escape from his misery, and, indeed, weakened as it is by the flesh, leaves the offender under the curse.

Article 6: The Saving Power of the Gospel

What, therefore, neither the light of nature nor the law can do, God accomplishes by the power of the Holy Spirit, through the Word or the ministry of reconciliation. This is the gospel about the Messiah, through which it has pleased God to save believers, in both the Old and the New Testament.

Article 7: God's Freedom in Revealing the Gospel

In the Old Testament, God revealed this secret of his will to a small number; in the New Testament (now without any distinction between peoples) he discloses it to a large number. The reason for this difference must not be ascribed to the greater worth of one nation over another, or to a better use of the light of nature, but to the free good pleasure and undeserved love of God. Therefore, those who receive so much grace, beyond and in spite of all they deserve, ought to acknowledge it with humble and thankful hearts; on the other hand, with the apostle they ought to adore (but certainly not inquisitively search into) the severity and justice of God's judgments on the others, who do not receive this grace.

Article 8: The Serious Call of the Gospel

Nevertheless, all who are called through the gospel are called seriously. For seriously and most genuinely God makes known in his Word what is pleasing to him: that those who are called should come to him. Seriously he also promises rest for their souls and eternal life to all who come to him and believe.

Article 9: Human Responsibility for Rejecting the Gospel

The fact that many who are called through the ministry of the gospel do not come and are not brought to conversion must not be blamed on the gospel, nor on Christ, who is offered through the gospel, nor on God, who calls them through the gospel and even bestows various gifts on them, but on the people themselves who are called. Some in self-assurance do not even entertain the Word of life; others do entertain it but do not take it to heart, and for that reason, after the fleeting joy of a temporary faith, they relapse; others choke the seed of the Word with the thorns of life's cares and with the pleasures of the world and bring forth no fruits. This our Savior teaches in the parable of the sower (Matt. 13).

Article 10: Conversion as the Work of God

The fact that others who are called through the ministry of the gospel do come and are brought to conversion must not be credited to man, as though one distinguishes himself by free choice from others who are furnished with equal or sufficient grace for faith and conversion (as the proud heresy of Pelagius maintains). No, it must be credited to God: just as from eternity he chose his own in Christ, so within time he effectively calls them, grants them faith and repentance, and, having rescued them from the dominion of darkness, brings them into the kingdom of his Son, in order that they may declare the wonderful deeds of him who called them out of darkness into this marvelous light, and may boast not in themselves, but in the Lord, as apostolic words frequently testify in Scripture.

Article 11: The Holy Spirit's Work in Conversion

Moreover, when God carries out this good pleasure in his chosen ones, or works true conversion in them, he not only sees to it that the gospel is proclaimed to them outwardly, and enlightens their minds powerfully by the

Holy Spirit so that they may rightly understand and discern the things of the Spirit of God, but, by the effective operation of the same regenerating Spirit, he also penetrates into the inmost being of man, opens the closed heart, softens the hard heart, and circumcises the heart that is uncircumcised. He infuses new qualities into the will, making the dead will alive, the evil one good, the unwilling one willing, and the stubborn one compliant; he activates and strengthens the will so that, like a good tree, it may be enabled to produce the fruits of good deeds.

Article 12: Regeneration a Supernatural Work

And this is the regeneration, the new creation, the raising from the dead, and the making alive so clearly proclaimed in the Scriptures, which God works in us without our help. But this certainly does not happen only by outward teaching, by moral persuasion, or by such a way of working that, after God has done his work, it remains in man's power whether or not to be reborn or converted. Rather, it is an entirely supernatural work, one that is at the same time most powerful and most pleasing, a marvelous, hidden, and inexpressible work, which is not lesser than or inferior in power to that of creation or of raising the dead, as Scripture (inspired by the author of this work) teaches. As a result, all those in whose hearts God works in this marvelous way are certainly, unfailingly, and effectively reborn and do actually believe. And then the will, now renewed, is not only activated and motivated by God but in being activated by God is also itself active. For this reason, man himself, by that grace which he has received, is also rightly said to believe and to repent.

Article 13: The Incomprehensible Way of Regeneration

In this life believers cannot fully understand the way this work occurs; meanwhile, they rest content with knowing and experiencing that by this grace of God they do believe with the heart and love their Savior.

Article 14: The Way God Gives Faith

In this way, therefore, faith is a gift of God, not in the sense that it is offered by God for man to choose, but that it is in actual fact bestowed on man, breathed and infused into him. Nor is it a gift in the sense that God bestows only the potential to believe, but then awaits assent—the act of believing—from man's choice; rather, it is a gift in the sense that he who works both willing and acting and, indeed, works all things in all people produces in man both the will to believe and the belief itself.

Article 15: Responses to God's Grace

God does not owe this grace to anyone. For what could God owe to one who has nothing to give that can be paid back? Indeed, what could God owe to one who has nothing of his own to give but sin and falsehood? Therefore the person who receives this grace owes and gives eternal thanks to God alone; the person who does not receive it either does not care at all about these spiritual things and is satisfied with himself in his condition, or else in self-assurance foolishly boasts about having something which he lacks. Furthermore, following the example of the apostles, we are to think and to speak in the most favorable way about those who outwardly profess their faith and better their lives, for the inner chambers of the heart are unknown to us. But for others who have not yet been called, we are to pray to the God who calls things that do not exist as though they did. In no way, however, are we to pride ourselves as better than they, as though we had distinguished ourselves from them.

Article 16: Regeneration's Effect

However, just as by the fall man did not cease to be man, endowed with intellect and will, and just as sin, which has spread through the whole human race, did not abolish the nature of the human race but distorted and spiritually killed it, so also this divine grace of regeneration does not act in people as if they were blocks and stones; nor does it abolish the will and its properties or coerce a reluctant will by force, but spiritually revives, heals, reforms, and—in a manner at once pleasing and powerful—bends it back. As a result, a ready and sincere obedience of the Spirit now begins to prevail where before the rebellion and resistance of the flesh were completely dominant. It is in this that the true and spiritual restoration and freedom of our will consists. Thus, if the marvelous Maker of every good thing were not dealing with us, man would have no hope of getting up from his fall by his free choice, by which he plunged himself into ruin when still standing upright.

Article 17: God's Use of Means in Regeneration

Just as the almighty work of God by which he brings forth and sustains our natural life does not rule out but requires the use of means, by which God, according to his infinite wisdom and goodness, has wished to exercise his power, so also the aforementioned supernatural work of God by which he regenerates us in no way rules out or cancels the use of the gospel, which God in his great wisdom has appointed to be the seed of regeneration and the food of the soul. For this reason, the apostles and the teachers who followed them taught the people in a godly manner about this grace of God, to give him the glory and to humble all pride, and yet did not neglect meanwhile to keep the people, by means of the holy admonitions of the gospel, under the administration of the Word, the sacraments, and discipline. So even today it is out of the question that the teachers or those taught in the church should presume to test God by separating what he in his good pleasure has wished to be closely joined together. For grace is bestowed through admonitions, and the more readily we perform our duty, the more lustrous the benefit of God working in us usually is and the better his work advances. To him alone, both for the means and for their saving fruit and effectiveness, all glory is owed forever. Amen.

REJECTION OF THE ERRORS

Having set forth the orthodox teaching, the Synod rejects the errors of those

I

Who teach that, properly speaking, it cannot be said that original sin in itself is enough to condemn the whole human race or to warrant temporal and eternal punishments.

For they contradict the apostle when he says: "Sin entered the world through one man, and death through sin, and in this way death passed on to all men because all sinned" (Rom. 5:12); also: "The guilt followed one sin and brought condemnation" (Rom. 5:16); likewise: "The wages of sin is death" (Rom. 6:23).

II

Who teach that the spiritual gifts or the good dispositions and virtues such as goodness, holiness, and righteousness could not have resided in man's will when

he was first created, and therefore could not have been separated from the will at the fall.

For this conflicts with the apostle's description of the image of God in Ephesians 4:24, where he portrays the image in terms of righteousness and holiness, which definitely reside in the will.

III

Who teach that in spiritual death the spiritual gifts have not been separated from man's will, since the will in itself has never been corrupted but only hindered by the darkness of the mind and the unruliness of the emotions, and since the will is able to exercise its innate free capacity once these hindrances are removed, which is to say, it is able of itself to will or choose whatever good is set before it—or else not to will or choose it.

This is a novel idea and an error and has the effect of elevating the power of free choice, contrary to the words of Jeremiah the prophet: "The heart itself is deceitful above all things and wicked" (Jer. 17:9); and of the words of the apostle: "All of us also lived among them [the sons of disobedience] at one time in the passions of our flesh, following the will of our flesh and thoughts" (Eph. 2:3).

IV

Who teach that unregenerate man is not strictly or totally dead in his sins or deprived of all capacity for spiritual good but is able to hunger and thirst for righteousness or life and to offer the sacrifice of a broken and contrite spirit which is pleasing to God.

For these views are opposed to the plain testimonies of Scripture: "You were dead in your transgressions and sins" (Eph. 2:1, 5); "The imagination of the thoughts of man's heart is only evil all the time" (Gen. 6:5; 8:21). Besides, to hunger and thirst for deliverance from misery and for life, and to offer God the sacrifice of a broken spirit is characteristic only of the regenerate and of those called blessed (Ps. 51:17; Matt. 5:6).

V

Who teach that corrupt and natural man can make such good use of common grace (by which they mean the light of nature) or of the gifts remaining after the fall that he is able thereby gradually to obtain a greater grace—evangelical or saving grace—as well as salvation itself; and that in this way God, for his part, shows himself ready to reveal Christ to all people, since he provides to all, to a sufficient extent and in an effective manner, the means necessary for the revealing of Christ, for faith, and for repentance.

For Scripture, not to mention the experience of all ages, testifies that this is false: "He makes known his words to Jacob, his statutes and his laws to Israel; he has done this for no other nation, and they do not know his laws" (Ps. 147:19–20); "In the past God let all nations go their own way" (Acts 14:16); "They [Paul and his companions] were kept by the Holy Spirit from speaking God's word in Asia"; and "When they had come to Mysia, they tried to go to Bithynia, but the Spirit would not allow them to" (Acts 16:6–7).

VI

Who teach that in the true conversion of man new qualities, dispositions, or gifts cannot be infused or poured into his will by God, and indeed that the faith [or believing] by which we first come to conversion and from which we receive the name "believers" is not a quality or gift infused by God, but only an act of man, and that it cannot be called a gift except in respect to the power of attaining faith.

For these views contradict the Holy Scriptures, which testify that God does infuse or pour into our hearts the new qualities of faith, obedience, and the experiencing of his love: "I will put my law in their minds, and write it on their hearts" (Jer. 31:33); "I will pour water on the thirsty land, and streams on the dry ground; I will pour out my Spirit on your offspring" (Isa. 44:3); "The love of God has been poured out in our hearts by the Holy Spirit, who has been given to us" (Rom. 5:5). They also conflict with the continuous practice of the church, which prays with the prophet: "Convert me, Lord, and I shall be converted" (Jer. 31:18).

VII

Who teach that the grace by which we are converted to God is nothing but a gentle persuasion, or (as others explain it) that the way of God's acting in man's conversion that is most noble and suited to human nature is that which happens by persuasion, and that nothing prevents this grace of moral suasion even by itself from making natural men spiritual; indeed, that God does not produce the assent of the will except in this manner of moral suasion, and that the effectiveness of God's work by which it surpasses the work of Satan consists in the fact that God promises eternal benefits while Satan promises temporal ones.

For this teaching is entirely Pelagian and contrary to the whole of Scripture, which recognizes besides this persuasion also another, far more effective and divine way in which the Holy Spirit acts in man's conversion. As Ezekiel 36:26 puts it: "I will give you a new heart and put a new spirit in you; and I will remove your heart of stone and give you a heart of flesh. . . ."

VIII

Who teach that God in regenerating man does not bring to bear that power of his omnipotence whereby he may powerfully and unfailingly bend man's will to faith and conversion, but that even when God has accomplished all the works of grace which he uses for man's conversion, man nevertheless can, and in actual fact often does, so resist God and the Spirit in their intent and will to regenerate him, that man completely thwarts his own rebirth; and, indeed, that it remains in his own power whether or not to be reborn.

For this does away with all effective functioning of God's grace in our conversion and subjects the activity of Almighty God to the will of man; it is contrary to the apostles, who teach that "we believe by virtue of the effective working of God's mighty strength" (Eph. 1:19), and that "God fulfills the undeserved good will of his kindness and the work of faith in us with power" (2 Thess. 1:11), and likewise that "his divine power has given us everything we need for life and godliness" (2 Peter 1:3).

IX

Who teach that grace and free choice are concurrent partial causes which cooperate to initiate conversion, and that grace does not precede—in the order of causality—the effective influence of the will; that is to say, that God does not effectively help man's will to come to conversion before man's will itself motivates and determines itself.

For the early church already condemned this doctrine long ago in the Pelagians, on the basis of the words of the apostle: "It does not depend on man's willing or running but on God's mercy" (Rom. 9:16); also: "Who makes you different from anyone else?" and "What do you have that you did not receive?" (1 Cor. 4:7); likewise: "It is God who works in you to will and act according to his good pleasure" (Phil. 2:13).

THE FIFTH MAIN POINT OF DOCTRINE: THE PERSEVERANCE OF THE SAINTS

Article 1: The Regenerate Not Entirely Free from Sin

Those people whom God according to his purpose calls into fellowship with his Son Jesus Christ our Lord and regenerates by the Holy Spirit, he also sets free from the reign and slavery of sin, though in this life not entirely from the flesh and from the body of sin.

Article 2: The Believer's Reaction to Sins of Weakness

Hence daily sins of weakness arise, and blemishes cling to even the best works of God's people, giving them continual cause to humble themselves before God, to flee for refuge to Christ crucified, to put the flesh to death more and more by the Spirit of supplication and by holy exercises of godliness, and to strain toward the goal of perfection, until they are freed from this body of death and reign with the Lamb of God in heaven.

Article 3: God's Preservation of the Converted

Because of these remnants of sin dwelling in them and also because of the temptations of the world and Satan, those who have been converted could not remain standing in this grace if left to their own resources. But God is faithful, mercifully strengthening them in the grace once conferred on them and powerfully preserving them in it to the end.

Article 4: The Danger of True Believers' Falling into Serious Sins

Although that power of God strengthening and preserving true believers in grace is more than a match for the flesh, yet those converted are not always so activated and motivated by God that in certain specific actions they cannot by their own fault depart from the leading of grace, be led astray by the desires of the flesh, and give in to them. For this reason they must constantly watch and pray that they may not be led into temptations. When they fail to do this, not only can they be carried away by the flesh, the world, and Satan into sins, even serious and outrageous ones, but also by God's just permission they sometimes are so carried away—witness the sad cases, described in Scripture, of David, Peter, and other saints falling into sins.

Article 5: The Effects of Such Serious Sins

By such monstrous sins, however, they greatly offend God, deserve the sentence of death, grieve the Holy Spirit, suspend the exercise of faith, severely wound the conscience, and sometimes lose the awareness of grace for a time—until, after they have returned to the way by genuine repentance, God's fatherly face again shines upon them.

Article 6: God's Saving Intervention

For God, who is rich in mercy, according to his unchangeable purpose of election does not take his Holy Spirit from his own completely, even when they fall grievously. Neither does he let them fall down so far that they forfeit the grace of adoption and the state of justification, or commit the sin which leads to death (the sin against the Holy Spirit), and plunge themselves, entirely forsaken by him, into eternal ruin.

Article 7: Renewal to Repentance

For, in the first place, God preserves in those saints when they fall his imperishable seed from which they have been born again, lest it perish or be dislodged. Secondly, by his Word and Spirit he certainly and effectively renews them to repentance so that they have a heartfelt and godly sorrow for the sins they have committed; seek and obtain, through faith and with a contrite heart, forgiveness in the blood of the Mediator; experience again the grace of a reconciled God; through faith adore his mercies; and from then on more eagerly work out their own salvation with fear and trembling.

Article 8: The Certainty of This Preservation

So it is not by their own merits or strength but by God's undeserved mercy that they neither forfeit faith and grace totally nor remain in their downfalls to the end and are lost. With respect to themselves this not only easily could happen, but also undoubtedly would happen; but with respect to God it cannot possibly happen, since his plan cannot be changed, his promise cannot fail, the calling according to his purpose cannot be revoked, the merit of Christ as well as his interceding and preserving cannot be nullified, and the sealing of the Holy Spirit can neither be invalidated nor wiped out.

Article 9: The Assurance of This Preservation

Concerning this preservation of those chosen to salvation and concerning the perseverance of true believers in faith, believers themselves can and do become assured in accordance with the measure of their faith, by which they firmly believe that they are and always will remain true and living members of the church, and that they have the forgiveness of sins and eternal life.

Article 10: The Ground of This Assurance

Accordingly, this assurance does not derive from some private revelation beyond or outside the Word, but from faith in the promises of God which he has very plentifully revealed in his Word for our comfort, from the testimony "of the Holy Spirit testifying with our spirit that we are God's children and heirs" (Rom. 8:16–17), and finally from a serious and holy pursuit of a clear conscience and of good works. And if God's chosen ones in this world did not have this well-founded comfort that the victory will be theirs and this reliable guarantee of eternal glory, they would be of all people most miserable.

Article 11: Doubts concerning This Assurance

Meanwhile, Scripture testifies that believers have to contend in this life with various doubts of the flesh and that under severe temptation they do not always experience this full assurance of faith and certainty of perseverance. But God, the Father of all comfort, "does not let them be tempted beyond what they can bear, but with the temptation he also provides a way out" (1 Cor. 10:13), and by the Holy Spirit revives in them the assurance of their perseverance.

Article 12: This Assurance as an Incentive to Godliness

This assurance of perseverance, however, so far from making true believers proud and carnally self-assured, is rather the true root of humility, of childlike respect, of genuine godliness, of endurance in every conflict, of fervent prayers, of steadfastness in crossbearing and in confessing the truth, and of well-founded joy in God. Reflecting on this benefit provides an incentive to a serious and continual practice of thanksgiving and good works, as is evident from the testimonies of Scripture and the examples of the saints.

Article 13: Assurance No Inducement to Carelessness

Neither does the renewed confidence of perseverance produce immorality or lack of concern for godliness in those put back on their feet after a fall, but it produces a much greater concern to observe carefully the ways of the Lord which he prepared in advance. They observe these ways in order that by walking in them they may maintain the assurance of their perseverance, lest, by their abuse of his fatherly goodness, the face of the gracious God (for the godly, looking upon his face is sweeter than life, but its withdrawal is more bitter than death) turn away from them again, with the result that they fall into greater anguish of spirit.

Article 14: God's Use of Means in Perseverance

And, just as it has pleased God to begin this work of grace in us by the proclamation of the gospel, so he preserves, continues, and completes his work by the hearing and reading of the gospel, by meditation on it, by its exhortations, threats, and promises, and also by the use of the sacraments.

Article 15: Contrasting Reactions to the Teaching of Perseverance

This teaching about the perseverance of true believers and saints, and about their assurance of it—a teaching which God has very richly revealed in his Word for the glory of his name and for the comfort of the godly and which he impresses on the hearts of believers—is something which the flesh does not understand, Satan hates, the world ridicules, the ignorant and the hypocrites abuse, and the spirits of error attack. The bride of Christ, on the other hand, has always loved this teaching very tenderly and defended it steadfastly as a priceless treasure; and God, against whom no plan can avail and no strength can prevail, will ensure that she will continue to do this. To this God alone, Father, Son, and Holy Spirit, be honor and glory forever. Amen.

REJECTION OF THE ERRORS

Having set forth the orthodox teaching, the Synod rejects the errors of those

I

Who teach that the perseverance of true believers is not an effect of election or a gift of God produced by Christ's death, but a condition of the new covenant which man, before what they call his "peremptory" election and justification, must fulfill by his free will.

For Holy Scripture testifies that perseverance follows from election and is granted to the chosen by virtue of Christ's death, resurrection, and intercession: "The chosen obtained it; the others were hardened" (Rom. 11:7); likewise, "He who did not spare his own Son, but gave him up for us all—how will he not, along with him, grant us all things? Who will bring any charge against those whom God has chosen? It is God who justifies. Who is he that condemns? It is Christ Jesus who died—more than that, who was raised—who also sits at the right hand of God, and is also interceding for us. Who shall separate us from the love of Christ?" (Rom. 8:32–35).

II

Who teach that God does provide the believer with sufficient strength to persevere and is ready to preserve this strength in him if he performs his duty, but that even with all those things in place which are necessary to persevere in faith and which God is pleased to use to preserve faith, it still always depends on the choice of man's will whether or not he perseveres.

For this view is obviously Pelagian; and though it intends to make men free it makes them sacrilegious. It is against the enduring consensus of evangelical teaching which takes from man all cause for boasting and ascribes the praise for this benefit only to God's grace. It is also against the testimony of the apostle: "It is God who keeps us strong to the end, so that we will be blameless on the day of our Lord Jesus Christ" (1 Cor. 1:8).

III

Who teach that those who truly believe and have been born again not only can forfeit justifying faith as well as grace and salvation totally and to the end, but also in actual fact do often forfeit them and are lost forever.

For this opinion nullifies the very grace of justification and regeneration as well as the continual preservation by Christ, contrary to the plain words of the apostle Paul: "If Christ died for us while we were still sinners, we will therefore much more be saved from God's wrath through him, since we have now been justified by his blood" (Rom. 5:8–9); and contrary to the apostle John: "No one who is born of God is intent on sin, because God's seed remains in him, nor can he sin, because he has been born of God" (1 John 3:9); also contrary to the words of Jesus Christ: "I give eternal life to my sheep, and they shall never perish; no one can snatch them out of my hand. My Father, who has given them to me, is greater than all; no one can snatch them out of my Father's hand" (John 10:28–29).

IV

Who teach that those who truly believe and have been born again can commit the sin that leads to death (the sin against the Holy Spirit).

For the same apostle John, after making mention of those who commit the sin that leads to death and forbidding prayer for them (1 John 5:16–17), immediately adds: "We know that anyone born of God does not commit sin" [that is, that kind of sin], "but the one who was born of God keeps himself safe, and the evil one does not touch him" (v. 18).

V

Who teach that apart from a special revelation no one can have the assurance of future perseverance in this life.

For by this teaching the well-founded consolation of true believers in this life is taken away and the doubting of the Romanists is reintroduced into the church. Holy Scripture, however, in many places derives the assurance not from a special and extraordinary revelation but from the marks peculiar to God's children and from God's completely reliable promises. So especially the apostle Paul: "Nothing in all creation can separate us from the love of God that is in Christ Jesus our Lord" (Rom. 8:39); and John: "They who obey his commands remain in him and he in them. And this is how we know that he remains in us: by the Spirit he gave us" (1 John 3:24).

VI

Who teach that the teaching of the assurance of perseverance and of salvation is by its very nature and character an opiate of the flesh and is harmful to godliness, good morals, prayer, and other holy exercises, but that, on the contrary, to have doubt about this is praiseworthy.

For these people show that they do not know the effective operation of God's grace and the work of the indwelling Holy Spirit, and they contradict the apostle John, who asserts the opposite in plain words: "Dear friends, now we are children of God, but what we will be has not yet been made known. But we know that when he is made known, we shall be like him, for we shall see him as he is. Everyone who has this hope in him purifies himself, just as he is pure" (1 John 3:2–3). Moreover, they are refuted by the examples of the saints in both the Old and the New Testament, who though assured of their perseverance and salvation yet were constant in prayer and other exercises of godliness.

VII

Who teach that the faith of those who believe only temporarily does not differ from justifying and saving faith except in duration alone.

For Christ himself in Matthew 13:20ff. and Luke 8:13ff. clearly defines these further differences between temporary and true believers: he says that the former receive the seed on rocky ground, and the latter receive it in good ground, or a good heart; the former have no root, and the latter are firmly rooted; the former have no fruit, and the latter produce fruit in varying measure, with steadfastness, or perseverance.

VIII

Who teach that it is not absurd that a person, after losing his former regeneration, should once again, indeed quite often, be reborn.

For by this teaching they deny the imperishable nature of God's seed by which we are born again, contrary to the testimony of the apostle Peter: "Born again, not of perishable seed, but of imperishable" (1 Peter 1:23).

IX

Who teach that Christ nowhere prayed for an unfailing perseverance of believers in faith.

For they contradict Christ himself when he says: "I have prayed for you, Peter, that your faith may not fail" (Luke 22:32); and John the gospel writer when he testifies in John 17 that it was not only for the apostles, but also for all those who were to believe by their message that Christ prayed: "Holy Father, preserve them in your name" (v. 11); and "My prayer is not that you take them out of the world, but that you preserve them from the evil one" (v. 15).

CONCLUSION

Rejection of False Accusations

And so this is the clear, simple, and straightforward explanation of the orthodox teaching on the five articles in dispute in the Netherlands, as well as the rejection of the errors by which the Dutch churches have for some time been disturbed. This explanation and rejection the Synod declares to be derived from God's Word and in agreement with the confessions of the Reformed churches. Hence it clearly appears that those of whom one could hardly expect it have shown no truth, equity, and charity at all in wishing to make the public believe:

- that the teaching of the Reformed churches on predestination and on the points associated with it by its very nature and tendency draws the minds of people away from all godliness and religion, is an opiate of the flesh and the devil, and is a stronghold of Satan where he lies in wait for all people, wounds most of them, and fatally pierces many of them with the arrows of both despair and self-assurance;

- that this teaching makes God the author of sin, unjust, a tyrant, and a hypocrite; and is nothing but a refurbished Stoicism, Manicheism, Libertinism, and Mohammedanism;

- that this teaching makes people carnally self-assured, since it persuades them that nothing endangers the salvation of the chosen, no matter how they live, so that they may commit the most outrageous crimes with self-assurance; and that on the other hand nothing is of use to the reprobate for salvation even if they have truly performed all the works of the saints;

- that this teaching means that God predestined and created, by the bare and unqualified choice of his will, without the least regard or consideration of any sin, the greatest part of the world to eternal condemnation; that in the same manner in which election is the source and cause of faith and good works, reprobation is the cause of unbelief and ungodliness; that many infant children of believers are snatched in their innocence from their mothers' breasts and cruelly cast into hell so that neither the blood of Christ nor their baptism nor the prayers of the church at their baptism can be of any use to them;

- and very many other slanderous accusations of this kind which the Reformed churches not only disavow but even denounce with their whole heart.

Therefore this Synod of Dort in the name of the Lord pleads with all who devoutly call on the name of our Savior Jesus Christ to form their judgment about the faith of the Reformed churches, not on the basis of false accusations gathered from here or there, or even on the basis of the personal statements of a number of ancient and modern authorities—statements which are also often either quoted out of context or misquoted and twisted to convey a different meaning—but on the basis of the churches' own official confessions and of the present explanation of the orthodox teaching which has been endorsed by the unanimous consent of the members of the whole Synod, one and all.

Moreover, the Synod earnestly warns the false accusers themselves to consider how heavy a judgment of God awaits those who give false testimony against so many churches and their confessions, trouble the consciences of the weak, and seek to prejudice the minds of many against the fellowship of true believers.

Finally, this Synod urges all fellow ministers in the gospel of Christ to deal with this teaching in a godly and reverent manner, in the academic institutions as well as in the churches; to do so, both in their speaking and writing, with a view to the glory of God's name, holiness of life, and the comfort of anxious souls; to think and also speak with Scripture according to the analogy of faith; and, finally, to refrain from all those ways of speaking which go beyond the bounds set for us by the genuine sense of the Holy Scriptures and which could give impertinent sophists a just occasion to scoff at the teaching of the Reformed churches or even to bring false accusations against it.

May God's Son Jesus Christ, who sits at the right hand of God and gives gifts to men, sanctify us in the truth, lead to the truth those who err, silence the mouths of those who lay false accusations against sound teaching, and equip faithful ministers of his Word with a spirit of wisdom and discretion, that all they say may be to the glory of God and the building up of their hearers. Amen.

16

Westminster Confession of Faith

(1646–47)

King Charles I of England had a problem. In 1640, he was in the middle of fighting a war with Scotland—precipitated by his attempt to impose the Anglican Book of Common Prayer on the fiercely Presbyterian Church of Scotland—and he needed to raise money. To raise money, he needed to call Parliament into session. In previous years, Parliament had often sought to use such financial asks as an opportunity to discuss grievances it had with the king. So beginning in 1629, Charles was determined to rule without Parliament. He was finally forced to call it in 1640 to pay his army, but he dissolved it after a few weeks. He had to call it again by the end of the year.

This time, Parliament was there to stay. It remained in session through 1653, and during this time it set about reforming the Church of England by stripping it of Arminian influence and reducing the power of church officials. Parliament soon came into conflict with Charles, leading to the English Civil War.

Parliament's desire to reform the church led it to call the Westminster Assembly. The assembly's divines, or theologians, were initially tasked with revising the Thirty-Nine Articles, but they soon embarked on drafting a new confession instead. The fruit of their work—the Westminster Confession of Faith, Larger and Shorter Catechisms, Directory of Public Worship, and Form of Church Government, collectively known as the Westminster Standards—became the foundational standards of Scottish Presbyterianism.

Westminster Confession of Faith

CHAPTER 1
OF THE HOLY SCRIPTURE

1. Although the light of nature, and the works of creation and providence do so far manifest the goodness, wisdom, and power of God, as to leave men unexcusable;[1] yet are they not sufficient to give that knowledge of God, and of his will, which is necessary unto salvation.[2] Therefore it pleased the Lord, at sundry times, and in divers manners, to reveal himself, and to declare that his will unto his church;[3] and afterwards, for the better preserving and propagating of the truth, and for the more sure establishment and comfort of the church against the corruption of the flesh, and the malice of Satan and of the world, to commit the same wholly unto writing:[4] which maketh the Holy Scripture to be most necessary;[5] those former ways of God's revealing his will unto his people being now ceased.[6]

2. Under the name of Holy Scripture, or the Word of God written, are now contained all the books of the Old and New Testament, which are these:

---

1 Rom. 2:14–15; Rom. 1:19–20; Ps. 19:1–4. (See Rom. 1:32–2:1.)
2 John 17:3; 1 Cor. 1:21; 1 Cor. 2:13–14.
3 Heb. 1:1–2.
4 Luke 1:3–4; Rom. 15:4; Matt. 4:4, 7, 10; Isa. 8:20.
5 2 Tim. 3:15; 2 Peter 1:19.
6 John 20:31; 1 Cor. 14:37; 1 John 5:13; 1 Cor. 10:11; Heb. 1:1–2; Heb. 2:2–4.

OF THE OLD TESTAMENT:

Genesis	II Chronicles	Daniel
Exodus	Ezra	Hosea
Leviticus	Nehemiah	Joel
Numbers	Esther	Amos
Deuteronomy	Job	Obadiah
Joshua	Psalms	Jonah
Judges	Proverbs	Micah
Ruth	Ecclesiastes	Nahum
I Samuel	The Song of Songs	Habakkuk
II Samuel	Isaiah	Zephaniah
I Kings	Jeremiah	Haggai
II Kings	Lamentations	Zechariah
I Chronicles	Ezekiel	Malachi

OF THE NEW TESTAMENT:

The Gospels	Galatians	The Epistle
according to	Ephesians	of James
Matthew	Philippians	The first and
Mark	Colossians	second Epistles
Luke	Thessalonians I	of Peter
John	Thessalonians II	The first, second,
The Acts of the	to Timothy I	and third Epistles
Apostles	to Timothy II	of John
Paul's Epistles	to Titus	The Epistle
to the Romans	to Philemon	of Jude
Corinthians I	The Epistle to	The Revelation
Corinthians II	the Hebrews	of John

All which are given by inspiration of God to be the rule of faith and life.[7]

3. The books commonly called Apocrypha, not being of divine inspiration, are no part of the canon of the Scripture, and therefore are of no authority in the church of God, nor to be any otherwise approved, or made use of, than other human writings.[8]

---

7 Luke 16:29, 31; Luke 24:27, 44; 2 Tim. 3:15–16; John 5:46–47.
8 Rev. 22:18–19; Rom. 3:2; 2 Peter 1:21.

4. The authority of the Holy Scripture, for which it ought to be believed, and obeyed, dependeth not upon the testimony of any man, or church; but wholly upon God (who is truth itself) the author thereof: and therefore it is to be received, because it is the Word of God.[9]

5. We may be moved and induced by the testimony of the church to an high and reverent esteem of the Holy Scripture.[10] And the heavenliness of the matter, the efficacy of the doctrine, the majesty of the style, the consent of all the parts, the scope of the whole (which is, to give all glory to God), the full discovery it makes of the only way of man's salvation, the many other incomparable excellencies, and the entire perfection thereof, are arguments whereby it doth abundantly evidence itself to be the Word of God: yet notwithstanding, our full persuasion and assurance of the infallible truth and divine authority thereof, is from the inward work of the Holy Spirit bearing witness by and with the Word in our hearts.[11]

6. The whole counsel of God concerning all things necessary for his own glory, man's salvation, faith and life, is either expressly set down in Scripture, or by good and necessary consequence may be deduced from Scripture: unto which nothing at any time is to be added, whether by new revelations of the Spirit, or traditions of men.[12] Nevertheless, we acknowledge the inward illumination of the Spirit of God to be necessary for the saving understanding of such things as are revealed in the Word:[13] and that there are some circumstances concerning the worship of God, and government of the church, common to human actions and societies, which are to be ordered by the light of nature, and Christian prudence, according to the general rules of the Word, which are always to be observed.[14]

7. All things in Scripture are not alike plain in themselves, nor alike clear unto all:[15] yet those things which are necessary to be known, believed, and

---

9 2 Peter 1:19–20; 2 Tim. 3:16; 1 John 5:9; 1 Thess. 2:13; Rev. 1:1–2.
10 1 Tim. 3:15.
11 1 Cor. 2:9–10; Heb. 4:12; John 10:35; Isa. 55:11 (see Rom. 11:36); Ps. 19:7–11 (see 2 Tim. 3:15); 1 Cor. 2:4–5; 1 Thess. 1:5; 1 John 2:20, 27 (see Isa. 59:2).
12 2 Tim. 3:16–17; Gal. 1:8–9; 2 Thess. 2:2.
13 John 6:45; 1 Cor. 2:12, 14–15; Eph. 1:18. (See 2 Cor. 4:6.)
14 1 Cor. 11:13–14; 1 Cor. 14:26, 40.
15 2 Peter 3:16.

observed for salvation, are so clearly propounded, and opened in some place of Scripture or other, that not only the learned, but the unlearned, in a due use of the ordinary means, may attain unto a sufficient understanding of them.[16]

8. The Old Testament in Hebrew (which was the native language of the people of God of old), and the New Testament in Greek (which, at the time of the writing of it, was most generally known to the nations), being immediately inspired by God, and, by his singular care and providence, kept pure in all ages, are therefore authentical;[17] so as, in all controversies of religion, the church is finally to appeal unto them.[18] But, because these original tongues are not known to all the people of God, who have right unto, and interest in the Scriptures, and are commanded, in the fear of God, to read and search them,[19] therefore they are to be translated into the vulgar language of every nation unto which they come,[20] that, the Word of God dwelling plentifully in all, they may worship him in an acceptable manner;[21] and, through patience and comfort of the Scriptures, may have hope.[22]

9. The infallible rule of interpretation of Scripture is the Scripture itself: and therefore, when there is a question about the true and full sense of any Scripture (which is not manifold, but one), it must be searched and known by other places that speak more clearly.[23]

10. The supreme judge by which all controversies of religion are to be determined, and all decrees of councils, opinions of ancient writers, doctrines of men, and private spirits, are to be examined, and in whose sentence we are to rest, can be no other but the Holy Spirit speaking in the Scripture.[24]

---

16 Ps. 119:105, 130; Deut. 29:29; Deut. 30:10–14; Acts 17:11.
17 Matt. 5:18; Ps. 119:89.
18 Isa. 8:20; Matt. 15:3, 6; Acts 15:15. (See Luke 16:31.)
19 John 5:39; Acts 17:11; Rev. 1:3. (See 2 Tim. 3:14–15.)
20 Matt. 28:19–20. (See 1 Cor. 14:6; Mark 15:34.)
21 Col. 3:16. (See Ex. 20:4–6; Matt. 15:7–9.)
22 Rom. 15:4.
23 Acts 15:15; John 5:46. (See 2 Peter 1:20–21.)
24 Matt. 22:29, 31; Acts 28:25. (See 1 John 4:1–6.)

CHAPTER 2

OF GOD, AND OF THE HOLY TRINITY

1. There is but one only,[1] living, and true God,[2] who is infinite in being and perfection,[3] a most pure spirit,[4] invisible,[5] without body, parts,[6] or passions;[7] immutable,[8] immense,[9] eternal,[10] incomprehensible,[11] almighty,[12] most wise,[13] most holy,[14] most free,[15] most absolute;[16] working all things according to the counsel of his own immutable and most righteous will,[17] for his own glory;[18] most loving,[19] gracious, merciful, long-suffering, abundant in goodness and truth, forgiving iniquity, transgression, and sin;[20] the rewarder of them that diligently seek him;[21] and withal, most just, and terrible in his judgments,[22] hating all sin,[23] and who will by no means clear the guilty.[24]

2. God hath all life,[25] glory,[26] goodness,[27] blessedness,[28] in and of himself; and is alone in and unto himself all-sufficient, not standing in need of any creatures

---

1 Deut. 6:4; 1 Cor. 8:4, 6. (See Gal. 3:20.)
2 1 Thess. 1:9; Jer. 10:10.
3 Job 11:7–9; Job 26:14. (See Ps. 139:6.)
4 John 4:24.
5 1 Tim. 1:17. (See John 1:18.)
6 Deut. 4:15–16. (Cf. John 4:24 with Luke 24:39.)
7 Acts 14:11, 15; James 1:17; Mal. 3:6; 1 Kings 8:27; Jer. 23:23–24.
8 Ps. 90:2. (See 1 Tim. 1:17.)
9 1 Kings 8:27; Jer. 23:23–24.
10 Ps. 90:2. (See 1 Tim. 1:17.)
11 Ps. 145:3. (See Rom. 11:34.)
12 Gen. 17:1; Rev. 4:8.
13 Rom. 16:27.
14 Isa. 6:3. (See Rev. 4:8.)
15 Ps. 115:3. (See Isa. 14:24.)
16 Isa. 45:5–6. (See Ex. 3:14.)
17 Eph. 1:11.
18 Prov. 16:4; Rom. 11:36. (See Rev. 4:11.)
19 1 John 4:8. (See 1 John 4:16; John 3:16.)
20 Ex. 34:6–7.
21 Heb. 11:6.
22 Neh. 9:32–33. (See Heb. 10:28–31.)
23 Rom. 1:18; Ps. 5:5–6. (See Ps. 11:5.)
24 Ex. 34:7a. (See Nah. 1:2–3, 6.)
25 Jer. 10:10. (See John 5:26.)
26 Acts 7:2.
27 Ps. 119:68.
28 1 Tim. 6:15. (See Rom. 9:5.)

which he hath made,[29] nor deriving any glory from them,[30] but only manifesting his own glory in, by, unto, and upon them. He is the alone fountain of all being, of whom, through whom, and to whom are all things;[31] and hath most sovereign dominion over them, to do by them, for them, or upon them whatsoever himself pleaseth.[32] In his sight all things are open and manifest,[33] his knowledge is infinite, infallible, and independent upon the creature,[34] so as nothing is to him contingent, or uncertain.[35] He is most holy in all his counsels, in all his works, and in all his commands.[36] To him is due from angels and men, and every other creature, whatsoever worship, service, or obedience he is pleased to require of them.[37]

3. In the unity of the Godhead there be three persons, of one substance, power, and eternity: God the Father, God the Son, and God the Holy Ghost:[38] the Father is of none, neither begotten, nor proceeding; the Son is eternally begotten of the Father;[39] the Holy Ghost eternally proceeding from the Father and the Son.[40]

---

29 Acts 17:24–25.
30 Luke 17:10.
31 Rom. 11:36.
32 Rev. 4:11; Dan. 4:25, 35. (See 1 Tim. 6:15.)
33 Heb. 4:13.
34 Rom. 11:33–34; Ps. 147:5.
35 Acts 15:18; Ezek. 11:5.
36 Ps. 145:17; Rom. 7:12.
37 Rev. 5:12–14.
38 Matt. 3:16–17; Matt. 28:19; 2 Cor. 13:14. (See Eph. 2:18.)
39 John 1:14, 18. (See Heb. 1:2–3; Col. 1:15.)
40 John 15:26; Gal. 4:6.

CHAPTER 3
OF GOD'S ETERNAL DECREE

1. God, from all eternity, did, by the most wise and holy counsel of his own will, freely, and unchangeably ordain whatsoever comes to pass:[1] yet so, as thereby neither is God the author of sin,[2] nor is violence offered to the will of the creatures; nor is the liberty or contingency of second causes taken away, but rather established.[3]

2. Although God knows whatsoever may or can come to pass upon all supposed conditions,[4] yet hath he not decreed anything because he foresaw it as future, or as that which would come to pass upon such conditions.[5]

3. By the decree of God, for the manifestation of his glory, some men and angels[6] are predestinated unto everlasting life; and others foreordained to everlasting death.[7]

4. These angels and men, thus predestinated, and foreordained, are particularly and unchangeably designed, and their number so certain and definite, that it cannot be either increased or diminished.[8]

5. Those of mankind that are predestinated unto life, God, before the foundation of the world was laid, according to his eternal and immutable purpose, and the secret counsel and good pleasure of his will, hath chosen, in Christ, unto everlasting glory,[9] out of his mere free grace and love, without any foresight of faith, or good works, or perseverance in either of them, or any other thing in the creature, as conditions, or causes moving him thereunto;[10] and all to the praise of his glorious grace.[11]

---

1 Ps. 33:11; Eph. 1:11; Heb. 6:17.
2 Ps. 5:4; James 1:13–14; 1 John 1:5. (See Hab. 1:13.)
3 Acts 2:23; Matt. 17:12; Acts 4:27–28; John 19:11; Prov. 16:33.
4 1 Sam. 23:11–12; Matt. 11:21, 23.
5 Rom. 9:11, 13, 16, 18.
6 1 Tim. 5:21; Jude 6; Matt. 25:31, 41.
7 Eph. 1:5–6; Rom. 9:22–23; Prov. 16:4.
8 John 13:18; 2 Tim. 2:19. (See John 10:14–16, 27–28; 17:2, 6, 9–12.)
9 Eph. 1:4, 9, 11; Rom. 8:28–30; 2 Tim. 1:9; 1 Thess. 5:9.
10 Rom. 9:11, 13, 15–16; Eph. 2:8–9. (See Eph. 1:5, 9, 11.)
11 Eph. 1:6, 12.

6. As God hath appointed the elect unto glory, so hath he, by the eternal and most free purpose of his will, foreordained all the means thereunto.[12] Wherefore, they who are elected, being fallen in Adam, are redeemed by Christ,[13] are effectually called unto faith in Christ by his Spirit working in due season, are justified, adopted, sanctified,[14] and kept by his power, through faith, unto salvation.[15] Neither are any other redeemed by Christ, effectually called, justified, adopted, sanctified, and saved, but the elect only.[16]

7. The rest of mankind God was pleased, according to the unsearchable counsel of his own will, whereby he extendeth or withholdeth mercy, as he pleaseth, for the glory of his sovereign power over his creatures, to pass by; and to ordain them to dishonor and wrath for their sin, to the praise of his glorious justice.[17]

8. The doctrine of this high mystery of predestination is to be handled with special prudence and care,[18] that men, attending the will of God revealed in his Word, and yielding obedience thereunto, may, from the certainty of their effectual vocation, be assured of their eternal election.[19] So shall this doctrine afford matter of praise, reverence, and admiration of God;[20] and of humility, diligence, and abundant consolation to all that sincerely obey the gospel.[21]

---

12 1 Peter 1:2; Eph. 2:10; 2 Thess. 2:13.
13 1 Thess. 5:9–10; Titus 2:14.
14 Rom. 8:30. (See Eph. 1:5; 2 Thess. 2:13.)
15 1 Peter 1:5.
16 John 10:14–15, 26; John 6:64–65; Rom. 8:28–39. (See John 8:47; 17:9; 1 John 2:19.)
17 Matt. 11:25–26; Rom. 9:17–18, 21–22; Jude 4; 1 Peter 2:8; 2 Tim. 2:19–20.
18 Rom. 9:20; Rom. 11:33; Deut. 29:29.
19 2 Peter 1:10; 1 Thess. 1:4–5.
20 Eph. 1:6. (See Rom. 11:33.)
21 Rom. 11:5–6, 20; Rom. 8:33; Luke 10:20. (See 2 Peter 1:10.)

CHAPTER 4
OF CREATION

1. It pleased God the Father, Son, and Holy Ghost,[1] for the manifestation of the glory of his eternal power, wisdom, and goodness,[2] in the beginning, to create, or make of nothing, the world, and all things therein whether visible or invisible, in the space of six days; and all very good.[3]

2. After God had made all other creatures, he created man, male and female,[4] with reasonable and immortal souls,[5] endued with knowledge, righteousness, and true holiness, after his own image;[6] having the law of God written in their hearts,[7] and power to fulfill it:[8] and yet under a possibility of transgressing, being left to the liberty of their own will, which was subject unto change.[9] Beside this law written in their hearts, they received a command, not to eat of the tree of the knowledge of good and evil; which while they kept, they were happy in their communion with God,[10] and had dominion over the creatures.[11]

1 Rom. 11:36; 1 Cor. 8:6; Heb. 1:2; John 1:2–3; Gen. 1:2; Job 33:4.
2 Rom. 1:20; Jer. 10:12; Ps. 104:24; Ps. 33:5.
3 Gen. 1:1–31; Ps. 33:6; Heb. 11:3; Col. 1:16; Acts 17:24; Ex. 20:11.
4 Gen. 1:27.
5 Gen. 2:7; Eccl. 12:7; Luke 23:43; Matt. 10:28.
6 Gen. 1:26; Col. 3:10; Eph. 4:24.
7 Rom. 2:14–15.
8 Gen. 2:17; Eccl. 7:29.
9 Gen. 3:6, 17.
10 Gen. 2:17; Gen. 2:15–3:24.
11 Gen. 1:28. (See Gen. 1:29–30; Ps. 8:6–8.)

CHAPTER 5

OF PROVIDENCE

1. God the great Creator of all things doth uphold,[1] direct, dispose, and govern all creatures, actions, and things,[2] from the greatest even to the least,[3] by his most wise and holy providence,[4] according to his infallible foreknowledge,[5] and the free and immutable counsel of his own will,[6] to the praise of the glory of his wisdom, power, justice, goodness, and mercy.[7]

2. Although, in relation to the foreknowledge and decree of God, the First Cause, all things come to pass immutably, and infallibly;[8] yet, by the same providence, he ordereth them to fall out, according to the nature of second causes, either necessarily, freely, or contingently.[9]

3. God, in his ordinary providence, maketh use of means,[10] yet is free to work without,[11] above,[12] and against them, at his pleasure.[13]

4. The almighty power, unsearchable wisdom, and infinite goodness of God so far manifest themselves in his providence, that it extendeth itself even to the first fall, and all other sins of angels and men;[14] and that not by a bare permission,[15] but such as hath joined with it a most wise and powerful bounding,[16] and otherwise ordering, and governing of them, in a manifold dispensation, to his own holy ends;[17] yet so, as the sinfulness thereof proceedeth only from

---

1 Neh. 9:6; Ps. 145:14–16; Heb. 1:3.
2 Dan. 4:34–35; Ps. 135:6; Acts 17:25–28; Job 38–41.
3 Matt. 10:29–31. (See Matt. 6:26–32.)
4 Prov. 15:3; 2 Chron. 16:9; Ps. 104:24; Ps. 145:17.
5 Acts 15:18; Isa. 42:9; Ezek. 11:5.
6 Eph. 1:11; Ps. 33:10–11.
7 Isa. 63:14; Eph. 3:10; Rom. 9:17; Gen. 45:7; Ps. 145:7.
8 Acts 2:23. (See Isa. 14:24, 27.)
9 Gen. 8:22; Jer. 31:35; Isa. 10:6–7. (See Ex. 21:13 and Deut. 19:5; 1 Kings 22:28–34.)
10 Acts 27:24, 31, 44b; Isa. 55:10–11.
11 Hos. 1:7; Matt. 4:4; Job 34:20.
12 Rom. 4:19–21.
13 2 Kings 6:6; Dan. 3:27.
14 Isa. 45:7; Rom. 11:32–34; 2 Sam. 16:10; Acts 2:23; Acts 4:27–28. (See 2 Sam. 24:1 and 1 Chron. 21:1; 1 Kings 22:22–23; 1 Chron. 10:4, 13–14.)
15 John 12:40; 2 Thess. 2:11.
16 Ps. 76:10; 2 Kings 19:28.
17 Gen. 50:20; Isa. 10:12. (See Isa. 10:6–7, 13–15.)

the creature, and not from God, who, being most holy and righteous, neither is nor can be the author or approver of sin.[18]

5. The most wise, righteous, and gracious God doth oftentimes leave, for a season, his own children to manifold temptations, and the corruption of their own hearts, to chastise them for their former sins, or to discover unto them the hidden strength of corruption and deceitfulness of their hearts, that they may be humbled;[19] and, to raise them to a more close and constant dependence for their support upon himself, and to make them more watchful against all future occasions of sin, and for sundry other just and holy ends.[20]

6. As for those wicked and ungodly men whom God, as a righteous Judge, for former sins, doth blind and harden,[21] from them he not only withholdeth his grace whereby they might have been enlightened in their understandings, and wrought upon in their hearts;[22] but sometimes also withdraweth the gifts which they had,[23] and exposeth them to such objects as their corruption makes occasions of sin;[24] and, withal, gives them over to their own lusts, the temptations of the world, and the power of Satan,[25] whereby it comes to pass that they harden themselves, even under those means which God useth for the softening of others.[26]

7. As the providence of God doth, in general, reach to all creatures; so, after a most special manner, it taketh care of his church, and disposeth all things to the good thereof.[27]

18 James 1:13–14, 17; 1 John 2:16; Ps. 50:21.
19 2 Chron. 32:25–26, 31; Deut. 8:2–3, 5; Luke 22:31–32. (See 2 Sam. 24:1, 25.)
20 2 Cor. 12:7–9. (See Ps. 73:1–28; 77:1–12; Mark 14:66–72; John 21:15–19.)
21 Rom. 1:24, 26, 28; Rom. 11:7–8.
22 Deut. 29:4; Mark 4:11–12.
23 Matt. 13:12; Matt. 25:29. (See Acts 13:10–11.)
24 Gen. 4:8; 2 Kings 8:12–13. (See Matt. 26:14–16.)
25 Ps. 109:6; Luke 22:3; 2 Thess. 2:10–12.
26 Ex. 8:15, 32; 2 Cor. 2:15–16; Isa. 8:14; 1 Peter 2:7–8. (See Ex. 7:3; Isa. 6:9–10; Acts 28:26–27.)
27 1 Tim. 4:10; Amos 9:8–9; Matt. 16:18; Rom. 8:28; Isa. 43:3–5, 14.

CHAPTER 6

OF THE FALL OF MAN, OF SIN,

AND OF THE PUNISHMENT THEREOF

1. Our first parents, being seduced by the subtilty and temptation of Satan, sinned, in eating the forbidden fruit.[1] This their sin, God was pleased, according to his wise and holy counsel, to permit, having purposed to order it to his own glory.[2]

2. By this sin they fell from their original righteousness and communion with God,[3] and so became dead in sin,[4] and wholly defiled in all the parts and faculties of soul and body.[5]

3. They being the root of all mankind, the guilt of this sin was imputed;[6] and the same death in sin, and corrupted nature, conveyed to all their posterity descending from them by ordinary generation.[7]

4. From this original corruption, whereby we are utterly indisposed, disabled, and made opposite to all good,[8] and wholly inclined to all evil,[9] do proceed all actual transgressions.[10]

5. This corruption of nature, during this life, doth remain in those that are regenerated;[11] and although it be, through Christ, pardoned, and mortified; yet both itself, and all the motions thereof, are truly and properly sin.[12]

---

1 Gen. 3:13; 2 Cor. 11:3.
2 See chapter 5, section 4.
3 Gen. 3:6–8; Rom. 3:23.
4 Gen. 2:17; Eph. 2:1–3. (See Rom. 5:12.)
5 Gen. 6:5; Jer. 17:9; Titus 1:15; Rom. 3:10–19.
6 Acts 17:26; Rom. 5:12, 15–19; 1 Cor. 15:21–22, 49.
7 Ps. 51:5; John 3:6; Gen. 5:3; Job 15:14.
8 Rom. 5:6; Rom. 7:18; Rom. 8:7; Col. 1:21.
9 Gen. 8:21. (See Gen. 6:5; Rom. 3:10–12.)
10 Matt. 15:19; James 1:14–15; Eph. 2:2–3.
11 Prov. 20:9; Eccl. 7:20; Rom. 7:14, 17–18, 21–23; 1 John 1:8, 10.
12 Rom. 7:7–8, 25; Gal. 5:17.

6. Every sin, both original and actual, being a transgression of the righteous law of God, and contrary thereunto,[13] doth, in its own nature, bring guilt upon the sinner,[14] whereby he is bound over to the wrath of God,[15] and curse of the law,[16] and so made subject to death,[17] with all miseries spiritual,[18] temporal,[19] and eternal.[20]

---

13 1 John 3:4.
14 Rom. 2:15; Rom. 3:9, 19.
15 Eph. 2:3.
16 Gal. 3:10.
17 Rom. 6:23.
18 Eph. 4:18.
19 Rom. 8:20; Lam. 3:39.
20 Matt. 25:41; 2 Thess. 1:9.

CHAPTER 7

OF GOD'S COVENANT WITH MAN

1. The distance between God and the creature is so great, that although reasonable creatures do owe obedience unto him as their Creator, yet they could never have any fruition of him as their blessedness and reward, but by some voluntary condescension on God's part, which he hath been pleased to express by way of covenant.[1]

2. The first covenant made with man was a covenant of works,[2] wherein life was promised to Adam; and in him to his posterity,[3] upon condition of perfect and personal obedience.[4]

3. Man, by his fall, having made himself uncapable of life by that covenant, the Lord was pleased to make a second,[5] commonly called the covenant of grace; wherein he freely offereth unto sinners life and salvation by Jesus Christ; requiring of them faith in him, that they may be saved,[6] and promising to give unto all those that are ordained unto eternal life his Holy Spirit, to make them willing, and able to believe.[7]

4. This covenant of grace is frequently set forth in Scripture by the name of a testament, in reference to the death of Jesus Christ the Testator, and to the everlasting inheritance, with all things belonging to it, therein bequeathed.[8]

5. This covenant was differently administered in the time of the law, and in the time of the gospel:[9] under the law, it was administered by promises, prophecies, sacrifices, circumcision, the paschal lamb, and other types and ordinances delivered to the people of the Jews, all foresignifying Christ to come;[10] which were, for that time, sufficient and efficacious, through the operation of the

---

1 Isa. 40:13–17; Job 9:32–33; Ps. 113:5–6; Job 22:2–3; Job 35:7–8; Luke 17:10; Acts 17:24–25.
2 Gen. 2:16–17; Hos. 6:7; Gal. 3:12.
3 Gen. 3:22; Rom. 10:5; Rom. 5:12–14. (See Rom. 5:15–20.)
4 Gen. 2:17; Gal. 3:10.
5 Gal. 3:21; Rom. 3:20–21; Rom. 8:3; Gen. 3:15. (See Isa. 42:6.)
6 John 3:16; Rom. 10:6, 9; Rev. 22:17.
7 Acts 13:48; Ezek. 36:26–27; John 6:37, 44–45; 1 Cor. 12:3.
8 Heb. 9:15–17.
9 2 Cor. 3:6–9.
10 Heb. 8–10; Rom. 4:11; Col. 2:11–12; 1 Cor. 5:7.

Spirit, to instruct and build up the elect in faith in the promised Messiah,[11] by whom they had full remission of sins, and eternal salvation; and is called the old testament.[12]

6. Under the gospel, when Christ, the substance,[13] was exhibited, the ordinances in which this covenant is dispensed are the preaching of the Word, and the administration of the sacraments of baptism and the Lord's Supper:[14] which, though fewer in number, and administered with more simplicity, and less outward glory, yet, in them, it is held forth in more fullness, evidence, and spiritual efficacy,[15] to all nations, both Jews and Gentiles;[16] and is called the new testament.[17] There are not therefore two covenants of grace, differing in substance, but one and the same, under various dispensations.[18]

---

11 1 Cor. 10:1–4; Heb. 11:13; John 8:56.
12 Gal. 3:7–9, 14; Ps. 32:1–2, 5.
13 Col. 2:17.
14 1 Cor. 1:21; Matt. 28:19–20; 1 Cor. 11:23–25.
15 Heb. 12:22–24; 2 Cor. 3:9–11; Jer. 31:33–34.
16 Luke 2:32; Acts 10:34; Eph. 2:15–19.
17 Luke 22:20.
18 Gal. 3:8–9, 14, 16; Rom. 3:21–22, 30; Rom. 4:3, 6–8 (see Gen. 15:6); Ps. 32:1–2; Rom. 4:16–17, 23–24; Heb. 4:2. (See Rom. 10:6–10; 1 Cor. 10:3–4.)

CHAPTER 8

OF CHRIST THE MEDIATOR

1. It pleased God, in his eternal purpose, to choose and ordain the Lord Jesus, his only begotten Son, to be the Mediator between God and man,[1] the Prophet,[2] Priest,[3] and King,[4] the Head and Savior of his church,[5] the Heir of all things,[6] and Judge of the world:[7] unto whom he did from all eternity give a people, to be his seed,[8] and to be by him in time redeemed, called, justified, sanctified, and glorified.[9]

2. The Son of God, the second person in the Trinity, being very and eternal God, of one substance and equal with the Father, did, when the fullness of time was come, take upon him man's nature,[10] with all the essential properties, and common infirmities thereof, yet without sin;[11] being conceived by the power of the Holy Ghost, in the womb of the virgin Mary, of her substance.[12] So that two whole, perfect, and distinct natures, the Godhead and the manhood, were inseparably joined together in one person, without conversion, composition, or confusion.[13] Which person is very God, and very man, yet one Christ, the only Mediator between God and man.[14]

3. The Lord Jesus, in his human nature thus united to the divine, was sanctified, and anointed with the Holy Spirit, above measure,[15] having in him all the treasures of wisdom and knowledge;[16] in whom it pleased the Father that

---

1 Isa. 42:1; 1 Peter 1:19–20; John 3:16; 1 Tim. 2:5.
2 Acts 3:20, 22. (See Deut. 18:15.)
3 Heb. 5:5–6.
4 Ps. 2:6; Luke 1:33. (See Isa. 9:5–6; Acts 2:29–36; Col. 1:13.)
5 Eph. 5:23.
6 Heb. 1:2.
7 Acts 17:31.
8 John 17:6; Ps. 22:30; Isa. 53:10; Eph. 1:4.
9 1 Tim. 2:6; Isa. 55:4–5; 1 Cor. 1:30; Rom. 8:30.
10 John 1:1, 14; 1 John 5:20; Phil. 2:6; Gal. 4:4.
11 Phil. 2:7; Heb. 2:14, 16–17; Heb. 4:15.
12 Luke 1:27, 31, 35; Gal. 4:4. (See Matt. 1:18, 20–21.)
13 Matt. 16:16; Col. 2:9; Rom. 9:5; 1 Tim. 3:16.
14 Rom. 1:3–4; 1 Tim. 2:5.
15 Ps. 45:7; John 3:34. (See Isa. 61:1; Luke 4:18; Heb. 1:8–9.)
16 Col. 2:3.

all fullness should dwell;[17] to the end that, being holy, harmless, undefiled, and full of grace and truth,[18] he might be thoroughly furnished to execute the office of a mediator, and surety.[19] Which office he took not unto himself, but was thereunto called by his Father,[20] who put all power and judgment into his hand, and gave him commandment to execute the same.[21]

4. This office the Lord Jesus did most willingly undertake;[22] which that he might discharge, he was made under the law,[23] and did perfectly fulfill it;[24] endured most grievous torments immediately in his soul,[25] and most painful sufferings in his body;[26] was crucified, and died,[27] was buried, and remained under the power of death, yet saw no corruption.[28] On the third day he arose from the dead,[29] with the same body in which he suffered,[30] with which also he ascended into heaven, and there sitteth at the right hand of his Father,[31] making intercession,[32] and shall return, to judge men and angels, at the end of the world.[33]

5. The Lord Jesus, by his perfect obedience, and sacrifice of himself, which he, through the eternal Spirit, once offered up unto God, hath fully satisfied the justice of his Father;[34] and purchased, not only reconciliation, but an everlasting inheritance in the kingdom of heaven, for all those whom the Father hath given unto him.[35]

---

17 Col. 1:19.
18 Heb. 7:26; John 1:14.
19 Acts 10:38; Heb. 12:24; Heb. 7:22.
20 Heb. 5:4–5.
21 John 5:22, 27; Matt. 28:18; Acts 2:36.
22 Ps. 40:7–8. (See Heb. 10:5–10; John 4:34; John 10:18; Phil. 2:8.)
23 Gal. 4:4.
24 Matt. 3:15; Matt. 5:17; Heb. 5:8–9.
25 Matt. 26:37–38; Luke 22:44; Matt. 27:46.
26 Matt. 26:67–68; Matt. 27:27–50.
27 Mark 15:24, 37; Phil. 2:8.
28 Matt. 27:60; Acts 2:24, 27; Acts 13:29, 37; Rom. 6:9.
29 1 Cor. 15:3–4.
30 Luke 24:39; John 20:25, 27.
31 Luke 24:50–51; 1 Peter 3:22.
32 Rom. 8:34; Heb. 7:25. (See Heb. 9:24.)
33 Acts 1:11; John 5:28–29; Rom. 14:10b; Acts 10:42; Matt. 13:40–42; Jude 6. (See 2 Peter 2:4.)
34 Rom. 5:19; Heb. 9:14; Heb. 10:14; Eph. 5:2; Rom. 3:25–26.
35 Dan. 9:24; 2 Cor. 5:18; Col. 1:20; Eph. 1:11, 14; Heb. 9:12, 15; John 17:2.

6. Although the work of redemption was not actually wrought by Christ till after his incarnation, yet the virtue, efficacy, and benefits thereof were communicated unto the elect, in all ages successively from the beginning of the world, in and by those promises, types, and sacrifices, wherein he was revealed, and signified to be the seed of the woman which should bruise the serpent's head; and the Lamb slain from the beginning of the world; being yesterday and today the same, and forever.[36]

7. Christ, in the work of mediation, acts according to both natures, by each nature doing that which is proper to itself;[37] yet, by reason of the unity of the person, that which is proper to one nature is sometimes in Scripture attributed to the person denominated by the other nature.[38]

8. To all those for whom Christ hath purchased redemption, he doth certainly and effectually apply and communicate the same;[39] making intercession for them,[40] and revealing unto them, in and by the Word, the mysteries of salvation;[41] effectually persuading them by his Spirit to believe and obey, and governing their hearts by his Word and Spirit;[42] overcoming all their enemies by his almighty power and wisdom, in such manner, and ways, as are most consonant to his wonderful and unsearchable dispensation.[43]

36 Gal. 4:4–5; Gen. 3:15; 1 Cor. 10:4; Rev. 13:8; Heb. 13:8. (See Rom. 3:25; Heb. 9:15.)
37 John 10:17–18; 1 Peter 3:18; Heb. 1:3. (See Heb. 9:14.)
38 Acts 20:28; Luke 1:43. (See Rom. 9:5.)
39 John 6:37, 39; John 10:15–16, 27–28.
40 1 John 2:1; Rom. 8:34.
41 John 15:15; Eph. 1:9; John 17:6.
42 John 14:26; 2 Cor. 4:13; Rom. 8:9, 14; Rom. 15:18–19; John 17:17.
43 Ps. 110:1; 1 Cor. 15:25–26; Col. 2:15; Luke 10:19.

CHAPTER 9
OF FREE WILL

1. God hath endued the will of man with that natural liberty, that it is neither forced, nor, by any absolute necessity of nature, determined to good, or evil.[1]

2. Man, in his state of innocency, had freedom, and power to will and to do that which was good and well pleasing to God;[2] but yet, mutably, so that he might fall from it.[3]

3. Man, by his fall into a state of sin, hath wholly lost all ability of will to any spiritual good accompanying salvation:[4] so as, a natural man, being altogether averse from that good,[5] and dead in sin,[6] is not able, by his own strength, to convert himself, or to prepare himself thereunto.[7]

4. When God converts a sinner, and translates him into the state of grace, he freeth him from his natural bondage under sin;[8] and, by his grace alone, enables him freely to will and to do that which is spiritually good;[9] yet so, as that by reason of his remaining corruption, he doth not perfectly, nor only, will that which is good, but doth also will that which is evil.[10]

5. The will of man is made perfectly and immutably free to good alone, in the state of glory only.[11]

---

1 James 1:13–14; Deut. 30:19; Isa. 7:11–12; Matt. 17:12; John 5:40; James 4:7.
2 Eccl. 7:29; Gen. 1:26, 31; Col. 3:10.
3 Gen. 2:16–17; Gen. 3:6, 17.
4 Rom. 8:7–8; John 6:44, 65; John 15:5; Rom. 5:5.
5 Rom. 3:9–10, 12, 23.
6 Eph. 2:1, 5; Col. 2:13.
7 John 6:44, 65; John 3:3, 5–6; 1 Cor. 2:14; Titus 3:3–5.
8 Col. 1:13; John 8:34, 36; Rom. 6:6–7.
9 Phil. 2:13; Rom. 6:14, 17–19, 22.
10 Gal. 5:17; Rom. 7:14–25; 1 John 1:8, 10.
11 Heb. 12:23; 1 John 3:2; Jude 24; Rev. 21:27.

CHAPTER 10
OF EFFECTUAL CALLING

1. All those whom God hath predestinated unto life, and those only, he is pleased, in his appointed and accepted time, effectually to call,[1] by his Word and Spirit,[2] out of that state of sin and death, in which they are by nature, to grace and salvation, by Jesus Christ;[3] enlightening their minds spiritually and savingly to understand the things of God,[4] taking away their heart of stone, and giving unto them a heart of flesh;[5] renewing their wills, and, by his almighty power, determining them to that which is good,[6] and effectually drawing them to Jesus Christ:[7] yet so, as they come most freely, being made willing by his grace.[8]

2. This effectual call is of God's free and special grace alone, not from anything at all foreseen in man,[9] who is altogether passive therein, until, being quickened and renewed by the Holy Spirit,[10] he is thereby enabled to answer this call, and to embrace the grace offered and conveyed in it.[11]

3. Elect infants, dying in infancy, are regenerated, and saved by Christ, through the Spirit,[12] who worketh when, and where, and how he pleaseth:[13] so also are all other elect persons who are uncapable of being outwardly called by the ministry of the Word.[14]

---

1 Acts 13:48; Rom. 8:28, 30; Rom. 11:7; Eph. 1:5, 11; 2 Tim. 1:9–10.
2 2 Thess. 2:13–14; James 1:18; 2 Cor. 3:3, 6; 1 Cor. 2:12.
3 2 Tim. 1:9–10; 1 Peter 2:9; Rom. 8:2; Eph. 2:1–10.
4 Acts 26:18; 1 Cor. 2:10, 12; Eph. 1:17–18; 2 Cor. 4:6.
5 Ezek. 36:26.
6 Ezek. 11:19; Deut. 30:6; Ezek. 36:27; John 3:5; Titus 3:5; 1 Peter 1:23.
7 John 6:44–45; Acts 16:14.
8 Ps. 110:3; John 6:37; Matt. 11:28; Rev. 22:17; Rom. 6:16–18; Eph. 2:8; Phil. 1:29.
9 2 Tim. 1:9; Eph. 2:8–9; Rom. 9:11.
10 1 Cor. 2:14; Rom. 8:7–9; Titus 3:4–5.
11 John 6:37; Ezek. 36:27; 1 John 5:1. (Cf. 1 John 3:9.)
12 Gen. 17:7; Luke 18:15–16; Acts 2:39; John 3:3, 5; 1 John 5:12. (See Luke 1:15.)
13 John 3:8.
14 John 16:7–8; 1 John 5:12; Acts 4:12.

4. Others, not elected, although they may be called by the ministry of the Word,[15] and may have some common operations of the Spirit,[16] yet they never truly come unto Christ, and therefore cannot be saved:[17] much less can men, not professing the Christian religion, be saved in any other way whatsoever, be they never so diligent to frame their lives according to the light of nature, and the laws of that religion they do profess.[18] And, to assert and maintain that they may, is very pernicious, and to be detested.[19]

---

15 Matt. 13:14–15; Acts 28:24 (cf. Acts 13:48); Matt. 22:14.
16 Matt. 13:20–21; Matt. 7:22; Heb. 6:4–5.
17 John 6:37, 64–66; John 8:44; John 13:18. (Cf. John 17:12.)
18 Acts 4:12; 1 John 4:2–3; 2 John 9; John 14:6; Eph. 2:12–13; John 4:22; John 17:3; Rom. 10:13–17.
19 2 John 9–11; 1 Cor. 16:22; Gal. 1:6–8.

CHAPTER 11

OF JUSTIFICATION

1. Those whom God effectually calleth, he also freely justifieth:[1] not by infusing righteousness into them, but by pardoning their sins, and by accounting and accepting their persons as righteous; not for anything wrought in them, or done by them, but for Christ's sake alone; nor by imputing faith itself, the act of believing, or any other evangelical obedience to them, as their righteousness; but by imputing the obedience and satisfaction of Christ unto them,[2] they receiving and resting on him and his righteousness, by faith; which faith they have not of themselves, it is the gift of God.[3]

2. Faith, thus receiving and resting on Christ and his righteousness, is the alone instrument of justification:[4] yet is it not alone in the person justified, but is ever accompanied with all other saving graces, and is no dead faith, but worketh by love.[5]

3. Christ, by his obedience and death, did fully discharge the debt of all those that are thus justified, and did make a proper, real, and full satisfaction to his Father's justice in their behalf.[6] Yet, inasmuch as he was given by the Father for them;[7] and his obedience and satisfaction accepted in their stead;[8] and both, freely, not for anything in them; their justification is only of free grace;[9] that both the exact justice and rich grace of God might be glorified in the justification of sinners.[10]

---

1   Rom. 8:30; Rom. 3:24; Rom. 5:15–16.
2   Rom. 4:5–8; 2 Cor. 5:19, 21; Rom. 3:22–28; Titus 3:5, 7; Eph. 1:7; Jer. 23:6; 1 Cor. 1:30–31; Rom. 5:17–19.
3   John 1:12; Acts 10:43; Acts 13:38–39; Phil. 3:9; Eph. 2:7–8; John 6:44–45, 65; Phil. 1:29.
4   John 3:18, 36; Rom. 3:28; Rom. 5:1.
5   James 2:17, 22, 26; Gal. 5:6.
6   Mark 10:45; Rom. 5:8–10, 18–19; Gal. 3:13; 1 Tim. 2:5–6; Heb. 1:3; Heb. 10:10, 14; Dan. 9:24, 26. (See Isa. 52:13–53:12.)
7   Rom. 8:32; John 3:16.
8   2 Cor. 5:21; Eph. 5:2; Phil. 2:6–9; Isa. 53:10–11.
9   Rom. 3:24; Eph. 1:7.
10   Rom. 3:26; Eph. 2:7; Zech. 9:9; Isa. 45:21.

4. God did, from all eternity, decree to justify all the elect,[11] and Christ did, in the fullness of time, die for their sins, and rise again for their justification:[12] nevertheless, they are not justified, until the Holy Spirit doth, in due time, actually apply Christ unto them.[13]

5. God doth continue to forgive the sins of those that are justified;[14] and, although they can never fall from the state of justification,[15] yet they may, by their sins, fall under God's fatherly displeasure, and not have the light of his countenance restored unto them, until they humble themselves, confess their sins, beg pardon, and renew their faith and repentance.[16]

6. The justification of believers under the old testament was, in all these respects, one and the same with the justification of believers under the new testament.[17]

---

11 Rom. 8:29–30; Gal. 3:8; 1 Peter 1:2, 19–20.
12 Gal. 4:4; 1 Tim. 2:6; Rom. 4:25.
13 Eph. 2:3; Titus 3:3–7; Gal. 2:16. (Cf. Col. 1:21–22.)
14 Matt. 6:12; 1 John 1:7, 9; 1 John 2:1–2.
15 Rom. 5:1–5; Rom. 8:30–39; Heb. 10:14 (cf. Luke 22:32); John 10:28.
16 Ps. 89:30–33; Ps. 51; Ps. 32:5; Matt. 26:75; Luke 1:20; 1 Cor. 11:30, 32.
17 Gal. 3:9, 13–14; Rom. 4:6–8, 22–24; Rom. 10:6–13; Heb. 13:8.

CHAPTER 12

OF ADOPTION

1. All those that are justified, God vouchsafeth, in and for his only Son Jesus Christ, to make partakers of the grace of adoption,[1] by which they are taken into the number, and enjoy the liberties and privileges of the children of God,[2] have his name put upon them,[3] receive the Spirit of adoption,[4] have access to the throne of grace with boldness,[5] are enabled to cry, Abba, Father,[6] are pitied,[7] protected,[8] provided for,[9] and chastened by him, as by a father:[10] yet never cast off,[11] but sealed to the day of redemption;[12] and inherit the promises,[13] as heirs of everlasting salvation.[14]

---

1 Eph. 1:5; Gal. 4:4–5.
2 Rom. 8:17; John 1:12.
3 Num. 6:24–26; Jer. 14:9; Amos 9:12; Acts 15:17; 2 Cor. 6:18; Rev. 3:12.
4 Rom. 8:15.
5 Eph. 3:12. (See Heb. 4:16.)
6 Rom. 8:15. (See Gal. 4:6; Rom. 8:16.)
7 Ps. 103:13.
8 Prov. 14:26.
9 Matt. 6:30, 32; 1 Peter 5:7.
10 Heb. 12:6.
11 Lam. 3:31–32. (See Ps. 89:30–35.)
12 Eph. 4:30.
13 Heb. 6:12.
14 1 Peter 1:3–4; Heb. 1:14.

CHAPTER 13
OF SANCTIFICATION

1. They, who are once effectually called, and regenerated, having a new heart, and a new spirit created in them, are further sanctified, really and personally, through the virtue of Christ's death and resurrection,[1] by his Word and Spirit dwelling in them:[2] the dominion of the whole body of sin is destroyed,[3] and the several lusts thereof are more and more weakened and mortified;[4] and they more and more quickened and strengthened in all saving graces,[5] to the practice of true holiness, without which no man shall see the Lord.[6]

2. This sanctification is throughout, in the whole man;[7] yet imperfect in this life, there abiding still some remnants of corruption in every part;[8] whence ariseth a continual and irreconcilable war, the flesh lusting against the Spirit, and the Spirit against the flesh.[9]

3. In which war, although the remaining corruption, for a time, may much prevail;[10] yet, through the continual supply of strength from the sanctifying Spirit of Christ, the regenerate part doth overcome;[11] and so, the saints grow in grace,[12] perfecting holiness in the fear of God.[13]

---

1   1 Thess. 5:23–24; 2 Thess. 2:13–14; Ezek. 36:22–28; Titus 3:5; Acts 20:32; Phil. 3:10; Rom. 6:5–6.
2   John 17:17, 19; Eph. 5:26; Rom. 8:13–14; 2 Thess. 2:13.
3   Rom. 6:6, 14.
4   Gal. 5:24; Rom. 8:13.
5   Col. 1:10–11; Eph. 3:16–19.
6   2 Cor. 7:1; Col. 1:28; Col. 4:12; Heb. 12:14.
7   1 Thess. 5:23; Rom. 12:1–2.
8   1 John 1:8–10; Rom. 7:14–25; Phil. 3:12.
9   Gal. 5:17.
10 Rom. 7:23.
11 Rom. 6:14; 1 John 5:4; Eph. 4:15–16. (See Rom. 8:2.)
12 2 Peter 3:18; 2 Cor. 3:18.
13 2 Cor. 7:1.

CHAPTER 14

OF SAVING FAITH

1. The grace of faith, whereby the elect are enabled to believe to the saving of their souls,[1] is the work of the Spirit of Christ in their hearts,[2] and is ordinarily wrought by the ministry of the Word,[3] by which also, and by the administration of the sacraments, and prayer, it is increased and strengthened.[4]

2. By this faith, a Christian believeth to be true whatsoever is revealed in the Word, for the authority of God himself speaking therein;[5] and acteth differently upon that which each particular passage thereof containeth; yielding obedience to the commands,[6] trembling at the threatenings,[7] and embracing the promises of God for this life, and that which is to come.[8] But the principal acts of saving faith are accepting, receiving, and resting upon Christ alone for justification, sanctification, and eternal life, by virtue of the covenant of grace.[9]

3. This faith is different in degrees, weak or strong;[10] may be often and many ways assailed, and weakened, but gets the victory:[11] growing up in many to the attainment of a full assurance, through Christ,[12] who is both the author and finisher of our faith.[13]

---

1 Titus 1:1; Heb. 10:39.
2 1 Cor. 12:3; John 3:5; Titus 3:5; John 6:44–45, 65; Eph. 2:8; Phil. 1:29; 2 Peter 1:1. (See 1 Peter 1:2.)
3 Matt. 28:19–20; Rom. 10:14, 17; 1 Cor. 1:21.
4 1 Peter 2:2; Acts 20:32; Rom. 1:16–17; Matt. 28:19 (see Acts 2:38); 1 Cor. 10:16; 1 Cor. 11:23–29; Luke 17:5; Phil. 4:6–7.
5 2 Peter 1:20–21; John 4:42; 1 Thess. 2:13; 1 John 5:9–10; Acts 24:14.
6 Ps. 119:10–11, 48, 97–98, 167–168; John 14:15.
7 Ezra 9:4; Isa. 66:2; Heb. 4:1.
8 Heb. 11:13; 1 Tim. 4:8.
9 John 1:12; Acts 16:31; Gal. 2:20; Acts 15:11; 2 Tim. 1:9–10.
10 Heb. 5:13–14; Rom. 14:1–2; Matt. 6:30; Rom. 4:19–20; Matt. 8:10.
11 Luke 22:31–32; Eph. 6:16; 1 John 5:4–5.
12 Heb. 6:11–12; Heb. 10:22; Col. 2:2.
13 Heb. 12:2.

CHAPTER 15
OF REPENTANCE UNTO LIFE

1. Repentance unto life is an evangelical grace,[1] the doctrine whereof is to be preached by every minister of the gospel, as well as that of faith in Christ.[2]

2. By it, a sinner, out of the sight and sense not only of the danger, but also of the filthiness and odiousness of his sins, as contrary to the holy nature, and righteous law of God; and upon the apprehension of his mercy in Christ to such as are penitent, so grieves for, and hates his sins, as to turn from them all unto God,[3] purposing and endeavoring to walk with him in all the ways of his commandments.[4]

3. Although repentance be not to be rested in, as any satisfaction for sin, or any cause of the pardon thereof,[5] which is the act of God's free grace in Christ;[6] yet it is of such necessity to all sinners, that none may expect pardon without it.[7]

4. As there is no sin so small, but it deserves damnation;[8] so there is no sin so great, that it can bring damnation upon those who truly repent.[9]

5. Men ought not to content themselves with a general repentance, but it is every man's duty to endeavor to repent of his particular sins, particularly.[10]

6. As every man is bound to make private confession of his sins to God, praying for the pardon thereof;[11] upon which, and the forsaking of them, he shall find mercy;[12] so, he that scandalizeth his brother, or the church of Christ, ought to be willing, by a private or public confession, and sorrow for his sin, to declare his repentance to those that are offended,[13] who are thereupon to be reconciled to him, and in love to receive him.[14]

---

1 Acts 11:18; 2 Cor. 7:10; Zech. 12:10.
2 Luke 24:47; Mark 1:15; Acts 20:21.
3 Ezek. 18:30–31; Ezek. 36:31; Isa. 30:22; Ps. 51:4; Jer. 31:18–19; Joel 2:12–13; Amos 5:15; Ps. 119:128; 2 Cor. 7:11; 1 Thess. 1:9.
4 Ps. 119:6, 59, 106; 2 Kings 23:25. (See Luke 1:6.)
5 Ezek. 36:31–32; Ezek. 16:61–63; Isa. 43:25.
6 Hos. 14:2, 4; Rom. 3:24; Eph. 1:7.
7 Luke 13:3, 5; Mark 1:4; Acts 17:30–31.
8 Rom. 6:23; Gal. 3:10; Matt. 12:36.
9 Isa. 55:7; Rom. 8:1; Isa. 1:16–18.
10 Ps. 19:13; Matt. 26:75; Luke 19:8; 1 Tim. 1:13, 15.
11 Ps. 32:5–6; Ps. 51:1–14.
12 Prov. 28:13; Isa. 55:7; 1 John 1:9.
13 James 5:16; Luke 17:3–4; Josh. 7:19. (See Matt. 18:15–18.)
14 2 Cor. 2:7–8. (See Gal. 6:1–2.)

CHAPTER 16

OF GOOD WORKS

1. Good works are only such as God hath commanded in his holy Word,[1] and not such as, without the warrant thereof, are devised by men, out of blind zeal, or upon any pretense of good intention.[2]

2. These good works, done in obedience to God's commandments, are the fruits and evidences of a true and lively faith:[3] and by them believers manifest their thankfulness,[4] strengthen their assurance,[5] edify their brethren,[6] adorn the profession of the gospel,[7] stop the mouths of the adversaries,[8] and glorify God,[9] whose workmanship they are, created in Christ Jesus thereunto,[10] that, having their fruit unto holiness, they may have the end, eternal life.[11]

3. Their ability to do good works is not at all of themselves, but wholly from the Spirit of Christ.[12] And that they may be enabled thereunto, beside the graces they have already received, there is required an actual influence of the same Holy Spirit, to work in them to will, and to do, of his good pleasure:[13] yet are they not hereupon to grow negligent, as if they were not bound to perform any duty unless upon a special motion of the Spirit; but they ought to be diligent in stirring up the grace of God that is in them.[14]

4. They who, in their obedience, attain to the greatest height which is possible in this life, are so far from being able to supererogate, and to do more than God requires, as that they fall short of much which in duty they are bound to do.[15]

---

1   Mic. 6:8; Rom. 12:2; Heb. 13:21.
2   Matt. 15:9; Isa. 29:13; 1 Peter 1:18; John 16:2; Rom. 10:2; 1 Sam. 15:21–23; Deut. 10:12–13; Col. 2:16–17, 20–23.
3   James 2:18, 22.
4   Ps. 116:12–14; Col. 3:15–17; 1 Peter 2:9.
5   1 John 2:3, 5; 2 Peter 1:5–10.
6   2 Cor. 9:2; Matt. 5:16; 1 Tim. 4:12.
7   Titus 2:5, 9–12; 1 Tim. 6:1.
8   1 Peter 2:15.
9   1 Peter 2:12; Phil. 1:11; John 15:8.
10 Eph. 2:10.
11 Rom. 6:22.
12 John 15:4–6; Rom. 8:4–14; Ezek. 36:26–27.
13 Phil. 2:13; Phil. 4:13; 2 Cor. 3:5; Eph. 3:16.
14 Phil. 2:12; Heb. 6:11–12; 2 Peter 1:3, 5, 10–11; Isa. 64:7; 2 Tim. 1:6; Acts 26:6–7; Jude 20–21.
15 Luke 17:10; Neh. 13:22; Rom. 8:21–25; Gal. 5:17.

5. We cannot by our best works merit pardon of sin, or eternal life at the hand of God, by reason of the great disproportion that is between them and the glory to come; and the infinite distance that is between us and God, whom, by them, we can neither profit, nor satisfy for the debt of our former sins,[16] but when we have done all we can, we have done but our duty, and are unprofitable servants:[17] and because, as they are good, they proceed from his Spirit;[18] and as they are wrought by us, they are defiled, and mixed with so much weakness and imperfection, that they cannot endure the severity of God's judgment.[19]

6. Notwithstanding, the persons of believers being accepted through Christ, their good works also are accepted in him;[20] not as though they were in this life wholly unblamable and unreprovable in God's sight;[21] but that he, looking upon them in his Son, is pleased to accept and reward that which is sincere, although accompanied with many weaknesses and imperfections.[22]

7. Works done by unregenerate men, although for the matter of them they may be things which God commands; and of good use both to themselves and others:[23] yet, because they proceed not from an heart purified by faith;[24] nor are done in a right manner, according to the Word;[25] nor to a right end, the glory of God,[26] they are therefore sinful, and cannot please God, or make a man meet to receive grace from God:[27] and yet, their neglect of them is more sinful and displeasing unto God.[28]

---

16 Rom. 3:20; Rom. 4:2, 4, 6; Eph. 2:8–9; Titus 3:5–7; Rom. 8:18, 22–24; Ps. 16:2; Job 22:2–3; Job 35:7–8.
17 Luke 17:10.
18 Rom. 8:13–14; Gal. 5:22–23.
19 Isa. 64:6; Gal. 5:17; Rom. 7:15, 18; Ps. 143:2; Ps. 130:3.
20 Eph. 1:6; 1 Peter 2:5. (See Ex. 28:38; Gen. 4:4; Heb. 11:4.)
21 Job 9:20; Ps. 143:2; 1 John 1:8.
22 Heb. 13:20–21; 2 Cor. 8:12; Heb. 6:10; Matt. 25:21, 23; 1 Cor. 3:14; 1 Cor. 4:5.
23 2 Kings 10:30–31; 1 Kings 21:27, 29; Luke 6:32–34; Luke 18:2–7. (See Rom. 13:4.)
24 Heb. 11:4, 6. (See Gen. 4:3–5.)
25 1 Cor. 13:3; Isa. 1:12.
26 Matt. 6:2, 5, 16; 1 Cor. 10:31.
27 Prov. 21:27; Hag. 2:14; Titus 1:15; Amos 5:21–22; Mark 7:6–7; Hos. 1:4; Rom. 9:16; Titus 3:5.
28 Ps. 14:4; Ps. 36:3; Matt. 25:41–45; Matt. 23:23. (See Rom. 1:21–32.)

CHAPTER 17
OF THE PERSEVERANCE OF THE SAINTS

1. They, whom God hath accepted in his Beloved, effectually called, and sanctified by his Spirit, can neither totally nor finally fall away from the state of grace, but shall certainly persevere therein to the end, and be eternally saved.[1]

2. This perseverance of the saints depends not upon their own free will, but upon the immutability of the decree of election, flowing from the free and unchangeable love of God the Father;[2] upon the efficacy of the merit and intercession of Jesus Christ,[3] the abiding of the Spirit, and of the seed of God within them,[4] and the nature of the covenant of grace:[5] from all which ariseth also the certainty and infallibility thereof.[6]

3. Nevertheless, they may, through the temptations of Satan and of the world, the prevalency of corruption remaining in them, and the neglect of the means of their preservation, fall into grievous sins;[7] and, for a time, continue therein:[8] whereby they incur God's displeasure,[9] and grieve his Holy Spirit,[10] come to be deprived of some measure of their graces and comforts,[11] have their hearts hardened,[12] and their consciences wounded;[13] hurt and scandalize others,[14] and bring temporal judgments upon themselves.[15]

---

1 Phil. 1:6; 2 Peter 1:10; Rom. 8:28–30; John 10:28–29; 1 John 3:9; 1 John 5:18; 1 Peter 1:5, 9.
2 Ps. 89:3–4, 28–33; 2 Tim. 2:18–19; Jer. 31:3.
3 Heb. 10:10, 14; Heb. 13:20–21; Heb. 9:12–15; Rom. 8:33–39; John 17:11, 24; Luke 22:32; Heb. 7:25.
4 John 14:16–17; 1 John 2:27; 1 John 3:9.
5 Jer. 32:40; Ps. 89:34–37. (See Jer. 31:31–34.)
6 John 6:38–40; John 10:28; 2 Thess. 3:3; 1 John 2:19.
7 Ex. 32:21; Jonah 1:3, 10; Ps. 51:14; Matt. 26:70, 72, 74.
8 2 Sam. 12:9, 13; Gal. 2:11–14.
9 Num. 20:12; 2 Sam. 11:27; Isa. 64:7, 9.
10 Eph. 4:30.
11 Ps. 51:8, 10, 12; Rev. 2:4; Matt. 26:75.
12 Isa. 63:17.
13 Ps. 32:3–4; Ps. 51:8.
14 Gen. 12:10–20; 2 Sam. 12:14; Gal. 2:13.
15 Ps. 89:31–32; 1 Cor. 11:32.

CHAPTER 18
OF THE ASSURANCE OF GRACE AND SALVATION

1. Although hypocrites and other unregenerate men may vainly deceive themselves with false hopes and carnal presumptions of being in the favor of God, and estate of salvation[1] (which hope of theirs shall perish[2]): yet such as truly believe in the Lord Jesus, and love him in sincerity, endeavoring to walk in all good conscience before him, may, in this life, be certainly assured that they are in the state of grace,[3] and may rejoice in the hope of the glory of God, which hope shall never make them ashamed.[4]

2. This certainty is not a bare conjectural and probable persuasion grounded upon a fallible hope;[5] but an infallible assurance of faith founded upon the divine truth of the promises of salvation,[6] the inward evidence of those graces unto which these promises are made,[7] the testimony of the Spirit of adoption witnessing with our spirits that we are the children of God,[8] which Spirit is the earnest of our inheritance, whereby we are sealed to the day of redemption.[9]

3. This infallible assurance doth not so belong to the essence of faith, but that a true believer may wait long, and conflict with many difficulties, before he be partaker of it:[10] yet, being enabled by the Spirit to know the things which are freely given him of God, he may, without extraordinary revelation, in the right use of ordinary means, attain thereunto.[11] And therefore it is the duty of everyone to give all diligence to make his calling and election sure,[12] that thereby his heart may be enlarged in peace and joy in the Holy Ghost, in love and thankfulness to God, and in strength and cheerfulness in the duties of

1 Mic. 3:11; Deut. 29:19; John 8:41.
2 Amos 9:10; Matt. 7:22–23.
3 1 John 5:13; 1 John 2:3; 1 John 3:14, 18–19, 21, 24.
4 Rom. 5:2, 5.
5 Heb. 6:11, 19.
6 Heb. 6:17–18.
7 2 Peter 1:4–11; 1 John 2:3; 1 John 3:14; 2 Cor. 1:12.
8 Rom. 8:15–16.
9 Eph. 1:13–14; Eph. 4:30; 2 Cor. 1:21–22.
10 1 John 5:13.
11 1 Cor. 2:12; 1 John 4:13; Heb. 6:11–12; Eph. 3:17–18.
12 2 Peter 1:10.

obedience, the proper fruits of this assurance;[13] so far is it from inclining men to looseness.[14]

4. True believers may have the assurance of their salvation divers ways shaken, diminished, and intermitted; as, by negligence in preserving of it, by falling into some special sin which woundeth the conscience and grieveth the Spirit; by some sudden or vehement temptation, by God's withdrawing the light of his countenance, and suffering even such as fear him to walk in darkness and to have no light:[15] yet are they never utterly destitute of that seed of God, and life of faith, that love of Christ and the brethren, that sincerity of heart, and conscience of duty, out of which, by the operation of the Spirit, this assurance may, in due time, be revived;[16] and by the which, in the meantime, they are supported from utter despair.[17]

---

13 Rom. 5:1–2, 5; Rom. 14:17; Rom. 15:13; Eph. 1:3–4; Ps. 4:6–7; Ps. 119:32.
14 1 John 2:1–2; Rom. 6:1–2; Titus 2:11–12, 14; 2 Cor. 7:1; Rom. 8:1, 12; 1 John 3:2–3; Ps. 130:4;
   1 John 1:6–7.
15 Ps. 51:8, 12, 14; Eph. 4:30–31; Ps. 77:1–10; Ps. 31:22. (Cf. Matt. 26:69–72 and Luke 22:31–34.)
16 1 John 3:9; Luke 22:32; Ps. 51:8, 12. (See Ps. 73:15.)
17 Mic. 7:7–9; Jer. 32:40; Isa. 54:7–14; 2 Cor. 4:8–10.

CHAPTER 19

OF THE LAW OF GOD

1. God gave to Adam a law, as a covenant of works, by which he bound him and all his posterity to personal, entire, exact, and perpetual obedience, promised life upon the fulfilling, and threatened death upon the breach of it, and endued him with power and ability to keep it.[1]

2. This law, after his fall, continued to be a perfect rule of righteousness; and, as such, was delivered by God upon Mount Sinai, in ten commandments, and written in two tables:[2] the first four commandments containing our duty towards God; and the other six, our duty to man.[3]

3. Beside this law, commonly called moral, God was pleased to give to the people of Israel, as a church under age, ceremonial laws, containing several typical ordinances, partly of worship, prefiguring Christ, his graces, actions, sufferings, and benefits;[4] and partly, holding forth divers instructions of moral duties.[5] All which ceremonial laws are now abrogated, under the new testament.[6]

4. To them also, as a body politic, he gave sundry judicial laws, which expired together with the State of that people; not obliging any other now, further than the general equity thereof may require.[7]

5. The moral law doth forever bind all, as well justified persons as others, to the obedience thereof;[8] and that, not only in regard of the matter contained in it, but also in respect of the authority of God the Creator, who gave it.[9] Neither doth Christ, in the gospel, any way dissolve, but much strengthen this obligation.[10]

---

1 Gen. 1:26–27; Gen. 2:17; Eph. 4:24; Rom. 2:14–15; Rom. 10:5; Rom. 5:12, 19; Gal. 3:10, 12; Eccl. 7:29.

2 James 1:25; James 2:8, 10–12; Rom. 3:19; Rom. 13:8–9; Deut. 5:32; Deut. 10:4; Ex. 34:1.

3 Ex. 20:3–17; Matt. 22:37–40.

4 Heb. 10:1; Gal. 4:1–3; Col. 2:17; Heb. 9:1–28.

5 Lev. 19:9–10, 19, 23, 27; Deut. 24:19–21. (See 1 Cor. 5:7; 2 Cor. 6:17; Jude 23.)

6 Col. 2:14, 16–17; Dan. 9:27; Eph. 2:15–16; Heb. 9:10; Acts 10:9–16; Acts 11:2–10.

7 Ex. 21:1–23:19 (cf. Gen. 49:10 with 1 Peter 2:13–14); 1 Cor. 9:8–10.

8 Rom. 13:8–10; Rom. 3:31; Rom. 7:25; 1 Cor. 9:21; Gal. 5:14; Eph. 6:2–3; 1 John 2:3–4, 7. (Cf. Rom. 3:20; Rom. 7:7–8 and 1 John 3:4 with Rom. 6:15.)

9 Deut. 6:4–5; Ex. 20:11; Rom. 3:19; James 2:8, 10–11; Matt. 19:4–6; Gen. 17:1.

10 Matt. 5:17–19; Rom. 3:31; 1 Cor. 9:21; Luke 16:17–18.

6. Although true believers be not under the law, as a covenant of works, to be thereby justified, or condemned;[11] yet is it of great use to them, as well as to others; in that, as a rule of life informing them of the will of God, and their duty, it directs and binds them to walk accordingly;[12] discovering also the sinful pollutions of their nature, hearts, and lives;[13] so as, examining themselves thereby, they may come to further conviction of, humiliation for, and hatred against sin,[14] together with a clearer sight of the need they have of Christ, and the perfection of his obedience.[15] It is likewise of use to the regenerate, to restrain their corruptions, in that it forbids sin:[16] and the threatenings of it serve to show what even their sins deserve; and what afflictions, in this life, they may expect for them, although freed from the curse thereof threatened in the law.[17] The promises of it, in like manner, show them God's approbation of obedience, and what blessings they may expect upon the performance thereof:[18] although not as due to them by the law as a covenant of works.[19] So as, a man's doing good, and refraining from evil, because the law encourageth to the one, and deterreth from the other, is no evidence of his being under the law; and, not under grace.[20]

7. Neither are the forementioned uses of the law contrary to the grace of the gospel, but do sweetly comply with it;[21] the Spirit of Christ subduing and enabling the will of man to do that freely, and cheerfully, which the will of God, revealed in the law, requireth to be done.[22]

---

11 Rom. 6:14; Rom. 7:4; Gal. 2:16; Gal. 3:13; Gal. 4:4–5; Acts 13:38–39; Rom. 8:1, 33.
12 Rom. 7:12, 22, 25; Ps. 119:1–6; 1 Cor. 7:19; Gal. 5:14–23.
13 Rom. 7:7, 13; Rom. 3:20.
14 James 1:23–25; Rom. 7:9, 14, 24.
15 Gal. 3:24; Rom. 7:24–25; Rom. 8:3–4.
16 James 2:11–12; Ps. 119:101, 104, 128.
17 Ezra 9:13–14; Ps. 89:30–34; Gal. 3:13.
18 Ex. 19:5–6; Deut. 5:33; Lev. 18:5; Matt. 19:17; Lev. 26:1–13; 2 Cor. 6:16; Eph. 6:2–3; Ps. 19:11; Ps. 37:11; Matt. 5:5.
19 Gal. 2:16; Luke 17:10.
20 Rom. 6:12–15; 1 Peter 3:8–12; With Ps. 34:12–16; Heb. 12:28–29.
21 Rom. 3:31; Gal. 3:21; Titus 2:11–14.
22 Ezek. 36:27; Heb. 8:10; With Jer. 31:33; Ps. 119:35, 47; Rom. 7:22.

CHAPTER 20
OF CHRISTIAN LIBERTY
AND LIBERTY OF CONSCIENCE

1. The liberty which Christ hath purchased for believers under the gospel consists in their freedom from the guilt of sin, the condemning wrath of God, the curse of the moral law;[1] and, in their being delivered from this present evil world, bondage to Satan, and dominion of sin;[2] from the evil of afflictions, the sting of death, the victory of the grave, and everlasting damnation;[3] as also, in their free access to God,[4] and their yielding obedience unto him, not out of slavish fear, but a childlike love and willing mind.[5] All which were common also to believers under the law.[6] But, under the new testament, the liberty of Christians is further enlarged, in their freedom from the yoke of the ceremonial law, to which the Jewish church was subjected;[7] and in greater boldness of access to the throne of grace,[8] and in fuller communications of the free Spirit of God, than believers under the law did ordinarily partake of.[9]

2. God alone is Lord of the conscience,[10] and hath left it free from the doctrines and commandments of men, which are, in anything, contrary to his Word; or beside it, if matters of faith, or worship.[11] So that, to believe such doctrines, or to obey such commands, out of conscience, is to betray true liberty of conscience:[12] and the requiring of an implicit faith, and an absolute and blind obedience, is to destroy liberty of conscience, and reason also.[13]

3. They who, upon pretense of Christian liberty, do practice any sin, or cherish any lust, do thereby destroy the end of Christian liberty, which is, that being

---

1 Titus 2:14; 1 Thess. 1:10; Gal. 3:13.
2 Gal. 1:4; Col. 1:13; Acts 26:18; Rom. 6:14.
3 Rom. 8:28; Ps. 119:71; 2 Cor. 4:15–18; 1 Cor. 15:54–57; Rom. 5:9; Rom. 8:1. (See 1 Thess. 1:10.)
4 Rom. 5:1–2.
5 Rom. 8:14–15; Gal. 4:6; 1 John 4:18.
6 Gal. 3:8–9, 14; Rom. 4:6–8; 1 Cor. 10:3–4; Heb. 11:1–40.
7 Gal. 4:1–7; Gal. 5:1; Acts 15:10–11.
8 Heb. 4:14–16; Heb. 10:19–22.
9 John 7:38–39; Acts 2:17–18; 2 Cor. 3:8, 13, 17–18. (See Jer. 31:31–34.)
10 James 4:12; Rom. 14:4, 10; 1 Cor. 10:29.
11 Acts 4:19; Acts 5:29; 1 Cor. 7:22–23; Matt. 15:1–6; Matt. 23:8–10; 2 Cor. 1:24; Matt. 15:9.
12 Col. 2:20–23; Gal. 1:10; Gal. 2:4–5; Gal. 4:9–10; Gal. 5:1.
13 Rom. 10:17; Isa. 8:20; Acts 17:11; John 4:22; Rev. 13:12, 16–17; Jer. 8:9; 1 Peter 3:15.

delivered out of the hands of our enemies, we might serve the Lord without fear, in holiness and righteousness before him, all the days of our life.[14]

4. And because the powers which God hath ordained, and the liberty which Christ hath purchased, are not intended by God to destroy, but mutually to uphold and preserve one another, they who, upon pretense of Christian liberty, shall oppose any lawful power, or the lawful exercise of it, whether it be civil or ecclesiastical, resist the ordinance of God.[15] And, for their publishing of such opinions, or maintaining of such practices, as are contrary to the light of nature, or to the known principles of Christianity (whether concerning faith, worship, or conversation), or to the power of godliness; or, such erroneous opinions or practices, as either in their own nature, or in the manner of publishing or maintaining them, are destructive to the external peace and order which Christ hath established in the church, they may lawfully be called to account, and proceeded against, by the censures of the church.[16]

---

14 Gal. 5:13; 1 Peter 2:16; 2 Peter 2:19; Rom. 6:15; John 8:34; Luke 1:74–75.

15 1 Peter 2:13–14, 16; Rom. 13:1–8; Heb. 13:17; 1 Thess. 5:12–13.

16 Rom. 1:32; 1 Cor. 5:1, 5, 11–13; 2 John 10–11; 2 Thess. 3:6, 14; 1 Tim. 6:3–4; Titus 1:10–11, 13–14; Titus 3:10; Rom. 16:17; Matt. 18:15–17; 1 Tim. 1:19–20; Rev. 2:2, 14–15, 20.

CHAPTER 21
OF RELIGIOUS WORSHIP AND THE SABBATH DAY

1. The light of nature showeth that there is a God, who hath lordship and sovereignty over all, is good, and doth good unto all, and is therefore to be feared, loved, praised, called upon, trusted in, and served, with all the heart, and with all the soul, and with all the might.[1] But the acceptable way of worshiping the true God is instituted by himself, and so limited by his own revealed will, that he may not be worshiped according to the imaginations and devices of men, or the suggestions of Satan, under any visible representation, or any other way not prescribed in the Holy Scripture.[2]

2. Religious worship is to be given to God, the Father, Son, and Holy Ghost; and to him alone;[3] not to angels, saints, or any other creature:[4] and, since the fall, not without a Mediator; nor in the mediation of any other but of Christ alone.[5]

3. Prayer, with thanksgiving, being one special part of religious worship,[6] is by God required of all men:[7] and, that it may be accepted, it is to be made in the name of the Son,[8] by the help of his Spirit,[9] according to his will,[10] with understanding, reverence, humility, fervency, faith, love, and perseverance;[11] and, if vocal, in a known tongue.[12]

---

1 Rom. 1:20; Ps. 19:1–4a; Ps. 50:6; Ps. 97:6; Ps. 145:9–12; Acts 14:17; Ps. 104:1–35; Ps. 86:8–10; Ps. 95:1–6; Ps. 89:5–7; Deut. 6:4–5.
2 Deut. 12:32; Matt. 15:9; Acts 17:23–25; Matt. 4:9–10; Deut. 4:15–20; Ex. 20:4–6; John 4:23–24; Col. 2:18–23.
3 John 5:23; Matt. 28:19; 2 Cor. 13:14; Eph. 3:14; Rev. 5:11–14; Acts 10:25–26.
4 Col. 2:18; Rev. 19:10; Rom. 1:25.
5 John 14:6; 1 Tim. 2:5; Eph. 2:18; Col. 3:17.
6 Phil. 4:6; 1 Tim. 2:1; Col. 4:2.
7 Ps. 65:2; Ps. 67:3; Ps. 96:7–8; Ps. 148:11–13; Isa. 55:6–7.
8 John 14:13–14; 1 Peter 2:5.
9 Rom. 8:26; Eph. 6:18.
10 1 John 5:14.
11 Ps. 47:7; Eccl. 5:1–2; Heb. 12:28; Gen. 18:27; James 5:16; James 1:6–7; Mark 11:24; Matt. 6:12, 14–15; Col. 4:2; Eph. 6:18.
12 1 Cor. 14:14.

4. Prayer is to be made for things lawful;[13] and for all sorts of men living, or that shall live hereafter:[14] but not for the dead,[15] nor for those of whom it may be known that they have sinned the sin unto death.[16]

5. The reading of the Scriptures with godly fear,[17] the sound preaching[18] and conscionable hearing of the Word, in obedience unto God, with understanding, faith, and reverence,[19] singing of psalms with grace in the heart;[20] as also, the due administration and worthy receiving of the sacraments instituted by Christ, are all parts of the ordinary religious worship of God:[21] beside religious oaths,[22] vows,[23] solemn fastings,[24] and thanksgivings upon special occasions,[25] which are, in their several times and seasons, to be used in an holy and religious manner.[26]

6. Neither prayer, nor any other part of religious worship, is now, under the gospel, either tied unto, or made more acceptable by any place in which it is performed, or towards which it is directed:[27] but God is to be worshiped everywhere,[28] in spirit and truth;[29] as, in private families[30] daily,[31] and in secret, each one by himself;[32] so, more solemnly in the public assemblies, which are not carelessly or willfully to be neglected, or forsaken, when God, by his Word or providence, calleth thereunto.[33]

---

13 1 John 5:14, 16; John 15:7.
14 1 Tim. 2:1–2; John 17:20; 2 Sam. 7:29; 2 Chron. 6:14–42.
15 Luke 16:25–26; Isa. 57:1–2; Ps. 73:24; 2 Cor. 5:8, 10; Phil. 1:21–24; Rev. 14:13.
16 1 John 5:16.
17 Luke 4:16–17; Acts 15:21; Col. 4:16; 1 Thess. 5:27; Rev. 1:3.
18 2 Tim. 4:2; Acts 5:42.
19 James 1:22; Acts 10:33; Matt. 13:19; Heb. 4:2; Isa. 66:2.
20 Col. 3:16; Eph. 5:19; James 5:13; 1 Cor. 14:15.
21 Matt. 28:19; 1 Cor. 11:23–29; Acts 2:42.
22 Deut. 6:13; Neh. 10:29; 2 Cor. 1:23.
23 Ps. 116:14; Isa. 19:21; Eccl. 5:4–5.
24 Joel 2:12; Est. 4:16; Matt. 9:15; Acts 14:23.
25 Ex. 15:1–21; Ps. 107:1–43; Neh. 12:27–43; Est. 9:20–22.
26 Heb. 12:28.
27 John 4:21.
28 Mal. 1:11; 1 Tim. 2:8.
29 John 4:23–24.
30 Jer. 10:25; Deut. 6:6–7; Job 1:5; 2 Sam. 6:18, 20.
31 Matt. 6:11. (See Job 1:5.)
32 Matt. 6:6, 16–18; Neh. 1:4–11; Dan. 9:3–4a.
33 Isa. 56:6–7; Heb. 10:25; Ps. 100:4; Ps. 122:1; Ps. 84:1–12; Luke 4:16; Acts 13:42, 44; Acts 2:42.

7. As it is the law of nature, that, in general, a due proportion of time be set apart for the worship of God; so, in his Word, by a positive, moral, and perpetual commandment binding all men in all ages, he hath particularly appointed one day in seven, for a Sabbath, to be kept holy unto him:[34] which, from the beginning of the world to the resurrection of Christ, was the last day of the week; and, from the resurrection of Christ, was changed into the first day of the week,[35] which, in Scripture, is called the Lord's Day,[36] and is to be continued to the end of the world, as the Christian Sabbath.[37]

8. This Sabbath is then kept holy unto the Lord, when men, after a due preparing of their hearts, and ordering of their common affairs beforehand, do not only observe an holy rest, all the day, from their own works, words, and thoughts about their worldly employments and recreations,[38] but also are taken up, the whole time, in the public and private exercises of his worship, and in the duties of necessity and mercy.[39]

---

34 Ex. 20:8–11; Isa. 56:2–7.
35 Gen. 2:2–3; 1 Cor. 16:1–2; Acts 20:7.
36 Rev. 1:10.
37 Matt. 5:17–18; Mark 2:27–28; Rom. 13:8–10; James 2:8–12.
38 Ex. 20:8; Ex. 16:23–30; Ex. 31:15–17; Isa. 58:13–14; Neh. 13:15–22.
39 Isa. 58:13–14; Luke 4:16; Matt. 12:1–13; Mark 3:1–5.

CHAPTER 22
OF LAWFUL OATHS AND VOWS

1. A lawful oath is a part of religious worship,[1] wherein, upon just occasion, the person swearing solemnly calleth God to witness what he asserteth, or promiseth, and to judge him according to the truth or falsehood of what he sweareth.[2]

2. The name of God only is that by which men ought to swear, and therein it is to be used with all holy fear and reverence.[3] Therefore, to swear vainly, or rashly, by that glorious and dreadful Name; or, to swear at all by any other thing, is sinful, and to be abhorred.[4] Yet, as in matters of weight and moment, an oath is warranted by the Word of God, under the new testament as well as under the old;[5] so a lawful oath, being imposed by lawful authority, in such matters, ought to be taken.[6]

3. Whosoever taketh an oath ought duly to consider the weightiness of so solemn an act, and therein to avouch nothing but what he is fully persuaded is the truth:[7] neither may any man bind himself by oath to anything but what is good and just, and what he believeth so to be, and what he is able and resolved to perform.[8]

4. An oath is to be taken in the plain and common sense of the words, without equivocation, or mental reservation.[9] It cannot oblige to sin; but in anything not sinful, being taken, it binds to performance, although to a man's own hurt.[10] Nor is it to be violated, although made to heretics, or infidels.[11]

5. A vow is of the like nature with a promissory oath, and ought to be made with the like religious care, and to be performed with the like faithfulness.[12]

---

1 Deut. 10:20; Isa. 45:23; Rom. 14:11; Phil. 2:10–11.
2 Ex. 20:7; Lev. 19:12; Rom. 1:9; 2 Cor. 1:23; 2 Cor. 11:31; Gal. 1:20; 2 Chron. 6:22–23.
3 Deut. 6:13; Josh. 23:7.
4 Ex. 20:7; Jer. 5:7; Matt. 5:33–37; James 5:12.
5 Heb. 6:16; 2 Cor. 1:23; Isa. 65:16.
6 1 Kings 8:31; Neh. 13:25; Ezra 10:5.
7 Ex. 20:7; Lev. 19:12; Jer. 4:2; Hos. 10:4.
8 Gen. 24:2–9; Neh. 5:12–13; Eccl. 5:2, 5.
9 Jer. 4:2; Ps. 24:4.
10 1 Sam. 25:22, 32–34; Ps. 15:4.
11 Ezek. 17:16–19; Josh. 9:18–19; 2 Sam. 21:1.
12 Num. 30:2; Isa. 19:21; Eccl. 5:4–6; Ps. 61:8; Ps. 66:13–14.

6. It is not to be made to any creature, but to God alone:[13] and, that it may be accepted, it is to be made voluntarily, out of faith, and conscience of duty, in way of thankfulness for mercy received, or for the obtaining of what we want, whereby we more strictly bind ourselves to necessary duties; or, to other things, so far and so long as they may fitly conduce thereunto.[14]

7. No man may vow to do anything forbidden in the Word of God, or what would hinder any duty therein commanded, or which is not in his own power, and for the performance whereof he hath no promise of ability from God.[15] In which respects, popish monastical vows of perpetual single life, professed poverty, and regular obedience, are so far from being degrees of higher perfection, that they are superstitious and sinful snares, in which no Christian may entangle himself.[16]

---

13 Ps. 50:14; Ps. 76:11; Ps. 116:14.

14 Deut. 23:21–23; Gen. 28:20–22; 1 Sam. 1:11; Ps. 66:13–14; Ps. 132:2–5.

15 Acts 23:12–14; Mark 6:26; Num. 30:5, 8, 12–13.

16 Matt. 19:11–12; 1 Cor. 7:2, 9; Heb. 13:4; Eph. 4:28; 1 Thess. 4:11–12; 1 Cor. 7:23.

CHAPTER 23
OF THE CIVIL MAGISTRATE

1. God, the supreme Lord and King of all the world, hath ordained civil magistrates, to be, under him, over the people, for his own glory, and the public good: and, to this end, hath armed them with the power of the sword, for the defense and encouragement of them that are good, and for the punishment of evildoers.[1]

2. It is lawful for Christians to accept and execute the office of a magistrate, when called thereunto:[2] in the managing whereof, as they ought especially to maintain piety, justice, and peace, according to the wholesome laws of each commonwealth;[3] so, for that end, they may lawfully, now under the new testament, wage war, upon just and necessary occasion.[4]

3. Civil magistrates may not assume to themselves the administration of the Word and sacraments; or the power of the keys of the kingdom of heaven;[5] or, in the least, interfere in matters of faith.[6] Yet, as nursing fathers, it is the duty of civil magistrates to protect the church of our common Lord, without giving the preference to any denomination of Christians above the rest, in such a manner that all ecclesiastical persons whatever shall enjoy the full, free, and unquestioned liberty of discharging every part of their sacred functions, without violence or danger.[7] And, as Jesus Christ hath appointed a regular government and discipline in his church, no law of any commonwealth should interfere with, let, or hinder, the due exercise thereof, among the voluntary members of any denomination of Christians, according to their own profession and belief.[8] It is the duty of civil magistrates to protect the person and good name of all their people, in such an effectual manner as that no person be suffered, either upon pretense of religion or of infidelity, to offer any indignity,

---

1 Rom. 13:1–4; 1 Peter 2:13–14.
2 Gen. 41:39–43; Neh. 12:26; Neh. 13:15–31; Dan. 2:48–49; Prov. 8:15–16; Rom. 13:1–4.
3 Ps. 2:10–12; 1 Tim. 2:2; Ps. 82:3–4; 2 Sam. 23:3; 1 Peter 2:13.
4 Luke 3:14; Rom. 13:4; Matt. 8:9–10; Acts 10:1–2.
5 2 Chron. 26:18; Matt. 18:17; Matt. 16:19; 1 Cor. 12:28–29; Eph. 4:11–12; 1 Cor. 4:1–2; Rom. 10:15; Heb. 5:4.
6 John 18:36; Acts 5:29; Eph. 4:11–12.
7 Isa. 49:23; Rom. 13:1–6.
8 Ps. 105:15.

violence, abuse, or injury to any other person whatsoever: and to take order, that all religious and ecclesiastical assemblies be held without molestation or disturbance.[9]

4. It is the duty of people to pray for magistrates,[10] to honor their persons,[11] to pay them tribute or other dues,[12] to obey their lawful commands, and to be subject to their authority, for conscience' sake.[13] Infidelity, or difference in religion, doth not make void the magistrates' just and legal authority, nor free the people from their due obedience to them:[14] from which ecclesiastical persons are not exempted,[15] much less hath the pope any power and jurisdiction over them in their dominions, or over any of their people; and, least of all, to deprive them of their dominions, or lives, if he shall judge them to be heretics, or upon any other pretense whatsoever.[16]

---

9 Rom. 13:4; 1 Tim. 2:2.

10 1 Tim. 2:1–3.

11 1 Peter 2:17.

12 Matt. 22:21; Rom. 13:6–7.

13 Rom. 13:5; Titus 3:1.

14 1 Peter 2:13–16.

15 Rom. 13:1; Acts 25:9–11; 2 Peter 2:1, 10–11; Jude 8–11.

16 Mark 10:42–44; Matt. 23:8–12; 2 Tim. 2:24; 1 Peter 5:3.

CHAPTER 24
OF MARRIAGE AND DIVORCE

1. Marriage is to be between one man and one woman: neither is it lawful for any man to have more than one wife, nor for any woman to have more than one husband, at the same time.[1]

2. Marriage was ordained for the mutual help of husband and wife,[2] for the increase of mankind with legitimate issue, and of the church with an holy seed;[3] and for preventing of uncleanness.[4]

3. It is lawful for all sorts of people to marry, who are able with judgment to give their consent.[5] Yet it is the duty of Christians to marry only in the Lord.[6] And therefore such as profess the true reformed religion should not marry with infidels, papists, or other idolaters: neither should such as are godly be unequally yoked, by marrying with such as are notoriously wicked in their life, or maintain damnable heresies.[7]

4. Marriage ought not to be within the degrees of consanguinity or affinity forbidden by the Word.[8] Nor can such incestuous marriages ever be made lawful by any law of man or consent of parties, so as those persons may live together as man and wife.[9]

5. Adultery or fornication committed after a contract, being detected before marriage, giveth just occasion to the innocent party to dissolve that contract.[10] In the case of adultery after marriage, it is lawful for the innocent party to sue out a divorce:[11] and, after the divorce, to marry another, as if the offending party were dead.[12]

---

1 Gen. 2:24; Matt. 19:4–6; Rom. 7:3; Prov. 2:17.
2 Gen. 2:18; Eph. 5:28; 1 Peter 3:7.
3 Gen. 1:28; Gen. 9:1; Mal. 2:15.
4 1 Cor. 7:2, 9.
5 Heb. 13:4; 1 Tim. 4:3; 1 Cor. 7:36–38; Gen. 24:57–58.
6 1 Cor. 7:39.
7 Gen. 34:14; Ex. 34:16; 2 Cor. 6:14. (See Deut. 7:3–4; 1 Kings 11:4; Neh. 13:25–27; Mal. 2:11–12.)
8 Lev. 18:6–17, 24–30; Lev. 20:19; 1 Cor. 5:1; Amos 2:7.
9 Mark 6:18; Lev. 18:24–28.
10 Matt. 1:18–20. (See Deut. 22:23–24.)
11 Matt. 5:31–32.
12 Matt. 19:9; Rom. 7:2–3.

6. Although the corruption of man be such as is apt to study arguments unduly to put asunder those whom God hath joined together in marriage: yet, nothing but adultery, or such willful desertion as can no way be remedied by the church, or civil magistrate, is cause sufficient of dissolving the bond of marriage:[13] wherein, a public and orderly course of proceeding is to be observed; and the persons concerned in it not left to their own wills, and discretion, in their own case.[14]

---

13 Matt. 19:8–9; 1 Cor. 7:15; Matt. 19:6.
14 Deut. 24:1–4.

CHAPTER 25

OF THE CHURCH

1. The catholic or universal church, which is invisible, consists of the whole number of the elect, that have been, are, or shall be gathered into one, under Christ the Head thereof; and is the spouse, the body, the fullness of him that filleth all in all.[1]

2. The visible church, which is also catholic or universal under the gospel (not confined to one nation, as before under the law), consists of all those throughout the world that profess the true religion;[2] and of their children:[3] and is the kingdom of the Lord Jesus Christ,[4] the house and family of God,[5] out of which there is no ordinary possibility of salvation.[6]

3. Unto this catholic visible church Christ hath given the ministry, oracles, and ordinances of God, for the gathering and perfecting of the saints, in this life, to the end of the world: and doth, by his own presence and Spirit, according to his promise, make them effectual thereunto.[7]

4. This catholic church hath been sometimes more, sometimes less visible.[8] And particular churches, which are members thereof, are more or less pure, according as the doctrine of the gospel is taught and embraced, ordinances administered, and public worship performed more or less purely in them.[9]

---

1   Eph. 1:10, 22–23; Eph. 5:23, 27, 32; Col. 1:18.
2   1 Cor. 1:2; 1 Cor. 12:12–13; Ps. 2:8; Rev. 7:9; Rom. 15:9–12.
3   1 Cor. 7:14; Acts 2:39; Gen. 17:7–12; Ezek. 16:20–21; Rom. 11:16. (See Gal. 3:7, 9, 14; Rom. 4:12, 16, 24.)
4   Matt. 13:47; Isa. 9:7; Luke 1:32–33; Acts 2:30–36; Col. 1:13.
5   Eph. 2:19; Eph. 3:15.
6   Acts 2:47.
7   1 Cor. 12:28; Eph. 4:11–13; Matt. 28:19–20; Isa. 59:21.
8   Rom. 11:3–5; Acts 9:31; Acts 2:41, 47; Acts 18:8–10.
9   Acts 2:41–42; 1 Cor. 5:6–7; Rev. 2–3.

5. The purest churches under heaven are subject both to mixture and error;[10] and some have so degenerated, as to become no churches of Christ, but synagogues of Satan.[11] Nevertheless, there shall be always a church on earth, to worship God according to his will.[12]

6. There is no other head of the church but the Lord Jesus Christ.[13] Nor can the pope of Rome, in any sense, be head thereof.[14]

---

10 1 Cor. 13:12; Rev. 2–3; Matt. 13:24–30, 47.
11 Matt. 23:37–39; Rom. 11:18–22.
12 Matt. 16:18; Ps. 45:16–17; Ps. 72:17; Matt. 28:19–20; 1 Cor. 15:51–52; 1 Thess. 4:17.
13 Col. 1:18; Eph. 1:22.
14 Matt. 23:8–10; 1 Peter 5:2–4.

CHAPTER 26
OF THE COMMUNION OF SAINTS

1. All saints, that are united to Jesus Christ their Head, by his Spirit, and by faith, have fellowship with him in his graces, sufferings, death, resurrection, and glory:[1] and, being united to one another in love, they have communion in each other's gifts and graces,[2] and are obliged to the performance of such duties, public and private, as do conduce to their mutual good, both in the inward and outward man.[3]

2. Saints by profession are bound to maintain an holy fellowship and communion in the worship of God, and in performing such other spiritual services as tend to their mutual edification;[4] as also in relieving each other in outward things, according to their several abilities and necessities. Which communion, as God offereth opportunity, is to be extended unto all those who, in every place, call upon the name of the Lord Jesus.[5]

3. This communion which the saints have with Christ, doth not make them in any wise partakers of the substance of his Godhead; or to be equal with Christ in any respect: either of which to affirm is impious and blasphemous.[6] Nor doth their communion one with another, as saints, take away, or infringe the title or propriety which each man hath in his goods and possessions.[7]

---

1   1 John 1:3; Eph. 3:16–18; John 1:16; Eph. 2:5–6; Phil. 3:10; Rom. 6:5–6; Rom. 8:17; 2 Tim. 2:12.
2   Eph. 4:15–16; 1 Cor. 12:7, 12; 1 Cor. 3:21–23; Col. 2:19.
3   1 Thess. 5:11, 14; Rom. 1:11–12, 14; 1 John 3:16–18; Gal. 6:10.
4   Heb. 10:24–25; Acts 2:42, 46; Isa. 2:3; 1 Cor. 11:20.
5   1 John 3:17; 2 Cor. 8–9; Acts 11:29–30. (See Acts 2:44–45.)
6   Col. 1:18–19; 1 Cor. 8:6; Ps. 45:6–7; Heb. 1:6–9; John 1:14; John 20:17.
7   Ex. 20:15; Eph. 4:28; Acts 5:4.

CHAPTER 27
OF THE SACRAMENTS

1. Sacraments are holy signs and seals of the covenant of grace,[1] immediately instituted by God,[2] to represent Christ, and his benefits; and to confirm our interest in him:[3] as also, to put a visible difference between those that belong unto the church, and the rest of the world;[4] and solemnly to engage them to the service of God in Christ, according to his Word.[5]

2. There is, in every sacrament, a spiritual relation, or sacramental union, between the sign and the thing signified: whence it comes to pass, that the names and effects of the one are attributed to the other.[6]

3. The grace which is exhibited in or by the sacraments rightly used, is not conferred by any power in them; neither doth the efficacy of a sacrament depend upon the piety or intention of him that doth administer it:[7] but upon the work of the Spirit,[8] and the word of institution, which contains, together with a precept authorizing the use thereof, a promise of benefit to worthy receivers.[9]

4. There be only two sacraments ordained by Christ our Lord in the gospel; that is to say, baptism, and the Supper of the Lord: neither of which may be dispensed by any, but by a minister of the Word lawfully ordained.[10]

5. The sacraments of the old testament, in regard of the spiritual things thereby signified and exhibited, were, for substance, the same with those of the new.[11]

---

1 Rom. 4:11; Gen. 17:7, 10–11.
2 Matt. 28:19; 1 Cor. 11:23.
3 Rom. 6:3–4; Col. 2:12; 1 Cor. 10:16; 1 Cor. 11:25–26; Gal. 3:27.
4 Ex. 12:48; Gen. 34:14; 1 Cor. 10:21.
5 Rom. 6:3–4; Gal. 3:27; 1 Peter 3:21; 1 Cor. 10:16. (See 1 Cor. 5:7–8.)
6 Gen. 17:10; Matt. 26:27–28; 1 Cor. 10:16–18.
7 Rom. 2:28–29; 1 Peter 3:21.
8 1 Cor. 12:13.
9 Matt. 26:26–28; Luke 22:19–20; Matt. 28:19–20; 1 Cor. 11:26.
10 Matt. 28:19; 1 Cor. 11:20, 23; 1 Cor. 4:1; Eph. 4:11–12.
11 1 Cor. 10:1–4; Rom. 4:11; Col. 2:11–12.

CHAPTER 28
OF BAPTISM

1. Baptism is a sacrament of the new testament, ordained by Jesus Christ,[1] not only for the solemn admission of the party baptized into the visible church;[2] but also, to be unto him a sign and seal of the covenant of grace,[3] of his ingrafting into Christ,[4] of regeneration,[5] of remission of sins,[6] and of his giving up unto God, through Jesus Christ, to walk in newness of life.[7] Which sacrament is, by Christ's own appointment, to be continued in his church until the end of the world.[8]

2. The outward element to be used in this sacrament is water, wherewith the party is to be baptized, in the name of the Father, and of the Son, and of the Holy Ghost, by a minister of the gospel, lawfully called thereunto.[9]

3. Dipping of the person into the water is not necessary; but baptism is rightly administered by pouring, or sprinkling water upon the person.[10]

4. Not only those that do actually profess faith in and obedience unto Christ,[11] but also the infants of one, or both, believing parents, are to be baptized.[12]

5. Although it be a great sin to contemn or neglect this ordinance,[13] yet grace and salvation are not so inseparably annexed unto it, as that no person can be regenerated, or saved, without it;[14] or, that all that are baptized are undoubtedly regenerated.[15]

---

1 Matt. 28:19.
2 1 Cor. 12:13; Gal. 3:27–28.
3 Rom. 4:11; Col. 2:11–12.
4 Gal. 3:27; Rom. 6:5.
5 John 3:5; Titus 3:5.
6 Mark 1:4; Acts 2:38; Acts 22:16.
7 Rom. 6:3–4.
8 Matt. 28:19–20.
9 Acts 10:47; Acts 8:36, 38; Matt. 28:19.
10 Heb. 9:10, 13, 19, 21; Mark 7:2–4; Luke 11:38.
11 Acts 2:41; Acts 8:12–13; Acts 16:14–15.
12 Gen. 17:7–14; Gal. 3:9, 14; Col. 2:11–12; Acts 2:38–39; Rom. 4:11–12; Matt. 19:13; Mark 10:13–16; Luke 18:15–17; Matt. 28:19; 1 Cor. 7:14.
13 Gen. 17:14; Matt. 28:19; Acts 2:38. (See Luke 7:30.)
14 Rom. 4:11; Acts 10:2, 4, 22, 31, 45, 47.
15 Acts 8:13, 23.

6. The efficacy of baptism is not tied to that moment of time wherein it is administered;[16] yet, notwithstanding, by the right use of this ordinance, the grace promised is not only offered, but really exhibited, and conferred, by the Holy Ghost, to such (whether of age or infants) as that grace belongeth unto, according to the counsel of God's own will, in his appointed time.[17]

7. The sacrament of baptism is but once to be administered unto any person.[18]

---

16 John 3:5, 8.
17 Rom. 6:3–6; Gal. 3:27; 1 Peter 3:21; Acts 2:38, 41.
18 Rom. 6:3–11.

CHAPTER 29
OF THE LORD'S SUPPER

1. Our Lord Jesus, in the night wherein he was betrayed, instituted the sacrament of his body and blood, called the Lord's Supper, to be observed in his church, unto the end of the world, for the perpetual remembrance of the sacrifice of himself in his death; the sealing all benefits thereof unto true believers, their spiritual nourishment and growth in him, their further engagement in and to all duties which they owe unto him; and, to be a bond and pledge of their communion with him, and with each other, as members of his mystical body.[1]

2. In this sacrament, Christ is not offered up to his Father; nor any real sacrifice made at all, for remission of sins of the quick or dead;[2] but only a commemoration of that one offering up of himself, by himself, upon the cross, once for all: and a spiritual oblation of all possible praise unto God, for the same:[3] so that the popish sacrifice of the Mass (as they call it) is most abominably injurious to Christ's one, only sacrifice, the alone propitiation for all the sins of his elect.[4]

3. The Lord Jesus hath, in this ordinance, appointed his ministers to declare his word of institution to the people; to pray, and bless the elements of bread and wine, and thereby to set them apart from a common to an holy use; and to take and break the bread, to take the cup, and (they communicating also themselves) to give both to the communicants;[5] but to none who are not then present in the congregation.[6]

4. Private Masses, or receiving this sacrament by a priest, or any other, alone;[7] as likewise, the denial of the cup to the people,[8] worshiping the elements, the lifting them up, or carrying them about, for adoration, and the reserving them for any pretended religious use; are all contrary to the nature of this sacrament, and to the institution of Christ.[9]

---

1   1 Cor. 11:23–26; 1 Cor. 10:16–17, 21; 1 Cor. 12:13.
2   Heb. 9:22, 25–26, 28; Heb. 10:10–14.
3   1 Cor. 11:24–26; Matt. 26:26–27; Luke 22:19–20.
4   Heb. 7:23–24, 27; Heb. 10:11–12, 14, 18.
5   Matt. 26:26–28; Mark 14:22–24; Luke 22:19–20; 1 Cor. 10:16–17; 1 Cor. 11:23–27.
6   Acts 20:7; 1 Cor. 11:20.
7   1 Cor. 10:16.
8   Matt. 26:27–28; Mark 14:23; 1 Cor. 11:25–29.
9   Matt. 15:9.

5. The outward elements in this sacrament, duly set apart to the uses ordained by Christ, have such relation to him crucified, as that, truly, yet sacramentally only, they are sometimes called by the name of the things they represent, to wit, the body and blood of Christ;[10] albeit, in substance and nature, they still remain truly and only bread and wine, as they were before.[11]

6. That doctrine which maintains a change of the substance of bread and wine, into the substance of Christ's body and blood (commonly called transubstantiation) by consecration of a priest, or by any other way, is repugnant, not to Scripture alone, but even to common sense, and reason; overthroweth the nature of the sacrament, and hath been, and is, the cause of manifold superstitions; yea, of gross idolatries.[12]

7. Worthy receivers, outwardly partaking of the visible elements, in this sacrament,[13] do then also, inwardly by faith, really and indeed, yet not carnally and corporally, but spiritually, receive, and feed upon, Christ crucified, and all benefits of his death: the body and blood of Christ being then, not corporally or carnally, in, with, or under the bread and wine; yet, as really, but spiritually, present to the faith of believers in that ordinance, as the elements themselves are to their outward senses.[14]

8. Although ignorant and wicked men receive the outward elements in this sacrament; yet, they receive not the thing signified thereby; but, by their unworthy coming thereunto, are guilty of the body and blood of the Lord, to their own damnation. Wherefore, all ignorant and ungodly persons, as they are unfit to enjoy communion with him, so are they unworthy of the Lord's table; and cannot, without great sin against Christ, while they remain such, partake of these holy mysteries,[15] or be admitted thereunto.[16]

---

10 Matt. 26:26–28.
11 1 Cor. 11:26–28; Matt. 26:29.
12 Acts 3:21; 1 Cor. 11:24–26; Luke 24:6, 39.
13 1 Cor. 11:28.
14 1 Cor. 10:16. (See 1 Cor. 10:3–4.)
15 1 Cor. 11:27–29; 2 Cor. 6:14–16; 1 Cor. 10:21.
16 1 Cor. 5:6–7, 13; 2 Thess. 3:6, 14–15; Matt. 7:6.

CHAPTER 30
OF CHURCH CENSURES

1. The Lord Jesus, as King and Head of his church, hath therein appointed a government, in the hand of church officers, distinct from the civil magistrate.[1]

2. To these officers the keys of the kingdom of heaven are committed; by virtue whereof, they have power, respectively, to retain, and remit sins; to shut that kingdom against the impenitent, both by the Word, and censures; and to open it unto penitent sinners, by the ministry of the gospel; and by absolution from censures, as occasion shall require.[2]

3. Church censures are necessary, for the reclaiming and gaining of offending brethren, for deterring of others from the like offenses, for purging out of that leaven which might infect the whole lump, for vindicating the honor of Christ, and the holy profession of the gospel, and for preventing the wrath of God, which might justly fall upon the church, if they should suffer his covenant, and the seals thereof, to be profaned by notorious and obstinate offenders.[3]

4. For the better attaining of these ends, the officers of the church are to proceed by admonition; suspension from the sacrament of the Lord's Supper for a season; and by excommunication from the church; according to the nature of the crime, and demerit of the person.[4]

---

1   Isa. 9:6–7; Col. 1:18; 1 Tim. 5:17; 1 Thess. 5:12; Acts 20:17, 28; Heb. 13:7, 17, 24; Eph. 4:11–12; 1 Cor. 12:28; Matt. 28:18–20; John 18:36.
2   Matt. 16:19; Matt. 18:17–18; John 20:21–23; 2 Cor. 2:6–8.
3   1 Cor. 5:1–13; 1 Tim. 5:20; Matt. 7:6; 1 Tim. 1:20; 1 Cor. 11:27–34; Jude 23.
4   1 Thess. 5:12; 2 Thess. 3:6, 14–15; 1 Cor. 5:4–5, 13; Matt. 18:17; Titus 3:10.

CHAPTER 31
OF SYNODS AND COUNCILS

1. For the better government, and further edification of the church, there ought to be such assemblies as are commonly called synods or councils:[1] and it belongeth to the overseers and other rulers of the particular churches, by virtue of their office, and the power which Christ hath given them for edification and not for destruction, to appoint such assemblies;[2] and to convene together in them, as often as they shall judge it expedient for the good of the church.[3]

2. It belongeth to synods and councils, ministerially to determine controversies of faith, and cases of conscience; to set down rules and directions for the better ordering of the public worship of God, and government of his church; to receive complaints in cases of maladministration, and authoritatively to determine the same: which decrees and determinations, if consonant to the Word of God, are to be received with reverence and submission; not only for their agreement with the Word, but also for the power whereby they are made, as being an ordinance of God appointed thereunto in his Word.[4]

3. All synods or councils, since the apostles' times, whether general or particular, may err; and many have erred. Therefore they are not to be made the rule of faith, or practice; but to be used as a help in both.[5]

4. Synods and councils are to handle, or conclude nothing, but that which is ecclesiastical: and are not to intermeddle with civil affairs which concern the commonwealth, unless by way of humble petition in cases extraordinary; or, by way of advice, for satisfaction of conscience, if they be thereunto required by the civil magistrate.[6]

---

1   Acts 15:2, 4, 6.
2   Acts 15:1–35.
3   Acts 15:1–35; Acts 20:17.
4   Acts 15:15, 19, 24, 27–31; Acts 16:4; Matt. 18:17–20.
5   Eph. 2:20; Acts 17:11; 1 Cor. 2:5; 2 Cor. 1:24; Cf. Isa. 8:19–20; Matt. 15:9.
6   Luke 12:13–14; John 18:36; Matt. 22:21.

CHAPTER 32

OF THE STATE OF MEN AFTER DEATH,
AND OF THE RESURRECTION OF THE DEAD

1. The bodies of men, after death, return to dust, and see corruption:[1] but their souls, which neither die nor sleep, having an immortal subsistence, immediately return to God who gave them:[2] the souls of the righteous, being then made perfect in holiness, are received into the highest heavens, where they behold the face of God, in light and glory, waiting for the full redemption of their bodies.[3] And the souls of the wicked are cast into hell, where they remain in torments and utter darkness, reserved to the judgment of the great day.[4] Beside these two places, for souls separated from their bodies, the Scripture acknowledgeth none.

2. At the last day, such as are found alive shall not die, but be changed:[5] and all the dead shall be raised up, with the selfsame bodies, and none other (although with different qualities), which shall be united again to their souls forever.[6]

3. The bodies of the unjust shall, by the power of Christ, be raised to dishonor: the bodies of the just, by his Spirit, unto honor; and be made conformable to his own glorious body.[7]

---

1 Gen. 3:19; Acts 13:36.
2 Luke 23:43; Eccl. 12:7.
3 Heb. 12:23; 2 Cor. 5:1, 6, 8; Phil. 1:23; Acts 3:21; Eph. 4:10; Rom. 8:23.
4 Luke 16:23–24; Acts 1:25; Jude 6–7; 1 Peter 3:19.
5 1 Thess. 4:17; 1 Cor. 15:51–52.
6 John 5:25–29; Acts 24:15; Job 19:26–27; Dan. 12:2; 1 Cor. 15:42–44.
7 Acts 24:15; John 5:25–29; 1 Cor. 15:43; Phil. 3:21.

CHAPTER 33
OF THE LAST JUDGMENT

1. God hath appointed a day, wherein he will judge the world, in righteousness, by Jesus Christ,[1] to whom all power and judgment is given of the Father.[2] In which day, not only the apostate angels shall be judged,[3] but likewise all persons that have lived upon earth shall appear before the tribunal of Christ, to give an account of their thoughts, words, and deeds; and to receive according to what they have done in the body, whether good or evil.[4]

2. The end of God's appointing this day is for the manifestation of the glory of his mercy, in the eternal salvation of the elect; and of his justice, in the damnation of the reprobate, who are wicked and disobedient. For then shall the righteous go into everlasting life, and receive that fullness of joy and refreshing, which shall come from the presence of the Lord: but the wicked, who know not God, and obey not the gospel of Jesus Christ, shall be cast into eternal torments, and be punished with everlasting destruction from the presence of the Lord, and from the glory of his power.[5]

3. As Christ would have us to be certainly persuaded that there shall be a day of judgment, both to deter all men from sin; and for the greater consolation of the godly in their adversity:[6] so will he have that day unknown to men, that they may shake off all carnal security, and be always watchful, because they know not at what hour the Lord will come; and may be ever prepared to say, Come Lord Jesus, come quickly, Amen.[7]

---

1 Acts 17:31.
2 John 5:22, 27.
3 Jude 6; 2 Peter 2:4.
4 2 Cor. 5:10; Eccl. 12:14; Rom. 2:16; Rom. 14:10, 12; Matt. 12:36–37.
5 Matt. 25:31–46; Rom. 2:5–6; Rom. 9:22–23; Matt. 25:21; Acts 3:19; 2 Thess. 1:7–10; Mark 9:48.
6 2 Peter 3:11, 14; 2 Cor. 5:10–11; 2 Thess. 1:5–7; Luke 21:27–28; Rom. 8:23–25.
7 Matt. 24:36, 42–44; Mark 13:35–37; Luke 12:35–36; Rev. 22:20.

17

Westminster Larger Catechism

(1646–47)

When Parliament called the Westminster Assembly, it asked not only for a confession but also for a means of catechizing the faithful. A committee of the assembly undertook this work but soon found it difficult to produce a catechism that was both deep enough for the learned in the faith and accessible to those unschooled in the faith. The committee thus decided to produce two catechisms.

The Larger Catechism was aimed at those who were already well acquainted with Christian doctrine. It is longer and more comprehensive than the Shorter Catechism, addressing subjects that are treated briefly in the Shorter (such as the means of salvation) or glossed over entirely (such as the doctrine of the church). At one time in many churches it was the expectation that adult believers would memorize or at least be conversant with the Larger Catechism.

For more background on the Westminster Assembly, see the introduction to the Westminster Confession of Faith.

Westminster Larger Catechism

Q. 1. What is the chief and highest end of man?

A. Man's chief and highest end is to glorify God,[1] and fully to enjoy him forever.[2]

Q. 2. How doth it appear that there is a God?

A. The very light of nature in man, and the works of God, declare plainly that there is a God;[1] but his Word and Spirit only do sufficiently and effectually reveal him unto men for their salvation.[2]

Q. 3. What is the Word of God?

A. The Holy Scriptures of the Old and New Testament are the Word of God,[1] the only rule of faith and obedience.[2]

Q. 4. How doth it appear that the Scriptures are the Word of God?

A. The Scriptures manifest themselves to be the Word of God, by their majesty[1] and purity;[2] by the consent of all the parts,[3] and the scope of the whole, which is to give all glory to God;[4] by their light and power to convince and

---

Q. 1
1   Rom. 11:36; 1 Cor. 6:20; 1 Cor. 10:31; Ps. 86:9, 12.
2   Ps. 73:24–28; John 17:21–23; Ps. 16:5–11; Rev. 21:3–4.
Q. 2
1   Rom. 1:19–20; Acts 17:28. (See Ps. 19:1–3.)
2   1 Cor. 2:9–10; 1 Cor. 1:20–21; 2 Tim. 3:15–17. (See Isa. 59:21.)
Q. 3
1   2 Tim. 3:16; 2 Peter 1:19–21; 2 Peter 3:2, 15–16; Matt. 19:4–5 (with Gen. 2:24).
2   Deut. 4:2; Eph. 2:20; Rev. 22:18–19; Isa. 8:20; Luke 16:29, 31; Gal. 1:8–9; 2 Tim. 3:15–16.
Q. 4
1   Hos. 8:12; 1 Cor. 2:6–7, 13; Ps. 119:18, 129.
2   Ps. 12:6; Ps. 119:140.
3   Luke 24:27; Acts 10:43; Acts 26:22.
4   Rom. 3:19, 27; Rom. 16:25–27. (See 2 Cor. 3:6–11.)

convert sinners, to comfort and build up believers unto salvation:[5] but the Spirit of God bearing witness by and with the Scriptures in the heart of man, is alone able fully to persuade it that they are the very Word of God.[6]

Q. 5. What do the Scriptures principally teach?

A. The Scriptures principally teach, what man is to believe concerning God,[1] and what duty God requires of man.[2]

WHAT MAN OUGHT TO BELIEVE CONCERNING GOD

Q. 6. What do the Scriptures make known of God?

A. The Scriptures make known what God is,[1] the persons in the Godhead,[2] his decrees,[3] and the execution of his decrees.[4]

Q. 7. What is God?

A. God is a Spirit,[1] in and of himself infinite in being,[2] glory,[3] blessedness,[4] and perfection;[5] all-sufficient,[6] eternal,[7] unchangeable,[8] incomprehensible,[9] every where present,[10] almighty,[11] knowing all things,[12] most wise,[13] most

5   Acts 18:28; Heb. 4:12; James 1:18; Ps. 19:7–9; Rom. 15:4; Acts 20:32.
6   John 16:13–14. (See 1 John 2:20, 27; John 20:31.)
Q. 5
1   Gen. 1:1; Ex. 34:5–7; Ps. 48:1; John 20:31. (See 2 Tim. 3:15.)
2   Deut. 10:12–13; 2 Tim. 3:15–17; Acts 16:30–31.
Q. 6
1   John 4:24; Ex. 34:6–7; Isa. 40:18, 21–23, 25, 28; Heb. 11:6.
2   Matt. 3:16–17; Deut. 6:4–6. (Cf. 1 Cor. 8:4, 6. See Matt. 28:19–20; 2 Cor. 13:14.)
3   Acts 15:14–15, 18; Isa. 46:9–10.
4   Acts 4:27–28.
Q. 7
1   John 4:24.
2   Ex. 3:14; Job 11:7–9; Ps. 145:3; Ps. 147:5.
3   Acts 7:2.
4   1 Tim. 6:15.
5   Matt. 5:48.
6   Ex. 3:14; Gen. 17:1; Rom. 11:35–36.
7   Ps. 90:2; Deut. 33:27.
8   Mal. 3:6.
9   1 Kings 8:27; Ps. 145:3. (See Rom. 11:34.)
10 Ps. 139:1–13.
11 Rev. 4:8; Gen. 17:1; Matt. 19:26.
12 Heb. 4:13. (See Ps. 147:5.)
13 Rom. 11:33–34; Rom. 16:27.

holy,[14] most just,[15] most merciful and gracious, long-suffering, and abundant in goodness and truth.[16]

Q. 8. Are there more Gods than one?

A. There is but one only,[1] the living and true God.[2]

Q. 9. How many persons are there in the Godhead?

A. There be three persons in the Godhead, the Father, the Son, and the Holy Ghost;[1] and these three are one true, eternal God, the same in substance, equal in power and glory; although distinguished by their personal properties.[2]

Q. 10. What are the personal properties of the three persons in the Godhead?

A. It is proper to the Father to beget the Son,[1] and to the Son to be begotten of the Father,[2] and to the Holy Ghost to proceed from the Father and the Son from all eternity.[3]

Q. 11. How doth it appear that the Son and the Holy Ghost are God equal with the Father?

A. The Scriptures manifest that the Son and the Holy Ghost are God equal with the Father, ascribing unto them such names,[1] attributes,[2] works,[3] and worship,[4] as are proper to God only.

---

14 1 Peter 1:15–16; Rev. 15:4; Isa. 6:3.

15 Deut. 32:4; Rom. 3:5, 26.

16 Ex. 34:6; Ps. 117:2; Deut. 32:4.

Q. 8

1   Deut. 6:4; 1 Cor. 8:4, 6; Isa. 45:21–22; Isa. 44:6.

2   Jer. 10:10; John 17:3; 1 Thess. 1:9; 1 John 5:20.

Q. 9

1   Matt. 3:16–17; Matt. 28:19; 2 Cor. 13:14.

2   John 1:1 (see Gen. 1:1–3); John 17:5; John 10:30; Ps. 45:6 (see Heb. 1:8–9); Acts 5:3–4; Rom. 9:5; Col. 2:9.

Q. 10

1   Heb. 1:5–6, 8.

2   John 1:14, 18.

3   John 15:26; Gal. 4:6.

Q. 11

1   Isa. 6:3, 5, 8; John 12:41; Acts 28:25; 1 John 5:20; Acts 5:3–4.

2   John 1:1; Isa. 9:6; John 2:24–25; 1 Cor. 2:10–11.

3   Col. 1:16; Gen. 1:2.

4   Matt. 28:19; 2 Cor. 13:14.

Q. 12. What are the decrees of God?

A. God's decrees are the wise, free, and holy acts of the counsel of his will,[1] whereby, from all eternity, he hath, for his own glory, unchangeably foreordained whatsoever comes to pass in time,[2] especially concerning angels and men.

Q. 13. What hath God especially decreed concerning angels and men?

A. God, by an eternal and immutable decree, out of his mere love, for the praise of his glorious grace, to be manifested in due time, hath elected some angels to glory;[1] and in Christ hath chosen some men to eternal life, and the means thereof:[2] and also, according to his sovereign power, and the unsearchable counsel of his own will, (whereby he extendeth or withholdeth favor as he pleaseth,) hath passed by and foreordained the rest to dishonor and wrath, to be for their sin inflicted, to the praise of the glory of his justice.[3]

Q. 14. How doth God execute his decrees?

A. God executeth his decrees in the works of creation and providence,[1] according to his infallible foreknowledge, and the free and immutable counsel of his own will.[2]

Q. 15. What is the work of creation?

A. The work of creation is that wherein God did in the beginning, by the word of his power, make of nothing the world, and all things therein, for himself, within the space of six days, and all very good.[1]

Q. 12
1 Isa. 45:6–7; Eph. 1:11; Rom. 11:33; Rom. 9:14–15, 18.
2 Ps. 33:11; Isa. 14:24; Acts 2:23; Acts 4:27–28; Rom. 9:22–23; Eph. 1:4, 11.
Q. 13
1 1 Tim. 5:21.
2 Eph. 1:4–6; Eph. 2:10; 2 Thess. 2:13–14; 1 Peter 1:2.
3 Rom. 9:17–18, 21–22; Matt. 11:25–26; 2 Tim. 2:20; Jude 4; 1 Peter 2:8.
Q. 14
1 Rev. 4:11. (See Isa. 40:12–31.)
2 Eph. 1:11; Ps. 148:8; Dan. 4:35; Acts 4:24–28.
Q. 15
1 Gen. 1:1 (see entire chapter); Ps. 33:6, 9; Heb. 11:3; Rev. 4:11. (See Rom. 11:36.)

Q. 16. How did God create angels?

A. God created all the angels[1] spirits,[2] immortal,[3] holy,[4] excelling in knowledge,[5] mighty in power,[6] to execute his commandments, and to praise his name,[7] yet subject to change.[8]

Q. 17. How did God create man?

A. After God had made all other creatures, he created man male and female;[1] formed the body of the man of the dust of the ground,[2] and the woman of the rib of the man,[3] endued them with living, reasonable, and immortal souls;[4] made them after his own image,[5] in knowledge,[6] righteousness, and holiness;[7] having the law of God written in their hearts,[8] and power to fulfill it,[9] and dominion over the creatures;[10] yet subject to fall.[11]

Q. 16

1. Col. 1:16.
2. Ps. 104:4.
3. Matt. 22:30; Luke 20:36.
4. Matt. 25:31.
5. 2 Sam. 14:17; Matt. 24:36.
6. 2 Thess. 1:7.
7. Ps. 91:11–12; Ps. 103:20–21.
8. 2 Peter 2:4.

Q. 17

1. Gen. 1:27; Matt. 19:4.
2. Gen. 2:7.
3. Gen. 2:22.
4. Gen. 2:7; Job 35:11; Eccl. 12:7; Matt. 10:28; Luke 23:43.
5. Gen. 1:26–27.
6. Col. 3:10.
7. Eph. 4:24.
8. Rom. 2:14–15.
9. Eccl. 7:29.
10. Gen. 1:28; Ps. 8:6–8.
11. Gen. 2:16–17; Gen. 3:6; Eccl. 7:29.

Q. 18. What are God's works of providence?

A. God's works of providence are his most holy,[1] wise,[2] and powerful preserving[3] and governing[4] all his creatures; ordering them, and all their actions,[5] to his own glory.[6]

Q. 19. What is God's providence towards the angels?

A. God by his providence permitted some of the angels, willfully and irrecoverably, to fall into sin and damnation,[1] limiting and ordering that, and all their sins, to his own glory;[2] and established the rest in holiness and happiness;[3] employing them all,[4] at his pleasure, in the administrations of his power, mercy, and justice.[5]

Q. 20. What was the providence of God toward man in the estate in which he was created?

A. The providence of God toward man in the estate in which he was created, was the placing him in paradise, appointing him to dress it, giving him liberty to eat of the fruit of the earth;[1] putting the creatures under his dominion,[2] and ordaining marriage for his help;[3] affording him communion with himself;[4] instituting the Sabbath;[5] entering into a covenant of life with him, upon condition of personal, perfect, and perpetual obedience,[6] of which the tree of life

Q. 18
1   Ps. 145:17; Lev. 21:8.
2   Ps. 104:24; Isa. 28:29.
3   Heb. 1:3; Ps. 36:6; Neh. 9:6.
4   Ps. 103:19. (See Job 38–41; Ps. 145:14–16.)
5   Matt. 10:29–31; Gen. 45:7; Ps. 135:6.
6   Rom. 11:36; Isa. 63:14.
Q. 19
1   Jude 6. (See 2 Peter 2:4; Heb. 2:16; John 8:44.)
2   Job 1:12; Matt. 8:31; Luke 10:17.
3   1 Tim. 5:21; Mark 8:38; Heb. 12:22.
4   Ps. 103:20; Ps. 104:4.
5   Heb. 1:14. (See 2 Kings 19:35.)
Q. 20
1   Gen. 2:8, 15–16.
2   Gen. 1:28.
3   Gen. 2:18. (See Matt. 19:3–9; Eph. 5:31.)
4   Gen. 1:26–29; Gen. 3:8.
5   Gen. 2:3. (Cf. Ex. 20:11.)
6   Gen. 2:16–17; Gal. 3:12; Rom. 10:5.

was a pledge;[7] and forbidding to eat of the tree of the knowledge of good and evil, upon the pain of death.[8]

Q. 21. Did man continue in that estate wherein God at first created him?

A. Our first parents being left to the freedom of their own will, through the temptation of Satan, transgressed the commandment of God in eating the forbidden fruit; and thereby fell from the estate of innocency wherein they were created.[1]

Q. 22. Did all mankind fall in that first transgression?

A. The covenant being made with Adam as a public person, not for himself only, but for his posterity, all mankind descending from him by ordinary generation,[1] sinned in him, and fell with him in that first transgression.[2]

Q. 23. Into what estate did the fall bring mankind?

A. The fall brought mankind into an estate of sin and misery.[1]

Q. 24. What is sin?

A. Sin is any want of conformity unto, or transgression of, any law of God, given as a rule to the reasonable creature.[1]

Q. 25. Wherein consisteth the sinfulness of that estate whereinto man fell?

A. The sinfulness of that estate whereinto man fell, consisteth in the guilt of Adam's first sin,[1] the want of that righteousness wherein he was created, and

---

7   Gen. 2:9; Gen. 3:22–24.
8   Gen. 2:17. (Cf. James 2:10.)
Q. 21
1   Gen. 3:6–8, 13; Eccl. 7:29; 2 Cor. 11:3.
Q. 22
1   Acts 17:26; Rom. 3:23.
2   Gen. 2:16–17; James 2:10 (cf. Rom. 5:12–20); 1 Cor. 15:21–22.
Q. 23
1   Gen. 3:16–19; Rom. 5:12; Eph. 2:1; Rom. 3:16, 23.
Q. 24
1   Lev. 5:17; James 4:17; 1 John 3:4. (See Gal. 3:10, 12.)
Q. 25
1   Rom. 5:12, 19. (See 1 Cor. 15:22.)

the corruption of his nature, whereby he is utterly indisposed, disabled, and made opposite unto all that is spiritually good, and wholly inclined to all evil, and that continually;[2] which is commonly called original sin, and from which do proceed all actual transgressions.[3]

Q. 26. How is original sin conveyed from our first parents unto their posterity?

A. Original sin is conveyed from our first parents unto their posterity by natural generation, so as all that proceed from them in that way are conceived and born in sin.[1]

Q. 27. What misery did the fall bring upon mankind?

A. The fall brought upon mankind the loss of communion with God,[1] his displeasure and curse;[2] so as we are by nature children of wrath,[3] bond slaves to Satan,[4] and justly liable to all punishments in this world, and that which is to come.[5]

Q. 28. What are the punishments of sin in this world?

A. The punishments of sin in this world are either inward, as blindness of mind,[1] a reprobate sense,[2] strong delusions,[3] hardness of heart,[4] horror of conscience,[5] and vile affections;[6] or outward, as the curse of God upon the

---

2 Rom. 3:10–12 (see vv. 13–19); Eph. 2:1–3; Rom. 5:6; Rom. 8:7–8; Gen. 6:5. (See Col. 3:10; Eph. 4:24.)
3 James 1:14–15; Ps. 53:1–3; Matt. 15:19. (See Rom. 3:10–18, 23; Gal. 5:19–21.)
Q. 26
1 Ps. 51:5; Job 14:4; John 3:6.
Q. 27
1 Gen. 3:8, 10, 24; John 8:34, 42, 44; Eph. 2:12.
2 Gen. 3:16–19; Job 5:7; Eccl. 2:22–23; Rom. 8:18–23.
3 Eph. 2:2–3; John 3:36; Rom. 1:18; Eph. 5:6.
4 2 Tim. 2:26.
5 Gen. 2:17; Lam. 3:39; Rom. 6:23; Matt. 25:41, 46; Jude 7.
Q. 28
1 Eph. 4:18.
2 Rom. 1:28.
3 2 Thess. 2:11.
4 Rom. 2:5.
5 Isa. 33:14; Gen. 4:13; Matt. 27:4.
6 Rom. 1:26.

creatures for our sakes,[7] and all other evils that befall us in our bodies, names, estates, relations, and employments;[8] together with death itself.[9]

Q. 29. What are the punishments of sin in the world to come?

A. The punishments of sin in the world to come, are everlasting separation from the comfortable presence of God, and most grievous torments in soul and body, without intermission, in hellfire forever.[1]

Q. 30. Doth God leave all mankind to perish in the estate of sin and misery?

A. God doth not leave all men to perish in the estate of sin and misery,[1] into which they fell by the breach of the first covenant, commonly called the covenant of works;[2] but of his mere love and mercy delivereth his elect out of it, and bringeth them into an estate of salvation by the second covenant, commonly called the covenant of grace.[3]

Q. 31. With whom was the covenant of grace made?

A. The covenant of grace was made with Christ as the second Adam, and in him with all the elect as his seed.[1]

Q. 32. How is the grace of God manifested in the second covenant?

A. The grace of God is manifested in the second covenant, in that he freely provideth and offereth to sinners a Mediator,[1] and life and salvation by him;[2] and requiring faith as the condition to interest them in him,[3] promiseth and

---

7   Gen. 3:17.
8   Deut. 28:15 (see vv. 16–68).
9   Rom. 6:21, 23.
Q. 29
1   2 Thess. 1:9; Mark 9:43–44, 46, 48; Luke 16:24, 26. (See Matt. 25:41, 46; Rev. 14:11; John 3:36.)
Q. 30
1   1 Thess. 5:9.
2   Gen. 3:17; Rom. 5:12, 15; Gal. 3:10, 12.
3   Titus 3:4–7; Gal. 3:21; Rom. 3:20–22; 2 Thess. 2:13–14. (See Acts 13:48; Eph. 1:4–5.)
Q. 31
1   Gal. 3:16; Rom. 5:15 (see vv. 16–21); Isa. 53:10–11; Isa. 59:20–21.
Q. 32
1   Gen. 3:15; Isa. 42:6; John 3:16; John 6:27; 1 Tim. 2:5.
2   1 John 5:11–12.
3   John 3:16, 36; John 1:12.

giveth his Holy Spirit[4] to all his elect, to work in them that faith,[5] with all other saving graces;[6] and to enable them unto all holy obedience,[7] as the evidence of the truth of their faith[8] and thankfulness to God,[9] and as the way which he hath appointed them to salvation.[10]

Q. 33. Was the covenant of grace always administered after one and the same manner?

A. The covenant of grace was not always administered after the same manner, but the administrations of it under the old testament were different from those under the new.[1]

Q. 34. How was the covenant of grace administered under the old testament?

A. The covenant of grace was administered under the old testament, by promises,[1] prophecies,[2] sacrifices,[3] circumcision,[4] the Passover,[5] and other types and ordinances, which did all foresignify Christ then to come, and were for that time sufficient to build up the elect in faith in the promised Messiah,[6] by whom they then had full remission of sin, and eternal salvation.[7]

4   Isa. 59:21; Luke 11:13; John 14:16–20; 1 Cor. 12:13; Rom. 8:9 (see vv. 4, 11, 14–16).
5   2 Cor. 4:13; 1 Cor. 12:3, 9; Eph. 2:8–10; Acts 16:14; 2 Peter 1:1.
6   Gal. 5:22–23.
7   Ezek. 36:27; Eph. 2:10.
8   James 2:18, 22.
9   2 Cor. 5:14–15.
10 Eph. 2:10; Titus 2:14.
Q. 33
1   2 Cor. 3:6–9. (See Heb. 8:7–13.)
Q. 34
1   Rom. 15:8. (See for example Gen. 3:15; 12:1–3; 15:5.)
2   Acts 3:20, 24. (See for example Isa. 52:13–53:12.)
3   Heb. 10:1. (See Lev. 1–7.)
4   Rom. 4:11. (See Gen. 17:1–14.)
5   1 Cor. 5:7; Ex. 12:14, 17, 24 (see entire chapter).
6   Heb. 8:1–2 (see chapters 8–10); Heb. 11:13.
7   Gal. 3:7–9, 14.

Q. 35. How is the covenant of grace administered under the new testament?

A. Under the new testament, when Christ the substance was exhibited, the same covenant of grace was and still is to be administered in the preaching of the Word,[1] and the administration of the sacraments of baptism[2] and the Lord's Supper;[3] in which grace and salvation are held forth in more fullness, evidence, and efficacy, to all nations.[4]

Q. 36. Who is the Mediator of the covenant of grace?

A. The only Mediator of the covenant of grace is the Lord Jesus Christ,[1] who, being the eternal Son of God, of one substance and equal with the Father,[2] in the fullness of time became man,[3] and so was and continues to be God and man, in two entire distinct natures, and one person, forever.[4]

Q. 37. How did Christ, being the Son of God, become man?

A. Christ the Son of God became man, by taking to himself a true body, and a reasonable soul,[1] being conceived by the power of the Holy Ghost in the womb of the virgin Mary, of her substance, and born of her,[2] yet without sin.[3]

Q. 38. Why was it requisite that the Mediator should be God?

A. It was requisite that the Mediator should be God, that he might sustain and keep the human nature from sinking under the infinite wrath of God, and the power of death;[1] give worth and efficacy to his sufferings, obedience,

Q. 35
1 Luke 24:47–48. (See Matt. 28:19–20.)
2 Matt. 28:19–20.
3 Matt. 26:28; 1 Cor. 11:23–25.
4 Rom. 1:16; 2 Cor. 3:6–9; Heb. 8:6, 10–11; Matt. 28:19. (See Eph. 3:1–12.)
Q. 36
1 1 Tim. 2:5; John 14:6; Acts 4:12.
2 John 1:1, 14, 18; John 10:30; Phil. 2:6; Ps. 2:7; Matt. 3:17; Matt. 17:5.
3 Gal. 4:4; Matt. 1:23. (See John 1:14.)
4 Luke 1:35; Acts 1:11; Rom. 9:5; Col. 2:9; Heb. 7:24–25; Heb. 13:8. (See Phil. 2:5–11.)
Q. 37
1 John 1:14; Matt. 26:38; Phil. 2:7; Heb. 2:14–17. (See Luke 2:40, 52; John 11:33.)
2 Luke 1:27, 31, 35; Gal. 4:4.
3 Heb. 4:15; Heb. 7:26; 2 Cor. 5:21; 1 John 3:5.
Q. 38
1 Acts 2:24–25; Rom. 1:4; Rom. 4:25; Heb. 9:14.

and intercession;[2] and to satisfy God's justice,[3] procure his favor,[4] purchase a peculiar people,[5] give his Spirit to them,[6] conquer all their enemies,[7] and bring them to everlasting salvation.[8]

Q. 39. Why was it requisite that the Mediator should be man?

A. It was requisite that the Mediator should be man, that he might advance our nature,[1] perform obedience to the law,[2] suffer and make intercession for us in our nature,[3] have a fellow feeling of our infirmities;[4] that we might receive the adoption of sons,[5] and have comfort and access with boldness unto the throne of grace.[6]

Q. 40. Why was it requisite that the Mediator should be God and man in one person?

A. It was requisite that the Mediator, who was to reconcile God and man, should himself be both God and man, and this in one person, that the proper works of each nature might be accepted of God for us,[1] and relied on by us, as the works of the whole person.[2]

Q. 41. Why was our Mediator called Jesus?

A. Our Mediator was called Jesus, because he saveth his people from their sins.[1]

2 Acts 20:28; Heb. 9:14; Heb. 7:25–28. (See John 17.)
3 Rom. 3:24–26.
4 Eph. 1:6; Matt. 3:17.
5 Titus 2:13–14.
6 Gal. 4:6; John 15:26. (See John 16:7; 14:26.)
7 Luke 1:68–69, 71, 74.
8 Heb. 5:8–9; Heb. 9:11–15.
Q. 39
1 Heb. 2:16; 2 Peter 1:4.
2 Gal. 4:4; Matt. 5:17; Rom. 5:19; Phil. 2:8.
3 Heb. 2:14; Heb. 7:24–25.
4 Heb. 4:15.
5 Gal. 4:5.
6 Heb. 4:16.
Q. 40
1 Matt. 1:21, 23; Matt. 3:17; Heb. 9:14.
2 1 Peter 2:6.
Q. 41
1 Matt. 1:21.

Q. 42. Why was our Mediator called Christ?

A. Our Mediator was called Christ, because he was anointed with the Holy Ghost above measure;[1] and so set apart, and fully furnished with all authority and ability,[2] to execute the offices of prophet,[3] priest,[4] and king of his church,[5] in the estate both of his humiliation and exaltation.

Q. 43. How doth Christ execute the office of a prophet?

A. Christ executeth the office of a prophet, in his revealing to the church,[1] in all ages, by his Spirit and Word,[2] in divers ways of administration,[3] the whole will of God,[4] in all things concerning their edification and salvation.[5]

Q. 44. How doth Christ execute the office of a priest?

A. Christ executeth the office of a priest, in his once offering himself a sacrifice without spot to God,[1] to be a reconciliation for the sins of his people;[2] and in making continual intercession for them.[3]

Q. 45. How doth Christ execute the office of a king?

A. Christ executeth the office of a king, in calling out of the world a people to himself,[1] and giving them officers,[2] laws,[3] and censures, by which he visibly

Q. 42
1   Matt. 3:16 (cf. Acts 10:37–38); John 3:34; Ps. 45:7.
2   John 6:27; Matt. 28:18–20; Rom. 1:3–4.
3   Acts 3:21–22; Luke 4:18, 21; Heb. 1:1–2; Deut. 18:18.
4   Heb. 5:5–7; Heb. 4:14–15.
5   Ps. 2:6; Luke 1:32–34; John 18:37; Matt. 21:5; Isa. 9:6–7; Phil. 2:8–11.
Q. 43
1   John 1:18.
2   1 Peter 1:10–12.
3   Heb. 1:1–2.
4   John 15:15.
5   Acts 20:32; Eph. 4:11–13; John 20:31.
Q. 44
1   Heb. 9:14, 28; Heb. 10:12. (See Isa. 53.)
2   Heb. 2:17; 2 Cor. 5:18; Col. 1:21–22.
3   Heb. 7:25; Heb. 9:24.
Q. 45
1   Acts 15:14–16; Gen. 49:10; Ps. 110:3; John 17:2.
2   Eph. 4:11–12; 1 Cor. 12:28.
3   Isa. 33:22.

governs them;[4] in bestowing saving grace upon his elect,[5] rewarding their obedience,[6] and correcting them for their sins,[7] preserving and supporting them under all their temptations and sufferings,[8] restraining and overcoming all their enemies,[9] and powerfully ordering all things for his own glory,[10] and their good;[11] and also in taking vengeance on the rest, who know not God, and obey not the gospel.[12]

Q. 46. What was the estate of Christ's humiliation?

A. The estate of Christ's humiliation was that low condition, wherein he for our sakes, emptying himself of his glory, took upon him the form of a servant,[1] in his conception[2] and birth,[3] life,[4] death,[5] and after his death,[6] until his resurrection.[7]

Q. 47. How did Christ humble himself in his conception and birth?

A. Christ humbled himself in his conception and birth, in that, being from all eternity the Son of God, in the bosom of the Father, he was pleased in the fullness of time to become the son of man, made of a woman of low estate, and to be born of her; with divers circumstances of more than ordinary abasement.[1]

4   Matt. 18:17–18; 1 Cor. 5:4–5.
5   Acts 5:31.
6   Rev. 22:12; Rev. 2:10.
7   Rev. 3:19.
8   Isa. 63:9.
9   1 Cor. 15:25; Ps. 110:1–2.
10 Rom. 14:10–11.
11 Rom. 8:28.
12 2 Thess. 1:8–9; Ps. 2:8–9.
Q. 46
1   Phil. 2:6–8.
2   Luke 1:31.
3   Luke 2:7.
4   Gal. 4:4; 2 Cor. 8:9; Luke 9:58; Heb. 2:18; Isa. 53:3.
5   Ps. 22:1 (cf. Matt. 27:46); Isa. 53:10; 1 John 2:2; Phil. 2:8.
6   Matt. 12:40; 1 Cor. 15:3–4.
7   Acts 2:24–27, 31.
Q. 47
1   John 1:14, 18; Gal. 4:4; Luke 2:7.

Q. 48. How did Christ humble himself in his life?

A. Christ humbled himself in his life, by subjecting himself to the law,[1] which he perfectly fulfilled;[2] and by conflicting with the indignities of the world,[3] temptations of Satan,[4] and infirmities in his flesh, whether common to the nature of man, or particularly accompanying that his low condition.[5]

Q. 49. How did Christ humble himself in his death?

A. Christ humbled himself in his death, in that having been betrayed by Judas,[1] forsaken by his disciples,[2] scorned and rejected by the world,[3] condemned by Pilate, and tormented by his persecutors;[4] having also conflicted with the terrors of death, and the powers of darkness, felt and borne the weight of God's wrath,[5] he laid down his life an offering for sin,[6] enduring the painful, shameful, and cursed death of the cross.[7]

Q. 50. Wherein consisted Christ's humiliation after his death?

A. Christ's humiliation after his death consisted in his being buried,[1] and continuing in the state of the dead, and under the power of death till the third day;[2] which hath been otherwise expressed in these words, *He descended into hell.*

Q. 48
1   Gal. 4:4.
2   Matt. 5:17; Rom. 5:19.
3   Ps. 22:6; Isa. 53:2–3; Heb. 12:2–3.
4   Matt. 4:1–11; Luke 4:13.
5   Heb. 2:17–18; Heb. 4:15; Isa. 52:13–14.
Q. 49
1   Matt. 27:4.
2   Matt. 26:56.
3   Isa. 53:2–3.
4   Matt. 27:26–50; John 19:34. (See Luke 22:63–64.)
5   Luke 22:44; Matt. 27:46.
6   Isa. 53:10; Matt. 20:28. (See Mark 10:45.)
7   Phil. 2:8; Heb. 12:2; Gal. 3:13.
Q. 50
1   1 Cor. 15:3–4.
2   Ps. 16:10; Acts 2:24–27, 31; Rom. 6:9; Matt. 12:40.

Q. 51. What was the estate of Christ's exaltation?

A. The estate of Christ's exaltation comprehendeth his resurrection,[1] ascension,[2] sitting at the right hand of the Father,[3] and his coming again to judge the world.[4]

Q. 52. How was Christ exalted in his resurrection?

A. Christ was exalted in his resurrection, in that, not having seen corruption in death, (of which it was not possible for him to be held,[1]) and having the very same body in which he suffered, with the essential properties thereof,[2] (but without mortality, and other common infirmities belonging to this life,) really united to his soul,[3] he rose again from the dead the third day by his own power;[4] whereby he declared himself to be the Son of God,[5] to have satisfied divine justice,[6] to have vanquished death, and him that had the power of it,[7] and to be Lord of quick and dead:[8] all which he did as a public person,[9] the head of his church,[10] for their justification,[11] quickening in grace,[12] support against enemies,[13] and to assure them of their resurrection from the dead at the last day.[14]

Q. 51
1   1 Cor. 15:4.
2   Ps. 68:18; Acts 1:11; Eph. 4:8.
3   Eph. 1:20; Ps. 110:1; Acts 2:33–34; Heb. 1:3.
4   Acts 1:11; Acts 17:31. (See Matt. 16:27.)
Q. 52
1   Acts 2:24, 27.
2   Luke 24:39.
3   Rom. 6:9; Rev. 1:18.
4   John 10:18.
5   Rom. 1:4.
6   Rom. 8:34; Rom. 3:25–26; Heb. 9:13–14.
7   Heb. 2:14.
8   Rom. 14:9.
9   1 Cor. 15:21–22; Isa. 53:10–11.
10 Eph. 1:20–23; Col. 1:18.
11 Rom. 4:25.
12 Eph. 2:1, 5–6; Col. 2:12.
13 1 Cor. 15:25–27; Ps. 2:7–9.
14 1 Cor. 15:20; 1 Thess. 4:14.

Q. 53. How was Christ exalted in his ascension?

A. Christ was exalted in his ascension, in that having after his resurrection often appeared unto and conversed with his apostles, speaking to them of the things pertaining to the kingdom of God,[1] and giving them commission to preach the gospel to all nations,[2] forty days after his resurrection, he, in our nature, and as our head,[3] triumphing over enemies,[4] visibly went up into the highest heavens, there to receive gifts for men,[5] to raise up our affections thither,[6] and to prepare a place for us,[7] where himself is, and shall continue till his second coming at the end of the world.[8]

Q. 54. How is Christ exalted in his sitting at the right hand of God?

A. Christ is exalted in his sitting at the right hand of God, in that as God-man he is advanced to the highest favor with God the Father,[1] with all fullness of joy,[2] glory,[3] and power over all things in heaven and earth;[4] and doth gather and defend his church, and subdue their enemies; furnisheth his ministers and people with gifts and graces,[5] and maketh intercession for them.[6]

Q. 55. How doth Christ make intercession?

A. Christ maketh intercession, by his appearing in our nature continually before the Father in heaven,[1] in the merit of his obedience and sacrifice on earth,[2]

Q. 53
1 Acts 1:2–3.
2 Matt. 28:19–20.
3 John 20:17; Heb. 6:20.
4 Eph. 4:8.
5 Acts 1:9–11; Eph. 4:7–8; Ps. 68:18; Eph. 4:10; Acts 2:33.
6 Col. 3:1–2.
7 John 14:3.
8 Acts 3:21.
Q. 54
1 Phil. 2:9.
2 Acts 2:28; Ps. 16:11.
3 John 17:5.
4 Dan. 7:13–14; Eph. 1:22; 1 Peter 3:22.
5 Eph. 4:10–12; Ps. 110:1; Heb. 10:12–14; Ezek. 37:24.
6 Rom. 8:34; 1 John 2:1; Heb. 7:25.
Q. 55
1 Heb. 9:12, 24.
2 Isa. 53:12; Heb. 1:3.

declaring his will to have it applied to all believers;[3] answering all accusations against them,[4] and procuring for them quiet of conscience, notwithstanding daily failings,[5] access with boldness to the throne of grace,[6] and acceptance of their persons[7] and services.[8]

Q. 56. How is Christ to be exalted in his coming again to judge the world?

A. Christ is to be exalted in his coming again to judge the world, in that he, who was unjustly judged and condemned by wicked men,[1] shall come again at the last day in great power,[2] and in the full manifestation of his own glory, and of his Father's, with all his holy angels,[3] with a shout, with the voice of the archangel, and with the trumpet of God,[4] to judge the world in righteousness.[5]

Q. 57. What benefits hath Christ procured by his mediation?

A. Christ, by his mediation, hath procured redemption,[1] with all other benefits of the covenant of grace.[2]

Q. 58. How do we come to be made partakers of the benefits which Christ hath procured?

A. We are made partakers of the benefits which Christ hath procured, by the application of them unto us,[1] which is the work especially of God the Holy Ghost.[2]

3 John 3:16; John 17:9, 20, 24.
4 Rom. 8:33–34.
5 Rom. 5:1–2; 1 John 2:1–2.
6 Heb. 4:16.
7 Eph. 1:6.
8 1 Peter 2:5.
Q. 56
1 Acts 3:14–15.
2 Matt. 24:30; 2 Thess. 1:9–10.
3 Luke 9:26; Matt. 25:31.
4 1 Thess. 4:16.
5 Acts 17:31; 2 Thess. 1:6–8.
Q. 57
1 1 Tim. 2:5–6; Heb. 9:12; Eph. 1:7.
2 2 Cor. 1:20; Eph. 1:3–6; 2 Peter 1:3–4.
Q. 58
1 John 1:11–12.
2 Titus 3:4–7; John 16:14–15. (See John 3:3–8.)

Q. 59. Who are made partakers of redemption through Christ?

A. Redemption is certainly applied, and effectually communicated, to all those for whom Christ hath purchased it;[1] who are in time by the Holy Ghost enabled to believe in Christ according to the gospel.[2]

Q. 60. Can they who have never heard the gospel, and so know not Jesus Christ, nor believe in him, be saved by their living according to the light of nature?

A. They who, having never heard the gospel,[1] know not Jesus Christ,[2] and believe not in him, cannot be saved,[3] be they never so diligent to frame their lives according to the light of nature,[4] or the laws of that religion which they profess;[5] neither is there salvation in any other, but in Christ alone,[6] who is the Savior only of his body the church.[7]

Q. 61. Are all they saved who hear the gospel, and live in the church?

A. All that hear the gospel, and live in the visible church, are not saved; but they only who are true members of the church invisible.[1]

Q. 62. What is the visible church?

A. The visible church is a society made up of all such as in all ages and places of the world do profess the true religion,[1] and of their children.[2]

Q. 59
1 Eph. 1:13–14; John 6:37, 39; John 10:15–16.
2 Rom. 10:17; 1 Cor. 2:12–16; Eph. 2:8; Rom. 8:9, 14.
Q. 60
1 Rom. 10:14.
2 2 Thess. 1:8–9; Eph. 2:12; John 1:10–12.
3 John 8:24; John 3:18.
4 1 Cor. 1:20–24.
5 John 4:22; Rom. 9:31–32; Phil. 3:4–9.
6 Acts 4:12.
7 Eph. 5:23.
Q. 61
1 John 12:38–40; Rom. 9:6; Matt. 22:14; Matt. 7:21; Rom. 11:7; 1 Cor. 10:2–5.
Q. 62
1 1 Cor. 1:2; 1 Cor. 12:13; Rom. 15:9–12; Rev. 7:9; Ps. 2:8; Ps. 22:27–31; Ps. 45:17; Matt. 28:19–20; Isa. 59:21.
2 1 Cor. 7:14; Acts 2:39; Rom. 11:16; Gen. 17:7.

Q. 63. What are the special privileges of the visible church?

A. The visible church hath the privilege of being under God's special care and government;[1] of being protected and preserved in all ages, notwithstanding the opposition of all enemies;[2] and of enjoying the communion of saints, the ordinary means of salvation,[3] and offers of grace by Christ to all the members of it in the ministry of the gospel, testifying, that whosoever believes in him shall be saved,[4] and excluding none that will come unto him.[5]

Q. 64. What is the invisible church?

A. The invisible church is the whole number of the elect, that have been, are, or shall be gathered into one under Christ the head.[1]

Q. 65. What special benefits do the members of the invisible church enjoy by Christ?

A. The members of the invisible church by Christ enjoy union and communion with him in grace and glory.[1]

Q. 66. What is that union which the elect have with Christ?

A. The union which the elect have with Christ is the work of God's grace,[1] whereby they are spiritually and mystically, yet really and inseparably, joined to Christ as their head and husband;[2] which is done in their effectual calling.[3]

Q. 63
1 Isa. 4:5–6; 1 Tim. 4:10; Eph. 4:11–13.
2 Ps. 115:1–2, 9; Isa. 31:4–5; Zech. 12:2–4, 8–9; Matt. 16:18.
3 Acts 2:39, 42; Matt. 28:19–20; 1 Cor. 12:12–13.
4 Ps. 147:19–20; Rom. 9:4; Eph. 4:11–12; Acts 22:16; Acts 2:21 (see Joel 2:32); Rom. 10:10–13, 17.
5 Matt. 11:28–29; John 6:37.
Q. 64
1 Eph. 1:10; Eph. 1:22–23; John 10:16; John 11:52; Eph. 5:23, 27, 32.
Q. 65
1 John 17:21; Eph. 2:5–6; John 17:24; 1 John 1:3; John 1:16; Eph. 3:16–19; Phil. 3:10; Rom. 6:5–6.
Q. 66
1 Eph. 2:6–7.
2 Eph. 1:22; 1 Cor. 6:17; John 10:28; Eph. 5:23, 30; John 15:5; Eph. 3:17.
3 1 Peter 5:10; 1 Cor. 1:9.

Q. 67. What is effectual calling?

A. Effectual calling is the work of God's almighty power and grace,[1] whereby (out of his free and special love to his elect, and from nothing in them moving him thereunto[2]) he doth, in his accepted time, invite and draw them to Jesus Christ, by his Word and Spirit;[3] savingly enlightening their minds,[4] renewing and powerfully determining their wills,[5] so as they (although in themselves dead in sin) are hereby made willing and able freely to answer his call, and to accept and embrace the grace offered and conveyed therein.[6]

Q. 68. Are the elect only effectually called?

A. All the elect, and they only, are effectually called;[1] although others may be, and often are, outwardly called by the ministry of the Word,[2] and have some common operations of the Spirit;[3] who, for their willful neglect and contempt of the grace offered to them, being justly left in their unbelief, do never truly come to Jesus Christ.[4]

Q. 69. What is the communion in grace which the members of the invisible church have with Christ?

A. The communion in grace which the members of the invisible church have with Christ, is their partaking of the virtue of his mediation, in their justification,[1] adoption,[2] sanctification, and whatever else, in this life, manifests their union with him.[3]

Q. 67
1   Ezek. 37:9, 14; John 5:25; Eph. 1:18–20; 2 Tim. 1:8–9.
2   Titus 3:4–5; Eph. 2:4–5, 7–9; Rom. 9:11; Deut. 9:5.
3   John 3:5; Titus 3:5; 2 Cor. 5:20; 2 Cor. 6:1–2; John 6:44–45; Acts 16:14; 2 Thess. 2:13–14.
4   Acts 26:18; 1 Cor. 2:10, 12; 2 Cor. 4:6; Eph. 1:17–18.
5   Ezek. 11:19; Ezek. 36:26–27; John 6:45.
6   Eph. 2:5; Phil. 2:13; Deut. 30:6; Isa. 45:22; Matt. 11:28–30; Rev. 22:17.
Q. 68
1   Acts 13:48.
2   Matt. 22:14; Acts 8:13, 20–21.
3   Matt. 7:22; Matt. 13:20–21; Heb. 6:4–6.
4   John 12:38–40; Acts 28:25–27; John 6:64–65; Ps. 81:11–12; Heb. 10:29; 1 John 2:19.
Q. 69
1   Rom. 8:30.
2   Eph. 1:5.
3   1 Cor. 1:30; 1 Cor. 6:11.

Q. 70. What is justification?

A. Justification is an act of God's free grace unto sinners,[1] in which he pardoneth all their sins, accepteth and accounteth their persons righteous in his sight;[2] not for anything wrought in them, or done by them,[3] but only for the perfect obedience and full satisfaction of Christ, by God imputed to them,[4] and received by faith alone.[5]

Q. 71. How is justification an act of God's free grace?

A. Although Christ, by his obedience and death, did make a proper, real, and full satisfaction to God's justice in the behalf of them that are justified;[1] yet inasmuch as God accepteth the satisfaction from a surety, which he might have demanded of them, and did provide this surety, his own only Son,[2] imputing his righteousness to them,[3] and requiring nothing of them for their justification but faith,[4] which also is his gift,[5] their justification is to them of free grace.[6]

Q. 72. What is justifying faith?

A. Justifying faith is a saving grace,[1] wrought in the heart of a sinner by the Spirit[2] and Word of God,[3] whereby he, being convinced of his sin and misery, and of the disability in himself and all other creatures to recover him out of his lost condition,[4] not only assenteth to the truth of the promise of the gospel,[5] but receiveth and resteth upon Christ and his righteousness, therein held

Q. 70

1   Rom. 3:22, 24–25; Rom. 4:5.
2   Jer. 23:6; Rom. 4:6–8; 2 Cor. 5:19, 21; Rom. 3:22, 24–25, 27–28.
3   Titus 3:5, 7; Eph. 1:7.
4   Rom. 4:6–8, 11; Rom. 5:17–19.
5   Acts 10:43; Gal. 2:16; Phil. 3:9.

Q. 71

1   Rom. 5:8–10, 19.
2   1 Tim. 2:5–6; Heb. 10:10; Matt. 20:28; Dan. 9:24, 26; Isa. 53:4–6, 10–12; Heb. 7:22; Rom. 8:32; 1 Peter 1:18–19.
3   2 Cor. 5:21; Rom. 4:6, 11.
4   Rom. 3:24–25.
5   Eph. 2:8.
6   Eph. 1:7; Rom. 3:24–25.

Q. 72

1   Heb. 10:39.
2   2 Cor. 4:13; Eph. 1:17–19; 1 Cor. 12:3; 1 Peter 1:2.
3   Rom. 10:14–17; 1 Cor. 1:21.
4   Acts 2:37; Acts 16:30; John 16:8–9; Rom. 6:6; Eph. 2:1; Acts 4:12.
5   Eph. 1:13; Heb. 11:13.

forth, for pardon of sin,[6] and for the accepting and accounting of his person righteous in the sight of God for salvation.[7]

Q. 73. How doth faith justify a sinner in the sight of God?

A. Faith justifies a sinner in the sight of God, not because of those other graces which do always accompany it, or of good works that are the fruits of it,[1] nor as if the grace of faith, or any act thereof, were imputed to him for his justification;[2] but only as it is an instrument by which he receiveth and applieth Christ and his righteousness.[3]

Q. 74. What is adoption?

A. Adoption is an act of the free grace of God,[1] in and for his only Son Jesus Christ,[2] whereby all those that are justified are received into the number of his children,[3] have his name put upon them,[4] the Spirit of his Son given to them,[5] are under his fatherly care and dispensations,[6] admitted to all the liberties and privileges of the sons of God, made heirs of all the promises, and fellow heirs with Christ in glory.[7]

Q. 75. What is sanctification?

A. Sanctification is a work of God's grace, whereby they whom God hath, before the foundation of the world, chosen to be holy, are in time, through the powerful operation of his Spirit[1] applying the death and resurrection of Christ unto them,[2]

6 John 1:12; Acts 16:31; Acts 10:43; Zech. 3:8–9.
7 Phil. 3:9; Acts 15:11.
Q. 73
1 Gal. 3:11; Rom. 3:28.
2 Rom. 4:5; Rom. 10:10.
3 John 1:12; Phil. 3:9; Gal. 2:16.
Q. 74
1 1 John 3:1.
2 Eph. 1:5; Gal. 4:4–5.
3 John 1:12; Rom. 8:15–16.
4 Num. 6:24–27; Amos 9:12; 2 Cor. 6:18; Rev. 3:12.
5 Gal. 4:6.
6 Ps. 103:13; Prov. 14:26; Matt. 6:32; Heb. 12:5–7, 11.
7 Heb. 6:12; Rom. 8:17; 1 Peter 1:3–4.
Q. 75
1 Ezek. 36:27; Phil. 2:13; 2 Thess. 2:13; Eph. 1:4; 1 Cor. 6:11.
2 Rom. 6:4–6; Col. 3:1–3; Phil. 3:10.

renewed in their whole man after the image of God;[3] having the seeds of repentance unto life, and all other saving graces, put into their hearts,[4] and those graces so stirred up, increased, and strengthened,[5] as that they more and more die unto sin, and rise unto newness of life.[6]

Q. 76. What is repentance unto life?

A. Repentance unto life is a saving grace,[1] wrought in the heart of a sinner by the Spirit[2] and Word of God,[3] whereby, out of the sight and sense, not only of the danger,[4] but also of the filthiness and odiousness of his sins,[5] and upon the apprehension of God's mercy in Christ to such as are penitent,[6] he so grieves for[7] and hates his sins,[8] as that he turns from them all to God,[9] purposing and endeavoring constantly to walk with him in all the ways of new obedience.[10]

Q. 77. Wherein do justification and sanctification differ?

A. Although sanctification be inseparably joined with justification,[1] yet they differ, in that God in justification imputeth the righteousness of Christ;[2] in sanctification his Spirit infuseth grace, and enableth to the exercise thereof;[3] in the former, sin is pardoned;[4] in the other, it is subdued:[5] the one doth equally free all believers from the revenging wrath of God, and that perfectly

3 2 Cor. 5:17; Eph. 4:23–24; 1 Thess. 5:23.
4 Acts 11:18; 1 John 3:9.
5 Jude 20; Heb. 6:11–12; Eph. 3:16–19; Col. 1:10–11.
6 Ezek. 36:25–27; Rom. 6:4, 6, 12–14; 2 Cor. 7:1; 1 Peter 2:24; Gal. 5:24.

Q. 76
1 2 Tim. 2:25; Acts 11:18.
2 Zech. 12:10.
3 Acts 11:18, 20–21.
4 Ezek. 18:28, 30, 32; Luke 15:17–18; Hos. 2:6–7.
5 Ezek. 36:31; Isa. 30:22; Phil. 3:7–8.
6 Joel 2:12–13; Ps. 51:1–4; Luke 15:7, 10; Acts 2:37.
7 Jer. 31:18–19; Ps. 32:5.
8 2 Cor. 7:11.
9 Luke 1:16–17; 1 Thess. 1:9; Acts 26:18; Ezek. 14:6; 1 Kings 8:47–48.
10 2 Chron. 7:14; Ps. 119:57–64; Matt. 3:8; 2 Cor. 7:10; Luke 1:6.

Q. 77
1 1 Cor. 6:11; 1 Cor. 1:30.
2 Rom. 4:6, 8.
3 Ezek. 36:27; Heb. 9:13–14.
4 Rom. 3:24–25.
5 Rom. 6:6, 14.

in this life, that they never fall into condemnation;[6] the other is neither equal in all,[7] nor in this life perfect in any,[8] but growing up to perfection.[9]

Q. 78. Whence ariseth the imperfection of sanctification in believers?

A. The imperfection of sanctification in believers ariseth from the remnants of sin abiding in every part of them, and the perpetual lustings of the flesh against the spirit; whereby they are often foiled with temptations, and fall into many sins,[1] are hindered in all their spiritual services,[2] and their best works are imperfect and defiled in the sight of God.[3]

Q. 79. May not true believers, by reason of their imperfections, and the many temptations and sins they are overtaken with, fall away from the state of grace?

A. True believers, by reason of the unchangeable love of God,[1] and his decree and covenant to give them perseverance,[2] their inseparable union with Christ,[3] his continual intercession for them,[4] and the Spirit and seed of God abiding in them,[5] can neither totally nor finally fall away from the state of grace,[6] but are kept by the power of God through faith unto salvation.[7]

6   Rom. 8:33–34.
7   1 John 2:12–14; Heb. 5:12–14.
8   1 John 1:8, 10.
9   2 Cor. 7:1; Phil. 3:12–14.
Q. 78
1   Rom. 7:18, 23 (see Mark 14:66–72); Gal. 2:11–12.
2   Heb. 12:1.
3   Isa. 64:6; Ex. 28:38; Gal. 5:16–18.
Q. 79
1   Jer. 31:3.
2   2 Tim. 2:19; Heb. 13:20–21; 2 Sam. 23:5.
3   1 Cor. 1:8–9.
4   Heb. 7:25; Luke 22:32.
5   1 John 3:9; 1 John 2:27.
6   Jer. 32:40; John 10:28.
7   1 Peter 1:5.

Q. 80. Can true believers be infallibly assured that they are in the estate of grace, and that they shall persevere therein unto salvation?

A. Such as truly believe in Christ, and endeavor to walk in all good conscience before him,[1] may, without extraordinary revelation, by faith grounded upon the truth of God's promises, and by the Spirit enabling them to discern in themselves those graces to which the promises of life are made,[2] and bearing witness with their spirits that they are the children of God,[3] be infallibly assured that they are in the estate of grace, and shall persevere therein unto salvation.[4]

Q. 81. Are all true believers at all times assured of their present being in the estate of grace, and that they shall be saved?

A. Assurance of grace and salvation not being of the essence of faith,[1] true believers may wait long before they obtain it;[2] and, after the enjoyment thereof, may have it weakened and intermitted, through manifold distempers, sins, temptations, and desertions;[3] yet are they never left without such a presence and support of the Spirit of God as keeps them from sinking into utter despair.[4]

Q. 82. What is the communion in glory which the members of the invisible church have with Christ?

A. The communion in glory which the members of the invisible church have with Christ, is in this life,[1] immediately after death,[2] and at last perfected at the resurrection and day of judgment.[3]

Q. 80

1 1 John 2:3; Heb. 10:19–23.
2 1 Cor. 2:12; 1 John 3:14, 18–19, 21, 24; 1 John 4:13, 16; Heb. 6:11–12.
3 Rom. 8:15–16.
4 1 John 5:13; Heb. 6:19–20. (See 2 Peter 1:5–11.)

Q. 81

1 Eph. 1:13.
2 Isa. 50:10; Ps. 88:1–3, 6–7, 9–10, 13–15.
3 Ps. 77:1–12; Ps. 51:8, 12; Ps. 31:22; Ps. 22:1; Eph. 4:30; Luke 22:31–34.
4 1 John 3:9; Ps. 73:15, 23; Isa. 54:7–10; 1 Peter 4:12–14.

Q. 82

1 2 Cor. 3:18.
2 Luke 23:43.
3 1 Thess. 4:17.

Q. 83. What is the communion in glory with Christ which the members of the invisible church enjoy in this life?

A. The members of the invisible church have communicated to them in this life the firstfruits of glory with Christ, as they are members of him their head, and so in him are interested in that glory which he is fully possessed of;[1] and, as an earnest thereof, enjoy the sense of God's love,[2] peace of conscience, joy in the Holy Ghost, and hope of glory;[3] as, on the contrary, sense of God's revenging wrath, horror of conscience, and a fearful expectation of judgment, are to the wicked the beginning of their torments which they shall endure after death.[4]

Q. 84. Shall all men die?

A. Death being threatened as the wages of sin,[1] it is appointed unto all men once to die;[2] for that all have sinned.[3]

Q. 85. Death being the wages of sin, why are not the righteous delivered from death, seeing all their sins are forgiven in Christ?

A. The righteous shall be delivered from death itself at the last day, and even in death are delivered from the sting and curse of it;[1] so that, although they die, yet it is out of God's love,[2] to free them perfectly from sin and misery,[3] and to make them capable of further communion with Christ in glory, which they then enter upon.[4]

Q. 83
1   Eph. 2:5–6.
2   Rom. 5:5; 2 Cor. 1:22.
3   Rom. 5:1–2; Rom. 14:17; 2 Peter 3:18.
4   Gen. 4:13; Matt. 27:4; Heb. 10:27; Rom. 2:9; Mark 9:44.
Q. 84
1   Rom. 6:23.
2   Heb. 9:27.
3   Rom. 5:12.
Q. 85
1   1 Cor. 15:26, 55–57; Heb. 2:15; John 11:25–26.
2   Isa. 57:1–2; 2 Kings 22:20.
3   Rev. 14:13; Eph. 5:27.
4   Luke 23:43; Phil. 1:23.

Q. 86. What is the communion in glory with Christ, which the members of the invisible church enjoy immediately after death?

A. The communion in glory with Christ, which the members of the invisible church enjoy immediately after death, is, in that their souls are then made perfect in holiness,[1] and received into the highest heavens,[2] where they behold the face of God in light and glory,[3] waiting for the full redemption of their bodies,[4] which even in death continue united to Christ,[5] and rest in their graves as in their beds,[6] till at the last day they be again united to their souls.[7] Whereas the souls of the wicked are at their death cast into hell, where they remain in torments and utter darkness, and their bodies kept in their graves, as in their prisons, till the resurrection and judgment of the great day.[8]

Q. 87. What are we to believe concerning the resurrection?

A. We are to believe, that at the last day there shall be a general resurrection of the dead, both of the just and unjust:[1] when they that are then found alive shall in a moment be changed; and the selfsame bodies of the dead which were laid in the grave, being then again united to their souls forever, shall be raised up by the power of Christ.[2] The bodies of the just, by the Spirit of Christ, and by virtue of his resurrection as their head, shall be raised in power, spiritual, incorruptible, and made like to his glorious body;[3] and the bodies of the wicked shall be raised up in dishonor by him, as an offended judge.[4]

Q. 86
1 Heb. 12:23; Acts 7:55, 59.
2 2 Cor. 5:1, 6, 8; Phil. 1:23; Acts 3:21; Eph. 4:10; Luke 23:43.
3 1 John 3:2; 1 Cor. 13:12.
4 Rom. 8:23; Ps. 16:9.
5 1 Thess. 4:14, 16.
6 Isa. 57:2.
7 Job 19:26–27.
8 Luke 16:23–24; Acts 1:25; Jude 6–7.
Q. 87
1 Dan. 12:2; Acts 24:15.
2 Job 19:26; 1 Cor. 15:51–53; 1 Thess. 4:15–17; John 5:28–29; Rom. 8:11.
3 1 Cor. 15:21–23, 42–44; Phil. 3:21.
4 John 5:27–29; Matt. 25:33.

Q. 88. What shall immediately follow after the resurrection?

A. Immediately after the resurrection shall follow the general and final judgment of angels and men;[1] the day and hour whereof no man knoweth, that all may watch and pray, and be ever ready for the coming of the Lord.[2]

Q. 89. What shall be done to the wicked at the day of judgment?

A. At the day of judgment, the wicked shall be set on Christ's left hand,[1] and, upon clear evidence, and full conviction of their own consciences,[2] shall have the fearful but just sentence of condemnation pronounced against them;[3] and thereupon shall be cast out from the favorable presence of God, and the glorious fellowship with Christ, his saints, and all his holy angels, into hell, to be punished with unspeakable torments, both of body and soul, with the devil and his angels forever.[4]

Q. 90. What shall be done to the righteous at the day of judgment?

A. At the day of judgment, the righteous, being caught up to Christ in the clouds,[1] shall be set on his right hand, and there openly acknowledged and acquitted,[2] shall join with him in the judging of reprobate angels and men,[3] and shall be received into heaven,[4] where they shall be fully and forever freed from all sin and misery;[5] filled with inconceivable joys,[6] made perfectly holy and happy both in body and soul, in the company of innumerable saints and holy angels,[7] but especially in the immediate vision and fruition of God the

---

Q. 88
1   Eccl. 12:14; 2 Peter 2:4, 6–7, 14–15; Matt. 25:46; 2 Cor. 5:10; Rom. 14:10, 12.
2   Matt. 24:36, 42, 44; Mark 13:35–37.
Q. 89
1   Matt. 25:33.
2   Rom. 2:15–16.
3   Matt. 25:41–43.
4   Luke 16:26; 2 Thess. 1:8–9.
Q. 90
1   1 Thess. 4:17; 1 Cor. 15:42–43.
2   Matt. 25:33; Matt. 10:32.
3   1 Cor. 6:2–3.
4   Matt. 25:34, 46.
5   Eph. 5:27; Rev. 14:13.
6   Ps. 16:11.
7   Heb. 12:22–23.

Father, of our Lord Jesus Christ, and of the Holy Spirit, to all eternity.[8] And this is the perfect and full communion, which the members of the invisible church shall enjoy with Christ in glory, at the resurrection and day of judgment.

HAVING SEEN WHAT THE SCRIPTURES PRINCIPALLY TEACH US TO BELIEVE CONCERNING GOD, IT FOLLOWS TO CONSIDER WHAT THEY REQUIRE AS THE DUTY OF MAN

Q. 91. What is the duty which God requireth of man?

A. The duty which God requireth of man, is obedience to his revealed will.[1]

Q. 92. What did God at first reveal unto man as the rule of his obedience?

A. The rule of obedience revealed to Adam in the estate of innocence, and to all mankind in him, besides a special command not to eat of the fruit of the tree of the knowledge of good and evil, was the moral law.[1]

Q. 93. What is the moral law?

A. The moral law is the declaration of the will of God to mankind, directing and binding everyone to personal, perfect, and perpetual conformity and obedience thereunto, in the frame and disposition of the whole man, soul and body,[1] and in performance of all those duties of holiness and righteousness which he oweth to God and man:[2] promising life upon the fulfilling, and threatening death upon the breach of it.[3]

---

8   1 John 3:2; Rom. 8:29; 1 Cor. 13:12; 1 Thess. 4:17–18.
Q. 91
1   Deut. 29:29; Mic. 6:8; 1 John 5:2–3; Rom. 12:1–2; 1 Sam. 15:22.
Q. 92
1   Gen. 1:26–27; Rom. 2:14–15; Rom. 10:5; Gen. 2:17.
Q. 93
1   Deut. 5:1–3, 31, 33; Luke 10:26–27; 1 Thess. 5:23; Eph. 4:24.
2   Luke 1:75; Acts 24:16; 1 Peter 1:15–16.
3   Rom. 10:5; Gal. 3:10, 12; Rom. 5:12.

Q. 94. Is there any use of the moral law to man since the fall?

A. Although no man, since the fall, can attain to righteousness and life by the moral law;[1] yet there is great use thereof, as well common to all men, as peculiar either to the unregenerate, or the regenerate.[2]

Q. 95. Of what use is the moral law to all men?

A. The moral law is of use to all men, to inform them of the holy nature and will of God,[1] and of their duty, binding them to walk accordingly;[2] to convince them of their disability to keep it, and of the sinful pollution of their nature, hearts, and lives;[3] to humble them in the sense of their sin and misery,[4] and thereby help them to a clearer sight of the need they have of Christ,[5] and of the perfection of his obedience.[6]

Q. 96. What particular use is there of the moral law to unregenerate men?

A. The moral law is of use to unregenerate men, to awaken their consciences to flee from wrath to come,[1] and to drive them to Christ;[2] or, upon their continuance in the estate and way of sin, to leave them inexcusable,[3] and under the curse thereof.[4]

Q. 97. What special use is there of the moral law to the regenerate?

A. Although they that are regenerate, and believe in Christ, be delivered from the moral law as a covenant of works,[1] so as thereby they are neither

Q. 94
1 Rom. 8:3; Gal. 2:16.
2 1 Tim. 1:8.
Q. 95
1 Rom. 1:20; Lev. 11:44–45; Lev. 20:7–8; Rom. 7:12.
2 Mic. 6:8; James 2:10–11; Rom. 1:32.
3 Ps. 19:11–12; Rom. 3:20; Rom. 7:7.
4 Rom. 3:9, 23.
5 Gal. 3:21–22, 24.
6 Rom. 10:4.
Q. 96
1 Ps. 51:13; 1 Tim. 1:9–11.
2 Gal. 3:24.
3 Rom. 1:20; Rom. 2:15.
4 Gal. 3:10.
Q. 97
1 Rom. 6:14; Rom. 7:4, 6; Gal. 4:4–5; Col. 2:13–14.

justified[2] nor condemned;[3] yet, besides the general uses thereof common to them with all men, it is of special use, to show them how much they are bound to Christ for his fulfilling it, and enduring the curse thereof in their stead, and for their good;[4] and thereby to provoke them to more thankfulness,[5] and to express the same in their greater care to conform themselves thereunto as the rule of their obedience.[6]

Q. 98. Where is the moral law summarily comprehended?

A. The moral law is summarily comprehended in the Ten Commandments, which were delivered by the voice of God upon Mount Sinai, and written by him in two tables of stone;[1] and are recorded in the twentieth chapter of Exodus: the four first commandments containing our duty to God, and the other six our duty to man.[2]

Q. 99. What rules are to be observed for the right understanding of the Ten Commandments?

A. For the right understanding of the Ten Commandments, these rules are to be observed:

1. That the law is perfect, and bindeth everyone to full conformity in the whole man unto the righteousness thereof, and unto entire obedience forever; so as to require the utmost perfection of every duty, and to forbid the least degree of every sin.[1]
2. That it is spiritual, and so reacheth the understanding, will, affections, and all other powers of the soul; as well as words, works, and gestures.[2]

---

2   Rom. 3:20.
3   Gal. 5:23; Rom. 8:1.
4   Rom. 7:24–25; Gal. 3:13–14; Rom. 8:3–4; Acts 13:38–39.
5   Luke 1:68–69, 74–75; Col. 1:12–14; Rom. 6:14.
6   Deut. 30:19–20; Rom. 7:22; Rom. 12:2; Titus 2:11–14; James 1:25.
Q. 98
1   Deut. 4:13; Deut. 10:4; Ex. 34:1–4; Rom. 13:8–10; James 2:8, 10–12.
2   Matt. 22:37–40; Matt. 19:17–19.
Q. 99
1   Ps. 19:7; James 2:10; Matt. 5:21–22.
2   Rom. 7:14; Deut. 6:5; Matt. 22:37–39; Matt. 5:21–22, 27–28, 33–34, 37–39, 43–44.

3. That one and the same thing, in divers respects, is required or forbidden in several commandments.[3]

4. That as, where a duty is commanded, the contrary sin is forbidden;[4] and, where a sin is forbidden, the contrary duty is commanded:[5] so, where a promise is annexed, the contrary threatening is included;[6] and, where a threatening is annexed, the contrary promise is included.[7]

5. That what God forbids, is at no time to be done;[8] what he commands, is always our duty;[9] and yet every particular duty is not to be done at all times.[10]

6. That under one sin or duty, all of the same kind are forbidden or commanded; together with all the causes, means, occasions, and appearances thereof, and provocations thereunto.[11]

7. That what is forbidden or commanded to ourselves, we are bound, according to our places, to endeavor that it may be avoided or performed by others, according to the duty of their places.[12]

8. That in what is commanded to others, we are bound, according to our places and callings, to be helpful to them;[13] and to take heed of partaking with others in what is forbidden them.[14]

Q. 100. What special things are we to consider in the Ten Commandments?

A. We are to consider, in the Ten Commandments, the preface, the substance of the commandments themselves, and several reasons annexed to some of them, the more to enforce them.[1]

---

3   Col. 3:5; Amos 8:5; Prov. 1:19; 1 Tim. 6:10.

4   Isa. 58:13; Deut. 6:13; Matt. 4:9–10; Matt. 15:4–6.

5   Matt. 5:21–25; Eph. 4:28.

6   Ex. 20:12; Prov. 30:17.

7   Jer. 18:7–8; Ex. 20:7; Ps. 15:1, 4–5; Ps. 24:4–5.

8   Job 13:7–8; Rom. 3:8; Job 36:21; Heb. 11:25.

9   Deut. 4:8–9; Luke 17:10.

10 Matt. 12:7.

11 Matt. 5:21–22, 27–28; Matt. 15:4–6; 1 Thess. 5:22; Jude 23; Gal. 5:26; Col. 3:21.

12 Ex. 20:10; Lev. 19:17; Gen. 18:19; Josh. 24:15; Deut. 6:6–7; Heb. 10:24–25.

13 2 Cor. 1:24.

14 1 Tim. 5:22; Eph. 5:11.

Q. 100

1   As an example, Eph. 6:1–3.

Q. 101. What is the preface to the Ten Commandments?

A. The preface to the Ten Commandments is contained in these words, *I am the LORD thy God, which have brought thee out of the land of Egypt, out of the house of bondage.*[1] Wherein God manifesteth his sovereignty, as being JEHOVAH, the eternal, immutable, and almighty God;[2] having his being in and of himself,[3] and giving being to all his words[4] and works:[5] and that he is a God in covenant, as with Israel of old, so with all his people;[6] who, as he brought them out of their bondage in Egypt, so he delivereth us from our spiritual thraldom;[7] and that therefore we are bound to take him for our God alone, and to keep all his commandments.[8]

Q. 102. What is the sum of the four commandments which contain our duty to God?

A. The sum of the four commandments containing our duty to God is, to love the Lord our God with all our heart, and with all our soul, and with all our strength, and with all our mind.[1]

Q. 103. Which is the first commandment?

A. The first commandment is, *Thou shalt have no other gods before me.*[1]

Q. 104. What are the duties required in the first commandment?

A. The duties required in the first commandment are, the knowing and acknowledging of God to be the only true God, and our God;[1] and to worship

Q. 101
1 Ex. 20:2. (Cf. Deut. 5:6.)
2 Isa. 44:6.
3 Ex. 3:14.
4 Ex. 6:3.
5 Acts 17:24, 28.
6 Gen. 17:7; Rom. 3:29.
7 Luke 1:74–75; Gal. 5:1.
8 1 Peter 1:15–19; Lev. 18:30; Lev. 19:37.
Q. 102
1 Luke 10:27; Matt. 22:37–40.
Q. 103
1 Ex. 20:3. (Cf. Deut. 5:7.)
Q. 104
1 1 Chron. 28:9; Deut. 26:7; Isa. 43:10. (See Jer. 14:22.)

and glorify him accordingly,[2] by thinking,[3] meditating,[4] remembering,[5] highly esteeming,[6] honoring,[7] adoring,[8] choosing,[9] loving,[10] desiring,[11] fearing of him;[12] believing him;[13] trusting,[14] hoping,[15] delighting,[16] rejoicing in him;[17] being zealous for him;[18] calling upon him, giving all praise and thanks,[19] and yielding all obedience and submission to him with the whole man;[20] being careful in all things to please him,[21] and sorrowful when in anything he is offended;[22] and walking humbly with him.[23]

Q. 105. What are the sins forbidden in the first commandment?

A. The sins forbidden in the first commandment are, atheism, in denying or not having a God;[1] idolatry, in having or worshiping more gods than one, or any with or instead of the true God;[2] the not having and avouching him for God, and our God;[3] the omission or neglect of anything due to him, required

2 Ps. 95:6–7; Matt. 4:10; Ps. 29:2.
3 Mal. 3:16.
4 Ps. 63:6.
5 Eccl. 12:1.
6 Ps. 71:19.
7 Mal. 1:6.
8 Isa. 45:23. (See Ps. 96.)
9 Josh. 24:15, 22.
10 Deut. 6:5.
11 Ps. 73:25.
12 Isa. 8:13.
13 Ex. 14:31.
14 Isa. 26:4.
15 Ps. 130:7.
16 Ps. 37:4.
17 Ps. 32:11.
18 Rom. 12:11. (See Num. 25:11.)
19 Phil. 4:6.
20 Jer. 7:23; James 4:7.
21 1 John 3:22.
22 Ps. 119:136; Jer. 31:18.
23 Mic. 6:8.
Q. 105
1 Ps. 14:1; Eph. 2:12.
2 Jer. 2:27–28; 1 Thess. 1:9.
3 Ps. 81:10–11. (See Rom. 1:21.)

in this commandment;[4] ignorance,[5] forgetfulness,[6] misapprehensions,[7] false opinions,[8] unworthy and wicked thoughts of him;[9] bold and curious searching into his secrets;[10] all profaneness,[11] hatred of God;[12] self-love,[13] self-seeking,[14] and all other inordinate and immoderate setting of our mind, will, or affections upon other things, and taking them off from him in whole or in part;[15] vain credulity,[16] unbelief,[17] heresy,[18] misbelief,[19] distrust,[20] despair,[21] incorrigibleness,[22] and insensibleness under judgments,[23] hardness of heart,[24] pride,[25] presumption,[26] carnal security,[27] tempting of God;[28] using unlawful means,[29] and trusting in lawful means;[30] carnal delights and joys;[31] corrupt, blind, and indiscreet zeal;[32] lukewarmness,[33] and deadness in the things of God;[34] estranging ourselves, and apostatizing from God;[35] praying, or giving any

4   Isa. 43:22–24.
5   Jer. 4:22; Hos. 4:1, 6.
6   Jer. 2:32.
7   Acts 17:23, 29.
8   Isa. 40:18.
9   Ps. 50:21.
10 Deut. 29:29.
11 Titus 1:16; Heb. 12:16.
12 Rom. 1:30.
13 2 Tim. 3:2.
14 Phil. 2:21.
15 1 John 2:15–16; Col. 3:2, 5. (See 1 Sam. 2:29.)
16 1 John 4:1.
17 Heb. 3:12.
18 Gal. 5:20; Titus 3:10.
19 Acts 26:9.
20 Ps. 78:22.
21 Gen. 4:13.
22 Jer. 5:3.
23 Isa. 42:25.
24 Rom. 2:5.
25 Jer. 13:15.
26 Ps. 19:13.
27 Zeph. 1:12.
28 Matt. 4:7.
29 Rom. 3:8.
30 Jer. 17:5.
31 2 Tim. 3:4.
32 Gal. 4:17; Rom. 10:2. (See John 16:2; Luke 9:54–55.)
33 Rev. 3:16.
34 Rev. 3:1.
35 Ezek. 14:5; Isa. 1:4–5.

religious worship, to saints, angels, or any other creatures;[36] all compacts and consulting with the devil,[37] and hearkening to his suggestions;[38] making men the lords of our faith and conscience;[39] slighting and despising God and his commands;[40] resisting and grieving of his Spirit,[41] discontent and impatience at his dispensations, charging him foolishly for the evils he inflicts on us;[42] and ascribing the praise of any good we either are, have, or can do, to fortune,[43] idols,[44] ourselves,[45] or any other creature.[46]

Q. 106. What are we specially taught by these words *before me* in the first commandment?

A. These words *before me* or *before my face*, in the first commandment, teach us, that God, who seeth all things, taketh special notice of, and is much displeased with, the sin of having any other God: that so it may be an argument to dissuade from it, and to aggravate it as a most impudent provocation:[1] as also to persuade us to do as in his sight, whatever we do in his service.[2]

Q. 107. Which is the second commandment?

A. The second commandment is, *Thou shalt not make unto thee any graven image, or any likeness of any thing that is in heaven above, or that is in the earth beneath, or that is in the water under the earth: thou shalt not bow down thyself to them, nor serve them: for I the LORD thy God am a jealous God, visiting the iniquity of the fathers upon the children unto the third and fourth generation of them that hate me; and shewing mercy unto thousands of them that love me, and keep my commandments.*[1]

36 Hos. 4:12; Acts 10:25–26; Rev. 19:10; Matt. 4:10; Col. 2:18; Rom. 1:25.
37 Lev. 20:6. (See 1 Sam. 28:7, 11; 1 Chron. 10:13–14.)
38 Acts 5:3.
39 2 Cor. 1:24. (See Matt. 23:9.)
40 Deut. 32:15; Prov. 13:13. (See 2 Sam. 12:9.)
41 Acts 7:51; Eph. 4:30.
42 Job 1:22; Ps. 73:2–3 (see vv. 13–15, 22).
43 1 Sam. 6:7–9; Luke 12:19.
44 Dan. 5:23.
45 Deut. 8:17. (See Dan. 4:30.)
46 Hab. 1:16.
Q. 106
1 Ps. 44:20–21. (See Deut. 30:17–18; Ezek. 8:5–6, 12.)
2 1 Chron. 28:9.
Q. 107
1 Ex. 20:4–6. (Cf. Deut. 5:8–10.)

Q. 108. What are the duties required in the second commandment?

A. The duties required in the second commandment are, the receiving, observing, and keeping pure and entire, all such religious worship and ordinances as God hath instituted in his Word;[1] particularly prayer and thanksgiving in the name of Christ;[2] the reading, preaching, and hearing of the Word;[3] the administration and receiving of the sacraments;[4] church government and discipline;[5] the ministry and maintenance thereof;[6] religious fasting;[7] swearing by the name of God,[8] and vowing unto him:[9] as also the disapproving, detesting, opposing all false worship;[10] and, according to each one's place and calling, removing it, and all monuments of idolatry.[11]

Q. 109. What are the sins forbidden in the second commandment?

A. The sins forbidden in the second commandment are, all devising,[1] counseling,[2] commanding,[3] using,[4] and anywise approving, any religious worship not instituted by God himself;[5] the making any representation of God, of all or of any of the three persons, either inwardly in our mind, or outwardly in any kind of image or likeness of any creature whatsoever;[6] all worshiping of it,[7] or God in it or by it;[8] the making of any representation of feigned deities,[9] and all worship

Q. 108
1   Deut. 12:32; Deut. 32:46–47; Matt. 28:20; 1 Tim. 6:13–14. (See Acts 2:42.)
2   Phil. 4:6; Eph. 5:20.
3   Deut. 17:18–19; Acts 15:21; 2 Tim. 4:2; James 1:21–22; Acts 10:33.
4   Matt. 28:19. (See 1 Cor. 11:23–30.)
5   Matt. 18:15–17; Matt. 16:19; 1 Cor. 12:28. (See 1 Cor. 5.)
6   Eph. 4:11–12; 1 Tim. 5:17–18. (See 1 Cor. 9:7–15.)
7   Joel 2:12–13; 1 Cor. 7:5.
8   Deut. 6:13.
9   Ps. 76:11; Isa. 19:21. (See Ps. 116:14, 18.)
10 Acts 17:16–17; Ps. 16:4.
11 Deut. 7:5; Isa. 30:22.
Q. 109
1   Num. 15:39.
2   Deut. 13:6–8.
3   Hos. 5:11; Mic. 6:16.
4   1 Kings 11:33; 1 Kings 12:33.
5   Deut. 12:30–32; Lev. 10:1–2; Jer. 19:5.
6   Deut. 4:15–16 (see vv. 17–19); Acts 17:29; Rom. 1:21–23, 25.
7   Gal. 4:8. (See Dan. 3:18.)
8   Ex. 32:5.
9   Ex. 32:8.

of them, or service belonging to them;[10] all superstitious devices,[11] corrupting the worship of God,[12] adding to it, or taking from it,[13] whether invented and taken up of ourselves,[14] or received by tradition from others,[15] though under the title of antiquity,[16] custom,[17] devotion,[18] good intent, or any other pretense whatsoever;[19] simony;[20] sacrilege;[21] all neglect,[22] contempt,[23] hindering,[24] and opposing the worship and ordinances which God hath appointed.[25]

Q. 110. What are the reasons annexed to the second commandment, the more to enforce it?

A. The reasons annexed to the second commandment, the more to enforce it, contained in these words, *For I the* LORD *thy God am a jealous God, visiting the iniquity of the fathers upon the children unto the third and fourth generation of them that hate me; and shewing mercy unto thousands of them that love me, and keep my commandments;*[1] are, besides God's sovereignty over us, and propriety in us,[2] his fervent zeal for his own worship,[3] and his revengeful indignation against all false worship, as being a spiritual whoredom;[4] accounting the breakers of this commandment such as hate him, and threatening to punish them unto divers generations;[5] and esteeming the observers of it such as love him and keep his commandments, and promising mercy to them unto many generations.[6]

10 1 Kings 18:26, 28. (See Isa. 65:11.)
11 Acts 17:22; Col. 2:21–23.
12 Mal. 1:7–8, 14.
13 Deut. 4:2.
14 Ps. 106:39.
15 Matt. 15:9.
16 1 Peter 1:18.
17 Jer. 44:17.
18 Isa. 65:3–5; Gal. 1:13–14.
19 1 Sam. 13:11–12; 1 Sam. 15:21.
21 Rom. 2:22; Mal. 3:8.
22 Ex. 4:24–26.
23 Matt. 22:5; Mal. 1:7, 13.
24 Matt. 23:13.
25 Acts 13:44–45. (See 1 Thess. 2:15–16.)
Q. 110
1 Ex. 20:5–6.
2 Ps. 45:11; Rev. 15:3–4. (See Ps. 95:2–3, 6–7; Ex. 19:5; Isa. 54:5.)
3 Ex. 34:13–14.
4 1 Cor. 10:20–22; Ezek. 16:26–27. (See Jer. 7:18–20; Deut. 32:16–20.)
5 Hos. 2:2–4.
6 Deut. 5:29.

Q. 111. Which is the third commandment?

A. The third commandment is, *Thou shalt not take the name of the* LORD *thy God in vain; for the Lord will not hold him guiltless that taketh his name in vain.*[1]

Q. 112. What is required in the third commandment?

A. The third commandment requires, that the name of God, his titles, attributes,[1] ordinances,[2] the Word,[3] sacraments,[4] prayer,[5] oaths,[6] vows,[7] lots,[8] his works,[9] and whatsoever else there is whereby he makes himself known, be holily and reverently used in thought,[10] meditation,[11] word,[12] and writing;[13] by an holy profession,[14] and answerable conversation,[15] to the glory of God,[16] and the good of ourselves,[17] and others.[18]

Q. 113. What are the sins forbidden in the third commandment?

A. The sins forbidden in the third commandment are, the not using of God's name as is required;[1] and the abuse of it in an ignorant,[2] vain,[3] irreverent,

---

Q. 111
1 Ex. 20:7. (Cf. Deut. 5:11.)
Q. 112
1 Matt. 6:9; Deut. 28:58; Ps. 68:4. (See Ps. 29:2; 1 Chron. 29:10–13; Rev. 15:3–4.)
2 Eccl. 5:1; Luke 1:6. (See Mal. 1:11, 14.)
3 Ps. 138:2.
4 1 Cor. 11:24–25, 28–29.
5 1 Tim. 2:8.
6 Jer. 4:2.
7 Eccl. 5:2, 4–6.
8 Acts 1:24, 26.
9 Job 36:24.
10 Mal. 3:16.
11 Ps. 8:1, 3–4.
12 Ps. 105:2, 5. (See Col. 3:17.)
13 Ps. 102:18.
14 1 Peter 3:15; Mic. 4:5.
15 Phil. 1:27.
16 1 Cor. 10:31.
17 Jer. 32:39.
18 1 Peter 2:12.
Q. 113
1 Mal. 2:2.
2 Acts 17:23.
3 Prov. 30:9.

profane,[4] superstitious,[5] or wicked mentioning or otherwise using his titles, attributes,[6] ordinances,[7] or works,[8] by blasphemy,[9] perjury;[10] all sinful cursings,[11] oaths,[12] vows,[13] and lots;[14] violating of our oaths and vows, if lawful,[15] and fulfilling them, if of things unlawful;[16] murmuring and quarreling at,[17] curious prying into,[18] and misapplying of God's decrees[19] and providences;[20] misinterpreting,[21] misapplying,[22] or anyway perverting the Word, or any part of it,[23] to profane jests,[24] curious or unprofitable questions, vain janglings, or the maintaining of false doctrines;[25] abusing it, the creatures, or anything contained under the name of God, to charms,[26] or sinful lusts and practices;[27] the maligning,[28] scorning,[29] reviling,[30] or anywise opposing of God's truth, grace, and ways;[31] making profession of religion in hypocrisy, or for sinister ends;[32]

4   Mal. 1:6–7, 12; Mal. 3:14.
5   1 Sam. 4:3–5; Jer. 7:4, 9–10, 14, 31; Col. 2:20–22.
6   2 Kings 18:30, 35; Ex. 5:2; Ps. 139:20.
7   Ps. 50:16–17.
8   Isa. 5:12.
9   2 Kings 19:22; Lev. 24:11.
10 Zech. 5:4; Zech. 8:17.
11 1 Sam. 17:43; 2 Sam. 16:5.
12 Jer. 5:7; Jer. 23:10.
13 Deut. 23:18; Acts 23:12, 14.
14 Est. 3:7; Est. 9:24; Ps. 22:18.
15 Ps. 24:4; Ezek. 17:16, 18–19.
16 Mark 6:26; 1 Sam. 25:22, 32–34.
17 Rom. 9:14, 19–20.
18 Deut. 29:29.
19 Rom. 3:5, 7; Rom. 6:1–2.
20 Eccl. 8:11; Eccl. 9:3. (See Ps. 39.)
21 Matt. 5:21–22, 27–28, 31–35, 38–39, 43–44.
22 Ezek. 13:22.
23 2 Peter 3:16. (See Matt. 22:24–31.)
24 Isa. 22:13; Jer. 23:34, 36, 38.
25 1 Tim. 1:4, 6–7; 1 Tim. 6:4–5, 20; 2 Tim. 2:14; Titus 3:9.
26 Deut. 18:10–14; Acts 19:13.
27 2 Tim. 4:3–4; 1 Kings 21:9–10; Jude 4. (See Rom. 13:13–14.)
28 Acts 13:45; 1 John 3:12.
29 Ps. 1:1; 2 Peter 3:3.
30 1 Peter 4:4.
31 Acts 13:45–46, 50; Acts 4:18; 1 Thess. 2:16; Heb. 10:29. (See Acts 19:9.)
32 2 Tim. 3:5; Matt. 23:14. (See Matt. 6:1–2, 5, 16.)

being ashamed of it,[33] or a shame to it, by unconformable,[34] unwise,[35] unfruitful,[36] and offensive walking,[37] or backsliding from it.[38]

Q. 114. What reasons are annexed to the third commandment?

A. The reasons annexed to the third commandment, in these words, *The* LORD *thy God,* and, *For the* LORD *will not hold him guiltless that taketh his name in vain,*[1] are, because he is the Lord and our God, therefore his name is not to be profaned, or anyway abused by us;[2] especially because he will be so far from acquitting and sparing the transgressors of this commandment, as that he will not suffer them to escape his righteous judgment,[3] albeit many such escape the censures and punishments of men.[4]

Q. 115. Which is the fourth commandment?

A. The fourth commandment is, *Remember the sabbath day, to keep it holy. Six days shalt thou labour, and do all thy work: but the seventh day is the sabbath of the* LORD *thy God: in it thou shalt not do any work, thou, nor thy son, nor thy daughter, thy manservant, nor thy maidservant, nor thy cattle, nor thy stranger that is within thy gates: for in six days the* LORD *made heaven and earth, the sea, and all that in them is, and rested the seventh day: wherefore the* LORD *blessed the sabbath day and hallowed it.*[1]

Q. 116. What is required in the fourth commandment?

A. The fourth commandment requireth of all men the sanctifying or keeping holy to God such set times as he hath appointed in his Word, expressly one whole day in seven; which was the seventh from the beginning of the world to

33 Mark 8:38.
34 Ps. 73:14–15.
35 Eph. 5:15–17. (See 1 Cor. 6:5–6.)
36 Isa. 5:4. (See 2 Peter 1:8–9.)
37 Rom. 2:23–24.
38 Gal. 3:1, 3. (See Heb. 6:6.)
Q. 114
1 Ex. 20:7.
2 Lev. 19:12.
3 Deut. 28:58–59. (See Ezek. 36:21–23.)
4 1 Sam. 2:29; 1 Sam. 3:13. (See 1 Sam. 2:12–17, 22–25.)
Q. 115
1 Ex. 20:8–11. (Cf. Deut. 5:12–15.)

the resurrection of Christ, and the first day of the week ever since, and so to continue to the end of the world; which is the Christian sabbath,[1] and in the New Testament called the Lord's Day.[2]

Q. 117. How is the Sabbath or the Lord's Day to be sanctified?

A. The Sabbath or Lord's Day is to be sanctified by an holy resting all the day,[1] not only from such works as are at all times sinful, but even from such worldly employments and recreations as are on other days lawful;[2] and making it our delight to spend the whole time (except so much of it as is to be taken up in works of necessity and mercy[3]) in the public and private exercises of God's worship:[4] and, to that end, we are to prepare our hearts, and with such foresight, diligence, and moderation, to dispose and seasonably dispatch our worldly business, that we may be the more free and fit for the duties of that day.[5]

Q. 118. Why is the charge of keeping the Sabbath more specially directed to governors of families, and other superiors?

A. The charge of keeping the Sabbath is more specially directed to governors of families, and other superiors, because they are bound not only to keep it themselves, but to see that it be observed by all those that are under their charge; and because they are prone ofttimes to hinder them by employments of their own.[1]

Q. 119. What are the sins forbidden in the fourth commandment?

A. The sins forbidden in the fourth commandment are, all omissions of the duties required,[1] all careless, negligent, and unprofitable performing of them,

---

Q. 116
1 Deut. 5:12–14; Gen. 2:2–3; 1 Cor. 16:1–2; Acts 20:7; John 20:19, 26. (See Matt. 5:17–18; Isa. 56:2, 4, 6–7.)
2 Rev. 1:10.
Q. 117
1 Ex. 20:8, 10.
2 Ex. 16:25–28; Jer. 17:21–22. (See Neh. 13:15–22.)
3 Matt. 12:1–5 (see vv. 6–13).
4 Isa. 58:13–14; Luke 4:16; Acts 20:7; 1 Cor. 16:1–2; Lev. 23:3. (See Ps. 92 title; Isa. 66:23.)
5 Ex. 20:8; Luke 23:54, 56; Ex. 16:22, 25–26, 29; Neh. 13:19.
Q. 118
1 Ex. 20:10; Ex. 23:12. (See Josh. 24:15; Neh. 13:15–17; Jer. 17:20–22.)
Q. 119
1 Ezek. 22:26.

and being weary of them;[2] all profaning the day by idleness, and doing that which is in itself sinful;[3] and by all needless works, words, and thoughts, about our worldly employments and recreations.[4]

Q. 120. What are the reasons annexed to the fourth commandment, the more to enforce it?

A. The reasons annexed to the fourth commandment, the more to enforce it, are taken from the equity of it, God allowing us six days of seven for our own affairs, and reserving but one for himself, in these words, *Six days shalt thou labour, and do all thy work:*[1] from God's challenging a special propriety in that day, *The seventh day is the sabbath of the LORD thy God:*[2] from the example of God, who *in six days . . . made heaven and earth, the sea, and all that in them is, and rested the seventh day:* and from that blessing which God put upon that day, not only in sanctifying it to be a day for his service, but in ordaining it to be a means of blessing to us in our sanctifying it; *Wherefore the LORD blessed the sabbath day, and hallowed it.*[3]

Q. 121. Why is the word *Remember* set in the beginning of the fourth commandment?

A. The word *Remember* is set in the beginning of the fourth commandment,[1] partly, because of the great benefit of remembering it, we being thereby helped in our preparation to keep it,[2] and, in keeping it, better to keep all the rest of the commandments,[3] and to continue a thankful remembrance of the two great benefits of creation and redemption, which contain a short abridgment of religion;[4] and partly, because we are very ready to forget it,[5] for that there is

2 Amos 8:5. (See Acts 20:7, 9; Ezek. 33:30–32; Mal. 1:13.)
3 Ezek. 23:38.
4 Jer. 17:24, 27. (See Isa. 58:13–14.)
Q. 120
1 Ex. 20:9.
2 Ex. 20:10.
3 Ex. 20:11.
Q. 121
1 Ex. 20:8.
2 Ex. 16:23; Luke 23:54, 56. (See Mark 15:42; Neh. 13:19.)
3 Ezek. 20:12, 19–20; Ps. 92:13–14. (See Ps. 92 title.)
4 Gen. 2:2–3; Ps. 118:22, 24; Rev. 1:10.
5 Ezek. 22:26.

less light of nature for it,[6] and yet it restraineth our natural liberty in things at other times lawful;[7] that it cometh but once in seven days, and many worldly businesses come between, and too often take off our minds from thinking of it, either to prepare for it, or to sanctify it;[8] and that Satan with his instruments much labor to blot out the glory, and even the memory of it, to bring in all irreligion and impiety.[9]

Q. 122. What is the sum of the six commandments which contain our duty to man?

A. The sum of the six commandments which contain our duty to man is, to love our neighbor as ourselves,[1] and to do to others what we would have them to do to us.[2]

Q. 123. Which is the fifth commandment?

A. The fifth commandment is, *Honour thy father and thy mother: that thy days may be long upon the land which the LORD thy God giveth thee.*[1]

Q. 124. Who are meant by *father* and *mother* in the fifth commandment?

A. By *father* and *mother,* in the fifth commandment, are meant, not only natural parents,[1] but all superiors in age[2] and gifts;[3] and especially such as, by God's ordinance, are over us in place of authority, whether in family,[4] church,[5] or commonwealth.[6]

---

6 Neh. 9:14.
7 Ex. 34:21.
8 Deut. 5:14–15; Amos 8:5.
9 Lam. 1:7; Jer. 17:21–23. (See Neh. 13:15–22.)
Q. 122
1 Matt. 22:39.
2 Matt. 7:12.
Q. 123
1 Ex. 20:12. (Cf. Deut. 5:16.)
Q. 124
1 Prov. 23:22, 25. (See Eph. 6:1–2.)
2 1 Tim. 5:1–2.
3 Gen. 4:20–21; Gen. 45:8.
4 2 Kings 5:13.
5 2 Kings 2:12; Gal. 4:19. (See 2 Kings 13:14.)
6 Isa. 49:23.

Q. 125. Why are superiors styled *father* and *mother*?

A. Superiors are styled *father* and *mother*, both to teach them in all duties toward their inferiors, like natural parents, to express love and tenderness to them, according to their several relations;[1] and to work inferiors to a greater willingness and cheerfulness in performing their duties to their superiors, as to their parents.[2]

Q. 126. What is the general scope of the fifth commandment?

A. The general scope of the fifth commandment is, the performance of those duties which we mutually owe in our several relations, as inferiors, superiors, or equals.[1]

Q. 127. What is the honor that inferiors owe to their superiors?

A. The honor which inferiors owe to their superiors is, all due reverence in heart,[1] word,[2] and behavior;[3] prayer and thanksgiving for them;[4] imitation of their virtues and graces;[5] willing obedience to their lawful commands and counsels;[6] due submission to their corrections;[7] fidelity to,[8] defense,[9] and maintenance of their persons and authority, according to their several ranks, and the nature of their places;[10] bearing with their infirmities, and covering them in love,[11] that so they may be an honor to them and to their government.[12]

Q. 125
1 Eph. 6:4; 2 Cor. 12:14; 1 Thess. 2:7–8, 11. (See Num. 11:11–12.)
2 1 Cor. 4:14–16. (See 2 Kings 5:13.)
Q. 126
1 Eph. 5:21; 1 Peter 2:17; Rom. 12:10. (See Rom. 13:1, 7; Eph. 5:22, 24; 6:1, 4–5, 9.)
Q. 127
1 Mal. 1:6; Lev. 19:3.
2 Prov. 31:28; 1 Peter 3:6.
3 Lev. 19:32; 1 Kings 2:19.
4 1 Tim. 2:1–2.
5 Heb. 13:7; Phil. 3:17.
6 Eph. 6:1–2, 5–7; 1 Peter 2:13–14; Heb. 13:17. (See Rom. 13:1–5; Prov. 4:3–4; 23:22; Ex. 18:19, 24.)
7 Heb. 12:9; 1 Peter 2:18–20.
8 Titus 2:9–10.
9 1 Sam. 26:15–16. (See 2 Sam. 18:3; Est. 6:2.)
10 Matt. 22:21; Rom. 13:6–7; 1 Tim. 5:17–18. (See Gal. 6:6; Gen. 45:11; 47:12.)
11 Gen. 9:23. (See 1 Peter 2:18; Prov. 23:22.)
12 Ps. 127:3–5; Prov. 31:23.

Q. 128. What are the sins of inferiors against their superiors?

A. The sins of inferiors against their superiors are, all neglect of the duties required toward them;[1] envying at,[2] contempt of,[3] and rebellion[4] against, their persons[5] and places,[6] in their lawful counsels,[7] commands, and corrections;[8] cursing, mocking,[9] and all such refractory and scandalous carriage, as proves a shame and dishonor to them and their government.[10]

Q. 129. What is required of superiors towards their inferiors?

A. It is required of superiors, according to that power they receive from God, and that relation wherein they stand, to love,[1] pray for,[2] and bless their inferiors;[3] to instruct,[4] counsel, and admonish them;[5] countenancing,[6] commending,[7] and rewarding such as do well;[8] and discountenancing,[9] reproving, and chastising such as do ill;[10] protecting,[11] and providing for them all things necessary for soul[12] and body:[13] and by grave, wise, holy, and exemplary

Q. 128
1 Matt. 15:4–6; Rom. 13:8.
2 Num. 11:28–29.
3 1 Sam. 8:7; Isa. 3:5.
4 2 Sam. 15:10 (see vv. 1–12).
5 Ex. 21:15.
6 1 Sam. 10:27.
7 1 Sam. 2:25.
8 Deut. 21:18–21.
9 Prov. 30:11, 17.
10 Prov. 19:26.
Q. 129
1 Col. 3:19; Titus 2:4.
2 1 Sam. 12:23; Job 1:5.
3 1 Kings 8:55–56; Heb. 7:7. (See Gen. 49:28.)
4 Deut. 6:6–7.
5 Eph. 6:4.
6 1 Peter 3:7.
7 1 Peter 2:14; Rom. 13:3.
8 Est. 6:3.
9 Rom. 13:3–4.
10 Prov. 29:15; 1 Peter 2:14.
11 Isa. 1:10, 17. (See Job 29:12–17.)
12 Eph. 6:4.
13 1 Tim. 5:8.

carriage, to procure glory to God,[14] honor to themselves,[15] and so to preserve that authority which God hath put upon them.[16]

Q. 130. What are the sins of superiors?

A. The sins of superiors are, besides the neglect of the duties required of them,[1] an inordinate seeking of themselves,[2] their own glory,[3] ease, profit, or pleasure;[4] commanding things unlawful,[5] or not in the power of inferiors to perform;[6] counseling,[7] encouraging,[8] or favoring them in that which is evil;[9] dissuading, discouraging, or discountenancing them in that which is good;[10] correcting them unduly;[11] careless exposing, or leaving them to wrong, temptation, and danger;[12] provoking them to wrath;[13] or anyway dishonoring themselves, or lessening their authority, by an unjust, indiscreet, rigorous, or remiss behavior.[14]

Q. 131. What are the duties of equals?

A. The duties of equals are, to regard the dignity and worth of each other,[1] in giving honor to go one before another;[2] and to rejoice in each other's gifts and advancement, as their own.[3]

14 1 Tim. 4:12. (See Titus 2:3–5.)
15 1 Kings 3:28.
16 Titus 2:15.
Q. 130
1 Ezek. 34:2–4.
2 Phil. 2:21.
3 John 5:44. (See John 7:18.)
4 Isa. 56:10–11. (See Deut. 17:17.)
5 Acts 4:17–18. (See Dan. 3:4–6.)
6 Ex. 5:18 (see vv. 10–19); Matt. 23:2, 4.
7 Matt. 14:8. (See Mark 6:24.)
8 2 Sam. 13:28.
9 Jer. 6:13–14; Judg. 20:13–14 (see entire chapter).
10 John 7:46–49. (See Col. 3:21; Ex. 5:17; John 9:28.)
11 1 Peter 2:18–20; Deut. 25:3.
12 Gen. 38:11, 26; Acts 18:17. (See 1 Sam. 23:15–17; Lev. 19:29; Isa. 58:7.)
13 Eph. 6:4.
14 Gen. 9:21; 1 Kings 12:13–16; 1 Kings 1:6. (See 1 Sam. 2:29–31; 3:13.)
Q. 131
1 1 Peter 2:17.
2 Rom. 12:10; Phil. 2:3.
3 Rom. 12:15–16; Phil. 2:3.

Q. 132. What are the sins of equals?

A. The sins of equals are, besides the neglect of the duties required,[1] the undervaluing of the worth,[2] envying the gifts,[3] grieving at the advancement of prosperity one of another;[4] and usurping preeminence one over another.[5]

Q. 133. What is the reason annexed to the fifth commandment, the more to enforce it?

A. The reason annexed to the fifth commandment, in these words, *That thy days may be long upon the land which the Lord thy God giveth thee,*[1] is an express promise of long life and prosperity, as far as it shall serve for God's glory and their own good, to all such as keep this commandment.[2]

Q. 134. Which is the sixth commandment?

A. The sixth commandment is, *Thou shalt not kill.*[1]

Q. 135. What are the duties required in the sixth commandment?

A. The duties required in the sixth commandment are, all careful studies, and lawful endeavors, to preserve the life of ourselves[1] and others[2] by resisting all thoughts and purposes,[3] subduing all passions,[4] and avoiding all occasions,[5] temptations,[6] and practices, which tend to the unjust taking away the life of any;[7]

Q. 132
1   Rom. 13:8.
2   2 Tim. 3:3. (See Prov. 14:21; Isa. 65:5.)
3   Acts 7:9; Gal. 5:26.
4   Num. 12:2.
5   3 John 9; Luke 22:24.
Q. 133
1   Ex. 20:12.
2   Eph. 6:2–3. (See Deut. 5:16; 1 Kings 8:25.)
Q. 134
1   Ex. 20:13. (Cf. Deut. 5:17.)
Q. 135
1   Eph. 5:28–29.
2   1 Kings 18:4.
3   Jer. 26:15–16. (See Acts 23:12, 16–17, 21, 27.)
4   Eph. 4:26–27.
5   2 Sam. 2:22–23; Deut. 22:8.
6   Matt. 4:6–7; Prov. 1:10–11, 15–16.
7   Gen. 37:21–22. (See 1 Sam. 24:12; 26:9–11.)

by just defense thereof against violence,[8] patient bearing of the hand of God,[9] quietness of mind,[10] cheerfulness of spirit;[11] a sober use of meat,[12] drink,[13] physic,[14] sleep,[15] labor,[16] and recreations;[17] by charitable thoughts,[18] love,[19] compassion,[20] meekness, gentleness, kindness;[21] peaceable,[22] mild, and courteous speeches and behavior;[23] forbearance, readiness to be reconciled, patient bearing and forgiving of injuries, and requiting good for evil;[24] comforting and succoring the distressed, and protecting and defending the innocent.[25]

Q. 136. What are the sins forbidden in the sixth commandment?

A. The sins forbidden in the sixth commandment are, all taking away the life of ourselves,[1] or of others,[2] except in case of public justice,[3] lawful war,[4] or necessary defense;[5] the neglecting or withdrawing the lawful and necessary means of preservation of life;[6] sinful anger,[7] hatred,[8] envy,[9] desire of revenge;[10] all excessive

8   Ps. 82:4; Prov. 24:11–12. (See 1 Sam. 14:45; Jer. 38:7–13.)
9   James 5:10–11; Heb. 12:9. (See 2 Sam. 16:10–12.)
10 1 Thess. 4:11; 1 Peter 3:3–4; Ps. 37:8, 11.
11 Prov. 17:22.
12 Prov. 23:20; Prov. 25:16, 27.
13 1 Tim. 5:23.
14 Isa. 38:21.
15 Ps. 127:2.
16 2 Thess. 3:12. (See Eccl. 5:12.)
17 Eccl. 3:4, 11; Mark 6:31.
18 1 Sam. 19:4–5. (See 1 Sam. 22:13–14.)
19 Rom. 13:10.
20 Luke 10:33–34.
21 Col. 3:12–13.
22 James 3:17.
23 1 Peter 3:8–11; 1 Cor. 4:12–13. (See Prov. 15:1; Judg. 8:1–3.)
24 Matt. 5:24; Eph. 4:2, 32; Rom. 12:17, 20–21.
25 1 Thess. 5:14; Matt. 25:35–36; Prov. 31:8–9. (See Job 31:19–20; Isa. 58:7.)
Q. 136
1   Acts 16:28.
2   Gen. 9:6.
3   Num. 35:31, 33; Rom. 13:4.
4   See Deut. 20 compared with Heb. 11:32–34.
5   Ex. 22:2.
6   Matt. 25:42–43; James 2:15–16.
7   Matt. 5:22.
8   1 John 3:15; Lev. 19:17.
9   Prov. 14:30.
10 Rom. 12:19.

passions,[11] distracting cares;[12] immoderate use of meat, drink,[13] labor,[14] and recreations;[15] provoking words,[16] oppression,[17] quarreling,[18] striking, wounding,[19] and whatsoever else tends to the destruction of the life of any.[20]

Q. 137. Which is the seventh commandment?

A. The seventh commandment is, *Thou shalt not commit adultery.*[1]

Q. 138. What are the duties required in the seventh commandment?

A. The duties required in the seventh commandment are, chastity in body, mind, affections,[1] words,[2] and behavior;[3] and the preservation of it in ourselves and others;[4] watchfulness over the eyes and all the senses;[5] temperance,[6] keeping of chaste company,[7] modesty in apparel;[8] marriage by those that have not the gift of continency,[9] conjugal love,[10] and cohabitation;[11] diligent labor in our callings;[12] shunning all occasions of uncleanness, and resisting temptations thereunto.[13]

11 Eph. 4:31.
12 Matt. 6:31, 34.
13 Luke 21:34; Rom. 13:13.
14 Eccl. 12:12; Eccl. 2:22–23.
15 Isa. 5:12.
16 Prov. 15:1; Prov. 12:18.
17 Ex. 1:14. (See Isa. 3:15.)
18 Gal. 5:15; Prov. 23:29.
19 Num. 35:16–17 (see vv. 18–21).
20 Ex. 21:29 (see vv. 18–36).
Q. 137
1   Ex. 20:14. (Cf. Deut. 5:18.)
Q. 138
1   1 Thess. 4:4–5; Job 31:1; 1 Cor. 7:34.
2   Eph. 4:29; Col. 4:6.
3   1 Peter 3:2.
4   1 Cor. 7:2–5, 34–36.
5   Matt. 5:28; Job 31:1.
6   Acts 24:24–25.
7   Prov. 2:16–20.
8   1 Tim. 2:9.
9   1 Cor. 7:2, 9.
10 Prov. 5:19–20.
11 1 Peter 3:7; 1 Cor. 7:5.
12 Prov. 31:11, 27–28.
13 Prov. 5:8. (See Gen. 39:8–10.)

Q. 139. What are the sins forbidden in the seventh commandment?

A. The sins forbidden in the seventh commandment, besides the neglect of the duties required,[1] are, adultery, fornication,[2] rape, incest,[3] sodomy, and all unnatural lusts;[4] all unclean imaginations, thoughts, purposes, and affections;[5] all corrupt or filthy communications, or listening thereunto;[6] wanton looks,[7] impudent or light behavior, immodest apparel;[8] prohibiting of lawful,[9] and dispensing with unlawful marriages;[10] allowing, tolerating, keeping of stews, and resorting to them;[11] entangling vows of single life,[12] undue delay of marriage,[13] having more wives or husbands than one at the same time;[14] unjust divorce,[15] or desertion;[16] idleness, gluttony, drunkenness,[17] unchaste company;[18] lascivious songs, books, pictures, dancings, stage plays;[19] and all other provocations to, or acts of uncleanness, either in ourselves or others.[20]

Q. 140. Which is the eighth commandment?

A. The eighth commandment is, *Thou shalt not steal.*[1]

Q. 139

1   Prov. 5:7. (See Prov. 4:23, 27.)
2   Heb. 13:4; Eph. 5:5. (See Gal. 5:19.)
3   2 Sam. 13:14; 1 Cor. 5:1; Mark 6:18.
4   Rom. 1:24, 26–27; Lev. 20:15–16.
5   Matt. 5:28; Matt. 15:19; Col. 3:5.
6   Eph. 5:3–4. (See Prov. 7:5, 21–22.)
7   Isa. 3:16; 2 Peter 2:14.
8   Prov. 7:10, 13.
9   1 Tim. 4:3.
10 Mark 6:18; Mal. 2:11–12. (See Lev. 18:1–21.)
11 1 Kings 15:12; 2 Kings 23:7; Lev. 19:29; Jer. 5:7. (See Deut. 23:17–18; Prov. 7:24–27.)
12 Matt. 19:10–11.
13 1 Cor. 7:7–9; Gen. 38:26.
14 Mal. 2:14–15; Matt. 19:5.
15 Mal. 2:16; Matt. 5:32; Matt. 19:8–9.
16 1 Cor. 7:12–13.
17 Ezek. 16:49. (See Prov. 23:30–33.)
18 Gen. 39:19. (See Prov. 5:8.)
19 Eph. 5:4; Rom. 13:13; 1 Peter 4:3. (See Ezek. 23:14–16; Isa. 3:16; 23:15–17; Mark 6:22.)
20 2 Kings 9:30; Jer. 4:30; Ezek. 23:40.

Q. 140

1   Ex. 20:15. (Cf. Deut. 5:19.)

Q. 141. What are the duties required in the eighth commandment?

A. The duties required in the eighth commandment are, truth, faithfulness, and justice in contracts and commerce between man and man;[1] rendering to everyone his due;[2] restitution of goods unlawfully detained from the right owners thereof;[3] giving and lending freely, according to our abilities, and the necessities of others;[4] moderation of our judgments, wills, and affections concerning worldly goods;[5] a provident care and study to get,[6] keep, use, and dispose these things which are necessary and convenient for the sustentation of our nature, and suitable to our condition;[7] a lawful calling,[8] and diligence in it;[9] frugality;[10] avoiding unnecessary lawsuits,[11] and suretyship, or other like engagements;[12] and an endeavor, by all just and lawful means, to procure, preserve, and further the wealth and outward estate of others, as well as our own.[13]

Q. 142. What are the sins forbidden in the eighth commandment?

A. The sins forbidden in the eighth commandment, besides the neglect of the duties required,[1] are, theft,[2] robbery,[3] manstealing,[4] and receiving anything that is stolen;[5] fraudulent dealing,[6] false weights and measures,[7] removing

---

Q. 141

1 Ps. 15:2, 4; Mic. 6:8; Zech. 8:16–17. (See Zech. 7:4, 10.)
2 Rom. 13:7.
3 Lev. 6:2–5. (See Luke 19:8.)
4 Luke 6:30, 38; 1 John 3:17; Eph. 4:28; Gal. 6:10.
5 1 Tim. 6:6–9. (See Gal. 6:14.)
6 1 Tim. 5:8.
7 Prov. 27:23 (see vv. 24–27); Eccl. 2:24; Eccl. 3:12–13; 1 Tim. 6:17–18. (See Isa. 38:1; Matt. 11:8.)
8 1 Cor. 7:20. (See Gen. 2:15; 3:19.)
9 Eph. 4:28; Prov. 10:4; Rom. 12:11.
10 John 6:12; Prov. 21:20.
11 1 Cor. 6:1 (see vv. 2–9).
12 Prov. 11:15. (See Prov. 6:1–6.)
13 Lev. 25:35; Phil. 2:4. (See Deut. 22:1–4; Ex. 23:4–5; Gen. 47:14, 20; Matt. 22:39.)

Q. 142

1 James 2:15–16; 1 John 3:17.
2 Eph. 4:28.
3 Ps. 62:10.
4 1 Tim. 1:10.
5 Prov. 29:24; Ps. 50:18.
6 1 Thess. 4:6; Lev. 19:13.
7 Prov. 11:1; Prov. 20:10.

landmarks,[8] injustice and unfaithfulness in contracts between man and man,[9] or in matters of trust;[10] oppression,[11] extortion,[12] usury,[13] bribery,[14] vexatious lawsuits,[15] unjust enclosures and depredation;[16] engrossing commodities to enhance the price;[17] unlawful callings,[18] and all other unjust or sinful ways of taking or withholding from our neighbor what belongs to him, or of enriching ourselves;[19] covetousness;[20] inordinate prizing and affecting worldly goods;[21] distrustful and distracting cares and studies in getting, keeping, and using them;[22] envying at the prosperity of others;[23] as likewise idleness,[24] prodigality, wasteful gaming; and all other ways whereby we do unduly prejudice our own outward estate,[25] and defrauding ourselves of the due use and comfort of that estate which God hath given us.[26]

Q. 143. Which is the ninth commandment?

A. The ninth commandment is, *Thou shalt not bear false witness against thy neighbour.*[1]

---

8 Deut. 19:14. (See Prov. 23:10.)

9 Amos 8:5; Ps. 37:21.

10 Luke 16:10–12.

11 Ezek. 22:29; Lev. 25:17.

12 Matt. 23:25; Ezek. 22:12.

13 Ps. 15:5.

14 Job 15:34.

15 1 Cor. 6:6–8; Prov. 3:29–30.

16 Isa. 5:8; Mic. 2:2.

17 Prov. 11:26.

18 Acts 19:19 (see vv. 24–25).

19 James 5:4; Prov. 21:6. (See Job 20:19.)

20 Luke 12:15.

21 1 Tim. 6:5; Col. 3:2; 1 John 2:15–16. (See Prov. 23:5; Ps. 62:10.)

22 Matt. 6:25, 31, 34; Eccl. 5:12.

23 Ps. 73:3. (See Ps. 37:1, 7.)

24 2 Thess. 3:10–11. (See Prov. 18:9.)

25 Prov. 21:17; Prov. 23:20–21. (See Prov. 28:19.)

26 Eccl. 4:8; Eccl. 6:2; 1 Tim. 4:3–5; 1 Tim. 5:8.

Q. 143

1 Ex. 20:16. (Cf. Deut. 5:20.)

Q. 144. What are the duties required in the ninth commandment?

A. The duties required in the ninth commandment are, the preserving and promoting of truth between man and man,[1] and the good name of our neighbor, as well as our own;[2] appearing and standing for the truth;[3] and from the heart,[4] sincerely,[5] freely,[6] clearly,[7] and fully,[8] speaking the truth, and only the truth, in matters of judgment and justice,[9] and in all other things whatsoever;[10] a charitable esteem of our neighbors;[11] loving, desiring, and rejoicing in their good name;[12] sorrowing for,[13] and covering of their infirmities;[14] freely acknowledging of their gifts and graces,[15] defending their innocency;[16] a ready receiving of a good report,[17] and unwillingness to admit of an evil report,[18] concerning them; discouraging talebearers,[19] flatterers,[20] and slanderers;[21] love and care of our own good name, and defending it when need requireth;[22] keeping of lawful promises;[23] studying and practicing of whatsoever things are true, honest, lovely, and of good report.[24]

Q. 144

1 Zech. 8:16; Eph. 4:25.
2 3 John 12.
3 Prov. 31:8–9.
4 Ps. 15:2.
5 2 Chron. 19:9.
6 1 Sam. 19:4–5.
7 Josh. 7:19 (see vv. 15–20).
8 2 Sam. 14:18 (see vv. 19–20); Acts 20:27.
9 Lev. 19:15; Prov. 14:5, 25.
10 2 Cor. 1:17–18; Eph. 4:25. (See Col. 3:9.)
11 Heb. 6:9; 1 Cor. 13:7.
12 Rom. 1:8; 2 John 4; 3 John 3–4.
13 2 Cor. 2:4; 2 Cor. 12:21. (See Ps. 119:158.)
14 Prov. 17:9; 1 Peter 4:8.
15 1 Cor. 1:4–5, 7. (See 2 Tim. 1:4–5.)
16 1 Sam. 22:14.
17 1 Cor. 13:6–7.
18 Ps. 15:3.
19 Prov. 25:23.
20 Prov. 26:24–25.
21 Ps. 101:5.
22 Prov. 22:1; John 8:49. (See 2 Cor. 11:1–12:13.)
23 Ps. 15:4.
24 Phil. 4:8.

Q. 145. What are the sins forbidden in the ninth commandment?

A. The sins forbidden in the ninth commandment are, all prejudicing the truth, and the good name of our neighbors, as well as our own,[1] especially in public judicature;[2] giving false evidence,[3] suborning false witnesses,[4] wittingly appearing and pleading for an evil cause, outfacing and overbearing the truth;[5] passing unjust sentence,[6] calling evil good, and good evil; rewarding the wicked according to the work of the righteous, and the righteous according to the work of the wicked;[7] forgery,[8] concealing the truth, undue silence in a just cause,[9] and holding our peace when iniquity calleth for either a reproof from ourselves,[10] or complaint to others;[11] speaking the truth unseasonably,[12] or maliciously to a wrong end,[13] or perverting it to a wrong meaning,[14] or in doubtful and equivocal expressions, to the prejudice of truth or justice;[15] speaking untruth,[16] lying,[17] slandering,[18] backbiting,[19] detracting,[20] talebearing,[21] whispering,[22] scoffing,[23] reviling,[24] rash,[25] harsh,[26] and partial censuring;[27]

Q. 145

1 Luke 3:14. (See 1 Sam. 17:28; 2 Sam. 16:3; 1:9–10, 15–16.)
2 Lev. 19:15. (See Hab. 1:4.)
3 Prov. 19:5. (See Prov. 6:16, 19.)
4 Acts 6:13.
5 Jer. 9:3, 5; Ps. 12:3–4. (See Acts 24:2, 5; Ps. 52:1–4.)
6 Prov. 17:15. (See 1 Kings 21:9–14.)
7 Isa. 5:23.
8 1 Kings 21:8.
9 Lev. 5:1; Acts 5:3 (see vv. 8–9). (See also Deut. 13:8; 2 Tim. 4:16.)
10 1 Kings 1:6; Lev. 19:17.
11 Isa. 59:4.
12 Prov. 29:11.
13 1 Sam. 22:9–10; Ps. 52:1–5.
14 Ps. 56:5; Matt. 26:60–61. (See John 2:19.)
15 Gen. 3:5. (See Gen. 26:7, 9.)
16 Isa. 59:13.
17 Col. 3:9. (See Lev. 19:11.)
18 Ps. 50:20.
19 Ps. 15:3.
20 James 4:11. (See Jer. 38:4.)
21 Lev. 19:16.
22 Rom. 1:29–30.
23 Gen. 21:9; Gal. 4:29.
24 1 Cor. 6:10.
25 Matt. 7:1.
26 Acts 28:4. (See James 2:13.)
27 Gen. 38:24; Rom. 2:1.

misconstructing intentions, words, and actions;[28] flattering,[29] vainglorious boasting;[30] thinking or speaking too highly or too meanly of ourselves or others;[31] denying the gifts and graces of God;[32] aggravating smaller faults;[33] hiding, excusing, or extenuating of sins, when called to a free confession;[34] unnecessary discovering of infirmities;[35] raising false rumors,[36] receiving and countenancing evil reports,[37] and stopping our ears against just defense;[38] evil suspicion;[39] envying or grieving at the deserved credit of any,[40] endeavoring or desiring to impair it,[41] rejoicing in their disgrace and infamy;[42] scornful contempt,[43] fond admiration;[44] breach of lawful promises;[45] neglecting such things as are of good report,[46] and practicing, or not avoiding ourselves, or not hindering what we can in others, such things as procure an ill name.[47]

Q. 146. Which is the tenth commandment?

A. The tenth commandment is, *Thou shalt not covet thy neighbour's house, thou shall not covet thy neighbour's wife, nor his manservant, nor his maidservant, nor his ox, nor his ass, nor any thing that is thy neighbour's.*[1]

28 Rom. 3:8; Ps. 69:10. (See Neh. 6:6–8; 1 Sam. 1:13–15; 2 Sam. 10:3.)
29 Ps. 12:2–3.
30 2 Tim. 3:2.
31 Luke 18:9, 11; Acts 12:22; Ex. 4:10–14. (See Rom. 12:16; Gal. 5:26; 1 Cor. 4:6.)
32 Luke 9:49–50; 2 Cor. 10:10; Acts 2:13. (See Job 27:5–6; 4:6.)
33 Matt. 7:3–5.
34 Prov. 28:13; Gen. 3:12–13. (See Prov. 30:20; Jer. 2:35; 2 Kings 5:25; Gen. 4:9.)
35 Prov. 25:9–10. (See Gen. 9:22.)
36 Ex. 23:1.
37 Prov. 29:12. (See Ps. 41:7–8.)
38 Acts 7:56–57; Job 31:13–14.
39 1 Cor. 13:5. (See 1 Tim. 6:4.)
40 Matt. 21:15. (See Num. 11:29.)
41 Ezra 4:12–13. (See Dan. 6:3–4.)
42 Jer. 48:27.
43 Matt. 27:28–29. (See Ps. 35:15–16, 21.)
44 Jude 16; Acts 12:22.
45 Rom. 1:31; 2 Tim. 3:3.
46 1 Sam. 2:24.
47 2 Sam. 13:12–13; Prov. 5:8–9; Prov. 6:33.
Q. 146
1 Ex. 20:17. (Cf. Deut. 5:21.)

Q. 147. What are the duties required in the tenth commandment?

A. The duties required in the tenth commandment are, such a full content-ment with our own condition,[1] and such a charitable frame of the whole soul toward our neighbor, as that all our inward motions and affections touching him, tend unto, and further all that good which is his.[2]

Q. 148. What are the sins forbidden in the tenth commandment?

A. The sins forbidden in the tenth commandment are, discontentment with our own estate;[1] envying[2] and grieving at the good of our neighbor,[3] together with all inordinate motions and affections to anything that is his.[4]

Q. 149. Is any man able perfectly to keep the commandments of God?

A. No man is able, either of himself,[1] or by any grace received in this life, perfectly to keep the commandments of God;[2] but doth daily break them in thought,[3] word, and deed.[4]

Q. 150. Are all transgressions of the law of God equally heinous in themselves, and in the sight of God?

A. All transgressions of the law of God are not equally heinous; but some sins in themselves, and by reason of several aggravations, are more heinous in the sight of God than others.[1]

Q. 147
1   Heb. 13:5; 1 Tim. 6:6. (See Phil. 4:11.)
2   Job 31:29; Rom. 12:15. (See Ps. 122:7–9; 1 Tim. 1:5; Est. 10:3; 1 Cor. 13:4–7.)
Q. 148
1   1 Cor. 10:10. (See 1 Kings 21:4; Est. 5:13.)
2   Gal. 5:26; James 3:14, 16.
3   Ps. 112:9–10. (See Neh. 2:10.)
4   Rom. 7:7–8; Rom. 13:9; Col. 3:5; Deut. 5:21.
Q. 149
1   James 3:2; John 15:5; Rom. 8:3.
2   Eccl. 7:20; 1 John 1:8, 10; Gal. 5:17; Rom. 7:18–19.
3   Gen. 6:5; Gen. 8:21; James 1:14.
4   Rom. 3:9 (see vv. 10–19). (See also James 3:2–13.)
Q. 150
1   John 19:11; 1 John 5:16; Heb. 2:2–3. (See Ps. 78:17, 32, 56; Ezek. 8:6, 13, 15.)

Q. 151. What are those aggravations that make some sins more heinous than others?

A. Sins receive their aggravations,

1. From the persons offending:[1] if they be of riper age,[2] greater experience or grace,[3] eminent for profession,[4] gifts,[5] place,[6] office,[7] guides to others,[8] and whose example is likely to be followed by others.[9]

2. From the parties offended:[10] if immediately against God,[11] his attributes,[12] and worship;[13] against Christ, and his grace;[14] the Holy Spirit,[15] his witness,[16] and workings;[17] against superiors, men of eminency,[18] and such as we stand especially related and engaged unto;[19] against any of the saints,[20] particularly weak brethren,[21] the souls of them, or any other,[22] and the common good of all or many.[23]

3. From the nature and quality of the offense:[24] if it be against the express letter of the law,[25] break many commandments, contain in

Q. 151
1   Jer. 2:8.
2   Job 32:7, 9; Eccl. 4:13.
3   1 Kings 11:4, 9.
4   2 Sam. 12:14; 1 Cor. 5:1.
5   James 4:17; Luke 12:47–48.
6   Jer. 5:4–5.
7   2 Sam. 12:7–9; Ezek. 8:11–12.
8   Rom. 2:17–24.
9   Gal. 2:11–14.
10 Ps. 2:12; Matt. 21:38–39.
11 1 Sam. 2:25; Acts 5:4; Ps. 5:4.
12 Rom. 2:4.
13 Mal. 1:8, 14.
14 Heb. 2:2–3; Heb. 12:25.
15 Heb. 10:28–29; Matt. 12:31–32.
16 Eph. 4:30.
17 Heb. 6:4–6.
18 Jude 8; Num. 12:8–9; Isa. 3:5.
19 Prov. 30:17; 2 Cor. 12:15; Ps. 55:12–15.
20 Zeph. 2:8, 10–11; Matt. 18:6; 1 Cor. 6:8; Rev. 17:6.
21 1 Cor. 8:11–12; Rom. 14:13, 15, 21.
22 Ezek. 13:19; 1 Cor. 8:12; Rev. 18:12–13; Matt. 23:15.
23 1 Thess. 2:15–16; Josh. 22:20.
24 Prov. 6:30–33.
25 Ezra 9:10–12; 1 Kings 11:9–10.

it many sins:[26] if not only conceived in the heart, but breaks forth in words and actions,[27] scandalize others,[28] and admit of no reparation:[29] if against means,[30] mercies,[31] judgments,[32] light of nature,[33] conviction of conscience,[34] public or private admonition,[35] censures of the church,[36] civil punishments;[37] and our prayers, purposes, promises,[38] vows,[39] covenants,[40] and engagements to God or men:[41] if done deliberately,[42] willfully,[43] presumptuously,[44] impudently,[45] boastingly,[46] maliciously,[47] frequently,[48] obstinately,[49] with delight,[50] continuance,[51] or relapsing after repentance.[52]

4. From circumstances of time[53] and place:[54] if on the Lord's Day,[55] or other times of divine worship;[56] or immediately before[57] or

26 Col. 3:5; 1 Tim. 6:10; Prov. 5:8–12; Prov. 6:32–33; Josh. 7:21.
27 James 1:14–15; Matt. 5:22; Mic. 2:1.
28 Matt. 18:7; Rom. 2:23–24.
29 Deut. 22:22, 28–29; Prov. 6:32–35.
30 Matt. 11:21–24; John 15:22.
31 Isa. 1:3; Deut. 32:6.
32 Amos 4:8–11; Jer. 5:3.
33 Rom. 1:26–27.
34 Rom. 1:32; Dan. 5:22; Titus 3:10–11.
35 Prov. 29:1.
36 Titus 3:10; Matt. 18:17.
37 Prov. 27:22; Prov. 23:35.
38 Ps. 78:34–37; Jer. 2:20; Jer. 13:5–6, 20–21.
39 Eccl. 5:4–6; Prov. 20:25.
40 Lev. 26:25.
41 Prov. 2:17; Ezek. 7:18–19.
42 Ps. 36:4.
43 Jer. 6:16.
44 Num. 15:30; Ex. 21:14.
45 Jer. 3:3; Prov. 7:13.
46 Ps. 52:1.
47 3 John 10.
48 Num. 14:22.
49 Zech. 7:11–12.
50 Prov. 2:14.
51 Isa. 57:17.
52 Jer. 34:8–11; 2 Peter 2:20–22.
53 2 Kings 5:26.
54 Jer. 7:10; Isa. 26:10.
55 Ezek. 23:37–39.
56 Isa. 58:3–5; Num. 25:6–7.
57 1 Cor. 11:20–21; Jer. 7:8–10.

after these,[58] or other helps to prevent or remedy such miscarriages:[59] if in public, or in the presence of others, who are thereby likely to be provoked or defiled.[60]

Q. 152. What doth every sin deserve at the hands of God?

A. Every sin, even the least, being against the sovereignty,[1] goodness,[2] and holiness of God,[3] and against his righteous law,[4] deserveth his wrath and curse,[5] both in this life,[6] and that which is to come;[7] and cannot be expiated but by the blood of Christ.[8]

Q. 153. What doth God require of us, that we may escape his wrath and curse due to us by reason of the transgression of the law?

A. That we may escape the wrath and curse of God due to us by reason of the transgression of the law, he requireth of us repentance toward God, and faith toward our Lord Jesus Christ,[1] and the diligent use of the outward means whereby Christ communicates to us the benefits of his mediation.[2]

Q. 154. What are the outward means whereby Christ communicates to us the benefits of his mediation?

A. The outward and ordinary means whereby Christ communicates to his church the benefits of his mediation, are all his ordinances; especially the Word, sacraments, and prayer; all which are made effectual to the elect for their salvation.[1]

58 Prov. 7:14–15; John 13:27, 30.
59 Ezra 9:13–14.
60 2 Sam. 16:22; 1 Sam. 2:22–24.
Q. 152
1   James 2:10–11.
2   Ex. 20:1–2.
3   Hab. 1:13; Lev. 10:3; Lev. 11:44–45.
4   1 John 3:4; Rom. 7:12.
5   Eph. 5:6; Gal. 3:10.
6   Lam. 3:39; Deut. 28:15–68.
7   Matt. 25:41.
8   Heb. 9:22; 1 Peter 1:18–19.
Q. 153
1   Acts 20:21; Matt. 3:7–8; Luke 13:3, 5; Acts 16:30–31; John 3:16, 18.
2   Prov. 2:1–5; Prov. 8:33–36.
Q. 154
1   Matt. 28:19–20; Acts 2:42, 46–47.

Q. 155. How is the Word made effectual to salvation?

A. The Spirit of God maketh the reading, but especially the preaching of the Word, an effectual means of enlightening,[1] convincing, and humbling sinners;[2] of driving them out of themselves, and drawing them unto Christ;[3] of conforming them to his image,[4] and subduing them to his will;[5] of strengthening them against temptations and corruptions;[6] of building them up in grace,[7] and establishing their hearts in holiness and comfort through faith unto salvation.[8]

Q. 156. Is the Word of God to be read by all?

A. Although all are not to be permitted to read the Word publicly to the congregation,[1] yet all sorts of people are bound to read it apart by themselves,[2] and with their families:[3] to which end, the Holy Scriptures are to be translated out of the original into vulgar languages.[4]

Q. 157. How is the Word of God to be read?

A. The Holy Scriptures are to be read with an high and reverent esteem of them;[1] with a firm persuasion that they are the very Word of God,[2] and that he only can enable us to understand them;[3] with desire to know, believe, and obey the will of God revealed in them;[4] with diligence,[5] and attention to the

Q. 155
1   Neh. 8:8; Acts 26:18; Ps. 19:8.
2   1 Cor. 14:24–25. (See 2 Chron. 34:18–19, 26–28.)
3   Acts 2:37, 41. (See Acts 8:27–38.)
4   2 Cor. 3:18. (See Col. 1:27.)
5   2 Cor. 10:4–6. (See Rom. 6:17–18.)
6   Eph. 6:16–17; Col. 1:28; Ps. 19:11. (See Matt. 4:4, 7, 10; 1 Cor. 10:11.)
7   Eph. 4:11–12; Acts 20:32. (See 2 Tim. 3:15–17.)
8   Rom. 16:25; 1 Thess. 3:2, 10–11, 13. (See Rom. 15:4; 10:13–17; 1:16.)

Q. 156
1   Deut. 31:9, 11–13. (See Neh. 8:2–3; 9:3–5.)
2   Deut. 17:19; Rev. 1:3; John 5:39; Isa. 34:16.
3   Deut. 6:6–9; Gen. 18:17, 19; Ps. 78:5–7.
4   1 Cor. 14:6, 9, 11–12, 15–16, 24, 27–28; Neh. 8:8.

Q. 157
1   Ps. 119:97; Ps. 19:10; Ex. 24:7; 2 Chron. 34:27; Isa. 66:2. (See Neh. 8:3–10.)
2   2 Peter 1:19–21; Matt. 4:4; 1 Thess. 2:13. (See Mark 7:13.)
3   Luke 24:45; 2 Cor. 3:13–16.
4   Deut. 17:10, 20.
5   Acts 17:11.

matter and scope of them;[6] with meditation,[7] application,[8] self-denial,[9] and prayer.[10]

Q. 158. By whom is the Word of God to be preached?

A. The Word of God is to be preached only by such as are sufficiently gifted,[1] and also duly approved and called to that office.[2]

Q. 159. How is the Word of God to be preached by those that are called thereunto?

A. They that are called to labor in the ministry of the Word, are to preach sound doctrine,[1] diligently,[2] in season and out of season;[3] plainly,[4] not in the enticing words of man's wisdom, but in demonstration of the Spirit, and of power;[5] faithfully,[6] making known the whole counsel of God;[7] wisely,[8] applying themselves to the necessities and capacities of the hearers;[9] zealously,[10] with fervent love to God[11] and the souls of his people;[12] sincerely,[13] aiming at his glory,[14] and their conversion,[15] edification,[16] and salvation.[17]

6   Acts 8:30, 34; Luke 10:26–28.
7   Ps. 1:2; Ps. 119:97.
8   2 Chron. 34:21.
9   Prov. 3:5; Deut. 33:3; Matt. 16:24. (See Luke 9:23; Gal. 1:15–16.)
10 Prov. 2:1–6; Ps. 119:18; Neh. 8:6, 8.
Q. 158
1   1 Tim. 3:2, 6; Eph. 4:8–11; Mal. 2:7; 2 Cor. 3:6; 2 Tim. 2:2.
2   Jer. 14:15; Rom. 10:15; Heb. 5:4; 1 Cor. 12:28–29; 1 Tim. 3:10; 1 Tim. 4:14; 1 Tim. 5:22.
Q. 159
1   Titus 2:1, 8.
2   Acts 18:25.
3   2 Tim. 4:2.
4   1 Cor. 14:9 (see vv. 10–19).
5   1 Cor. 2:4.
6   Jer. 23:28; 1 Cor. 4:1–2.
7   Acts 20:27.
8   Col. 1:28; 2 Tim. 2:15.
9   1 Cor. 3:2; Heb. 5:12–14; Luke 12:42.
10 Acts 18:25; Ps. 119:139; 2 Tim. 4:5.
11 2 Cor. 5:13–14; Phil. 1:15–17.
12 Col. 4:12; 2 Cor. 12:15.
13 2 Cor. 2:17; 2 Cor. 4:2.
14 1 Thess. 2:4–6; John 7:18.
15 1 Cor. 9:19–22.
16 2 Cor. 12:19; Eph. 4:12.
17 1 Tim. 4:16; Acts 26:16–18.

Q. 160. What is required of those that hear the Word preached?

A. It is required of those that hear the Word preached, that they attend upon it with diligence,[1] preparation,[2] and prayer;[3] examine what they hear by the Scriptures;[4] receive the truth with faith,[5] love,[6] meekness,[7] and readiness of mind,[8] as the Word of God;[9] meditate,[10] and confer of it;[11] hide it in their hearts,[12] and bring forth the fruit of it in their lives.[13]

Q. 161. How do the sacraments become effectual means of salvation?

A. The sacraments become effectual means of salvation, not by any power in themselves, or any virtue derived from the piety or intention of him by whom they are administered, but only by the working of the Holy Ghost, and the blessing of Christ, by whom they are instituted.[1]

Q. 162. What is a sacrament?

A. A sacrament is an holy ordinance instituted by Christ in his church,[1] to signify, seal, and exhibit[2] unto those that are within the covenant of grace,[3] the benefits of his mediation;[4] to strengthen and increase their faith, and all

Q. 160
1 Prov. 8:34.
2 1 Peter 2:1–2; Luke 8:18.
3 Ps. 119:18; Eph. 6:18–19.
4 Acts 17:11.
5 Heb. 4:2.
6 2 Thess. 2:10.
7 James 1:21.
8 Acts 17:11.
9 1 Thess. 2:13.
10 Luke 9:44; Heb. 2:1.
11 Luke 24:14; Deut. 6:6–7.
12 Prov. 2:1; Ps. 119:11.
13 Luke 8:15; James 1:25.
Q. 161
1 1 Peter 3:21; Acts 8:13, 23; 1 Cor. 3:5–7 (cf. 1 Cor. 1:12–17); 1 Cor. 12:13; 1 Cor. 6:11.
Q. 162
1 Gen. 17:7, 10; Ex. 12 (containing the institution of the Passover); Matt. 28:19; Matt. 26:26–28. (See Mark 14:22–25; Luke 22:19–20; 1 Cor. 11:22–26.)
2 Rom. 4:11; 1 Cor. 11:24–25.
3 Rom. 15:8; Ex. 12:48; Rom. 9:8; Gal. 3:27, 29.
4 Acts 2:38; 1 Cor. 10:16.

other graces;[5] to oblige them to obedience;[6] to testify and cherish their love and communion one with another;[7] and to distinguish them from those that are without.[8]

Q. 163. What are the parts of a sacrament?

A. The parts of a sacrament are two; the one an outward and sensible sign, used according to Christ's own appointment; the other an inward and spiritual grace thereby signified.[1]

Q. 164. How many sacraments hath Christ instituted in his church under the new testament?

A. Under the new testament Christ hath instituted in his church only two sacraments, baptism and the Lord's Supper.[1]

Q. 165. What is baptism?

A. Baptism is a sacrament of the new testament, wherein Christ hath ordained the washing with water in the name of the Father, and of the Son, and of the Holy Ghost,[1] to be a sign and seal of ingrafting into himself,[2] of remission of sins by his blood,[3] and regeneration by his Spirit;[4] of adoption,[5] and resurrection unto everlasting life;[6] and whereby the parties baptized are solemnly admitted into the visible church,[7] and enter into an open and professed engagement to be wholly and only the Lord's.[8]

5   Rom. 4:11; Gal. 3:27.
6   Rom. 6:3–4; 1 Cor. 10:21.
7   Eph. 4:2–5; 1 Cor. 12:13; 1 Cor. 10:16–17.
8   Eph. 2:11–12; Gen. 34:14.
Q. 163
1   Matt. 3:11; 1 Peter 3:21; Titus 3:5. (Cf. Confession of Faith 27.2 and the passages cited thereunder. Cf. also Deut. 10:16; 30:6; Jer. 4:4.)
Q. 164
1   Matt. 28:19; 1 Cor. 11:20, 23; Matt. 26:26–28.
Q. 165
1   Matt. 28:19.
2   Gal. 3:27; Rom. 6:3.
3   Mark 1:4; Rev. 1:5; Acts 2:38; Acts 22:16; 1 Peter 3:21.
4   Titus 3:5; Eph. 5:26. (See Acts 2:38.)
5   Gal. 3:26–27.
6   1 Cor. 15:29; Rom. 6:5.
7   1 Cor. 12:13; Acts 2:41.
8   Rom. 6:4. (See Acts 2:38–42.)

Q. 166. Unto whom is baptism to be administered?

A. Baptism is not to be administered to any that are out of the visible church, and so strangers from the covenant of promise, till they profess their faith in Christ, and obedience to him,[1] but infants descending from parents, either both, or but one of them, professing faith in Christ, and obedience to him, are in that respect within the covenant, and to be baptized.[2]

Q. 167. How is our baptism to be improved by us?

A. The needful but much neglected duty of improving our baptism, is to be performed by us all our life long, especially in the time of temptation, and when we are present at the administration of it to others;[1] by serious and thankful consideration of the nature of it, and of the ends for which Christ instituted it, the privileges and benefits conferred and sealed thereby, and our solemn vow made therein;[2] by being humbled for our sinful defilement, our falling short of, and walking contrary to, the grace of baptism, and our engagements;[3] by growing up to assurance of pardon of sin, and of all other blessings sealed to us in that sacrament;[4] by drawing strength from the death and resurrection of Christ, into whom we are baptized, for the mortifying of sin, and quickening of grace;[5] and by endeavoring to live by faith,[6] to have our conversation in holiness and righteousness,[7] as those that have therein given up their names to Christ;[8] and to walk in brotherly love, as being baptized by the same Spirit into one body.[9]

Q. 166
1 Acts 2:38–39, 41; Acts 8:12, 36, 38; Acts 16:15.
2 Col. 2:11–12; Acts 2:38–39; Rom. 4:11–12; 1 Cor. 7:14; Luke 18:15–16. (See Gen. 17:7–9; Gal. 3:9–14; Rom. 11:16.)
Q. 167
1 Col. 2:11–12; Rom. 6:4, 6, 11.
2 Rom. 6:3–5; 1 Peter 3:21.
3 1 Cor. 1:11–13; Rom. 6:2–3.
4 Rom. 6:4–7, 22; 1 Peter 3:21; Rom. 5:1–2; Jer. 33:8.
5 Rom. 6:3–5.
6 Gal. 3:26–27.
7 Rom. 6:22.
8 Acts 2:38 (cf. Gal. 2:20). (See also Rev. 2:17.)
9 1 Cor. 12:13, 25.

Q. 168. What is the Lord's Supper?

A. The Lord's Supper is a sacrament of the new testament,[1] wherein, by giving and receiving bread and wine according to the appointment of Jesus Christ, his death is showed forth; and they that worthily communicate feed upon his body and blood, to their spiritual nourishment and growth in grace;[2] have their union and communion with him confirmed;[3] testify and renew their thankfulness,[4] and engagement to God,[5] and their mutual love and fellowship each with other, as members of the same mystical body.[6]

Q. 169. How hath Christ appointed bread and wine to be given and received in the sacrament of the Lord's Supper?

A. Christ hath appointed the ministers of his Word, in the administration of this sacrament of the Lord's Supper, to set apart the bread and wine from common use, by the word of institution, thanksgiving, and prayer; to take and break the bread, and to give both the bread and the wine to the communicants: who are, by the same appointment, to take and eat the bread, and to drink the wine, in thankful remembrance that the body of Christ was broken and given, and his blood shed, for them.[1]

Q. 170. How do they that worthily communicate in the Lord's Supper feed upon the body and blood of Christ therein?

A. As the body and blood of Christ are not corporally or carnally present in, with, or under the bread and wine in the Lord's Supper,[1] and yet are spiritually present to the faith of the receiver, no less truly and really than the elements themselves are to their outward senses;[2] so they that worthily communicate in

---

Q. 168
1   Luke 22:20.
2   Matt. 26:26–28; 1 Cor. 11:23–26.
3   1 Cor. 10:16.
4   1 Cor. 11:24.
5   1 Cor. 10:14–16, 21. (Cf. Rom. 7:4.)
6   1 Cor. 10:17.
Q. 169
1   1 Cor. 11:23–24. (See Matt. 26:26–28; Mark 14:22–24; Luke 22:19–20.)
Q. 170
1   Acts 3:21.
2   Matt. 26:26, 28.

the sacrament of the Lord's Supper, do therein feed upon the body and blood of Christ, not after a corporal and carnal, but in a spiritual manner; yet truly and really,[3] while by faith they receive and apply unto themselves Christ crucified, and all the benefits of his death.[4]

Q. 171. How are they that receive the sacrament of the Lord's Supper to prepare themselves before they come unto it?

A. They that receive the sacrament of the Lord's Supper are, before they come, to prepare themselves thereunto, by examining themselves[1] of their being in Christ,[2] of their sins and wants;[3] of the truth and measure of their knowledge,[4] faith,[5] repentance;[6] love to God and the brethren,[7] charity to all men,[8] forgiving those that have done them wrong;[9] of their desires after Christ,[10] and of their new obedience;[11] and by renewing the exercise of these graces,[12] by serious meditation,[13] and fervent prayer.[14]

Q. 172. May one who doubteth of his being in Christ, or of his due preparation, come to the Lord's Supper?

A. One who doubteth of his being in Christ, or of his due preparation to the sacrament of the Lord's Supper, may have true interest in Christ, though he be not yet assured thereof;[1] and in God's account hath it, if he be duly affected with the apprehension of the want of it,[2] and unfeignedly desires to be found

3 1 Cor. 11:24–29. (Cf. Confession of Faith 27.2. Cf. also John 6:51, 53.)
4 1 Cor. 10:16.
Q. 171
1 1 Cor. 11:28.
2 2 Cor. 13:5.
3 1 Cor. 5:7; Ex. 12:15.
4 1 Cor. 11:29.
5 2 Cor. 13:5; Matt. 26:28.
6 Zech. 12:10; 1 Cor. 11:31.
7 1 Cor. 10:16–17; Acts 2:46–47.
8 1 Cor. 5:8; 1 Cor. 11:18, 20.
9 Matt. 5:23–24.
10 Isa. 55:1; John 7:37.
11 1 Cor. 5:7–8.
12 1 Cor. 11:25–26, 28; Heb. 10:21–22, 24; Ps. 26:6.
13 1 Cor. 11:24–25.
14 2 Chron. 30:18–19; Matt. 26:26.
Q. 172
1 Isa. 50:10; 1 John 5:13; Ps. 88; Ps. 77:1–4, 7–10; Jonah 2:4.
2 Isa. 54:7–10; Matt. 5:3–4; Ps. 31:22; Ps. 73:13, 22–23.

in Christ,[3] and to depart from iniquity:[4] in which case (because promises are made, and this sacrament is appointed, for the relief even of weak and doubting Christians[5]) he is to bewail his unbelief,[6] and labor to have his doubts resolved;[7] and, so doing, he may and ought to come to the Lord's Supper, that he may be further strengthened.[8]

Q. 173. May any who profess the faith, and desire to come to the Lord's Supper, be kept from it?

A. Such as are found to be ignorant or scandalous, notwithstanding their profession of the faith, and desire to come to the Lord's Supper, may and ought to be kept from that sacrament, by the power which Christ hath left in his church,[1] until they receive instruction, and manifest their reformation.[2]

Q. 174. What is required of them that receive the sacrament of the Lord's Supper in the time of the administration of it?

A. It is required of them that receive the sacrament of the Lord's Supper, that, during the time of the administration of it, with all holy reverence and attention they wait upon God in that ordinance,[1] diligently observe the sacramental elements and actions,[2] heedfully discern the Lord's body,[3] and affectionately meditate on his death and sufferings,[4] and thereby stir up themselves to a vigorous exercise of their graces;[5] in judging themselves,[6] and sorrowing for sin;[7]

3 Phil. 3:8–9; Ps. 10:17; Ps. 42:1–2, 5, 11.
4 2 Tim. 2:19; Isa. 50:10; Ps. 66:18–20.
5 Isa. 40:11, 29, 31; Matt. 11:28; Matt. 12:20; Matt. 26:28.
6 Mark 9:24.
7 Acts 2:37; Acts 16:30.
8 Rom. 4:11; 1 Cor. 11:28.
Q. 173
1 1 Cor. 11:27–34; Matt. 7:6; 1 Cor. 5; Jude 23; 1 Tim. 5:22.
2 2 Cor. 2:7.
Q. 174
1 Lev. 10:3; Heb. 12:28; Ps. 5:7; 1 Cor. 11:17, 26–27.
2 Ex. 24:8; Matt. 26:28.
3 1 Cor. 11:29.
4 Luke 22:19.
5 1 Cor. 11:26; 1 Cor. 10:3–5, 11, 14.
6 1 Cor. 11:31.
7 Zech. 12:10.

in earnest hungering and thirsting after Christ,[8] feeding on him by faith,[9] receiving of his fullness,[10] trusting in his merits,[11] rejoicing in his love,[12] giving thanks for his grace;[13] in renewing of their covenant with God,[14] and love to all the saints.[15]

Q. 175. What is the duty of Christians, after they have received the sacrament of the Lord's Supper?

A. The duty of Christians, after they have received the sacrament of the Lord's Supper, is seriously to consider how they have behaved themselves therein, and with what success;[1] if they find quickening and comfort, to bless God for it,[2] beg the continuance of it,[3] watch against relapses,[4] fulfill their vows,[5] and encourage themselves to a frequent attendance on that ordinance:[6] but if they find no present benefit, more exactly to review their preparation to, and carriage at, the sacrament;[7] in both which, if they can approve themselves to God and their own consciences, they are to wait for the fruit of it in due time:[8] but, if they see they have failed in either, they are to be humbled,[9] and to attend upon it afterwards with more care and diligence.[10]

8 Rev. 22:17. (See Matt. 5:6.)
9 John 6:35 (see vv. 47–58).
10 John 1:16.
11 Phil. 3:9.
12 Ps. 63:4–5; 2 Chron. 30:21.
13 Ps. 22:26. (See 1 Cor. 10:16.)
14 Jer. 50:5; Ps. 50:5.
15 Acts 2:42.
Q. 175
1 Ps. 28:7; Ps. 85:8; 1 Cor. 11:17, 30–31.
2 2 Chron. 30:21–23, 25–26; Acts 2:42, 46–47.
3 Ps. 36:10; Song 3:4; 1 Chron. 29:18.
4 1 Cor. 10:3–5, 12.
5 Ps. 50:14.
6 1 Cor. 11:25–26; Acts 2:42, 46.
7 Eccl. 5:1–6; Ps. 139:23–24.
8 Ps. 123:1–2; Ps. 42:5, 8; Ps. 43:3–5.
9 2 Chron. 30:18–19.
10 2 Cor. 7:11; 1 Chron. 15:12–14.

Q. 176. Wherein do the sacraments of baptism and the Lord's Supper agree?

A. The sacraments of baptism and the Lord's Supper agree, in that the author of both is God;[1] the spiritual part of both is Christ and his benefits;[2] both are seals of the same covenant,[3] are to be dispensed by ministers of the gospel, and by none other;[4] and to be continued in the church of Christ until his second coming.[5]

Q. 177. Wherein do the sacraments of baptism and the Lord's Supper differ?

A. The sacraments of baptism and the Lord's Supper differ, in that baptism is to be administered but once, with water, to be a sign and seal of our regeneration and ingrafting into Christ,[1] and that even to infants;[2] whereas the Lord's Supper is to be administered often, in the elements of bread and wine, to represent and exhibit Christ as spiritual nourishment to the soul,[3] and to confirm our continuance and growth in him,[4] and that only to such as are of years and ability to examine themselves.[5]

Q. 178. What is prayer?

A. Prayer is an offering up of our desires unto God,[1] in the name of Christ,[2] by the help of his Spirit;[3] with confession of our sins,[4] and thankful acknowledgment of his mercies.[5]

Q. 176
1 Matt. 28:19; 1 Cor. 11:23.
2 Rom. 6:3–4; 1 Cor. 10:16.
3 Rom. 4:11 (cf. Col. 2:12); Matt. 26:27–28.
4 John 1:33; Matt. 28:19; 1 Cor. 11:23; 1 Cor. 4:1; Heb. 5:4.
5 Matt. 28:19–20; 1 Cor. 11:26.
Q. 177
1 Matt. 3:11; Titus 3:5; Gal. 3:27.
2 Gen. 17:7, 9; Acts 2:38–39; 1 Cor. 7:14.
3 1 Cor. 11:23–26.
4 1 Cor. 10:16.
5 1 Cor. 11:28–29.
Q. 178
1 Ps. 10:17; Ps. 62:8; Matt. 7:7–8.
2 John 16:23.
3 Rom. 8:26.
4 Ps. 32:5–6; 1 John 1:9. (See Dan. 9:4–19.)
5 Phil. 4:6; Ps. 103:1–5. (See Ps. 136.)

Q. 179. Are we to pray unto God only?

A. God only being able to search the hearts,[1] hear the requests,[2] pardon the sins,[3] and fulfill the desires of all;[4] and only to be believed in,[5] and worshiped with religious worship;[6] prayer, which is a special part thereof,[7] is to be made by all to him alone,[8] and to none other.[9]

Q. 180. What is it to pray in the name of Christ?

A. To pray in the name of Christ is, in obedience to his command, and in confidence on his promises, to ask mercy for his sake;[1] not by bare mentioning of his name,[2] but by drawing our encouragement to pray, and our boldness, strength, and hope of acceptance in prayer, from Christ and his mediation.[3]

Q. 181. Why are we to pray in the name of Christ?

A. The sinfulness of man, and his distance from God by reason thereof, being so great, as that we can have no access into his presence without a mediator;[1] and there being none in heaven or earth appointed to, or fit for, that glorious work but Christ alone,[2] we are to pray in no other name but his only.[3]

Q. 182. How doth the Spirit help us to pray?

A. We not knowing what to pray for as we ought, the Spirit helpeth our infirmities, by enabling us to understand both for whom, and what, and how prayer

Q. 179
1   1 Kings 8:39; Acts 1:24; Rom. 8:27.
2   Ps. 65:2.
3   Mic. 7:18.
4   Ps. 145:18.
5   Rom. 10:14.
6   Matt. 4:10.
7   1 Cor. 1:2.
8   Isa. 45:22; Matt. 6:9; Ps. 50:15.
9   Isa. 43:11; Isa. 46:9 (see entire chapter).
Q. 180
1   John 14:13–14; John 16:24; Dan. 9:17.
2   Matt. 7:21.
3   Heb. 4:14–16; 1 John 5:13–15.
Q. 181
1   John 14:6; Isa. 59:2; Eph. 3:12.
2   John 6:27; Heb. 7:25–27; 1 Tim. 2:5.
3   Col. 3:17; Heb. 13:15.

is to be made; and by working and quickening in our hearts (although not in all persons, nor at all times, in the same measure) those apprehensions, affections, and graces which are requisite for the right performance of that duty.[1]

Q. 183. For whom are we to pray?

A. We are to pray for the whole church of Christ upon earth;[1] for magistrates,[2] and ministers;[3] for ourselves,[4] our brethren,[5] yea, our enemies;[6] and for all sorts of men living,[7] or that shall live hereafter;[8] but not for the dead,[9] nor for those that are known to have sinned the sin unto death.[10]

Q. 184. For what things are we to pray?

A. We are to pray for all things tending to the glory of God,[1] the welfare of the church,[2] our own[3] or others' good;[4] but not for anything that is unlawful.[5]

Q. 185. How are we to pray?

A. We are to pray with an awful apprehension of the majesty of God,[1] and deep sense of our own unworthiness,[2] necessities,[3] and sins;[4] with penitent,[5]

Q. 182
1 Rom. 8:26–27; Ps. 10:17; Zech. 12:10.
Q. 183
1 Eph. 6:18; Ps. 28:9.
2 1 Tim. 2:1–2.
3 Col. 4:3.
4 Gen. 32:11.
5 James 5:16.
6 Matt. 5:44.
7 1 Tim. 2:1–2.
8 John 17:20; 2 Sam. 7:29.
9 2 Sam. 12:21–23.
10 1 John 5:16.
Q. 184
1 Matt. 6:9.
2 Ps. 51:18; Ps. 122:6.
3 Matt. 7:11.
4 Ps. 125:4.
5 1 John 5:14.
Q. 185
1 Ps. 33:8; Ps. 95:6; Ps. 145:5.
2 Gen. 18:27; Gen. 32:10.
3 Luke 15:17–19.
4 Luke 18:13–14.
5 Ps. 51:17.

thankful,[6] and enlarged hearts;[7] with understanding,[8] faith,[9] sincerity,[10] fervency,[11] love,[12] and perseverance,[13] waiting upon him,[14] with humble submission to his will.[15]

Q. 186. What rule hath God given for our direction in the duty of prayer?

A. The whole Word of God is of use to direct us in the duty of prayer;[1] but the special rule of direction is that form of prayer which our Savior Christ taught his disciples, commonly called the Lord's Prayer.[2]

Q. 187. How is the Lord's Prayer to be used?

A. The Lord's Prayer is not only for direction, as a pattern, according to which we are to make other prayers; but may also be used as a prayer, so that it be done with understanding, faith, reverence, and other graces necessary to the right performance of the duty of prayer.[1]

Q. 188. Of how many parts doth the Lord's Prayer consist?

A. The Lord's Prayer consists of three parts; a preface, petitions, and a conclusion.

Q. 189. What doth the preface of the Lord's Prayer teach us?

A. The preface of the Lord's Prayer (contained in these words, *Our Father which art in heaven,*[1]) teacheth us, when we pray, to draw near to God with

---

6   Phil. 4:6.
7   1 Sam. 1:15; 1 Sam. 2:1.
8   1 Cor. 14:15.
9   Mark 11:24; James 1:6.
10 Ps. 145:18; Ps. 17:1.
11 James 5:16.
12 Ps. 116:1–2; Rom. 15:30.
13 Eph. 6:18.
14 Mic. 7:7.
15 Matt. 26:39.
Q. 186
1   1 John 5:14.
2   Matt. 6:9–13; Luke 11:2–4.
Q. 187
1   Matt. 6:9; Luke 11:2.
Q. 189
1   Matt. 6:9. (Cf. Luke 11:2.)

confidence of his fatherly goodness, and our interest therein;[2] with reverence, and all other childlike dispositions,[3] heavenly affections,[4] and due apprehensions of his sovereign power, majesty, and gracious condescension:[5] as also, to pray with and for others.[6]

Q. 190. What do we pray for in the first petition?

A. In the first petition, (which is, *Hallowed be thy name*,[1]) acknowledging the utter inability and indisposition that is in ourselves and all men to honor God aright,[2] we pray, that God would by his grace enable and incline us and others to know, to acknowledge, and highly to esteem him,[3] his titles,[4] attributes,[5] ordinances, Word,[6] works, and whatsoever he is pleased to make himself known by;[7] and to glorify him in thought, word,[8] and deed:[9] that he would prevent and remove atheism,[10] ignorance,[11] idolatry,[12] profaneness,[13] and whatsoever is dishonorable to him;[14] and, by his overruling providence, direct and dispose of all things to his own glory.[15]

Q. 191. What do we pray for in the second petition?

A. In the second petition, (which is, *Thy kingdom come*,[1]) acknowledging ourselves and all mankind to be by nature under the dominion of sin and

2   Ps. 103:13; Luke 11:13; Rom. 8:15.
3   Isa. 64:9.
4   Col. 3:1–2; Ps. 123:1; Lam. 3:41.
5   Isa. 63:15–16; Neh. 1:4–6. (See Ps. 113:4–6.)
6   Acts 12:5; 1 Tim. 2:1–2; Eph. 6:18.
Q. 190
1   Matt. 6:9. (Cf. Luke 11:2.)
2   2 Cor. 3:5; Ps. 51:15.
3   Ps. 67:2–3; Ps. 99:1–3.
4   Ps. 83:18.
5   Ps. 86:10–13, 15.
6   2 Thess. 3:1; Ps. 147:19–20; Ps. 138:1–3; 2 Cor. 2:14–15.
7   Ps. 145; Ps. 8.
8   Ps. 103:1; Ps. 19:14.
9   Phil. 1:9, 11; Ps. 100:3–4.
10 Ps. 67:1–4.
11 Eph. 1:17–18.
12 Ps. 97:7.
13 Ps. 74:18, 22–23.
14 2 Kings 19:15–16.
15 2 Chron. 20:6 (see vv. 10–12); Rom. 11:33–36; Rev. 4:11. (See Pss. 83; 140:4, 8.)
Q. 191
1   Matt. 6:10. (Cf. Luke 11:2.)

Satan,[2] we pray, that the kingdom of sin and Satan may be destroyed,[3] the gospel propagated throughout the world,[4] the Jews called,[5] the fullness of the Gentiles brought in;[6] the church furnished with all gospel officers and ordinances,[7] purged from corruption,[8] countenanced and maintained by the civil magistrate:[9] that the ordinances of Christ may be purely dispensed, and made effectual to the converting of those that are yet in their sins, and the confirming, comforting, and building up of those that are already converted:[10] that Christ would rule in our hearts here,[11] and hasten the time of his second coming, and our reigning with him forever:[12] and that he would be pleased so to exercise the kingdom of his power in all the world, as may best conduce to these ends.[13]

Q. 192. What do we pray for in the third petition?

A. In the third petition, (which is, *Thy will be done in earth, as it is in heaven*,[1]) acknowledging, that by nature we and all men are not only utterly unable and unwilling to know and do the will of God,[2] but prone to rebel against his Word,[3] to repine and murmur against his providence,[4] and wholly inclined to do the will of the flesh, and of the devil:[5] we pray, that God would by his Spirit take away from ourselves and others all blindness,[6] weakness,[7] indisposedness,[8]

2 Eph. 2:2–3.
3 Ps. 68:1, 18; Rev. 12:10–11.
4 Ps. 67:1–2; 2 Thess. 3:1.
5 Rom. 10:1.
6 John 17:9, 20; Rom. 11:25–26. (See Ps. 67.)
7 Matt. 9:38; 2 Thess. 3:1.
8 Mal. 1:11; Zeph. 3:9.
9 1 Tim. 2:1–2; Isa. 49:23.
10 Acts 4:29–30; Eph. 6:18–20; Rom. 15:29–30, 32; 2 Thess. 1:11; 2 Thess. 2:16–17.
11 Eph. 3:14–20; Col. 3:15.
12 Rev. 22:20; 2 Tim. 2:12; 2 Peter 3:12.
13 Isa. 64:1–2; Rev. 4:8–11.
Q. 192
1 Matt. 6:10. (Cf. Luke 11:2.)
2 Rom. 7:18; Job 21:14; 1 Cor. 2:14.
3 Rom. 8:7.
4 Ex. 17:7; Num. 14:2.
5 Eph. 2:2.
6 Eph. 1:17–18.
7 Eph. 3:16.
8 Matt. 26:40–41.

and perverseness of heart;[9] and by his grace make us able and willing to know, do, and submit to his will in all things,[10] with the like humility,[11] cheerfulness,[12] faithfulness,[13] diligence,[14] zeal,[15] sincerity,[16] and constancy,[17] as the angels do in heaven.[18]

Q. 193. What do we pray for in the fourth petition?

A. In the fourth petition, (which is, *Give us this day our daily bread*,[1]) acknowledging, that in Adam, and by our own sin, we have forfeited our right to all the outward blessings of this life, and deserve to be wholly deprived of them by God, and to have them cursed to us in the use of them;[2] and that neither they of themselves are able to sustain us,[3] nor we to merit,[4] or by our own industry to procure them;[5] but prone to desire,[6] get,[7] and use them unlawfully:[8] we pray for ourselves and others, that both they and we, waiting upon the providence of God from day to day in the use of lawful means, may, of his free gift, and as to his fatherly wisdom shall seem best, enjoy a competent portion of them;[9] and have the same continued and blessed unto us in our holy and comfortable use of them,[10] and contentment in them;[11] and be kept from all things that are contrary to our temporal support and comfort.[12]

9 Jer. 31:18–19.
10 Ps. 19:14; Acts 21:14. (See Ps. 119; 1 Thess. 5:23; Heb. 13:20–21.)
11 Mic. 6:8.
12 Ps. 100:2; Job 1:21; 2 Sam. 15:25–26.
13 Isa. 38:3.
14 Ps. 119:4–5.
15 Ps. 69:9; John 2:17; Rom. 12:11.
16 Josh. 24:14; Ps. 119:80; 1 Cor. 5:8. (See 2 Cor. 1:12.)
17 Ps. 119:112.
18 Isa. 6:2–3; Ps. 103:20–21; Matt. 18:10.
Q. 193
1 Matt. 6:11. (Cf. Luke 11:3.)
2 Gen. 2:17; Gen. 3:17; Rom. 8:20–22; Jer. 5:25; Deut. 28:15–68.
3 Deut. 8:3.
4 Gen. 32:10.
5 Deut. 8:17–18.
6 Jer. 6:13; Mark 7:21–22.
7 Hos. 12:7.
8 James 4:3.
9 Gen. 43:12–14; Gen. 28:20; Eph. 4:28; 2 Thess. 3:11–12; Phil. 4:6.
10 1 Tim. 4:3–5.
11 1 Tim. 6:6–8.
12 Prov. 30:8–9.

Q. 194. What do we pray for in the fifth petition?

A. In the fifth petition, (which is, *Forgive us our debts, as we forgive our debtors,*[1]) acknowledging, that we and all others are guilty both of original and actual sin, and thereby become debtors to the justice of God; and that neither we, nor any other creature, can make the least satisfaction for that debt:[2] we pray for ourselves and others, that God of his free grace would, through the obedience and satisfaction of Christ, apprehended and applied by faith, acquit us both from the guilt and punishment of sin,[3] accept us in his Beloved;[4] continue his favor and grace to us,[5] pardon our daily failings,[6] and fill us with peace and joy, in giving us daily more and more assurance of forgiveness;[7] which we are the rather emboldened to ask, and encouraged to expect, when we have this testimony in ourselves, that we from the heart forgive others their offenses.[8]

Q. 195. What do we pray for in the sixth petition?

A. In the sixth petition, (which is, *And lead us not into temptation, but deliver us from evil,*[1]) acknowledging, that the most wise, righteous, and gracious God, for divers holy and just ends, may so order things, that we may be assaulted, foiled, and for a time led captive by temptations;[2] that Satan,[3] the world,[4] and the flesh, are ready powerfully to draw us aside, and ensnare us;[5] and that we, even after the pardon of our sins, by reason of our corruption,[6]

Q. 194
1 Matt. 6:12. (Cf. Luke 11:4.)
2 Rom. 3:9–22; Matt. 18:24–25; Ps. 130:3–4.
3 Rom. 3:24–26; Heb. 9:22.
4 Eph. 1:6–7.
5 2 Peter 1:2.
6 Hos. 14:2; Jer. 14:7; 1 John 1:9. (See Dan. 9:17–19.)
7 Rom. 15:13; Ps. 51:7–10, 12.
8 Luke 11:4; Matt. 6:14–15; Eph. 4:32; Col. 3:13. (See Matt. 18:21–35.)
Q. 195
1 Matt. 6:13. (Cf. Luke 11:4.)
2 2 Chron. 32:31.
3 1 Chron. 21:1.
4 Luke 21:34; Mark 4:19.
5 James 1:14.
6 Gal. 5:17.

weakness, and want of watchfulness,[7] are not only subject to be tempted, and forward to expose ourselves unto temptations,[8] but also of ourselves unable and unwilling to resist them, to recover out of them, and to improve them;[9] and worthy to be left under the power of them:[10] we pray, that God would so overrule the world and all in it,[11] subdue the flesh,[12] and restrain Satan,[13] order all things,[14] bestow and bless all means of grace,[15] and quicken us to watchfulness in the use of them, that we and all his people may by his providence be kept from being tempted to sin;[16] or, if tempted, that by his Spirit we may be powerfully supported and enabled to stand in the hour of temptation;[17] or when fallen, raised again and recovered out of it,[18] and have a sanctified use and improvement thereof:[19] that our sanctification and salvation may be perfected,[20] Satan trodden under our feet,[21] and we fully freed from sin, temptation, and all evil, forever.[22]

Q. 196. What doth the conclusion of the Lord's Prayer teach us?

A. The conclusion of the Lord's Prayer, (which is, *For thine is the kingdom, and the power, and the glory, for ever. Amen.*[1]) teacheth us to enforce our petitions with arguments,[2] which are to be taken, not from any worthiness in ourselves, or in any other creature, but from God;[3] and with our prayers to join praises,[4]

---

7 Matt. 26:41.
8 Matt. 26:69–72; Gal. 2:11–14; 2 Chron. 18:3; 2 Chron. 19:2.
9 Rom. 7:23–24; 1 Chron. 21:1–4; 2 Chron. 16:7–10.
10 Ps. 81:11–12.
11 John 17:15.
12 Ps. 51:10; Ps. 119:133.
13 2 Cor. 12:7–8.
14 1 Cor. 10:12–13.
15 Heb. 13:20–21.
16 Matt. 26:41; Ps. 19:13.
17 Eph. 3:14–17; 1 Thess. 3:13; Jude 24.
18 Ps. 51:12.
19 1 Peter 5:8–10.
20 2 Cor. 13:7, 9.
21 Rom. 16:20; Luke 22:31–32.
22 John 17:15; 1 Thess. 5:23.
Q. 196
1 Matt. 6:13.
2 Rom. 15:30.
3 Dan. 9:4, 7–9, 16–19.
4 Phil. 4:6.

ascribing to God alone eternal sovereignty, omnipotency, and glorious excellency;[5] in regard whereof, as he is able and willing to help us,[6] so we by faith are emboldened to plead with him that he would,[7] and quietly to rely upon him, that he will fulfill our requests.[8] And, to testify this our desire and assurance, we say, *Amen.*[9]

5   1 Chron. 29:10–13; 1 Tim. 1:17; Rev. 5:11–13.
6   Eph. 3:20–21; Luke 11:13.
7   2 Chron. 20:6, 11.
8   2 Chron. 14:11.
9   1 Cor. 14:16; Rev. 22:20–21.

18

Westminster Shorter Catechism

(1646–47)

When Parliament called the Westminster Assembly, it asked not only for a confession but also for a means of catechizing the faithful. A committee of the assembly undertook this work but soon found it difficult to produce a catechism that was both deep enough for the learned in the faith and accessible to those unschooled in the faith. The committee thus decided to produce two catechisms.

The Shorter Catechism was based on the Larger Catechism but was aimed at those who were newer in the faith, including covenant children and adult converts. It presents a clear and simple introduction to the Reformed faith, and it has been used and memorized in Presbyterian churches and households for generations.

For more background on the Westminster Assembly, see the introduction to the Westminster Confession of Faith.

Westminster Shorter Catechism

Q. 1. What is the chief end of man?

A. Man's chief end is to glorify God,[1] and to enjoy him forever.[2]

Q. 2. What rule hath God given to direct us how we may glorify and enjoy him?

A. The Word of God, which is contained in the Scriptures of the Old and New Testaments,[1] is the only rule to direct us how we may glorify and enjoy him.[2]

Q. 3. What do the Scriptures principally teach?

A. The Scriptures principally teach, what man is to believe concerning God,[1] and what duty God requires of man.[2]

Q. 1

1 Ps. 86:9; Isa. 60:21; Rom. 11:36; 1 Cor. 6:20; 1 Cor. 10:31; Rev. 4:11.
2 Ps. 16:5–11; Ps. 144:15; Isa. 12:2; Luke 2:10; Phil. 4:4; Rev. 21:3–4.

Q. 2

1 Matt. 19:4–5 (with Gen. 2:24); Luke 24:27, 44; 1 Cor. 2:13; 1 Cor. 14:37; 2 Peter 1:20–21; 2 Peter 3:2, 15–16.
2 Deut. 4:2; Ps. 19:7–11; Isa. 8:20; John 15:11; John 20:30–31; Acts 17:11; 2 Tim. 3:15–17; 1 John 1:4.

Q. 3

1 Gen. 1:1; John 5:39; John 20:31; Rom. 10:17; 2 Tim. 3:15.
2 Deut. 10:12–13; Josh. 1:8; Ps. 119:105; Mic. 6:8; 2 Tim. 3:16–17.

Q. 4. What is God?

A. God is a Spirit,[1] infinite,[2] eternal,[3] and unchangeable,[4] in his being,[5] wisdom,[6] power,[7] holiness,[8] justice,[9] goodness,[10] and truth.[11]

Q. 5. Are there more Gods than one?

A. There is but one only,[1] the living and true God.[2]

Q. 6. How many persons are there in the Godhead?

A. There are three persons in the Godhead; the Father, the Son, and the Holy Ghost;[1] and these three are one God, the same in substance, equal in power and glory.[2]

Q. 7. What are the decrees of God?

A. The decrees of God are, his eternal purpose, according to the counsel of his will, whereby, for his own glory, he hath foreordained whatsoever comes to pass.[1]

Q. 8. How doth God execute his decrees?

A. God executeth his decrees in the works of creation and providence.[1]

Q. 4
1 Deut. 4:15–19; Luke 24:39; John 1:18; John 4:24; Acts 17:29.
2 1 Kings 8:27; Ps. 139:7–10; Ps. 145:3; Ps. 147:5; Jer. 23:24; Rom. 11:33–36.
3 Deut. 33:27; Ps. 90:2; Ps. 102:12, 24–27; Rev. 1:4, 8.
4 Ps. 33:11; Mal. 3:6; Heb. 1:12; Heb. 6:17–18; Heb. 13:8; James 1:17.
5 Ex. 3:14; Ps. 115:2–3; 1 Tim. 1:17; 1 Tim. 6:15–16.
6 Ps. 104:24; Rom. 11:33–34; Heb. 4:13; 1 John 3:20.
7 Gen. 17:1; Ps. 62:11; Jer. 32:17; Matt. 19:26; Rev. 1:8.
8 Hab. 1:13; 1 Peter 1:15–16; 1 John 3:3, 5; Rev. 15:4.
9 Gen. 18:25; Ex. 34:6–7; Deut. 32:4; Ps. 96:13; Rom. 3:5, 26.
10 Ps. 103:5; Ps. 107:8; Matt. 19:17; Rom. 2:4.
11 Ex. 34:6; Deut. 32:4; Ps. 86:15; Ps. 117:2; Heb. 6:18.
Q. 5
1 Deut. 6:4; Isa. 44:6; Isa. 45:21–22; 1 Cor. 8:4–6.
2 Jer. 10:10; John 17:3; 1 Thess. 1:9; 1 John 5:20.
Q. 6
1 Matt. 3:16–17; Matt. 28:19; 2 Cor. 13:14; 1 Peter 1:2.
2 Ps. 45:6; John 1:1; John 17:5; Acts 5:3–4; Rom. 9:5; Col. 2:9; Jude 24–25.
Q. 7
1 Ps. 33:11; Isa. 14:24; Acts 2:23; Eph. 1:11–12.
Q. 8
1 Ps. 148:8; Isa. 40:26; Dan. 4:35; Acts 4:24–28; Rev. 4:11.

Q. 9. What is the work of creation?

A. The work of creation is, God's making all things of nothing, by the word of his power,[1] in the space of six days, and all very good.[2]

Q. 10. How did God create man?

A. God created man male and female, after his own image,[1] in knowledge,[2] righteousness, and holiness,[3] with dominion over the creatures.[4]

Q. 11. What are God's works of providence?

A. God's works of providence are, his most holy,[1] wise,[2] and powerful[3] preserving[4] and governing[5] all his creatures, and all their actions.[6]

Q. 12. What special act of providence did God exercise towards man in the estate wherein he was created?

A. When God had created man, he entered into a covenant of life with him, upon condition of perfect obedience; forbidding him to eat of the tree of the knowledge of good and evil, upon pain of death.[1]

Q. 13. Did our first parents continue in the estate wherein they were created?

A. Our first parents, being left to the freedom of their own will, fell from the estate wherein they were created, by sinning against God.[1]

Q. 9
1   Gen. 1:1; Ps. 33:6, 9; Heb. 11:3.
2   Gen. 1:31.
Q. 10
1   Gen. 1:27.
2   Col. 3:10.
3   Eph. 4:24.
4   Gen. 1:28. (See Ps. 8.)
Q. 11
1   Ps. 145:17.
2   Ps. 104:24.
3   Heb. 1:3.
4   Neh. 9:6.
5   Eph. 1:19–22.
6   Ps. 36:6; Prov. 16:33; Matt. 10:30.
Q. 12
1   Gen. 2:16–17; James 2:10.
Q. 13
1   Gen. 3:6–8, 13; 2 Cor. 11:3.

Q. 14. What is sin?

A. Sin is any want of conformity unto, or transgression of, the law of God.[1]

Q. 15. What was the sin whereby our first parents fell from the estate wherein they were created?

A. The sin whereby our first parents fell from the estate wherein they were created, was their eating the forbidden fruit.[1]

Q. 16. Did all mankind fall in Adam's first transgression?

A. The covenant being made with Adam,[1] not only for himself, but for his posterity; all mankind, descending from him by ordinary generation, sinned in him, and fell with him, in his first transgression.[2]

Q. 17. Into what estate did the fall bring mankind?

A. The fall brought mankind into an estate of sin and misery.[1]

Q. 18. Wherein consists the sinfulness of that estate whereinto man fell?

A. The sinfulness of that estate whereinto man fell, consists in the guilt of Adam's first sin,[1] the want of original righteousness,[2] and the corruption of his whole nature,[3] which is commonly called original sin; together with all actual transgressions which proceed from it.[4]

Q. 14
1   Lev. 5:17; James 4:17; 1 John 3:4.
Q. 15
1   Gen. 3:6.
Q. 16
1   Gen. 2:16–17; James 2:10.
2   Rom. 5:12–21; 1 Cor. 15:22.
Q. 17
1   Gen. 3:16–19, 23; Rom. 3:16; Rom. 5:12; Eph. 2:1.
Q. 18
1   Rom. 5:12, 19.
2   Rom. 3:10; Col. 3:10; Eph. 4:24.
3   Ps. 51:5; John 3:6; Rom. 3:18; Rom. 8:7–8; Eph. 2:3.
4   Gen. 6:5; Ps. 53:1–3; Matt. 15:19; Rom. 3:10–18, 23; Gal. 5:19–21; James 1:14–15.

Q. 19. What is the misery of that estate whereinto man fell?

A. All mankind by their fall lost communion with God,[1] are under his wrath[2] and curse,[3] and so made liable to all the miseries of this life,[4] to death[5] itself, and to the pains of hell forever.[6]

Q. 20. Did God leave all mankind to perish in the estate of sin and misery?

A. God, having out of his mere good pleasure, from all eternity, elected some to everlasting life,[1] did enter into a covenant of grace to deliver them out of the estate of sin and misery, and to bring them into an estate of salvation by a Redeemer.[2]

Q. 21. Who is the Redeemer of God's elect?

A. The only Redeemer of God's elect is the Lord Jesus Christ,[1] who, being the eternal Son of God,[2] became man,[3] and so was, and continueth to be, God and man in two distinct natures, and one person, forever.[4]

Q. 22. How did Christ, being the Son of God, become man?

A. Christ, the Son of God, became man, by taking to himself a true body, and a reasonable soul,[1] being conceived by the power of the Holy Ghost, in the womb of the Virgin Mary, and born of her,[2] yet without sin.[3]

Q. 19
1   Gen. 3:8, 24; John 8:34, 42, 44; Eph. 2:12; Eph. 4:18.
2   John 3:36; Rom. 1:18; Eph. 2:3; Eph. 5:6.
3   Gal. 3:10; Rev. 22:3.
4   Gen. 3:16–19; Job 5:7; Eccl. 2:22–23; Rom. 8:18–23.
5   Ezek. 18:4; Rom. 5:12; Rom. 6:23.
6   Matt. 25:41, 46; 2 Thess. 1:9; Rev. 14:9–11.
Q. 20
1   Acts 13:48; Eph. 1:4–5; 2 Thess. 2:13–14.
2   Gen. 3:15; Gen. 17:7; Ex. 19:5–6; Jer. 31:31–34; Matt. 20:28; 1 Cor. 11:25; Heb. 9:15.
Q. 21
1   John 14:6; Acts 4:12; 1 Tim. 2:5–6.
2   Ps. 2:7; Matt. 3:17; Matt. 17:5; John 1:18.
3   Isa. 9:6; Matt. 1:23; John 1:14; Gal. 4:4.
4   Acts 1:11; Heb. 7:24–25.
Q. 22
1   Phil. 2:7; Heb. 2:14, 17.
2   Luke 1:27; 31, 35.
3   2 Cor. 5:21; Heb. 4:15; Heb. 7:26; 1 John 3:5.

Q. 23. What offices doth Christ execute as our Redeemer?

A. Christ, as our Redeemer, executeth the offices of a prophet,[1] of a priest,[2] and of a king,[3] both in his estate of humiliation and exaltation.

Q. 24. How doth Christ execute the office of a prophet?

A. Christ executeth the office of a prophet, in revealing to us, by his Word[1] and Spirit,[2] the will of God for our salvation.[3]

Q. 25. How doth Christ execute the office of a priest?

A. Christ executeth the office of a priest, in his once offering up of himself a sacrifice to satisfy divine justice,[1] and reconcile us to God,[2] and in making continual intercession for us.[3]

Q. 26. How doth Christ execute the office of a king?

A. Christ executeth the office of a king, in subduing us to himself, in ruling and defending us,[1] and in restraining and conquering all his and our enemies.[2]

Q. 27. Wherein did Christ's humiliation consist?

A. Christ's humiliation consisted in his being born, and that in a low condition,[1] made under the law,[2] undergoing the miseries of this life,[3] the wrath

---

Q. 23
1 Deut. 18:18; Acts 2:33; Acts 3:22–23; Heb. 1:1–2.
2 Heb. 4:14–15; Heb. 5:5–6.
3 Isa. 9:6–7; Luke 1:32–33; John 18:37; 1 Cor. 15:25.
Q. 24
1 Luke 4:18–19, 21; Acts 1:1–2; Heb. 2:3.
2 John 15:26–27; Acts 1:8; 1 Peter 1:11.
3 John 4:41–42; John 20:30–31.
Q. 25
1 Isa. 53; Acts 8:32–35; Heb. 9:26–28; Heb. 10:12.
2 Rom. 5:10–11; 2 Cor. 5:18; Col. 1:21–22.
3 Rom. 8:34; Heb. 7:25; Heb. 9:24.
Q. 26
1 Ps. 110:3; Matt. 28:18–20; John 17:2; Col. 1:13.
2 Ps. 2:6–9; Ps. 110:1–2; Matt. 12:28; 1 Cor. 15:24–26; Col. 2:15.
Q. 27
1 Luke 2:7; 2 Cor. 8:9; Gal. 4:4.
2 Gal. 4:4.
3 Isa. 53:3; Luke 9:58; John 4:6; John 11:35; Heb. 2:18.

of God,[4] and the cursed death of the cross;[5] in being buried, and continuing under the power of death for a time.[6]

Q. 28. Wherein consisteth Christ's exaltation?

A. Christ's exaltation consisteth in his rising again from the dead on the third day,[1] in ascending up into heaven,[2] in sitting at the right hand of God the Father,[3] and in coming to judge the world at the last day.[4]

Q. 29. How are we made partakers of the redemption purchased by Christ?

A. We are made partakers of the redemption purchased by Christ, by the effectual application of it to us by his Holy Spirit.[1]

Q. 30. How doth the Spirit apply to us the redemption purchased by Christ?

A. The Spirit applieth to us the redemption purchased by Christ, by working faith in us,[1] and thereby uniting us to Christ in our effectual calling.[2]

Q. 31. What is effectual calling?

A. Effectual calling is the work of God's Spirit, whereby, convincing us of our sin and misery, enlightening our minds in the knowledge of Christ,[1] and renewing our wills,[2] he doth persuade and enable us to embrace Jesus Christ,[3] freely offered to us in the gospel.[4]

---

4 Ps. 22:1; Matt. 27:46; Isa. 53:10; 1 John 2:2.
5 Gal. 3:13; Phil. 2:8.
6 Matt. 12:40; 1 Cor. 15:3–4.
Q. 28
1 1 Cor. 15:4.
2 Ps. 68:18; Acts 1:11; Eph. 4:8.
3 Ps. 110:1; Acts 2:33–34; Heb. 1:3.
4 Matt. 16:27; Acts 17:31.
Q. 29
1 Titus 3:4–7.
Q. 30
1 Rom. 10:17; 1 Cor. 2:12–16; Eph. 2:8; Phil. 1:29.
2 John 15:5; 1 Cor. 1:9; Eph. 3:17.
Q. 31
1 Acts 26:18; 1 Cor. 2:10, 12; 2 Cor. 4:6; Eph. 1:17–18.
2 Deut. 30:6; Ezek. 36:26–27; John 3:5; Titus 3:5.
3 John 6:44–45; Acts 16:14.
4 Isa. 45:22; Matt. 11:28–30; Rev. 22:17.

Q. 32. What benefits do they that are effectually called partake of in this life?

A. They that are effectually called do in this life partake of justification, adoption, and sanctification, and the several benefits which in this life do either accompany or flow from them.[1]

Q. 33. What is justification?

A. Justification is an act of God's free grace,[1] wherein he pardoneth all our sins,[2] and accepteth us as righteous in his sight,[3] only for the righteousness of Christ imputed to us,[4] and received by faith alone.[5]

Q. 34. What is adoption?

A. Adoption is an act of God's free grace,[1] whereby we are received into the number, and have a right to all the privileges, of the sons of God.[2]

Q. 35. What is sanctification?

A. Sanctification is the work of God's free grace,[1] whereby we are renewed in the whole man after the image of God,[2] and are enabled more and more to die unto sin, and live unto righteousness.[3]

Q. 32
1 Rom. 8:30; 1 Cor. 1:30; 1 Cor. 6:11; Eph. 1:5.
Q. 33
1 Rom. 3:24.
2 Rom. 4:6–8; 2 Cor. 5:19.
3 2 Cor. 5:21.
4 Rom. 4:6, 11; Rom. 5:19.
5 Gal. 2:16; Phil. 3:9.
Q. 34
1 1 John 3:1.
2 John 1:12; Rom. 8:17.
Q. 35
1 Ezek. 36:27; Phil. 2:13; 2 Thess. 2:13.
2 2 Cor. 5:17; Eph. 4:23–24; 1 Thess. 5:23.
3 Ezek. 36:25–27; Rom. 6:4, 6, 12–14; 2 Cor. 7:1; 1 Peter 2:24.

Q. 36. What are the benefits which in this life do accompany or flow from justification, adoption, and sanctification?

A. The benefits which in this life do accompany or flow from justification, adoption, and sanctification, are, assurance of God's love,[1] peace of conscience,[2] joy in the Holy Ghost,[3] increase of grace,[4] and perseverance therein to the end.[5]

Q. 37. What benefits do believers receive from Christ at death?

A. The souls of believers are at their death made perfect in holiness,[1] and do immediately pass into glory;[2] and their bodies, being still united to Christ,[3] do rest in their graves, till the resurrection.[4]

Q. 38. What benefits do believers receive from Christ at the resurrection?

A. At the resurrection, believers, being raised up in glory,[1] shall be openly acknowledged and acquitted in the day of judgment,[2] and made perfectly blessed in the full enjoying of God[3] to all eternity.[4]

Q. 39. What is the duty which God requireth of man?

A. The duty which God requireth of man, is obedience to his revealed will.[1]

Q. 36
1 Rom. 5:5.
2 Rom. 5:1.
3 Rom. 14:17.
4 2 Peter 3:18.
5 Phil. 1:6; 1 Peter 1:5.
Q. 37
1 Heb. 12:23.
2 Luke 23:43; 2 Cor. 5:6, 8; Phil. 1:23.
3 1 Thess. 4:14.
4 Dan. 12:2; John 5:28–29; Acts 24:15.
Q. 38
1 1 Cor. 15:42–43.
2 Matt. 25:33–34, 46.
3 Rom. 8:29; 1 John 3:2.
4 Ps. 16:11; 1 Thess. 4:17.
Q. 39
1 Deut. 29:29; Mic. 6:8; 1 John 5:2–3.

Q. 40. What did God at first reveal to man for the rule of his obedience?

A. The rule which God at first revealed to man for his obedience, was the moral law.[1]

Q. 41. Wherein is the moral law summarily comprehended?

A. The moral law is summarily comprehended in the Ten Commandments.[1]

Q. 42. What is the sum of the Ten Commandments?

A. The sum of the Ten Commandments is, to love the Lord our God with all our heart, with all our soul, with all our strength, and with all our mind; and our neighbor as ourselves.[1]

Q. 43. What is the preface to the Ten Commandments?

A. The preface to the Ten Commandments is in these words, *I am the LORD thy God, which have brought thee out of the land of Egypt, out of the house of bondage.*[1]

Q. 44. What doth the preface to the Ten Commandments teach us?

A. The preface to the Ten Commandments teacheth us, that because God is the Lord, and our God, and Redeemer, therefore we are bound to keep all his commandments.[1]

Q. 45. Which is the first commandment?

A. The first commandment is, *Thou shalt have no other gods before me.*[1]

Q. 40
1 Rom. 2:14–15; Rom. 10:5.
Q. 41
1 Deut. 4:13; Matt. 19:17–19.
Q. 42
1 Matt. 22:37–40.
Q. 43
1 Ex. 20:2; Deut. 5:6.
Q. 44
1 Luke 1:74–75; 1 Peter 1:14–19.
Q. 45
1 Ex. 20:3; Deut. 5:7.

Q. 46. What is required in the first commandment?

A. The first commandment requireth us to know and acknowledge God to be the only true God, and our God; and to worship and glorify him accordingly.[1]

Q. 47. What is forbidden in the first commandment?

A. The first commandment forbiddeth the denying,[1] or not worshiping and glorifying, the true God as God,[2] and our God;[3] and the giving of that worship and glory to any other, which is due to him alone.[4]

Q. 48. What are we specially taught by these words, *before me*, in the first commandment?

A. These words, *before me*, in the first commandment teach us, that God, who seeth all things, taketh notice of, and is much displeased with, the sin of having any other God.[1]

Q. 49. Which is the second commandment?

A. The second commandment is, *Thou shalt not make unto thee any graven image, or any likeness of any thing that is in heaven above, or that is in the earth beneath, or that is in the water under the earth: thou shalt not bow down thyself to them, nor serve them: for I the LORD thy God am a jealous God, visiting the iniquity of the fathers upon the children unto the third and fourth generation of them that hate me; and shewing mercy unto thousands of them that love me, and keep my commandments.*[1]

Q. 46
1   1 Chron. 28:9; Isa. 45:20–25; Matt. 4:10.
Q. 47
1   Ps. 14:1.
2   Rom. 1:20–21.
3   Ps. 81:10–11.
4   Ezek. 8:16–18; Rom. 1:25.
Q. 48
1   Deut. 30:17–18; Ps. 44:20–21; Ezek. 8:12.
Q. 49
1   Ex. 20:4–6; Deut. 5:8–10.

Q. 50. What is required in the second commandment?

A. The second commandment requireth the receiving, observing, and keeping pure and entire, all such religious worship and ordinances as God hath appointed in his Word.[1]

Q. 51. What is forbidden in the second commandment?

A. The second commandment forbiddeth the worshiping of God by images,[1] or any other way not appointed in his Word.[2]

Q. 52. What are the reasons annexed to the second commandment?

A. The reasons annexed to the second commandment are, God's sovereignty over us,[1] his propriety in us,[2] and the zeal he hath to his own worship.[3]

Q. 53. Which is the third commandment?

A. The third commandment is, *Thou shalt not take the name of the* LORD *thy God in vain: for the Lord will not hold him guiltless that taketh his name in vain.*[1]

Q. 54. What is required in the third commandment?

A. The third commandment requireth the holy and reverent use of God's names, titles,[1] attributes,[2] ordinances,[3] Word,[4] and works.[5]

Q. 50
1 Deut. 12:32; Matt. 28:20.
Q. 51
1 Deut. 4:15–19; Rom. 1:22–23.
2 Lev. 10:1–2; Jer. 19:4–5; Col. 2:18–23.
Q. 52
1 Ps. 95:2–3, 6–7; Ps. 96:9–10.
2 Ex. 19:5; Ps. 45:11; Isa. 54:5.
3 Ex. 34:14; 1 Cor. 10:22.
Q. 53
1 Ex. 20:7; Deut. 5:11.
Q. 54
1 Deut. 10:20; Ps. 29:2; Matt. 6:9.
2 1 Chron. 29:10–13; Rev. 15:3–4.
3 Acts 2:42; 1 Cor. 11:27–28.
4 Ps. 138:2; Rev. 22:18–19.
5 Ps. 107:21–22; Rev. 4:11.

Q. 55. What is forbidden in the third commandment?

A. The third commandment forbiddeth all profaning or abusing of anything whereby God maketh himself known.[1]

Q. 56. What is the reason annexed to the third commandment?

A. The reason annexed to the third commandment is, that however the breakers of this commandment may escape punishment from men, yet the Lord our God will not suffer them to escape his righteous judgment.[1]

Q. 57. Which is the fourth commandment?

A. The fourth commandment is, *Remember the sabbath day, to keep it holy. Six days shalt thou labour, and do all thy work: but the seventh day is the sabbath of the* LORD *thy God: in it thou shalt not do any work, thou, nor thy son, nor thy daughter, thy manservant, nor thy maidservant, nor thy cattle, nor thy stranger that is within thy gates: for in six days the* LORD *made heaven and earth, the sea, and all that in them is, and rested the seventh day: wherefore the* LORD *blessed the sabbath day, and hallowed it.*[1]

Q. 58. What is required in the fourth commandment?

A. The fourth commandment requireth the keeping holy to God such set times as he hath appointed in his Word; expressly one whole day in seven, to be a holy Sabbath to himself.[1]

Q. 55
1   Lev. 19:12; Matt. 5:33–37; James 5:12.
Q. 56
1   Deut. 28:58–59; 1 Sam. 3:13; 1 Sam. 4:11.
Q. 57
1   Ex. 20:8–11; Deut. 5:12–15.
Q. 58
1   Ex. 31:13, 16–17.

Q. 59. Which day of the seven hath God appointed to be the weekly Sabbath?

A. From the beginning of the world to the resurrection of Christ, God appointed the seventh day of the week to be the weekly Sabbath;[1] and the first day of the week ever since, to continue to the end of the world, which is the Christian Sabbath.[2]

Q. 60. How is the Sabbath to be sanctified?

A. The Sabbath is to be sanctified by a holy resting all that day, even from such worldly employments and recreations as are lawful on other days;[1] and spending the whole time in the public and private exercises of God's worship,[2] except so much as is to be taken up in the works of necessity and mercy.[3]

Q. 61. What is forbidden in the fourth commandment?

A. The fourth commandment forbiddeth the omission, or careless performance, of the duties required, and the profaning the day by idleness, or doing that which is in itself sinful, or by unnecessary thoughts, words, or works, about our worldly employments or recreations.[1]

Q. 62. What are the reasons annexed to the fourth commandment?

A. The reasons annexed to the fourth commandment are, God's allowing us six days of the week for our own employments,[1] his challenging a special propriety in the seventh, his own example, and his blessing the Sabbath day.[2]

Q. 59
1 Gen. 2:2–3; Ex. 20:11.
2 Mark 2:27–28; Acts 20:7; 1 Cor. 16:2; Rev. 1:10.
Q. 60
1 Ex. 20:10; Neh. 13:15–22; Isa. 58:13–14.
2 Ex. 20:8; Lev. 23:3; Luke 4:16; Acts 20:7.
3 Matt. 12:1–13.
Q. 61
1 Neh. 13:15–22; Isa. 58:13–14; Amos 8:4–6.
Q. 62
1 Ex. 20:9; Ex. 31:15; Lev. 23:3.
2 Gen. 2:2–3; Ex. 20:11; Ex. 31:17.

Q. 63. Which is the fifth commandment?

A. The fifth commandment is, *Honour thy father and thy mother: that thy days may be long upon the land which the* LORD *thy God giveth thee.*[1]

Q. 64. What is required in the fifth commandment?

A. The fifth commandment requireth the preserving the honor, and performing the duties, belonging to everyone in their several places and relations, as superiors, inferiors, or equals.[1]

Q. 65. What is forbidden in the fifth commandment?

A. The fifth commandment forbiddeth the neglecting of, or doing anything against, the honor and duty which belongeth to everyone in their several places and relations.[1]

Q. 66. What is the reason annexed to the fifth commandment?

A. The reason annexed to the fifth commandment is, a promise of long life and prosperity (as far as it shall serve for God's glory and their own good) to all such as keep this commandment.[1]

Q. 67. Which is the sixth commandment?

A. The sixth commandment is, *Thou shalt not kill.*[1]

Q. 68. What is required in the sixth commandment?

A. The sixth commandment requireth all lawful endeavors to preserve our own life, and the life of others.[1]

Q. 63
1   Ex. 20:12; Deut. 5:16.
Q. 64
1   Rom. 13:1, 7; Eph. 5:21–22, 24; Eph. 6:1, 4–5, 9; 1 Peter 2:17.
Q. 65
1   Matt. 15:4–6; Rom. 13:8.
Q. 66
1   Ex. 20:12; Deut. 5:16; Eph. 6:2–3.
Q. 67
1   Ex. 20:13; Deut. 5:17.
Q. 68
1   Eph. 5:28–29.

Q. 69. What is forbidden in the sixth commandment?

A. The sixth commandment forbiddeth the taking away of our own life, or the life of our neighbor unjustly, or whatsoever tendeth thereunto.[1]

Q. 70. Which is the seventh commandment?

A. The seventh commandment is, *Thou shalt not commit adultery.*[1]

Q. 71. What is required in the seventh commandment?

A. The seventh commandment requireth the preservation of our own and our neighbor's chastity, in heart, speech, and behavior.[1]

Q. 72. What is forbidden in the seventh commandment?

A. The seventh commandment forbiddeth all unchaste thoughts, words, and actions.[1]

Q. 73. Which is the eighth commandment?

A. The eighth commandment is, *Thou shalt not steal.*[1]

Q. 74. What is required in the eighth commandment?

A. The eighth commandment requireth the lawful procuring and furthering the wealth and outward estate of ourselves and others.[1]

Q. 69
1   Gen. 9:6; Matt. 5:22; 1 John 3:15.
Q. 70
1   Ex. 20:14; Deut. 5:18.
Q. 71
1   1 Cor. 7:2–3, 5; 1 Thess. 4:3–5.
Q. 72
1   Matt. 5:28; Eph. 5:3–4.
Q. 73
1   Ex. 20:15; Deut. 5:19.
Q. 74
1   Lev. 25:35; Eph. 4:28b; Phil. 2:4.

Q. 75. What is forbidden in the eighth commandment?

A. The eighth commandment forbiddeth whatsoever doth, or may, unjustly hinder our own, or our neighbor's, wealth or outward estate.[1]

Q. 76. Which is the ninth commandment?

A. The ninth commandment is, *Thou shalt not bear false witness against thy neighbour.*[1]

Q. 77. What is required in the ninth commandment?

A. The ninth commandment requireth the maintaining and promoting of truth between man and man, and of our own and our neighbor's good name,[1] especially in witness bearing.[2]

Q. 78. What is forbidden in the ninth commandment?

A. The ninth commandment forbiddeth whatsoever is prejudicial to truth, or injurious to our own, or our neighbor's, good name.[1]

Q. 79. Which is the tenth commandment?

A. The tenth commandment is, *Thou shalt not covet thy neighbour's house, thou shalt not covet thy neighbour's wife, nor his manservant, nor his maidservant, nor his ox, nor his ass, nor any thing that is thy neighbour's.*[1]

Q. 75
1 Prov. 28:19ff.; Eph. 4:28a; 2 Thess. 3:10; 1 Tim. 5:8.
Q. 76
1 Ex. 20:16; Deut. 5:20.
Q. 77
1 Zech. 8:16; Acts 25:10; 3 John 12.
2 Prov. 14:5, 25.
Q. 78
1 Lev. 19:16; Ps. 15:3; Prov. 6:16–19; Luke 3:14.
Q. 79
1 Ex. 20:17; Deut. 5:21.

Q. 80. What is required in the tenth commandment?

A. The tenth commandment requireth full contentment with our own condition,[1] with a right and charitable frame of spirit toward our neighbor, and all that is his.[2]

Q. 81. What is forbidden in the tenth commandment?

A. The tenth commandment forbiddeth all discontentment with our own estate,[1] envying or grieving at the good of our neighbor, and all inordinate motions and affections to anything that is his.[2]

Q. 82. Is any man able perfectly to keep the commandments of God?

A. No mere man, since the fall, is able in this life perfectly to keep the commandments of God, but doth daily break them in thought, word, and deed.[1]

Q. 83. Are all transgressions of the law equally heinous?

A. Some sins in themselves, and by reason of several aggravations, are more heinous in the sight of God than others.[1]

Q. 84. What doth every sin deserve?

A. Every sin deserveth God's wrath and curse, both in this life, and that which is to come.[1]

Q. 80
1 Ps. 34:1; Phil. 4:11; 1 Tim. 6:6; Heb. 13:5.
2 Luke 15:6, 9, 11–32; Rom. 12:15; Phil. 2:4.
Q. 81
1 1 Cor. 10:10; James 3:14–16.
2 Gal. 5:26; Col. 3:5.
Q. 82
1 Gen. 8:21; Rom. 3:9ff., 23.
Q. 83
1 Ezek. 8:6, 13, 15; Matt. 11:20–24; John 19:11.
Q. 84
1 Matt. 25:41; Gal. 3:10; Eph. 5:6; James 2:10.

Q. 85. What doth God require of us, that we may escape his wrath and curse, due to us for sin?

A. To escape the wrath and curse of God, due to us for sin, God requireth of us faith in Jesus Christ, repentance unto life,[1] with the diligent use of all the outward means whereby Christ communicateth to us the benefits of redemption.[2]

Q. 86. What is faith in Jesus Christ?

A. Faith in Jesus Christ is a saving grace,[1] whereby we receive and rest upon him alone for salvation, as he is offered to us in the gospel.[2]

Q. 87. What is repentance unto life?

A. Repentance unto life is a saving grace,[1] whereby a sinner, out of a true sense of his sin, and apprehension of the mercy of God in Christ,[2] doth, with grief and hatred of his sin, turn from it unto God,[3] with full purpose of, and endeavor after, new obedience.[4]

Q. 88. What are the outward and ordinary means whereby Christ communicateth to us the benefits of redemption?

A. The outward and ordinary means whereby Christ communicateth to us the benefits of redemption are, his ordinances, especially the Word, sacraments, and prayer; all which are made effectual to the elect for salvation.[1]

Q. 85
1   Mark 1:15; Acts 20:21.
2   Acts 2:38; 1 Cor. 11:24–25; Col. 3:16.
Q. 86
1   Eph. 2:8–9. (Cf. Rom. 4:16.)
2   John 20:30–31; Gal. 2:15–16; Phil. 3:3–11.
Q. 87
1   Acts 11:18; 2 Tim. 2:25.
2   Ps. 51:1–4; Joel 2:13; Luke 15:7, 10; Acts 2:37.
3   Jer. 31:18–19; Luke 1:16–17; 1 Thess. 1:9.
4   2 Chron. 7:14; Ps. 119:57–64; Matt. 3:8; 2 Cor. 7:10.
Q. 88
1   Matt. 28:18–20; Acts 2:41–42.

Q. 89. How is the Word made effectual to salvation?

A. The Spirit of God maketh the reading, but especially the preaching, of the Word, an effectual means of convincing and converting sinners, and of building them up in holiness and comfort, through faith, unto salvation.[1]

Q. 90. How is the Word to be read and heard, that it may become effectual to salvation?

A. That the Word may become effectual to salvation, we must attend thereunto with diligence, preparation, and prayer;[1] receive it with faith and love, lay it up in our hearts, and practice it in our lives.[2]

Q. 91. How do the sacraments become effectual means of salvation?

A. The sacraments become effectual means of salvation, not from any virtue in them, or in him that doth administer them; but only by the blessing of Christ, and the working of his Spirit in them that by faith receive them.[1]

Q. 92. What is a sacrament?

A. A sacrament is a holy ordinance instituted by Christ;[1] wherein, by sensible signs, Christ, and the benefits of the new covenant, are represented, sealed, and applied to believers.[2]

Q. 93. Which are the sacraments of the New Testament?

A. The sacraments of the New Testament are, baptism,[1] and the Lord's Supper.[2]

Q. 89
1   Neh. 8:8–9; Acts 20:32; Rom. 10:14–17; 2 Tim. 3:15–17.
Q. 90
1   Deut. 6:16ff.; Ps. 119:18; 1 Peter 2:1–2.
2   Ps. 119:11; 2 Thess. 2:10; Heb. 4:2; James 1:22–25.
Q. 91
1   1 Cor. 3:7. (Cf. 1 Cor. 1:12–17.)
Q. 92
1   Matt. 28:19; Matt. 26:26–28; Mark 14:22–25; Luke 22:19–20; 1 Cor. 1:22–26.
2   Gal. 3:27; 1 Cor. 10:16–17.
Q. 93
1   Matt. 28:19.
2   1 Cor. 11:23–26.

Q. 94. What is baptism?

A. Baptism is a sacrament, wherein the washing with water in the name of the Father, and of the Son, and of the Holy Ghost,[1] doth signify and seal our ingrafting into Christ, and partaking of the benefits of the covenant of grace, and our engagement to be the Lord's.[2]

Q. 95. To whom is baptism to be administered?

A. Baptism is not to be administered to any that are out of the visible church, till they profess their faith in Christ, and obedience to him;[1] but the infants of such as are members of the visible church are to be baptized.[2]

Q. 96. What is the Lord's Supper?

A. The Lord's Supper is a sacrament, wherein, by giving and receiving bread and wine, according to Christ's appointment, his death is showed forth;[1] and the worthy receivers are, not after a corporal and carnal manner, but by faith, made partakers of his body and blood, with all his benefits, to their spiritual nourishment, and growth in grace.[2]

Q. 97. What is required for the worthy receiving of the Lord's Supper?

A. It is required of them that would worthily partake of the Lord's Supper, that they examine themselves of their knowledge to discern the Lord's body, of their faith to feed upon him, of their repentance, love, and new obedience; lest, coming unworthily, they eat and drink judgment to themselves.[1]

Q. 94
1   Matt. 28:19.
2   Acts 2:38–42; Acts 22:16; Rom. 6:3–4; Gal. 3:26–27; 1 Peter 3:21.
Q. 95
1   Acts 2:41; Acts 8:12, 36, 38; Acts 18:8.
2   Gen. 17:7, 9–11; Acts 2:38–39; Acts 16:32–33; Col. 2:11–12.
Q. 96
1   Luke 22:19–20; 1 Cor. 11:23–26.
2   1 Cor. 10:16–17.
Q. 97
1   1 Cor. 11:27–32.

Q. 98. What is prayer?

A. Prayer is an offering up of our desires unto God,[1] for things agreeable to his will,[2] in the name of Christ,[3] with confession of our sins,[4] and thankful acknowledgment of his mercies.[5]

Q. 99. What rule hath God given for our direction in prayer?

A. The whole Word of God is of use to direct us in prayer;[1] but the special rule of direction is that form of prayer which Christ taught his disciples, commonly called the Lord's Prayer.[2]

Q. 100. What doth the preface of the Lord's Prayer teach us?

A. The preface of the Lord's Prayer, which is, *Our Father which art in heaven*, teacheth us to draw near to God with all holy reverence[1] and confidence,[2] as children to a father,[3] able and ready to help us;[4] and that we should pray with and for others.[5]

Q. 101. What do we pray for in the first petition?

A. In the first petition, which is, *Hallowed be thy name*, we pray that God would enable us, and others, to glorify him in all that whereby he maketh himself known;[1] and that he would dispose all things to his own glory.[2]

Q. 98
1 Ps. 10:17; Ps. 62:8; Matt. 7:7–8.
2 1 John 5:14.
3 John 16:23–24.
4 Ps. 32:5–6; Dan. 9:4–19; 1 John 1:9.
5 Ps. 103:1–5; Ps. 136; Phil. 4:6.
Q. 99
1 1 John 5:14.
2 Matt. 6:9–13.
Q. 100
1 Ps. 95:6.
2 Eph. 3:12.
3 Matt. 7:9–11 (cf. Luke 11:11–13); Rom. 8:15.
4 Eph. 3:20.
5 Eph. 6:18; 1 Tim. 2:1–2.
Q. 101
1 Ps. 67:1–3; Ps. 99:3; Ps. 100:3–4.
2 Rom. 11:33–36; Rev. 4:11.

Q. 102. What do we pray for in the second petition?

A. In the second petition, which is, *Thy kingdom come*, we pray that Satan's kingdom may be destroyed;[1] and that the kingdom of grace may be advanced,[2] ourselves and others brought into it, and kept in it;[3] and that the kingdom of glory may be hastened.[4]

Q. 103. What do we pray for in the third petition?

A. In the third petition, which is, *Thy will be done in earth, as it is in heaven*, we pray that God, by his grace, would make us able and willing to know, obey, and submit to his will in all things,[1] as the angels do in heaven.[2]

Q. 104. What do we pray for in the fourth petition?

A. In the fourth petition, which is, *Give us this day our daily bread*, we pray that of God's free gift we may receive a competent portion of the good things of this life, and enjoy his blessing with them.[1]

Q. 105. What do we pray for in the fifth petition?

A. In the fifth petition, which is, *And forgive us our debts, as we forgive our debtors*, we pray that God, for Christ's sake, would freely pardon all our sins;[1] which we are the rather encouraged to ask, because by his grace we are enabled from the heart to forgive others.[2]

Q. 102
1 Matt. 12:25–28; Rom. 16:20; 1 John 3:8.
2 Ps. 72:8–11; Matt. 24:14; 1 Cor. 15:24–25.
3 Ps. 119:5; Luke 22:32; 2 Thess. 3:1–5.
4 Rev. 22:20.
Q. 103
1 Ps. 19:14; Ps. 119; 1 Thess. 5:23; Heb. 13:20–21.
2 Ps. 103:20–21; Heb. 1:14.
Q. 104
1 Prov. 30:8–9; Matt. 6:31–34; Phil. 4:11, 19; 1 Tim. 6:6–8.
Q. 105
1 Ps. 51:1–2, 7, 9; Dan. 9:17–19; 1 John 1:7.
2 Matt. 18:21–35; Eph. 4:32; Col. 3:13.

Q. 106. What do we pray for in the sixth petition?

A. In the sixth petition, which is, *And lead us not into temptation, but deliver us from evil*, we pray that God would either keep us from being tempted to sin,[1] or support and deliver us when we are tempted.[2]

Q. 107. What doth the conclusion of the Lord's Prayer teach us?

A. The conclusion of the Lord's Prayer, which is, *For thine is the kingdom, and the power, and the glory, for ever. Amen*, teacheth us to take our encouragement in prayer from God only,[1] and in our prayers to praise him, ascribing kingdom, power, and glory to him;[2] and, in testimony of our desire, and assurance to be heard, we say, *Amen*.[3]

Q. 106
1 Ps. 19:13; Matt. 26:41; John 17:15.
2 Luke 22:31–32; 1 Cor. 10:13; 2 Cor. 12:7–9; Heb. 2:18.
Q. 107
1 Dan. 9:4, 7–9, 16–19; Luke 18:1, 7–8.
2 1 Chron. 29:10–13; 1 Tim. 1:17; Rev. 5:11–13.
3 1 Cor. 14:16; Rev. 22:20.

19

Savoy Declaration

(1658)

The religious landscape of England in the seventeenth century was marked by differences over worship, theology, piety, and more, but especially controversial was church polity. For every committed Episcopalian there was a divine-right Presbyterian who believed presbyterian polity was instituted by God for the church and a Congregationalist who asserted that the Scriptures taught absolute local church autonomy.

The Savoy Declaration represents the definitive statement of English Puritan Congregationalism. It is a revision of the Westminster Confession of Faith, and it was drafted by a group that included John Owen, one of the most important theologians of the Reformed tradition of Christianity.

The reestablishment of the monarchy and of episcopacy meant that the Savoy Declaration was largely rendered insignificant in England by the end of the seventeenth century, but it enjoyed greater reception in New England.

Savoy Declaration

PREFACE

Confession of the Faith that is in us, when justly called for, is so indispensable a due all owe to the Glory of the Sovereign God, that it is ranked among the Duties of the first Commandment, such as Prayer is; and therefore by Paul yoked with Faith itself, as necessary to salvation: with the heart man believeth unto righteousness, and with the mouth confession is made unto salvation. Our Lord Christ himself, when he was accused of his Doctrine, considered simply as a matter of fact by Preaching, refused to answer; because, as such, it lay upon evidence, and a matter of testimony of others; unto whom therefore he refers himself: But when both the High-Priest and Pilate expostulate his Faith, and what he held himself to be; he without any demur at all, cheerfully makes his Declaration, That he was the Son of God; so to the High-Priest: and that he was a King, and born to be a King; thus to Pilate. Though upon the uttering of it his life lay at stake; Which holy Profession of his is celebrated for our example, 1 Tim. 6:13.

Confessions, when made by a company of Professors of Christianity jointly meeting to that end, the most genuine and natural use of such Confessions is, That under the same form of words, they express the substance of the same common salvation or unity of their faith; whereby speaking the same things, they show themselves perfectly joined in the same mind, and in the same judgment, 1 Cor. 1:10.

And accordingly such a transaction is to be looked upon but as a meet or fit medium or means whereby to express that their common faith and salvation, and no way to be made use of as an imposition upon any: Whatever is of force or constraint in matters of this nature, causeth them to degenerate from the name and nature of Confessions, and turns them from being Confessions of Faith, into Exactions and Impositions of Faith.

And such common Confessions of the Orthodox faith, made in simplicity of heart by any such body of Christians, with concord among themselves, ought to be entertained by all others that love the truth as it is in Jesus, with an answerable rejoicing: For if the unanimous opinions and assertions but in some few points of Religion, and that when by two Churches, namely, that of Jerusalem, and the Messengers of Antioch met, assisted by some of the Apostles, were by the Believers of those times received with so much joy, (as it is said, They rejoiced for the consolation) much more this is to be done, when the whole substance of Faith, and form of wholesome words shall be declared by the Messengers of a multitude of Churches, though wanting those advantages of Counsel and Authority of the Apostles, which that Assembly had.

Which acceptation is then more specially due, when these shall (to choose) utter and declare their Faith, in the same substance for matter, yea, words, for the most part, that other Churches and Assemblies, reputed the most Orthodox, have done before them: For upon such a correspondency, all may see that actually accomplished, which the Apostle did but exhort unto, and pray for, in those two more eminent Churches of the Corinthians and the Romans, (and so in them for all the Christians of his time) that both Jew and Gentile, that is, men of different persuasions, (as they were) might glorify God with one mind and with one mouth. And truly, the very turning of the Gentiles to the owning of the same Faith, in the substance of it, with the Christian Jew (though differing in greater points than we do from our Brethren) is presently after dignified by the Apostle with this style, That it is the Confession of Jesus Christ himself; not as the Object only, but as the Author and Maker thereof: I will confess to thee (saith Christ to God) among the Gentiles. So that in all such accords, Christ is the great and first Confessor; and we, and all our Faith uttered by Us, are but the Epistles, (as Paul) and Confessions (as Isaiah there) of their Lord and ours; He, but expressing what is written in his heart, through their hearts and mouths, to the glory of God the Father: And shall we not all rejoice herein, when as Christ himself is said to do it upon this occasion: as it there also follows, I will sing unto thy Name.

Further, as the soundness and wholesomeness of the matter gives the vigor and life to such Confessions, so the inward freeness, willingness, and readiness of the Spirits of the Confessors do contribute to the beauty and loveliness thereunto: As it is in Prayer to God, so in Confessions made to men. If two or three met, do agree, it renders both, to either the more acceptable. The

Spirit of Christ is in himself too free, great and generous a Spirit, to suffer himself to be used by any human arm, to whip men into belief; he drives not, but gently leads into all truth, and persuades men to dwell in the tents of like precious Faith; which would lose of its preciousness and value, if that sparkle of freeness shone not in it: The Character of his People, is to be a willing people in the day of his power (not Man's) in the beauties of holiness, which are the Assemblings of the Saints: one glory of which Assemblings in that first Church, is said to have been, They met with one accord; which is there in that Psalm prophesied of, in the instance of that first Church, for all other that should succeed.

And as this great Spirit is in himself free, when, and how far, and in whom to work, so where and when he doth work, he carrieth it with the same freedom, and is said to be a free Spirit, as he both is, and works in us: And where this Spirit of the Lord is, there is liberty.

Now as to this Confession of ours, besides, that a conspicuous conjunction of the particulars mentioned, hath appeared therein: There are also four remarkable Attendants thereon, which added, might perhaps in the eyes of sober and indifferent Spirits, give the whole of this Transaction a room and rank amongst other many good and memorable things of this Age; at least all set together, do cast as clear a gleam and manifestation of God's Power and Presence, as hath appeared in any such kind of Confessions, made by so numerous a company these later years.

The first, is the Temper (or distemper rather) of the Times, during which, these Churches have been gathering, and which they have run through. All do (out of a general sense) complain that these times have been perilous, or difficult times (as the Apostle foretold); and that in respect to danger from seducing spirits, more perilous than the hottest seasons of Persecution.

We have failed through an Aestuation, Fluxes and Refluxes of great varieties of Spirits, Doctrines, Opinions and Occurrences, and especially in the matter of Opinions, which have been accompanied in their several seasons, with powerful persuasions and temptations, to seduce those of our way. It is known, men have taken the freedom (notwithstanding what Authority hath interposed to the contrary) to vent and vend their own vain and accursed imaginations, contrary to the great and fixed Truths of the Gospel, insomuch, as to take the whole Round and Circle of Delusions, the Devil hath in this small time, ran; it will be found, that every Truth, of greater or lesser weight, hath by one or the other hand, at one time or another, been questioned and called to the Bar amongst us, yea, and impleaded, under the pretext (which hath some degree of Justice in it) that all should not be bound up to the Traditions of former times, nor take Religion upon trust.

Whence it hath come to pass, that many of the soundest Professors were put upon a new search and disquisition of such Truths, as they had taken for granted, and yet had lived upon the comfort of: to the end they might be able to convince others, and establish their own hearts against that darkness and unbelief, that is ready to close with error, or at least to doubt of the truth, when error is speciously presented. And hereupon we do professedly account it one of the greatest advantages gained out of the Temptations of these Times, yea the honor of the Saints and Ministers of these Nations, That after they had sweetly been exercised in, and had improved practical and experimental Truths, this should be their further Lot, to examine and discuss, and indeed anew to learn over every Doctrinal Truth, both out of the Scriptures, and also with a fresh taste thereof in their own hearts; which is no other than what the Apostle exhorts to, Try all things, hold fast that which is good. Conversion unto God at first, what is it else than a savory and affectionate application, and the bringing home to the heart with spiritual light and life, all truths that are necessary to salvation, together with other lesser Truths? All which we had afore conversion taken in but notionally from common Education and Tradition.

Now that after this first gust those who have been thus converted should be put upon a new probation and search out the Scriptures, not only of all principles explicitly ingredients to Conversion; (unto which the Apostle referreth the Galatians when they had diverted from them) but of all other superstructures as well as fundamentals; and together therewith, anew to experiment the power and sweetness of all these in their own souls: What is this but tried Faith indeed? And equivalent to a new conversion unto the truth? An Anchor that is proved to be sure and steadfast, that will certainly hold in all contrary storms. This was the eminent seal and commendation which those holy Apostles that lived and wrote last (Peter, John and Jude in their Epistles) did set and give to the Christians of the latter part of those primitive times. And besides, it is clear and evident by all the other Epistles, from first to last, that it cost the Apostles as much, and far more care and pains to preserve them they had converted, in the truth, than they had taken to turn them thereunto at first: And it is in itself as great a work and instance of the power of God, that keeps, yea, guards us through faith unto salvation.

Secondly, let this be added (or superadded rather) to give full weight and measure, even to running over, that we have all along this season, held forth (though quarreled with for it by our brethren) this great principle of these times, That amongst all Christian States and Churches, there ought to be vouchsafed a forbearance and mutual indulgence unto Saints of all persuasions, that keep unto, and hold fast the necessary foundations of faith and holiness, in all other matters extra fundamental, whether of Faith or Order.

This to have been our constant principle, we are not ashamed to confess to the whole Christian world. Wherein yet we desire we may be understood, not as if in the abstract we stood indifferent to falsehood or truth, or were careless whether faith or error, in any Truths but fundamental, did obtain or not, so we had our liberty in our petty and smaller differences; or as if to make sure of that, we had cut out this wide cloak for it: No, we profess that the whole, and every particle of that Faith delivered to the Saints (the substance of which we have according to our light here professed) is, as to the propagation and furtherance of it by all Gospel means, as precious to us as our lives; or what can be supposed dear to us; and in our sphere we have endeavored to promote them accordingly: But yet withal, we have and do contend for this, That in the concrete, the persons of all such gracious Saints, they and their errors, as they are in them, when they are but such errors as do and may stand with communion with Christ, though they should not repent of them, as not being convinced of them to the end of their days; that those, with their errors (that are purely spiritual, and intrench and overthrow not civil societies,) as concrete with their persons, should for Christ's sake be borne withal by all Christians in the world; and they notwithstanding be permitted to enjoy all Ordinances and spiritual Privileges according to their light, as freely as any other of their brethren that pretend to the greatest Orthodoxy; as having as equal, and as fair a right in and unto Christ, and all the holy things of Christ, that any other can challenge to themselves.

And this doth afford a full and invincible testimony on our behalf, in that whiles we have so earnestly contended for this just liberty of Saints in all the

Churches of Christ, we ourselves have no need of it: that is, as to the matter of the profession of Faith which we have maintained together with others: and of this, this subsequent Confession of Faith gives sufficient evidence. So as we have the confidence in Christ, to utter in the words of those two great Apostles, That we have stood fast in the liberty wherewith Christ hath made us free (in the behalf of others, rather than ourselves) and having been free, have not made use of our liberty for a cloak of error or maliciousness in ourselves. And yet, lo, whereas from the beginning of the rearing of these Churches, that of the Apostle hath been (by some) prophesied of us, and applied to us, That while we promised (unto others) liberty, we ourselves would become servants of corruption, and be brought in bondage to all sorts of fancies and imaginations, yet the whole world may now see after the experience of many years ran through (and it is manifest by this Confession) that the great and gracious God hath not only kept us in that common unity of the Faith and Knowledge of the Son of God, which the whole Community of Saints have and shall in their Generations come unto, but also in the same Truths, both small and great, that are built thereupon, that any other of the best and more pure Reformed Churches in their best times (which were their first times) have arrived unto: This Confession withal holding forth a professed opposition unto the common errors and heresies of these times.

These two considerations have been taken from the seasons we have gone through.

Thirdly, let the space of time itself, or days, wherein from first to last the whole of this Confession was framed and consented to by the whole of us, be duly considered by sober and ingenious spirits: the whole of days in which we had meetings about it (set aside the two Lord's days, and the first day's meeting, in which we considered and debated what to pitch upon) were but 11 days, part of which also was spent by some of us in Prayer, others in consulting; and in the end all agreeing. We mention this small circumstance but to this end (which still adds unto the former) That it gives demonstration, not of our freeness and willingness only, but of our readiness and preparedness unto so great a work; which otherwise, and in other Assemblies, hath ordinarily taken up long and great debates, as in such a variety of matters of such concernment, may well be supposed to fall out. And this is no other than what the Apostle Peter exhorts unto, Be ready always to give an answer to every man that asketh you a reason, or account of the hope that is in you. The Apostle Paul saith of the spiritual Truths of the Gospel, That God hath prepared them for those that love him. The inward and innate constitution of the new Creature being in itself such as is suited to all those Truths, as congenial thereunto: But although there be this mutual adaptness between these two, yet such is the mixture of ignorance, darkness and unbelief, carnal reason, pre-occupation of judgment, interest of parties, wantonness in opinion, proud adhering to our own persuasions, and perverse oppositions and averseness to agree with others, and a multitude of such like distempers common to believing man: All which are not only mixed with, but at times (especially in such times as have passed over our heads) are ready to overcloud our judgments, and to cause our eyes to be double, and sometimes prevail as well as lusts, and do bias our wills and affections: And such is their mixture, that although there may be existent an habitual preparedness in men's spirits, yet not always a present readiness to be found, specially not in such a various multitude of men, to make a solemn and deliberate profession of all truths, it being as great a work to find the spirits of the just (perhaps the best of Saints) ready for every truth, as to be prepared to every good work.

It is therefore to be looked at, as a great and special work of the Holy Ghost, that so numerous a company of Ministers, and other principal brethren, should so readily, speedily, and jointly give up themselves unto such a whole Body of Truths that are after godliness.

This argues that they had not their faith to seek; but, as is said of Ezra, that they were ready Scribes, and (as Christ) instructed unto the Kingdom of Heaven, being as the good householders of so many families of Christ, bringing forth of their store and treasury New and Old. It shows these truths had been familiar to them, and they acquainted with them, as with their daily food and provision (as Christ's allusion there insinuates): In a word, that so they had preached, and that so their people had believed, as the Apostle speaks upon one like particular occasion. And the Apostle Paul considers (in cases of this nature) the suddenness or length of time, either one way or the other; whether it were in men's forsaking of learning of the truth. Thus the suddenness in the Galatians' case in leaving the truth, he makes a wonder of it: I marvel that you are so soon (that is, in so short a time) removed from the true Gospel unto another. Again on the contrary, in the Hebrews he aggravates their backwardness, That when for the first time you ought to be Teachers, you had need that one teach you the very first principles of the Oracles of God. The Parallel contrary to both these having fallen out in this transaction, may have some ingredient and weight with ingenious spirits in its kind, according to the proportion is put upon either of these forementioned in their adverse kind, and obtain the like special observation.

This accord of ours hath fallen out without having held any correspondency together, or prepared consultation, by which we might come to be advised of one another's minds. We allege this not as a matter of commendation in us; no, we acknowledge it to have been a great neglect: And accordingly one of the first proposals for union amongst us was, That there might be a constant correspondence held among the Churches for counsel and mutual edification, so for time to come to present the like omission.

We confess that from the first, every [one], or at least the generality of our Churches, have been in a manner like so many Ships (though holding forth the same general colors) launched singly, and sailing apart and alone on the vast Ocean of these tumultuating times, and they exposed to every wind of Doctrine, under no other conduct than the Word and Spirit, and their particular Elders and principal Brethren, without Associations among ourselves, or so much as holding out common lights to others, whereby to know where we are.

But yet whilst we thus confess to our own shame this neglect, let all acknowledge, that God hath ordered it for his high and greater glory, in that his singular care and power should have watched over each of these, as that all should be found to have steered their course by the same Chart, and to have been bound for one and the same Port, and that upon this general search now made, that the same holy and blessed truths of all sorts, which are current and warrantable amongst all the other Churches of Christ in the world, should be found to be our Lading.

The whole, and every [one] of these things when put together, do cause us (whatever men of prejudiced and opposite spirits may find out to slight them) with a holy admiration, to say, That this is no other than the Lord's doing; and which we with thanksgiving do take from his hand as a special token upon us for good, and doth show that God is faithful and upright towards those that are planted in his house: And that as the Faith was but once for all, and intentionally first delivered unto the Saints; so the Saints, when not abiding scattered, but gathered under their respective Pastors according to God's heart into an house, and Churches unto the living God, such together are, as Paul forspake it, the most steady and firm pillar and seat of Truth that God hath any where appointed to himself on earth, where his truth is best conserved, and publicly held forth; there being in such Assemblies weekly a rich dwelling of the Word amongst them, that is, a daily open house kept by the means of those good Householders, their Teachers and other Instructors respectively appropriated to them, whom Christ in the virtue of his Ascension, continues to give as gifts to his people, himself dwelling amongst them; to the end that by this, as the most sure standing permanent means, the Saints might be perfected, till we all (even all the Saints in present and future ages) do come by this constant and daily Ordinance of his unto the unity of the Faith and Knowledge of the Son of God unto a perfect man, unto the measure of the stature of the fullness of Christ (which though growing on by parts and piece-meal, will yet appear complete, when that great and general Assembly shall be gathered, then when this world is ended, and these dispensations have had their fullness and period) and so that from henceforth (such a provision being made for us) we be no more children tossed to and fro, and carried about with every wind of Doctrine.

And finally, this doth give a fresh and recent demonstration, that the great Apostle and High-Priest of our profession is indeed ascended into heaven, and continues there with power and care, faithful as a son over his own house, whose house are we, if we hold fast the confidence and the rejoicing of the hope firm unto the end: and shows that he will, as he hath promised, be with his own Institutions to the end of the world.

It is true, that many sad miscarriages, and divisions, breaches, fallings off from holy Ordinances of God, have along this time of tentation (especially in the beginning of it) been found in some of our Churches; and no wonder, if what hath been said be fully considered: Many reasons might further be given hereof, that would be a sufficient Apology, without the help of a retortion upon other Churches (that promised themselves peace) how that more destroying ruptures have befallen them, and that in a wider sphere and compass; which though it should not justify us, yet may serve to stop others' mouths.

Let Rome glory of the peace in, and obedience of her Children, against the Reformed Churches for their divisions which occurred (especially in the first rearing of them) whilst we all know the causes of their dull and stupid peace to have been carnal interests, worldly correspondencies, and coalitions, strengthened by gratifications of all sorts of men by that Religion, the principles of blind Devotion, Traditional Faith, Ecclesiastical Tyranny, by which she keeps her Children in bondage to this day. We are also certain, that the very same prejudices that from hence they would cast upon the Reformed (if they were just) do lie as fully against those pure Churches raised up by the Apostles themselves in those first times: for as we have heard of their patience, sufferings, consolations, and the transcending gifts poured out, and graces shining in them, so we have heard complaints of their divisions too, of the forsakings of their Assemblies, as the custom or manner of some was (which later were in that respect felo de se, and needed no other delivering up to Satan as their punishment, than what they executed upon themselves). We read of the shipwreck also of Faith and a good Conscience, and overthrowings of the faith of some; and still but of some not all, nor the most: which is one piece of an Apology the Apostle again and again inserts to future ages, and through mercy we have the same to make.

And truly we take the confidence professedly to say, that these tentations common to the purest Churches of Saints separated from the mixture of the world, though they grieve us (for who is offended, and we burn not?), yet they do not at all stumble us, as to the truth of our way, had they been many more: We say it again, these stumble us no more (as to that point) than it doth offend us against the power of Religion itself, to have seen, and to see daily in particular persons called out and separated from the world by an effectual work of conversion, that they for a while do suffer under disquietments, vexations, turmoils, unsettlements of spirit, that they are tossed with tempests and horrid tentations, such as they had not in their former estate, whilst they walked according to the course of this world: For Peter hath sufficiently instructed us whose business it is to raise such storms, even the Devil's; and also whose design it is, that after they have suffered a while, thereby they shall be settled, perfected, established, that have so suffered, even the God of all Grace. And look what course of dispensation God holds to Saints personally, he doth the like to bodies of Saints in Churches and the Devil the same for his part too: And that consolatory Maxim of the Apostle, God shall tread down Satan under your feet shortly, which Paul uttereth concerning the Church of Rome, shows how both God and Satan have this very hand therein; for he speaks that very thing in reference unto their divisions, as the coherence clearly manifests; and so you have both designs expressed at once.

Yea, we are not a little induced to think, that the divisions, breaches, etc., of those primitive Churches would not have been so frequent among the people themselves, and not the Elders only, had not the freedom, liberties, and rights of Members (the Brethren, we mean) been stated and exercised in those Churches, the same which we maintain and contend for to be in ours.

Yea (which perhaps may seem more strange to many) had not those Churches been constituted of members enlightened further than with notional and traditional knowledge, by a new and more powerful light of the Holy Ghost, wherein they had been made partakers of the Holy Ghost and the heavenly gift, and their hearts had tasted the good Word of God, and the Powers of the world to come, and of such Members at lowest, there had not fallen out those kinds of divisions among them.

For Experience hath shown, that the common sort of mere Doctrinal Professors (such as the most are nowadays), whose highest education is but freedom from moral scandal, joined with devotion to Christ through mere Education, such as in many Turks is found towards Mohammed, that these finding and feeling themselves not much concerned in the active part of Religion, so they may have the honor (especially upon a Reformation of a new Refinement) that themselves are approved Members, admitted to the Lord's Supper, and their Children to the Ordinance of Baptism; they regard not other matters (as Gallio did not), but do easily and readily give up themselves unto their Guides, being like dead fishes carried with the common stream; whereas those that have a further renewed Light by a work of the Holy Ghost, whether saving or temporary, are upon the quite contrary grounds apt to be busy about, and inquisitive into, what they are to receive and practice, or wherein their Consciences are professedly concerned and involved: And thereupon they take the freedom to examine and try the spirits, whether of God or no: And from hence are more apt to dissatisfaction, and from thence to run into division, and many of such proving to be enlightened but with a temporary, not saving Faith (who have such a work of the Spirit upon them, and profession in them, as will and doth approve itself to the judgment of the Saints, and ought to be so judged, until they be otherwise discovered) who at long-run, prove hypocrites, through indulgence unto Lusts, and then out of their Lusts persist to hold up these divisions unto breach of, or departings from, Churches, and the Ordinances of God, and God is even with them for it, they waxing worse and worse, deceiving and being deceived; and even many of those that are sincere, through a mixture of darkness and erroneousness in their Judgments, are for a season apt out of Conscience to be led away with the error of others, which lie in wait to deceive.

Insomuch as the Apostle upon the example of those first times, forseeing also the like events in following generations upon the causes, hath been bold to set this down as a ruled Case, that likewise in other Churches so constituted and de facto emprivileged as that of the Church of Corinth was (which single Church, in the Sacred Records about it, is the completest Mirror of Church Constitution, Order, and Government, and Events thereupon ensuing, of any one Church whatever that we have a story of), his Maxim is, There must be also divisions amongst you; he setly inserts an [also] in the case, as that which had been his own observation, and that which would be ἐπὶ τὸ πολὺ the fate of the other Churches like thereunto, so prophesieth he: And he speaks this as peremptorily, as he doth elsewhere in that other, We must through tribulations enter into the Kingdom of Heaven: Yea, and that all that will live godly in Christ Jesus, shall suffer persecution: There is a [must] upon both alike; and we bless God, that we have run through both, and do say, and we say no more, That as it was then, so it is now, in both respects.

However, such hath been the powerful hand of God's providence in these, which have been the worst of our Trials, That out of an approved Experience and Observation of the Issue, we are able to add that other part of the Apostle's Prediction, That therefore such rents must be, that they which are approved may be made manifest among you; which holy issue God (as having aimed at it therein) doth frequently and certainly bring about in Churches, as he doth bring upon them that other fate of division, Let them therefore look unto it, that are the Authors of such disturbances, as the Apostle warneth, Gal. 5:10. The experiment is this, That we have seen, and do daily see, that multitudes of holy and precious souls, and (in the Holy Ghost's word) approved Saints, have been, and are the more rooted and grounded by means of these shakings, and do continue to cleave the faster to Christ, and the purity of his Ordinances, and value them the more by this cost God hath put them to for the enjoying of them, Who having been planted in the House of the Lord, have flourished in the Courts of our God, in these evil times, to show that the Lord is upright. And this experimented event from out of such divisions, hath more confirmed us, and is a louder Apology for us, than all that our opposites are able from our breaches to allege to prejudice us.

We will add a few words for conclusion, and give a more particular account of this our Declaration. In drawing up this Confession of Faith, we have had before us the Articles of Religion, approved and passed by both Houses of Parliament, after advice had with an Assembly of Divines, called together by them for that purpose. To which Confession, for the substance of it, we fully assent, as do our Brethren of New England, and the Churches also of Scotland, as each in their general Synods have testified.

A few things we have added for obviating some erroneous Opinions, that have been more broadly and boldly here of late maintained by the Asserters, than in former times; and made other additions and alterations in method, here and there, and some clearer Explanations, as we found occasion.

We have endeavored throughout, to hold such Truths in this our Confession, as are more properly termed matters of Faith; and what is of Church-order, we dispose in certain Propositions by itself. To this course we are led by the Example of the Honorable Houses of Parliament, observing what was established, and what omitted by them in that Confession the Assembly presented to them. Who thought it is not convenient to have matters of Discipline and Church Government put into a Confession of Faith, especially the particulars thereof, as then were, and still are controverted and under dispute by men Orthodox and found in Faith. The 30th chap. Therefore of that Confession, as it was presented to them by the Assembly, which is of Church Censures, their Use, Kinds, and in whom placed: As also chap. 31, of Synods and Councils, by whom to be called, of what force in their Decrees and Determinations. And the 4th Paragr. of the 20th chap., which determines what Opinions and Practices disturb the peace of the Church, and how such Disturbers ought to be proceeded against by the Censures of the Church, and punished by the Civil Magistrate. Also a great part of the 24th chap. of Marriage and Divorce. These were such doubtful assertions, and so unsuitable to a Confession of

Faith, as the Honorable Houses in their great Wisdom thought fit to lay them aside: There being nothing that tends more to heighten Dissensions among Brethren, than to determine and adopt the manner of their difference, under so high a Title, as to be an Article of our Faith: So that there are two whole Chapters, and some Paragraphs in other Chapters in their Confession, that we have upon this account omitted; and the rather do we give this notice, because that Copy of the Parl. followed by us, is in few men's hands; the other as it came from the Assembly, being approved of in Scotland, was printed and hastened into the world, before the Parl. had declared their Resolutions about it; which was not till June 20, 1648, and yet had been, and continueth to be the Copy (ordinarily) only sold, printed, and reprinted for these 11 years.

After the 19th chap. of the Law, we have added a cap. of the Gospel, it being a Title that may not well be omitted in a Confession of Faith: In which Chapter, what is dispersed, and by intimation in the Assemblies' Confession, with some little addition, is here brought together, and more fully, under one head.

That there are not Scriptures annexed, as in some Confessions (though in divers others it's otherwise), we give the same account as did the Reverend Assembly in the same case; which was this: "The Confession being large, and so framed, as to meet with the common errors, if the Scriptures should have been alleged with any clearness, and by showing where the strength of the proof lieth, it would have required a Volume."

We say further, it being our utmost end in this (as it is indeed of a Confession) humbly to give an account what we hold and assert in these matters; that others, especially the Churches of Christ may judge of us accordingly: This we aimed at, and not so much to instruct others, or convince gainsayers. These are the proper works of other Institutions of Christ, and are to be done in the strength of express Scripture. A Confession is an Ordinance of another nature.

What we have laid down and asserted about Churches and their Government, we humbly conceive to be the Order which Christ himself hath appointed to be observed, we have endeavored to follow Scripture light; and those also that went before us according to that Rule, desirous of nearest uniformity with Reforming Churches, as with our Brethren in New England, so with others, that differ from them and us.

The Models and Platforms of this subject laid down by learned men, and practiced by Churches, are various: We do not judge it brotherly, or grateful, to insist upon comparisons, as some have done; but this Experience teacheth, That the variety, and possibly the Disputes and Emulations arising thence, have much strengthened, if not fixed, this unhappy persuasion in the minds of some learned and good men, namely, That there is no settled Order laid down in Scripture; but it's left to the Prudence of the Christian Magistrate, to compose or make a choice of such a Form as is most suitable and consistent with their Civil Government. Where this Opinion is entertained in the persuasion of Governors, there, Churches asserting their Power and Order to be jure divino, and the appointment of Jesus Christ, can have no better nor more honorable Entertainment, than a Toleration or Permission.

Yet herein there is this remarkable advantage to all parties that differ, about what is in Government is of Christ's appointment; in that such Magistrates have a far greater latitude in conscience, to tolerate and permit the several forms of each so bound up in their persuasion, than they have to submit unto what the Magistrate shall impose: And thereupon the Magistrate exercising and indulgency and forbearance, with protection and encouragement to the people of God, so differing from him, and amongst themselves: Doth therein discharge as great a faithfulness to Christ, and love to his people, as can any way be supposed and expected from any Christian Magistrate, of what persuasion soever he is. And where this clemency from Governors is shown to any sort of persons, or Churches of Christ, upon such a principle, it will in equity produce this just effect, That all that so differ from him, and amongst themselves, standing in equal and alike difference from the principle of such a Magistrate, he is equally free to give alike liberty to them, one as well as the other.

This faithfulness in our Governors we do with thankfulness to God acknowledge, and to their everlasting honor, which appeared much in the late Reformation. The Hierarchy, Common Prayer-Book, and all other things grievous to God's People, being removed, they made choice of an Assembly of learned men, to advise what Government and Order is meet to be established in the room of these things; and because it was known there were different opinions (as always hath been among godly men) about forms of Church Government, there was by the Ordinance first sent forth to call an Assembly, not only a choice made of persons of several persuasions, to sit as Members there, but liberty given, to a lesser number, if dissenting, to report their Judgments and Reasons, as well and as freely as the major part.

Hereupon the Honorable House of Commons (an Indulgence we hope will never be forgotten) finding by Papers received from them, that the Members of the Assembly were not like to compose differences among themselves, so as to join in the same Rule for Church Government, did order further as followeth: That a Committee of Lords and Commons, etc., do take into consideration the differences of the Opinions in the Assembly of Divines in point of Church government, and to endeavor a union if it be possible; and in case that cannot be done, to endeavor the finding out some way, how far tender consciences, who can not in all things submit to the same Rule which that be established, may be born according to the Word, and as may stand with the Public Peace.

By all which it is evident, the Parliament purposed not to establish the Rule of Church Government with such rigor, as might not permit and bear with a practice different from what they had established: In persons and Churches of different principles, if occasion were. And this Christian Clemency and indulgence in our Governors, hath been the foundation of that Freedom and Liberty, in the managing of Church affairs, which our Brethren, as well as WE, that differ from them, do now, and have many years enjoyed.

The Honorable Houses by several Ordinances of Parliament after much consultation, having settled Rules for Church Government, and such an Ecclesiastical Order as they judged would best joint with the Laws and Government of the Kingdom, did publish them, requiring the practice hereof throughout the Nation; and in particular, by the Min. of the Pr. of Lon. But (upon the former reason, or the like charitable consideration) these Rules were not imposed by them under any Penalty, or rigorous enforcement, though frequently urged thereunto by some.

Our Reverend Brethren of the Province of London, having considered of these Ordinances, and the Church Government laid down in them, declared their Opinions to be, That there is not a complete Rule in those Ordinances; also that there are many necessary things not yet established, and some things wherein their consciences are not so fully satisfied. These Brethren, in the same Paper, have published also their joint Resolution to practice in all things according to the Rule of the Word, and according to these Ordinances, so far as they conceive them [to] correspond to it, and in so doing, they trust they shall not grieve the Spirit of the truly godly, nor give any just occasion to them that are contrary minded, to blame their proceedings.

We humbly conceive that (we being dissatisfied in these things as our Brethren) the like liberty was intended by the Honorable Houses, and may be taken by us of the Congregational way (without blame or grief to the spirits of those Brethren at least), to resolve, or rather to continue in the same Resolution and Practice in these matters, which indeed were our practices in times of greatest opposition, and before this Reformation was begun.

And as our Brethren the Ministers of London, drew up and published their opinions and apprehensions about Church Government into an entire System; so we now give the like public account of our Consciences, and the Rules by which we have constantly practiced hitherto; which we have here drawn up, and do present. Whereby it will appear how much or how little we differ in these things from our Presbyterian Brethren.

And we trust there is no just cause by which any man, either for our differing from the present settlement, it being out of Conscience, and not out of contempt, or our differences one from another, being not willful, should charge either of us with that odious reproach of Schism. And indeed, if not for our differing from the State settlement, much less because we differ from our Brethren, our differences being in some lesser things, and circumstances only, as themselves acknowledge. And let it be further considered, that we have not broken from them or their Order by these differences (but rather they from us), and in that respect we less deserve their censure; our practice being no other than what it was in our breaking from Episcopacy, and long before Presbytery, or any such form as now they are in, was taken up by them; and we will not say how probable it is, that the yoke of Episcopacy had been upon our neck to this day, if some such way (as formerly, and now is, and hath been termed Schism) had not with much suffering been then practiced, and since continued in.

For *Novelty* wherewith we are likewise both charged by the Enemies of both, it is true, in respect of the public and open Profession, either of Presbytery or Independency, this Nation hath been a stranger to each way, it's possible, ever since it hath been Christian; though for ourselves we are able to trace the footsteps of an Independent Congregational way in the ancientest customs of the Churches; as also in the Writings of our soundest Protestant Divines, and (that which we are much satisfied in) a full concurrence throughout all in the substantial parts of Church Government, with our Reverend Brethren in the old Puritan Non-conformists, who being instant in Prayer and much sufferings, prevailed in the Lord, and we reap with joy what they sowed in tears. Our Brethren also that are for Presbyterial Subordinations, profess what is of weight against Novelty for their way.

And now therefore seeing the Lord, in whose hand is the heart of Princes, hath put into the hearts of our Governors, to tolerate and permit (as they have done many years) persons of each persuasion, to enjoy their Consciences, though neither come up to the Rule established by Authority: And that which is more, to give us both Protection, and the same encouragement, that the most devoted Conformists in those former Superstitious Times enjoyed; yea, and by a public Law to establish this Liberty for time to come; and yet further, in the midst of our fears, to set over us a Prince that owns this Establishment, and cordially resolves to secure our Churches in the enjoyment of these Liberties, if we abuse them not to the disturbance of the Civil Peace.

This should be a very great engagement upon the hearts of all, though of different persuasions, to endeavor our utmost, jointly to promote the honor and prosperity of such a Government and Governors by whatsoever means, which in our Callings as Ministers of the Gospel, and as Churches of Jesus Christ the Prince of Peace, we are any way able to do; as also to be peaceably disposed one towards another, and with mutual toleration to love as brethren, notwithstanding such differences: remembering, as it's very equal we should, the differences that are between Presbyterians and Independents being differences between fellow-servants, and neither of them having authority given from God or Man, to impose their Opinions, one more than the other. That our Governors after so solemn an establishment, should thus bear with us both, in our greater differences from their Rule: and after this, for any of us to take a fellow-servant by the throat, upon the account of a lesser reckoning, and nothing due to him upon it, is to forget, at least not to exercise, that compassion and tenderness we have found, where we had less ground to challenge or expect it.

Our prayer unto God is, That whereto we have already attained, we all may walk by the same rule, and that wherein we are otherwise minded, God would reveal it to us in his due time.

CHAPTER 1
OF THE HOLY SCRIPTURE

1. Although the light of nature, and the works of creation and providence, do so far manifest the goodness, wisdom and power of God, as to leave men unexcusable; yet are they not sufficient to give that knowledge of God and of his will, which is necessary unto salvation: therefore it pleased the Lord at sundry times, and in divers manners, to reveal himself, and to declare that his will unto his church; and afterwards for the better preserving and propagating of the truth, and for the more sure establishment and comfort of the church against the corruption of the flesh, and the malice of Satan and of the world, to commit the same wholly unto writing: which maketh the Holy Scripture to be most necessary; those former ways of God's revealing his will unto his people, being now ceased.

2. Under the name of Holy Scripture, or the Word of God written, are now contained all the books of the Old and New Testament; which are these:

OF THE OLD TESTAMENT:

Genesis	II Chronicles	Daniel
Exodus	Ezra	Hosea
Leviticus	Nehemiah	Joel
Numbers	Esther	Amos
Deuteronomy	Job	Obadiah
Joshua	Psalms	Jonah
Judges	Proverbs	Micah
Ruth	Ecclesiastes	Nahum
I Samuel	The Song of Songs	Habakkuk
II Samuel	Isaiah	Zephaniah
I Kings	Jeremiah	Haggai
II Kings	Lamentations	Zechariah
I Chronicles	Ezekiel	Malachi

OF THE NEW TESTAMENT:

The Gospels	Galatians	The Epistle
according to	Ephesians	of James
Matthew	Philippians	The first and
Mark	Colossians	second Epistles
Luke	Thessalonians I	of Peter
John	Thessalonians II	The first, second,
The Acts of the	to Timothy I	and third Epistles
Apostles	to Timothy II	of John
Paul's Epistles	to Titus	The Epistle
to the Romans	to Philemon	of Jude
Corinthians I	The Epistle to	The Revelation
Corinthians II	the Hebrews	of John

All which are given by the inspiration of God to be the rule of faith and life.

3. The books commonly called Apocrypha, not being of divine inspiration, are no part of the canon of the Scripture; and therefore are of no authority in the church of God, nor to be any otherwise approved or made use of, than other human writings.

4. The authority of the Holy Scripture, for which it ought to be believed and obeyed, dependeth not upon the testimony of any man or church; but wholly upon God (who is truth itself) the Author thereof: and therefore it is to be received, because it is the Word of God.

5. We may be moved and induced by the testimony of the church, to an high and reverent esteem of the Holy Scripture; and the heavenliness of the matter, the efficacy of the doctrine, the majesty of the style, the consent of all the parts, the scope of the whole (which is, to give all glory to God), the full discovery it makes of the only way of man's salvation, the many other incomparable excellencies, and the entire perfection thereof, are arguments whereby it doth abundantly evidence itself to be the Word of God; yet notwithstanding, our full persuasion and assurance of the infallible truth and divine authority thereof, is from the inward work of the Holy Spirit, bearing witness by and with the Word in our hearts.

6. The whole counsel of God concerning all things necessary for his own glory, man's salvation, faith and life, is either expressly set down in Scripture,

or by good and necessary consequence may be deduced from Scripture; unto which nothing at any time is to be added, whether by new revelations of the Spirit, or traditions of men. Nevertheless we acknowledge the inward illumination of the Spirit of God to be necessary for the saving understanding of such things as are revealed in the Word: and that there are some circumstances concerning the worship of God and government of the church, common to human actions and societies, which are to be ordered by the light of nature and Christian prudence, according to the general rules of the Word, which are always to be observed.

7. All things in Scripture are not alike plain in themselves, nor alike clear unto all: yet those things which are necessary to be known, believed and observed for salvation, are so clearly propounded and opened in some place of Scripture or other, that not only the learned, but the unlearned, in a due use of the ordinary means, may attain unto a sufficient understanding of them.

8. The Old Testament in Hebrew (which was the native language of the people of God of old) and the New Testament in Greek (which at the time of writing of it was most generally known to the nations) being immediately inspired by God, and by his singular care and providence kept pure in all ages, are therefore authentical; so as in all controversies of religion the church is finally to appeal unto them. But because these original tongues are not known to all the people of God, who have right unto and interest in the Scriptures, and are commanded in the fear of God to read and search them; therefore they are to be translated into the vulgar language of every nation unto which they come, that the Word of God dwelling plentifully in all, they may worship him in an acceptable manner, and through patience and comfort of the Scriptures may have hope.

9. The infallible rule of interpretation of Scripture, is the Scripture itself; and therefore when there is a question about the true and full sense of any Scripture (which is not manifold, but one) it must be searched and known by other places, that speak more clearly.

10. The supreme judge by which all controversies of religion are to be determined, and all decrees of councils, opinions of ancient writers, doctrines of

men and private spirits, are to be examined, and in whose sentence we are to rest, can be no other, but the Holy Scripture delivered by the Spirit; into which Scripture so delivered, our faith is finally resolved.

CHAPTER 2
OF GOD, AND OF THE HOLY TRINITY

1. There is but one only living and true God; who is infinite in being and perfection, a most pure spirit, invisible, without body, parts or passions, immutable, immense, eternal, incomprehensible, almighty, most wise, most holy, most free, most absolute, working all things according to the counsel of his own immutable and most righteous will, for his own glory, most loving, gracious, merciful, long-suffering, abundant in goodness and truth, forgiving iniquity, transgression and sin, the rewarder of them that diligently seek him; and withal most just and terrible in his judgments, hating all sin, and who will by no means clear the guilty.

2. God hath all life, glory, goodness, blessedness, in, and of himself; and is alone, in, and unto himself, all-sufficient, not standing in need of any creatures, which he hath made, nor deriving any glory from them, but only manifesting his own glory in, by, unto, and upon them. He is the alone fountain of all being, of whom, through whom, and to whom are all things; and hath most sovereign dominion over them, to do by them, for them, or upon them, whatsoever himself pleaseth. In his sight all things are open and manifest, his knowledge is infinite, infallible, and independent upon the creature, so as nothing is to him contingent or uncertain. He is most holy in all his counsels, in all his works, and in all his commands. To him is due from angels and men, and every other creature, whatsoever worship, service or obedience, as creatures, they owe unto the Creator, and whatever he is further pleased to require of them.

3. In the unity of the Godhead there be three persons, of one substance, power and eternity. God the Father, God the Son, and God the Holy Ghost. The Father is of none, neither begotten, nor proceeding; the Son is eternally begotten of the Father; the Holy Ghost eternally proceeding from the Father and the Son. Which doctrine of the Trinity is the foundation of all our communion with God, and comfortable dependence upon him.

CHAPTER 3
OF GOD'S ETERNAL DECREE

1. God from all eternity did by the most wise and holy counsel of his own will, freely and unchangeably ordain whatsoever comes to pass: yet so, as thereby neither is God the author of sin, nor is violence offered to the will of the creatures, nor is the liberty or contingency of second causes taken away, but rather established.

2. Although God knows whatsoever may or can come to pass upon all supposed conditions, yet hath he not decreed any thing, because he foresaw it as future, or as that which would come to pass upon such conditions.

3. By the decree of God for the manifestation of his glory, some men and angels are predestinated unto everlasting life, and others foreordained to everlasting death.

4. These angels and men thus predestinated, and foreordained, are particularly and unchangeably designed, and their number is so certain and definite, that it cannot be either increased or diminished.

5. Those of mankind that are predestinated unto life, God, before the foundation of the world was laid, according to his eternal and immutable purpose, and the secret counsel and good pleasure of his will, hath chosen in Christ unto everlasting glory, out of his mere free grace and love, without any foresight of faith or good works, or perseverance in either of them, or any other thing in the creature, as conditions or causes moving him thereunto, and all to the praise of his glorious grace.

6. As God hath appointed the elect unto glory, so hath he by the eternal and most free purpose of his will foreordained all the means thereunto. Wherefore they who are elected, being fallen in Adam, are redeemed by Christ, are effectually called unto faith in Christ by his Spirit working in due season, are justified, adopted, sanctified, and kept by his power, through faith, unto salvation. Neither are any other redeemed by Christ, or effectually called, justified, adopted, sanctified and saved, but the elect only.

7. The rest of mankind God was pleased, according to the unsearchable counsel of his own will, whereby he extendeth or withholdeth mercy, as he pleaseth,

for the glory of his sovereign power over his creatures, to pass by and to ordain them to dishonor and wrath for their sin, to the praise of his glorious justice.

8. The doctrine of this high mystery of predestination is to be handled with special prudence and care, that men attending the will of God revealed in his Word, and yielding obedience thereunto, may from the certainty of their effectual vocation, be assured of their eternal election. So shall this doctrine afford matter of praise, reverence and admiration of God, and of humility, diligence, and abundant consolation to all that sincerely obey the gospel.

CHAPTER 4
OF CREATION

1. It pleased God the Father, Son and Holy Ghost, for the manifestation of the glory of his eternal power, wisdom and goodness, in the beginning, to create or make out of nothing the world, and all things therein, whether visible or invisible, in the space of six days, and all very good.

2. After God had made all other creatures, he created man, male and female, with reasonable and immortal souls, endued with knowledge, righteousness and true holiness, after his own image, having the law of God written in their hearts, and power to fulfill it; and yet under a possibility of transgressing, being left to the liberty of their own will, which was subject unto change. Besides this law written in their hearts, they received a command not to eat of the tree of the knowledge of good and evil; which while they kept, they were happy in their communion with God, and had dominion over the creatures.

CHAPTER 5
OF PROVIDENCE

1. God the great Creator of all things, doth uphold, direct, dispose and govern all creatures, actions and things from the greatest even to the least by his most wise and holy providence, according to his infallible foreknowledge, and the free and immutable counsel of his own will, to the praise of the glory of his wisdom, power, justice, goodness and mercy.

2. Although in relation to the foreknowledge and decree of God, the first cause, all things come to pass immutably and infallibly; yet by the same providence

he ordereth them to fall out according to the nature of second causes, either necessarily, freely, or contingently.

3. God in his ordinary providence maketh use of means, yet is free to work without, above, and against them at his pleasure.

4. The almighty power, unsearchable wisdom, and infinite goodness of God, so far manifest themselves in his providence, in that his determinate counsel extendeth itself even to the first fall, and all other sins of angels and men (and that not by a bare permission) which also he most wisely and powerfully boundeth, and otherwise ordereth and governeth in a manifold dispensation to his own most holy ends; yet so, as the sinfulness thereof proceedeth only from the creature, and not from God, who being most holy and righteous, neither is, nor can be the author or approver of sin.

5. The most wise, righteous and gracious God doth oftentimes leave for a season his own children to manifold temptations, and the corruption of their own hearts, to chastise them for their former sins, or to discover unto them the hidden strength of corruption, and deceitfulness of their hearts, that they may be humbled; and to raise them to a more close and constant dependence for their support upon himself, and to make them more watchful against all future occasions of sin, and for sundry other just and holy ends.

6. As for those wicked and ungodly men, whom God as a righteous judge, for former sins, doth blind and harden, from them he not only withholdeth his grace, whereby they might have been enlightened in their understandings, and wrought upon in their hearts; but sometimes also withdraweth the gifts which they had, and exposeth them to such objects, as their corruption makes occasions of sin; and withal gives them over to their own lusts, the temptations of the world, and the power of Satan; whereby it comes to pass that they harden themselves, even under those means which God useth for the softening of others.

7. As the providence of God doth in general reach to all creatures, so after a most special manner it taketh care of his church, and disposeth all things to the good thereof.

CHAPTER 6
OF THE FALL OF MAN, OF SIN,
AND OF THE PUNISHMENT THEREOF

1. God having made a covenant of works and life, thereupon, with our first parents and all their posterity in them, they being seduced by the subtlety and temptation of Satan did willfully transgress the law of their creation, and break the covenant in eating the forbidden fruit.

2. By this sin they, and we in them, fell from original righteousness and communion with God, and so became dead in sin, and wholly defiled in all the faculties and parts of soul and body.

3. They being the root, and by God's appointment standing in the room and stead of all mankind, the guilt of this sin was imputed, and corrupted nature conveyed to all their posterity descending from them by ordinary generation.

4. From this original corruption, whereby we are utterly indisposed, disabled and made opposite to all good, and wholly inclined to all evil, do proceed all actual transgressions.

5. This corruption of nature during this life, doth remain in those that are regenerated; and although it be through Christ pardoned and mortified, yet both itself and all the motions thereof are truly and properly sin.

6. Every sin, both original and actual, being a transgression of the righteous law of God, and contrary thereunto, doth in its own nature bring guilt upon the sinner, whereby he is bound over to the wrath of God, and curse of the law, and so made subject to death, with all miseries, spiritual, temporal and eternal.

CHAPTER 7
OF GOD'S COVENANT WITH MAN

1. The distance between God and the creature is so great, that although reasonable creatures do owe obedience unto him as their Creator, yet they could never have attained the reward of life, but by some voluntary condescension on God's part, which he hath been pleased to express by way of covenant.

2. The first covenant made with man, was a covenant of works, wherein life was promised to Adam, and in him to his posterity, upon condition of perfect and personal obedience.

3. Man by his fall having made himself incapable of life by that covenant, the Lord was pleased to make a second, commonly called the covenant of grace; wherein he freely offereth unto sinners life and salvation by Jesus Christ, requiring of them faith in him that they may be saved, and promising to give unto all those that are ordained unto life, his Holy Spirit, to make them willing and able to believe.

4. This covenant of grace is frequently set forth in the Scripture by the name of a testament, in reference to the death of Jesus Christ the Testator, and to the everlasting inheritance, with all things belonging to it, therein bequeathed.

5. Although this covenant hath been differently and variously administered in respect of ordinances and institutions in the time of the law, and since the coming of Christ in the flesh; yet for the substance and efficacy of it, to all its spiritual and saving ends, it is one and the same; upon the account of which various dispensations, it is called the Old and New Testament.

CHAPTER 8
OF CHRIST THE MEDIATOR

1. It pleased God, in his eternal purpose, to choose and ordain the Lord Jesus his only begotten Son, according to a covenant made between them both, to be the Mediator between God and man; the Prophet, Priest, and King, the Head and Savior of his church, the Heir of all things and Judge of the world; unto whom he did from all eternity give a people to be his seed, and to be by him in time redeemed, called, justified, sanctified, and glorified.

2. The Son of God, the second person in the Trinity, being very and eternal God, of one substance and equal with the Father, did, when the fullness of time was come, take upon him man's nature, with all the essential properties and common infirmities thereof, yet without sin, being conceived by the power of the Holy Ghost, in the womb of the virgin Mary, of her substance: So that two whole perfect and distinct natures, the Godhead and the manhood, were inseparably joined together in one person, without conversion,

composition, or confusion; which person is very God and very man, yet one Christ, the only Mediator between God and man.

3. The Lord Jesus in his human nature, thus united to the divine in the person of the Son, was sanctified and anointed with the Holy Spirit above measure, having in him all the treasures of wisdom and knowledge, in whom it pleased the Father that all fullness should dwell; to the end that being holy, harmless, undefiled, and full of grace and truth, he might be thoroughly furnished to execute the office of a mediator and surety; which office he took not unto himself, but was thereunto called by his Father, who also put all power and judgment into his hand, and gave him commandment to execute the same.

4. This office the Lord Jesus did most willingly undertake; which that he might discharge, he was made under the law, and did perfectly fulfil it, and underwent the punishment due to us, which we should have borne and suffered, being made sin and a curse for us, enduring most grievous torments immediately from God in his soul, and most painful sufferings in his body, was crucified, and died; was buried, and remained under the power of death, yet saw no corruption. On the third day he arose from the dead with the same body in which he suffered, with which also he ascended into heaven, and there sitteth at the right hand of his Father, making intercession; and shall return to judge men and angels at the end of the world.

5. The Lord Jesus by his perfect obedience and sacrifice of himself, which he through the eternal Spirit, once offered up unto God, hath fully satisfied the justice of God, and purchased not only reconciliation, but an everlasting inheritance in the kingdom of heaven, for all those whom the Father hath given unto him.

6. Although the work of redemption was not actually wrought by Christ, till after his incarnation; yet the virtue, efficacy and benefits thereof were communicated to the elect in all ages, successively from the beginning of the world, in and by those promises, types and sacrifices wherein he was revealed and signified to be the seed of the woman, which should bruise the serpent's head, and the Lamb slain from the beginning of the world, being yesterday and today the same, and for ever.

7. Christ in the work of mediation acteth according to both natures; by each nature doing that which is proper to itself; yet by reason of the unity of the person, that which is proper to one nature, is sometimes in Scripture attributed to the person denominated by the other nature.

8. To all those for whom Christ hath purchased redemption, he doth certainly and effectually apply and communicate the same; making intercession for them; and revealing unto them in and by the Word, the mysteries of salvation; effectually persuading them by his Spirit to believe and obey, and governing their hearts by his Word and Spirit; overcoming all their enemies by his almighty power and wisdom, and in such manner and ways as are most consonant to his most wonderful and unsearchable dispensation.

CHAPTER 9
OF FREE WILL

1. God hath endued the will of man with that natural liberty and power of acting upon choice that it is neither forced, nor by any absolute necessity of nature determined to do good or evil.

2. Man in his state of innocency had freedom and power to will and to do that which was good and well-pleasing to God; but yet mutably, so that he might fall from it.

3. Man by his fall into a state of sin, hath wholly lost all ability of will to any spiritual good accompanying salvation; so as a natural man being altogether averse from that good, and dead in sin, is not able by his own strength to convert himself, or to prepare himself thereunto.

4. When God converts a sinner, and translates him into the state of grace, he freeth him from his natural bondage under sin, and by his grace alone enables him freely to will and to do that which is spiritually good; yet so as that, by reason of his remaining corruption, he doth not perfectly nor only will that which is good, but doth also will that which is evil.

5. The will of man is made perfectly and immutably free to do good alone in the state of glory only.

CHAPTER 10
OF EFFECTUAL CALLING

1. All those whom God hath predestinated unto life, and those only, he is pleased in his appointed and accepted time effectually to call by his Word and Spirit, out of that state of sin and death in which they are by nature, to grace and salvation by Jesus Christ; enlightening their minds spiritually and savingly to understand the things of God, taking away their heart of stone, and giving unto them an heart of flesh; renewing their wills, and by his almighty power determining them to that which is good; and effectually drawing them to Jesus Christ; yet so, as they come most freely, being made willing by his grace.

2. This effectual call is of God's free and special grace alone, not from any thing at all foreseen in man, who is altogether passive therein, until being quickened and renewed by the Holy Spirit he is thereby enabled to answer this call, and to embrace the grace offered and conveyed in it.

3. Elect infants dying in infancy, are regenerated and saved by Christ, who worketh when, and where, and how he pleaseth: so also are all other elect persons who are incapable of being outwardly called by the ministry of the Word.

4. Others not elected, although they may be called by the ministry of the Word, and may have some common operations of the Spirit, yet not being effectually drawn by the Father, they neither do nor can come unto Christ, and therefore cannot be saved: much less can men not professing the Christian religion, be saved in any other way whatsoever, be they never so diligent to frame their lives according to the light of nature, and the law of that religion they do profess: and to assert and maintain that they may, is very pernicious, and to be detested.

CHAPTER 11
OF JUSTIFICATION

1. Those whom God effectually calleth, he also freely justifieth; not by infusing righteousness into them, but by pardoning their sins, and by accounting and accepting their persons as righteous; not for anything wrought in them, or

done by them, but for Christ's sake alone; nor by imputing faith itself, the act of believing, or any other evangelical obedience to them, as their righteousness; but by imputing Christ's active obedience to the whole law, and passive obedience in his death for their whole and sole righteousness, they receiving and resting on him and his righteousness by faith; which faith they have not of themselves, it is the gift of God.

2. Faith thus receiving and resting on Christ, and his righteousness, is the alone instrument of justification; yet it is not alone in the person justified, but is ever accompanied with all other saving graces, and is no dead faith, but worketh by love.

3. Christ by his obedience and death did fully discharge the debt of all those that are justified, and did by the sacrifice of himself, in the blood of his cross, undergoing in their stead the penalty due unto them make a proper, real, and full satisfaction to God's justice in their behalf. Yet in as much as he was given by the Father for them, and his obedience and satisfaction accepted in their stead, and both freely, not for any thing in them, their justification is only of free grace, that both the exact justice and rich grace of God might be glorified in the justification of sinners.

4. God did from all eternity decree to justify all the elect, and Christ did in the fulness of time die for their sins, and rise again for their justification: nevertheless, they are not justified personally, until the Holy Spirit doth in due time actually apply Christ unto them.

5. God doth continue to forgive the sins of those that are justified; and although they can never fall from the state of justification, yet they may by their sins fall under God's fatherly displeasure: and in that condition they have not usually the light of his countenance restored unto them, until they humble themselves, confess their sins, beg pardon, and renew their faith and repentance.

6. The justification of believers under the Old Testament, was in all these respects one and the same with the justification of believers under the New Testament.

CHAPTER 12
OF ADOPTION

1. All those that are justified, God vouchsafeth in and for his only Son Jesus Christ to make partakers of the grace of adoption, by which they are taken into the number, and enjoy the liberties and privileges of the children of God, have his name put upon them, receive the Spirit of adoption; have access to the throne of grace with boldness, are enabled to cry, Abba Father; are pitied, protected, provided for, and chastened by him as by a father; yet never cast off, but sealed to the day of redemption, and inherit the promises as heirs of everlasting salvation.

CHAPTER 13
OF SANCTIFICATION

1. They that are united to Christ, effectually called and regenerated, having a new heart and a new spirit created in them, through the virtue of Christ's death and resurrection, are also further sanctified really and personally through the same virtue, by his Word and Spirit dwelling in them; the dominion of the whole body of sin is destroyed and the several lusts thereof are more and more weakened, and mortified, and they more and more quickened, and strengthened in all saving graces, to the practice of all true holiness, without which no man shall see the Lord.

2. This sanctification is throughout in the whole man, yet imperfect in this life; there abideth still some remnants of corruption in every part; whence ariseth a continual and irreconcilable war, the flesh lusting against the Spirit, and the Spirit against the flesh.

3. In which war, although the remaining corruption for a time may much prevail, yet through the continual supply of strength from the sanctifying Spirit of Christ, the regenerate part doth overcome, and so the saints grow in grace, perfecting holiness in the fear of God.

CHAPTER 14
OF SAVING FAITH

1. The grace of faith, whereby the elect are enabled to believe to the saving of their souls, is the work of the Spirit of Christ in their hearts, and is ordinarily

wrought by the ministry of the Word; by which also, and by the administration of the seals, prayer, and other means, it is increased and strengthened.

2. By this faith a Christian believeth to be true whatsoever is revealed in the Word, for the authority of God himself speaking therein, and acteth differently upon that which each particular passage thereof containeth; yielding obedience to the commands, trembling at the threatenings, and embracing the promises of God for this life, and that which is to come. But the principal acts of saving faith are, accepting, receiving, and resting upon Christ alone, for justification, sanctification, and eternal life, by virtue of the covenant of grace.

3. This faith, although it be different in degrees, and may be weak or strong yet it is in the least degree of it different in the kind or nature of it (as is all other saving grace) from the faith and common grace of temporary believers; and therefore, though it may be many times assailed and weakened, yet it gets the victory, growing up in many to the attainment of a full assurance through Christ, who is both the author and finisher of our faith.

CHAPTER 15
OF REPENTANCE UNTO LIFE AND SALVATION

1. Such of the elect as are converted at riper years, having sometime lived in the state of nature, and therein served divers lusts and pleasures, God in their effectual calling giveth them repentance unto life.

2. Whereas there is none that doth good, and sinneth not, and the best of men may through the power and deceitfulness of their corruptions dwelling in them, with the prevalency of temptation, fall into great sins and provocations; God hath in the covenant of grace mercifully provided, that believers so sinning and falling, be renewed through repentance unto salvation.

3. This saving repentance is an evangelical grace, whereby a person being by the Holy Ghost made sensible of the manifold evils of his sin, doth by faith in Christ humble himself for it with godly sorrow, detestation of it, and self-abhorrence, praying for pardon and strength of grace, with a purpose, and endeavor by supplies of the Spirit, to walk before God unto all well-pleasing in all things.

4. As repentance is to be continued through the whole course of our lives, upon the account of the body of death, and the motions thereof; so it is every man's duty to repent of his particular known sins particularly.

5. Such is the provision which God hath made through Christ in the covenant of grace, for the preservation of believers unto salvation, that although there is no sin so small, but it deserves damnation; yet there is no sin so great, that it shall bring damnation on them who truly repent; which makes the constant preaching of repentance necessary.

CHAPTER 16
OF GOOD WORKS

1. Good works are only such as God hath commanded in his holy Word, and not such as without the warrant thereof are devised by men out of blind zeal, or upon pretense of good intentions.

2. These good works done in obedience to God's commandments, are the fruits and evidences of a true and lively faith; and by them believers manifest their thankfulness, strengthen their assurance, edify their brethren, adorn the profession of the gospel, stop the mouths of the adversaries, and glorify God, whose workmanship they are, created in Christ Jesus thereunto; that having their fruit unto holiness, they may have the end, eternal life.

3. Their ability to do good works is not at all of themselves, but wholly from the Spirit of Christ. And that they may be enabled thereunto, besides the graces they have already received, there is required an actual influence of the same Holy Spirit to work in them to will and to do of his good pleasure; yet are they not hereupon to grow negligent, as if they were not bound to perform any duty unless upon a special motion of the Spirit; but they ought to be diligent in stirring up the grace of God that is in them.

4. They who in their obedience attain to the greatest height which is possible in this life, are so far from being able to supererogate, and to do more than God requires, as that they fall short of much which in duty they are bound to do.

5. We cannot by our best works merit pardon of sin, or eternal life at the hand of God, by reason of the great disproportion that is between them and the glory to come; and the infinite distance that is between us and God, whom

by them we can neither profit, nor satisfy for the debt of our former sins; but when we have done all we can, we have done but our duty, and are unprofitable servants; and because, as they are good, they proceed from the Spirit, and as they are wrought by us, they are defiled and mixed with so much weakness and imperfection, that they cannot endure the severity of God's judgment.

6. Yet notwithstanding, the persons of believers being accepted through Christ, their good works also are accepted in him; not as though they were in this life wholly unblameable and unreproveable in God's sight; but that he looking upon them in his Son is pleased to accept and reward that which is sincere, although accompanied with many weaknesses and imperfections.

7. Works done by unregenerate men, although for the matter of them they may be things which God commands, and of good use both to themselves and to others: yet because they proceed not from a heart purified by faith; nor are done in a right manner, according to the Word; nor to a right end, the glory of God; they are therefore sinful, and cannot please God, nor make a man meet to receive grace from God; and yet their neglect of them is more sinful, and displeasing unto God.

CHAPTER 17
OF THE PERSEVERANCE OF THE SAINTS

1. They whom God hath accepted in his Beloved, effectually called and sanctified by his Spirit, can neither totally nor finally fall away from the state of grace; but shall certainly persevere therein to the end, and be eternally saved.

2. This perseverance of the saints depends not upon their own free will, but upon the immutability of the decree of election; from the free and unchangeable love of God the Father; upon the efficacy of the merit and intercession of Jesus Christ, and union with him; the oath of God; the abiding of his Spirit; and of the seed of God within them; and the nature of the covenant of grace; from all which ariseth also the certainty and infallibility thereof.

3. And though they may, through the temptation of Satan, and of the world, the prevalency of corruption remaining in them, and the neglect of the means of their preservation, fall into grievous sins; and for a time continue therein, whereby they incur God's displeasure, and grieve his Holy Spirit; come to have their graces and

comforts impaired; have their hearts hardened, and their consciences wounded; hurt and scandalize others, and bring temporal judgments upon themselves; yet they are and shall be kept by the power of God through faith unto salvation.

CHAPTER 18
OF THE ASSURANCE OF GRACE AND SALVATION

1. Although temporary believers and other unregenerate men may vainly deceive themselves with false hopes, and carnal presumptions of being in the favor of God, and state of salvation, which hope of theirs shall perish; yet such as truly believe in the Lord Jesus, and love him in sincerity, endeavoring to walk in all good conscience before him, may in this life be certainly assured that they are in the state of grace, and may rejoice in the hope of the glory of God, which hope shall never make them ashamed.

2. This certainty is not a bare conjectural and probable persuasion, grounded upon a fallible hope; but an infallible assurance of faith, founded on the blood and righteousness of Christ, revealed in the gospel, and also upon the inward evidence of those graces unto which promises are made, and on the immediate witness of the Spirit, testifying our adoption, and as a fruit thereof, leaving the heart more humble and holy.

3. This infallible assurance doth not so belong to the essence of faith, but that a true believer may wait long, and conflict with many difficulties before he be partaker of it; yet being enabled by the Spirit to know the things which are freely given him of God, he may, without extraordinary revelation, in the right use of ordinary means attain thereunto. And therefore it is the duty of every one to give all diligence to make his calling and election sure; that thereby his heart may be enlarged in peace and joy in the Holy Ghost, in love and thankfulness to God, and in strength and cheerfulness in the duties of obedience, the proper fruits of this assurance; so far is it from inclining men to looseness.

4. True believers may have the assurance of their salvation divers ways shaken, diminished and intermitted; as by negligence in preserving of it; by falling into some special sin, which woundeth the conscience, and grieveth the Spirit; by some sudden or vehement temptation; by God's withdrawing the light of his countenance; suffering even such as fear him to walk in darkness, and to have no light; yet are they neither utterly destitute of that seed of God, and life of faith,

that love of Christ and the brethren, that sincerity of heart and conscience of duty, out of which by the operation of the Spirit this assurance may in due time be revived, and by the which in the meantime they are supported from utter despair.

CHAPTER 19
OF THE LAW OF GOD

1. God gave to Adam a law of universal obedience written in his heart, and a particular precept of not eating the fruit of the tree of knowledge of good and evil, as a covenant of works, by which he bound him and all his posterity to personal, entire, exact and perpetual obedience; promised life upon the fulfilling, and threatened death upon the breach of it; and endued him with power and ability to keep it.

2. This law, so written in the heart, continued to be a perfect rule of righteousness after the fall of man; and was delivered by God upon Mount Sinai in ten commandments, and written in two tables; the four first commandments containing our duty towards God, and the other six our duty to man.

3. Beside this law, commonly called moral, God was pleased to give to the people of Israel ceremonial laws, containing several typical ordinances; partly of worship, prefiguring Christ, his graces, actions, sufferings and benefits, and partly holding forth divers instructions of moral duties. All which ceremonial laws being appointed only to the time of reformation, are by Jesus Christ the true Messiah and only Lawgiver, who was furnished with power from the Father for that end, abrogated and taken away.

4. To them also he gave sundry judicial laws, which expired together with the state of that people, not obliging any now by virtue of that institution, their general equity only being still of moral use.

5. The moral law doth for ever bind all, as well justified persons as others, to the obedience thereof; and that not only in regard of the matter contained in it, but also in respect of the authority of God the Creator, who gave it: neither doth Christ in the gospel any way dissolve, but much strengthen this obligation.

6. Although true believers be not under the law, as a covenant of works, to be thereby justified or condemned; yet it is of great use to them as well as to others, in that, as a rule of life, informing them of the will of God, and their duty, it

directs and binds them to walk accordingly; discovering also the sinful pollutions of their nature, hearts and lives; so as examining themselves thereby, they may come to further conviction of, humiliation for, and hatred against sin; together with a clearer sight of the need they have of Christ, and the perfection of his obedience. It is likewise of use to the regenerate, to restrain their corruptions, in that it forbids sin; and the threatenings of it serve to show what even their sins deserve, and what afflictions in this life they may expect for them, although freed from the curse thereof threatened in the law. The promises of it in like manner show them God's approbation of obedience, and what blessings they may expect upon the performance thereof, although not as due to them by the law, as a covenant of works; so as a man's doing good, and refraining from evil, because the law encourageth to the one, and deterreth from the other, is no evidence of his being under the law, and not under grace.

7. Neither are the forementioned uses of the law contrary to the grace of the gospel, but do sweetly comply with it; the Spirit of Christ subduing and enabling the will of man to do that freely and cheerfully, which the will of God revealed in the law required to be done.

CHAPTER 20
OF THE GOSPEL, AND OF THE EXTENT
OF THE GRACE THEREOF

1. The covenant of works being broken by sin, and made unprofitable unto life, God was pleased to give unto the elect the promise of Christ, the seed of the woman, as the means of calling them, and begetting in them faith and repentance: in this promise the gospel, as to the substance of it, was revealed, and was therein effectual for the conversion and salvation of sinners.

2. This promise of Christ, and salvation by him, is revealed only in and by the Word of God; neither do the works of creation or providence, with the light of nature, make discovery of Christ, or of grace by him, so much as in a general or obscure way; much less that men destitute of the revelation of him by the promise or gospel, should be enabled thereby to attain saving faith or repentance.

3. The revelation of the gospel unto sinners, made in divers times, and by sundry parts, with the addition of promises and precepts for the obedience required therein, as to the nations and persons to whom it is granted, is merely

of the sovereign will and good pleasure of God, not being annexed by virtue of any promise to the due improvement of men's natural abilities, by virtue of common light received without it, which none ever did make or can so do. And therefore in all ages the preaching of the gospel hath been granted unto persons and nations, as to the extent or straitening of it, in great variety, according to the counsel of the will of God.

4. Although the gospel be the only outward means of revealing Christ and saving grace, and is as such abundantly sufficient thereunto; yet that men who are dead in trespasses, may be born again, quickened or regenerated, there is moreover necessary an effectual, irresistible work of the Holy Ghost upon the whole soul, for the producing in them a new spiritual life, without which no other means are sufficient for their conversion unto God.

CHAPTER 21
OF CHRISTIAN LIBERTY AND LIBERTY OF CONSCIENCE

1. The liberty which Christ hath purchased for believers under the gospel, consists in their freedom from the guilt of sin, the condemning wrath of God, the rigor and curse of the law; and in their being delivered from this present evil world, bondage to Satan, and dominion of sin, from the evil of afflictions, the fear and sting of death, the victory of the grave, and everlasting damnation; as also in their free access to God, and their yielding obedience unto him, not out of slavish fear, but a childlike love and willing mind. All which were common also to believers under the law, for the substance of them; but under the New Testament the liberty of Christians is further enlarged in their freedom from the yoke of the ceremonial law, the whole legal administration of the covenant of grace, to which the Jewish church was subjected; and in greater boldness of access to the throne of grace, and in fuller communications of the free Spirit of God, than believers under the law did ordinarily partake of.

2. God alone is Lord of the conscience, and hath left it free from the doctrines and commandments of men which are in any thing contrary to his Word, or not contained in it; so that to believe such doctrines, or to obey such commands out of conscience, is to betray true liberty of conscience; and the requiring of an implicit faith, and an absolute and blind obedience, is to destroy liberty of conscience, and reason also.

3. They who upon pretense of Christian liberty do practice any sin, or cherish any lust, as they do thereby pervert the main design of the grace of the gospel to their own destruction; so they wholly destroy the end of Christian liberty, which is, that being delivered out of the hands of our enemies, we might serve the Lord without fear, in holiness and righteousness before him all the days of our life.

CHAPTER 22
OF RELIGIOUS WORSHIP AND THE SABBATH-DAY

1. The light of nature showeth that there is a God, who hath lordship and sovereignty over all, is just, good, and doth good unto all, and is therefore to be feared, loved, praised, called upon, trusted in, and served with all the heart, and all the soul, and with all the might. But the acceptable way of worshiping the true God is instituted by himself, and so limited by his own revealed will, that he may not be worshiped according to the imaginations and devices of men, or the suggestions of Satan, under any visible representations, or any other way not prescribed in the Holy Scripture.

2. Religious worship is to be given to God the Father, Son, and Holy Ghost, and to him alone; not to angels, saints, or any other creatures; and since the fall, not without a Mediator, nor in the mediation of any other but of Christ alone.

3. Prayer, with thanksgiving, being one special part of natural worship, is by God required of all men; but that it may be accepted, it is to be made in the name of the Son by the help of his Spirit, according to his will, with understanding, reverence, humility, fervency, faith, love, and perseverance; and when with others in a known tongue.

4. Prayer is to be made for things lawful, and for all sorts of men living, or that shall live hereafter; but not for the dead, nor for those of whom it may be known that they have sinned the sin unto death.

5. The reading of the Scriptures, preaching, and hearing the Word of God, singing of psalms; as also the administration of baptism and the Lord's Supper, are all parts of religious worship of God, to be performed in obedience unto God with understanding, faith, reverence, and godly fear. Solemn

humiliations, with fastings and thanksgivings upon special occasions, are in their several times and seasons to be used in a holy and religious manner.

6. Neither prayer, nor any other part of religious worship, is now under the gospel either tied unto, or made more acceptable by any place in which it is performed, or towards which it is directed; but God is to be worshiped every-where in spirit and in truth, as in private families daily, and in secret each one by himself, so more solemnly in the public assemblies, which are not carelessly nor wilfully to be neglected, or forsaken, when God by his Word or provi-dence calleth thereunto.

7. As it is of the law of nature, that in general a proportion of time by God's appointment be set apart for the worship of God; so by his Word in a positive, moral, and perpetual commandment, binding all men in all ages, he hath par-ticularly appointed one day in seven for a Sabbath to be kept holy unto him; which from the beginning of the world to the resurrection of Christ, was the last day of the week; and from the resurrection of Christ was changed into the first day of the week, which in Scripture is called the Lord's Day, and is to be continued to the end of the world as the Christian Sabbath, the observation of the last day of the week being abolished.

8. This Sabbath is then kept holy unto the Lord, when men after a due prepar-ing of their hearts, and ordering their common affairs beforehand, do not only observe an holy rest all the day from their own works, words, and thoughts about their worldly employments and recreations; but also are taken up the whole time in the public and private exercises of his worship, and in the duties of necessity and mercy.

CHAPTER 23
OF LAWFUL OATHS AND VOWS

1. A lawful oath is a part of religious worship, wherein the person swearing in truth, righteousness and judgment, solemnly calleth God to witness what he asserteth or promiseth, and to judge him according to the truth or falsehood of what he sweareth.

2. The name of God only is that by which men ought to swear, and therein it is to be used with all holy fear and reverence. Therefore to swear vainly, or

rashly, by that glorious or dreadful name, or to swear at all by any other thing, is sinful and to be abhorred. Yet as in matters of weight and moment an oath is warranted by the Word of God under the New Testament, as well as under the Old; so a lawful oath, being imposed by lawful authority in such matters, ought to be taken.

3. Whosoever taketh an oath, warranted by the Word of God, ought duly to consider the weightiness of so solemn an act, and therein to avouch nothing but what he is fully persuaded is the truth: neither may any man bind himself by oath to any thing, but what is good and just, and what he believeth so to be, and what he is able and resolved to perform. Yet it is a sin to refuse an oath touching any thing that is good and just, being lawfully imposed by authority.

4. An oath is to be taken in the plain and common sense of the words, without equivocation or mental reservation. It cannot oblige to sin, but in any thing not sinful, being taken it binds to performance, although to a man's own hurt; nor is it to be violated, although made to heretics or infidels.

5. A vow, which is not to be made to any creature, but God alone, is of the like nature with a promissory oath, and ought to be made with the like religious care, and to be performed with the like faithfulness.

6. Popish monastical vows of perpetual single life, professed poverty, and regular obedience, are so far from being degrees of higher perfection, that they are superstitious and sinful snares, in which no Christian may entangle himself.

CHAPTER 24
OF THE CIVIL MAGISTRATE

1. God the supreme Lord and King of all the world, hath ordained civil magistrates to be under him, over the people for his own glory and the public good; and to this end hath armed them with the power of the sword, for the defence and encouragement of them that do good, and for the punishment of evildoers.

2. It is lawful for Christians to accept and execute the office of a magistrate, when called thereunto: in the management whereof, as they ought specially to maintain justice and peace, according to the wholesome laws of each

commonwealth; so for that end they may lawfully now under the New Testament wage war upon just and necessary occasion.

3. Although the magistrate is bound to encourage, promote, and protect the professors and profession of the gospel, and to manage and order civil administrations in a due subserviency to the interest of Christ in the world, and to that end to take care that men of corrupt minds and conversations do not licentiously publish and divulge blasphemy and errors, in their own nature subverting the faith and inevitably destroying the souls of them that receive them: yet in such differences about the doctrines of the gospel, or ways of the worship of God, as may befall men exercising a good conscience, manifesting it in their conversation, and holding the foundation, not disturbing others in their ways or worship that differ from them; there is no warrant for the magistrate under the gospel to abridge them of their liberty.

4. It is the duty of people to pray for magistrates, to honor their persons, to pay them tribute and other dues, to obey their lawful commands, and to be subject to their authority for conscience' sake. Infidelity, or difference in religion, doth not make void the magistrate's just and legal authority, nor free the people from their obedience to him: from which ecclesiastical persons are not exempted, much less hath the pope any power or jurisdiction over them in their dominions, or over any of their people, and least of all to deprive them of their dominions or lives, if he shall judge them to be heretics, or upon any other pretense whatsoever.

CHAPTER 25
OF MARRIAGE

1. Marriage is to be between one man and one woman: neither is it lawful for any man to have more than one wife, nor for any woman to have more than one husband at the same time.

2. Marriage was ordained for the mutual help of husband and wife; for the increase of mankind with a legitimate issue, and of the church with an holy seed, and for preventing of uncleanness.

3. It is lawful for all sorts of people to marry, who are able with judgment to give their consent. Yet it is the duty of Christians to marry in the Lord;

and therefore such as profess the true reformed religion, should not marry with infidels, papists, or other idolaters: neither should such as are godly, be unequally yoked by marrying with such as are wicked in their life, or maintain damnable heresies.

4. Marriage ought not to be within the degrees of consanguinity or affinity forbidden in the Word; nor can such incestuous marriages ever be made lawful by any law of man, or consent of parties, so as those persons may live together as man and wife.

CHAPTER 26
OF THE CHURCH

1. The catholic or universal church, which is invisible, consists of the whole number of the elect, that have been, are, or shall be gathered into one under Christ, the Head thereof, and is the spouse, the body, the fulness of him that filleth all in all.

2. The whole body of men throughout the world, professing the faith of the gospel and obedience unto God by Christ according to it, not destroying their own profession by any errors everting the foundation, or unholiness of conversation, are, and may be called the visible catholic church of Christ; although as such it is not entrusted with the administration of any ordinances, or have any officers to rule or govern in, or over the whole body.

3. The purest churches under heaven are subject both to mixture and error, and some have so degenerated as to become no churches of Christ, but synagogues of Satan: nevertheless Christ always hath had, and ever shall have, a visible kingdom in this world, to the end thereof, of such as believe in him, and make profession of his name.

4. There is no other head of the church but the Lord Jesus Christ; nor can the pope of Rome in any sense be head thereof; but is that antichrist, that man of sin, and son of perdition, that exalteth himself in the church against Christ, and all that is called God, whom the Lord shall destroy with the brightness of his coming.

5. As the Lord in his care and love towards his church, hath in his infinite wise providence exercised it with great variety in all ages, for the good of them that

love him, and his own glory; so according to his promise, we expect that in the latter days, antichrist being destroyed, the Jews called, and the adversaries of the kingdom of his dear Son broken, the churches of Christ being enlarged, and edified through a free and plentiful communication of light and grace, shall enjoy in this world a more quiet, peaceable and glorious condition than they have enjoyed.

CHAPTER 27
OF THE COMMUNION OF SAINTS

1. All saints that are united to Jesus Christ their Head, by his Spirit and faith, although they are not made thereby one person with him, have fellowship in his graces, sufferings, death, resurrection and glory: and being united to one another in love, they have communion in each other's gifts and graces, and are obliged to the performance of such duties, public and private, as do conduce to their mutual good, both in the inward and outward man.

2. All saints are bound to maintain an holy fellowship and communion in the worship of God, and in performing such other spiritual services as tend to their mutual edification; as also in relieving each other in outward things, according to their several abilities and necessities: which communion, though especially to be exercised by them in the relations wherein they stand, whether in families or churches, yet as God offereth opportunity, is to be extended unto all those who in every place call upon the name of the Lord Jesus.

CHAPTER 28
OF THE SACRAMENTS

1. Sacraments are holy signs and seals of the covenant of grace, immediately instituted by Christ, to represent him and his benefits, and to confirm our interest in him, and solemnly to engage us to the service of God in Christ, according to his Word.

2. There is in every sacrament a spiritual relation, or sacramental union, between the sign and the thing signified; whence it comes to pass that the names and effects of the one are attributed to the other.

3. The grace which is exhibited in or by the sacraments rightly used, is not conferred by any power in them; neither doth the efficacy of a sacrament depend

upon the piety or intention of him that doth administer it, but upon the work of the Spirit, and the word of institution; which contains, together with a precept authorising the use thereof, a promise of benefit to worthy receivers.

4. There be only two sacraments ordained by Christ our Lord in the gospel, that is to say, baptism and the Lord's Supper; neither of which may be dispensed by any but a minister of the Word lawfully called.

5. The sacraments of the Old Testament, in regard of the spiritual things thereby signified and exhibited, were for substance the same with those of the New.

CHAPTER 29
OF BAPTISM

1. Baptism is a sacrament of the New Testament, ordained by Jesus Christ to be unto the party baptized a sign and seal of the covenant of grace, of his ingrafting into Christ, of regeneration, of remission of sins, and of his giving up unto God through Jesus Christ to walk in newness of life; which ordinance is by Christ's own appointment to be continued in his church until the end of the world.

2. The outward element to be used in this ordinance, is water, wherewith the party is to be baptized in the name of the Father, and of the Son, and of the Holy Ghost, by a minister of the gospel lawfully called.

3. Dipping of the person into the water is not necessary; but baptism is rightly administered by pouring or sprinkling water upon the person.

4. Not only those that do actually profess faith in and obedience unto Christ, but also the infants of one or both believing parents are to be baptized, and those only.

5. Although it be a great sin to contemn or neglect this ordinance, yet grace and salvation are not so inseparably annexed unto it, as that no person can be regenerated or saved without it; or that all that are baptized are undoubtedly regenerated.

6. The efficacy of baptism is not tied to that moment of time wherein it is administered; yet notwithstanding, by the right use of this ordinance, the grace promised is not only offered, but really exhibited and conferred by the

Holy Ghost to such (whether of age or infants) as that grace belongeth unto, according to the counsel of God's own will in his appointed time.

7. Baptism is but once to be administered to any person.

CHAPTER 30
OF THE LORD'S SUPPER

1. Our Lord Jesus in the night wherein he was betrayed, instituted the sacrament of his body and blood, called the Lord's Supper, to be observed in his churches to the end of the world, for the perpetual remembrance, and showing forth of the sacrifice of himself in his death, the sealing of all benefits thereof unto true believers, their spiritual nourishment, and growth in him, their further engagement in and to all duties which they owe unto him, and to be a bond and pledge of their communion with him, and with each other.

2. In this sacrament Christ is not offered up to his Father, nor any real sacrifice made at all for remission of sin of the quick or dead, but only a memorial of that one offering up of himself upon the cross once for all, and a spiritual oblation of all possible praise unto God for the same; so that the popish sacrifice of the Mass (as they call it) is most abominable, injurious to Christ's own only sacrifice, the alone propitiation for all the sins of the elect.

3. The Lord Jesus hath in this ordinance appointed his ministers to pray and bless the elements of bread and wine, and thereby to set them apart from a common to an holy use; and to take and break the bread, to take the cup, and (they communicating also themselves) to give both to the communicants; but to none who are not then present in the congregation.

4. Private Masses, or receiving the sacrament by a priest, or any other, alone; as likewise the denial of the cup to the people; worshiping the elements, the lifting them up, or carrying them about for adoration, and the reserving them for any pretended religious use; are contrary to the nature of this sacrament, and to the institution of Christ.

5. The outward elements in this sacrament duly set apart to the uses ordained by Christ, have such relation to him crucified, as that truly, yet sacramentally

only, they are sometimes called by the name of the things they represent, to wit, the body and blood of Christ; albeit, in substance and nature, they still remain truly and only bread and wine as they were before.

6. The doctrine which maintains a change of the substance of bread and wine into the substance of Christ's body and blood (commonly called transubstantiation) by consecration of a priest, or by any other way, is repugnant not to Scripture alone, but even to common sense and reason; overthroweth the nature of the sacrament; and hath been and is the cause of manifold superstitions, yea, of gross idolatries.

7. Worthy receivers outwardly partaking of the visible elements in this sacrament, do then also inwardly by faith, really and indeed, yet not carnally and corporally, but spiritually, receive and feed upon Christ crucified, and all benefits of his death; the body and blood of Christ being then not corporally or carnally in, with, or under the bread or wine; yet as really, but spiritually present to the faith of believers in that ordinance, as the elements themselves are to their outward senses.

8. All ignorant and ungodly persons, as they are unfit to enjoy communion with Christ, so are they unworthy of the Lord's table, and cannot without great sin against him, while they remain such, partake of these holy mysteries, or be admitted thereunto; yea, whosoever shall receive unworthily, are guilty of the body and blood of the Lord, eating and drinking judgment to themselves.

CHAPTER 31

OF THE STATE OF MAN AFTER DEATH, AND OF THE RESURRECTION OF THE DEAD

1. The bodies of men after death return to dust, and see corruption; but their souls (which neither die nor sleep) having an immortal subsistence, immediately return to God who gave them. The souls of the righteous being then made perfect in holiness, are received into the highest heavens, where they behold the face of God in light and glory, waiting for the full redemption of their bodies: and the souls of the wicked are cast into hell, where they remain

in torment and utter darkness, reserved to the judgment of the great day: Besides these two places for souls separated from their bodies, the Scripture acknowledgeth none.

2. At the last day such as are found alive shall not die, but be changed; and all the dead shall be raised up with the selfsame bodies, and none other, although with different qualities, which shall be united again to their souls for ever.

3. The bodies of the unjust shall by the power of Christ be raised to dishonor; the bodies of the just, by his Spirit unto honor, and to be made conformable to his own glorious body.

CHAPTER 32
OF THE LAST JUDGMENT

1. God hath appointed a day wherein he will judge the world in righteousness by Jesus Christ, to whom all power and judgment is given of the Father. In which day, not only the apostate angels shall be judged, but likewise all persons that have lived upon earth shall appear before the tribunal of Christ, to give an account of their thoughts, words and deeds, and to receive according to what they have done in the body, whether good or evil.

2. The end of God's appointing this day is for the manifestation of the glory of his mercy in the eternal salvation of the elect, and of his justice in the damnation of the reprobate, who are wicked and disobedient. For then shall the righteous go into everlasting life, and receive that fulness of joy and glory, with everlasting reward in the presence of the Lord; but the wicked who know not God, and obey not the gospel of Jesus Christ, shall be cast into eternal torments, and be punished with everlasting destruction from the presence of the Lord, and from the glory of his power.

3. As Christ would have us to be certainly persuaded that there shall be a judgment, both to deter all men from sin, and for the greater consolation of the godly in their adversity; so will he have that day unknown to men, that they may shake off all carnal security, and be always watchful, because they know not at what hour the Lord will come, and may be ever prepared to say, Come Lord Jesus, come quickly, Amen.

THE INSTITUTION OF CHURCHES, AND THE ORDER APPOINTED IN THEM BY JESUS CHRIST

1. By the appointment of the Father all power for the calling, institution, order, or government of the church, is invested in a supreme and sovereign manner in the Lord Jesus Christ, as King and Head thereof.

2. In the execution of this power wherewith he is so entrusted, the Lord Jesus calleth out of the world unto communion with himself, those that are given unto him by his Father, that they may walk before him in all the ways of obedience, which he prescribeth to them in his Word.

3. Those thus called (through the ministry of the Word by his Spirit) he commandeth to walk together in particular societies or churches, for their mutual edification, and the due performance of that public worship, which he requireth of them in this world.

4. To each of these churches thus gathered, according to his mind declared in his Word, he hath given all that power and authority, which is any way needful for their carrying on that order in worship and discipline, which he hath instituted for them to observe, with commands and rules for the due and right exerting and executing of that power.

5. These particular churches thus appointed by the authority of Christ, and entrusted with power from him for the ends before expressed, are each of them as unto those ends, the seat of that power which he is pleased to communicate to his saints or subjects in this world, so that as such they receive it immediately from himself.

6. Besides these particular churches, there is not instituted by Christ any church more extensive or catholic entrusted with power for the administration of his ordinances, or the execution of any authority in his name.

7. A particular church gathered and completed according to the mind of Christ, consists of officers and members. The Lord Christ having given to his called ones (united according to his appointment in church-order) liberty and power to choose persons fitted by the Holy Ghost for that purpose, to be over them, and to minister to them in the Lord.

8. The members of these churches are saints by calling, visibly manifesting and evidencing (in and by their profession and walking) their obedience unto that call of Christ; who, being further known to each other by their confession of the faith wrought in them by the power of God, declared by themselves or otherwise manifested, do willingly consent to walk together according to the appointment of Christ; giving up themselves to the Lord, and to one another by the will of God in professed subjection to the ordinances of the gospel.

9. The officers appointed by Christ, to be chosen and set apart by the church so called, and gathered for the peculiar administration of ordinances, and execution of power and duty which he entrusts them with, or calls them to, to be continued to the end of the world, are pastors, teachers, elders and deacons.

10. Churches thus gathered and assembling for the worship of God, are thereby visible and public, and their assemblies (in whatever place they are, according as they have liberty or opportunity) are therefore church or public assemblies.

11. The way appointed by Christ for the calling of any person, fitted and gifted by the Holy Ghost, unto the office of pastor, teacher or elder in a church, is, that he be chosen thereunto by the common suffrage of the church itself, and solemnly set apart by fasting and prayer, with imposition of hands of the eldership of that church, if there be any before constituted therein. And of a deacon, that he be chosen by the like suffrage, and set apart by prayer, and the like imposition of hands.

12. The essence of this call of a pastor, teacher or elder unto office, consists in the election of the church, together with his acceptance of it, and separation by fasting and prayer. And those who are so chosen, though not set apart by imposition of hands, are rightly constituted ministers of Jesus Christ, in whose name and authority they exercise the ministry to them so committed. The calling of deacons consisteth in the like election and acceptation with separation by prayer.

13. Although it be incumbent on the pastors and teachers of the churches to be instant in preaching the Word, by way of office; yet the work of preaching the Word is not so peculiarly confined to them, but that others also gifted and fitted by the Holy Ghost for it, and approved (being by lawful ways and means

in the providence of God called thereunto) may publicly, ordinarily and constantly perform it; so that they give themselves up thereunto.

14. However, they who are engaged in the work of public preaching, and enjoy the public maintenance upon that account, are not thereby obliged to dispense the seals to any other than such as (being saints by calling, and gathered according to the order of the gospel) they stand related to, as pastors or teachers. Yet ought they not to neglect others living within their parochial bounds, but besides their constant public preaching to them, they ought to enquire after their profiting by the Word, instructing them in, and pressing upon them (whether young or old) the great doctrines of the gospel, even personally and particularly, so far as their strength and time will admit.

15. Ordination alone without the election or precedent consent of the church, by those who formerly have been ordained by virtue of that power they have received by their ordination, doth not constitute any person a church-officer, or communicate office-power to him.

16. A church furnished with officers (according to the mind of Christ) hath full power to administer all his ordinances; and where there is want of any one or more officers required, that officer, or those which are in the church, may administer all the ordinances proper to their particular duty and offices; but where there are no teaching officers, none may administer the seals, nor can the church authorize any so to do.

17. In the carrying on of church-administrations, no person ought to be added to the church, but by the consent of the church itself; that so love (without dissimulation) may be preserved between all the members thereof.

18. Whereas the Lord Jesus Christ hath appointed and instituted as a means of edification, that those who walk not according to the rules and laws appointed by him (in respect of faith and life, so that just offence doth arise to the church thereby) be censured in his name and authority. Every church hath power in itself to exercise and execute all those censures appointed by him in the way and order prescribed in the gospel.

19. The censures so appointed by Christ, are admonition and excommunication. And whereas some offences are or may be known only to some, it is

appointed by Christ, that those to whom they are so known, do first admonish the offender in private: in public offences where any sin, before all. Or in case of non-amendment upon private admonition, the offence being related to the church, and the offender not manifesting his repentance, he is to be duly admonished in the name of Christ by the whole church, by the ministry of the elders of the church; and if this censure prevail not for his repentance, then he is to be cast out by excommunication with the consent of the church.

20. As all believers are bound to join themselves to particular churches, when and where they have opportunity so to do, so none are to be admitted unto the privileges of the churches, who do not submit themselves to the rule of Christ in the censures for the government of them.

21. This being the way prescribed by Christ in case of offence, no church-members upon any offences taken by them, having performed their duty required of them in this matter, ought to disturb any church-order, or absent themselves from the public assemblies, or the administration of any ordinances upon that pretense, but to wait upon Christ in the further proceeding of the church.

22. The power of censures being seated by Christ in a particular church, is to be exercised only towards particular members of each church respectively as such; and there is no power given by him unto any synods or ecclesiastical assemblies to excommunicate, or by their public edicts to threaten excommunication, or other church-censures against churches, magistrates, or their people upon any account, no man being obnoxious to that censure, but upon his personal miscarriage, as a member of a particular church.

23. Although the church is a society of men, assembling for the celebration of the ordinances according to the appointment of Christ, yet every society assembling for that end or purpose, upon the account of cohabitation within any civil precincts and bounds, is not thereby constituted a church, seeing there may be wanting among them, what is essentially required thereunto; and therefore a believer living with others in such a precinct, may join himself with any church for his edification.

24. For the avoiding of differences that may otherwise arise, for the greater solemnity in the celebration of the ordinances of Christ, and the opening a way

for the larger usefulness of the gifts and graces of the Holy Ghost; saints living in one city or town, or within such distances as that they may conveniently assemble for divine worship, ought rather to join in one church for their mutual strengthening and edification, than to set up many distinct societies.

25. As all churches and all the members of them are bound to pray continually for the good or prosperity of all the churches of Christ in all places, and upon all occasions to further it; (every one within the bounds of their places and callings, in the exercise of their gifts and graces). So the churches themselves (when planted by the providence of God, so as they may have opportunity and advantage for it) ought to hold communion amongst themselves for their peace, increase of love, and mutual edification.

26. In cases of difficulties or differences, either in point of doctrine or in administrations, wherein either the churches in general are concerned, or any one church in their peace, union, and edification, or any member or members of any church are injured in, or by any proceeding in censures, not agreeable to truth and order: it is according to the mind of Christ, that many churches holding communion together, do by their messengers meet in a synod or council, to consider and give their advice in, or about that matter in difference, to be reported to all the churches concerned. Howbeit, these synods so assembled are not entrusted with any church-power, properly so called, or with any jurisdiction over the churches themselves, to exercise any censures, either over any churches or persons, or to impose their determinations on the churches or officers.

27. Besides these occasional synods or councils, there are not instituted by Christ any stated synods in a fixed combination of churches, or their officers in lesser or greater assemblies; nor are there any synods appointed by Christ in a way of subordination to one another.

28. Persons that are joined in church-fellowship, ought not lightly or without just cause to withdraw themselves from the communion of the church whereunto they are so joined. Nevertheless, where any person cannot continue in any church without his sin, either for want of the administration of any ordinances instituted by Christ, or by his being deprived of his due privileges, or compelled to anything in practice not warranted by the Word, or in case of

persecution, or upon the account of conveniency of habitation; he consulting with the church, or the officer or officers thereof, may peaceably depart from the communion of the church, wherewith he hath so walked, to join himself with some other church, where he may enjoy the ordinances in the purity of the same, for his edification and consolation.

29. Such reforming churches as consist of persons sound in the faith and of conversation becoming the gospel, ought not to refuse the communion of each other, so far as may consist with their own principles respectively, though they walk not in all things according to the same rules of church-order.

30. Churches gathered and walking according to the mind of Christ, judging other churches (though less pure) to be true churches, may receive unto occasional communion with them, such members of those churches as are credibly testified to be godly, and live without offence.

20

Second London Baptist Confession of Faith

(1689)

As the Savoy Declaration was a revision of the Westminster Confession of Faith along Congregationalist lines, so the Second London Baptist Confession was a revision along Particular (Calvinistic) Baptist lines. In this, the Baptists expressed their solidarity with the Westminster divines and the Congregationalists over much of the theology of the Reformation while asserting their own convictions regarding baptism.

This confession follows the First London Baptist Confession of 1644. That confession was aimed at providing doctrinal unity in the face of continued persecution and at distinguishing the Particular Baptists from the General (Arminian) Baptists and from the Continental Anabaptists.

This new confession was drafted in 1677, but the religious situation in England precluded public endorsement. Things changed in 1689 with the Act of Toleration, which allowed for a measure of religious freedom, allowing the Particular Baptists to adopt a revised version of the confession that year. A slightly revised version was adopted by American Particular Baptists in 1742 as the Philadelphia Confession of Faith.

Second London Baptist Confession of Faith

PREFACE

To the judicial and impartial reader

Courteous Reader: It is now many years since divers of us (with other sober Christians then living and walking in the way of the Lord that we profess) did conceive ourselves to be under a necessity of publishing a Confession of our Faith, for the information and satisfaction of those, that did not thoroughly understand what our principles were, or had entertained prejudices against our Profession, by reason of the strange representation of them, by some men of note, who had taken very wrong measures, and accordingly led others into misapprehensions, of us, and them: and this was first put forth about the year, 1643, in the name of seven Congregations then gathered in London; since which time, divers impressions thereof have been dispersed abroad, and our end proposed, in good measure answered, inasmuch as many (and some of those men eminent, both for piety and learning) were thereby satisfied, that we were no way guilty of those Heterodoxies and fundamental errors, which had too frequently been charged upon us without ground, or occasion given on our part. And forasmuch as that Confession is not now commonly to be had; and also that many others have since embraced the same truth which is owned therein: it was judged necessary by us to join together in giving a testimony to the world; of our firm adhering to those wholesome Principles, by the publication of this which is now in your hand.

And forasmuch as our method, and manner of expressing our sentiments in this doth vary from the former (although the substance of this matter is the same), we shall freely impart to you the reason and occasion thereof. One thing that greatly prevailed with us to undertake this work, was (not only to give a full account of ourselves to those Christians that differ from us about the subject of baptism, but also) the profit that might from thence arise unto those that have any account of our labors, in their instruction and establishment in the great truths of the gospel; in the clear understanding and steady belief of which our comfortable walking with God, and fruitfulness before him in all our ways is most nearly concerned. And therefore we did conclude it necessary to express ourselves the more fully and distinctly, and also to fix on such a method as might be most comprehensive of those things we designed to explain our sense and belief of; and finding no defect in this regard in that fixed on by the Assembly, and after them by those of the Congregational way, we did readily conclude it best to retain the same order in our present Confession. And also when we observed that those last mentioned did, in their Confessions (for reasons which seemed of weight both to themselves and others), choose not only to express their mind in words concurrent with the former in sense, concerning all those articles wherein they were agreed, but also for the most part without any variation of the terms, we did in like manner conclude it best to follow their example, in making use of the very same words with them both, in these articles (which are very many) wherein our faith and doctrine are the same with theirs. And this we did, the more abundantly to manifest our consent with both, in all the fundamental articles of the Christian religion, as also with many others whose orthodox confessions have been published to the World, on the behalf of the Protestants in diverse nations and cities; and also to convince all that we have no itch to clog religion with new words, but do readily acquiesce in that form of sound words which hath been, in consent with the Holy Scriptures, used by others before us; hereby declaring, before God, angels, and men, our hearty agreement with them, in that wholesome Protestant doctrine, which, with so clear evidence of Scriptures they have asserted. Some things, indeed, are in some places added, some terms omitted, and some few changed; but these alterations are of that nature, as that we need not doubt any charge or suspicion of unsoundness in the faith, from any of our brethren upon the account of them.

In those things wherein we differ from others, we have expressed ourselves with all candor and plainness, that none might entertain Jealousy of aught secretly lodged in our breasts, that we would not the world should be acquainted with; yet we hope we have also observed those rules of modesty and humility as will render our freedom in this respect inoffensive, even to those whose sentiments are different from ours.

We have also taken care to affix texts of Scripture, for the confirmation of each article in our Confession; in which work we have studiously endeavored to select such as are most clear and pertinent for the proof of what is asserted by us; and our earnest desire is, that all into whose hands this may come would follow that (never enough commended) example of the noble Bereans, who searched the Scriptures daily that they might find out whether the things preached to them were so or not.

There is one thing more which we sincerely profess, and earnestly desire credence in, viz., that contention is most remote from our design in all that we have done in this matter; and we hope that the liberty of an ingenuous unfolding our principles and opening our hearts unto our brethren, with the scriptural grounds on which our faith and practice leans, will by none of them be either denied to us, or taken ill from us. Our whole design is accomplished if we may have attained that justice, as to be measured in our principles and practice and the judgment of both by others, according to what we have now published; which the Lord (whose eyes are as a flame of fire) knoweth to be the doctrine, which with our hearts we most firmly believe and sincerely endeavor to conform our lives to. And oh that other contentions being laid asleep, the only care and contention of all upon whom the name of our blessed Redeemer is called, might for the future be, to walk humbly with their God, and in the exercise of all Love and Meekness towards each other, to perfect holiness in the fear of the Lord, each one endeavoring to have his conversation such as becometh the Gospel; and also, suitable to his place and capacity, vigorously to promote in others the practice of true Religion and undefiled in the sight of God our Father. And that in this backsliding day, we might not spend our breath in fruitless complaints of the evils of others; but may every one begin at home, to reform in the first place our own hearts, and ways; and then to quicken all that we may have influence upon, to the same work; that if the will of God were so, none might deceive themselves, by resting in, and trusting to, a form of Godliness without the power of it, and inward experience of the efficacy of those truths that are professed by them.

And verily there is one spring and cause of the decay of Religion in our day, which we cannot but touch upon, and earnestly urge a redress of; and that is the neglect of the worship of God in Families, by those to whom the charge and conduct of them is committed. May not the gross ignorance, and instability of many; with the profaneness of others, be justly charged upon their

Parents and Masters, who have not trained them up in the way wherein they ought to walk when they were young; but have neglected those frequent and solemn commands which the Lord hath laid upon them, so to catechize, and instruct them, that their tender years might be seasoned with the knowledge of the truth of God as revealed in the Scriptures; and also by their own omission of Prayer, and other duties of Religion in their families, together with the ill example of their loose conversation, having inured them first to a neglect, and then contempt of all Piety and Religion? We know this will not excuse the blindness, or wickedness of any; but certainly it will fall heavy upon those that have been thus the occasion thereof; they indeed die in their sins; but will not their blood be required of those under whose care they were, who yet permitted them to go on without warning—yea, led them into the paths of destruction? And will not the diligence of Christians with respect to the discharge of these duties, in ages past, rise up in judgment against, and condemn many of those who would be esteemed such now?

We shall conclude with our earnest prayer that the God of all grace, will pour out those measures of his Holy Spirit upon us, that the profession of truth may be accompanied with the sound belief, and diligent practice of it by us; that his name may in all things be glorified, through Jesus Christ our Lord, *Amen*.

CHAPTER 1
OF THE HOLY SCRIPTURE

1. The Holy Scripture is the only sufficient, certain, and infallible rule of all saving knowledge, faith, and obedience:[1] although the light of nature, and the works of creation and providence do so far manifest the goodness, wisdom, and power of God, as to leave men unexcusable; yet are they not sufficient to give that knowledge of God and his will, which is necessary unto salvation.[2] Therefore it pleased the Lord at sundry times, and in divers manners, to reveal himself, and to declare that his will unto his church;[3] and afterward for the better preserving, and propagating of the truth, and for the more sure establishment and comfort of the church against the corruption of the flesh, and the malice of Satan, and of the world, to commit the same wholly unto writing; which maketh the Holy Scriptures to be most necessary, those former ways of God's revealing his will unto his people being now ceased.[4]

2. Under the name of Holy Scripture, or the Word of God written; are now contained all the books of the Old and New Testaments, which are these:

OF THE OLD TESTAMENT:

Genesis	II Chronicles	Daniel
Exodus	Ezra	Hosea
Leviticus	Nehemiah	Joel
Numbers	Esther	Amos
Deuteronomy	Job	Obadiah
Joshua	Psalms	Jonah
Judges	Proverbs	Micah
Ruth	Ecclesiastes	Nahum
I Samuel	The Song of Songs	Habakkuk
II Samuel	Isaiah	Zephaniah
I Kings	Jeremiah	Haggai
II Kings	Lamentations	Zechariah
I Chronicles	Ezekiel	Malachi

---

1 2 Tim. 3:15–17; Isa. 8:20; Luke 16:29, 31; Eph. 2:20.
2 Rom. 1:19–21; Rom. 2:14–15; Ps. 19:1–3.
3 Heb. 1:1.
4 Prov. 22:19–21; Rom. 15:4; 2 Peter 1:19–20.

OF THE NEW TESTAMENT:

The Gospels	Galatians	The Epistle
according to	Ephesians	of James
Matthew	Philippians	The first and
Mark	Colossians	second Epistles
Luke	Thessalonians I	of Peter
John	Thessalonians II	The first, second,
The Acts of the	to Timothy I	and third Epistles
Apostles	to Timothy II	of John
Paul's Epistles	to Titus	The Epistle
to the Romans	to Philemon	of Jude
Corinthians I	The Epistle to	The Revelation
Corinthians II	the Hebrews	of John

All of which are given by the inspiration of God, to be the rule of faith and life.[5]

3. The books commonly called Apocrypha, not being of divine inspiration, are no part of the canon (or rule) of the Scripture, and therefore are of no authority to the church of God, nor to be any otherwise approved or made use of, than other human writings.[6]

4. The authority of the Holy Scripture, for which it ought to be believed, dependeth not upon the testimony of any man, or church; but wholly upon God (who is truth itself), the author thereof; therefore it is to be received, because it is the Word of God.[7]

5. We may be moved and induced by the testimony of the church of God, to a high and reverent esteem of the Holy Scriptures; and the heavenliness of the matter, the efficacy of the doctrine, and the majesty of the style, the consent of all the parts, the scope of the whole (which is to give all glory to God), the full discovery it makes of the only way of man's salvation, and many other incomparable excellencies, and entire perfections thereof, are arguments whereby it doth abundantly evidence itself to be the Word of God; yet, notwithstanding, our full persuasion, and assurance of the infallible truth, and divine authority

---

5   2 Tim. 3:16.
6   Luke 24:27, 44; Rom. 3:2.
7   2 Peter 1:19–21; 2 Tim. 3:16; 2 Thess. 2:13; 1 John 5:9.

thereof, is from the inward work of the Holy Spirit, bearing witness by and with the Word in our hearts.[8]

6. The whole counsel of God concerning all things necessary for his own glory, man's salvation, faith and life, is either expressly set down or necessarily contained in the Holy Scripture; unto which nothing at any time is to be added, whether by new revelation of the Spirit, or traditions of men.[9] Nevertheless, we acknowledge the inward illumination of the Spirit of God to be necessary for the saving understanding of such things as are revealed in the Word,[10] and that there are some circumstances concerning the worship of God, and government of the church common to human actions and societies; which are to be ordered by the light of nature, and Christian prudence, according to the general rules of the Word, which are always to be observed.[11]

7. All things in Scripture are not alike plain in themselves, nor alike clear unto all;[12] yet those things which are necessary to be known, believed, and observed for salvation, are so clearly propounded, and opened in some place of Scripture or other, that not only the learned, but the unlearned, in a due use of ordinary means, may attain to a sufficient understanding of them.[13]

8. The Old Testament in Hebrew (which was the native language of the people of God of old),[14] and the New Testament in Greek (which at the time of the writing of it was most generally known to the nations), being immediately inspired by God, and by his singular care and providence kept pure in all ages, are therefore authentical; so as in all controversies of religion, the church is finally to appeal to them.[15] But because these original tongues are not known to all the people of God, who have a right unto, and interest in the Scriptures, and are commanded in the fear of God to read and search them,[16] therefore they are to be translated into the vulgar language of every nation, unto which

8   John 16:13–14; 1 Cor. 2:10–12; 1 John 2:20, 27.
9   2 Tim. 3:15–17; Gal. 1:8–9.
10 John 6:45; 1 Cor. 2:9–12.
11 1 Cor. 11:13–14; 1 Cor. 14:26, 40.
12 2 Peter 3:16.
13 Ps. 19:7; Ps. 119:130.
14 Rom. 3:2.
15 Isa. 8:20; Acts 15:15.
16 John 5:39.

they come,[17] that the Word of God dwelling plentifully in all, they may worship him in an acceptable manner, and through patience and comfort of the Scriptures may have hope.[18]

9. The infallible rule of interpretation of Scripture is the Scripture itself:[19] and therefore when there is a question about the true and full sense of any Scripture (which is not manifold but one), it must be searched by other places that speak more clearly.

10. The supreme judge, by which all controversies of religion are to be determined, and all decrees of councils, opinions of ancient writers, doctrines of men, and private spirits, are to be examined, and in whose sentence we are to rest, can be no other but the Holy Scripture delivered by the Spirit, into which Scripture so delivered, our faith is finally resolved.[20]

---

17 1 Cor. 14:6, 9, 11–12, 24, 28.
18 Col. 3:16.
19 2 Peter 1:20–21; Acts 15:15–16.
20 Matt. 22:29, 31–32; Eph. 2:20; Acts 28:23.

CHAPTER 2
OF GOD, AND OF THE HOLY TRINITY

1. The Lord our God is but one only living and true God;[1] whose subsistence is in and of himself,[2] infinite in being and perfection; whose essence cannot be comprehended by any but himself;[3] a most pure spirit,[4] invisible, without body, parts, or passions, who only hath immortality, dwelling in the light, which no man can approach unto,[5] who is immutable,[6] immense,[7] eternal,[8] incomprehensible, almighty,[9] every way infinite, most holy,[10] most wise, most free, most absolute, working all things according to the counsel of his own immutable and most righteous will,[11] for his own glory,[12] most loving, gracious, merciful, long-suffering, abundant in goodness and truth, forgiving iniquity, transgression and sin, the rewarder of them that diligently seek him,[13] and withal most just and terrible in his judgments,[14] hating all sin,[15] and who will by no means clear the guilty.[16]

2. God having all life,[17] glory,[18] goodness,[19] blessedness, in and of himself: is alone in and unto himself all-sufficient, not standing in need of any creature which he hath made, nor deriving any glory from them,[20] but only manifesting his own glory in, by, unto, and upon them; he is the alone fountain of all

---

1 1 Cor. 8:4, 6; Deut. 6:4.
2 Jer. 10:10; Isa. 48:12.
3 Ex. 3:14.
4 John 4:24.
5 1 Tim. 1:17; Deut. 4:15–16.
6 Mal. 3:6.
7 1 Kings 8:27; Jer. 23:23.
8 Ps. 90:2.
9 Gen. 17:1.
10 Isa. 6:3.
11 Ps. 115:3; Isa. 46:10.
12 Prov. 16:4; Rom. 11:36.
13 Ex. 34:6–7; Heb. 11:6.
14 Neh. 9:32–33.
15 Ps. 5:5–6.
16 Ex. 34:7; Nah. 1:2–3.
17 John 5:26.
18 Ps. 148:13.
19 Ps. 119:68.
20 Job 22:2–3.

being, of whom, through whom, and to whom are all things,[21] and he hath most sovereign dominion over all creatures, to do by them, for them, or upon them, whatsoever himself pleaseth;[22] in his sight all things are open and manifest,[23] his knowledge is infinite, infallible, and independent upon the creature, so as nothing is to him contingent or uncertain;[24] he is most holy in all his counsels, in all his works,[25] and in all his commands; to him is due from angels and men, whatsoever worship,[26] service, or obedience, as creatures they owe unto the Creator, and whatever he is further pleased to require of them.

3. In this divine and infinite Being there are three subsistences, the Father, the Word (or Son), and Holy Spirit,[27] of one substance, power, and eternity, each having the whole divine essence, yet the essence undivided,[28] the Father is of none neither begotten nor proceeding, the Son is eternally begotten of the Father,[29] the Holy Spirit proceeding from the Father and the Son,[30] all infinite, without beginning, therefore but one God, who is not to be divided in nature and being; but distinguished by several peculiar, relative properties, and personal relations; which doctrine of the Trinity is the foundation of all our communion with God, and comfortable dependence on him.

---

21 Rom. 11:34–36.
22 Dan. 4:25, 34–35.
23 Heb. 4:13.
24 Ezek. 11:5; Acts 15:18.
25 Ps. 145:17.
26 Rev. 5:12–14.
27 1 John 5:7; Matt. 28:19; 2 Cor. 13:14.
28 Ex. 3:14; John 14:11; 1 Cor. 8:6.
29 John 1:14, 18.
30 John 15:26; Gal. 4:6.

CHAPTER 3
OF GOD'S ETERNAL DECREE

1. God hath decreed in himself from all eternity, by the most wise and holy counsel of his own will, freely and unchangeably, all things whatsoever comes to pass;[1] yet so as thereby is God neither the author of sin, nor hath fellowship with any therein;[2] nor is violence offered to the will of the creature, nor yet is the liberty, or contingency of second causes taken away, but rather established;[3] in which appears his wisdom in disposing all things, and power and faithfulness in accomplishing his decree.[4]

2. Although God knoweth whatsoever may, or can come to pass upon all supposed conditions;[5] yet hath he not decreed anything, because he foresaw it as future, or as that which would come to pass upon such conditions.[6]

3. By the decree of God, for the manifestation of his glory, some men and angels are predestinated, or foreordained to eternal life, through Jesus Christ,[7] to the praise of his glorious grace;[8] others being left to act in their sin to their just condemnation,[9] to the praise of his glorious justice.

4. These angels and men thus predestinated, and foreordained, are particularly, and unchangeably designed, and their number so certain, and definite, that it cannot be either increased, or diminished.[10]

5. Those of mankind that are predestinated to life, God, before the foundation of the world was laid, according to his eternal and immutable purpose, and the secret counsel and good pleasure of his will, hath chosen in Christ

1 Isa. 46:10; Eph. 1:11; Heb. 6:17; Rom. 9:15, 18.
2 James 1:13; 1 John 1:5.
3 Acts 4:27–28; John 19:11.
4 Num. 23:19; Eph. 1:3–5.
5 Acts 15:18.
6 Rom. 9:11, 13, 16, 18.
7 1 Tim. 5:21; Matt. 25:34.
8 Eph. 1:5–6.
9 Rom. 9:22–23; Jude 4.
10 2 Tim. 2:19; John 13:18.

unto everlasting glory, out of his mere free grace and love;[11] without any other thing in the creature as a condition or cause moving him thereunto.[12]

6. As God hath appointed the elect unto glory, so he hath, by the eternal and most free purpose of his will, foreordained all the means thereunto,[13] wherefore they who are elected, being fallen in Adam, are redeemed by Christ,[14] are effectually called unto faith in Christ, by his Spirit working in due season, are justified, adopted, sanctified,[15] and kept by his power through faith unto salvation;[16] neither are any other redeemed by Christ, or effectually called, justified, adopted, sanctified, and saved, but the elect only.[17]

7. The doctrine of this high mystery of predestination, is to be handled with special prudence and care; that men attending the will of God revealed in his Word, and yielding obedience thereunto, may from the certainty of their effectual vocation, be assured of their eternal election;[18] so shall this doctrine afford matter of praise,[19] reverence, and admiration of God, and of humility,[20] diligence, and abundant consolation, to all that sincerely obey the gospel.[21]

11 Eph. 1:4, 9, 11; Rom. 8:30; 2 Tim. 1:9; 1 Thess. 5:9.
12 Rom. 9:13, 16; Eph. 2:5, 12.
13 1 Peter 1:2; 2 Thess. 2:13.
14 1 Thess. 5:9–10.
15 Rom. 8:30; 2 Thess. 2:13.
16 1 Peter 1:5.
17 John 10:26; John 17:9; John 6:64.
18 1 Thess. 1:4–5; 2 Peter 1:10.
19 Eph. 1:6; Rom. 11:33.
20 Rom. 11:5–6.
21 Luke 10:20.

CHAPTER 4
OF CREATION

1. In the beginning it pleased God the Father, Son, and Holy Spirit,[1] for the manifestation of the glory of his eternal power,[2] wisdom, and goodness, to create or make the world, and all things therein, whether visible or invisible, in the space of six days, and all very good.[3]

2. After God had made all other creatures, he created man, male and female,[4] with reasonable and immortal souls,[5] rendering them fit unto that life to God, for which they were created; being made after the image of God, in knowledge, righteousness, and true holiness;[6] having the law of God written in their hearts,[7] and power to fulfill it; and yet under a possibility of transgressing, being left to the liberty of their own will, which was subject to change.[8]

3. Besides the law written in their hearts, they received a command not to eat of the tree of knowledge of good and evil;[9] which while they kept, they were happy in their communion with God, and had dominion over the creatures.[10]

---

1 John 1:2–3; Heb. 1:2; Job 26:13.
2 Rom. 1:20.
3 Col. 1:16; Gen. 1:31.
4 Gen. 1:27.
5 Gen. 2:7.
6 Eccl. 7:29; Gen. 1:26.
7 Rom. 2:14–15.
8 Gen. 3:6.
9 Gen. 2:17; Gen. 3:8–10.
10 Gen. 1:26, 28.

CHAPTER 5
OF DIVINE PROVIDENCE

1. God, the good Creator of all things, in his infinite power and wisdom, doth uphold, direct, dispose, and govern all creatures, and things,[1] from the greatest even to the least,[2] by his most wise and holy providence, to the end for the which they were created; according unto his infallible foreknowledge, and the free and immutable counsel of his own will; to the praise of the glory of his wisdom, power, justice, infinite goodness, and mercy.[3]

2. Although in relation to the foreknowledge and decree of God, the First Cause, all things come to pass immutably and infallibly;[4] so that there is not anything befalls any by chance, or without his providence;[5] yet by the same providence he ordereth them to fall out, according to the nature of second causes, either necessarily, freely, or contingently.[6]

3. God, in his ordinary providence maketh use of means;[7] yet is free to work without,[8] above,[9] and against them[10] at his pleasure.

4. The almighty power, unsearchable wisdom, and infinite goodness of God, so far manifest themselves in his providence, that his determinate counsel extendeth itself even to the first fall, and all other sinful actions both of angels and men;[11] (and that not by a bare permission) which also he most wisely and powerfully boundeth, and otherwise ordereth, and governeth,[12] in a manifold dispensation to his most holy ends:[13] yet so, as the sinfulness of their acts

---

1 Heb. 1:3; Job 38:11; Isa. 46:10–11; Ps. 135:6.
2 Matt. 10:29–31.
3 Eph. 1:11.
4 Acts 2:23.
5 Prov. 16:33.
6 Gen. 8:22.
7 Acts 27:31, 44; Isa. 55:10–11.
8 Hos. 1:7.
9 Rom. 4:19–21.
10 Dan. 3:27.
11 Rom. 11:32–34; 2 Sam. 24:1; 1 Chron. 21:1.
12 2 Kings 19:28; Ps. 76:10.
13 Gen. 50:20; Isa. 10:6–7, 12.

proceeds only from the creatures, and not from God; who being most holy and righteous, neither is nor can be, the author or approver of sin.[14]

5. The most wise, righteous, and gracious God, doth oftentimes, leave for a season his own children to manifold temptations, and the corruptions of their own hearts, to chastise them for their former sins, or to discover unto them the hidden strength of corruption and deceitfulness of their hearts, that they may be humbled; and to raise them to a more close, and constant dependence for their support, upon himself; and to make them more watchful against all future occasions of sin, and for other just and holy ends.[15] So that whatsoever befalls any of his elect is by his appointment, for his glory, and their good.[16]

6. As for those wicked and ungodly men, whom God as a righteous judge, for former sin doth blind and harden;[17] from them he not only withholdeth his grace, whereby they might have been enlightened in their understanding, and wrought upon in their hearts:[18] but sometimes also withdraweth the gifts which they had,[19] and exposeth them to such objects as their corruptions make occasion of sin;[20] and withal, gives them over to their own lusts, the temptations of the world, and the power of Satan,[21] whereby it comes to pass, that they harden themselves, even under those means which God useth for the softening of others.[22]

7. As the providence of God doth in general reach to all creatures, so after a more special manner it taketh care of his church, and disposeth of all things to the good thereof.[23]

14 Ps. 50:21; 1 John 2:16.
15 2 Chron. 32:25–26, 31; 2 Sam. 24:1; 2 Cor. 12:7–9.
16 Rom. 8:28.
17 Rom. 1:24–26, 28; Rom. 11:7–8.
18 Deut. 29:4.
19 Matt. 13:12.
20 Deut. 2:30; 2 Kings 8:12–13.
21 Ps. 81:11–12; 2 Thess. 2:10–12.
22 Ex. 8:15, 32; Isa. 6:9–10; 1 Peter 2:7–8.
23 1 Tim. 4:10; Amos 9:8–9; Isa. 43:3–5.

CHAPTER 6

OF THE FALL OF MAN, OF SIN,
AND OF THE PUNISHMENT THEREOF

1. Although God created man upright and perfect, and gave him a righteous law, which had been unto life had he kept it, and threatened death upon the breach thereof;[1] yet he did not long abide in this honor; Satan using the subtlety of the serpent to seduce Eve, then by her seducing Adam, who, without any compulsion, did willfully transgress the law of their creation, and the command given unto them, in eating the forbidden fruit;[2] which God was pleased, according to his wise and holy counsel to permit, having purposed to order it, to his own glory.

2. Our first parents, by this sin, fell from their original righteousness and communion with God, and we in them, whereby death came upon all;[3] all becoming dead in sin,[4] and wholly defiled in all the faculties, and parts, of soul, and body.[5]

3. They being the root, and by God's appointment, standing in the room, and stead of all mankind; the guilt of the sin was imputed, and corrupted nature conveyed, to all their posterity descending from them by ordinary generation,[6] being now conceived in sin,[7] and by nature children of wrath,[8] the servants of sin, the subjects of death,[9] and all other miseries, spiritual, temporal and eternal, unless the Lord Jesus set them free.[10]

---

1 Gen. 2:16–17.
2 Gen. 3:12–13; 2 Cor. 11:3.
3 Rom. 3:23.
4 Rom. 5:12ff.
5 Titus 1:15; Gen. 6:5; Jer. 17:9; Rom. 3:10–19.
6 Rom. 5:12–19; 1 Cor. 15:21–22, 45, 49.
7 Ps. 51:5; Job 14:4.
8 Eph. 2:3.
9 Rom. 6:20; Rom. 5:12.
10 Heb. 2:14–15; 1 Thess. 1:10.

4. From this original corruption, whereby we are utterly indisposed, disabled, and made opposite to all good, and wholly inclined to all evil,[11] do proceed all actual transgressions.[12]

5. The corruption of nature, during this life, doth remain in those that are regenerated;[13] and although it be through Christ pardoned and mortified, yet both itself, and the first motions thereof, are truly and properly sin.[14]

11 Rom. 8:7; Col. 1:21.
12 James 1:14–15; Matt. 15:19.
13 Rom. 7:18, 23; Eccl. 7:20; 1 John 1:8.
14 Rom. 7:23–25; Gal. 5:17.

CHAPTER 7
OF GOD'S COVENANT

1. The distance between God and the creature is so great, that although reasonable creatures do owe obedience to him as their Creator, yet they could never have attained the reward of life, but by some voluntary condescension on God's part, which he hath been pleased to express, by way of covenant.[1]

2. Moreover, man having brought himself under the curse of the law by his fall, it pleased the Lord to make a covenant of grace,[2] wherein he freely offereth unto sinners, life and salvation by Jesus Christ, requiring of them faith in him, that they may be saved;[3] and promising to give unto all those that are ordained unto eternal life, his Holy Spirit, to make them willing, and able to believe.[4]

3. This covenant is revealed in the gospel; first of all to Adam in the promise of salvation by the seed of the woman,[5] and afterwards by farther steps, until the full discovery thereof was completed in the New Testament;[6] and it is founded in that eternal covenant transaction, that was between the Father and the Son, about the redemption of the elect;[7] and it is alone by the grace of this covenant, that all the posterity of fallen Adam, that ever were saved, did obtain life and blessed immortality; man being now utterly incapable of acceptance with God upon those terms, on which Adam stood in his state of innocency.[8]

---

1 Luke 17:10; Job 35:7–8.
2 Gen. 2:17; Gal. 3:10; Rom. 3:20–21.
3 Rom. 8:3; Mark 16:15–16; John 3:16.
4 Ezek. 36:26–27; John 6:44–45; Ps. 110:3.
5 Gen. 3:15.
6 Heb. 1:1.
7 2 Tim. 1:9; Titus 1:2.
8 Heb. 11:6, 13; Rom. 4:1–2ff; Acts 4:12; John 8:56.

CHAPTER 8
OF CHRIST THE MEDIATOR

1. It pleased God, in his eternal purpose, to choose and ordain the Lord Jesus his only begotten Son, according to the covenant made between them both, to be the Mediator between God and man;[1] the Prophet,[2] Priest,[3] and King;[4] Head and Savior of his church,[5] the Heir of all things,[6] and Judge of the world;[7] unto whom he did from all eternity give a people to be his seed, and to be by him in time redeemed, called, justified, sanctified, and glorified.[8]

2. The Son of God, the second person in the Holy Trinity, being very and eternal God, the brightness of the Father's glory, of one substance and equal with him who made the world, who upholdeth and governeth all things he hath made: did when the fullness of time was come take upon him man's nature, with all the essential properties, and common infirmities thereof,[9] yet without sin:[10] being conceived by the Holy Spirit in the womb of the virgin Mary, the Holy Spirit coming down upon her, and the power of the Most High overshadowing her, and so was made of a woman, of the tribe of Judah, of the seed of Abraham, and David according to the Scriptures:[11] so that two whole, perfect, and distinct natures, were inseparably joined together in one person: without conversion, composition, or confusion: which person is very God and very man; yet one Christ, the only Mediator between God and man.[12]

3. The Lord Jesus, in his human nature thus united to the divine, in the person of the Son, was sanctified, anointed with the Holy Spirit, above measure;[13]

---

1 Isa. 42:1; 1 Peter 1:19–20.
2 Acts 3:22.
3 Heb. 5:5–6.
4 Ps. 2:6; Luke 1:33.
5 Eph. 1:22–23.
6 Heb. 1:2.
7 Acts 17:31.
8 Isa. 53:10; John 17:6; Rom. 8:30.
9 John 1:14; Gal. 4:4.
10 Rom. 8:3; Heb. 2:14, 16–17; Heb. 4:15.
11 Luke 1:27, 31, 35.
12 Rom. 9:5; 1 Tim. 2:5
13 Ps. 45:7; Acts 10:38; John 3:34.

having in him all the treasures of wisdom and knowledge;[14] in whom it pleased the Father that all fullness should dwell:[15] to the end that being holy, harmless, undefiled,[16] and full of grace, and truth,[17] he might be thoroughly furnished to execute the office of a mediator and surety;[18] which office he took not upon himself, but was thereunto called by his Father;[19] who also put all power and judgment in his hand, and gave him commandment to execute the same.[20]

4. This office the Lord Jesus did most willingly undertake,[21] which that he might discharge he was made under the law,[22] and did perfectly fulfill it, and underwent the punishment due to us, which we should have born and suffered,[23] being made sin and a curse for us:[24] enduring most grievous sorrows in his soul; and most painful sufferings in his body;[25] was crucified, and died, and remained in the state of the dead; yet saw no corruption:[26] on the third day he arose from the dead,[27] with the same body in which he suffered;[28] with which he also ascended into heaven:[29] and there sitteth at the right hand of his Father, making intercession;[30] and shall return to judge men and angels, at the end of the world.[31]

5. The Lord Jesus by his perfect obedience and sacrifice of himself, which he through the eternal Spirit once offered up unto God,[32] hath fully satisfied the justice of God, procured reconciliation, and purchased an everlasting

---

14 Col. 2:3.
15 Col. 1:19.
16 Heb. 7:26.
17 John 1:14.
18 Heb. 7:22.
19 Heb. 5:5.
20 John 5:22, 27; Matt. 28:18; Acts 2:36.
21 Ps. 40:7–8; Heb. 10:5–10; John 10:18.
22 Gal 4:4; Matt. 3:15.
23 Gal. 3:13; Isa. 53:6; 1 Peter 3:18.
24 2 Cor. 5:21.
25 Matt. 26:37–38; Luke 22:44; Matt. 27:46.
26 Acts 13:37.
27 1 Cor. 15:3–4.
28 John 20:25, 27.
29 Mark 16:19; Acts 1:9–11.
30 Rom. 8:34; Heb. 9:24.
31 Acts 10:42; Rom. 14:9–10; Acts 1:11.
32 Heb. 9:14; Heb. 10:14; Rom. 3:25–26.

inheritance in the kingdom of heaven, for all those whom the Father hath given unto him.[33]

6. Although the price of redemption was not actually paid by Christ, till after his incarnation, yet the virtue, efficacy, and benefit thereof were communicated to the elect in all ages successively, from the beginning of the world, in and by those promises, types, and sacrifices, wherein he was revealed, and signified to be the seed of the woman, which should bruise the serpent's head;[34] and the Lamb slain from the foundation of the world:[35] being the same yesterday, and today and forever.[36]

7. Christ, in the work of mediation, acteth according to both natures, by each nature doing that which is proper to itself; yet by reason of the unity of the person, that which is proper to one nature is sometimes in Scripture, attributed to the person denominated by the other nature.[37]

8. To all those for whom Christ hath obtained eternal redemption, he doth certainly, and effectually apply, and communicate the same; making intercession for them,[38] uniting them to himself by his Spirit, revealing unto them, in and by the Word, the mystery of salvation; persuading them to believe, and obey,[39] governing their hearts by his Word and Spirit,[40] and overcoming all their enemies by his almighty power, and wisdom;[41] in such manner, and ways as are most consonant to his wonderful, and unsearchable dispensation; and all of free, and absolute grace, without any condition foreseen in them, to procure it.[42]

---

33 John 17:2; Heb. 9:15.

34 1 Cor. 4:10; Heb. 4:2; 1 Peter 1:10–11.

35 Rev. 13:8.

36 Heb. 13:8.

37 John 3:13; Acts 20:28.

38 John 6:37; John 10:15–16; John 17:9.

39 John 17:6; Eph. 1:9; 1 John 5:20.

40 Rom. 8:9, 14.

41 Ps. 110:1; 1 Cor. 15:25–26.

42 John 3:8; Eph. 1:8.

9. This office of Mediator between God and man, is proper only to Christ, who is the Prophet, Priest, and King of the church of God; and may not be either in whole, or any part thereof transferred from him to any other.[43]

10. This number and order of offices is necessary; for in respect of our ignorance, we stand in need of his prophetical office;[44] and in respect of our alienation from God, and imperfection of the best of our services, we need his priestly office, to reconcile us, and present us acceptable unto God:[45] and in respect to our averseness, and utter inability to return to God, and for our rescue, and security from our spiritual adversaries, we need his kingly office, to convince, subdue, draw, uphold, deliver, and preserve us to his heavenly kingdom.[46]

---

43 1 Tim. 2:5.
44 John 1:18.
45 Col. 1:21; Gal. 5:17.
46 John 16:8; Ps. 110:3; Luke 1:74–75.

CHAPTER 9
OF FREE WILL

1. God hath endued the will of man, with that natural liberty, and power of acting upon choice; that it is neither forced, nor by any necessity of nature determined to do good or evil.[1]

2. Man, in his state of innocency, had freedom, and power, to will and to do that which was good, and well-pleasing to God,[2] but yet was mutable, so that he might fall from it.[3]

3. Man by his fall into a state of sin hath wholly lost all ability of will, to any spiritual good accompanying salvation;[4] so as a natural man, being altogether averse from that good, and dead in sin,[5] is not able, by his own strength, to convert himself; or to prepare himself thereunto.[6]

4. When God converts a sinner, and translates him into the state of grace, he freeth him from his natural bondage under sin,[7] and by his grace alone, enables him freely to will and to do that which is spiritually good;[8] yet so as that by reason of his remaining corruptions he doth not perfectly nor only will that which is good; but doth also will that which is evil.[9]

5. This will of man is made perfectly, and immutably free to good alone, in the state of glory only.[10]

---

1 Matt. 17:12; James 1:14; Deut. 30:19.
2 Eccl. 7:29.
3 Gen. 3:6.
4 Rom. 5:6; Rom. 8:7.
5 Eph. 2:1, 5.
6 Titus 3:3–5; John 6:44.
7 Col. 1:13; John 8:36.
8 Phil. 2:13.
9 Rom. 7:15, 18–19, 21, 23.
10 Eph. 4:13.

CHAPTER 10

OF EFFECTUAL CALLING

1. Those whom God hath predestinated unto life, he is pleased, in his appointed, and accepted time, effectually to call,[1] by his Word, and Spirit, out of that state of sin, and death, in which they are by nature, to grace and salvation by Jesus Christ;[2] enlightening their minds, spiritually, and savingly to understand the things of God;[3] taking away their heart of stone, and giving to them a heart of flesh;[4] renewing their wills, and by his almighty power determining them to that which is good, and effectually drawing them to Jesus Christ;[5] yet so as they come most freely, being made willing by his grace.[6]

2. This effectual call is of God's free, and special grace alone, not from anything at all foreseen in man, nor from any power, or agency in the creature, coworking with his special grace,[7] the creature being wholly passive therein, being dead in sins and trespasses, until being quickened and renewed by the Holy Spirit;[8] he is thereby enabled to answer this call, and to embrace the grace offered and conveyed in it, and that by no less power, than that which raised up Christ from the dead.[9]

3. Elect infants dying in infancy, are regenerated and saved by Christ through the Spirit;[10] who works when, and where, and how he pleaseth;[11] so also are all other elect persons, who are incapable of being outwardly called by the ministry of the Word.

4. Others not elected, although they may be called by the ministry of the Word, and may have some common operations of the Spirit,[12] yet not being

---

1 Rom. 8:30; Rom. 11:7; Eph. 1:10–11; 2 Thess. 2:13–14.
2 Eph. 2:1–6.
3 Acts 26:18; Eph. 1:17–18.
4 Ezek. 36:26.
5 Deut. 30:6; Ezek. 36:27; Eph. 1:19.
6 Ps. 110:3; Song 1:4.
7 2 Tim. 1:9; Eph. 2:8.
8 1 Cor. 2:14; Eph. 2:5; John 5:25.
9 Eph. 1:19–20.
10 John 3:3, 5–6.
11 John 3:8.
12 Matt. 22:14; Matt. 13:20–21; Heb. 6:4–5.

effectually drawn by the Father, they neither will nor can truly come to Christ, and therefore cannot be saved:[13] much less can men that receive not the Christian religion be saved; be they never so diligent to frame their lives according to the light of nature and the law of that religion they do profess.[14]

---

13 John 6:44–45, 65; 1 John 2:24–25.
14 Acts 4:12; John 4:22; John 17:3.

CHAPTER 11

OF JUSTIFICATION

1. Those whom God effectually calleth, he also freely justifieth,[1] not by infusing righteousness into them, but by pardoning their sins, and by accounting, and accepting their persons as righteous;[2] not for anything wrought in them, or done by them, but for Christ's sake alone;[3] not by imputing faith itself, the act of believing, or any other evangelical obedience to them, as their righteousness; but by imputing Christ's active obedience unto the whole law, and passive obedience in his death for their whole and sole righteousness, they receiving, and resting on him, and his righteousness, by faith,[4] which faith they have not of themselves; it is the gift of God.[5]

2. Faith thus receiving and resting on Christ, and his righteousness, is the alone instrument of justification:[6] yet is not alone in the person justified, but is ever accompanied with all other saving graces, and is no dead faith, but worketh by love.[7]

3. Christ, by his obedience, and death, did fully discharge the debt of all those that are justified; and did by the sacrifice of himself, in the blood of his cross, undergoing in their stead, the penalty due unto them: make a proper, real, and full satisfaction to God's justice in their behalf:[8] yet in as much as he was given by the Father for them, and his obedience and satisfaction accepted in their stead, and both freely, not for anything in them;[9] their justification is only of free grace, that both the exact justice and rich grace of God, might be glorified in the justification of sinners.[10]

---

1   Rom. 3:24; Rom. 8:30.
2   Rom. 4:5–8; Eph. 1:7.
3   1 Cor. 1:30–31; Rom. 5:17–19.
4   Phil. 3:8–9; Eph. 2:8–10.
5   John 1:12; Rom. 5:17.
6   Rom. 3:28.
7   Gal.5:6; James 2:17, 22, 26.
8   Heb. 10:14; 1 Peter 1:18–19; Isa. 53:5–6.
9   Rom. 8:32; 2 Cor. 5:21.
10 Rom. 3:26; Eph. 1:6–7; Eph. 2:7.

4. God did from all eternity decree to justify all the elect,[11] and Christ did in the fullness of time die for their sins, and rise again for their justification;[12] nevertheless, they are not justified personally, until the Holy Spirit, doth in due time actually apply Christ unto them.[13]

5. God doth continue to forgive the sins of those that are justified,[14] and although they can never fall from the state of justification;[15] yet they may, by their sins, fall under God's fatherly displeasure;[16] and in that condition, they have not usually the light of his countenance restored unto them, until they humble themselves, confess their sins, beg pardon, and renew their faith, and repentance.[17]

6. The justification of believers under the Old Testament was, in all these respects, one and the same with the justification of believers under the New Testament.[18]

---

11 Gal. 3:8; 1 Peter 1:2; 1 Tim. 2:6.
12 Rom. 4:25.
13 Col. 1:21–22; Titus 3:4–7.
14 Matt. 6:12; 1 John 1:7, 9.
15 John 10:28.
16 Ps. 89:31–33.
17 Ps. 32:5; Ps. 51; Matt. 26:75.
18 Gal. 3:9; Rom. 4:22–24.

CHAPTER 12
OF ADOPTION

1. All those that are justified, God vouchsafed, in and for the sake of his only Son Jesus Christ, to make partakers of the grace of adoption,[1] by which they are taken into the number, and enjoy the liberties, and privileges of children of God,[2] have his name put on them,[3] receive the Spirit of adoption,[4] have access to the throne of grace with boldness, are enabled to cry, Abba, Father,[5] are pitied,[6] protected,[7] provided for,[8] and chastened by him as by a father;[9] yet never cast off;[10] but sealed to the day of redemption,[11] and inherit the promises as heirs of everlasting salvation.[12]

---

1 Eph. 1:5; Gal. 4:4–5.
2 John 1:12; Rom. 8:17.
3 2 Cor. 6:18; Rev. 3:12.
4 Rom. 8:15.
5 Gal. 4:6; Eph. 2:18.
6 Ps. 103:13.
7 Prov. 14:26
8 1 Peter 5:7.
9 Heb. 12:6.
10 Isa. 54:8–9; Lam. 3:31.
11 Eph. 4:30.
12 Heb. 1:14; Heb. 6:12.

CHAPTER 13

OF SANCTIFICATION

1. They who are united to Christ, effectually called, and regenerated, having a new heart, and a new spirit created in them, through the virtue of Christ's death and resurrection; are also farther sanctified, really, and personally,[1] through the same virtue, by his Word and Spirit dwelling in them;[2] the dominion of the whole body of sin is destroyed,[3] and the several lusts thereof are more and more weakened, and mortified,[4] and they more and more quickened and strengthened in all saving graces,[5] to the practice of all true holiness, without which no man shall see the Lord.[6]

2. This sanctification is throughout, in the whole man,[7] yet imperfect in this life; there abideth still some remnants of corruption in every part,[8] whence arises a continual and irreconcilable war; the flesh lusting against the Spirit, and the Spirit against the flesh.[9]

3. In which war, although the remaining corruption for a time may much prevail;[10] yet through the continual supply of strength from the sanctifying Spirit of Christ, the regenerate part doth overcome;[11] and so the saints grow in grace, perfecting holiness in the fear of God, pressing after a heavenly life, in evangelical obedience to all the commands which Christ as Head and King, in his Word hath prescribed to them.[12]

---

1   Acts 20:32; Rom. 6:5–6.
2   John 17:17; Eph. 3:16–19; 1 Thess. 5:21–23.
3   Rom. 6:14.
4   Gal. 5:24.
5   Col. 1:11.
6   2 Cor. 7:1; Heb. 12:14.
7   1 Thess. 5:23.
8   Rom. 7:18, 23.
9   Gal. 5:17; 1 Peter 2:11.
10   Rom. 7:23.
11   Rom. 6:14.
12   Eph. 4:15–16; 2 Cor. 3:18; 2 Cor. 7:1.

CHAPTER 14

OF SAVING FAITH

1. The grace of faith, whereby the elect are enabled to believe to the saving of their souls, is the work of the Spirit of Christ in their hearts;[1] and is ordinarily wrought by the ministry of the Word;[2] by which also, and by the administration of baptism, and the Lord's Supper, prayer, and other means appointed of God, it is increased and strengthened.[3]

2. By this faith a Christian believeth to be true, whatsoever is revealed in the Word, for the authority of God himself;[4] and also apprehendeth an excellency therein, above all other writings; and all things in the world:[5] as it bears forth the glory of God in his attributes, the excellency of Christ in his nature and offices, and the power and fullness of the Holy Spirit in his workings, and operations; and so is enabled to cast his soul upon the truth thus believed;[6] and also acteth differently, upon that which each particular passage thereof containeth; yielding obedience to the commands,[7] trembling at the threatenings,[8] and embracing the promises of God, for this life, and that which is to come:[9] but the principal acts of saving faith have immediate relation to Christ, accepting, receiving, and resting upon him alone, for justification, sanctification, and eternal life, by virtue of the covenant of grace.[10]

3. This faith although it be in different degrees, and may be weak, or strong;[11] yet it is in the least degree of it, different in the kind, or nature of it (as is all other saving grace) from the faith, and common grace of temporary believers;[12]

---

1 2 Cor. 4:13; Eph. 2:8.
2 Rom. 10:14, 17.
3 Luke 17:5; 1 Peter 2:2; Acts 20:32.
4 Acts 24:14.
5 Ps. 19:7–10; Ps. 119:72.
6 2 Tim 1:12.
7 John 15:14.
8 Isa. 66:2.
9 Heb. 11:13.
10 John 1:12; Acts 16:31; Gal. 2:20; Acts 15:11.
11 Heb. 5:13–14; Matt. 6:30; Rom. 4:19–20.
12 2 Peter 1:1.

and therefore though it may be many times assailed, and weakened; yet it gets the victory;[13] growing up in many, to the attainment of a full assurance through Christ,[14] who is both the author and finisher of our faith.[15]

---

13 Eph. 6:16; 1 John 5:4–5.
14 Heb. 6:11–12; Col. 2:2.
15 Heb. 12:2.

CHAPTER 15

OF REPENTANCE UNTO LIFE AND SALVATION

1. Such of the elect that are converted at riper years, having for sometimes lived in the state of nature, and therein served divers lusts and pleasures, God in their effectual calling giveth them repentance unto life.[1]

2. Whereas there is none that doth good, and sinneth not,[2] and the best of men may, through the power, and deceitfulness of their corruption dwelling in them, with the prevalency of temptation, fall into great sins and provocations; God hath in the covenant of grace, mercifully provided that believers so sinning and falling, be renewed through repentance unto salvation.[3]

3. This saving repentance is an evangelical grace,[4] whereby a person, being by the Holy Spirit made sensible of the manifold evils of his sin, doth, by faith in Christ, humble himself for it, with godly sorrow, detestation of it, and self-abhorrency,[5] praying for pardon and strength of grace, with a purpose and endeavor by supplies of the Spirit, to walk before God unto all well pleasing in all things.[6]

4. As repentance is to be continued through the whole course of our lives, upon the account of the body of death, and the motions thereof; so it is every man's duty to repent of his particular known sins particularly.[7]

5. Such is the provision which God hath made through Christ in the covenant of grace, for the preservation of believers unto salvation, that although there is no sin so small, but it deserves damnation;[8] yet there is no sin so great, that it shall bring damnation on them that repent;[9] which makes the constant preaching of repentance necessary.

---

1 Titus 3:2–5.
2 Eccl. 7:20.
3 Luke 22:31–32.
4 Zech. 12:10; Acts 11:18.
5 Ezek. 36:31; 2 Cor. 7:11.
6 Ps. 119:6, 128.
7 Luke 19:8; 1 Tim. 1:13, 15.
8 Rom. 6:23.
9 Isa. 1:16–18; Isa. 55:7.

CHAPTER 16
OF GOOD WORKS

1. Good works are only such as God hath commanded in his Holy Word;[1] and not such as without the warrant thereof, are devised by men out of blind zeal, or upon any pretense of good intentions.[2]

2. These good works, done in obedience to God's commandments, are the fruits, and evidences of a true and lively faith;[3] and by them believers manifest their thankfulness,[4] strengthen their assurance,[5] edify their brethren, adorn the profession of the gospel,[6] stop the mouths of the adversaries, and glorify God,[7] whose workmanship they are, created in Christ Jesus thereunto,[8] that having their fruit unto holiness, they may have the end eternal life.[9]

3. Their ability to do good works, is not at all of themselves, but wholly from the Spirit of Christ;[10] and that they may be enabled thereunto, besides the graces they have already received, there is necessary an actual influence of the same Holy Spirit, to work in them and to will, and to do of his good pleasure;[11] yet they are not hereupon to grow negligent, as if they were not bound to perform any duty, unless upon a special motion of the Spirit; but they ought to be diligent in stirring up the grace of God that is in them.[12]

4. They who in their obedience attain to the greatest height which is possible in this life, are so far from being able to supererogate, and to do more than God requires, as that they fall short of much which in duty they are bound to do.[13]

1 Mic. 6:8; Heb. 13:21.
2 Matt. 15:9; Isa. 29:13.
3 James 2:18, 22.
4 Ps. 116:12–13.
5 1 John 2:3, 5; 2 Peter 1:5–11.
6 Matt. 5:16.
7 1 Tim. 6:1; 1 Peter 2:15; Phil. 1:11.
8 Eph. 2:10.
9 Rom. 6:22.
10 John 15:4, 6.
11 2 Cor. 3:5; Phil. 2:13.
12 Phil. 2:12; Heb. 6:11–12; Isa. 64:7.
13 Job 9:2–3; Gal. 5:17; Luke 17:10.

5. We cannot by our best works merit pardon of sin or eternal life at the hand of God, by reason of the great disproportion that is between them and the glory to come; and the infinite distance that is between us and God, whom by them we can neither profit, nor satisfy for the debt of our former sins;[14] but when we have done all we can, we have done but our duty, and are unprofitable servants; and because as they are good they proceed from his Spirit,[15] and as they are wrought by us they are defiled and mixed with so much weakness and imperfection, that they cannot endure the severity of God's judgment.[16]

6. Yet notwithstanding the persons of believers being accepted through Christ, their good works also are accepted in him;[17] not as though they were in this life wholly unblamable and unreprovable in God's sight; but that he looking upon them in his Son is pleased to accept and reward that which is sincere although accompanied with many weaknesses and imperfections.[18]

7. Works done by unregenerate men, although for the matter of them they may be things which God commands, and of good use, both to themselves and others;[19] yet because they proceed not from a heart purified by faith,[20] nor are done in a right manner according to the Word,[21] nor to a right end, the glory of God;[22] they are therefore sinful and cannot please God; nor make a man meet to receive grace from God;[23] and yet their neglect of them is more sinful and displeasing to God.[24]

---

14 Rom. 3:20; Eph. 2:8–9; Rom. 4:6.
15 Gal. 5:22–23.
16 Isa. 64:6; Ps. 143:2.
17 Eph. 1:6; 1 Peter 2:5.
18 Matt. 25:21, 23; Heb. 6:10.
19 2 Kings 10:30; 1 Kings 21:27, 29.
20 Gen. 4:5; Heb. 11:4, 6.
21 1 Cor. 13:1.
22 Matt. 6:2, 5.
23 Amos 5:21–22; Rom. 9:16; Titus 3:5.
24 Job 21:14–15; Matt. 25:41–43.

CHAPTER 17
OF THE PERSEVERANCE OF THE SAINTS

1. Those whom God hath accepted in the Beloved, effectually called and sanctified by his Spirit, and given the precious faith of his elect unto, can neither totally nor finally fall from the state of grace; but shall certainly persevere therein to the end, and be eternally saved, seeing the gifts and callings of God are without repentance (whence he still begets and nourishes in them faith, repentance, love, joy, hope, and all the graces of the Spirit unto immortality);[1] and though many storms and floods arise and beat against them, yet they shall never be able to take them off that foundation and rock which by faith they are fastened upon: notwithstanding, through unbelief and the temptations of Satan, the sensible sight of the light and love of God, may for a time be clouded, and obscured from them,[2] yet he is still the same, and they shall be sure to be kept by the power of God unto salvation, where they shall enjoy their purchased possession, they being engraven upon the palms of his hands, and their names having been written in the book of life from all eternity.[3]

2. This perseverance of the saints depends not upon their own free will; but upon the immutability of the decree of election,[4] flowing from the free and unchangeable love of God the Father; upon the efficacy of the merit and intercessions of Jesus Christ and union with him,[5] the oath of God,[6] the abiding of his Spirit, and the seed of God within them,[7] and the nature of the covenant of grace;[8] from all which ariseth also the certainty and infallibility thereof.

3. And though they may, through the temptation of Satan and of the world, the prevalency of corruption remaining in them, and the neglect of means of their preservation, fall into grievous sins, and for a time continue therein;[9]

---

1   John 10:28–29; Phil. 1:6; 2 Tim. 2:19; 1 John 2:19.
2   Ps. 89:31–32; 1 Cor. 11:32.
3   Mal. 3:6.
4   Rom. 8:30; Rom. 9:11, 16.
5   Rom. 5:9–10; John 14:19.
6   Heb. 6:17–18.
7   1 John 3:9.
8   Jer. 32:40.
9   Matt. 26:70, 72, 74.

whereby they incur God's displeasure, and grieve his Holy Spirit,[10] come to have their graces and comforts impaired,[11] have their hearts hardened, and their consciences wounded,[12] hurt and scandalize others, and bring temporal judgments upon themselves:[13] yet they shall renew their repentance and be preserved through faith in Christ Jesus to the end.[14]

---

10 Isa. 64:5, 9; Eph. 4:30.
11 Ps. 51:10, 12.
12 Ps. 32:3–4.
13 2 Sam. 12:14.
14 Luke 22:32, 61–62.

CHAPTER 18
OF THE ASSURANCE OF GRACE AND SALVATION

1. Although temporary believers, and other unregenerate men, may vainly deceive themselves with false hopes, and carnal presumptions of being in the favor of God, and in a state of salvation, which hope of theirs shall perish;[1] yet such as truly believe in the Lord Jesus, and love him in sincerity, endeavoring to walk in all good conscience before him, may in this life be certainly assured that they are in the state of grace; and may rejoice in the hope of the glory of God,[2] which hope shall never make them ashamed.[3]

2. This certainty is not a bare conjectural and probable persuasion, grounded upon a fallible hope; but an infallible assurance of faith,[4] founded on the blood and righteousness of Christ revealed in the gospel;[5] and also upon the inward evidence of those graces of the Spirit unto which promises are made,[6] and on the testimony of the Spirit of adoption, witnessing with our spirits that we are the children of God;[7] and as a fruit thereof, keeping the heart both humble and holy.[8]

3. This infallible assurance doth not so belong to the essence of faith, but that a true believer, may wait long, and conflict with many difficulties before he be partaker of it;[9] yet being enabled by the Spirit to know the things which are freely given him of God, he may without extraordinary revelation in the right use of means attain thereunto:[10] and therefore it is the duty of every one, to give all diligence to make his calling and election sure, that thereby his heart may be enlarged in peace and joy in the Holy Spirit, in love and thankfulness to God, and in strength and cheerfulness in the duties of

---

1 Job 8:13–14; Matt. 7:22–23.
2 1 John 2:3; 1 John 3:14, 18–19, 21, 24; 1 John 5:13.
3 Rom. 5:2, 5.
4 Heb. 6:11, 19.
5 Heb. 6:17–18.
6 2 Peter 1:4–5, 10–11.
7 Rom. 8:15–16.
8 1 John 3:1–3.
9 Isa. 50:10; Ps. 88; Ps. 77:1–12.
10 1 John 4:13; Heb. 6:11–12.

obedience, the proper fruits of this assurance;[11] so far is it from inclining men to looseness.[12]

4. True believers may have the assurance of their salvation divers ways shaken, diminished, and intermitted; as by negligence in preserving of it,[13] by falling into some special sin, which woundeth the conscience, and grieveth the Spirit;[14] by some sudden or vehement temptation,[15] by God's withdrawing the light of his countenance and suffering even such as fear him to walk in darkness and to have no light;[16] yet are they never destitute of the seed of God[17] and life of faith,[18] that love of Christ and the brethren, that sincerity of heart and conscience of duty, out of which by the operation of the Spirit, this assurance may in due time be revived:[19] and by the which in the meantime they are preserved from utter despair.[20]

---

11 Rom. 5:1–2, 5; Rom. 14:17; Ps. 119:32.
12 Rom. 6:1–2; Titus 2:11–12, 14.
13 Song 5:2–3, 6.
14 Ps. 51:8, 12, 14.
15 Ps. 116:11; Ps. 77:7–8; Ps. 31:22.
16 Ps. 30:7.
17 1 John 3:9.
18 Luke 22:32.
19 Ps. 42:5, 11.
20 Lam. 3:26–31.

CHAPTER 19
OF THE LAW OF GOD

1. God gave to Adam a law of universal obedience, written in his heart, and a particular precept of not eating the fruit of the tree of knowledge of good and evil;[1] by which he bound him, and all his posterity to personal, entire, exact, and perpetual obedience;[2] promised life upon the fulfilling, and threatened death upon the breach of it, and endued him with power and ability to keep it.[3]

2. The same law that was first written in the heart of man, continued to be a perfect rule of righteousness after the fall;[4] and was delivered by God upon Mount Sinai, in ten commandments, and written in two tables; the four first containing our duty towards God, and the other six our duty to man.[5]

3. Besides this law commonly called moral, God was pleased to give to the people Israel ceremonial laws, containing several typical ordinances, partly of worship, prefiguring Christ, his graces, actions, sufferings, and benefits;[6] and partly holding forth divers instructions of moral duties,[7] all which ceremonial laws being appointed only to the time of reformation, are by Jesus Christ the true Messiah and only Lawgiver, who was furnished with power from the Father, for that end, abrogated and taken away.[8]

4. To them also he gave sundry judicial laws, which expired together with the state of that people, not obliging any now by virtue of that institution; their general equity only, being of moral use.[9]

5. The moral law doth forever bind all, as well justified persons as others, to the obedience thereof,[10] and that not only in regard of the matter contained

---

1 Gen. 1:27; Eccl. 7:29.
2 Rom. 10:5.
3 Gal. 3:10, 12.
4 Rom. 2:14–15.
5 Deut. 10:4.
6 Heb. 10:1; Col. 2:17.
7 1 Cor. 5:7.
8 Col. 2:14, 16–17; Eph. 2:14, 16.
9 1 Cor. 9:8–10.
10 Rom. 13:8–10; James 2:8, 10–12.

in it, but also in respect of the authority of God the Creator, who gave it:[11] neither doth Christ in the gospel any way dissolve, but much strengthen this obligation.[12]

6. Although true believers be not under the law, as a covenant of works, to be thereby justified or condemned;[13] yet it is of great use to them as well as to others: in that as a rule of life, informing them of the will of God, and their duty, it directs and binds them, to walk accordingly; discovering also the sinful pollutions of their natures, hearts, and lives; so as examining themselves thereby, they may come to further conviction of, humiliation for, and hatred against sin;[14] together with a clearer sight of the need they have of Christ and the perfection of his obedience: it is likewise of use to the regenerate to restrain their corruptions, in that it forbids sin; and the threatenings of it serve to show what even their sins deserve; and what afflictions in this life they may expect for them, although freed from the curse and unallayed rigor thereof. The promises of it likewise show them God's approbation of obedience, and what blessings they may expect upon the performance thereof, though not as due to them by the law as a covenant of works; so as man's doing good and refraining from evil, because the law encourageth to the one and detereth from the other, is no evidence of his being under the law and not under grace.[15]

7. Neither are the aforementioned uses of the law contrary to the grace of the gospel; but do sweetly comply with it;[16] the Spirit of Christ subduing and enabling the will of man, to do that freely and cheerfully, which the will of God revealed in the law, requireth to be done.[17]

---

11 James 2:10–11.
12 Matt. 5:17–19; Rom. 3:31.
13 Rom. 6:14; Gal. 2:16; Rom. 8:1; Rom. 10:4.
14 Rom. 3:20; Rom. 7:7ff.
15 Rom. 6:12–14; 1 Peter 3:8–13.
16 Gal. 3:21.
17 Ezek. 36:27.

CHAPTER 20

OF THE GOSPEL, AND OF THE EXTENT OF THE GRACE THEREOF

1. The covenant of works being broken by sin, and made unprofitable unto life; God was pleased to give forth the promise of Christ, the seed of the woman, as the means of calling the elect, and begetting in them faith and repentance;[1] in this promise, the gospel, as to the substance of it, was revealed, and therein effectual, for the conversion and salvation of sinners.[2]

2. This promise of Christ, and salvation by him, is revealed only by the Word of God;[3] neither do the works of creation, or providence, with the light of nature, make discovery of Christ, or of grace by him; so much as in a general, or obscure way;[4] much less that men destitute of the revelation of him by the promise, or gospel; should be enabled thereby, to attain saving faith or repentance.[5]

3. The revelation of the gospel unto sinners, made in divers times, and by sundry parts; with the addition of promises, and precepts for the obedience required therein, as to the nations, and persons to whom it is granted, is merely of the sovereign will and good pleasure of God;[6] not being annexed by virtue of any promise, to the due improvement of men's natural abilities, by virtue of common light received without it; which none ever did make, or can do so:[7] and therefore in all ages the preaching of the gospel hath been granted unto persons and nations, as to the extent, or straitening of it, in great variety, according to the counsel of the will of God.

4. Although the gospel be the only outward means, of revealing Christ, and saving grace; and is, as such, abundantly sufficient thereunto; yet that men who are dead in trespasses, may be born again, quickened or regenerated; there is moreover necessary, an effectual, insuperable work of the Holy Spirit, upon the whole soul, for the producing in them a new spiritual life;[8] without which no other means will effect their conversion unto God.[9]

---

1 Gen. 3:15.
2 Rev. 13:8.
3 Rom. 1:17.
4 Rom. 10:14–15, 17.
5 Prov. 29:18; Isa. 25:7; Isa. 60:2–3.
6 Ps. 147:20; Acts 16:7.
7 Rom. 1:18ff.
8 Ps. 110:3; 1 Cor. 2:14; Eph. 1:19–20.
9 John 6:44; 2 Cor. 4:4, 6.

CHAPTER 21

OF CHRISTIAN LIBERTY AND LIBERTY OF CONSCIENCE

1. The liberty which Christ hath purchased, for believers under the gospel, consists in their freedom from the guilt of sin, the condemning wrath of God, the rigor and curse of the law;[1] and in their being delivered from this present evil world,[2] bondage to Satan,[3] and dominion of sin;[4] from the evil of afflictions;[5] the fear, and sting of death, the victory of the grave,[6] and everlasting damnation:[7] as also in their free access to God; and their yielding obedience unto him not out of slavish fear,[8] but a childlike love and willing mind.[9] All which were common also to believers under the law for the substance of them;[10] but under the New Testament the liberty of Christians is further enlarged in their freedom from the yoke of the ceremonial law, to which the Jewish church was subjected; and in greater boldness of access to the throne of grace; and in fuller communications of the free Spirit of God, than believers under the law did ordinarily partake of.[11]

2. God alone is Lord of the conscience,[12] and hath left it free from the doctrines and commandments of men which are in anything contrary to his Word, or not contained in it.[13] So that to believe such doctrines, or obey such commands out of conscience, is to betray true liberty of conscience;[14] and the requiring of an implicit faith, and absolute and blind obedience, is to destroy liberty of conscience, and reason also.[15]

---

1 Gal. 3:13.
2 Gal. 1:4.
3 Acts 26:18.
4 Rom. 8:3.
5 Rom. 8:28.
6 1 Cor. 15:54–57.
7 2 Thess. 1:10.
8 Rom. 8:15.
9 Luke 1:74–75; 1 John 4:18.
10 Gal. 3:9, 14.
11 John 7:38–39; Heb. 10:19–21.
12 James 4:12; Rom. 14:4.
13 Acts 4:19; Acts 5:29; 1 Cor. 7:23; Matt. 15:9.
14 Col. 2:20, 22–23.
15 1 Cor. 3:5; 2 Cor. 1:24.

3. They who upon pretense of Christian liberty do practice any sin, or cherish any sinful lust; as they do thereby pervert the main design of the grace of the gospel to their own destruction;[16] so they wholly destroy the end of Christian liberty, which is, that being delivered out of the hands of all our enemies we might serve the Lord without fear, in holiness, and righteousness before him, all the days of our lives.[17]

16 Rom. 6:1–2.
17 Gal. 5:13; 2 Peter 2:18, 21.

CHAPTER 22

OF RELIGIOUS WORSHIP AND THE SABBATH DAY

1. The light of nature shows that there is a God, who hath lordship and sovereignty over all; is just, good, and doth good unto all; and is therefore to be feared, loved, praised, called upon, trusted in, and served, with all the heart, and all the soul, and with all the might.[1] But the acceptable way of worshiping the true God, is instituted by himself,[2] and so limited by his own revealed will, that he may not be worshiped according to the imaginations, and devices of men, or the suggestions of Satan, under any visible representations, or any other way, not prescribed in the Holy Scriptures.[3]

2. Religious worship is to be given to God the Father, Son, and Holy Spirit, and to him alone;[4] not to angels, saints, or any other creatures;[5] and since the fall, not without a Mediator,[6] nor in the mediation of any other but Christ alone.[7]

3. Prayer, with thanksgiving, being one special part of natural worship, is by God required of all men.[8] But that it may be accepted, it is to be made in the name of the Son,[9] by the help of the Spirit,[10] according to his will;[11] with understanding, reverence, humility, fervency, faith, love, and perseverance; and when with others, in a known tongue.[12]

4. Prayer is to be made for things lawful, and for all sorts of men living, or that shall live hereafter;[13] but not for the dead,[14] nor for those of whom it may be known that they have sinned the sin unto death.[15]

---

1   Jer. 10:7; Mark 12:33.
2   Deut. 12:32.
3   Ex. 20:4–6.
4   Matt. 4:9–10; John 6:23; Matt. 28:19.
5   Rom. 1:25; Col. 2:18; Rev. 19:10.
6   John 14:6.
7   1 Tim. 2:5.
8   Ps. 95:1–7; Ps. 65:2.
9   John 14:13–14.
10 Rom. 8:26.
11 1 John 5:14.
12 1 Cor. 14:16–17.
13 1 Tim. 2:1–2; 2 Sam. 7:29.
14 2 Sam. 12:21–23.
15 1 John 5:16.

5. The reading of the Scriptures,[16] preaching, and hearing the Word of God,[17] teaching and admonishing one another in psalms, hymns, and spiritual songs, singing with grace in our hearts to the Lord;[18] as also the administration of baptism,[19] and the Lord's Supper,[20] are all parts of religious worship of God, to be performed in obedience to him, with understanding, faith, reverence, and godly fear; moreover, solemn humiliation, with fastings,[21] and thanksgivings, upon special occasions, ought to be used in an holy and religious manner.[22]

6. Neither prayer, nor any other part of religious worship, is now under the gospel tied unto, or made more acceptable by, any place in which it is performed, or towards which it is directed; but God is to be worshiped everywhere in spirit, and in truth;[23] as in private families[24] daily,[25] and in secret each one by himself;[26] so more solemnly in the public assemblies, which are not carelessly nor willfully to be neglected, or forsaken, when God by his word, or providence calleth thereunto.[27]

7. As it is the law of nature, that in general a proportion of time by God's appointment, be set apart for the worship of God, so by his Word, in a positive moral, and perpetual commandment, binding all men, in all ages, he hath particularly appointed one day in seven for a Sabbath to be kept holy unto him,[28] which from the beginning of the world to the resurrection of Christ, was the last day of the week; and from the resurrection of Christ, was changed into the first day of the week, which is called the Lord's Day;[29] and is to be continued to the end of the world, as the Christian Sabbath; the observation of the last day of the week being abolished.

---

16 1 Tim. 4:13.
17 2 Tim. 4:2; Luke 8:18.
18 Col. 3:16; Eph. 5:19.
19 Matt. 28:19–20.
20 1 Cor. 11:26.
21 Esth. 4:16; Joel 2:12.
22 Exod. 15:1ff.; Ps. 107.
23 John 4:21; Mal. 1:11; 1 Tim. 2:8.
24 Acts 10:2.
25 Matt. 6:11; Ps. 55:17.
26 Matt. 6:6.
27 Heb. 10:25; Acts 2:42.
28 Ex. 20:8.
29 1 Cor. 16:1–2; Acts 20:7; Rev. 1:10.

8. The Sabbath is then kept holy unto the Lord, when men after a due preparing of their hearts, and ordering their common affairs aforehand, do not only observe a holy rest all the day, from their own works, words and thoughts, about their worldly employment and recreations,[30] but are also taken up the whole time in the public and private exercises of his worship, and in the duties of necessity and mercy.[31]

30 Isa. 58:13; Neh. 13:15–22.
31 Matt. 12:1–13.

CHAPTER 23
OF LAWFUL OATHS AND VOWS

1. A lawful oath is a part of religious worship, wherein the person swearing in truth, righteousness, and judgment, solemnly calleth God to witness what he sweareth;[1] and to judge him according to the truth or falseness thereof.[2]

2. The name of God only is that by which men ought to swear; and therein it is to be used, with all holy fear and reverence; therefore to swear vainly or rashly by that glorious, and dreadful name, or to swear at all by any other thing, is sinful, and to be abhorred;[3] yet as in matter of weight and moment for confirmation of truth, and ending all strife, an oath is warranted by the Word of God;[4] so a lawful oath being imposed, by lawful authority, in such matters, ought to be taken.[5]

3. Whosoever taketh an oath warranted by the Word of God, ought duly to consider the weightiness of so solemn an act; and therein to avouch nothing, but what he knoweth to be truth; for that by rash, false, and vain oaths, the Lord is provoked, and for them this land mourns.[6]

4. An oath is to be taken in the plain, and common sense of the words; without equivocation or mental reservation.[7]

5. A vow, which is not to be made to any creature, but to God alone, is to be made and performed with all religious care and faithfulness;[8] but popish monastical vows, of perpetual single life,[9] professed poverty,[10] and regular obedience, are so far from being degrees of higher perfection, that they are superstitious, and sinful snares, in which no Christian may entangle himself.[11]

---

1 Ex. 20:7; Deut. 10:20; Jer. 4:2.
2 2 Chron. 6:22–23.
3 Matt. 5:34, 37; James 5:12.
4 Heb. 6:16; 2 Cor. 1:23.
5 Neh. 13:25.
6 Lev. 19:12; Jer. 23:10.
7 Ps. 24:4.
8 Ps. 76:11; Gen. 28:20–22.
9 1 Cor. 7:2, 9.
10 Eph. 4:28.
11 Matt. 19:11.

CHAPTER 24

OF THE CIVIL MAGISTRATE

1. God, the supreme Lord, and King of all the world, hath ordained civil magistrates to be under him, over the people, for his own glory, and the public good; and to this end hath armed them with the power of the sword, for defense and encouragement of them that do good, and for the punishment of evildoers.[1]

2. It is lawful for Christians to accept and execute the office of a magistrate, when called thereunto; in the management whereof, as they ought especially to maintain justice, and peace,[2] according to the wholesome laws of each kingdom, and commonwealth: so for that end they may lawfully now under the New Testament wage war upon just and necessary occasions.[3]

3. Civil magistrates being set up by God, for the ends aforesaid; subjection in all lawful things commanded by them, ought to be yielded by us, in the Lord, not only for wrath but for conscience's sake;[4] and we ought to make supplications and prayers for kings, and all that are in authority, that under them we may live a quiet and peaceable life, in all godliness and honesty.[5]

---

1 Rom. 13:1–4.
2 2 Sam. 23:3; Ps. 82:3–4.
3 Luke 3:14.
4 Rom. 13:5–7; 1 Peter 2:17.
5 1 Tim. 2:1–2.

CHAPTER 25
OF MARRIAGE

1. Marriage is to be between one man and one woman; neither is it lawful for any man to have more than one wife, nor for any woman to have more than one husband at the same time.[1]

2. Marriage was ordained for the mutual help of husband and wife,[2] for the increase of mankind with a legitimate issue,[3] and the preventing of uncleanness.[4]

3. It is lawful for all sorts of people to marry, who are able with judgment to give their consent;[5] yet it is the duty of Christians to marry in the Lord,[6] and therefore such as profess the true religion, should not marry with infidels, or idolaters; neither should such as are godly be unequally yoked, by marrying with such as are wicked in their life, or maintain damnable heresy.[7]

4. Marriage ought not to be within the degrees of consanguinity, or affinity forbidden in the Word;[8] nor can such incestuous marriages ever be made lawful, by any law of man or consent of parties, so as those persons may live together as man and wife.[9]

---

1 Gen. 2:24; Mal. 2:15; Matt. 19:5–6.
2 Gen. 2:18.
3 Gen. 1:28.
4 1 Cor. 7:2, 9.
5 Heb. 13:4; 1 Tim. 4:3.
6 1 Cor. 7:39.
7 Neh. 13:25–27.
8 Lev. 18.
9 Mark 6:18; 1 Cor. 5:1.

CHAPTER 26

OF THE CHURCH

1. The catholic or universal church, which (with respect to the internal work of the Spirit, and truth of grace) may be called invisible, consists of the whole number of the elect, that have been, are, or shall be gathered into one, under Christ, the Head thereof; and is the spouse, the body, the fullness of him that filleth all in all.[1]

2. All persons throughout the world, professing the faith of the gospel, and obedience unto God by Christ, according unto it, not destroying their own profession by any errors everting the foundation, or unholiness of conversation, are and may be called visible saints;[2] and of such ought all particular congregations to be constituted.[3]

3. The purest churches under heaven are subject to mixture and error;[4] and some have so degenerated as to become no churches of Christ, but synagogues of Satan;[5] nevertheless Christ always hath had, and ever shall have a kingdom, in this world, to the end thereof, of such as believe in him, and make profession of his name.[6]

4. The Lord Jesus Christ is the Head of the church, in whom, by the appointment of the Father, all power for the calling, institution, order, or government of the church, is invested in a supreme and sovereign manner;[7] neither can the pope of Rome in any sense be head thereof, but is that antichrist, that man of sin, and son of perdition, that exalts himself in the church against Christ, and all that is called God; whom the Lord shall destroy with the brightness of his coming.[8]

5. In the execution of this power wherewith he is so entrusted, the Lord Jesus calleth out of the world unto himself, through the ministry of his Word, by his

---

1. Heb. 12:23; Col. 1:18; Eph. 1:10, 22–23; Eph. 5:23, 27, 32.
2. 1 Cor. 1:2; Acts 11:26.
3. Rom. 1:7; Eph. 1:20–22.
4. 1 Cor. 5; Rev. 2:1–3:22.
5. Rev. 18:2; 2 Thess. 2:11–12.
6. Matt. 16:18; Ps. 72:17; Ps. 102:28; Rev. 12:17.
7. Col. 1:18; Matt. 28:18–20; Eph. 4:11–12.
8. 2 Thess. 2:3–9.

Spirit, those that are given unto him by his Father;[9] that they may walk before him in all the ways of obedience, which he prescribeth to them in his Word.[10] Those thus called, he commandeth to walk together in particular societies, or churches, for their mutual edification; and the due performance of that public worship, which he requireth of them in the world.[11]

6. The members of these churches are saints by calling, visibly manifesting and evidencing (in and by their profession and walking) their obedience unto that call of Christ;[12] and do willingly consent to walk together according to the appointment of Christ, giving up themselves, to the Lord and one to another by the will of God, in professed subjection to the ordinances of the gospel.[13]

7. To each of these churches thus gathered, according to his mind, declared in his Word, he hath given all that power and authority, which is in any way needful, for their carrying on that order in worship, and discipline, which he hath instituted for them to observe; with commands, and rules for the due and right exerting, and executing of that power.[14]

8. A particular church, gathered and completely organized, according to the mind of Christ, consists of officers, and members; and the officers appointed by Christ to be chosen and set apart by the church (so called and gathered) for the peculiar administration of ordinances, and execution of power, or duty, which he entrusts them with, or calls them to, to be continued to the end of the world, are bishops or elders and deacons.[15]

9. The way appointed by Christ for the calling of any person, fitted, and gifted by the Holy Spirit, unto the office of bishop or elder, in a church, is, that he be chosen thereunto by the common suffrage of the church itself;[16] and solemnly set apart by fasting and prayer, with imposition of hands of the eldership of the church, if there be any before constituted therein;[17] and of a deacon that

---

9 John 10:16; John 12:32.
10 Matt. 28:20.
11 Matt. 18:15–20.
12 Rom. 1:7; 1 Cor. 1:2.
13 Acts 2:41–42; Acts 5:13–14; 2 Cor. 9:13.
14 Matt. 18:17–18; 1 Cor. 5:4–5, 13; 2 Cor. 2:6–8.
15 Acts 20:17, 28; Phil. 1:1.
16 Acts 14:23.
17 1 Tim. 4:14.

he be chosen by the like suffrage, and set apart by prayer, and the like imposition of hands.[18]

10. The work of pastors being constantly to attend the service of Christ, in his churches, in the ministry of the Word, and prayer, with watching for their souls, as they that must give an account to him;[19] it is incumbent on the churches to whom they minister, not only to give them all due respect, but also to communicate to them of all their good things according to their ability,[20] so as they may have a comfortable supply, without being themselves entangled in secular affairs;[21] and may also be capable of exercising hospitality towards others;[22] and this is required by the law of nature, and by the express order of our Lord Jesus, who hath ordained that they that preach the gospel, should live of the gospel.[23]

11. Although it be incumbent on the bishops or pastors of the churches to be instant in preaching the Word, by way of office; yet the work of preaching the Word, is not so peculiarly confined to them; but that others also gifted, and fitted by the Holy Spirit for it, and approved, and called by the church, may and ought to perform it.[24]

12. As all believers are bound to join themselves to particular churches, when and where they have opportunity so to do; so all that are admitted unto the privileges of a church, are also under the censures and government thereof, according to the rule of Christ.[25]

13. No church members, upon any offense taken by them, having performed their duty required of them towards the person they are offended at, ought to disturb any church order, or absent themselves from the assemblies of the church, or administration of any ordinances, upon the account of such offense at any of their fellow members, but to wait upon Christ, in the further proceeding of the church.[26]

---

18 Acts 6:3, 5–6.
19 Acts 6:4; Heb. 13:17.
20 1 Tim. 5:17–18; Gal. 6:6–7.
21 2 Tim. 2:4.
22 1 Tim. 3:2.
23 1 Cor. 9:6–14.
24 Acts 11:19–21; 1 Peter 4:10–11.
25 1 Thess. 5:14; 2 Thess. 3:6, 14–15.
26 Matt. 18:15–17; Eph. 4:2–3.

14. As each church, and all the members of it, are bound to pray continually for the good and prosperity of all the churches of Christ,[27] in all places; and upon all occasions to further it (every one within the bounds of their places and callings, in the exercise of their gifts and graces) so the churches (when planted by the providence of God so as they may enjoy opportunity and advantage for it) ought to hold communion among themselves for their peace, increase of love, and mutual edification.[28]

15. In cases of difficulties or differences, either in point of doctrine, or administration; wherein either the churches in general are concerned, or any one church in their peace, union, and edification; or any member, or members, of any church are injured, in or by any proceedings in censures not agreeable to truth, and order: it is according to the mind of Christ, that many churches holding communion together, do by their messengers, meet to consider, and give their advice in, or about that matter in difference, to be reported to all the churches concerned;[29] howbeit these messengers assembled, are not entrusted with any church-power properly so called; or with any jurisdiction over the churches themselves, to exercise any censures either over any churches or persons: or to impose their determination on the churches, or officers.[30]

---

27 Eph. 6:18; Ps. 122:6.
28 Rom. 16:1–2; 3 John 8–10.
29 Acts 15:2, 4, 6, 22–23, 25.
30 2 Cor. 1:24; 1 John 4:1.

CHAPTER 27
OF THE COMMUNION OF SAINTS

1. All saints that are united to Jesus Christ, their Head, by his Spirit, and faith; although they are not made thereby one person with him, have fellowship in his graces, sufferings, death, resurrection, and glory;[1] and, being united to one another in love, they have communion in each other's gifts, and graces;[2] and obliged to the performance of such duties, public and private, in an orderly way, as do conduce to their mutual good, both in the inward and outward man.[3]

2. Saints by profession are bound to maintain a holy fellowship and communion in the worship of God, and in performing such other spiritual services, as tend to their mutual edification;[4] as also in relieving each other in outward things according to their several abilities, and necessities;[5] which communion, according to the rule of the gospel, though especially to be exercised by them, in the relation wherein they stand, whether in families,[6] or churches;[7] yet as God offereth opportunity, is to be extended to all the household of faith, even all those who in every place call upon the name of the Lord Jesus; nevertheless their communion one with another as saints, doth not take away or infringe the title or propriety which each man hath in his goods and possessions.[8]

1 1 John 1:3; John 1:16; Phil. 3:10; Rom. 6:5–6.
2 Eph. 4:15–16; 1 Cor. 12:7; 1 Cor. 3:21–23.
3 1 Thess. 5:11, 14; Rom. 1:12; 1 John 3:17–18; Gal. 6:10.
4 Heb. 10:24–25; Heb. 3:12–13.
5 Acts 11:29–30.
6 Eph. 6:4.
7 1 Cor. 12:14–27.
8 Acts 5:4; Eph. 4:28.

CHAPTER 28

OF BAPTISM AND THE LORD'S SUPPER

1. Baptism and the Lord's Supper are ordinances of positive, and sovereign institution; appointed by the Lord Jesus, the only Lawgiver, to be continued in his church to the end of the world.[1]

2. These holy appointments are to be administered by those only, who are qualified and thereunto called, according to the commission of Christ.[2]

---

1   Matt. 28:19–20; 1 Cor. 11:26.
2   Matt. 28:19; 1 Cor. 4:1.

CHAPTER 29
OF BAPTISM

1. Baptism is an ordinance of the New Testament, ordained by Jesus Christ, to be unto the party baptized, a sign of his fellowship with him, in his death, and resurrection; of his being engrafted into him;[1] of remission of sins;[2] and of his giving up unto God, through Jesus Christ, to live and walk in newness of life.[3]

2. Those who do actually profess repentance towards God, faith in, and obedience to, our Lord Jesus Christ, are the only proper subjects of this ordinance.[4]

3. The outward element to be used in this ordinance is water, wherein the party is to be baptized, in the name of the Father, and of the Son, and of the Holy Spirit.[5]

4. Immersion, or dipping of the person in water, is necessary to the due administration of this ordinance.[6]

---

1   Rom. 6:3–5; Col. 2:12; Gal. 3:27.
2   Mark 1:4; Acts 22:16.
3   Rom. 6:2, 4.
4   Mark 16:16; Acts 8:36–37.
5   Matt. 28:19–20; Acts 8:38.
6   Matt. 3:16; John 3:23.

CHAPTER 30
OF THE LORD'S SUPPER

1. The supper of the Lord Jesus was instituted by him the same night wherein he was betrayed, to be observed in his churches, unto the end of the world, for the perpetual remembrance, and showing forth the sacrifice in his death,[1] confirmation of the faith of believers in all the benefits thereof, their spiritual nourishment, and growth in him, their further engagement in, and to all duties which they owe to him; and to be a bond and pledge of their communion with him, and with each other.[2]

2. In this ordinance Christ is not offered up to his Father, nor any real sacrifice made at all, for remission of sin of the quick or dead; but only a memorial of that one offering up of himself, by himself, upon the cross, once for all;[3] and a spiritual oblation of all possible praise unto God for the same;[4] so that the popish sacrifice of the Mass (as they call it) is most abominable, injurious to Christ's own only sacrifice the alone propitiation for all the sins of the elect.

3. The Lord Jesus hath, in this ordinance, appointed his ministers to pray, and bless the elements of bread and wine, and thereby to set them apart from a common to an holy use, and to take and break the bread; to take the cup, and (they communicating also themselves) to give both to the communicants.[5]

4. The denial of the cup to the people, worshiping the elements, the lifting them up, or carrying them about for adoration, and reserving them for any pretended religious use, are all contrary to the nature of this ordinance, and to the institution of Christ.[6]

5. The outward elements in this ordinance, duly set apart to the uses ordained by Christ, have such relation to him crucified, as that truly, although in terms used figuratively, they are sometimes called by the names of the things they

---

1 1 Cor. 11:23–26.
2 1 Cor. 10:16–17, 21.
3 Heb. 9:25–26, 28.
4 1 Cor. 11:24; Matt. 26:26–27.
5 1 Cor. 11:23–26ff.
6 Matt. 26:26–28; Matt. 15:9; Ex. 20:4–5.

represent, to wit, the body and blood of Christ;[7] albeit, in substance, and nature, they still remain truly, and only bread, and wine, as they were before.[8]

6. That doctrine which maintains a change of the substance of bread and wine, into the substance of Christ's body and blood (commonly called transubstantiation) by consecration of a priest, or by any other way, is repugnant not to Scripture alone,[9] but even to common sense and reason; overthroweth the nature of the ordinance, and hath been, and is the cause of manifold superstitions, yea, of gross idolatries.[10]

7. Worthy receivers, outwardly partaking of the visible elements in this ordinance, do then also inwardly by faith, really and indeed, yet not carnally, and corporally, but spiritually receive, and feed upon Christ crucified, and all the benefits of his death: the body and blood of Christ, being then not corporally, or carnally, but spiritually present to the faith of believers, in that ordinance, as the elements themselves are to their outward senses.[11]

8. All ignorant and ungodly persons, as they are unfit to enjoy communion with Christ; so are they unworthy of the Lord's table; and cannot without great sin against him, while they remain such, partake of these holy mysteries, or be admitted thereunto:[12] yea, whosoever shall receive unworthily, are guilty of the body and blood of the Lord, eating and drinking judgment to themselves.[13]

---

7 1 Cor. 11:27.
8 1 Cor. 11:26–28.
9 Acts 3:21; Luke 24:6, 39.
10 1 Cor. 11:24–25.
11 1 Cor. 10:16; 1 Cor. 11:23–26.
12 2 Cor. 6:14–15.
13 1 Cor. 11:29; Matt. 7:6.

CHAPTER 31

OF THE STATE OF MAN AFTER DEATH, AND OF THE RESURRECTION OF THE DEAD

1. The bodies of men after death return to dust, and see corruption;[1] but their souls (which neither die nor sleep) having an immortal subsistence, immediately return to God who gave them;[2] the souls of the righteous being then made perfect in holiness, are received into paradise where they are with Christ, and behold the face of God, in light and glory; waiting for the full redemption of their bodies;[3] and the souls of the wicked, are cast into hell; where they remain in torment and utter darkness, reserved to the judgment of the great day;[4] besides these two places for souls separated from their bodies, the Scripture acknowledgeth none.

2. At the last day such of the saints as are found alive shall not sleep, but be changed;[5] and all the dead shall be raised up with the selfsame bodies, and none other;[6] although with different qualities, which shall be united again to their souls forever.[7]

3. The bodies of the unjust shall by the power of Christ, be raised to dishonor; the bodies of the just by his Spirit unto honor, and be made conformable to his own glorious body.[8]

---

1   Gen. 3:19; Acts 13:36.
2   Eccl. 12:7.
3   Luke 23:43; 2 Cor. 5:1, 6, 8; Phil. 1:23; Heb. 12:23.
4   Jude 6–7; 1 Peter 3:19; Luke 16:23–24.
5   1 Cor. 15:51–52; 1 Thess. 4:17.
6   Job 19:26–27.
7   1 Cor. 15:42–43.
8   Acts 24:15; John 5:28–29; Phil. 3:21.

CHAPTER 32

OF THE LAST JUDGMENT

1. God hath appointed a day wherein he will judge the world in righteousness, by Jesus Christ;[1] to whom all power and judgment is given of the Father; in which day not only the apostate angels shall be judged;[2] but likewise all persons that have lived upon the earth, shall appear before the tribunal of Christ; to give an account of their thoughts, words, and deeds, and to receive according to what they have done in the body, whether good or evil.[3]

2. The end of God's appointing this day, is for the manifestation of the glory of his mercy, in the eternal salvation of the elect; and of his justice in the eternal damnation of the reprobate, who are wicked and disobedient;[4] for then shall the righteous go into everlasting life, and receive that fullness of joy, and glory, with everlasting reward, in the presence of the Lord: but the wicked, who do not know God, and obey not the gospel of Jesus Christ, shall be cast into eternal torments,[5] and punished with everlasting destruction, from the presence of the Lord, and from the glory of his power.[6]

3. As Christ would have us to be certainly persuaded that there shall be a day of judgment, both to deter all men from sin,[7] and for the greater consolation of the godly in their adversity;[8] so will he have the day unknown to men, that they may shake off all carnal security, and be always watchful, because they know not at what hour, the Lord will come;[9] and may ever be prepared to say, *Come Lord Jesus, come quickly, Amen.*[10]

---

1 Acts 17:31; John 5:22, 27.
2 1 Cor. 6:3; Jude 6.
3 2 Cor. 5:10; Eccl. 12:14; Matt. 12:36; Rom. 14:10, 12; Matt. 25:32ff.
4 Rom. 9:22–23.
5 Matt. 25:21, 34; 2 Tim. 4:8.
6 Matt. 25:46; Mark 9:48; 2 Thess. 1:7–10.
7 2 Cor. 5:10–11.
8 2 Thess. 1:5–7.
9 Mark 13:35–37; Luke 12:35–40.
10 Rev. 22:20.

About Ligonier

Ligonier Ministries is an international Christian discipleship organization founded by Dr. R.C. Sproul in 1971 to proclaim, teach, and defend the holiness of God in all its fullness to as many people as possible. Dr. Sproul dedicated his life to helping people grow in their knowledge of God and His holiness, and our desire is to support the church of Jesus Christ by helping Christians know what they believe, why they believe it, how to live it, and how to share it. If you would like to learn more about Ligonier or discover more resources like this one, please visit Ligonier.org.